THROUGH FIRE AND WATER

Mark Higgitt is a 48-year-old journalist who lives in South Warwickshire with his wife. They have two daughters. *Through Fire and Water* is his first book.

THROUGH FIRE
AND WATER

**HMS *ARDENT*: THE FORGOTTEN FRIGATE
OF THE FALKLANDS**

Mark Higgitt

MAINSTREAM
PUBLISHING

EDINBURGH AND LONDON

This edition, 2007

Copyright © Mark Higgitt, 2000
All rights reserved
The moral right of the author has been asserted

First published in Great Britain in 2000 by
MAINSTREAM PUBLISHING COMPANY (EDINBURGH) LTD
7 Albany Street
Edinburgh EH1 3UG

ISBN 9781845962722

A catalogue record for this book is available from the British Library

Typeset in Ariel and Times

Printed and bound in Great Britain by
William Clowes Ltd, Beccles, Suffolk

CONTENTS

Acknowledgements   7
Author's Note   9
The Bright Side of Life   11
South   71
The Thin Grey Line   117
Thoughts of Home   279
The Benefit of Hindsight   315
A Kind of Homecoming   333
HMS *Ardent* Ship's Company (21 May 1982)   401
HMS *Ardent* Roll of Honour (21 May 1982)   405
Appendix: HMS *Ardent* Plan   407
Further Reading   409
Glossary   411

ACKNOWLEDGEMENTS

It wouldn't have been possible to write this book without the advice, support and encouragement of the many people who, like me, believe that the Ardents and their ship must not remain forgotten.

First and foremost, my thanks and love go to Maggie, Katie and Jacqui, for understanding what drove me to cover the long miles and hours of research and writing, and why. Thanks also to the Defence Attaché at the Argentine Embassy in London, for help in tracing Capitan Alberto Philippi; to David Brown and Jock Gardner, Naval Historical Branch, for help and advice; to the Captain and ship's company, HMS *Chatham*, December 1996, for taking me on a Thursday War; the officers and men of the Damage Repair Instructional Unit, HMS *Raleigh*, for taking me into the firebox and simulator, and bringing me out again; the Fleet Photographic Units, HMS *Drake*, Plymouth, and HM Naval Base, Portsmouth, for their assistance with pictures; the Imperial War Museum Visitors' Centre, London, for help with picture research; Flag Lt Andy Lamb and colleagues, Commander UK Task Group staff, HM Naval Base Portsmouth (1996) for their assistance; the editor, *Navy News*, for spreading the word; and Andrew Lownie, my agent, for taking on a half-read manuscript and helping to bring *Ardent* back to the British public.

In addition, my gratitude goes to Surg.-Capt Morgan O'Connell, for his careful counselling; the Serrells and Rays, for providing food and a place to lay my head; Bill Mitchell, Yarrow Shipbuilders, Glasgow, and Gerry Butcher, Ministry of Defence, London, for providing Type 21 layout drawings, an invaluable aid to following the footsteps of Ardents in dozens of interviews; Gerry Gunning, for his Spanish translation service; Roy Pierce-Jones and Mike Walton, my first readers, for four years of objectivity and judgement; and Mick Bishop, Andy Churchill and Vaughan Willcox for services rendered.

My particular gratitude goes to Rick Jolly, for his vital words of advice and encouragement from the early days. His South Atlantic Medal Association 82 has a Garden of Remembrance website which pays tribute to the lost Ardents, among many others, on www.sama82.org.uk.

Finally, my deepest thanks go to Admiral Sir Alan West, GCB, DSC, Commanding Officer HMS *Ardent*, Falklands 1982, and his ship's company, for their co-operation in making this book possible; and to Tony Ray, MBE, BEM, and Lenny Yeatman, of the HMS *Ardent* Association, their fellow members and all the *Ardent* families, for having faith that their story could be told after all these years. It could. Now it has been.

AUTHOR'S NOTE

At around 10 a.m. on Whit Sunday every year, a motley collection of twenty or thirty middle-aged men haul their weary legs and baggy heads onto a pleasure boat at Plymouth's Phoenix Wharf and set off on a two-hour cruise up the Tamar Estuary to Devonport Naval Base.

Some find company with their families, others seek it in a can of beer. They shoot the breeze about this and that: who lost his trousers at their reunion the night before, who slipped quietly into the Service of Remembrance on the Saturday afternoon, who didn't turn up at all, and why. When the boat passes Wharf 13, more often than not the conversation is replaced by the chug of a diesel engine and the sound of water.

When HMS *Ardent* slipped her line from that very small piece of England's edge at 1000Z on Monday, 19 April 1982, heading south to remove the Argentinians from the Falkland Islands, the average age of the 200 men on board was 23. Few believed it would come to shooting. Thirty-two days later, twenty-two of them were dead, another thirty wounded.

Close to the sanctuary of darkness, after leading the British amphibious group into Falkland Sound and defending the landings from air attack, *Ardent* had been hit 17 times in the space of 22 minutes. She sank a few hours later. Within a day or two, as the breakout for Stanley began, her name had disappeared from the headlines.

For each of her men, there's a story of those grim hours, and the years that followed. There's another for every mother, father, brother, sister, wife, lover, son and daughter who sat at home and waited for news. This is just one more, an unofficial account of *Ardent*'s last months, the story of men whose memories have stretched to fill the gaps with the passing of the years, or found that time has distorted them instead.

It's the story of men who prefer to be cautious with their recollections after so long, and those who've simply forgotten. Most of all, it's the story of ordinary men from the classrooms and factories of Britain who did something extraordinary and remember enough of the experience to wish two things: that these weren't their memories, and that their ship wasn't the forgotten frigate of the Falklands War.

This is my small effort to repay our nation's debt to them, their families and the rest of the Thin Grey Line. They're my heroes.

Mark Higgitt

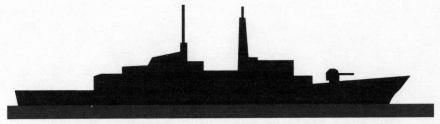

THE BRIGHT SIDE OF LIFE

One   Amsterdam (11–13 December 1981)   13

Two   Portland Naval Base to Portland Naval Base
           (10 January – 4 February 1982)   21

Three   Rosyth Naval Base, Scotland, to Cardigan Bay,
           Wales (19 February – 21 March 1982)   35

Four   Devonport Naval Base, Plymouth
           (24 March – 10 April 1982)   49

Five   Devonport Naval Base, Plymouth
           (11–18 April 1982)   57

ONE

AMSTERDAM

(11–13 DECEMBER 1981)

Scouse Phillips was freezing, 'chuffing freezing'. The side of his face was numb as the North Sea wind drilled deeper and the snow grew thicker. Some wise arse had decided the Ardents should turn out in Procedure Alpha, standing on the Upper Deck in Number 1 or Number 2 rig, as the frigate nudged towards Amsterdam that bitter December morning. The 19-year-old weapons engineer just wanted warmth. A bar. A pint. Or two. But snow was all there was.

The last place Leading Medical Assistant Bob Young wanted to be was beside the sleek Type 21's 4.5-inch gun turret, head on to the icy blast. He didn't see the point. No one ashore could see what they were wearing on *Ardent* or her three sister ships, up ahead. But that was where he was, with the rest of his shipmates. Freezing their nuts off. From that day, he made it his policy not to turn up for Procedure Alpha. He'd always have some pressing medical thing to do in the Sickbay.

As *Ardent* berthed, electrician Andy Cox was holding a metal T-bar, trying to drive the capstan with hands he couldn't feel. They turned white, then blue. It was a horrible sensation. The Navy-issue gloves were about as useful as a teabag.

For Petty Officer of the Fo'c'sle Richie Gough, staring into a white void, it was the most ridiculous thing the Ardents had ever done. Snow wasn't what any of them wanted. It was evil.

In the relative snug of the Bridge, Commander Alan West surveyed the same wintry scene and felt a thrill, not a shiver. He heard the faint hum of *Ardent*'s Tyne engines behind the textbook conversation of his officers and men as they executed one move after the next to bring her to rest outboard of HMS *Arrow*. With HMS *Alacrity* outboard of HMS *Amazon*, the Flight Decks of four proud Type 21s were tied together for the first time.

The four ships of the Fourth Frigate Squadron had been hard at work for months, either protecting Britain's interests in waters as warm and divided as the Caribbean and the Gulf, or training to plug the North Atlantic route from the USSR. Now, for the next few days, the routines of tropical guardship duty and Cold War manoeuvres were being interrupted by an icy and ceremonial peace.

Ardent had been on the Armilla Patrol, escorting tankers through the volatile seas of the Middle East, a deployment not without its moments, or its memories. The run up the Channel hadn't been without them either. As the squadron's junior member, courtesy of having the youngest frigate captain in

the Royal Navy, *Ardent* had assumed her traditional Canteen Boat station at the end of the line through the busy Straits of Dover, working desperately to avoid traffic in the sprint or Holland. It was a task Alan West relished.

'Going into Amsterdam, with everything covered in snow, it looked beautiful,' he recalls. 'We were berthed at the same jetty, two and two, and all the ship's companies knew each other. Christmas was coming. It was just very special.'

Phillips, Young, Gough, Cox and most of the others shivering on F184 didn't share the view, not yet anyway. Their thrills would come later.

◆ ◆ ◆

At action stations, the sparse surroundings of the Junior Ratings Dining Hall doubled as *Ardent*'s Aft Damage Control Section Base, not a place for the faint-hearted. In a few frantic moments, though, the space had been transformed for *Ardent*'s traditional party for local youngsters, a gift for the weekend host that always went down well. Now it was full of excited young Dutch schoolchildren having a party amid the pipes and cables running overhead and down the bulkheads. Fourteen days before Christmas, damage and control were at risk elsewhere.

On 2 Deck, the knock on the door of *Ardent*'s Chiefs' Mess hadn't been unexpected. The door opened and there stood Mick Brain, HMS *Amazon*'s Deputy Marine Engineering Officer. Behind him marched her Chiefs' Mess with a barrel of beer suspended from a pole between two of his men.

Lunchtime was a little early to start a Chiefs' Mess night, but who would notice? Not Tony Ray, Brain's *Ardent* counterpart. Not Lenny Yeatman, her Master at Arms. Nor Chief Stoker Andy Andrew, Chief Petty Officer Ken Enticknap, on his first foreign run ashore with this bunch, or anyone else girding themselves for the inevitable.

Ray's eyes lit up when he saw the barrel and the confident look on Mick Brain's face. Barrel-pulling was *Amazon*'s party piece. But Brain had forgotten something: Ray had taught him all he knew of the black art. And he hadn't accounted for one other factor in the equation: CPO Andy Lee, 'Big Tansy'.

'You just couldn't break his grip,' Ray laughs years later. 'So we won the barrel-pulling. Everyone was falling arse over breakfast-time.' One up to *Ardent*.

It's unclear exactly what else happened that afternoon, but there are faint recollections that bottle-walking – taking a bottle in each hand with your feet behind a fixed line, then walking with your bottles as far as possible – and blow football – using a table tennis ball on a pitch crafted by Andy Andrew from cardboard and sticky tape – were part of the fun. So might have been the three-man lift, which starts with one man bidding to prove his strength and ends with one unsuspecting soul having his trousers opened and a pint of water or beer poured over him. And spoons, a noble tradition in which two protagonists, blindfolded by tea towels, take it in turns to hit each other over the head with spoons held in their mouths – except that the sharp crack of Sheffield steel on the skull of the game's 'green' player is applied by a third contestant he doesn't know is playing.

If *Amazon* misjudged expectations on barrel-pulling, they wouldn't make the same mistake on one of the day's final encounters, the Duck Run Derby. In Tony Ray, *Ardent* had a man with a special talent for squeezing 24 tuppence pieces between the cheeks of his backside and dropping them, after a short walk, into a pint pot.

'It took years to practise,' Ray recalls. 'By this time, we were quite happy.'

◆ ◆ ◆

Master at Arms Lenny Yeatman, the ship's policeman, had been a stoker long before the Royal Navy reorganised and gave the job a new name, Marine Engineering Mechanic, or MEM for short. So he knew the score long before the Ship's Doctor, Bob Young, started his walk through *Ardent*'s three Junior Ratings messdecks, dishing Durex out like confetti.

Amsterdam, the drugs capital of the world. A very young ship's company. No surprise, then, that Yeatman and the First Lieutenant – otherwise known as the Jimmy – had discussed this moment long before the vague outline of Holland loomed through the snow.

'Drunkenness was an occupational hazard,' Master at Arms Yeatman says. 'What we really had to worry about wasn't them misbehaving when they were drunk but getting back down the Mess, falling asleep and vomiting and choking.'

The young Ardents knew the score too, even before he handed out his docket on the passage from Devonport. At 27, after ten years in the Junior Rates Messdeck and now a leading hand, Andy Cox was as familiar with the bars of the Mediterranean, North America and Africa, and many more points east and west as those in his native Redditch, probably more.

'On one page of Lenny's docket,' he explains, 'it has a list of where you're not supposed to go, which is where you're going. They know you're going there, because they're going to find you there for a recall.'

◆ ◆ ◆

The 25 Ikkies Bar wasn't a place Scouse Phillips would have taken his mother. So instead, he went with WEM Simon Lawson. The pair were kindred spirits who maintained the radars which governed *Ardent*'s weapons systems when they weren't on a run ashore. In Norfolk, Virginia, an ikkie was a dollar. In Haifa, a shekel. In France, a franc. Thus, in Holland you needed guilders to put the 25 Ikkies Bar to the test. Phillips speaks on behalf of many matelots who willingly did that weekend.

'You paid 25 guilders to get in and you could drink as much as you wanted in 30 minutes. It was about a fiver,' he says. 'We drank Bacardi and Coke until it was coming out of our ears. By the time the three naked girls behind the bar decided it was time to play, we were 25 minutes into the half-hour session. We could hardly see. We took turns trying to throw coins at certain parts of their bodies. To see if they'd stick. They wiggled. I hit a girl in the eye. Her box was only a foot and a half away, but I hit her in the eye.'

Some perspectives were different.

'There was a recess behind the bar,' Chief Electrician Taff Lovidge smiles. 'This lady would put a little headrest on the bar and a coin on your nose, and she'd step down with her legs apart and pluck the coin off.' He laughs and leaves the story there.

At 18, on his first foreign run ashore, Wyatt Earp was about to sample the kind of delights that would make the genteel folk of Malvern blanche. After ten minutes taking some culture at a museum, he and a couple of others headed for a bar. He walked in and the first person the young, impressionable Marine Engineer saw was one of his senior rates on a table, banana in one hand, baby oil in the other.

'If this is the Navy,' he thought, 'I'm glad I joined!'

Geordie weapons engineer Buck Taylor wasn't far behind. Since joining *Ardent* a couple of months before, he'd been taken under the wing of Knocker White, a fellow North-Easterner with a well-tuned talent for finding fun. Just a couple of weeks away from his 21st birthday, White was an old hand at the run ashore. If he hadn't been ready to extend Taylor's education, someone else would have. With Bernie Berntsen in tow, one of the oldest old hands in the Stokers' Mess, the aim of the evening was to see as much as they could. They succeeded.

'I was dragged from bar to bar. The Schooner and The Three Musketeers and The Jolly Sailor,' Taylor recalls. 'One young lady must have made a fortune. Three or four lads on *Alacrity* went with her, and then seven or eight lads from *Arrow* afterwards. Our ship was last,' as a good Canteen Boat would be. 'We ducked out. She must have been in tatters by the time they were finished.'

He threw up at some point. Kebabs. Lager. But he did live to tell the tale. So did all the other Ardents. One night down. Two to go.

The only change Saturday brought was a hangover or two. The memories of those who ventured to the Upper Deck are sketchy, but it seems that the snow was still falling. Just after stand-easy, about 1000, Lenny Yeatman nudged his cap back and surveyed the snowman competition. As he did, *Arrow*'s Master at Arms emerged on the Flight Deck of F173 and lifted his cap in greeting. Cold or not, something told Yeatman this was a morning to be glad you were alive.

He nodded and waited until his counterpart's back was turned before he bent down. The snowball hit *Arrow*'s man square on the back of the head. That was it.

'Snowball fight!' *Ardent*'s Tannoy called for reinforcements. Within minutes, there was chaos. Men on duty had abandoned their stations as *Ardent* and *Arrow* pitched in battle against *Amazon* and *Alacrity*, 400 grown men launching volley after volley across the wide jetty.

By the time Alan West and his fellow commanding officers returned from a visit ashore, the *Ardent–Arrow* alliance was moving slowly up the jetty, Zulu-style – 'Front rank fire! Rear rank advance! Front rank fire!' – and a massive public gallery had gathered beside the railway line. The four COs did the only thing they could. They joined in.

Only one thing was going to stop the slaughter: running out of snow. Or some hapless Dutchman walking his dog, minding his own business. He escaped, eventually. But only after a 500-snowball salvo had greeted him.

◆ ◆ ◆

Bob Young had been ashore but, as the only medic on the ship, he knew the worst thing he could do would be to have a skinful, then have an emergency to deal with, a case of hypothermia, for instance. What's more, within hours he'd be celebrating his 26th birthday, and wouldn't there be one more run ashore before they slipped away from the jetty and headed home for Devonport? Of course there would.

Little did he know, though he might have guessed, but the seeds of doom had been sown the previous night by 19-year-old MEM (L) Stephen Coates – 'Ralph' to his mates; 'Sinus' to Lenny Yeatman, 'because he used to get right up your nose'. The young electrician still insists it could have happened to anyone.

'The Jolly Sailor.' Scouse Phillips shakes his head. 'He was dancing and he couldn't dance. His legs were all over the show. He just kicked out and accidentally kicked this lad in the face. Big lad.'

The big lad stood up. Even though their tracks hadn't taken them to The Three Musketeers, the pint-sized Coates was surrounded by a stack of big lads of his own. All for one, and so on.

It's unclear whether this one incident was to blame, or whether the final straw came when the Ardents debagged him, but he was still barred. It was meant as punishment but taken as a challenge.

'Next night,' Phillips goes on, 'the lads went back in and got him a beer and put it on the bar. Ralph was walking up and down outside, then he tried to sneak in on all-fours, got to the bar and this little hand came up, trying to get the beer.'

This time, the rest of the Ardents were shown the door with him.

With The Jolly Sailor struck off their list for the rest of the weekend, and the night still promisingly young at 2300, they walked on to Kanalstrasse and paused. Snow might have been falling, but it was the last thing on their minds.

Ken Dodds looked at Bernie Berntsen. 'Where are we going next?' he asked.

'Over there!' Bernie pointed across the canal. Whether Dodds or Coates set off first is open to speculation. Whoever, one of them disappeared first, attempting to cross a bridge that was ten short strides further up the street. Bernie recalls that he heard Dodds shout and, registering Ralph's sympathetic laugh, jumped in to save his mate. On the lip of the canal, Buck Taylor did the noble thing too. Oblivious to any boat hidden a few feet away, he pushed Ralph in after them.

As Bernie gasped for air, he realised there were now three of them thrashing for dear life, the icy, condom-littered water like a clamp round their chests. All they could hear above was laughter and the sound of disappearing feet.

'When I looked up, all of them had gone.' Ralph is still annoyed by it. 'Some Dutch bloke got me out on the other side of the canal. He put me in a taxi that took me back to the ship.'

Bernie and Dodds found their own temporary solution: a radiator in a sex shop that hissed as they thawed. Then they took a taxi back to the jetty and waddled, steaming, down to 3 Deck, stripping off where they stood in the Mess Square and climbing into their pits.

By that time, an ordinary Saturday had become Bob Young's 26th birthday. He had the ideal means of revenge for being stirred from his bunk at that godforsaken hour.

'Ken was extremely manky,' Young says, so he hit him with a tetanus jab. As soon as Bernie woke, he was hit with the big needle too.

As Ralph snored in his grot the next morning, Lenny Yeatman was in his Regulating Office, just across the flat on 1 Deck from the Electrical Workshop, receiving reports of the night's activities. Swimming in an ice-covered canal hadn't been at the top of the list of dos and don'ts handed out on the passage from Devonport, but he was relatively unconcerned.

'We were expecting a lot worse,' he laughs now, though he doesn't mention the cook's ID card that went missing with a young lady at a blue movie, or four ratings spending most of the night in the cells, something that started with an orange in a bar but moved on to a brawl and ended with them howling the police station down before they were freed. They crept back on board.

◆ ◆ ◆

Expecting worse? They'd almost had it. With *Ardent*'s helicopter Flight still somewhere in the Gulf, based on an oil tanker, F184 had HMS *Antelope*'s Flight on board. While some slept off their excesses, and those on duty did their rounds, an alarm had gone off in the Hangar. The first on the scene was Lt Cdr Tim MacMahon, *Antelope*'s Flight Commander. The second was *Ardent*'s First Lieutenant, Andrew Gordon Lennox. He arrived to see MacMahon playing a hose on an oily rag. The scare was quickly dealt with, but it only served to sharpen the edge on board.

With the IRA active on mainland Europe seeking soft military targets, vigilance was vital. So rhythmic tapping on the ship's hull wasn't music to Mick Cox's ears as he worked on a pump in the Aft Engine Room some hours later. He didn't need two invitations to report what he'd heard.

'We were just going to move the propeller blades,' the softly spoken Scot, a Marine Engineering Artificer, then 34, recalls. He went to the Ship Control Centre and asked his stocky, bespectacled boss, Lt Cdr Terry Pendrous, if any divers were down.

'Why?' asked Pendrous, turning round.

'I heard banging on the hull.'

The ship moved to Operation Awkward State 3, a high state of defence against attack from land or sea when a ship is berthed or at anchor. The Duty Petty Officer of the Day, Richie Gough, posted unarmed sentries to the Upper Deck.

On the jetty, Coates, Cox and co. were off in search of another wet. Behind them, the Tannoy barked into life, ordering Duty Watch – about a quarter of the

ship's company – to muster on the Flight Deck. The stokers began running, but not towards the ship. As the same call echoed on 2 Deck, preparations were being made in the POs' Mess to entertain officers from *Arrow*, *Amazon* and *Alacrity*. With barely a word, the bar was shut and the off-duty POs disembarked through the snow too.

In the Diving Store, outside the Hangar on *Ardent*'s port side, Diving Officer Lt Nigel Langhorn gathered himself to probe the murky shallows. The conditions couldn't have been less inviting.

Langhorn and one of *Ardent*'s other divers searched both flanks of the ship and then inched along the length of *Arrow*. When they were certain there was nothing there, they surfaced, cold.

'You bastard!' Langhorn muttered as Mick Cox appeared. He'd found nothing except a loose rope, rapping the ship's side with every pulsing rise of the waves lapping between *Ardent* and *Arrow*. The sentries were stood down. On the Flight Deck, PO Richie Gough went back to his duties, preparing for a few drunken matelots as they came back from the delights of Amsterdam. Again.

In a passageway later on, Alan West took Cox to one side. That rhythmic beat had escalated, step by step, until the entire northern NATO intelligence chain knew about it.

◆ ◆ ◆

No one can remember where the Christmas tree came from, or whose idea it was to pass a gallon bottle of whisky around, or even whether the four ships' companies were gathered on *Arrow*'s Flight Deck or alongside it on the jetty which, 24 hours before, had witnessed the snowball battle. But the most unsentimental old soaks remember the Carol Service on the afternoon of Sunday, 13 December, even if they can't recall the carols. Whichever they were, they put their own words to them anyway.

'It was a happy sing-song,' PO Wacker Payne recalls.

'It was just very special,' Alan West adds. It was, too.

A day later, Andy Cox sacrificed his hands to the elements as he drove the capstan, Scouse Phillips and Richie Gough steeled themselves for the icy North Sea wind and other figures busied themselves in the art of seamanship. Bob Young doesn't remember where he was as *Ardent* slipped away from *Arrow* for the short run home to families and Christmas, though it's a fair bet he found something more pressing in the Sickbay.

Naafi manager John Leake braved *Ardent*'s Upper Deck to take one last look at Amsterdam. Scattered on the jetty was a pile of bikes. He didn't know who their owners were, but he had an idea where he'd find the last people who rode them.

It's a little after six on the morning of Friday, 21 May 1982. Showered and dressed, Lt Cdr Alberto Philippi, second in command of the Rio Grande Naval

Air Base in the southern reaches of Argentina, sits down for breakfast: orange juice, coffee with milk, toast and marmalade laid out in front of him.

The radio's on and, while he listens for the latest news of the Malvinas crisis, Philippi chats with his wife, Graciela. He's 43, maybe the oldest fighter pilot on both sides. She's 40, a primary-school teacher in the town of Rio Grande.

At work, home's always far from his mind. One hundred per cent concentration until after the post-flight debrief, then relax. That's the way it's been since the start of his career. But at home, his thoughts are devoted to his family, Alberto junior – a 15 year old studying in Bahia Blanca and living with his grandmother – 13-year-old Verónica, Cristina, 11, and Manfred Otto, aged two, who are sleeping in their rooms. This morning, though, it's difficult not to let his mind stray. Impossible, almost.

TWO

PORTLAND NAVAL BASE TO PORTLAND NAVAL BASE

(10 JANUARY – 4 FEBRUARY 1982)

Plymouth was thick with snow, and First Lieutenant Andrew Gordon Lennox wasn't a happy man.

'You came aboard last night, Master at Arms, why didn't they?' he asked Lenny Yeatman.

That rankled. The Jimmy was insisting men should be punished because they were adrift in the foul weather. The Joss thought they'd made the effort. But Christmas had gone. Goodwill to all men didn't stretch as far as a Sunday morning in Devonport dockyard, not when four weeks of hell beckoned.

Portland was worse. There were some who felt a slight glow of satisfaction as Alan West brought *Ardent* alongside a deserted Q Pier characteristically early. But it didn't warm many hearts on board.

Continuation Operational Sea Training is designed to keep a ship at full readiness for war or any peacetime emergency – fire, flood, hurricane or salvage. There was no enemy for the Ardents to fight, unless you counted the so-called wreckers from Flag Officer Sea Training who'd make the next few weeks of their lives hell, waking and sleeping.

The wreckers' plan was simple: to help West 'work up' his team and test the ability and ingenuity of the ship's company, from the likes of MEM Stephen 'Florrie' Ford, maybe the youngest rating, to the Jimmy and everyone in between. No one would be spared. No one ever was. No one could hide.

So, the aim of every Ardent was to put ticks in all the right boxes, a measure of pride in themselves, pride in each other, pride in their young teams, pride in the ship, pride in the face of the Enemy, even if, as the days passed, many would wind up willing to trade any tick for an end to it all.

If Portland was going to prove anything, it was a feeling that had emerged in Amsterdam. The key, ironically, was the departure of so many men who'd served on the Armilla Patrol. The Navy's system of trickle drafting – a set period on one ship before being moved on, like an Army tour of duty – took men out a few at a time and avoided a wholesale change of skills decimating a ship's fighting capability. But, during Armilla, there'd been little or no chance for drafts. So, once she'd pulled alongside again in Devonport – on Thursday, 23 April 1981, to be exact – there'd been a massive intake of new men. A new team.

Sonar operator Dave Croft had been good mates with Mick Newby since

he'd joined in November, six months on from Armilla, proud of his 21 draft and his leading seaman's rate as he arrived from Leigh. Newby, already a killick – and leading hand – in the radar branch, had shown him to the 2 Deck Junior Ratings Mess in traditional style, by hurling his bag down the ladder. Now, on a cold January night, they anticipated what the wreckers would throw at them.

'Anything can happen at any moment.' Croft draws a clear picture. He'd only just left sonar training school, a new pin who feared being found wanting. That night, every bunk harboured similar thoughts.

'These bastards,' Newby remembers well, 'would come along and, five minutes after you was asleep, you got a fire alarm. Which takes four or five hours, because they decide you haven't done it right, so you'll do it again. You're back on watch in another hour. That's stress.'

◆ ◆ ◆

The 21 Club was nine units – *Amazon*, *Antelope*, *Active*, *Ambuscade*, *Arrow*, *Alacrity*, *Ardent*, *Avenger* and the Type 21 support group at Devonport. They were stopgap ships, built to a civilian design: a slick, sleek sportscar of a 3,500-ton fighting machine to some; to others a cheap and cheerful Woolworths frigate. They had big problems with weight and corrosion between the aluminium superstructure and steel hull. They also had severe operational limitations. Most of *Ardent*'s older hands knew what that meant: a weapon which didn't reach its maximum effective range until most attacking aircraft had already fired their weapons. Not good.

But 21s were quick and relatively easy to run. On a steam turbine ship, like a Leander, you had to run the machinery up the day before you wanted to go anywhere. With two Tyne and two Olympus gas turbine engines, *Ardent* could leave at ten minutes' notice. That meant a 21 could play on while other ships worked. The downside was that there were a hundred fewer hands. That meant no passengers.

So, as the gangway was removed that cold Portland Monday morning, and the First Lieutenant handed the ship over to him – 'Ready for sea, sir.' 'Thank you, Number One. Let go aft.' – Alan West placed his faith in four departments: Operations, Weapons Engineering, Marine Engineering, and Supply and Secretariat. More importantly, he handed his reputation over to the 174 officers and men working, sleeping and occasionally playing on seven decks, 1 to 4 below her Upper Deck, 01 to 03 above it.

On the typewritten daily Watch and Station Bill hanging on the wall of Lenny Yeatman's office, *Ardent*'s hierarchy looked clinical and soulless. The black and white of it was this. The typical Type 21 captain would be a Commander, probably in his late thirties after around 20 years' service, almost certainly on his first and only drive before promotion. Alan West was an exception. At 33, he was the Navy's youngest frigate commanding officer.

His second-in-command, First Lieutenant Andrew Gordon Lennox – known as the Jimmy below decks and the Executive Officer by his peers – was in charge of the Lieutenant Commander or Lieutenant heading each department. They, in turn, had their own chain, with chief petty officers one step below and

sub-departments run by petty officers and leading hands, their co-ordinators. Below them were the young men of the Junior Ratings Mess at the beginning of their careers, learning their trades and doing their taskbooks. The whole organisation was run by Master at Arms Lenny Yeatman.

From department to department, a picture just as bland and functional could be painted. The Operations Department was the Jimmy's individual responsibility. In it, 80 ratings in the Missile, Sonar, Radar and Electronic Warfare divisions rubbed shoulders with radio operators of the Communications division and air engineers of the Flight, all of them trained to man and fight the sensors and weapons of the Type 21, as well as look after the inside and outside of the ship, to handle it in harbour and execute replenishments at sea, under the watchful eye of the Chief Bosun's Mate.

There was also the Supply and Secretariat Department. In a nutshell, if a spare helicopter engine was needed, or a tin of brass polish, they found it; a never-ending demand met by the never-ending business of ordering, storing, stocktaking and issuing, 24 hours a day, 365 days of the year. The S&S was also home to the men responsible, ultimately, for the ship's morale, the cooks.

In the Weapons Engineering Department, old heads and young hands of eight sub-sections maintained the weapons, sensors, computers or communications. Their task would be simple in the coming four weeks – to give Alan West the weapons he wanted, when he wanted them, no ifs or buts.

Terry Pendrous's Marine Engineering Department was a curious mix of the very old and the very new. Fifty or so 'stokers' tended technology unknown to previous Grey Funnel Line generations, but they still wielded spanners and scrubbed deckplates. And they still carried out safety rounds that stood a chance of being recognised by the ghosts of warships from the beginning of the century, but done now in the Forward and Aft Engine Rooms, two decks high on 3 and 4 Deck, or the Auxiliary Machine Rooms forward and aft of them on 3 Deck, from where a mass of systems, electrical supplies, lighting, ventilation, firemain, fresh water and sundry domestics stretched through the ship.

A Type 21 Watch and Station Bill. Cold, clinical, functional, formal? Not if the Jimmy's judgement was sound. The 34 year old had joined two days before a trip to *Ardent*'s affiliated town, Milford Haven, the previous July, his first appointment as an Executive Officer. Standing on the Flight Deck, soon after, he'd watched a party of sailors going ashore. Seconds later, one came running back.

'Where are you going?' he asked.

'The killick sent me to sort out some ropes hanging over the side of the Fo'c'sle.'

Gordon Lennox watched the seaman dash off. He was impressed.

Immediately below the Bridge in the Ops Room, *Ardent*'s two Principal Warfare Officers, Lieutenants Mike Knowles and Tom Williams, would be vital to many of the COST ticks F184 hoped to score. But directing the minute-by-minute running of the ship in its fighting mode would bring an added stress, because Alan West had carved out his reputation in Ops Rooms as a PWO too.

The Chief Gunner, Pete Rowe, and 23-year-old Weapons Director Richie Gough would be Tom Williams' first resort once the call came for pretend air

defence or NGS, naval gunfire support. Gough worked opposite Rowe. He was newly qualified, the Navy's youngest Weapons Director, a man turned on by the multimillion-pound technology at fingertips that were capable of unleashing a Seacat missile or a 4.5-inch shell, a man happy with his gung-ho reputation.

By contrast, at 35, Rowe was the Ops Room co-ordinator, responsible for the radar and sonar rates, like Dave Croft and Mick Newby, the Electronic Warfare rates, the missilemen and day-to-day manning. He was also fresh out of a year back at gunnery school, retraining to take his place in a Type 21 Ops Room.

Rowe's culture shock was one PO Mike Lewis understood on the opposite side of *Ardent*'s green-tinged Ops Room. After 20 years relying on a chinagraph pencil and brainpower, Lewis was also coming to the conclusion that adjusting to *Ardent*'s new Electronic Warfare equipment would take time. His was perhaps the smallest department, but it suited this quiet man down to the ground. He was happy to spend hours at the screen, twiddling knobs, waiting to play his part, unconcerned that much of the EW operator's work went unseen, veiled in secrecy from all but a handful of Ops Room officers.

The only evidence on *Ardent*'s radar-packed foremast of his presence was a discreet collection of cotton-reel-like horns, the ship's ears, which picked up radar frequencies from ships and aircraft. Where the likes of Gough and Rowe could respond to a threat by launching a missile, a passive role like EW called for patience. Lots of it. You listened, identified and reported to the Captain what you thought it was you'd heard. But, unlike radar, it didn't tell anybody else you were there.

Lewis was expecting moments when Alan West would shout 'What's that ship on the starboard quarter?' Four hours on watch, three hours 50 minutes of utter boredom, then he could come back and say 'It's so-and-so, and she has this sort of missile.' Then, in his dark corner, he could be smug.

Among the young men who shared his diligent nature, if not always his quiet manner, were Steve Earnshaw and John Goddard. This was the first chance they'd had to work as a team under pressure. None was expecting an easy ride. But, then, Portland wasn't meant to be fun. Not most of the time.

The men of Lt Cdr Rick Banfield's S&S Department would readily take up that challenge, PO Cook Cliff Goldfinch most of all, even if COST meant action snacks, with everything served from the same stewpot rather than the gourmet fayre the Ardents had become accustomed to. Since they'd returned from Armilla, he'd slowly transformed the Ardents' eating habits. After cooking for captains and admirals, he'd begun to wonder why the ratings couldn't have the same. So he'd changed it. They still had sausage and mash, omelettes, salads and so on for lunch. But, in the evening, there was a roast, chops, a three-choice menu, and often a cheese board. No mean feat on about £1.40 per man, per day.

Jon Major's life was a little different. After an Amsterdam christening in the ways of the S&S Mess, the 19 year old's typical week started: 'Day One, normal duty watch, eight till after the evening meal; Day Two, morning watch, rise about four to do breakfast, take an hour off, then spend a couple more cleaning before lunch; Day Three, long standby, helping and cleaning . . .' and so on. What it amounted to most, though, was doing the spuds and keeping the

sink down. After a day in a humid atmosphere, it took just one thing to make it worthwhile, one person in 200 saying, 'Cheers, I really did enjoy that!'

COST was no exception. At action stations, Major's job was action-messing, cooking a piping hot meal and watching it disappear in seconds before men dashed back to their posts. Other cooks turned their hands to firefighting as part of Damage Control, or working with a First Aid Party. No passengers.

For an 18 year old having his first taste of the sea, like Buck Taylor, or a 20 year old finding it hard to adjust to the ways of the in-crowd on a 21 Messdeck, like Buck Ryan, that meant good days and bad.

PO Ian Jacobs, hardly old and bold at 26, knew what the two weapons engineers were going through.

'All sections on a 21 had a heavy load. You had to train your junior rates quickly and trust them to carry out a lot of routine maintenance,' he reflects. 'Buck Ryan was quick to learn and always willing to help. He did the work of a leading hand. He was a good talker, which meant he was often classed as cocky.' His Geordie sidekick was quiet until Ryan loosened him up, and they soon had their own equipment to maintain. Taylor looked to Ryan. Ryan looked to Jacobs. That's how the Navy ran.

'If you were a naughty boy,' Ryan explains, 'you were hit with a screwdriver. The more senior you get, the bigger screwdriver you get.'

It was the same among the stokers who shared the two 3 Deck Messes with Taylor and Ryan and the rest of the WEMs. Unlike the Leanders most had served on, a 21's main Mess Square was in the centre of each Messdeck, with four-bunk sleeping cubicles – grots and gulches to their tenants – lining the perimeter. In the most forward of the two Messes, there was room for 44 men to sleep, drink, brag and break wind. In the one just aft, 48 others could do the same.

The Junior Marine Engineering Mechanics were the youngest and least experienced of the 30-odd stokers. They looked to the Marine Engineering Mechanics, who were maybe a year older. The MEMs looked to their Leading Marine Engineering Mechanics, the so-called 'killicks' who might be working towards promotion to the POs' Mess.

It filtered on down beyond that. The Electrical (L) Department, for instance, was a sub-section of the stokers branch, ten 'greenies' under the guidance of Chief Electrician Taff Lovidge. PO Wacker Payne's section, he suggests, was an example of the spirit that drove *Ardent*. Wacker had joined her to do a PO's job. Suddenly, he was in charge of L2 section and clutched water for a long time.

'One day we had a problem with the diesels and we were working late, really, really late. Wacker solved it. It was a Chief's job really. From that day, he became a brilliant PO. Leader of his guys.'

He needed to be. 'We had people like Coxie, who were larger than life, animals ashore, and Ralphie, who didn't like to do much work and was always a bit of a whinger. But he'd work for Wacker.'

And, if he didn't, Coxie would thump him. That's also the way the Navy ran.

Lenny Yeatman had been a stoker before switching to the Regulatory branch. Now, armed with the Naval Discipline Act instead of a spanner, he maintained

law and order, not engines. The Messdecks regarded it as a challenge.

'He knew all the tricks,' says LMEM Jan Joyce, the Beer Bosun, the leading hand responsible for the consumption of beer on the Messdeck. Unsurprisingly, in a service that taught its young men to eat, fight and drink, beer was at the heart of the relationship. It wasn't always kept in the fridges. It turned up in the ventilation shafts and underneath the seats where the fuel tanks below kept it cool. At three cans per man per day, the game was played for high stakes, and it was played when Yeatman did his evening rounds with the Jimmy. The young ratings had to learn the rules quickly.

The greatest respect afforded to the Joss, a man who'd been one of their own, was that, if someone overstepped the mark, he'd face the judgement of his colleagues first.

'We'd go to Lenny and say, "We've given him a rollicking. He knows he's done wrong." Sometimes that would be it. Other times he'd say, "I can't let it go because so-and-so's seen what happened."'

Along with the Galley, the divisional system also maintained morale. Divisional Petty Officers worked closely with the leading hands of the messes. A conversation by the SCC might be 'He's not happy, his wife's left him,' or 'He needs advancement.' The Divisional Officer would pass the word on to his Head of Department. The system's been in the Navy for 300 years and it's the best.

It was during evening rounds that the ritual was played out most religiously.

'I had a tradition,' Yeatman laughs softly. 'Rounds were a method of keeping in contact with the men, the link between Command and the Lower Deck. Go out, get a feeling for the ship, make sure everything was secured. There was a pipe, 'Hands shift into night clothing.' It was leisure time so, instead of lounging around in overalls, you had to get yourself clean. Hygiene at sea's most important.'

Walking round the Mess, the Joss and Jimmy used to sit and chat. If something was happening, and Yeatman had a twig of it, he'd have a can with them and say: 'Look, what's going on?' He didn't necessarily want to know why or who. But nipping it in the bud paid dividends and, if a lad had incurred his wrath, he'd wait until the First Lieutenant was out of sight and execute his party piece – off with the glasses, 'Hold these young man,' and drop the nut. He laughs again.

He loved the ship, and its men. Knocker White was the one who'd brought the fact home one day.

'A young stoker came to join. He was only 18 and Knocker had given him his bits and pieces and I said 'Will you take him down to the Divisional Officer?' Knocker stuck his hand out and said, 'Welcome to *Ardent*. You'll enjoy this ship. It's a great ship's company. Skipper's a cracker. We all pull together and people look after you.' That just about summed it up for me.'

At sea one night, the Jimmy was on his rounds with Yeatman, and Buck Ryan neglected to take his Walkman off.

'Ryan, what are you listening to?'

'Depeche Mode. You're too old for that!' The lads laughed and Ralph Coates couldn't resist putting his oar in. Two seconds later, off came the Joss's glasses.

But Ryan also knew the other side to the double act. He was married with a

young child and living in Portland. If he wasn't on duty, and the ship was at anchor, the Jimmy would organise a boat to take him home for the evening.

'I didn't have a very good marriage,' he admits. 'I think that actually got to Gordon Lennox, and that's why he did it.'

Take John Foster too. The 22-year-old Liverpudlian general radio operator recalls finishing for a week at Portland. He went to see the Joss and asked if he could leave the ship there, to save him going all the way back to Plymouth, simply to return to Portland.

'He squared it with the First Lieutenant. It made you feel right. He'd done me a favour, so when I'm next doing my job, I'll push it all the way. You get to ships where you just do enough to get by, whereas everyone wanted to do their bit.'

It illustrated one of the Jimmy's firmest beliefs: 'The First Lieutenant and the Master at Arms need to be like that,' he crosses his fingers, 'no daylight between them. They need to get on together, respect each other, know each other's capabilities and limitations and, between them, move to fill the gaps. Lenny and I had that sort of relationship.'

For Taff Lovidge, though, their strengths reflected the character of the man at the top. In short, if his men hadn't begun to devote themselves to Alan West before Portland, they soon did.

'Lenny was very instrumental, when he came on board, in changing the image of the ship in a big way,' the Chief Electrician, then 36, insists. 'But I think Alan West was the guy who got the ship into the spirit. Then it came all the way down the line.'

Nineteen-year-old Scouse Phillips thought West was sometimes too aloof, though he accepts the Naval hierarchy was probably watching his progress so closely that 'if he'd farted, they'd have known'. The view from the Ops Room was no different.

'Because there were never any tantrums,' says PWO Mike Knowles, 'people always wanted to give their best. Very quickly the spirit in the ship developed. Maybe because the ship was junior we felt no one was going to get the better of us. We always wanted to be up there.'

The FOST wreckers would be determined to find out just how 'up there' the Ardents were.

It might have been hard to believe as the month of hell began, but Bernie Berntsen's experienced view was probably the best to take. He knew action stations in Portland was a game they played, and that the better you played it their way, the bigger the laugh you could have. Jan Joyce didn't need two invitations to prove it. He'd learnt to always have a piece of chalk in his pocket. It came in useful sooner than he'd thought.

'They draw these blinking great holes in the decks and they say, "You can't go past there."'

They did it on the Fo'c'sle one morning. So Joyce took his chalk out and drew.

'Plank!' he replied, and walked across the hole. The die was cast.

Shorn of his Ops Room EW duties one morning, John Goddard was enlisted to test the fibre of one of *Ardent*'s junior officers on the Fo'c'sle.

'What I want you to do,' a FOST man told him, 'is throw a real wobbly.'
Goddard was happy to oblige.

'You're talking fucking bollocks!' he ranted. 'I'm not going to do that!' It went on for ten minutes.

The junior officer responded as FOST had hoped. Goddard was hauled away and locked up. Then it was a case of waiting for the FOST staff to turn up and confess to the charade. They did, eventually.

It went on. 'The individual knows most of what's going to happen with damage control,' says Berntsen, who worked in the Forward Auxiliary Machine Room alongside two of *Ardent*'s youngest stokers, Stephen Ford and Alistair Leighton. 'There's going to be fire, bomb blasts, shrapnel. Bodies. All your training's pointed that way, so all through the years you go balls out. You've got to when you play their war games. The quicker you can get back on line, you're a fighting ship. There's nowhere to run and if your weapons or radar have gone, you've got to get them back on before you get hit again.'

Deciding when the next 'attack' would come in was, perhaps, the toughest of the tough jobs when FOST was breathing down your neck.

'If we could, we were determined to piss these people off,' says Scouse Phillips, 'because they weren't going to get us down.'

One morning, the Officer of the Day heard there was going to be a fire exercise. On the basis of prepare for the worst, hope for the best, the Duty Watch mustered in the Hangar with fearnought firefighting suits on. Phillips was in the attack party. In his mind, the job was simple. Wherever he was, he'd grab an extinguisher, run to the fire, 'put the bugger out', then go back to bed.

The broadcast pipe came, pointing the Damage Control Party somewhere aft. Phillips shot down the ladder, legged towards the Dining Hall, grabbed the extinguisher and ran on. At the other end of the Dining Hall, heading aft, was a doorway hatch. Behind that was a small flat and a ladder going up to the rear of the Quarterdeck. Behind that ladder were two hatches going down, the left one to the Tiller Flat, the right to the Storeroom and the Avcat Pump Space. There was smoke everywhere and a Fleet Chief from FOST.

'Right,' he told Phillips, 'the fire's in the Avcat Pump Space.'

Phillips went straight down, a big Triple F extinguisher dangling through his legs. He reached the space, turned round 'like this man of action' and realised there was no smoke. It was the wrong hatch.

'Shit!' By the time he staggered back up again, there was smoke everywhere, and he couldn't breathe. A familiar voice echoed from behind the dense cloud.

'Where's Scouse Phillips?' It was Coxie. There was so much smoke that the rest of the DCP had put all the clips on the door to contain the smoke and imaginary fire.

'Where's Scouse?'

'I'm in here!'

'Where's Scouse?'

'Here!'

Then he heard Wacker Payne yell, 'Get the clips off the door!'

Scouse staggered through the door, retching, and looked at the rest of the DCP.

'Well, we stuffed that one, then!'

There were others for whom the 'fun' passed by so infrequently it was almost unnoticed. PO Mike Lewis hardly recalls looking up from his EW screens. He never thought too far ahead.

'It was absolute hell. Anyone who says it wasn't is lying. You didn't get any sleep. They did everything apart from beat you about the head with a big stick.'

It was one thing to think that way with the best part of 20 years' service behind you, another for the newest Ardents experiencing FOST for the first time. By this time, Buck Taylor's permanent draft had come through. He hadn't been on the Gun Section long when he was drafted as a messman.

'What a pig of a life,' he says. 'All you were supposed to do was go down to the Dining Hall and look after the Chiefs and POs. The PO Caterer, who was ultimately your boss, is saying 'There's no clean plates, there's no cutlery,' and the Fleet Chief, Jim Watts, is saying, 'Get your arse in here – you're not supposed to be there.' You're getting shot from both sides. Before the exercise, we still had to stack the tables and get it cleared for action. Then you'd be down the Magazine for six hours. Then you'd have to come back and set up all the tables. It was shit. You'd be coming back into Portland and everybody would be getting ready to go ashore, and I'd be cleaning a gun barrel. By the time you're showered, all the lads are coming back, pissed. I was on the verge of cracking. Put a kid in a position like that . . .'

Dickie Henderson and Errol Flynn, all of 21, would look across the gulch at the likes of Taylor, and Florrie Ford, and recall their own baptisms of fire.

'You've got to adapt to it. You had to pull along,' says Flynn, a pint-sized Brummie.

In the Seamen's Mess, Wyatt Earp, Barry Muncer and Paul Behagg, all teenagers who'd done their initial training at Raleigh around the same time, were going through it too. Brand new, just bad timing to join a ship heading for a COST. The old hands knew the periods of resentment were simply part of grinding off the rough edges.

◆ ◆ ◆

On a Friday morning, even if you'd finished at 0600, even if the weather had abated for a few teasing hours, you weren't allowed to go on leave until 1600.

One Friday, Dave Croft and Mick Newby had both finished watches early. Stay on board? Not if they could help it. In their curtained gulches, the pair furtively crammed civvies into gashbags, then sauntered ashore and headed straight for a toilet block. They walked in in their 8s – their working overalls – walked out in civvies, jumped in Croft's car and, having arranged with PO Clem Clements to field the occasional precautionary phone call, drove off.

'I was going to see this girl in Chatham and Mick was going to Southampton,' Croft admits.

The plan worked until they reached Dorchester and phoned the ship.

'You'd better come back,' Clements told them. 'You've been stitched!'

They thought he was winding them up. He wasn't. They drove back to

Portland, back into the dockyard, concocting alibis. They changed back into their 8s and went back on board.

'The Joss wants to see you,' the Quartermaster told them. It was about three by this time, anyway, so they hadn't gained a thing. Lenny Yeatman took them straight in.

'I don't know what you two've been up to. Tell me.'

'We've been in the dockyard.'

'You haven't been in the dockyard.'

'We've been in the rigging shed.'

'I phoned the rigging shed.'

'We've been in the paint shop.'

'I phoned the paint shop.' The pair felt their chests tighten, but Yeatman couldn't prove anything.

'Get out.' It would be 15 years before he knew the truth.

If Portland was about work hard, it was also about play hard. Sometimes, the two overlapped.

'It was all good-natured fun,' reflects Wacker Payne, at 24 a man of the Forest of Dean whose swift rise to petty officer hadn't dulled his preference for the company of the Junior Rates' Messdeck.

'They put the whaler in by the arse end and, overnight, it developed a leak and sunk to the gunnels. Ralph and Coxie were on duty. I told the rest to bugger off, and I stayed behind.'

That afternoon, the whole L Department turned up on the Flight Deck.

'In 12 hours, we got the boat out, drained it, changed every component, engine, batteries, rewired her, cleaned it and it was ready to go. From that day on, I knew we were getting it right.'

Work hard, play hard, work hard.

'You'd come alongside,' says Bernie Berntsen, 'and the first thing on your mind was going ashore. Everyone would be there. Not just one or two. We'd be out till two in the morning.' And up at five.

Most nights invariably ended at The Breakwater. By this time, too, the youngsters were beginning to find the pace of *Ardent*'s social way of life, though some were more successful at it than others. One night, 18-year-old Wyatt Earp found himself at a Portland club with Florrie Ford, a 'scally' he's always regarded as his little brother. Florrie drank too much and was thrown down the steps.

Earp walked over to him and suggested he walk away. But the 17 year old had other ideas.

'No, I'm going to have him!'

There was a bouncer at the top of the steps and, every time Florrie went up, he was pushed down.

'It was like a comedy,' Earp laughs.

It might have been the same night when Mick Cox, Ken Enticknap, Bernie Berntsen, Coxie, Ralph, Buck Taylor, JJ Smith, Cliff Sharp, Joe Laidlaw and Eddie Edwards were bimbling back from a wet ashore, passing a graveyard. It seemed reasonable that someone should be thrown over the wall.

The thud of well-oiled Mick Cox came after a longer pause than they might

have anticipated, if they'd stopped to think. It was followed by a call on the icy breeze.

'I need a hand!' They looked. The drop was huge. Their amusement was interrupted as a Royal Navy patrol wagon approached slowly, so they did the only thing they could. They threw Ken Enticknap over to help him back.

◆ ◆ ◆

A week before the end of the COST ordeal, Alan West called PO Cook Cliff Goldfinch and told him to organise a Burns' Night Supper. He was planning to entertain guests from 2 Battalion Scots Guards, *Ardent*'s affiliated regiment, and half of the FOST inspection team. Goldfinch can't remember what the menu was that night – in fact, it was Saturday, 30 January, and it was haggis and mashed neeps – but the rest of the evening's etched in his memory.

It was going well. Goldfinch had 'done the old spiel' and was ready to offer Cdr West's guests crêpes Suzette, over which he was ready to pour a vodka and Grand Marnier sauce. A flaming vodka and Grand Marnier sauce. There was one other detail to his plan. At a pre-arranged signal, LMEM Bob Lewis and another member of *Ardent*'s well-practised Portland Damage Control Party men were primed to enter in firefighting suits. But there was one flaw. They didn't have enough stewards.

The lights were dimmed and all went well, until one of Goldfinch's stand-ins somehow managed to pour the flaming sauce over Terry Pendrous's head. Goldfinch whipped his apron off and smothered the flames on the Marine Engineering Officer's face. With an immaculately poor sense of timing, Lewis and his attack party came crashing in, extinguishers primed, yelling, 'Fire! Fire! Fire!'

Goldfinch doesn't remember Terry Pendrous's reaction, but he can still picture the delicate look on Alan West's face the next morning.

'He looked like a shower of shit! He called us a bunch of bastards! Until then he was very aloof. But that morning he won the ship's company.'

As Portland neared its close, the ship's company were beginning to win their skipper too.

'We thought if we can get our jobs done and all of us, all branches, get good marks, maybe Whitehall will think "great ship's company here", and they might give us a little bonus by sending us somewhere nice and warm to show the ship off,' Jan Joyce says.

The time that happened eventually arrived. The afternoon of Thursday, 4 February 1982, brought the promise of sleep and seeing the back of the Enemy. *Ardent*'s COST was over.

There's a faint recollection that she came out with a 'satisfactory', but they knew the final exercise hadn't gone well. In the moments after it, though, with the ship's company gathering in the Junior Ratings' Dining Hall, Knocker White was coming to the conclusion that the scorecard didn't matter.

Though some older hands resented the fact that, at just 21, White was on a fast track to promotion, he laughed it off. Like he laughed off most things.

'When you had a damage control exercise, or anything like that, if you wanted anything done, Knocker was the man to get it done,' PO Eddie Edwards says.

'He was always happy,' according to Jon Major. 'Things like that rub off.'

'He was going to do his own thing,' says Buck Ryan, who slept below his mate in 7 Gulch, with John Bullock at the bottom and Bob Lewis in between.

Buck Taylor could testify what 'his own thing' meant. For Buck's 18th birthday – Saturday, 14 November 1981– Knocker had bought the Geordie a bib and everyone at *Ardent*'s local, the Grand Theatre, had signed it. He treasures it still. But the pair's rapport had begun while Taylor was still 17.

'I'd been on board a week and Knocker's brother Ian, and the *Alacrity*, was in. There were two or three lads from the *Alacrity*, and we went into the Long Bar and got into an almighty fight with lads from 42 Commando.

'I remember getting hold of this Marine and hitting him, and he said, "It wasn't me, mate!" So I let him go, and he chinned us one. Fred Heggarty was still on board at the time. Champion boxer. He just picked us up and put me behind him, and he was just knocking this Marine about.'

Taylor might have been slightly the worse for wear, but the White brothers ended up in hospital. While Brenda White received a phone call from worried doctors and packed little sister Mandy, wrapped in a sleeping bag, into her Robin Reliant for the long drive from Washington, Taylor, Paul Behagg and Fred Heggarty made their way back on board. The next morning, all hell broke loose.

'I knew Ian was badly hurt. He had a fractured skull,' Taylor explains. He was in the Messdeck, aware that Special Investigations Branch was on board, when the Main Broadcast broke his thoughts.

'WEM Taylor to the Regulating Office immediately.' He looked at his new mates.

'Where's the Regulating Office?' Everybody burst out laughing.

At 17, a week into an emergency draft on his first ship, he feared his career was in jeopardy, but he escaped punishment. Fortunately, too, the White brothers both made full recoveries.

◆ ◆ ◆

Tuesday, 4 February, then. After four long, tortuous weeks, they had their ticks in the right boxes.

Earlier during the ordeal, it hadn't looked like happening. On their first Major Fire Exercise, they'd fouled up. At 1700 on the Thursday in question, the FOST staff had walked into the Junior Ratings' Dining Hall to tell them how badly. Maybe they weren't as good as they thought.

'All these guys were sitting there rattling off how they had thought it should be done,' Scouse Phillips recalls. 'And somebody said "Any questions?"'

The FOST staff looked around for takers but didn't find any. Instead, from a group at the back, Knocker began whistling. The Ardents quickly picked up the tune. Within seconds, everyone was singing 'Always Look on the Bright Side of Life'.

'It cracked these people up,' Deputy Marine Engineering Officer Tony Ray, White's Divisional Officer, smiles. 'OK, we hadn't done well, but we'd get it together. They could never do us down.'

Or, as MEM Brum Serrell has it: 'Everyone was walking around with big cheesy grins. They buggered off and that was that. Always look on the bright side of life.' From then on, they did.

THREE

ROSYTH NAVAL BASE, SCOTLAND, TO CARDIGAN BAY, WALES

(19 FEBRUARY – 21 MARCH 1982)

As *Ardent* crept cautiously into the murky Firth of Forth on Friday, 19 February 1982, after a week of shore training, she'd seen the lot. Coxie, Ralph, Bernie, Knocker and the rest of the crowd who called the Grand Theatre home in Plymouth had been banned from The Cochrane Club for using Eddie Edwards as a bowling ball on the dance floor. They could hardly complain. The Cochrane was a ratings' club so, as a PO, he should never have been in there.

Steve Kent, aged 19 and just three months into his first draft as a Tactical Radio Operator, was finding the going hard, spending more time on the Bridge than the one-in-two watches he'd become accustomed to. There should have been three like him sharing the duties but, shortly before sailing, one Ardent had gone ashore to dump the rubbish and never returned.

On the Bridge, Alan West turned to Lt Alan Maunder. 'We're going! Are you confident?'

Maunder nodded, but was quietly growing more nervous. Three months before, he'd abandoned the pursuit of a flying career as an observer and returned to general service. To be appointed as a Frigate Navigator was the natural alternative, but he hadn't banked on the fog blanketing Rosyth – or West's willingness to be the only ship sailing out in it – for his first test. Now here he was, with a commanding officer who didn't know him from Adam, yet was willing to put his ship, his trust and his reputation in an untried Navigator's hands. It set the scene for the rest of Maunder's brief *Ardent* career.

If the plan they'd worked on together was good, the first significant landmark would be the Forth Bridge. Maunder was in radio contact with freezing lookouts, straining to catch the first reassuring glimpses of the massive structure marked on the map.

'Can you see it?' Maunder's anxious voice echoed in the fog.

It was a Bridge Wing lookout who answered.

'Here it is!'

'Which side?'

'No! Look up!' They did.

With a four-week COST gone, what *Ardent* needed now was time in a big team. The Joint Maritime Course was a week of submarine-chasing, Naval

Gunfire Support amid the deceptive beauty of Cape Wrath, and work with Combat Air Patrols. She simply slotted back into Portland mode. The weather was dreadful but nothing they hadn't seen before, even if work on the Upper Deck was still unbearably foul, whatever protection the ratings wore. The only hitch of note came when the Lynx helicopter developed a series of radar faults and flew back to RNAS Yeovilton, leaving *Ardent* to sail from Rosyth for good on Friday, 26 February, with half the Flight missing.

◆ ◆ ◆

Three days after leaving the Forth behind, Alan West turned *Ardent* on a sixpence and took her alongside a jetty in Stavanger, the ship's first port of call at the start of another demanding three-week stint fine-tuning its fighting systems and rehearsing the role NATO had for it in the event of a Russian advance through Norway or via the North Atlantic gap.

On a junior rating's wages, Stavanger was an expensive place to relax. After a raucous, costly night at a disco, 10 or 12 members of the Stokers' Mess ended up at a party. Karoly Nagy can't remember exactly who else was there, but the names Buck Ryan, Andy Cox and Les Pearce bring a flickering smile. He'd joined *Ardent* in Portsmouth 24 hours after the COST ended. His first day had started with a traditional *Ardent* welcome – by being dangled by his nipples down the ladder between 2 and 3 Decks – and had ended in a flat with two dubious-looking women and Knocker White after a run ashore with Ralph Coates in Beasties – a cockroach-infested club – had gone sour. Now, in Norway, by the time Naggers and Buck Ryan arrived, Knocker and Ralph were already in a bedroom, entertaining. The two eventually emerged to find food all over the kitchen, and a distinct lack of Ardents and house plants.

The next morning, Ralph woke, peeled back the curtain in 8 Gulch and saw flowerpots hanging from the vents. With Lenny Yeatman in tow, it wasn't long before the Jimmy was staring at the foliage.

'Where have these come from?' he asked.

'What?' Ralph played the bemused card.

'Is he involved, Master?' Andrew Gordon Lennox turned to Yeatman

The Joss stared at Ralph, unconvinced by the innocent look. 'My office, tomorrow, Sinus.'

The following morning, the Main Broadcast barked, 'MEM Coates to the Regulating Office.'

'Where did you get the plants?' Yeatman asked after Ralph had made the familiar walk.

'Why do you always assume I'm involved?'

'Sinus, I work on the basis that if you're not responsible, you know who is.'

Ralph didn't realise, but the Joss already knew. Minutes before, Karoly Nagy had trodden the same path to explain how one of the larger specimens had found its way into the Regulating Office, with a tag reading, 'From Stavanger, with love, Naggers.'

'Naggers, is it?' Yeatman had enquired.

'That's right!'

The Joss took his glasses off and slid them in his pocket. A second later, Nags was rubbing his forehead. He paused only to ask the Joss a final question.

'Can I have my plant back?'

At the lip of a fjord, the sea becomes shallower and can be mountainous. Waves with 400 yards between peaks and 15 feet tall move ten times closer and tower 50 feet. A south-westerly gale was blowing into the fjord at about 1000 as they left Stavanger for Narvik on Wednesday, 3 March. Alan West had rung his engines down to Slow, but the wave coming their way was still horrifying, a towering wall of green. He stopped both engines, jumped off his chair and braced himself. Around him, men turned their backs and waited for the Bridge windows to crash in.

It was like a bomb going off, but the noise Alan West recalls most came from the two Naval construction experts who were on board to investigate cracks appearing between *Ardent*'s steel hull and aluminium superstructure. He watched daylight emerge and saw the petrified look on their faces.

Below, it sounded as if they'd hit something. In the confines of his cabin, CPO Ken Enticknap had been robbed of his senses. A ship has a natural roll period, and he knew *Ardent*'s. But, as she hovered over the void left by this wave, he had no idea whether they were travelling sidewards or down. All he had in the pit of his stomach, as cupboards crashed open and kit flew across the cabin, was the dread that *Ardent* wouldn't make it back.

In the open Hangar, MEM Wyatt Earp and the rest of the Fire Party were waiting for the Lynx to return after her Yeovilton repairs. As Alan West tried to ride the wave, the aft end had dropped and a second wave was heading for them.

'Fucking grab hold of something!' someone yelled. Earp seized the Hangar door as the wave broke round their feet. Someone lost their footing and slid into the safety netting edging the Flight Deck. In the Lynx, pilot John Sephton made several attempts to land, holding his nerve as his frightened crew rode the roller coaster.

While the Ardents gathered their wits and checked for damage, the main worry was the Exocet containers on the Fo'c'sle and the radar aerials on the communications mast. Below, the Wardroom and Alan West's cabin were taking water, but up top it was a different story. The Bridge screen door was buckled and twisted. Much worse, though, was that the Mark 8 4.5-inch gun was damaged. The turret's umbilical power cord had twisted off its winding gear and locked. Two days before they were due to use it in anger, that was a disaster.

On the Thursday night, a day out of Narvik, CPO Dave Lee sat back in his cabin and began writing.

Thursday, 4 March

My darling Catherine, – sorry – Katy,

At last there is another period of reasonable peace on board after the hassle of the past few days. It may be a lot colder outside now but at least the sea has calmed enough to ensure a reasonable sleep tonight. Whilst we were fuelling today the snow was blowing nearly parallel to the sea.

The ship left the FORACS range yesterday late afternoon after achieving nothing at all because of the weather. We then hit a tremendous sea blown up by the same gale that had raised 100 m.p.h. winds in Scotland. It was frightening to see these huge waves towering up when the ship went into a trough.

I came off the Bridge as it started to get too crowded; shortly afterwards the ship went into a trough and apparently a giant of a wave appeared, towering above the height of the Bridge which was so steep that the ship could never have rode over it. It crashed down on to the ship, even the skipper and the Jimmy ducked as it hit the Bridge windows but all I felt was this big shudder down below.

When we were through the worst of it we then went at 25 knots to meet the *Invincible*, causing us to throw about everywhere and another cat-napping sleep throughout the night.

I didn't have much of a chance to get ashore at FORACS, apart from going to a meeting on Monday morning. It was mainly my gear and radars that were being checked there and most of the work, of course, was on my section.

Also Stavanger was two miles away, it was pouring with rain and those that did go said that there was nothing there anyway, apart from a few expensive shops. £80 for a woolly jumper.

I hope to have a walk ashore in Narvik if the weather isn't too Arctic, but it will just be to stretch the legs and attempt to phone you.

The *Ardent* was the only ship to sail from Rosyth on Saturday morning, much to the disbelief of the other ships there.

I was glad to hear that you say that you are feeling better after your week in Scotland. Don't go drinking all my Johnnie Walker or else I shall keep the brandy all to myself and drink it in front of you out of my crystal glass.

I wish I could give you some advice of my own to help you with Stuart and Sharon but as I am out here away from it all I can only say follow the doctor's advice and let the school stew. As for Sharon, I think the only thing you can do is to be firm and tell her she's going whatever as it only seems to be the mornings she plays up. But I'm not there, so I can't be sure that's the right way to treat her problem.

So, my love, Narvik tomorrow, at sea on Monday and maybe somewhere else the weekend after.

To appreciate these places, imagine that the whole population of

Norway is only four million so wherever we go along the northern coast there isn't much life in these places.

So, goodnight, my lovely, looking forward to three weeks' time and two weeks' leave with you. Sleep tight. Goodnight, my darling.

David. XXXXXXXXXX

I love you Katy

XXXXX Stuart XXXXX Sharon

A day later, *Ardent* met *Invincible* at Narvik. To qualify for Local Overseas Allowance, where pay goes up for the ship's company to live in that country, *Ardent* needed an official excuse to send men ashore. Alan West quickly arranged a sports team.

On board, medic Bob Young always made it a rule to stash his fishing gear away on a foreign run, and so did a number of others. So, after a trip to the Galley, Young and Pete Brouard, *Ardent*'s popular Flight maintainer, had bacon on their hooks and lines dangling in the patch of water melted from the frozen sea by the heat from *Ardent*'s cooling service outlets. The chefs were rewarded for their bait with a mighty cod.

From there, Young recalls, he and Brummie canteen manager John Leake trudged through the Narvik snow to the local museum. For a few minutes, it put life into perspective.

'They've got a German tank outside,' Young remembers. 'It was sad, all these relics of the occupation and the story of the little Norwegian ships that went out and faced the Germans and probably lasted about five seconds.'

Not all was well, though. Behind the happy-go-lucky nature that drove his friendship with Joe Laidlaw and Blood Reed, Eddie Edwards was niggled in the POs' Mess. The married men, who normally lived at home, were running the Mess for their own social purposes, he says, bringing their wives on board when the single men wanted a quiet night in, watching the telly. Before leaving Devonport, he'd decided to run for President of the POs' Mess against the Buffer, Chief Bosun's Mate Mal Crane. But the two had a face-to-face in his cabin one night in Narvik and sorted it out.

For someone like Naggers, only on board a month, it was a frustrating mix of all-for-one and every man for himself, not the camaraderie he recalled from his last frigate, *Galatea. Ardent* was too serious.

Buck Ryan felt even more uneasy during the Ardents' first hours ashore. There's a moral code among matelots, but he watched in horror as messmates stepped over the line.

'I don't know whether it was the frustration of the Joint Maritime Course or the expense. Everyone was stealing. Characters I'd never seen do it before. It's all right to see off someone's pint. That doesn't belong to anybody really. That's not going into shops and having that.'

In particular, the population of stuffed toys in the gulches on *Ardent*'s Junior

Messdeck exploded during the 48 hours the ship was in Narvik. But there was legitimate fun, too. The Ardents met their match in the obligatory snowball fight, this time against a group of local children who repaid their hosts for jelly, ice cream and a Mickey Mouse film in the Junior Ratings' Dining Hall by pounding Bernie Berntsen, Knocker and the rest of the Duty Watch on the jetty.

Elsewhere, while the locals lined up at the chairlift in their colourful fashion statements, skis leaning confidently against their shoulders, gloves tightened against the chilly Norwegian air, the Ardents took their place in the queue. Mick Newby was in a bright-orange once-only suit, the kind that's meant to promote survival if you have to go into water, while Bob Young took a black bin liner and others improvised with blue foulies, standard issue foul-weather gear for the Upper Deck.

At the top of the freezing mountain, some minutes later, Wyatt Earp stepped off the lift in a grey Crombie jacket, Levi's and Dr Martens. It took a lad brought up in the shadow of Elgar's majestic Malvern Hills to realise that Franz Klammer had met Frank Spencer.

Once they were up the mountain, of course, they had to find a way down. It wasn't long before the locals, Gucci people who could transfer weight gracefully from one leg to the other on a treacherous 45-degree slope, stood open-mouthed as Newby's Belisha beacon and tables stripped of their Martini umbrellas flew past on a series of suicide runs. The Stokers' Mess took first prize, John Goddard insists, for the three or four they managed to pack on a snow shovel.

In general, the only concern most of the ship's company had was the cost of maintaining the standard set in Amsterdam, though for some it didn't start well. Free of his Quartermaster duties – in charge of the gangway, checking that everything was secure in compartments and spaces, wrapped against minus 14 in heated suits loaned by the Gunnery section – Dave Croft went ashore that night, found a burger van on the side of the road, bought £5 worth of chips, turned round and fell over. The chips went everywhere.

Fleet Chief Tony Ray and *Ardent*'s other Warrant Officer, Jim Watts, had taken up an invitation to join a party of Marines on the other side of the fjord. The heated bus ride there made perfect sense of the decision to leave their coats on board, but the back of a truck, tail-sheet flapping in the breeze on the way home, didn't.

Back on board, the night still enticingly young, their only remedy was a whisky, followed by another, and another, before going ashore with the rest of the Chiefs' Mess. Hours later, brim-full, the only thing separating them from the Junior Ratings was style. No bin liners or table tops for them. Ray and Watts tobogganed down the hill on their Naval raincoats.

Back in the Chiefs' Mess, warmed inside and out, the night went on. One deck above, MEO Terry Pendrous soon gave up trying to sleep. Instead, he sat on the edge of his bunk and joined in the singing from below. At about the same time, most of his young stokers were staggering through the snowy Narvik streets, heading home. Below, picked out by moonlight, was *Ardent*. Errol Flynn looked down to the sea, then the pint-sized Brummie's tired eyes happened upon a sledge, discarded by the side of the road. That's how he remembers it, anyway.

'As I came to the top of the hill, it was just sat there,' he says. 'I honestly . . .

I'd had a few beers, but it was just there. At that time of night, I thought someone had forgot it.'

Before long, while Ralph Coates, Knocker White, Buck Taylor and Wacker Payne were taking it in turns to ride down the hill, Errol was engrossed by the thought of how it might handle the flat pavements of Castle Vale.

'We liked this sledge a lot. Well, I did,' he admits. So a plan was hatched. The returning hands pushed the sledge to the edge of the jetty, leaving two rail tracks carved in the snow, to give the impression they'd pushed it into the water. Instead, they carried it to the end of the Fo'c'sle and handed it up to JJ Smith.

While the young Ardents toed the tenuous line between rogue and wrong, in the relative warmth of the Chief's Mess Dave Lee penned his second letter home in three days.

Saturday 6 March

My dearest darling Catherine,

My heart is with you tonight on this otherwise boring night in the upper reaches of the world at Narvik. I didn't think at first that I could write to you because when this so familiar mood sets in there is very little I can do but sit in the Mess and stare at the ceiling.

I have been ashore here today, but Saturday is early closing, apart from a couple of gift shops, so there was nothing much at all ashore to buy or talk about. But oh! So expensive.

I had a letter from you yesterday which has settled my mind a lot about you and the children at home. It isn't easy for me either to wonder how you and the children are coming along.

Today ashore it was freezing. I had two pairs of socks plus my steaming boots but the cold still got through to my toes. It snowed continually all day yesterday but although the sky was clear today and sunny there is no sign of the snow melting because of the temperature.

Even if the shops had been open, there was nowhere that I saw that I could buy some seeds or a plant for Stuart. I was looking for a phone box today – which I found – but all I have at the moment is a 100 Kroner note (£9) and change is difficult to come by. I will try again tomorrow if I can face the cold.

It is now midnight here and I have this terrible need at the moment for a feel of your right breast so before you think that I am totally unromantic or just plain crude I will now go to bed and keep my thoughts to myself.

Goodnight, my lovely. Keep the bed warm. Loving you as always.

David. XXXXXXXXXX

XXXXX Stuart XXXXX Sharon X Patch X Snowy

The next morning, Errol Flynn had barely dragged his thumping head off the pillow before the Tannoy boomed, 'MEM Flynn to the Regulating Office!'

He hauled himself up to Lenny Yeatman's office and closed the door.

'It won't go any further, but if you don't tell me where that sledge is . . .' the Joss started.

'What sledge?'

'You've been seen throwing it over the jetty. Before we leave, I want that sledge found. Go down the Bosun's Store, get a grappling hook and some rope . . .'

On his way back from the Stores, he stopped by the Ship Control Centre. Terry Pendrous walked in with a smile brimming.

'Where's the sledge?' he asked. Errol realised they couldn't keep the subterfuge going. They took him up to the Funnel, through a small hatch, and showed him where it was hidden.

Later that morning, Yeatman's deputy, Leading Regulator Ken Chapman, took the sledge back to its owner, an old lady, and offered his apologies.

◆ ◆ ◆

On Sunday, 7 March, like most mornings, *Ardent* sailed early. But, this time, she left Narvik for good. The sledge, the ski slopes, the clubs, the mortgage-sized drink prices; the little house at the end of the jetty where the light was always on, the place the Quarterdeck party had wanted to live these past few days because it looked so cosy. Most Ardents remember what happened soon after that, and where they were, though at the time the event was unimportant.

Radio Operator John Foster was on her starboard Bridge wing, PO Cook Cliff Goldfinch was on the Bridge, the two young Bucks and Jake Jacobs were on Upper Deck, swathed in heated suits, soldering electronics on the Seacat system. The list goes on.

John Sephton and his observer, Brian Murphy, were in the Lynx, capturing an image of the Type 21, sleek, powerful, purposeful, racing north to join the other ships on Operation Alloy Express. It would be three months before any of them saw Murphy's picture, but it remains the one Ardents treasure.

In the following days, they honed their skills in Naval Gunfire Support, escorted *Invincible* and the USS *Guadalcanal*, supported amphibious landings involving the Royal and US Marines, and found out more about how they'd reinforce the left flank of NATO from an over-the-top Russian advance.

It was as if barely a moment had passed since Knocker White's rendition of 'Always Look on the Bright Side of Life' a month before.

'We were probably 99.9 per cent there,' says Mick Newby. 'Everyone else was 95 per cent, but we'd just been through these weeks of sheer hell. We went up there and knocked the socks off them.'

'The main point for me,' Weapons Director Richie Gough recalls, 'was the amount of time we spent doing NGS. We were working with the Americans and we'd done a good job.'

The Ops Room was buzzing.

'You trained for everything, gunnery or anti-surface warfare,' PWO Tom

Williams adds. 'John Sephton had won the ASW Trophy and I wanted to win it again. To do that you have to exercise with the helicopter a lot. Whenever we had an opportunity, we did.'

The work was hard, though. JMC was one of the toughest exercises. The hours were long, six on and six off at Defence Watches, a big learning curve where you either caved in or came up smiling, where new men had a chance to gel, where ratings could work towards their killick rate, where a leading hand could pass on his experience, and a PO worth his salt would do the same.

The weather was grim, but *Ardent* pressed on. Not that she wasn't allowed to forget that she was the Canteen Boat. She still found herself going 20 miles down-screen to 20 miles up, heavy seas all the way, playing handmaiden to the likes of *Invincible*.

Among other things, it presented Cliff Goldfinch with a particular problem because, when the seas were high, fat-fried chips were off the menu. He had the perfect solution.

'We didn't get many for a midnight meal. I thought "Sod it! We'll do a candlelight dinner."'

He swiped candles from the Wardroom Galley and set to. As men came off watch, his cooks welcomed the guests into the Dining Hall, showed them the menu and read out the day's offering – 'It's stew, stew, stew or stew!'

Goldfinch sat them down and fetched a mug of tea or coffee. Such distractions were priceless. For most of their off-watch time, however, the Ardents did what matelots do. They set time aside to sit down and write a letter, and think of home. Then, when it was written, it was time to forget about what they couldn't control and concentrate on what they could.

◆ ◆ ◆

The final week of Alloy Express went in the same manner – foul weather, hard work, the warm feeling of a job well done. At the end of it, the name mentioned most, by his young ratings above all, was Alan West's.

'When the guy was on that Bridge, everyone was aware he was special,' was how Leading Seaman Dave Croft saw it.

'There was this aura around him,' Mick Newby adds. 'If he congratulated you, the old hairs on the back of your neck would come up. If I got one in all the time I was on the *Ardent*, that was it.'

The bright side of life?

'We were superior,' Newby says.

The 13th HMS *Ardent* was a 2,750-ton Type 21 Amazon-class frigate, built at Yarrow Shipyard in Glasgow, launched by the Duchess of Gloucester on Friday, 9 May 1975, and commissioned on Friday, 14 October 1977. She bore her motto, *Through Fire and Water*, proudly, and with good reason.

The 981-ton First World War destroyer, costing £116,335, was launched on

Monday, 8 September 1913. Just before midnight on Wednesday, 31 May 1916, she was the eighth in a line of 11 4th Flotilla destroyers closest to the German Battle Fleet, steaming south-east off the north Danish coast.

Ship by ship, in a rapid sequence of disasters shaped by coincidence and error, the Flotilla was mauled by German battleships in what became known as the Battle of Jutland. *Ardent* survived, but all she had saved herself for was a sickeningly one-sided final encounter.

At 0120 on Thursday, 1 June, separated from the remnants of the Flotilla, moments after witnessing the end of the *Black Prince*, *Ardent* sighted smoke while searching for her division. She turned to it. By the time her crew realised she was heading for the leading German battleships, 900 yards away, it was too late. One of them, the 18,569-ton Nassau-class dreadnought battleship *Westfalen*, lit up *Ardent* with her searchlights. Twenty-two rounds of 5.9-inch and eighteen 3.5-inch shells turned her into an inferno. Even by the events of a night on which 13 other British warships were lost, it was overkill. Only a wreck remained when the German ships switched off their searchlights and slid into darkness.

At 0930, Admiral Jellicoe, aboard *Iron Duke*, passed through the wreckage. Moments before, lifebelts from *Ardent* had been discovered among it. Seventy-eight men were dead and one wounded.

At 1,350 tons, the Acasta-class destroyer built for £228,783 and launched on Wednesday, 26 June 1929, was a bigger ship, yet still half the size of Alan West's, minuscule compared with the heavy German battlecruisers she faced on Saturday, 8 June 1940, four weeks after being sent to protect the evacuation of Norway.

At 1600 that day, the *Scharnhorst* was looking for a group of British warships north-west of the Andfjord when a masthead lookout sighted smoke on the starboard bow. It was the aircraft carrier *Glorious*, making for home ahead of her strongest defences, it was officially explained, because of a lack of fuel. Escorting her, 200 miles from the mutual safety of the main convoy, were *Ardent* and *Acasta*.

Decisively, *Scharnhorst* positioned herself so that *Glorious* would have steam towards the enemy to launch her planes into wind. At about 1720, *Scharnhorst* opened fire with her secondary armament at 28,000 yards. Not at *Glorious*, but at her escorts. Then she turned her main guns on the carrier.

Ardent and *Acasta* did all they could to protect *Glorious*, laying down smoke screens. *Glorious* did what she could, too, but her 4.7-inch shells were useless against the German ship. Her Forward Upper Hangar was soon hit, destroying her Hurricane Flight. Then *Gneisenau* opened up, hitting her Bridge.

The two destroyers laid more smoke but, when *Glorious* emerged from their screen, both German warships opened up again. She was soon listing and on fire.

Ardent emerged from the smoke twice to attack *Gneisenau*. Briefly, it seemed her final torpedo would claim its victim. But it didn't. For her impudence, *Scharnhorst* and *Gneisenau* ripped into her too. She sank in four minutes. Moments later, *Glorious* sank as well. Despite striking the torpedo blows that sent *Scharnhorst* skulking inshore for repairs, *Acasta* was sent down

too. The final entry in the Ministry of Defence's *Record of Ship Movements* for the day is chillingly short: '*Glorious* was last heard of on 8/6 and since that date all attempts to get in touch with her and her escort have failed. The three ships are therefore presumed lost.'

Of the 1,515 men aboard the three ships, 45 were saved. Two were Ardents. Only one survived the war.

◆ ◆ ◆

Around mid-morning on Wednesday, 17 March 1982, the lines drawn on a chart of the Norwegian Sea south-west of the Lofoten Islands brought *Ardent* to the spot where, almost 42 years earlier, the last *Ardent* had gone down. The Flight Deck was solemn and cold as Cdr West was handed a wreath procured in Rosyth. With her engines idling and the hum of her auxiliaries riding the sharp breeze, he recited their predecessors' history, explaining what had taken them there and the sacrifice made without thought.

'If we're faced with the same problem, I hope we'll take the same difficult decision,' he told them.

As Ken Enticknap blew his bugle, and 'Last Post' echoed round the Flight Deck, the Ardents paid their respects in silence.

'Obviously he wasn't a bugle player by trade,' says Buck Taylor, who was among them. 'But it was poignant.'

As he played, Enticknap's mind went back 40-odd years. They all knew the fate of anyone who fell in the water and wasn't rescued within ten minutes. Fewer, probably. Bob Young was thinking the same. So were most of them, staring into a Force 6 wind, wondering if it was only being a sailor that could make you feel that way, thinking of their namesake – a happy ship? – and of life in a blue suit.

Radio Operator John Foster lifted his gaze and looked at Lenny Yeatman. There were tears rolling down the Master at Arms' cheeks.

◆ ◆ ◆

Commodore Mike Clapp hadn't met Alan West before discovering *Ardent* would be on Operation Alloy Express and under his direction from his Amphibious Command Ship, HMS *Fearless*. Neither had he rubbed shoulders with Cdr Nick Tobin or his Antelopes.

'Everybody was saying he was an up-and-coming star,' he remembers of West. 'I liked them both. I went on board both ships, and spent pretty well a day with them, and you got a feel immediately. Once you've been around a few ships you walk on board and, in seconds, you know if you like it or not.'

He didn't come away from Alloy Express with the view that *Ardent* or her skipper were any better than anyone else, but what did capture his attention was the ship's companies' willingness to come up with ideas, and their enthusiasm.

'We explored one or two things about the defence of ships in fjords and stuff, which was good fun.'

They learnt, in particular, how to station ships near land to make it so hard

for fast jets to fly the right lines and tight circles that an attack was almost impossible.

By Thursday, 18 March, though, Alloy Express was history, lessons learnt, filed away. What lay ahead for *Ardent* was Operation Larder, off the north of Scotland, trailing a Soviet Primorye spy ship that had been shadowing them for a couple of days. Leading Seaman Dave Croft recalls it being around every time duty took him to the Bridge. Eventually, Alan West had enough.

'Wind him in,' he ordered.

He stepped on to the Bridge Wing and saluted the Primorye's captain. The enemy saluted back and, as he did, West gave his command: 'Lever nine-zero!'

Ardent's nose rose, smoke punched from her funnel and the Primorye was left in her wake.

'It was brilliant,' Croft remembers.

A day later, as *Ardent* made her way towards the Western Isles, Argentinian scrap merchants raised their national flag in Leith, South Georgia. A day after that, as she navigated the shallow Kyles of Lochalsh, a Royal Marine party was heading for South Georgia from the Falkland Islands capital, Stanley, on board HMS Endurance. The ice patrol vessel was commanded by Capt Nick Barker, the son of Lt Cdr Chris Barker, the brave commanding officer of the last *Ardent*.

All this passed *Ardent* by, however, for every man on board had their minds 8,000 miles closer still, the Exocet range off the Welsh coast at Aberporth. Then home for Easter.

For Chief GI Pete Rowe, Aberporth was all-consuming. He'd spent a month worrying; about the complex series of keystrokes he'd have to make in the heart of *Ardent*'s Ops Room; about not having time to read that sequence off a cue card; about his peers heaping pressure on him to do it right; about his 23-year-old Weapons Director itching to do it instead; that it would all have to be perfect, that half-a-million pounds of lethal missile would be at his fingertip.

He'd been worrying so much, his Chiefs' Mess colleagues had given their moral support by telling him a VIP was coming on board to do it instead. He feared the weather would be against him. But that didn't matter. *Ardent* could control the system. Lt Tom Williams had even been hand-picked to liaise by radio in Welsh with the man in the range hut.

By the time *Ardent* went to action stations, closed down in case the Exocet left its container just beneath the Bridge and punched an expensive hole in a Type 21 rather than a barge covered in lattice metalwork, the tension had reached every last flat and space. Every man had been told how to behave: don't breathe the fumes of it, the fumes will kill you; don't look at the flash, the flash will blind you; face away from the Bridge.

The range hut gave the all-clear, the drills were followed, Rowe pushed the button and, from his position in the Ops Room, Principal Warfare Officer Mike Knowles thought it had all gone perfectly.

Wyatt Earp recalls the explicit warning not to stray near the Upper Deck: 'We all stayed at the door, and this thing went shooting off. It dropped down, 15 feet or something above the water, and the noise . . . we all just shot back in!'

'Everyone was walking round the Bridge like this, with anti-flash gloves on,'

Dave Croft peeps through his fingers. 'It just went woof! What a noise. But it was gone.' Gone, but not where intended.

'I think we were the first ship to miss with one,' First Lieutenant Andrew Gordon Lennox shrugs.

'I couldn't believe it. How the bloody hell could we miss?' Mike Knowles remains disconcerted.

'Bit of a damp squib,' Pete Rowe puts a brave face on it. 'We had the weather against us.'

The data showed that a switch drill hadn't been done properly. Otherwise, the exercise had been a success. *Ardent* could fire a missile and do it quickly.

Not everyone read it the same way. The Stokers' Mess was already planning a hard time for the gunners on their way back to Devonport. Devonport and Easter leave. And major repairs to the gun and Forward Citadel door.

It was only as they steamed out of Cardigan Bay on Sunday, 21 March, that news of South Georgia and the Falklands began to filter through. For many young Ardents, most thinking of two weeks at home, at least 14 planning to invade the Norfolk Broads, the puzzle was why a bunch of Argentinian scrap merchants had landed on a string of islands off Scotland.

◆ ◆ ◆

Lt Cdr Alberto Philippi looks in on his three sleeping children, gives his wife Graciela a kiss goodbye and pulls off the drive on his daily journey to the Rio Grande base. But, after driving 20 yards, he remembers the woollen gloves and scarf he's taken home to be washed. His mother, Margarethe Zander, has knitted them for the cold southern weather and he doesn't want to fly without them. Graciela's still at the front door as he goes back.

Minutes later, now Skyhawk pilot, no longer husband, father or son, he's being briefed about the British invasion at San Carlos and the first division's early sortie. Then, with his wingmen, Lt Marcelo 'Loro' Marquez and Lt Jose Arca, he begins planning their own mission: sifting intelligence, learning the enemy force's deployment, checking communications and identification codes.

The squadron pilots have been preparing themselves for the mission since the Argentinian aircraft carrier *25 de Mayo* returned to Puerto Belgrano suffering mechanical failures thirteen days ago – Saturday, 8 May 1982 – six days after the sinking of the cruiser *ARA General Belgrano*. During the next three days, its Third Attack Squadron had flown 2,000 miles south to Rio Grande Naval Air Station, Tierra del Fuego.

From that day on, the squadron's pilots had been preparing themselves for the coming fight. The tension could almost be wrung between their hands. Now, Friday, 21 May 1982, the day has come. Philippi knows his flight to the target area will last 58 minutes. The flight plan, designed to avoid enemy radar, will take them to 30,000 feet until they're a hundred miles from the island shore. An easy descent over the next 50 will put them 100 feet from the wave tops, 450 knots, deployed for anti-ship attack.

FOUR

DEVONPORT NAVAL BASE, PLYMOUTH

(24 MARCH – 10 APRIL 1982)

The start of *Ardent*'s Assisted Maintenance Period on Wednesday, 24 March, brought good news or bad, depending on your outlook. The damage caused to her 4.5-inch gun would take nine weeks to repair. Nine weeks. So half of the ship's company hurried off on leave, desperate for a rest, anticipating the long stay in Devonport before heading back for the Clyde, then touring the islands looking for submarines and meeting up with the 2nd Battalion Scots Guards, *Ardent*'s affiliated regiment.

PO Cook Cliff Goldfinch was among the first 20 or so to discover that even those plans might be fluid. He was preparing Alan West's dinner party for the Scots Guards when *Ardent* was tugged clear to let two other 21s come alongside. As she was being pulled away, any doubts he had about the South Atlantic were swept aside as ammunition trucks began arriving through the Naval Dockyard's St Leven's Gate. Ammunition was normally loaded from a buoy in the channel.

If Lt Mike Knowles had doubts about his posting as Naval Liaison Officer at the Royal Military Academy, Sandhurst, they were reinforced before he even met his replacement, an Australian.

'If anything happens,' Andrew Gordon Lennox took him to one side, 'we want you back. And by the way,' he added, 'the Captain's going if he gets half a chance.'

Chief Stoker Andy Andrew, not long married, was another with a draft chit in his hand, two *Ardent* years done, looking forward to finishing with the sea and painting the house.

For Chief GI Pete Rowe, the frustration was different. From the moment he found out his Mark 8 gun would take nine weeks to fix, he felt as if he was missing out. He needn't have worried.

'Dockyard matey usually did the square root of bugger all,' Scouse Phillips explains. 'Give them their due, the buggers pulled their finger out. Twenty-five hours a day to fix the stuff in two weeks.' Suddenly, *Ardent*'s immediate future looked less certain.

Whatever the Argentinian dictator, General Leopoldo Galtieri, had in mind for the Falklands, he did Norfolk a favour. Fourteen Ardents were going on holiday to the Broads, Mick Foote, Bernie Berntsen, Knocker White, Soapy Watson, Tug Wilson, Mark Bramwell, Andy Cox, Paddy Samson, Ralph

Coates, Jan Joyce and Scouse among them, seven each in two boats. They'd put £40 each in the beer kitty and Foote was due to be in charge of reheating 14 cases of stew. They'd even decided who would do colours and sunset.

One of them was deployed to write a letter apologising for the cancellation. 'We weren't allowed to say where we were going,' Phillips explains. 'So the letter went something along the lines of "Due to operational circumstances . . ."'

So much for security. A perfumed letter arrived by return: 'We understand you're going to the Falklands. Would you like us to postpone the holiday for your return?' They didn't.

◆ ◆ ◆

With the gun being fixed rapidly, some hands were taking their draft chits and leaving, and new faces were arriving. Buck Taylor's pub-fight saviour, Fred Heggarty, was one who went. As he left, his relief came on board, Acting Leading Marine Engineering Mechanic Garry Whitford.

One man absolutely convinced that *Ardent* was going nowhere was Lt David Searle. Convinced, even though an Argentinian invasion force had left Puerto Belgrano on Sunday, 28 March. Two things made him certain. One, the gun still wasn't ready. Two, he was due to marry the next Saturday.

Four days later – Thursday, 1 April – the Argentinians invaded the Falklands and, 8,000 miles away, the British Government made public what Devonport had known for days, that preparations had started to send a Task Force to take them back. In the privacy of his cabin, Alan West was thumbing through *Jane's* and coming to a rapid conclusion. The main threat would come from the air.

◆ ◆ ◆

Buck Ryan and Karoly Nagy were on a 125 heading to Dorchester, Ryan going home to Portland, Naggers heading to see his parents in Hemel Hempstead. That's as much as either are sure about. What isn't clear is where the duty-frees came from, even if it was good to be celebrating their escape.

'Naggers doesn't drink spirits,' Buck explains. 'He generally sneezes after it. We was singing and being particularly obnoxious and I'm sure all these people were totally pissed off with us.'

'We was trying to get everyone to sing,' Nags adds. 'I'm one of those . . . I only know the first line of every song. That's as far as I go.' It wasn't, however, as far as either of them went in search of fun.

'Getting out and trying to climb on top of the train was obviously not a good idea,' Ryan concedes. 'I don't remember why the fuck we done that.' They both made it home in one piece, somehow.

◆ ◆ ◆

The first Lenny Yeatman heard of the invasion was on the Saturday morning as he loaded the car to take Beryl and the children to the in-laws in the Cotswolds.

His neighbour shouted the news to him. He thought no more about it.

On the other side of the world, about the same time, after a battle with the Royal Marine party put ashore by Nick Barker's *Endurance*, Argentinian forces took Grytviken, South Georgia.

In a car park in Reigate, the Radio 4 time check announced 11 as David Searle and a couple of friends listened to the Emergency Debate in the House of Commons. Wearing his dress uniform and a ceremonial sword borrowed from *Ardent*'s Lynx observer, Brian Murphy, he was about to walk into church for his wedding, remarkably cool.

'But if your ship's not going to sea,' he shrugs, 'it's not hard to be cool.'

Three hours later, Andrew Gordon Lennox was weeding his garden, a radio in the wheelbarrow, listening to the same debate. But he didn't share his junior officer's outlook. Within a couple of hours, Alan West had phoned and they'd decided it was time to go back. He was upset that *Ardent* couldn't sail with the Task Force. But his men knew exactly what they were doing. If one leave party was recalled, the other could have the weekend. Then they'd be ready if the call came.

The next day, the aircraft carriers *Hermes* and *Invincible* sailed from Portsmouth under escort. Politically, the United States demanded Argentina's withdrawal from the islands. It had no effect.

At ten o'clock, Lenny Yeatman was digging the garden at his in-laws' near Bourton-on-the-Hill when a CB-user called. The ship had been bouncing a message from breaker to breaker across the Cotswolds, trying to locate the family. Lenny put his spade down and rang the ship.

'What's it about?' he asked Duty Officer Richie Gough moments later.

'The Falklands. You've got to come back.' That was it. For Gough, it would be a long, hard day.

Ken and Frankie Enticknap were about to decorate the nursery in their Plymouth home. She was three months pregnant. They'd been watching the news. She thought the United Nations would have it sorted out before *Ardent* was anywhere near, even if the ship sailed. The phone went. He was gone.

Carole Leake was in Birmingham with husband-to-be John, *Ardent*'s civilian Naafi canteen manager, visiting his mum, thinking of him going back to Civvie Street.

A neighbour told the former Devon & Dorsets squaddie that he had to phone Plymouth. In minutes, they were heading south, his mind on stores, but not before he'd scribbled a will and given it to his brother David. Carole? She saw no reason to worry about something that might not happen.

Errol Flynn was decorating his bedroom in Castle Vale, on Birmingham's northern suburban fringe, when a policeman rang the doorbell. His mum called him down.

'You know what I've come for, don't you?' the bobby said.

Errol turned to his folks and shrugged. 'I've got to go guys!' They were worried. A couple of hours later, he was on the train to Plymouth.

In Rotherham, Eddie Edwards's mum rang him at a mate's house. 'They want you to go back,' she told him.

He thought she was joking. 'I'll go back tomorrow.'

She wasn't having any of it. He caught the eight o'clock Sunday night train from Sheffield. They said goodbye on the platform.

◆ ◆ ◆

Pete and Renee Hanson still have a photo in their house of Shaun as a five year old, with a Navy cap on. Not long into his apprenticeship at a Sheffield engineering company, he arrived home one day and told his folks he'd joined up. Mum didn't say a lot. He hadn't completed his shore training before a temporary draft took him to *Ardent*. He loved it.

On his weekend leave, the young steward rang the Duty Officer and was told they'd call him back later. As a relief, only 20, he didn't have to go if *Ardent* sailed.

'But he said he wanted to, so he did,' Pete recalls. Shaun finally went back on the Sunday evening. They weren't worried. It would blow over.

The day before, *Ardent*'s Deputy Marine Engineering Officer, Tony Ray, had driven his family through the gates at Sandhurst, for a wedding, not knowing the police were looking for him. The gate sentry had asked him why he wasn't off fighting in the Falklands.

'Why?' Ray asked in return.

'They've invaded.'

In the back seat, Stuart Ray knew something was wrong. His dad called the ship. Within hours, the nine year old was back in the car with his sisters, Liz and Helen, and his mum was telling them it might not come to anything. The ship was only on standby. Deep down, though, Stuart didn't believe her. On the A38, they passed the Yeatmans. Soon after, they encountered a convoy of 40-ton trucks, full of troops and supplies. He craned his neck to look, as the mood in the car grew sombre.

The recalls went on. John Foster and his fiancée Jane had just arrived at a hotel in West Chiltingdon, on the Sussex Downs, oak beams and whitewashed walls, when the hotel owner greeted them.

'Are you Mr Foster?' Scouse nodded. The Joss was on the phone. A few hours later, they were at Jane's parents' in London. He threw some kit into a bag, then they drove to Paddington.

'If you don't come back, I'll kill you,' were her final tearful words.

Buck Ryan's folks were down from Chatham when the Regulator knocked on his door, ready to drive him to the station. But his dad insisted on running him all the way to the dockyard. When they arrived there, Ryan's wife, Teresa, climbed out and gave him a kiss.

In Malvern, Wyatt Earp was painting his brother's bathroom when his dad walked in with a plan hatched as near as matters 40 years before.

'You need to go back,' he told the 18 year old. 'I've told them you're away.'

It had worked once before. But Earp wouldn't follow his father's Second World War cycle tracks.

'No, I'd better get back,' he told him. It wasn't bravado. He was convinced they'd reach Ascension and turn home. Typical. No commitments, no imagination, no worries. That attitude would come to test the fuses of some older colleagues. But not yet.

Newlywed Lt David Searle had been convinced he ran the risk of hitting a foreign air-traffic-control strike, or a ferry work-to-rule, so he'd booked a honeymoon in Wales. He rang in every morning, but the First Lieutenant gave him a few days' grace.

Distant memories of Rosyth were conjured for Steve Kent, when his 22-year-old mate Jeff Gullick arrived from Yorkshire, via HMS *Mercury*, to replace the radio operator whose short walk to ditch gash bags hadn't stopped at the dockyard gates.

Fate wasn't as kind to Dickie Henderson. Still stunned at going home the previous summer and finding his wife had packed her bags, the big stoker was celebrating his 21st at his mother-in-law's on Tuesday, 6 April, when his dad phoned.

It's safe to assume their short conversation didn't include the fact that Francis Pym had succeeded Lord Carrington as Foreign Secretary, or that US Secretary of State Al Haig had begun a shuttle diplomacy mission, desperate to broker a deal to keep allies Argentina and Britain from war. The same day, at about 1100, Cliff Goldfinch wandered on board in civvies. Lenny Yeatman asked him what he was doing.

'I'm on leave.' No one had told him.

Within 24 hours, Alan West's recall had been answered in full. It had been a breathless few days. But it would become more frantic. With every returning man, the job of storing the ship, making her ready for the unknown, gathered momentum. All each could see were people and trucks everywhere. The dockyard mateys had been busy.

On *Ardent*, Goldfinch was told to start restoring provisions for 48 days, the maximum she could hold. He went through the books and began his task. Big John Leake wasn't far behind, his search for a settled life in Civvie Street on hold. As he walked towards South Yard's Wharf 13, the canteen manager glanced up at the activity on board. One of the lads spotted him.

'Are you going to come with us?' came the call.

'I'm going to have to come with you. I wouldn't be able to sleep at night thinking of you all!'

He knew the first thing to order. Beer. He had a space for all the spirits and tobacco, anything that would keep morale high, biscuits, as much nutty as he could find. He didn't expect to sell many gifts.

Supply Officer Rick Banfield was the busiest man on board, as storing went on round the clock. Everyone brought the food, drink, cans of soft drink, cold stores and fresh veg on board. Fresh water was handled by the stokers. So was fuel, oil and grease, and other engine room materials. After the week of NGS at Cape Wrath, the Magazine was also in need of replenishment. If there was a hole, they were filling it. In the end, the passageways were stacked with tins of beans, and tins of peas, and steak and kidney pies. The Fridge Flat, on 3 Deck, was stacked three boxes high with corned beef. Argentinian corned beef. Then

they'd go home, or relax in the Mess, and watch the politicians shuttle between Argentina and America on the news. But *Ardent* still had no orders. Instead, some of them would sit on the Flight Deck during the evening, and others would wander ashore, all trying to fill in the missing pieces.

By Wednesday, 7 April, the War Cabinet had launched Operation Paraquet to retake South Georgia. On Thursday, 8 April, Britain gave Argentina four days' notice of a 200-mile Maritime Exclusion Zone around the Falklands, Buenos Aires responded with its own South Atlantic Operations Zone, and those Ardents who'd been on board over Easter began a long weekend leave.

Atlantic Conveyor came into the basin one day, opposite *Ardent*, and work began on equipping her to carry eight Sea Harriers, six Harriers, eight Wessex choppers and five Chinooks. At 696 feet long, she dwarfed the 384-foot frigate. She was going but, on *Ardent*, there was still uncertainty.

◆ ◆ ◆

The dark-blue sky of early dawn was giving way to a lighter shade over Dartmoor when Lt Tom Williams, *Ardent*'s Ops Officer, strode into Plymouth's Roborough Airport shortly before 0700 on Friday, 9 April, Good Friday. In minutes, he'd joined Alan West and the commanding officer of the frigate HMS *Argonaut,* Capt Kit Layman, and his Ops Officer, on a flight to Heathrow. From there, a car drove them straight to HQ CinC Fleet, in Northwood. As soon as Alan West stepped inside, his belief that Britain was entering a shooting war became a conviction.

'I didn't believe the Argentinians would step down,' he says, 'and it was quite clear . . . you can tell when the Government starts releasing the money.'

Ardent's first role soon became apparent. Submarines had already sailed in secret, and the vanguard of the Task Force had gone in full media glare, but they had no intelligence on the Argentinian surface threat. *Ardent* would take that to *Ascension*. The outlook for the rest of her deployment was laid out in front of them too. Then West asked an unexpected question.

'What about Stingrays?'

Stingray torpedoes were in development. After a short delay, the answer came back. There were some pre-production versions available, and they'd be with *Ardent* by the Monday.

At the end of the briefing, West and the two others set off for Heathrow while Williams waited for the intelligence material. An RAF corporal brought it, stuffed in a briefcase, then Williams took the Tube, aware that everyone was reading their paper or talking about the crisis, little knowing the man opposite was carrying the material which might play a part in bringing it to an end. When the train pulled into Plymouth, Williams headed straight for *Ardent*. Understandably.

◆ ◆ ◆

Cliff Goldfinch walked towards the waitress. He'd been allowed a weekend with his parents, and he'd watched *Canberra* leave Southampton after a two-day refit. He went to pay the bill.

'What ship are you on?'

'HMS *Ardent.*'

'Why aren't you there?'

'We go soon,' he said, then touched the crest on his *Ardent* sweater, a flaming torch, discreet on his chest. 'Take note. You'll hear a lot of that.'

It was the first time he'd had a premonition, he says. It wasn't the last.

In Wiltshire, that weekend, Alan West paid his parents a visit. They were at dinner, discussing the prospect of war, when his mother asked exactly what he expected.

'Well,' he drew a breath, choosing to paint a picture that wouldn't alarm her. 'If we have a couple of aircraft coming at us . . . in open water, it isn't a problem. Start getting more than that and we have a problem.'

His mind didn't have to go back far to know the wisdom of his assessment and, after his Northwood briefing, its implications. Alloy Express was a very recent memory, and he knew his ship was the best Type 21, a boast backed by hard evidence, the Plessey Trophy for underwater warfare, the Gunnery Trophy, and others besides. But he also knew the one area a 21 was not good at, any 21, was defence against fast ground-attack aircraft close in to shore. Portland had proved it time and time again.

'Our radars were not optimised,' he admits. 'Anti-submarine warfare, we were good at. Open ocean against long-range missiles, we were very competent at. Surface-to-surface warfare, we were extremely good at, probably best of all. But the area we were not very good at was inshore anti-air warfare.'

◆ ◆ ◆

It was a knock at the door, not a phone call, that brought Easter leave to an end for Bill Bailey, the Flight's radar engineer. It came one afternoon. It was Allan McAulay, his Senior Flight Maintainer.

'Change of plan,' Mac announced to the 35 year old. 'Get your kit!'

In the village of Preston, near Weymouth, pilot John Sephton was moving just as hastily. The Flight gathered at Yeovilton for a swift course about the new Stingray torpedo. This meant business.

Around the same time, John Dillon, a lanky south Londoner, walked on board *Ardent*. Richie Gough was Duty Petty Officer, again, so he had the 18 year old, fresh out of radar school, shown to his gulch and set him to work.

'I remember him being very keen, doing jobs and coming back for more,' Gough recalls. 'Typical young sailor. He was a nice, likeable guy, but quiet.'

The lads of the Junior Messdeck stayed busy too that uncertain weekend, then hit the Grand Theatre and the clubs. Buck Ryan had arranged to go home on the Sunday, so Saturday night was free.

'Knocker White got his leg over, like he always did. Donna,' he says.

Ralph Coates was in Boobs with Knocker that night. A woman approached him.

'You're going to the Falklands,' she said.

'She knew more than I did,' the young electrician admits. More now, but not for long.

FIVE

DEVONPORT NAVAL BASE, PLYMOUTH

(11–18 APRIL 1982)

Scouse Phillips made a beeline for the Ship Control Centre as soon as he arrived on board after weekend leave. His mate Mark Bramwell, the on-watch weapons engineer, was in the MEO's seat.

'Are we going, or what?'

'Yeah!' It was that short.

While Phillips had been on leave, as Quartermaster, Topsy Turner had taken a call for the Captain on the external telephone. It struck him as unusual, because Alan West had a line in his cabin. The caller asked for the First Lieutenant when Turner told him Cdr West wasn't on board. Then, after a long, one-sided conversation, Turner 'accidentally' heard Andrew Gordon Lennox say, 'You'll confirm this by signal.' As soon as he put the phone down, the Jimmy piped on the Main Broadcast for the Heads of Department to go to his cabin. Turner kept the content of the call secret for two seconds.

Phillips didn't know this, or whether to believe Bramwell's news, but he started thinking.

'Christ. This is it.'

Preparations went on. By Sunday, 11 April, three British nuclear submarines were off the Falklands. Closer to home, in particular at Bernie Berntsen's mum's house, the crisis was invading every corner too. By day, he'd watch flight decks grow on *Atlantic Conveyor*. By night, he'd drive back to Grenville Road and stow more of the gear the Ardents had been told to move, those whose homes were too far to lug much. Scouse's music centre, Buck Taylor's kit, Knocker's kit. Some of Coxie's too.

Ardent was as hectic as ever. While Yugoslav Riesling was secreted under the seats in the Chiefs' Mess, Fleet Maintenance was welding brackets to mount Light Machine Guns round the ship.

With PO Johnno Johnson and Leading Seaman Tony Langridge's help, Richie Gough persuaded the Stores and Armament Depot to deliver grenades and a spare General Purpose Machine-Gun. He was checking the GPMG in its box on the Flight Deck, before signing for it, when John Leake wandered over and idly mentioned that he'd used one in the Army. Gough made a mental note.

The ship was fuelled to the limit. Her freshwater tanks were the same. Every day, someone would deliver something else. There were modifications, too, in the shape of Satnav.

'Suddenly, someone was drilling holes in the roof,' Navigating Officer Alan Maunder explains. 'Every day, the Captain was "We've got to have this." If anything was up for grabs, we were to have it.' He spent hours on the phone.

PO Mike Lewis found himself buried in his Electronic Warfare books, sifting through facts on Argentinian radar with newly returned and disgruntled Lt Mike Knowles. If you'd asked him about a Russian ship, he could name everything. But Argentina? It was a tough time for them all, and not just on board.

In Portsmouth on Monday, 12 April, PO Pete Brierley was visiting his wife Christine and three-year-old daughter Karen for the umpteenth time since their separation, trying for a final reconciliation. It was difficult, but in the end fruitless. He returned to the Home Club, in Pompey, and was told to ring the ship. Brierley asked for another 24 hours' leave and it was granted. He'd decided to start divorce proceedings. On Friday, 21 May, after being on *Ardent* for almost three years, he'd leave the ship too.

Back on board, he threw his energy into the Ops Room sonar team. It was a man short, so he called HMS *Vernon* and asked if any ratings were ready for a draft. The only youngster they could send was still training, but he was the best of the class. He was Sean Hayward, from Barrow.

'Train him as best you can on the way down,' Brierley turned to LS Dave Croft.

Croft knew the fresh face would have no trouble fitting in. The sonar crew had a reputation for being friendly, two in particular.

'Andy Barr was a big lad,' Croft recalls of the 20 year old from Bridgwater. 'He always tried to exhibit this fearsome expression, cropped hair, Doc Martens, cut-offs, but he was as soft as a tomato,' while Geordie Derek Armstrong, 22, 'were a nice quiet lad too'.

Later that night, as Britain's 200-mile Maritime Exclusion Zone took force around the Falklands, a covered wagon pulled up on Wharf 13 and its driver stepped out. Tom Williams and Pete Rowe oversaw his delivery. One by one, four long black boxes were lashed in the Hangar. Then the truck left.

Scouse Phillips watched. Word spread. Alan West's experimental Stingray torpedoes had arrived.

'I remember thinking, "This is for real, if they're putting those buggers on here,"' Phillips says.

◆ ◆ ◆

Most of what Stuart Ray knew about his dad's impending departure came from his best friend, John Perry. They'd taken to standing in the playground at Langley Primary School talking about those first encounters between the Argentine soldiers and the Royal Marines.

'He knew a fair bit, but I didn't really take much notice,' he admits. Not many nine year olds did. Nor many adults. If most Ardents thought the Falklands were off the Scottish coast when the crisis erupted, few had troubled a geography or history book since. There really was no point.

They didn't need to know that the first recorded landing was by Capt John Strong, in 1690, or that he named them after the Treasurer of the British Navy.

Or that, in the years after, the French visited the islands regularly. Or that Les Iles Malouines, after St Malo, became Las Malvinas in Spanish.

They didn't know the French had sold their claim on the Falklands to the Spanish crown in 1766, or that, after negotiations to avoid war, Port Egmont – cleared of British settlers that same year – was restored to the British in 1771, even if the Spanish made it clear they hadn't yielded sovereignty. So the plaque left as a token of British ownership at Port Egmont three years later had passed them by, as had Argentina's split from Spain's authority in 1816, and its formal takeover of the islands in 1820. So, most likely, had the diplomatic hand-wringing and the lobbying of the islanders in the 1960s, and every claim and counter-claim in between. They didn't know. And, if they didn't care, that didn't matter a jot, one way or the other, because on the morning of Tuesday, 13 April, Cdr West cleared Lower Deck to the Hangar and told his men that on Monday, 19 April, they were going south. The news was greeted with silence.

'You may or may not like this next bit of news,' he added, 'but I've managed to persuade their Lordships that I'm coming with you.' The Hangar erupted.

'I was due to have handed over on 17 April,' West recalls. 'I was asked by the Appointer if I wanted to go. I said "You must be joking!" She was a very happy ship. There was a special thing about them.'

As he spoke, he felt a weight on his shoulders. Since Aden, the Navy hadn't seen much fighting and he knew the men in front of him had taken the Queen's Shilling, never reckoning on this happening.

'As a Captain, they're your family. People who aren't in the Navy don't understand, but that's how you see them. You have good boys and bad boys, but you're family, so you love the lot of 'em.'

A million thoughts raced through 199 minds. The Ardents still didn't know much. The politicians were still talking, but it stood to reason that, as a frigate with a Mk 8 gun, they'd be providing escort and Naval Gunfire Support. Most important, though, was that West was going with them.

'He was young, good looking; he had a gorgeous wife. He had two little nippers who'd come on board and run riot,' Master at Arms Lenny Yeatman recalls. 'He was never too busy to say good morning or have a smile. And he knew absolutely everyone else's job. That's why he commanded respect. They worshipped the ground he walked on.'

Deputy Marine Engineering Officer Tony Ray also vividly remembers apprehension turn to relief.

'We'd thought, "Here we go. New skipper. What's it going to be like?" It wasn't only the fact that he was liked, it was also the fact that we hadn't got the unknown.' The sentiment rippled down the ranks.

'We devoured Portland, utterly devoured Portland,' Ralph Coates insists. 'They'd never seen any 21 crew that good. *Always look on the bright side of life*. No matter what they threw at us, they got the self-same thing thrown back.'

MEM Jessie Owens agrees. 'He made that ship tick. He expected the best. His best was the best 21.'

Karoly Nagy was strangely excited. 'At 21, I had no mortgage and no kids. I didn't even think about the consequences. I just wanted to get down there.'

Richie Gough's relief, though, had as much to do with unleashing missiles

as anything else. He wasn't worried. He was 23. He'd been in the Navy since he was 16. He was on a Type 21. He was a Weapons Director. He wanted it and wrote to his sister Theresa saying so. She didn't share his view.

For MEM Brum Serrell, the fact was that the islands were British and 'someone had walked over us, so we had to go and walk over them'.

'There was apprehension,' he says. 'Not so much fear, but apprehension of the unknown.'

Fear, relief, duty; it didn't matter. With the informed exception of Alan West, they all thought *Ardent* would reach Ascension, then turn back.

'Once round the island, then home by nine for tea and biscuits,' LMEM Andy Cox laughs.

During the next few days, preparations intensified. Spare parts ordered by Rick Banfield weeks before suddenly appeared. Departments planned and worked as one to make sure *Ardent* would leave Devonport with everything working at 100 per cent. But the preparations weren't confined to equipment.

Karoly Nagy remembers phoning his parents, caught in a dilemma.

'I'm one of those,' Naggers explains, 'if I'm told not to say nothing, I don't say nothing. I said "We're going somewhere where it isn't exactly tropical." It was like a code. I did take it a bit serious.'

Preparations were also reaching a peak at the Grand Theatre on Union Street. Dave and Val Wopling had been there eight years, first running the pub for his ex-matelot brother-in-law, who also had the Clarence, then taking it over when the brewery decided one pub was enough for one landlord.

In that time, they'd turned the Grand from the haunt of local crooks into the Lower Deck's local.

Leander's ratings had been the first to venture in. Soon, matelots from the *Fearless*, *Ark Royal* and *Charybdes* were calling it home from home. The Ardents had stayed loyal longer than most.

'They were there when the pub opened,' Dave says, 'and they were there for the evening. Then they'd go off clubbing, unless they were too drunk. They were so young.'

But the Grand became more than just a watering hole. If they ever had a problem, a fallout with the girlfriend, for instance, they'd confide in Val. And she always knew if they were up to no good.

There was plenty of fun too. If any of them misbehaved, there was the soda syphon, or six of the best from the business end of a paddle brought back from some foreign jaunt and kept behind the bar.

Every night, almost without fail, Dave would sneak out with a dozen Ardents for a ritual walkabout, three or four pints in the Royal Adelaide, the Sovereign and the Clarence, then home. And, on those frequent occasions when they were too tired and emotional to find the ship, Val wouldn't let them go. Instead, bed was a carpet in the ladies' loo.

The open door traditionally extended to a Christmas night party in the couple's private quarters above the pub, for those lads staying on board. So,

when the young Ardents walked in that Tuesday night and told the Woplings they were heading south, the idea was logical. They'd hold a Christmas party.

◆ ◆ ◆

Wyatt Earp was washing up when Gilly Williams told him south was the last place he wanted to go.

'I lent him a bit of money because he was in that Britannia Music thing,' Earp explains. 'They'd been sending him tapes and, of course, you're meant to send them back . . . I suppose he was a bit of a loner.'

Before long, Earp realised how much the 20-year-old misfit stoker was convinced he wasn't coming back to Plymouth, or Kidlington, his home town. 'I remember him going down the Forward Engine Room and getting some rag and he tried to set fire to it,' Earp says. It left a lasting impression.

Dickie Henderson had joined up with Williams, but the incident didn't surprise him. 'He was frightened of any shadow. He got ribbed. Nobody wanted him in their part of the ship.'

His boss, Chief Stoker Andy Andrew, maintains the rag was a token. 'He wasn't that sort. He was an outsider and didn't fit into the Naval way of life – certainly not the Engine Room way of life. He was quiet. They made fun of him. I used to try to get his confidence. We couldn't quite straighten him out. I don't think that the lads hated him. It was a giggle.'

Like the Joss, Andrew hadn't forgotten his own time on the Junior Messdeck. He had those rules he wanted obeyed and, if they were, he wouldn't trouble them much about the others. Balance. He wouldn't have it any other way, even if he thought *Ardent* wasn't always as laid-back as she needed to be.

'It isn't like Civvie Street. Every day you've got to push this 3,000 tonnes of metal round the sea. A little town on the move. A lot of them are shift workers, like in the Engine Room, sleeping, washing, eating, back on shift. But the day workers, you can't expect them to finish at five, wash and sit reading a book. No. They'll sneak a few cans of beer. They'll do silly little things.'

Silly? Maybe not. They were just young lads, some younger than others, like Florrie Ford. He didn't have to go south. After chatting with the 17 year old, his dad visited the ship.

'He wants to go,' Charlie Ford told the Chief Stoker.

'Well, we'll look after him,' Andrew promised.

◆ ◆ ◆

With their immediate future clearer, they also faced writing wills. Some found it grim, some funny, some just difficult.

'I remember filling out the form with Gilly,' Wyatt Earp recalls. 'I put my mum and dad. Gilly signed his and said "I'm leaving it all to my dog."'

Williams was called up in front of the Joss.

'You can't leave it to the dog,' Lenny Yeatman told him.

'I've got no one else.'

Most hadn't counted on naming an executor either, but, true to form, the solution was close at hand.

'We were passing it to the left,' Scouse Phillips remembers. '"Sign that!" Pass-the-will. It wasn't worth a friggin' crate. Jessie Owens was one of mine and I'm stuffed if I know who the other was.'

◆ ◆ ◆

As the main vessels of the Task Force departed Ascension for the South Atlantic, for the Ardents it was Saturday and Sunday at home, sail on Monday. Radio Operator Steve Kent travelled most of the way back to Lincolnshire with Shaun Hanson, who was heading for Ecclesfield, in Sheffield. Kent remembers only feeling 'honoured' to be taking part.

On his way home, Nags's mind replayed his short time on board and then forgot about it. He spent his final leave at the Dorchester flat his girlfriend had rented, trying to escape to the pub.

In Washington, Tyne and Wear, Knocker White stayed at home with his mum, Brenda, and younger sister, Mandy, 13, while his elder brother, Ian – who'd just left *Ardent*'s Type 21 sister *Alacrity* – and Dawn, a 24-year-old nurse at South Cleveland Hospital, went camping. Brenda's aim was to keep the weekend as normal as possible. So it included shopping and a trip to Sunderland for a DIY will.

'He wasn't going to fill it in,' she says. But he did. 'We made a joke of what would happen to all his records if anything happened. It sounds so silly now.'

The family was close. Brenda had brought them up single-handedly so, beyond agreeing that the crisis might pass quickly, the rest of the weekend was a blur of activity. No time for deep thought.

'I prayed and just expected him to be safe,' she says. 'We knew he had a job to do. He was indestructible.'

Back in Plymouth, the thought of Dad going away hung over the Ray children, despite the distraction of relatives visiting from Canada. Nine-year-old Stuart often slid onto the back seat when his mum, Carol, took *Ardent*'s Deputy Marine Engineering Officer to work. The military kit on display was exciting, but the gargantuan sight of *Atlantic Conveyor* left the biggest impression.

For CPO Jeff Curran, Galtieri had intervened in some important plans. Curran had been due a draft at the end of May, but he knew *Ardent* like the back of his hand after 30 months on board and, with a possible run ashore in South America, he volunteered his services – even though it would leave his wedding day with a bride but no bridegroom. His fiancée, Diane, managed to slot them in with the Plymouth Register Office on the Saturday.

The weekend didn't turn out the way he expected. On the Friday, to his dismay, a machinery check showed that *Ardent*'s starboard controllable-pitch propeller was faulty. The problem was easily identified – a shaft within the propeller shaft that took hydraulic fluid to pistons and changed the pitch of the propeller blades – but finding a solution was another matter. The SCC readings said one thing, but something else entirely was happening underwater. In

essence, if Alan West wanted *Ardent* to stand still, she'd be creeping along. What's more, the noise would have been like phoning an Argentinian sonar rating and saying, 'We're over here.'

While a few friends watched Curran and his bride do the honest thing, Mick Cox worked with Eddie Edwards, Tony Ray and others to find a cure. There weren't many others on board with them. In the Ops Room, still not totally adjusted to his Sandhurst disappointment, Lt Mike Knowles was digesting Alan West's post-Northwood briefings, casting his eye over a map of the Falklands and a chart of intelligence summaries on Argentinian aircraft and ship numbers brought on by the skipper. With Tom Williams, the three had already done some homework and agreed on one thing.

'The worst situation is if we come under sustained air attack close to land,' West had told them. 'If we've got a single plane, then we stand a reasonable chance of shooting it down with the Seacat or the close-range weapons. Two in close sequence is going to be a real challenge, probably more than we can handle. Three or more, we'll probably take hits. If I'm not in the Ops Room, I don't want you to ask me. If you need to fire, I want you to fire straight away.'

On the Upper Deck, about the same time, Dave Lee had an equally sobering experience. In the hurly-burly of storing, thousands of items had arrived on board, but there was no disguising one delivery.

'How many?' the CPO looked at the driver and nodded towards his goods.

'One each' he replied, whoever he was. They were body bags.

◆ ◆ ◆

At the start of April, Surg Lt Simon Ridout had watched the carriers *Hermes* and *Invincible* being stored in Portsmouth. On Sunday, 18 April, he arrived in Devonport as the two ships prepared to depart again, this time from Ascension, 4,000 miles away. The two events seemed an age apart.

The unimaginable scale of what he'd witnessed in Pompey had left so deep an impression that he'd realised how ashamed he'd be if he wasn't part of it.

'I don't think there's anything,' the Medical Appointer shook his head when he asked for a ship. But while they were talking, the phone rang. In the coded conversation that followed, Ridout realised one was sailing and needed a doc. Twenty-four hours later, he was told to join *Ardent* on the Sunday. They'd sail on Monday. He rushed home, packed and left for Plymouth. Life was never the same again.

There was one person on board who knew Ridout's bearded face, and the stammer, as well as a little of the expertise he'd gained in two years at the Naval Hospital in Plymouth, and seven months as a casualty officer in an Accident and Emergency department. That was Lt Nigel Langhorn. By chance, Ridout had given Alan West's Correspondence Officer a second opinion on a car-crash knee injury that had kept him from David Searle's wedding and threatened to strand him at home.

'Bugger me, before we sailed, Simon Ridout turned up,' he recalls. 'He said "You're all right now. I can personally tend to your knee on the way down."'

If Ridout was a welcome face on the Bridge, though, he wasn't in the

Sickbay. Leading Medical Assistant Bob Young's happy to admit that all he saw was a 'tall, untidy chap who had a severe stammer' and little in common with him. By the time Ridout began acquainting himself with *Ardent*'s medical preparations, Young had already distributed the extra shipment of medical stores from RNH Plymouth, six large packing cases of dressings and pharmaceutical supplies.

With baked beans and corned beef filling most orifices already – and beer apparently filling what was left – he broke them into packs and dispersed them. The principle, like so much of the preparations, was simple: if the Sickbay was burnt out, or the Medical Store was flooded, there'd be a box of kit elsewhere for the chefs, writers and stewards of the First Aid Parties to use.

The ship carried a set of tools, life-support equipment and 'some things for collecting blood, so you could give a transfusion', extra shell dressings, sticking tapes, airways for the First Aid Posts, splints . . . the list was almost endless.

Young understood his responsibility at sea was just the basics – stabilising casualties for the people who'd mend them, if they were available. He could either treat ten people for primary injuries or one person for major injuries. Not everything was kept close to hand, though.

They carried instruments like a brace bit bone hudson. Years before, some Surgeon Captain had told a dit about a guy with an injury who'd had his head drilled with one, under local anaesthetic. Young had already decided what his medical advice would be, faced with similar circumstances – 'You're on your own, buddy' – so the 'hudson' had hit the back of the cupboard. But he also knew that, if an Ardent was doing a dangerous job, one of the things that made him do it well was believing in the medical back-up waiting to catch him.

'I'd like to think I was the best that was available,' he adds. 'In theory, you could cope.' It was Simon Ridout's job to make sure Young was right.

◆ ◆ ◆

On the Sunday morning, Chief Petty Officer and Mrs Jeff Curran dropped in while the stokers and dockyard mateys recalibrated *Ardent*'s rogue starboard prop shaft. A diver had gone down, but it was too late to do anything other than cut a hole between the Aft and Forward Engine Rooms to install a huge spring to rectify the problem. This was how they'd sail. The rest of Sunday was like a social.

◆ ◆ ◆

Garry Whitford had joined *Ardent* three weeks before, and elder brother Alan remembers him being proud of his new ship. Before that final weekend leave, the family knew only what the TV had brought into their modest Blackburn home. War or a diplomatic alternative. The 23 year old didn't give them any more. He kept it low-key. So did the family. *Ardent* was coming back. Look on the bright side. So, typically, the brothers didn't see much of each other that

weekend. Garry went to the Lord Raglan, a backstreet pub, or Audley Working Men's Club just behind it.

The day Garry left, Alan called at his parents' for lunch, but when Garry was ready to go their father, Jack, asked him to wait for his mother, Teresa. It would only be a matter of minutes, but Garry was anxious to go back early. They presumed it was to see fiancée Isabel, who was also in the Navy.

'I don't think he wanted to face the goodbyes,' Alan says now. 'Mum would have preferred it if he hadn't gone, but she let it happen. She thought it was for the best.'

The boys had a game of pool and a couple of pints at the Raglan and, as they watched the news, Garry turned to his brother and said, 'We'll sort 'em out.'

Minutes later, they pulled up on double-yellow lines amid the terraced buildings either side of Mill Hill station. Garry handed Alan three tapes and stepped out of the car. He was wearing just a jumper.

'I'll see you later,' Alan said deliberately, then watched Garry bimble down the steps. He waited and waited to see him walk onto the platform and was about to move off when the fresh-faced Ardent appeared.

'I waved and saw him turning towards me as I left.' He doesn't know whether Garry saw him.

Pete and Renee Hanson had planned to make the long haul from Sheffield to Plymouth to see Shaun off, but the young steward went home instead. His sister Carol was looking forward to her 18th on 10 May. Lisa was 13. The 20 year old planned to go back south on the Sunday, promising to call the next morning. He asked his folks if they were going for a drink. They did, then they took him to Midland Road station. After they said goodbye, Shaun sat down with a cuppa as he waited for Jon Major.

'We were other side. He'd gone through ticket barrier,' Pete says. 'It were me last sighting of him.'

In Newcastle, Knocker White met Buck Taylor. As they stepped onto the train, Brenda White told them to look after each other.

'I was fine until it pulled out,' she says. She didn't know that, before they'd left, Knocker had taken his brother Ian to one side and told him they might lose the ship.

In Redditch, killick electrician Andy Cox was aware of an edge.

'They're trying to put your mind at ease, I suppose, saying it'll probably be solved by talks. It was what I was paid for, as simple as that. But the family wasn't.'

He went out for a jar with his mates, then kept his departure low-key. His Aunt Joan and Uncle Tom took him to Birmingham's New Street station with his mother, Valerie.

'You're thinking, "I might never see this place again." Mum didn't show it when I was there but probably did later. On the train, you get a can of beer and relax. All you're thinking about then is getting back to your mates.'

His mother remembers it differently.

'Outside, he walked away, then turned and gave me a kiss, which wasn't like him. I said "What's that for?" He said "Because I might not come back."'

On board *Ardent*, meanwhile, the Navy was finding some limits and exploring others. John Sephton's Flight might have been on their crash course at Yeovilton to learn how to deploy Alan West's Stingray torpedoes, but one thing was missing. The instructions. So part of Lt Tom Williams's final weekend was spent lifting pieces of paper from a fax and piecing a makeshift manual together.

PO Richie Gough and his leading hand, Tony Langridge, were also testing their ingenuity. Langridge shared his boss' gung-ho love of missiles and they had a plan if they trod Falkland soil. Langridge had borrowed a metal tube from the dockyard and hidden it in his Messdeck, waiting for the moment to convert it into an anti-tank weapons launcher, using the three-inch chaff rockets as ammunition.

If you listened to most Ardents, it would be a wasted effort. The vanguard of the fleet had sailed on 4 April, a showpiece departure with all the machinery in the wrong order and a common expectation that they'd unfold the sunbeds at Ascension, sort themselves out, wait for everyone else, then leave. That's not to say that, in some quarters, at particular times of the day, thoughts didn't run deep.

Steve Heyes had only just joined PO Mike Lewis's Electronic Warfare team. At 22, he knew little of *Ardent*, her capability or the spirit that Amsterdam, Portland, Cape Wrath, Narvik and Aberporth – even Aberporth – had generated. He knew even less of what she faced. He turned to John Goddard.

'I was only 23 myself,' the Londoner recalls. 'He asked me if they were going to sort it out. I said, "Yeah, they might," but I didn't know any different.'

The name Thatcher surfaced occasionally too.

'It didn't matter if we were going to rescue one Briton or fight a whole continent,' was PO Pete Brierley's opinion. 'It was what our leaders said was needed. It was something that had to be done.'

Not that there was much time to agonise over politics because, while Gen Haig continued his diplomatic shuttling and a strident Margaret Thatcher ran her War Cabinet, while husbands, sons, brothers and lovers were preparing for a deployment that they insisted would be like any other, and the world saw war in the offing, life had to go on.

Lenny Yeatman and Andrew Gordon Lennox had already set the ball rolling in one key respect. The Joss returned home one night and presented wife Beryl with all the names and addresses of the ship's company. They spread them out on the carpet and began dividing 200 names into groups of six. *Ardent*'s Link Wives group would keep information flowing on the home front and provide support for those who lived far from the hurly-burly of Plymouth.

The village of Preston, near Weymouth, might as well have been a million miles from Devon, so far as Lesley Sephton was concerned. If the Flight lived a life separate from the rest of the ship's company, by necessity, effectively on 24-hour call, the life of this Flight Commander's wife was even more remote. By her own admission, she had never adjusted to John's long absences, but it wasn't until their daughter, Harriet, was born that he began to question it too.

'Although he outwardly didn't say, "I don't wish to go," there were little inferences.'

At 35, he was even talking about leaving the Service, and she was looking forward to those days when 'you've just come back from somewhere, choose me' was a thing of the past. But, that weekend, she accepted him going again.

'I think we both knew it wasn't going to be a jolly,' she says. 'This was what they'd trained for. The last morning, I was standing here at seven and someone was giving him a lift up there. I always remember, I was looking out of the window and he never looked up to wave. I was quite upset.'

◆ ◆ ◆

In Plymouth, John Foster and his fiancée, Jane, had spent the weekend with John Newton and his wife, Jan. They took pictures on the Sunday then, as the two Ardents left, Jan turned to Foster. 'You must look after him,' she said. That was his task and Newton's.

Back on board, men were returning to join those who'd stayed on duty.

'I don't think anxiety came into it for me,' young Brummie Errol Flynn remembers. 'I was that age.'

For young Geordie Buck Taylor, it was still a big game. Understandable. With Knocker White's expert help, he'd just acquired a taste for lager and women.

On his way back to Devonport with Shaun Hanson, cook Jon Major knew it wasn't a case of not wanting to be involved. Neither of the young Ardents had talked much about what might follow.

'It was just another trip,' he says. 'We was looking forward to getting away.'

All but the most essential personal items had been cleared from lockers, but there would still be enough to occupy them when training didn't keep them from their grots. There'd be reading, listening to music, watching videos, playing Uckers – a version of Ludo with fluid rules – and retracing their steps over the Gronk Board, the Messdeck photo collection of conquests, a few gorgeous, others clearly not, all with a story attached, some of them true.

Micky Mullen was a small, fair-haired, stocky 24-year-old Scouser with a reputation as a quiet man who found it difficult to be one of the boys but was always willing to do people a favour. Where Dave Croft's girlfriend Denise Collins was concerned, it wasn't so much a favour as a money-making service. Whenever Crofty was on watch, he and Mick Newby would charge messmates for five minutes viewing the pictures of the Page 3 model that were plastered all over his grot, kit on and kit off.

'Whether you're going to COST or Florida, the routine was the same,' Newby also recalls. 'You'd have your usual groups go ashore. But, in the end, you'd all meet up.'

That night, it was the Grand Theatre and Boobs. Val and Dave Wopling had promised their *Ardent* regulars they'd have a Christmas party, and they didn't let them down. But Dave hadn't told them there was going to be a Santa. At 8.30, the bell rang and in came Reg, a regular, with a sack.

'They loved it,' he says. 'We got a sack and he gave them all little presents, sat on his lap. It was ever so funny.'

All the talk that night was about the Falklands, but Val didn't like it.

'They kept saying, "We'll soon sort them out,"' she recalls. 'I used to say, "Don't keep on."'

Amid all the laughing, though, one Ardent in particular worried her: Gilly Williams.

'I felt sorry for him because he was only a young lad,' she says. 'They used to treat him horribly.'

It was late as they prepared to move on. Before they left, she made them promise to look after the young stoker.

It was way gone closing time when Knocker White, the last Ardent, left. He was leaning on the jukebox when Dave strolled up to him.

'Goodnight and good luck,' the landlord said. The 21-year-old Geordie turned and shook his hand.

'I might never see you again!' he smiled. Then they headed off clubbing.

◆ ◆ ◆

Some didn't make it to Boobs. But Andy Barr, Fluff Garnham, John Goddard, Jon Major, Ralph, Knocker, Buck Taylor, Shaun Hanson, Mick Newby, Eddie Edwards and Joe Laidlaw did, among others. A normal Boobs night would involve Knocker meeting Donna – 'She thought the world of Knocker,' Goddard explains – and end up with Ardents running around in their underpants.

'We were all doing the same thing,' Newby says. 'We were having drinks, we were trying to get laid, we were trying to have a good time. Most of us probably succeeded in doing all three. I didn't.'

At about one in the morning, drunk, he slipped away and found a phone. In Essex, his mother picked up the receiver and heard crying.

'Mum,' he said. 'What am I going to do? I haven't signed up for this sort of thing.'

'Get back on board. That's what you signed up for,' she told him abruptly. It sobered him up.

'I signed up because they came round saying, "Look, you can see the world." Forget the wars, you didn't sign up for that. But my mother was right,' he realised. 'I had to go. Then it wasn't beer talking, it was adrenaline. Let's have another couple and then go and do the business.'

One by one, men wandered off to phone home too.

◆ ◆ ◆

At about three that morning, as Ardents were drifting back on board, Crofty arrived after the long drive from Lancashire. He parked his car in the dockyard, thinking he'd need it again in a couple of weeks, and slipped the key into his pocket. His optimism was shared. Despite Newby's aberration, life in a blue suit was about lager and ladies, and training for a war off Norway that would never come.

'People were only on *Ardent* because they were the best of the bunch,' Newby insists still. 'That may not have been the consensus of the Admiralty, or

the *Invincible*, or the rest. But, in the eyes of everybody on board, we were the best in the Fleet. Nobody was going to take that away.'

A fighting force in Alan West's image? Andrew Gordon Lennox doesn't like such ethereal things.

'Yes,' he draws a breath, 'we tried very hard to live up to his obvious capability. He led from the front. He didn't like second best, and he required us all to produce the tops."

Rio Grande Air Base, Friday, 21 May 1982: While Lt Cdr Alberto Philippi and his wingmen update their maps and navigation charts, the first division of the Aviacion Naval's Third Attack Squadron takes off and heads for San Carlos Water. Two hours later, at 1210, the six planes return, having failed to reach their target. They're refuelled and rearmed, ready for Philippi's mission.

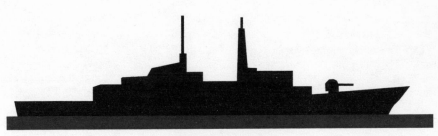

SOUTH

One	Devonport Naval Base to Atlantic Ocean (19–29 April 1982)	73
Two	Ascension Island (29 April – 3 May 1982)	81
Three	Ascension Island (4–6 May 1982)	89
Four	Atlantic Ocean (7–9 May 1982)	99
Five	Atlantic Ocean (10–15 May 1982)	107

ONE

DEVONPORT NAVAL BASE TO ATLANTIC OCEAN

(19–29 APRIL 1982)

A thousand and one goodbyes had already been said in homes across Britain, and on railway platforms and bus stations. Now it was Plymouth's turn, and the day delivered for it was grey.

At six in the morning on Monday, 19 April, Steward Shaun Hanson stood in a phonebox outside the Naval Base and dialled a Sheffield number, to say he'd arrived safely and that *Ardent* would sail in the next few hours. It was the last time Pete Hanson heard his son's voice.

In their married quarters at Crownhill, overlooking the dockyard, Carol Serrell was preparing to drive her husband, Brum, to work, uncertain whether he'd be back just as she settled into her routine, or when life had begun to drag from a long separation. Whichever, as usual, she put a pair of his slippers by the stairs so that, if anyone came to the door, they'd look in and see them.

Chief Gunner Pete Rowe's wife Christine drove him in to Devonport too – not the way to celebrate a 13th wedding anniversary. They made it simple. A quick kiss, then gone. No misgivings.

About the same time, Frankie Enticknap drove alongside the ship and dropped husband Ken, the man in charge of *Ardent*'s Aft Auxiliary Machine Room. She waved and turned for work in the Met Office at RAF Mount Batten, high above Plymouth Sound. Not everyone braved it past the doorstep, though.

Carole Leake was one, convinced *Ardent*'s NAAFI manager would soon be trotting home but with a nagging thought that, if it came to shooting, Big John wouldn't be able to resist the call.

'The night before, I said to John, "Look, don't be a hero," because I knew what he was like.' She knew it was a pointless thing to say.

◆◆◆

As *Ardent*'s special duties seamen prepared her to slip out of South Yard, there was an understandable edge to the familiar routine: men harbouring final thoughts of family, men nursing hangovers after a final night on Plymouth's tiles, men uttering quiet words of suspicion at the low-key departure and at provenance and providence.

Every watch on board was set to Zulu time, synchronised with the clocks in

Northwood, Downing Street and 200 other mantelpieces around the country, so 10 a.m. at home was always 1000Z on board.

So, at 1000Z, the 13th *Ardent* slipped her line from Wharf 13 and, with her ship's company standing ceremonially in Procedure Alpha along her decks, she moved slowly out into the basin. How many had worked out that her pennant number – 184 – added up to 13 too is uncertain.

The dockyard mateys weren't known for their farewells but, having repaired *Ardent*'s broken gun in record time, the 'ninth frigate' of the Fourth Frigate Squadron were lining the yard, cheering.

Beneath the White Ensign flying from her main mast was *Ardent*'s new RAS flag, flown during replenishments at sea, the £5 prize-winner picked from a host of X-rated entries in a competition run by the Jimmy. It was in the style of an Access credit card, with a capital A followed by 'Ardent' and the legend 'Your Flexible Friend' underneath, the work of PO Pete Brierley.

Then, with the strains of the England World Cup song, 'We're On Our Way', predictably reworded and retitled 'Club 21', coming from the ship's Tannoy, they did a sharp left and headed south.

'We thought it was brilliant,' killick electrician Andy Cox recalls. 'I was so proud to be English and in the Royal Navy. A good mix of young lads and older lads. We were ready to drag them through.'

Not everyone was swept by euphoria, though. Buck Ryan was on the Flight Deck. He presumed Naggers was on the Fo'c'sle. He wasn't. He was feet away, being as ill as he'd ever been, calculating the scale of the mistake he'd made helping to polish off six bottles of Ryan's dad's rhubarb wine on the train the night before.

Not much further away, newly-wed Jeff Curran waved in the direction of Devil's Point, hoping Diane would pick him out. In the weekend's rush to marry, he'd forgotten to pack his Number One uniform. So he'd borrowed Allan McAulay's and run masking tape over his close friend's ribbons. Mac wouldn't need it. The Senior Flight Maintainer would arrive with the rest of the Flight – *Ardent*'s self-contained, 24-hour team-within-a-team – in the Lynx once they were at sea.

Those families who did maintain the ritual of seeing the ship off were scattered along the shore.

With Mum tied up at her Tavistock hairdressing salon, young Stuart Ray had been taken to Mount Wise with one of his sisters and their relatives from Canada. It was a well-trodden path but if, this time, he was a little more upset than normal, his young heart swelled with pride and he felt like telling everyone it was his dad's ship. Except that everyone with him already knew.

As *Ardent* nudged on into the Sound, CPO Ken Enticknap rolled the focusing ring on his binoculars. As greys, greens and browns sharpened, he fixed his gaze on RAF Mount Batten. Among the entire Met Office staff, he caught a fleeting glimpse of Frankie. He wondered if there was anyone left answering the phone. Then the movement of the ship took her behind a hedge.

Back on the Hoe, Beryl Yeatman turned to a playschool colleague who'd joined her for the send-off. 'Some of those aren't going to come back,' she said. To this day, she doesn't know why.

On board, there was a faint echo of her thoughts. Bob Young had been given an answer to his Amsterdam Procedure Alpha prayer – something pressing to attend to in the Sickbay. Before they'd even reached Drake Island, Russ Goble had been taken ill with 'a fluttering thing' in his heart.

On the Upper Deck, Pete Brierley had a tear in his eye. He probably wasn't the only one. It's probably as well he didn't know that at Ascension, 4,000 miles away, Admiral Sandy Woodward was on *Hermes*, preparing to tell his commanders two facts dressed in darker tones. War was inevitable. And, if the Naval Staff's calculation was sound, they should be ready to lose eight ships to the Argentinian Air Force.

❖❖❖

Ardent had barely cleared the breakwater before her men set about ensuring they wouldn't be among them. With the fading whiff of Cornwall's cliffside fields hanging on the breeze, the main broadcast ordered everyone to Defence Watches. This time, for some, the call had a feel they'd never experienced at Portland, no matter how hard the wreckers had tried.

If *Ardent*'s Funnel of Fate had begun with its Naval Gunfire Support off the Norwegian coast six short weeks before, if it was destined to taper out with a lap or two of sun-licked Ascension, far beyond the horizon, or further south . . . well, who could say?

Whichever, they had to be ready. So, two hours after slipping away from Wharf 13, Navigating Officer Lt Alan Maunder took a notebook from his breast pocket and pencilled in the first of the rough notes he'd transfer to the log, when time allowed. From now till they saw Devonport again, God only knew when, everything would be measured in time or distance. His first lines were short but functional: '1200Z–1300Z: Gunex 19 aircraft tracking' and '1300Z–1330Z: Gun functioning'.

❖❖❖

From the vantage point of his Bridge, decorated with silhouettes of Skyhawks, Daggers, Pucaras and Super Etendards, Alan West was already backing his judgement that the greatest threat to *Ardent* would come from the air, even if the majority of his men didn't yet have the benefit of his calculations.

The air-defence exercise made perfect sense to Principal Warfare Officer Mike Knowles, and the Cornish landscape was ideal to confirm the dilemma they might face if the politicians didn't prevent them steaming the full 8,000 miles south – *Ardent*'s 992 middle-frequency radar would have difficulty picking out low-flying planes from the Ops Room's cluttered picture of land.

That night, soon after *Ardent* made her 1900 rendezvous with HMS *Argonaut*, the fleet replenishment ship *Regent* and the support oiler *Plumleaf*, Lt Tom Williams identified another problem. He'd been prepared to go to Alloy Express with *Ardent*'s existing General Communications Radio Supervisor, but war was a different matter. Williams went to Alan West and said as much, then

wrote a signal to Commander Task Group and said he wanted him replaced. They agreed. The man would leave at Ascension.

The salty Bay of Biscay was quick to add to their troubles. Within a day of leaving Devonport, *Ardent*'s newly installed, pristine Satnav system failed. No matter what Chief Electrician Taff Lovidge tried, it refused to work. Alan Maunder resigned himself to finding the dot that was Ascension using something a little less sophisticated – the stars. If Alan West was worried, he didn't show it.

At 1030 the next day, John Sephton and Brian Murphy flew him and Knowles to join Capt Kit Layman on *Argonaut* for a three-hour briefing. At around the same time, the two commanding officers received a fresh signal from Admiral Woodward, telling them that the fleet must be ready for war by 2000 on Friday, 23 April, four days hence. The two ships would still be a week north of Ascension, but that meant little. Preparations would be intensified. Alan Maunder's pencil was about to take a pounding.

The drills that night were mainly the loading of depth charges, torpedoes and Sea Skua missiles, but the Flight carried them out wearing full NBCD outfits. No one minded. Morale was still high, engagingly full of bravado.

On Wednesday, 21 April, a Sea Harrier intercepted and warned off an Argentinian 707 snooping around the Task Force, the first contact between the two sides – not that that affected life on *Ardent*.

There was one rare break from routine, though. Alan West's 34th birthday. The Ardents didn't forget it. On a pretext, he was lured aft. When he arrived in the Dining Hall, most of the ship's company was there, with a birthday cake. 'They were sparky,' he recalls. 'It was a very special day.'

So it went on, a routine of work, rest, play, exercise in their confined grey box and, once or twice a day, tuning in for the wider picture from the World Service. Some events in the Task Force, inevitably, took the headlines – World Service, Thursday, 22 April, two British Sea Kings crashed on South Georgia as SBS units put ashore.

Busy days, busy nights. That night, CPO Dave Lee picked up a pen and began writing:

> Thursday, 22 April
>
> My dearest darling Catherine,
>
> It is really a Friday now as I have just finished my Middle Watch rounds. I was turned in at nine o'clock, up again at 1.30 a.m. so there is little point in trying to sleep again until seven o'clock because I know that I would just be lying awake until then.
>
> I think it is the sea time more than anything else which is the hardest thing to take about this trip (disregarding the separation aspect of course).
>
> What makes it worse is the fact that nobody knows how long it will be for.
>
> Most of us feel that the best thing will be for the government to bring the situation over as soon as possible. What we don't want to happen is

to have the Argentinians brought to their knees by a long, slow, and drawn-out process. This would involve keeping ships in the area for many months, which we feel the government won't want. One thing is for sure, whatever way it happens we will bring them to their knees because we are more than capable of that.

The past two days have been quite warm and will get steadily warmer as we steam south.

One thing I have to tell you is that after we reach the Ascension Island there will be official censorship on all the mail going off.

It is an MOD decision; not a ship decision. It we will mean that the First Lieutenant and the Master at Arms will read all out-going mail so that nothing about what the ship is doing or where it is going will be written down in anybody's mail.

So if you want to know what is happening you will have to ask pertinent questions in your letters (and remember them) as I can answer them in a way that you will know what is going on without me being specific. In that way they should pass the censor.

Suffice to say that you have realised now that we are going further south after Ascension Island, which is the limit of my knowledge.

On Wednesday the Captain had all the Chiefs in the Mess to explain the situation and give us as much information as he could. Apart from letting you know that we are going south after Ascension Island there is nothing else to let you know. I only wish I knew. I think you are going to be well informed of the situation through the news media anyway which will be more free of censorship than we will be I feel . . .

He left the letter unfinished. Forty-eight hours on, on what passed for a day of rest, he picked up his unfinished bluey.

Sunday, 25 April

. . . How things change so from day to day. Tonight we have been told that there will not be any official censorship – we are to be relied upon until there is evidence of links to the press from a talkative wife or whatever.

Here's hoping that all is well your end my lovely. I wish that I could tell you that I will be coming home in a couple of weeks but there is still no hint from anywhere of how long we shall be away. We really should be sharing the summer together instead of all this. Not that I think we are doing the wrong thing by retaking the Falklands, it is just the timing of it all that is wrong.

Everyone onboard is quite confident that we can look after ourselves if we should be attacked but I don't think that the Argentinian Navy is anywhere near willing to engage our forces so they will have to be hard pressed to attempt to any attack. A last-ditch stand, so to speak. Anyway, the sooner we get down there and sort them out the sooner we can come home and that is the general opinion of our mess.

I spent my first hour on the Upper Deck this afternoon to take in some sun. An hour was enough because it was really hot on the Fo'c'sle, even with a reasonable breeze blowing across the deck.

This week will be a busy week of exercises for us to tune us all up. Not that we need all that much tuning up with what we have done this year so far.

We are all due at Ascension Island on Thursday and as planned at the moment we sail the following day. If there is any mail going off after that I just don't know . . .

Quiet confidence. Tuning up. He slipped the bluey away again. It could be finished another day. There were other things to do. The whole ship had other things to do.

In that first week out of Devonport, LMA Bob Young's frosty relationship with Surg. Lt Simon Ridout had warmed to cool. Even though he admits it was arrogant, Young didn't like the new arrival invading his Sickbay, leaving his 'crap' everywhere, like all docs. Ridout knew how his colleague was feeling so, for the time being, home was the CO's Sea Cabin.

Other routines had changed as well. Cliff Goldfinch, for one. He was already running his cooks out of one Galley and serving the main meal at midnight. Further south they'd have to eat late anyway, when it was dark and the air raid threat had subsided, when they could chew over the Jimmy's evening sitreps – the ship's position, the fact that they'd used 36.5 tons of fresh water that day, things like that.

There was a lot of painting too. Everything on the Upper Deck had a coat of grey. Not that Wyatt Earp wanted to hear about grey. The 18-year-old MEM's memory of those days is of him and Barry Muncer painting under the Tynes in the Aft Engine Room. Why? Who'd go down there? 'You could eat in there, it was immaculate,' he says. 'The whole ship was.' That was the point.

At 24, Buck Ryan was a little older than both, but still considered himself naïve and, at times, a little resentful of the stokers in his 3 Deck Junior Ratings' Messdeck who, he calculated, had an easier mix of normal working duties and watchkeeping.

Ironically, he'd taken to immersing himself in extra work anyway. It saved his mind wandering to his failing marriage, or his young son Kevin. With his closest friends on board, Karoly Nagy and John Bullock, he'd also taken to keeping a diary. At breaks, and in the evening, they'd talk about the day, then Bullock would apply his literary skills and jot a few lines. The diary was kept at his action station, in the Torpedo Magazine.

Not everyone found it as easy to cope, despite the efforts of the old hands. In the Dining Hall party, Stoker Gilly Williams was still unhappy. And PO Eddie Edwards spent some of his time keeping an eye on Buzz Leighton's task-book training. The 18 year old was a willing student, but the thought of what lay ahead was rarely far from his mind.

'What's all the point of this? We could all get killed,' he said to Edwards one night.

'No, don't be stupid!' the pint-sized PO reassured him. 'Nothing'll happen.'

In general, though, spirits were high. Why not? Ascension was four days

away. The Lower Deck knew that meant breaking out the sunbeds and doing a couple of laps before calling the whole thing off.

If the next day – Monday, 26 April – was to end with news that simply backed up that view, the fact that Lt Col Alfredo Astiz had surrendered South Georgia, the bits in between hardly dented the Ardents' confidence that, if push did come to shove, they'd be more than equal. No worries.

Alan Maunder's pencil had another busy day. So did John Sephton's Lynx. The bulk of his time had been spent flying 'Skutacs' at the ship from this angle and that, doing his best to mimic a fast Argentinian jet, going round again and coming in from some unknown direction outside radar range, seeing how quickly Mike Knowles's Ops Room teams could pick up the threat.

At 50 feet above the Atlantic waves, doing 120 knots, the detection rate was sometimes worryingly late, fatally late. Sephton would give Knowles the benefit of his opinion – 'What the bloody hell were you doing?' – then go round again. And again.

Had he been a 450kt wave-top Skyhawk, detection would have been one thing, hitting it another.

Even though the rapid fire exercise was a vital hour, good though the Mark 8 was, deadly accurate over 17 miles and fast with it, Knowles knew the chances of taking a jet out with a 4.5-inch brick in anti-aircraft mode were remote. What *Ardent* needed for that was either a clever missile system or a close-in weapon system with a high rate of fire putting up an impenetrable wall of lead. What she had were 20mm Oerlikons on each Bridge Wing, sundry light and General Purpose Machine-Guns, and Seacat at the back end.

In the open sea, *Ardent* had few concerns – fewer concerns – but the thought of land-clutter on her radar screens had already convinced Alan West that they'd need eyes on the Upper Deck, as well as the cool head of the Seacat's Ped Site operator, if the missile was even going to have time to be a deterrent.

Some people might have mulled deeply on such a thin defence against air attack. Not Knowles. It was a fact of life. Type 21s were interim, so no one was going to waste money bolting close-range Sea Wolf systems or the longer range Sea Darts to them. Make the best of it. Meanwhile, regular Wardroom briefings – and *Jane's Fighting Ships* – would keep the concentration high.

◆◆◆

The various preparations had taken the Ardents to a peak, but the one thing they were short on was NBCD (nuclear, biological, chemical defence). The Jimmy called Deputy Marine Engineering Officer Tony Ray to his cabin and told him to put it right.

As she exercised – stewards and cooks ditching ladles for field dressings and First-Aid Parties, stokers standing by in firefighting suits and breathing apparatus to tackle make-believe fires, the Mobile Repair Party ready to shore phantom holes made by phantom missiles – Britain's Maritime Exclusion Zone became a Total Exclusion Zone. If any ship or plane ventured within 200 miles of the Falklands, whatever their nationality, they'd need a good excuse or impressive firepower to support them.

Within hours, *Ardent*'s continuing preparations took a fresh turn. The defence intelligence staff had lost track of one of Argentina's submarines. A swift calculation of its last-known position and a check on her potential speed persuaded Whitehall there was a chance she could be near Ascension. *Ardent* was signalled to make best speed there so, leaving *Argonaut* with the fleet oiler *Tidepool*, she disappeared over the horizon with the support oiler *Plumleaf*. Her NBCD exercise went on.

On the way, the big picture remained just as disjointed. On the Bridge one day, Alan West turned to Lt David Searle and asked what latitude, specifically, was Ascension in relation to eight degrees south?

Searle was puzzled. What he didn't know was that the criteria for any South Atlantic campaign medal were being worked out. Eight degrees south, Searle later figured, included all the sunbathers at Ascension.

In the Chiefs' Mess that night, Dave Lee completed his letter home. On *Ardent*'s scale of secrets, it would hardly trouble the censors:

Wednesday

. . . The end of a very busy 28 hours for us came today – exercises and yet more exercises. Not that we have done anything that we have not done many times before, but it is all in the cause of tuning us up.

The worst part about it all was the heat generated inside (mainly because of the heat outside) making it most uncomfortable when the ventilation was stopped for fire exercises etc.

Ten days away means that it will take at least ten days from here to get home.

I only wish I was home at the moment. It annoys me sometimes when I think of the number of days that I have spent at sea on this ship. Especially when I think of the number of days that could have been spent in the garden or relaxing indoors – or just generally living a normal life.

Oh! My darling it is so difficult to find things to say to you just now. I will close now hoping that you are as happy as possible in the circumstances. Good night my lovely.

Your ever loving husband.
David XXXXXXXXX

I love you Katy

XXXXX Stuart XXXXX Sharon

TWO

ASCENSION ISLAND

(29 APRIL – 3 MAY 1982)

After straining at the leash to stay within *Plumleaf*'s 15kt top speed for the best part of a day, *Ardent* arrived at Ascension late on Thursday, 29 April. Apart from evidence that microbiological growth had contaminated fuel taken from the oiler three days before, she could hardly have been in better shape.

If the majority of her men were right, their stay would be a bearable mix of the mundane and the expected, more exercising, more hanging around, then a slow steam home.

On Friday, 30 April, 11 days from Plymouth, the Ardents woke to a piece of the moon in the middle of the ocean, something out of *Thunderbirds*. Ascension. That and the news that the Task Force was at six hours' notice to sail and that the Argentinians had introduced their own 200-mile Total Exclusion Zone after rejecting the Americans' latest peace deal. Maybe twice round the island then home for tea was a little optimistic.

Ardent quickly slipped into a new routine too, staying at anchor during the day and shadowing a Soviet Primorye auxiliary intelligence-gathering vessel by night. 'We used to show films on the Flight Deck,' Bob Young recalls. 'Me and a couple of guys were on the Gun Direction Platform, looking at this ship, and they were watching a film as well. We shadowed them, watching them watching us watching them.' The pennant number SSV501 would become familiar.

At home in Britain, if the 'shoes-in-the-cupboard', 'toilet-seat-lid-down' routine of other trips had returned, the passing of ten days had brought an edge that was easy to explain but virtually impossible to smooth. Weekly Link Wives meetings handed out what information there was, but wanting to know where the ship was at any moment was an urge most hadn't experienced before. And they could never find out. So the rhythm of life in Plymouth found a familiar beat: up, breakfast, school, work, home for lunch, work, tea, wait. Wait for news. Wherever most went, the radio went with them. Televisions would run simultaneously in living rooms, kitchens and bedrooms to guard against key words being missed.

In Sheffield, the Hansons had helped to form an impromptu organisation to pass information on. There were hundreds of families like them, with sons down south, but no news coming through.

On *Ardent*, beyond describing the sight of helicopters cross-decking stores from ship to ship to airfield, and the breath-taking panorama of ships on a Tracy Island canvas, there wasn't much to say. They were training every day, but then they trained most days. The men looked well. They had fresh food. The Chiefs' Mess was constantly briefed by the Captain and the First Lieutenant, and the

Chiefs briefed their lads. The greatest difference was not being able to talk to families and receive mail. The Navy's priority was ammunition, stores, food, hospital equipment and God knows what else.

In the absence of hard information, there was always the Buzz. The ship was awash with stories. A civilian female employee on *Canberra* had been flown home for running a brothel. A Marine leaping to a landing craft had slipped in the water and lost chunks of his leg to piranha-like fish hunting the clear blue water. Everyone suspected they were false, but they helped pass the time. Time was dragging.

While *Ardent* shadowed SSV501 anti-clockwise round Ascension, 30 miles off, there was plenty to listen to on the World Service on Saturday, 1 May: British ships and aircraft launched their first attack on East Falkland, Sea Harriers downing one enemy Mirage fighter and a Canberra reconnaissance plane, with a second Argentinian Mirage accidentally shot by friendly fire; HMS *Arrow* was slightly damaged; Operation Black Buck saw Vulcans from Wideawake crater Stanley Airfield, with Harriers conducting bomb and rocket attacks round Stanley and Goose Green airstrips in their wake; and the *QE2* was requisitioned as a troop carrier.

As significantly, the War Cabinet detailed almost unlimited rules of engagement and, on *Fearless*, Commodore Mike Clapp, Commander Amphibious Warfare, and Brigadier Julian Thompson, Commander Land Forces, narrowed the landing date to between Tuesday, 18 May and Tuesday, 25 May.

For Clapp, the man who'd witnessed *Ardent* and *Antelope* playing a vital part in an amphibious landing off Norway two months before, the decision ended days of frustration. His Operational Orders from Commander Task Force in London hadn't survived even a superficial scrutiny:

1) Blockade.
2) Special Forces recces and action.
3) Amphibious landings and minesweepers.
4) Landing operations before arrival of 5 Brigade.
5) CLFFI to join *Fearless* and 5 Brigade to land.
6) Repossession of whole of Islands.

'They were ringing me saying, "We've got these instructions and it's going to say this that and the other. Have you any comments?"' Clapp explains. 'And so we were getting either no instructions or instructions which really didn't make a great deal of sense.'

Clapp didn't have to run his finger far down CTF's timetable to back up his argument. Point 3: he didn't have any minesweepers, which either meant that no minesweeping would be needed, or that something other than a minesweeper would have to do the job.

Point 4: what sense was there in launching an amphibious landing before 5 Brigade was available as rapid back-up to the men digging in ashore? The Marines and Paras packing *Canberra*'s decks surely couldn't strike out from the beaches without someone in support. And then there was putting men

ashore – and keeping them there – before sea and air superiority had been achieved. It beggared belief.

While he was rushing from ship to ship, looking for a feel for how sharpened the operation was becoming, Clapp could see that communication had become the biggest threat to his plans; not the kit, but the Naval pomposity that said you didn't consult a junior officer. 'When I tried to get hold of them, they were thinking along one channel and I was thinking along another. In between, Sandy Woodward' – on board *Hermes* – 'would be along another channel down there. The Royal Marines would be wanting something else. Nobody could get a straight answer.'

Knowing Julian Thompson was just as unhappy, he did the only thing he could. If 300 years of pomposity had helped to cause the problem, he'd employ as much tradition to solve it.

'I decided to do the old Naval trick of observing the last pipe, taking the last signal and following it, trying to keep as quiet as I could,' he says. 'We just got on with it.'

It was just a case of which last order to pick. It didn't take long. West Falkland had been touted as the place to land first. But not any more. The pair began looking for a beachhead on East Falkland.

Not that their tribulations meant anything to *Ardent*. Not yet. It had been another routine day but there were signs, for those who cared to read them, that this wasn't as far south as they'd go. While Mike Knowles watched the RAF's Vulcan bombers lumber overhead on their way to bomb Stanley airfield, a delivery on the opposite end of the military scale caused Lenny Yeatman and assorted members of the Marine Engineering branch to sit up.

The gash disposal unit (GDU) in the Scullery had been unserviceable since a seal failed, letting water into its electric motor. They were notoriously temperamental machines, particularly prone to being fed knives and forks, accidentally. The offending seal was only three inches across. So, when its replacement was helicoptered on to the Flight Deck in a box six-feet square, word soon spread. A new GDU. The stops were being pulled out.

Richie Gough was told he'd be Bombardment Officer and met the Special Forces teams who'd sit in some ditch and call in *Ardent*'s 4.5-inch bricks, an arduous, high stakes version of *The Golden Shot*, if she reached the gunline.

Gough was delighted that he, not his boss Pete Rowe, would be in control.

'They trusted me,' he says. 'Listen, report, co-ordinate, input all the stuff in the computer. It would happen. Pete couldn't talk and listen. He was an old-style gunner. The job's aimed at young men.'

The F184 on *Ardent*'s flanks, and the '4' of the Fourth Frigate Squadron on her funnel were painted out, but they weren't the only things removed. Beards went too, in the name of a tight fit for their air gas respirators (AGRs). There were suddenly some ugly men on board.

'There was a lot of laughing, the thing we did best,' killick electrician Andy Cox recalls, 'although, deep down, everyone was wondering if peace would happen. Either way, we were prepared.'

But, when men gathered on the Quarterdeck that night, shooting the breeze with the setting sun, the sight of the armada played both ways. Was a wave of

the stick all Britain needed? Or would it swing in anger? Will we, won't we? The coming 24 hours would bring Alan West's men no closer to agreeing.

◆◆◆

Sunday, 2 May was hardly a day of rest but, as the pressure was cranked up, some Ardents made an effort.

Put a party of stokers near the 4.5-inch gun, with Knocker White in the middle and a camera in Brum Serrell's hands and the outcome was inevitable. While they 'partied' for a few hours on the Fo'c'sle, Brum lay back looking forward to seeing the recorded evidence of his young Geordie messmate sitting astride the Mark 8, 'giving it this'.

By now, Dave Croft had become PO Clem Clements's Killick of the Boats – on this Sunday a Gemini – and had won a reputation as a boy racer.

'Come here!' the Jimmy called before the boat was lowered. 'See that there?' he pointed to a buoy and a floating pipe used by tankers offloading oil for Wideawake airfield. 'You go anywhere near that and I'll have that hook off your shoulder before you get back!'

He meant it. Croft did the only thing he could in the circumstances.

'We were winding him up. We were going, "Look! Fifty yards away from it" and doing turns!'

The fun only stopped when a huge head reared up from the sea. Croft thought the giant turtle was some kind of sea monster. He threw the tiller over and the young rating acting as his bowman went flying. He survived. It wasn't the only mishap with boats, and far from the most painful.

Young stoker J.J. Smith had stretched out in the Whaler and fallen asleep. When he woke, all he could do was stagger as far as Bernie Berntsen with blisters hanging off his chest. He resisted all of the old hand's efforts to visit Bob Young in the Sickbay, fearing he'd be trooped.

'He'd have his overalls on with a white T-shirt,' Berntsen recalls the excruciating routine they adopted instead. 'When he came off rounds, he'd take his overalls down and you'd see a mass of pus. And every night, after going off watch, he'd get in the shower and I'd pull it off.' He survived too.

Even if the depth of J.J. Smith's tan hadn't troubled him, though, Bob Young had other matters on his mind. Though niggled at being 'cut out of the loop' by Ridout's late arrival, Young accepted it. Ridout would continue telling him things he'd already thought of but, stuck in their compartment with little else to do, they talked to each other: about the great what-ifs, what extra training the First-Aid parties needed, whether they'd pick up survivors from other ships.

Using *Ardent*'s huge medical library on survival medicine, they gave mini health lectures and went over and over the buddy care system. If it came to it, they'd all need to know about buddy care, how to keep the wounded man alongside you alive and do your job until a medical person provided care.

'You could be a million miles from help and, really, you are,' Young explains. 'There's other things going on around which may be a higher priority than you.' The evidence that he'd been heeded would come with every dressing taped to every lifejacket.

Will we, won't we? There were moments when it didn't even enter the equation, moments so routine that *Ardent* could have been anywhere in the world.

On *Fearless*, with questions about the East Falkland landing site in his mind, Cdre Mike Clapp was about to renew an old acquaintance. His amphibious force would need escorts and ships capable of long-range Naval Gunfire Support. He knew all this from experience, but it had been confirmed only weeks before.

So, when Admiral Woodward allocated him *Ardent* and *Antelope*, he was a happy man. 'When I found they were with me, I was so pleased because there was no one else I could talk to on the same sort of general basis on amphibious operations,' he says. 'I was probably way ahead in certain respects, but at least they'd done a lot of shore bombardment, stuff like that. I knew they'd be as worked up as any Naval ship was going to be for that role. I had faith in them.'

The intelligence briefing for officers, that afternoon, did little to settle the 'will we, won't we' debate. Mike Knowles and Tom Williams, Alan West's Warfare Officers, pored over the latest from the defence intelligence staff about the enemy threat and viewed it from the light of their warning that Britain stood to lose eight ships. On the Lower Deck, the thinking was less pessimistic: American Second World War surplus equipment, ex-British carrier, most in a fairly poor state of repair.

On the hour, every hour, all they wanted to hear was 'Lilliburlero' heralding the next news bulletin, to have more of their thoughts fuelled, not the least wishful thinking.

'Morale varied depending on who you were talking to,' PO Pete Brierley believes, though he accepts he wasn't placed to make the best judgement. The effort he'd made to save his marriage in the days before leaving was weighing more heavily on his mind than anything General Galtieri might throw his way.

He watched extroverts in the Mess and knew the façade hid deep fears. But there were others who were convinced the Argentinians couldn't hurt them. They were eating three good meals a day. They had their beer at night. They weren't thinking of war. It was 1982, and it wasn't going to happen.

At 2000, Errol Flynn wandered from the SCC into the Junior Ratings' Dining Hall to stoke up on news. He didn't expect what came next. No one did. The cruiser *General Belgrano* had been sunk.

Lenny Yeatman had been hoping that General Al Haig's shuttle diplomacy had produced a last-minute, if unexpected, solution. The name *Belgrano* came instead, like a thunderbolt. He went straight to Alan West's cabin and knocked on the door.

'Yes, Master?' the Captain said.

'The *Belgrano*'s been sunk.' Yeatman walked away without waiting for West's reaction. 'I was shocked,' he says now. 'I thought, "Bloody hell, it's going all the way." He'd been trying to convince us all from the day we sailed.' Instead of 'That'll show the bastards,' all he felt was remorse.

The glee of the SCC was short-lived. MEO Terry Pendrous reminded his men that, as they rejoiced, there were men dying.

'We started to think about the 120, whatever it was, who died,' Russ Goble reflects. 'They were all sailors. It doesn't become a ship, then. It becomes a steel tomb.'

Brum Serrell looked around the Mess and the mood changed. 'For me, it

wasn't fear, it was apprehension at going into a situation you'd never been in before. Fair enough, you're trained for it to happen, but you never think it's going to.'

But still waters ran deep. 'It's very difficult to explain,' says Ken Enticknap. 'You have confidence in your training and that you're a major force. But how on earth did troops go over the top during the First World War knowing that, two days before, they did it and they didn't like it much?

'I could calm myself thinking that I'm in a position of trust and leadership. And I'm going to have to make some unpopular decisions. Unpopular with myself and my shipmates. Am I able to step over a dying shipmate to do something I perceive to be a higher priority? I certainly thought a lot about that.'

What no one knew was what the consequences would be. Not in Whitehall, not along the Link Wives chain, not on board *Ardent*. What they did know was simple, for Mick Newby, at least. The never-ending inquests began – why had we torpedoed the ship which was meant to be sailing away from the islands?

'We're saying, "Well, guys, who gives a flying fuck whether it's going away or not? It's an Argentinian!" If they'd come closer and sunk one of our ships, what would have happened? There are times that we go off the rails. We act like 12 year olds. It was about having fun, when you had the chance, and working bloody hard. Those times made you look at the wider picture. It was about saving grace. Saving the country. The Falklanders. They belonged to Britain.'

That night, people began to seek out Joe Laidlaw's view as a former submariner – the certainty that *Belgrano* shouldn't have been in the area but was, and the fact that it was probably taken out with a Mark 8, the cheapest, most old-fashioned torpedo the Navy had.

In his cabin, Alan West's beliefs were reinforced. The main threat would be the Argentinian Air Force. From now on, he expected General Galtieri's surface ships to stay out of the game.

On the Quarterdeck, near the double-hose connection they used for shooting a cooling gush of water on a hot day, John Foster was in a group, chewing over the turn of events. Lenny Yeatman joined them. 'Those poor bastards,' the Joss uttered.

'It was the depths of winter down there,' Foster says now. 'Their ship had been sunk in this black, freezing environment and we felt nothing but pity for them.'

The sea was never far from Scouse Phillips's thoughts, either. The biggest battle wasn't with each other, the sea would 'pick you up and throw you away without thinking about it'.

Tony Ray remembers sitting on the Gun Direction Platform above the Bridge, feeling very, very moody and depressed, looking at Ascension and thinking 'Bloody hell, I've spent all these years in the Navy, I've managed to survive so far. Am I going to survive this?' If he were to fall and break a leg, he'd be sent home. The thought was fleeting. If he did, he'd never live with himself.

Will we, won't we? Ray was left with one certainty: 'This is it. This is war.'

Monday, 3 May, unsurprisingly, was partly spent shadowing SSV501. That and conducting an early morning Naval Gunfire Support exercise off North Ascension with a spotter ashore, taking fresh oil from *Plumleaf*, then practising

how they'd use the 4.5-inch gun if the loss of computers and radar left only eyeballs on the GDP and Seacat Pedestal Site looking for fast jets. And thinking of *Belgrano*.

At 1800, *Ardent* was relieved by *Argonaut* and set off on a new patrol, south of Ascension.

During the day, Andrew Gordon Lennox had taken a signal explaining the background to *Belgrano*'s sinking, the theory of an Argentinian pincer movement, how HMS *Conqueror* had nailed the threat, and why. That night, before giving his daily account of life on board, what was planned for tomorrow, and a few little fun ditties, he told the ship's company. After listening, the Ardents set about their normal evening routine.

THREE

ASCENSION ISLAND

(4–6 MAY 1982)

The moment John Leake had touched a General Purpose Machine-Gun again at Devonport after seven or eight years, it was as if he'd just put one down. Richie Gough had made a mental note of the look on the Brummie NAAFI Canteen Manager's face. Gough mentioned it to Pete Rowe, Leake talked about it with Tony Ray so, when the Lynx arrived from Wideawake airfield one morning with broad smiles and an extra GPMG, there was an inevitability about who'd end up with it. The former Devon and Dorset squaddie.

Cliff Goldfinch hadn't had the benefit of the same grounding as his drinking partner when Rowe wandered into the Chiefs' Mess, soon after, and explained the new arrangement. He's not sure that his first thought was whether there were enough cooks below to feed the ship's company, or that there was nobody else who could have released themselves to be Leake's loader, but it's academic. 'I'll load the bastard for you,' he told Rowe. Later on, alone in his cabin, he realised what he'd done. By that time, it was too late.

Leake took the GPMG from Rowe and dismantled it and put it back together again quicker than the Chief GI could. It would stay in the Canteen. The fact that Leake was a civilian and couldn't pick up a weapon if it came to shooting was something they could address later. Until then, they'd train, train and train to the point where they could strip it, clean it, fire it and strip it again blindfold.

The team's first test came at 1600 on Tuesday, 4 May, with a rapid fire exercise from the Gun Direction Platform, the trailing end of another busy day for Alan Maunder's pencil, one marked by four alien words on a fresh page of his notebook: 'My Birthday! 28 today!'

The rest of it was a little more conventional, if just as brief in its use of English: '0400Z: Conducted sonar sweep of anchorage; Gunex 31 NGS firing against a smoke flare in the open ocean north of Ascension using spotting procedures from a helicopter and Beacon MIP on a danbuoy; 1200Z: Midday position 7 51S 14 24W; RAS (L) Tidepool to stretch rigs and to RAS Avcat; 1800Z: Shadow Primorye.'

On the wider front, the Task Force suffered its first significant loss with the death of Sea Harrier pilot Lt Nicholas Turner, shot down attacking Goose Green airfield. Elsewhere, Vulcans from Wideawake flew a second marathon mission in as many days to pound Stanley airfield.

◆◆◆

So *Ardent's* close-quarters gun crews were taking shape, even if PO Richie Gough still couldn't work out how the Flight had spirited John Leake's GPMG away from Wideawake.

Suddenly, they were on a roll. Somebody came up with the bright idea of using the Ship Torpedo Weapon System launching tubes (the STWS or Stews) as a Chaff dispenser. Why not?

Joe Laidlaw and Fleet Chief Jim Watts cut paper up into small pieces, stuffed them into the tube and triggered the compressed air which, ordinarily, would spear a torpedo into the water. They hoped to see the scraps fly high enough to alarm an incoming pilot. But they just fluttered. That was the end of that.

Undeterred, Gough joined John Sephton's men and Chippy Roger Fenton in trying to work out how to put a spare GPMG in the Lynx. What the plan lacked in science, it made up for in improvisation. They relieved a swivel chair of its seat and, using the skills Fenton had already applied to knocking up machine-gun brackets on the GDP, fixed the pedestal to the helicopter's Sea Skua torpedo mounting. The GPMG was fitted and they admired the way it could now move.

To stop the whole contraption revolving beyond reach, they commandeered bungee straps and stretched them from all four corners of the airframe to the new GPMG mount. That left one problem. The gun would spew spent cartridges over the cabin floor. This was where it could become dangerous.

Gough doesn't recall whose overalls were sacrificed but, with the cuff of one dismembered arm sewn and Velcro strips attaching the open shoulder to the side of the GPMG, they had their cartridge-catcher.

'It worked perfectly,' he insists, though he doesn't say how they tested it.

◆◆◆

At 1700, Alan Maunder slipped the notebook from his pocket and began writing. As he did, *Ardent* weighed anchor and began its ritual moonlight tour, shadowing the Soviet AGI.

The all-seeing sweep of the 992 surveillance radar made World Service reception fuzzy but, even so, the strains of 'Lilliburlero' heralding the 2000 news were unmistakable. In the Stokers' Mess, Brum Serrell was sinking a can of beer after a hard day. Knocker White was there, so were Dickie Henderson, Naggers, Jessie Owens, possibly Cliff Sharpe. Sport, beer and women always gave them enough in common to fill any spare moment. This night, as the BBC announcer began his bulletin, they shared something new. HMS *Sheffield* had been hit by an Exocet.

It didn't dwell on the fact that 19 men had been killed. Or that the missile had slammed through the destroyer's starboard side. Or that its unspent fuel – not its 370lb warhead – had ignited, heated by a deceleration equal to 75-ton locomotive being halted from 60 m.p.h. in the space of ten yards. They knew none of that. The bare facts were enough to make the Stokers' Mess fall silent. She'd been hit.

In the S&S Mess, one deck above, Jon Major was with fellow cook Mick Foote, Frank Gilmour, Shaun Hanson and PTI Gary Nelson. As the same news echoed off the walls, he watched faces change.

In the Wardroom, on 1 Deck, dinner was about to be served. PO Cook Cliff

Goldfinch's head appeared through the hatch. They turned. 'Gentlemen, I have some bad news. I've just heard that *Sheffield* has been hit.'

It was an age before anyone broke the silence. When they did, the feeling was shared: 'Jesus, if one of our ships has been sunk, then we'd definitely be going down there,' Andrew Gordon Lennox remembers. 'Then we talked through that meal about the consequences.'

Back in the Stokers' Mess, Brum Serrell watched everyone disappear to a quiet corner. In the POs' Mess, Wacker Payne had already made his mind up. 'Fucking hell. It's happening.'

If Mick Newby's watch was correct, they had minutes to take in the news.

'Standby, general broadcast.' The Tannoy snapped them from their thoughts.

Alan West's voice was firm. 'He said, "Right, this is what we're going to do . . ." and that was it,' Newby remembers.

It was what the Ardents needed. 'He was telling us we had a job to do. He's playing on our spirits, on the fact that we're as good as we think we are. All the work we'd put in. All right, we've just lost however many. Accept it. Gone. There's nothing you can do. Let's start thinking about what we can do for ourselves and this operation. He was up front and told us black was black. That's what we liked about him.' And this was black.

'I could tell from chaps I spoke to, they thought it's going to stop. That's human nature,' West says. 'I don't think they believed me until *Sheffield* got sunk. I was convinced, having seen the money, that if the Argentinians didn't withdraw . . . governments didn't release that many billions of pounds.

'It did give you a sinking feeling that she'd gone. Then you thought, right, you've really got to get on with the job now. We have to sort these blighters out. That's a step change. You can have danger in training, and you do. But it's not the same as having someone trying to kill you, and keep on trying. They hadn't had that.' He began to feel a responsibility he'd not experienced before.

So, *Sheffield* had gone. One down, seven to go, if Whitehall's grim calculation was right. Now, indeed, he'd see if his Ardents were as good as they thought they were.

◆◆◆

Rio Grande, Friday, 21 May. While the returned Skyhawks are refuelled and repaired, Lt Cdr Alberto Philippi and his wingmen sit in as his old friend Lt Cdr Rodolfo Castro Fox, and the other pilots who accompanied him in the first strike, are debriefed. Any information will be useful. What they learn is that the weather's bad at the southern entrance to Falkland Sound.

◆◆◆

Exocet was everybody's fear. *Sheffield* was the first ship hit by one in anger. So, let's think about this. Argentinians played a good game of polo, Fangio was a remarkable racing driver, and their pilots weren't too bad. The simple fact was that they didn't have to come anywhere near to end *Ardent*'s war as

swiftly as they'd ended the *Sheffield*'s. It frightened them. They had guns that could fire a few hundred yards and a 4.5 that could fire 17 miles. Seacat could only fire a few miles. But an Etendard could be 25 miles away and hit them. Minds ran.

For Bill Bailey, the Flight's 35-year-old radar engineer, it was the most disturbing night. He found himself chatting to his old friend Pete Brouard. They'd shared many highs and lows over the months, but this night the conversation was about survival, and Brouard was troubled.

'Peter's wife was pregnant with their first child after nine years constantly trying,' Bailey says. 'He seemed really low. Perhaps he had a fear he'd never see the child he'd wanted for so long.' But Bailey was convinced his own time hadn't come. So the 31 year old had nothing to fear either.

Russ Goble replayed every escape drill he could imagine: 'If we get bombed there, my escape route would be here. What would you do if they came through here, and that door was blocked? Would you help people? Could you help people?' He didn't know, and he wouldn't, unless it happened.

The Jimmy, Andrew Gordon Lennox, banished all thoughts of home from his mind. They'd be too painful. His attitude was simple: 'I've married a girl who's quite capable and there's nothing I can do from 8,000 miles away, worrying about it. So I don't.'

At 18, 'just a bairn', the loss of *Sheffield* didn't register with Buck Taylor until snippets of news became something he could string together. His working partner Buck Ryan, six crucial years older, found himself trying to put it into perspective for his younger messmates.

In the coming days, John Leake would notice the difference at the NAAFI counter. No chat. Few sales.

But evenings. Evenings were different, 'especially if you're lying on your bunk, writing a letter', Brum Serrell remembers. The first night was probably the worst.

'When you join up, you sign on the line, and that's it. All of a sudden, you're hit with the realisation, "Bloody hell, I'm going to have to go through with it." Your thought process tends to swing.'

In the S&S Mess, young writer Mark Bogard's mind went to cook Kevin Williams, one of his mates on HMS *Sheffield*. Until the casualty list arrived on board, all he could do was hope he was all right.

In the Chiefs' Mess, at the same time, Dave Lee found a fresh bluey.

'An hour ago we heard the bad news about Sheffield,' he wrote to Cathy. 'Although this news has jolted us a bit, brought things home, it hasn't dampened the morale of the mess, which remains fairly high. It would be a lie to say it hasn't made me feel a little apprehensive but I will just have to put those thoughts to the back of my mind. Thoughts of 'it could happen to us' I mean.'

After swapping thoughts of typewriters, Sharon's withdrawn mood and marigolds in the garden, the letter was interrupted for a few minutes. When he came back to it, he continued: 'We have just heard that up to 30 lives may have been lost on the *Sheffield*. My heart goes out to all the wives, children and parents of those missing. She was on her way back from the Gulf as well, so

she had been away a long time. Don't let it distress you too much My Lovely that it could happen to us.'

He put the letter down gone midnight. Unfinished.

◆◆◆

Tony Ray's wife, Carol, was doing well. In Derriford – like St Budeaux, Milehouse, Crownhill, Liskeard, Portland, Hemel Hempstead, Ecclesfield, Washington, Redditch – a hunger for news had long since consumed her. If that hunger couldn't be satisfied, at least the children were blissfully unaware. For them, Mum was the provider of the school-run, the lift to the sports club, the manic woman obsessed with decorating anything with a wall, and wiping out the Devon ironing mountain in one go, who spent the evenings on the phone saying things like 'Are they in that part of it?' to the latest caller.

That morning, Stuart, Liz and Helen had taken her breakfast in bed. As she was eating, the name *Sheffield* drifted from the radio. Stuart looked at his mum as two indelible facts entered his thoughts: one, *Sheffield* had been hit; two, she was a Royal Navy ship. 'I felt useless not being able to do anything to make her feel better,' he says.

The power of mind over matter, a child's instinct for wishful thinking, quickly threw a protective screen around the nine year old. Whatever had happened to *Sheffield*, his dad's ship wouldn't be affected. If ever he felt a moment's doubt, all he had to do was look at Mum, a picture of normality.

So Carol Ray was doing well. Doing well until she turned on the TV and watched slow-motion library film of an Exocet ripping through the side of a ship and heard the latest news of *Sheffield*'s fate.

'I thought "Oh God. Who could get out of that alive?" I think that was a low point,' she admits.

Shielded from the unexpected, the children had their own alternative to ironing. At 16, Helen was in with the college crowd and could proudly say 'My dad's gone down to the Falklands'. At 14, Liz had come to the conclusion that 'No one will tell me off because my dad's down at the Falklands'. Stuart? He had Air Training Corps knowledge. As Carol knew already, 'he just took things in'.

Beryl Yeatman didn't just wash and iron, she weeded the garden and mowed the lawn. She also lived by the phone, 'in case it rang', and wrote to Lenny. *Belgrano* had convinced her this was more than just a high-powered game of bluff but, when the credits rolled on the last news programme of any night, she mentally ticked another day off. If *Ardent* hadn't been mentioned, everything was all right.

Not for Joanne Yeatman, though. She'd already been faced by playground bullies – 'Your dad's not going to come back again' – but she didn't trouble Mum by sharing the news.

Routine kept mum-to-be Frankie Enticknap going too, the housework, shifts at the Met Office – with the TV on, depending on who the boss was – talking with parents, seeing the other Link Wives. Even if the news became more depressing every day, she wasn't frightened. It would still be sorted out.

Carole Leake shared her optimism, but not the support. A NAAFI wife had no connection with the Navy, or *Ardent*'s Link network. But she had reasons to

be cheerful, even if information was hard to come by. Soon after John had gone, she'd learned she was pregnant. A letter was on its way south.

In Blackburn, though, the news of *Sheffield* had made the Whitfords anxious. 'That was when it became real,' Alan Whitford admits. 'Now they'd done something like that, they'd see sense. Maybe Thatcher would see sense. My dad definitely blamed her.'

Otherwise, there were the kind of irreconcilable thoughts that perplexed families across the country. Alan was still hoping for a compromise – 'Naïve, or what?' – but he knew that, in *Ardent*'s Forward Damage Control Party, his little brother Garry would be in the thick of it if the ship had to fight.

In her house overlooking the sea at Weymouth, Lesley Sephton was numb. Busy looking after her shop in Dorchester, busy swapping news of little Harriet's latest landmark and Lynx sorties with her pilot husband John, busy walking the dog, busy trying to remain positive. Busy, but numb.

'I don't think I was scared, for the first time,' she confesses. 'But I didn't like it because it was going to be for real. Before that, I was the one doing all the work. I was the one with the problems.'

And she was addicted to information too, not that news of such an 'unnecessary escapade' gave her much comfort. The Task Force. The people. The amount of money being spent. It was ridiculous. 'This tinpot little place that no one wanted to know anyway, just to appease Margaret Thatcher's credibility.'

Val and Dave Wopling weren't happy either but, if folk in Plymouth had read the *Herald*, they'd have known by then that life in the Grand Theatre was strangely quiet. A reporter had called, out of the blue. 'I'm phoning because it was the pub the *Ardent* lads came in,' he said. 'What d'you think about it?'

'Well, I'm not very happy about my boys going,' Val replied.

'I like the way you call them "your boys",' he said.

'Well, they are. When they're in Plymouth, they are.'

How they wished they still were. Alan Maunder doubtless knew the longitude and latitude of that magnetic slice of Union Street but, instead, at noon on Wednesday, 5 May, they were at 8 08S 14 26.5W, wherever that was. They'd shadowed the Primorye that morning. They'd shadow it in the afternoon. In between, Allan McAulay's Flight Engineers serviced the Lynx, and Terry Pendrous's Marine Engineers did the same for *Ardent*'s starboard Tyne. The dirty fuel taken from *Plumleaf* shortly before the final 'sprint' had given them a few headaches, but bright orange drums had arrived on board and the chemical concoction inside them had been dumped in her fuel tanks to sort the problem out.

At 1800, just as Dave Wopling opened to another empty bar at the Grand Theatre, the Ardents were relieved by *Argonaut* and F184 set off on patrol south-west of Ascension, still feeling raw from the devastating news 22 hours before, but glad there was routine maintenance to escape to.

If Naval training had done its job right, whether that was one year before or 20, they'd provide each other with a way out of their gloom. Alan West would depend on some simple beliefs; that young men's minds can be directed to tasks, away from reality; that mates didn't let each other down. And he'd be crucial, too, as long as someone occasionally reminded him how his men looked up to him.

None of it would be easy. When the *Sheffield* casualty list went up, men

94

pored over it in the hope of not seeing a familiar name. For Mark Bogard, the news wasn't good. His mate Kevin Williams, just 20, had been killed. For the Jimmy, Andrew Gordon Lennox, the grim list was equally depressing. *Sheffield*'s Supply Officer, Lt Cdr David Balfour, a close friend, had also died.

◆◆◆

Chief GI Pete Rowe didn't take long to muster his Ops Room team and start refocusing minds. 'You've heard the news, you've heard what happened,' he told them. Then he cranked up the training routine. In small corners and vast machinery spaces around the ship, the same was going on.

In his cabin, Alan West made a promise to Rowe, and Master at Arms Lenny Yeatman, and extracted one in return. When any news came through, the ship's company would be told. Until then, above all, he didn't want the Dining Hall gossip shop filling any gaps.

In the Chiefs' Mess, according to Chief Electrician Taff Lovidge, there were the Tories, the Labours, and the I-don't-give-a-shits – those who were justifying why they should be heading south, Maggie's boys; the Labour guys saying, 'This is a complete waste of time'; and those who couldn't give a damn. Lovidge was an I-don't-give-a-shit, and carried on circuit training with Jim Watts.

As photos of home began to appear on bulkheads, there was lots to talk about: the expectation of losses; the rumours that Argentina had sent young, ill-equipped boys to defend the Falklands; Mrs Thatcher's motives; the responsibilities of a family and mortgage.

'There were political animals and I was one,' Chief Stoker Andy Andrew admits. 'We all thought the Government should sort it out. I thought we were going to paste the Argentinians. But, Mrs Thatcher. I've got no quick gripes. She knew what she wanted.'

One room forward, PO Joe Laidlaw still detected a certain spirit, a vital spirit. 'We were the *Ardent*,' he shrugs his shoulders. 'That was it. "We can do whatever we wish. No one can hurt us." We could fly to the moon. You were what you were.'

It wasn't over-confidence, he says, or complacency. The 19 names on *Sheffield*'s roll of honour wouldn't allow that. It was arrogance. Arrogance, 'in the belief that we were superior', he adds. 'The training and the ship's company. Who you were with. That was understood. We didn't really care what other people thought. We knew what we did was the best and, if other people chose to differ, so be it.'

Across the Burma Way on 2 Deck, if Radio Operator John Foster had it right, everybody was looking at themselves and thinking, 'Can we do this?' 'I hoped maybe not to be totally involved,' he admits. 'We'll get down there and it'll be all over.'

In the S&S Mess, Bob Young and PTI Gary Nelson chewed the fat that night. For the popular club-swinger, that shocking World Service bulletin threatened to be a lifelong reminder of how he'd spent the final hours of his 25th birthday. Young was anticipating his wedding anniversary the next day. To mark it, they talked about the chances of survival if the ship was hit. And Nelson confessed

he wasn't happy to be away from home. The Doc knew the feeling. The Stokers' Mess was no different.

Fear? 'You don't understand fear,' Karoly Nagy says. 'I mean, the biggest fear you have is when you're in a bar and someone tries to hit you over the head with a bottle.'

Confidence? 'When the *Sheffield* got sunk I never thought . . . I don't know, I thought we'd fight a Naval battle,' Bernie Berntsen nods. 'If that was the case, there was no way anybody could touch us.'

Troubled? 'I was upset,' the old hand adds, replaying his advice when young Alistair Leighton confided his worry about how far the crisis might go. 'I was telling him it couldn't, and it has.' And the Buzz was filling the information gap.

First there was a suspicion that *Sheffield* was transmitting on Scot (satellite communications) and had its war radars off when the Super Etendard launched its missile at the Type 42. And, the rumour was that it had been fired from four miles away, not 40, so it should have gone straight through, yet hadn't.

'We had heard, mind you, this is speculation,' Scouse Phillips shrugs, 'that it burned its fuel off and that's what put up the smoke, then it went bang. That scared us.'

Then there was a crude assessment of *Sheffield*'s isolation. 'Out on a limb. Nothing going on,' Mick Newby recalls. 'Bad weather. This, that and the other.'

It could add up whichever way you wanted. But, for Jan Joyce, the maths was simple. 'They'd had one of ours, we'd hit one of theirs. They aren't going to get any more of ours because we've learned our lesson now.'

Maybe. Maybe not. Not if the *Sun* and the BBC continued passing on vital information.

'It came out on the World Service. "Oh yes, they haven't primed their bombs properly and they're bouncing off,"' Berntsen continues. 'I thought, "The bastards! All they've got to do now is reprime them. Just what we need. Our side snookering us."'

'I would've hung 'em,' Andy Cox adds.

But there were other things to test the hopes and fears of the men inside that sleek grey warship. Dickie Henderson recalls being told to go to the Workshop and make dog-tags. 'I thought, "Why do you make a dog-tag?" To take them off bodies.'

The *Sheffield* effect was clear from where Alan West stood. 'It had given them quite a thump,' he admits. 'It was quite clear they were a competent country in terms of jets.' It left him more convinced than ever that there would be losses.

The Ardents, like it or not, had taken the Queen's Shilling, signed up to an insurance policy with unlimited liability. No way out. Alan West had to hope that, whatever Lower Deck's feelings, his men would resolve to be ready for anything, and meet it when it came. His own part would be pivotal. In moments of crisis, a ship's company looks to its commanding officer, makes a value judgement. If they like what they see, they have confidence. They tick the box. Close the book. Crack on.

◆◆◆

After starting the day patrolling to the west of Ascension, *Ardent* dropped seven shackles of anchor off Pyramid Point at 0900 on Thursday, 6 May, and joined the other amphibious ships in a day-long switch of supplies to put things hurriedly stored at home where they should be.

When Lt Nigel Langhorn, Alan West's Diving Officer, slid into the crystal clear water at 1300, to scrape the sonar dome clear of contaminating marine biology, he knew that, within minutes of coming out again, *Ardent* would be on her way.

This wasn't murky Amsterdam or Plymouth. This was a joy. He could see the nose in front of his face, and from the 21's propellers all the way to the anchor chain, 350 or more feet away.

In seconds, the debris being scraped off the dome attracted hundreds of tiny black fish, snappy little bastards with very thin, sharp teeth.

On the Flight Deck, it had become a relaxing ritual for various Ardents to lob the odd morsel over the side, to drop an organopolypropylene line and a little float in after it, and wait for the inevitable bounty. But, this time, the trigger fish and dorados weren't biting, they had sonar dome scrapings instead. Then someone – no one admits it – arrived with engineers' putty. Ten feet below, Langhorn watched it sink slowly and his joy departed. There was a taker for this tasty scrap. A hammerhead shark.

While Langhorn and his colleague clambered back on board in swift and orderly manner, the shark was caught. The young Lieutenant engaged the chefs in a one-way conversation of short words. The duped hammerhead was hauled into the sunshine via the 182 radar winch on the Quarterdeck. And Mr Wong, the laundryman, was engaged by Joe Laidlaw to create a mouth-watering shark's fin soup.

The diversion was welcome but short. At 1600, the ship's company did recognition training. They already knew their most vital role in the coming days would be looking after *Canberra*, all 44,807 tons and 818ft 6ins of her. From hammerhead shark to Great White Whale. The thought ran a bristle of pride through the ship. Within the hour, she weighed anchor and departed for the Falklands.

◆◆◆

On HMS *Fearless*, still following the last pipe, still searching for the right landing site, the Commodore Amphibious Warfare – COMAW Mike Clapp – was facing difficulty. The frantic race to put a fleet to sea in a blaze of media attention had been calculated to show that, if the politicians and diplomats couldn't change General Galtieri's mind, a show of force might. It didn't matter if equipment was stored haphazardly. The priority was putting to sea, and being seen there.

With the collapse of Peru's peace efforts, the impetus had switched again from the pen to the sword. But the sequence of moves on this particular chessboard had exacted its price. Clapp hadn't been able to use the Ascension stopover for fine-tuning his Rapier missile batteries, not when the minds around the War Cabinet table and in Northwood's chess rooms had left him perpetually uncertain about what the next signal would demand, maybe an immediate departure north, maybe south.

Not that Rapier would be of any practical use to the Royal Navy for the first few days of any counter-invasion. The short-range weapon would be dotted to cover the landing soldiers, distributed by Brigadier Julian Thompson, Clapp's partner in the Last Pipe routine. Clapp had to accept it. So he'd need a gun with a 17-mile reach to act as a deterrent while Rapier was taken ashore and bedded in.

The job could be done by the Mark 8 4.5-inch gun on a Type 42 destroyer, but Clapp knew he didn't have one, they were with the Battle Group. The destroyer Clapp did have was *Antrim*, with a Mark 6 gun. Not good enough. Likewise the venerable Type 12s *Yarmouth* and *Plymouth*. It had to be a 21.

It didn't take Clapp and his right-hand man, Capt. Jeremy Larken, *Fearless*'s commanding officer, long to trim the field. HMS *Arrow*, still recovering from tending the stricken *Sheffield*, had suffered weather damage and was being nursed. It left *Antelope* and *Ardent*. Both, of course, knew them well. Spirited ships. There may have been an element of Hobson's choice, but both were more than satisfied. 'I don't think I could have asked for more,' Clapp reflects.

◆◆◆

On *Ardent*'s Bridge, six minutes after she actually began moving at 1654, Alan Maunder opened his notebook again and wrote: '1700Z: Sailed for Falklands in company with *Canberra*, *Elk* and *Tidepool*.' At 2359, after an Engine Room leak forced Canberra to stop pumping her share of *Tidepool*'s precious cargo, *Ardent* took station beside the fleet oiler and replenished her tanks too.

The Funnel of Fate was narrowing.

FOUR

ATLANTIC OCEAN

(7–9 MAY 1982)

On Friday, 7 May, Britain widened the Total Exclusion Zone to Argentina's horizon, 12 miles off the coast. In New York, United Nations Secretary General Javier Perez de Cuellar picked up the peace baton dropped by Peru. And, on *Canberra*, 252 nautical miles south-west of Ascension, doctors called for volunteers to build up a blood bank. The donors would need ten days to recuperate.

At 0330, her RAS (L) duties complete, *Tidepool* had detached from the group with *Argonaut*. *Canberra* had set off on a zig-zag course south with the tiny *Ardent* and the P&O roll-on roll-off cargo ship *Elk* as her constant companions, between six and 12 miles away.

Having tracked the Soviet AGI round Ascension, the Task Force assumed that the Argentinians were being fed information about their positions from Russian Bear flights. That might mean submarines. And the best way to thwart a submarine was to stop it finding them. So Alan West ran a dog-leg track to make it impossible for the Argentinians or the Russians to work out who was where, three small dots of grey and white in an unfathomable expanse of sea.

At 0420, *Ardent*'s course was 290, her speed a stately 16kts, the best *Elk* could manage packed to the gunnels with ammunition, three Sea Kings and three Scout helicopters. At 0540, her heading was 240. And so it would continue. Another routine day, a day to refocus, a day to train, and train again.

At 0924, John Sephton and Brian Murphy used a delivery service to *Canberra* as a test flight, and Mike Knowles and Pete Rowe ran their Ops Room and GDP teams through a gun direction exercise.

Midday found the three dots at or near 10 42S 17 43W, edging further from the heat of Ascension. At 1400, the call to action stations echoed round *Ardent*'s cold, functional metal interior and her men sprinted to their pre-planned positions, a race against time, desperate to stop the clock before the second hand started its third sweep.

While they ran, despite the Chief Electrician's protests, the First Lieutenant had Taff Lovidge and Tony Ray, his roving senior rates, switching off machinery.

'I can't do that!' Lovidge had Portland in his mind.

But the Jimmy was insistent. 'It might happen if we go to war,' he told them.

So there were make-believe fires, make-believe floods, make-believe rocket attacks. Training, training, training, with breathing apparatus, firehose nozzles, bungs, timber wedges, shoring. Damage control parties ran cables from A to B,

B to C, C to D and back. Stores men and cooks toiled behind red crosses, under Bob Young and Simon Ridout's gaze, treating make-believe casualties.

If the worst came to the worst, bodies wouldn't mean anything. Their priority would be to keep the ship moving. Firefighters going to a burning house don't care about the house, they want to save lives. In a ship, it's different. If there's a fire and two men are down below, they'll die. Lose two people, save the ship. The first priority. Always.

In the Ops Room, newly arrived Radio Operator Supervisor Pete Saward was coming to terms with life as an Ardent, learning to rely upon his two killicks, Phil Udy and John Newton. It didn't take him long. They had reputations for being switched-on, very particular, very methodical.

The radar team's drills continued as ever, tweaked to keep them interested. Pete Brierley kept Task Book training going, too. For the ratings spending long nights researching intelligence, the sudden call to action stations was the last thing they needed. Still, the enemy wouldn't time a strike to suit them.

It was tiring, as Pete Rowe recalls. 'You're in a coffin. Let's face it, that's what it is if anything happens. It's teamwork, teamwork, teamwork from day one. You've got to have your wits about you, 24 hours a day.'

It was worth it, if only to put Tuesday, 4 May, behind them.

As Mike Lewis watched his Ops Room EW ratings priming their eyes to recognise the telltale radar signature of Super Etendards, Exocets and all, he knew training would do something else too.

'The *Sheffield* had made mistakes and we weren't going to be caught out. It was within us. Do the best possible job so they don't get you.'

It wasn't all taken as seriously as intended, though.

At 1400, Master at Arms Lenny Yeatman and the Jimmy, Andrew Gordon Lennox, began an exercise to identify the problems *Ardent* might have handling prisoners: How many sentries they'd need, where they'd be posted, how Cliff Goldfinch would feed an unknown number of extra mouths.

If the exercise started from an optimistic assumption – that they'd be the ones taking prisoners – it allowed Alan West's younger Ardents to prepare for the alternative. Despite the provisions of the Geneva Convention, and the ID cards they all carried, the Stokers' Mess had settled on their own course of action, should the worst come to the worst. 'If we were taken prisoner, it was going to be name rank, number and "Him officer",' Andy Cox recalls. It wasn't the point of the Joss's careful planning. So what? It was a laugh.

That night, though, not everyone was able to concentrate on what the Jimmy had to tell them on the main broadcast. As they departed Ascension, *Ardent* had gone to EMCON silence (emission control silence) with all radars, sonars and communications switched to stand-by and the UWT (underwater telephone) on loudspeaker to monitor and record any sounds.

The principle was simple. Low-frequency signals spread far and wide but are hard to pinpoint. High-frequency transmissions fall short of distant ears, but they're easy to follow back to a source. Reducing the emissions of *Ardent*'s sensor or communications equipment would keep her hidden.

At 1830, *Ardent* thought she'd picked up something unexpected. The Lynx was sent aloft for a surface search. For some minutes, the Ops Room watched

its screens and waited on tenterhooks for news. John Sephton and Brian Murphy came back, eventually, but none the wiser.

◆◆◆

At 1200 on Saturday, 8 May – position 13 18S 22 36W – Alan West and Tom Williams flew to meet *Elk*'s Senior Naval Officer, Cdr Andrew Ritchie, and her skipper, Capt John Morton, for a briefing. The 495ft walk from her bow to stern was enough to have Williams craving the stop-off on *Canberra* on the way back. Big, white and unmissable the liner may have been, but she wasn't bursting with ammunition. John Sephton soon had them there.

The day had already been busy for the 35-year-old pilot and his observer, Brian Murphy. After its surface search the night before, the Lynx had been back in the air at 0853 for a delivery service to *Canberra* and to drop flares for a Seacat shoot in 'emergency' mode.

Seacat. It still hardly filled the Lower Deck with optimism.

Its principle was easy but, then, so was the thinking behind arcade games the Knocker Whites, Buck Taylors and Ralph Coates had played on Union Street.

If *Ardent*'s 912 radar picked up a plane, the Ops Room Seacat Controller in the hotseat next to Richie Gough had some rapid choices to make. He could let the system's closed-circuit TV camera gather the target and follow it until the moment a proximity fuse, or impact, detonated the high explosive warhead. Or he could take over with a joystick soon after he'd unleashed the 63kg missile. Or play the whole 'game' alone from the word go.

Or he could let the rating manning the Launch Control Room, on the Upper Deck overlooking the Seacat launcher, flick a switch to emergency control, and hand the whole job over to another rating holding a joystick on the Ped Site, above the Hangar.

Whichever man was at the controls and following the pictures, once the missile's fins had unlocked in the first milliseconds of flight, the game was simple. He'd lock on to flares at the back of the missile, put the cross-wires on to the target, then slowly bring the two together in the centre of his screen, knowing that every minuscule movement of the joystick would send an adjusting radio signal to the missile. If the target moved, so did the joystick. Then – bang! That was the theory.

There was one problem. Seacat had a range of a shade over three miles, not a lot of time to spot the threat and see it all the way through. It was a high-risk arcade game, but the only one *Ardent* would have at hand if Alan West's hunch was right.

As *Ardent* kept *Canberra* and *Elk* company 570nm, or thereabouts, south south-west of Ascension, Richie Gough wasn't happy with the choice of player if *Ardent*'s future rested on the Ped Site operator. Pete Rowe wanted young missileman Scouse Wharton. Gough thought PO Johnno Johnson was better qualified. Both admit there was tension.

'I was losing faith in him,' Gough recalls.

'The hanging around was beginning to tell,' Rowe says. He invited the 23 year old in for a beer.

'You know your job inside out,' the chat stretched beyond Seacat. 'If you try to do it too fast you're going to make mistakes and your mate's going to end up dead! Get it through to the lads!'

In the end, what PWO Mike Knowles saw was Gough's rapid mind, Rowe's old head. The perfect combination. 'Team gels.' Johnson was restored.

Ardent fired two live missiles from the Ped Site that afternoon. Both hit. In the Ops Room, Lt Tom Williams noted the firings as 'satisfactory'. For Knowles, it had been 'all right'. Hardly great optimism, considering emergency control was all they'd have if COMAW Mike Clapp sent F184 to hug the radar-baffling Falkland coastline, laying down Naval Gunfire Support on the big day.

For Alan West, which ship and what part of the rugged coast were the only questions.

On *Fearless*, Clapp and right-hand man Jeremy Larken already knew both answers. But the value of their chosen Amphibious Objective Area wasn't their only calculation. For almost three weeks, they'd had an idea of how much punishment they might take in making the landings a success.

'All ships faced risks,' Larken explains, 'an inescapable feature of serious warfare. The aim was to get the troops and equipment and stores ashore safely and then take and hold the beachhead. The whole would add up to the sum of the parts.'

In fact, it needed to add up to more, and for two reasons: first, Larken knew that any team had to boast that kind of strength; second, Clapp and he expected to lose ships. If they did, what was left had to match the task.

The thinking was that the Argentinian pilots would be sent to hit the Task Force's 'power-projection cutting edge', the troops and their amphibious, troop and stores ships, the HVUs (high value units). All that the escorts, the *Ardent* and *Antelope*, had to do was what they were designed for and trained to do. Put themselves in the way. Most pilots would surely want to avoid being taken out by an escort. If Clapp had done his sums correctly, his thin grey line of Royal Navy frigates and destroyers was less likely to be attacked than the HVUs. Exposed, yes, but not exceptionally at risk.

On *Ardent*, Taff Lovidge was assessing risks too. Leading hand Bob Lewis and MEM Ralph Coates were good cable-runners. It made no sense to have both in Ken Enticknap's Aft DCP, so Lewis moved forward. There was no point having PO Wacker Payne and his killick electrician, Andy Cox, aft either. So Cox went forward to even the experience in CPO Geoff Hart's section base. Garry Whitford, an acting leading hand but not an electrics specialist, switched from the forward Comms position to go aft.

Whitford would be equal to whatever Ken Enticknap threw at him. In his short time on board, he'd gained a reputation as a quiet man, quiet but clever and determined. A dishwasher that had resisted every effort to mend it was testimony to his patience too.

Slowly but surely, then, *Ardent* was heading for war and Sunday, 9 May, was anything but a day of rest. At some point, the news-watchers at home would see more of the big picture – *Narwal*, a fishing vessel and spy ship, was strafed by two Harriers, killing one and injuring 13; an enemy helicopter was downed by a missile from a British warship; and the garrison round Stanley was bombarded.

The pictures wouldn't arrive home for weeks, but *Ardent* was about to make its newsreel debut too. For some days, the morale of the Paras and Marines had worried *Canberra*'s Senior Naval Officer, Capt Chris 'Beagle' Burne. So, with RO Steve Kent flashing Morse signals to the liner from her port Bridge Wing, *Ardent* set about providing everyone with a badly needed boost.

At 0800, now 700nm south-west of Ascension, with her nameplates and pennant numbers as grey as the Atlantic swell, she closed *Canberra*'s starboard quarter and began painting herself into one of the war's most memorable pictures. As she did, she went through her party pieces. At full power, her 4.5 spat five HE rounds into the air and, with LS Leigh Slatter strapped in, her starboard 20mm Oerlikon ripped through 1.5-inch parachute flares, like ducks on a fairground stall.

Surg. Lt Cdr Morgan O'Connell, the Navy's psychiatrist on *Canberra*, had joined the hundreds lining *Canberra*'s starboard rail and smiled broadly as *Ardent* did her bit, typical Type 21 Club. 'It had a tremendous effect on morale, to see this little ship's demonstration of firepower and then, suddenly, they put the handle down. Very dramatic. *Ardent* had become our chummy ship.'

For a short while at least, O'Connell had been able to put a worrying thought to the back of his mind. How were they going to defuse the Royal Marines and Paras if it never came to shooting? More importantly, how would the Navy cope with the losses he'd been told to expect?

By the time *Ardent* did its flypast, he'd already woken up to the fact that the people he had most in common with on *Canberra* were the chaplains. And he'd already incurred Beagle Burne's wrath for talking in the bar, one night, to the *Telegraph*'s Charles Laurence about bereavement and the need to anticipate grief if the trauma was going to be kept to a minimum, a chat which had turned up in print.

To Burne, O'Connell recalls, it was forbidden territory. To him, it was not. 'What's so terrible talking about it?' he asked his superior. 'This is normal stuff.'

❖❖❖

They didn't talk about death much on *Ardent*, unless there was a joke at the end of the conversation. But they did think about it. At night. They thought about an Exocet attack.

'Initially, you don't think how people had died,' Andy Cox says. 'Then your mind wanders. You lie there thinking about how you'd get out if the ship turns turtle.'

The thought at least brushed their minds at that Sunday's 1100 church service, where the victims of the *Belgrano* and *Sheffield* were remembered. An invigorating demonstration of lethal firepower and a solemn remembrance of the devastation of modern warfare, all in the space of a morning.

In the wake of *Sheffield*, Wyatt Earp found himself with nowhere to run in the SCC, a place looking like something from *Star Trek* to the 18-year-old stoker. He had no option but to walk in from the Aft Engine Room. There was a conversation going on, but MEO Terry Pendrous swung around in his chair.

'I'll tell you now, there's only two ways you're coming back, and that's either in a box or as a hero,' he told the Malvern lad. 'You didn't join for that, did you?' Pendrous waited for his reply.

'No, I must admit,' Earp said, finally. 'They mentioned about seeing the world and all that, but no one mentioned you might get killed!'

In the Seamen's Mess, the news of 4 May had concentrated minds. The buck stopped with Scouse Flynn, the Killick of the Mess, to make sure it was always ready for action. Watching over the Junior Mess members, to make sure their kit was stowed away, or they weren't loafing, was always a full-time task. After *Sheffield*, it had become easier, much easier.

Newly-wed CPO Jeff Curran noticed how some men were starting to show the signs of fear and anxiety, questioning the Navy's involvement in such a crazy scheme. He recalls Chief Stoker Andy Andrew asking what he thought of it. Curran told him it was his job. He was being paid for it. 'That caused him to hit the roof. He thought I should be thinking of my wife,' Curran says.

PO Joe Laidlaw immersed himself in work, content that a regular mental sprint through the ship, from hatch to hatch, exit to exit, would keep him ready for whatever lay beyond the horizon.

Where most people buried themselves in a book to unwind, or otherwise, Karoly Nagy's decision to start reading did the opposite. His mother had always dabbled in fortune-telling. Two or three generations had.

'Her Auntie Nell done it,' he explains. 'So she wrote me a letter.'

It read: 'I have a feeling that your ship is going to be engaged in an activity and it's going to sink . . . but if you keep your head down you'll be okay!'

Receiving the letter wasn't a mistake. But reading it out was.

'It was a bit of a giggle. I didn't think anything of it.' He was in the minority. Word spread.

'He was going to be all right, but the ship wasn't going to be all right!' Jessie Owens remembers. 'You knew something was going to happen, but you didn't want to admit it.'

The helo delivery service on to *Ardent*'s Flight Deck, of course, had meant the chance of one off it, and Dave Lee had taken out his pen again:

> Sunday, 9 May, same address
>
> My darling Catherine,
>
> Something of a surprise to have some more mail leaving the ship today so here is a quick 'Hello' to you to take advantage of it. It is obviously a ship going the other way that is taking the mail off us, the same direction that I hope we will be going soon.
>
> Nothing has changed at all my lovely, so very little to add to what I told you in my last letter. There should be a mail drop today as well so I hope to have a letter from you later on.
>
> I continue to hope that you and the children are still well and happy. Are you still managing to take the children out at the weekends? I feel sure that it will be of help to you to take your mind off things and keep

them happier as well if you can get out when weather permits.

No doubt you have given the new shed a coat of preserver by now and the children have found it like a great playhouse.

Everyone in the Mess is getting ready for a film: the Sunday matinee. I haven't watched one all week and I won't be watching this one either unless it meets my requirement level.

The weather here is the lumpiest since we left UK. But nowhere near as rough as I feel it is going to get. That is the one big thing I will never, ever miss about the Navy when I come outside – rough weather. I always pray that nothing goes wrong with the equipment in rough weather.

A pay rise is through – nearly £13 a week before tax. Not a great deal, but nothing more or less than expected. I haven't drawn any money as yet nor should I need to for a couple of weeks. And I shall do my spending when I am home again (unless of course you do it all for me my petal).

No mail on board today but perhaps tomorrow maybe. This letter is still going tonight if we make our rendezvous. I watched most of the film this afternoon only missing half a reel when I was called out. Brass Target not a bad film. I have been working steadily most of the day, which isn't a bad thing on a Sunday at sea. I shall save my time off for the rough weather.

I'm sorry this letter is so short my lovely but there really isn't much more to say. I said it all in my last letter to you but at least this quick Hello might help to brighten up a morning for you. I am off for a bath now and to read a book. Goodnight then my darling, sleep tight. Missing you very much, your ever loving husband.

David XXXXX

I love you Katy

XXXXX Stuart XXXXX Sharon

At 2359, *Ardent* rendezvoused with *Antelope* and launched the Lynx to transfer mail, and collect two Skua missiles.

FIVE

ATLANTIC OCEAN

(10–15 MAY 1982)

Monday, 10 May: It had taken ten days to reach Ascension's sun. Now they were four days south of that lump of rock in the middle of the grey Atlantic, and the crystal-clear waters seemed far away. But not as far away as home.

It was cold and rough and, if anyone on board was still trying to convince themselves that it wouldn't come to shooting, the first nine and a half hours of the day would demand to know how, and why.

At 0220, while their families slept, the Ardents brought *Canberra* and *Elk* back to COMAW Mike Clapp's *Fearless* group, around 1,000nm north-west of Tristan da Cuñha. Using the stores ship *Stromness* as a guide, the three joined *Intrepid, Norland, Atlantic Conveyor* and *Europic Ferry*, and the escorts *Antrim* and *Argonaut*, on a course of 190 at 17kts. Forty minutes later, they changed tack to Co 213 and slowed to 15kts. Half-an-hour after that, the four-day zig-zag stopped.

For Navigating Officer Alan Maunder, new company doubtless prompted a sigh of relief. Since *Ardent* had split off with *Canberra* and *Elk*, he'd been exchanging positions with the Great White Whale's Navigating Officer, the liner's man using Satnav, Maunder the heavens.

With *Ardent*'s Satnav long since giving up the ghost, and her navigation lights on only as necessary – and even then on a narrow sweep – they'd experienced a few hairy moments. Not long before the rendezvous, one Morning Watch, he'd stepped on the Bridge Wing and thought it odd that he couldn't see the sky. Then he saw the outline of a ship. Two hundred yards away. It was *Elk*, huge, on the beam. He grabbed one of Pete Saward's radio operators and flashed an Aldis light warning to the giant ammunition carrier. The moment was tense, but suddenly *Elk* was gone.

◆◆◆

At 0730, John Sephton and Brian Murphy were scrambled for a surface search, not an exercise this time. At 0830 the main broadcast called the Ardents to action stations, their pounding hearts hoping the tinny 'Exocet! Exocet! Exocet!' wasn't for real.

It was one topic allowed out of cabins and gulches in the past four days. They'd discussed all the options carefully, and had different plans for different situations; where it was heading from, whether it was Mike Lewis's Electronic Warfare team who'd detected it, whatever. They could handle most

permutations, but Tony Ray, Taff Lovidge and Terry Pendrous had already agreed that there was no point having all their eggs in one basket. After *Sheffield*, Mick Cox would be the Action Marine Engineering Officer of the Watch in the SCC, with a stoker PO or a leading stoker on the throttles. CPO Andy Lee would be in the Aft Switchboard, across the SCC Flat. The other Chiefs would scatter.

Fourteen seconds was how long they'd have to react. *Sheffield* had had three.

Lovidge and Ray practised charging out of the SCC at the clap of someone's hands, to see how far forward they could thud before an imaginary Exocet exploded. Forty-somethings, steaming boot feet, racing a 700 m.p.h. missile. They agreed to leave the doors open, but it was academic. They could run, but they wouldn't have had time to close the doors anyway. It was the best they could do.

In the Tiller Flat, the emergency steering position beneath the Quarterdeck at the stern, PTI Gary 'Ginger' Nelson was rehearsing too. At the best of times, you had to bend double to work in the space.

In normal service, rudders were connected to the Bridge. If the connections were broken, the tiller man would pump them vigorously by hand to midships, so they could steer using the main engines.

God forbid, but Nelson and Ken Chapman had to account for it. They had three escape routes from the Tiller Flat: up to the Quarterdeck; up to the 2 Deck Paint Store; or into the 3 Deck air lock. Ginger was a broad man, so he practised, practised, practised. The alternative wasn't worth contemplating.

On the Flight Deck, Radar Engineer Bill Bailey had chewed over the same question with Scouse Lacey, Pete Brouard, Speedy Ball, Rick Schofield and Wally Wallington and concluded that, apart from going over the side, there were few escape routes. They'd also discussed how their families would fare if anything happened, although, Bailey concedes, it was a bit late, wasn't it?

◆◆◆

In Cruising Watches, the worst risk was a collision, or a grounding. If something caught fire, Alan West would need enough people to deal with it. In Cruising Watches, he'd be pushed to make action stations, because his Ardents would be doing other things, maybe on one of the day's six watches, or at work, or grabbing a couple of hours sleep before the next watch.

In Defence Watches, they'd need to move to action stations rapidly. Closed down to Damage Control State 2 Yankee, doors and hatches shut to create smoke boundaries and blast routes, moving about would be difficult in any case. So half the ship's company would be on-watch and half off-watch. The men standing down would be lying on their bunks, in dry clothing, waiting for his 'Hands to action stations' pipe, on the blocks and ready to go. After eight hours, they'd swap.

In short, if a ship's in Defence Watches, it's operating in a dangerous area. Or it's going to war.

At 0930, the anti-Exocet drill ended. And *Ardent* changed to Defence Watches.

The rest of the day was textbook, except there'd be no night out at the Grand Theatre. Under Pete Rowe's critical eye, young Sub-Lieutenant Richie Barker ran John Leake and Cliff Goldfinch through a GPMG rapid fire exercise. Above the Hangar, Russ Goble and Scouse Wharton squeezed their LMG triggers again and again.

At the other end of 02 Deck, just aft of the door to the Bridge, Mick Newby and Topsy Turner worked at squeezing every last round of 20mm ammunition out of their Oerlikons. At 400 rounds a minute, a 60-round magazine crammed with 66 pressure-fed bullets wouldn't last long.

That was the routine in the morning. And in the afternoon. If the 992 radar couldn't alert Seacat quickly enough to something hugging the waves or grass at 450kts, then human eyes would have to.

On rounds that night, as every night since 'Lilliburlero' had broken the *Sheffield* news, the Jimmy was tuned to the atmosphere, his eyes to people's faces, his ears to any hint that morale had fallen beyond the instinctive fear that comes with being in a grey box, heading, in choppy grey seas, to a war zone.

'If you felt there was a problem, you'd have done something about it already,' he shrugs. 'My job was to keep the ship happy about what they had to do, ready for what the Captain wanted.' He looked round the Messes that night and sensed everything was as well as could be expected, maybe better.

'Lilliburlero' appeared briefly in quiet corners as Monday, 10 May, rolled to an end. She told them that *Sheffield* had sunk while under tow by *Yarmouth*. The same day, *Ardent*'s sister *Alacrity* had ventured inside Falkland Sound for the first time and blown up the Argentinian supply ship *Isla de los Estados*.

◆◆◆

Tuesday, 11 May: At 0300, now 930nm north-west of Tristan da Cunha, west of the Cape of Good Hope, RFA *Tidepool* stretched the fleet to 11 ships. A few hours later, *Ardent* received a signal from *Stromness* to take position at the supply vessel's Station 9, ready for a RAS – five loads of food to replenish Cliff Goldfinch's cupboard.

In the morning, a bright day with brilliant blue skies, Alan West flew to *Fearless* for a briefing with COMAW Mike Clapp. Otherwise, there were anti-Exocet drills before noon and anti-Exocet drills after. More make-believe, more lung-bursting races, more mouth-drying anticipation. Then, at 1432, the odd rhythm of life was shattered for real.

'Hands to action stations! Hands to action stations!' The Ardents ran and waited, not knowing what had sent the Damage Control parties to their section bases, the gunnery teams to their weapons.

In the Ops Room they did. *Intrepid* thought she'd detected a submarine and put out a cert sub alert, the highest classification for a possible contact. Someone must have seen something. In textbook fashion, the convoy broke up, altered course and increased speed.

Lt David Searle was on the Bridge as John Sephton and Brian Murphy took the Lynx up. Nerves were jangling away when, suddenly, he saw a spout of water. 'You realised you were speaking now on behalf of the entire Task Force,'

Searle recalls. 'So I decided, "I'll take this really seriously. It's a whale!"'

A returning Brian Murphy described a fabulous piece of sealife, and Searle sighed. But not for long.

At 1713, they were back at action stations. *Argonaut*, this time, had picked up a surface contact and wasn't taking any chances. A helicopter was launched but the contact turned out to be a friendly trawler. More sighs of relief. However, the tension had been cranked up another notch.

In the grey, functional confines of their Type 21, it could often have been any time of day or night. It was the metronomic, disciplined Defence Watch routine, the rhythm of exercises, the anticipation of food or sleep, that had provided the constant. Now they couldn't even rely on that.

Now, with each unexpected call, the rhythm was being broken. Body clocks were shot. The capacity for some men to remember events by the minute but not the day, and others by the day, not the time, had rarely mattered. So, apart from being 'pretty hyped up', Pete Brierley doesn't remember exactly when he switched on to a series of transmissions coming from the UWT, the underwater telephone being used to record any noise while they were in EMCON silence, their sensors switched off. By the time Lt Tom Williams, the Officer of the Watch, arrived on his shoulder to check if there were enemy units around, he'd classified it as SQS 23, an American sonar system fitted to Argentinian ships and running in 'acute' mode, in other words, ready for attack.

The tape-recorder was started, and the noise came again. But then it became erratic.

Confused, Brierley sent a couple of his sonar lads to search the ship for noises. In minutes, they were back with a young stoker in tow. He'd been chipping floor tiles in his Mess. They laughed. Eventually.

◆◆◆

'As it got further, you definitely had a difference between the old and the young generation,' Naggers recalls. 'The youngsters just got on with it.'

'We had nothing to lose,' Buck Taylor adds. But weren't they sensitive towards the others?

'Not at all,' Nags shrugs.

You didn't modify your behaviour?

'Not at all,' Taylor confirms.

Chief Tiff Ken Enticknap can vouch for that. He was on watch with Naggers, PO Stoker Paddy McGinnis, Dickie Henderson and Errol Flynn in the SCC, the roll of the ship in choppy seas broken by the occasional bang of a wave against the starboard side.

After one odd thud, Nagy and Henderson hit the deck, yelling 'Exocet! Exocet!' Enticknap threw a wobbly and banned Naggers from the SCC for the rest of the watch. Mind you, it hadn't surprised him.

'My watch was labelled a bit of a doom watch. Paddy and Dickie were always concocting gloomy tales. That was typical . . . probably a way for nervous people to come to terms with the unknown.'

Maybe. But it didn't matter to the young stokers. Barry Muncer was having a gulch party with Wyatt Earp and three or four others one night when he asked what sort of injury they'd like to go home with.

'If anything, it'd be nice to be shot through the arm,' Earp replied. 'It'd be a good party piece!' The curtain ripped back and someone let them have it. He had to be dragged off. He was in tears.

'Other people take it badly,' a second stoker told the 18 year old. It stopped Earp in his tracks. 'I thought, "Fuck! If you're going to get shot, you're going to be dead."'

◆◆◆

The deployment was going well for Pete Brierley. His sonar team was feeling the uncertainty, like everyone, but the food was good, the training solid, there was time to sleep and time to have fun with Mal Crane, often at the expense of Richie Gough, six years Brierley's junior and so gung-ho it hurt.

Crane would mumble so the 23 year old had to ask him to repeat. Brierley would interpret. Gough's head would swivel, trying to decipher the rubbish one was speaking, trying to make sense of the translation the other was fabricating. It took him ages to twig.

Tom Williams walked into the Ops Room after dinner late that night – Tuesday, 11 May – and called to Brierley: 'Go down and see the Captain.'

Brierley had forgotten that he'd become eligible for his third badge, '12 years undetected crime'. As he knocked on Alan West's cabin door, he realised. Alongside in Devonport, they'd have been dressed in No. 1 uniforms. Now, they were in full anti-flash and action working rig.

West presented the badge and asked about home, then offered the ship's help again. Brierley was grateful. He'd already received a Family Services signal saying his wife needed cash for the gas bill.

Whatever news 'Lilli' brought each night, it had no effect on the 29 year old. No one on board could control the outcome of the crisis, not the political, not the diplomatic, certainly not the military. Whatever would happen would happen. It was more the thinking of a man heading for a divorce than one heading for war. It meant that, whatever was on the others' minds, he never thought of dying. 'If I did, it wouldn't matter. I'd lost everything.' It was a grim shield against a grimmer threat.

Wednesday, 12 May: The preparations went on. At 0500, around 770nm west north-west of Tristan da Cunha, *Ardent* split off in line abreast with *Argonaut* to practise surface action group (SAG) procedures, fighting as a team in a high-speed, fuel-burning zig-zag designed to allow each ship to hit the enemy before the enemy could hit them. The theory was simple. Capt Kit Layman and Alan West would take their ships to the edge of their Exocet range, fire at the same time, then dash away while they assessed the damage they'd inflicted.

At 2230, 12 hours after topping up her half-empty tanks from *Tidepool*, she did it again. As they did so, in lounges and bedrooms around the country, *News at Ten* recapped *QE2*'s departure from Southampton with 5 Brigade, like

Canberra's sailing, 34 days earlier, an occasion stage-managed for news-junkies on the home front and whoever cared to watch overseas. Its real significance was lost on most onlookers.

If Commander Task Group's Operation Order of 1 May was to be stuck to – Clapp and Thompson's Last Pipe – it meant the Amphibious Landing Force would be ashore for days before back-up arrived. Thus, whoever made up Clapp's thin grey line of Naval escorts would have a long, hard task ahead.

The next day maintained the pattern. And so did the next day, though Tristan da Cunha had been replaced in the minds of the Amphibious Group by a name of greater significance, for *Ardent, Fearless, Intrepid, Canberra, Atlantic Conveyor, Norland, Elk, Europic Ferry, Stromness, Tidepool* and *Argonaut* were now 1,146nm east north-east of Port Stanley.

At 0700, visibility was 1.5 miles. At 1200, Maunder recorded a position of 40 48S 34 25W. At 1345, on the basis of never passing a petrol pump, *Ardent* lined up at *Tidepool*'s Station 8 for more fuel. At 1700, after most of the day at Alert 15 – take-off at 15 minutes notice – Sephton and Murphy took the Lynx up for a surface probe. At 1815, the ship received two deliveries. At 1913, the Lynx came home.

If no news was good news, it was also an invitation for the social heart of the ship, the Junior Ratings' Dining Hall beneath the Hangar, to fill the void. Tradition. And, if there were some – like John Foster, Dave Croft, Mick Newby and their Ops Room colleagues – who were privy to certain information, and determined to keep it to themselves, there were others who couldn't help nudging gossip along.

'Chinese whispers,' says Newby. 'When you're in a position of responsibility, the last thing you need to do is talk. By the time it gets to the thirteenth person, it's a ballistic missile-carrying submarine.'

In his quest for information, Karoly Nagy was regarded by many as the biggest buzz-carrier. 'Some of the shit he used to come out with,' Bernie Berntsen recalls. 'He'd come down the Mess with some buzz and get whacked for it.' It didn't stop it happening.

The old man of the Junior Messdeck, 33-year-old Berntsen kept the young ratings on an even keel. It was a task he was ably qualified for. There were so many things for the world's best lovers, referees and politicians to chat about.

'Let's get down there and start kicking arse now,' or 'There's a chance he might eff-off home,' or 'If anything happens, it happens,' or 'If it doesn't happen, we've enjoyed ourselves.' The Flight Deck echoed to similar conversations. About the same time, Cliff Goldfinch paid one of his regular visits to his boss, Rick Banfield, a man whose company he enjoyed, as most people did. 'I bet you we go in on the 20th,' Goldfinch told the Supply Officer.

'Don't be stupid!' But the PO Cook was insistent. Banfield told him to bugger off.

On his wanderings from the Sickbay, in his unequal effort to match Bob Young's knowledge of every corner of the Type 21, Surg. Lt Simon Ridout had lent an ear to those Ardents who needed it.

He spotted a few signs of stress in some, and also had a word with those

who'd caught Young's eye. In many ways, Ridout was less well-off than the men he tried to reassure. They had their mates around them. Ridout still felt an outsider. He would face his fear – the fear of being afraid – alone.

At 2330, as the cooks in *Ardent's* Galley prepared another midnight meal, north of East Falkland two Sea King 4 helicopters left *Hermes* with 45 men of D Squadron SAS, heading for a Pucara airbase at Pebble Island, on the north coast of West Falkland. It would be a decisive raid. All 45 returned unscathed but for a few scratches. Twenty-two of the men, however, would be dead within five days.

Half-an-hour after the Sea Kings took off, at 0000, active service was declared. Everyone at sea was now subject to service discipline, and covered by the provisions of the Geneva Convention. There was also the comfort of knowing that, if the worst came to the worst, everyone's estate would be free from death duties. For the media men, particularly, this was an odd kind of bargain.

◆◆◆

Saturday, 15 May. In the Roaring Forties, the grey expanse from 42 to 48 degrees south, you can expect storms at any time. To escape the most evil, you'd have to run to the southern Indian Ocean. But *Ardent* was heading the other way, now comfortably within 1,000 miles of Port Stanley.

From the Seacat Pedestal Site above the Hangar, Russ Goble was on Comms to Bagsy Baker on the LAS sight above the Bridge when a flash across the black sky on the port side silenced him. Missile!

On the Bridge, Alan Maunder saw the flash and feared the same. While Goble tried to log in to the Ops Room, Maunder guessed this bright-tailed projectile was only miles away. And closing.

Then, as soon as it had appeared, it disintegrated.

On his headset, Goble heard the skipper's voice cut in: 'That's a meteor.'

Goble breathed a deep sigh of relief. So did Maunder.

◆◆◆

In the confines of *Fearless's* Maritime Ops Room, COMAW Mike Clapp and Capt Jeremy Larken had spent hours with Brig Julian Thompson turning the Last Pipe into a blueprint for retaking the islands. All that remained was for Clapp to tell his commanding officers how. How and where.

From its single command position, via its antiquated Action Information System, Clapp would play manager, conductor and nervous parent: delegating command duties for the surface, sub-surface and air wars to the more modern *Antrim*; controlling the landing forces; studying the unfolding canvas, then handing over to Thompson for the breakout from his beachhead. Job done. That was the theory.

In the middle of that Saturday morning, he gathered his commanding officers on *Fearless*. He didn't need to tell them some things. Each already knew, for instance, that to suit its limited resources the UK fleet had specialised

in open ocean roles, particularly anti-submarine warfare. Thus it hadn't needed to invest in radars which could track aircraft confidently over land. So it hadn't. Defence cuts had also killed the Navy's carrier-borne airborne long-range early warning capability.

That had left Clapp with a mix of Sea Harrier jets and Sea Dart, Sea Slug, Seacat, Rapier and Stinger missiles to fight the coming inshore surface-to-air battle; and 20mm Oerlikons, GPMGs and LMGs; and self-loading rifles and 9mm Browning service revolvers. It would leave his thin grey line ill-equipped for the task ahead. But it was all he had. His commanding officers knew that too.

On the plus side, just two months before, Operation Alloy Express had taught Clapp, Larken and Alan West vital lessons about placing ships near land masses so that fast jets would find too little space to identify a target, fly straight for about ten seconds to aim and release a bomb, then flee. Fifteen seconds, tops. And all in the midst of a distracting hail of fire, some well-directed.

All the COs needed to know was who and where. Clapp put up a map of Falkland Sound on the wall. At the centre of it was San Carlos Water. Then he added the detail. Alan West looked and listened.

On the basis of conjecture and Special Forces intelligence, Brig Julian Thompson believed the Argentinians could counter-attack the San Carlos landing sites from Darwin settlement, to the south-west. He'd received reports of helicopters being stored there. It was an obvious place. His plan was to send the SAS on a high-powered shooting spree, pretending they were a huge force. Any target, though, would need the Navy. Goose Green airfield, a mile south, had to be eliminated too. Someone had to pick that ticket up.

But the submarine threat meant that, whichever ship Clapp chose for the naval gunfire role, it would be impossible to provide a second ship in close mutual support.

Clapp had weighed the odds with Larken. The risk his NGS ship ran was neither out of order nor balance. The Argentinians would surely go for the high value targets, the troopships. So, they either sent someone to the gunline in Grantham Sound alone, or not at all – leaving the landings unprotected.

The ship needed a Mark 8 gun. So, it had to be a Type 21. Clapp looked at West and assumed he was already filling the gaps. Whichever ship Clapp chose would lead the amphibians into Falkland Sound late on Thursday, 20 May.

West caught Principal Warfare Officer Tom Williams's eye. Williams still hasn't forgotten the look on West's face. He knew instinctively what it meant. They'd have to start preparing to be that ship. The Funnel of Fate was about to narrow once more.

Clapp had made it very clear that *Hermes* and *Invincible* would stay east, beyond the range of enemy fighters, but leaving her patrolling Sea Harriers little flying time above the imaginary Falkland Sound no-go safety box – above because anything fast and menacing inside it would be taken as a target.

West knew that losing *Hermes* or *Invincible* would stop the whole war. Losing an escort wouldn't. 'When I saw we were going to be right down, I realised we were going to be exposed,' he admits. 'The best way of killing

enemy fighters is with your own fighters. Then you use missiles. Guns last.'

So Combat Air Patrol was compromised by distance, radar ruined by land, and Seacat restricted by a short range. The odds didn't look favourable. Yet one thing still took priority. 'Someone had to bugger up Goose Green. It made sense that we should be there.'

On the return flight to *Ardent*, West turned to Williams and told him he didn't want to paint a picture to the ship's company the way it had been painted on *Fearless*. Back in his cabin, he said it again. Williams knew why, because what he'd seen on Clapp's map had already frightened him. If anyone else was going to be worried, they could worry after fathoming it out for themselves.

Then they began to work on the details Clapp had left unplanned. Like the run-in. They didn't know when they'd detach. They didn't know whether they'd have to fight their way in. Where exactly would West place *Ardent* to provide her NGS? And what, exactly, would they be shelling?

While West pondered his task, John Sephton and Brian Murphy were back in the air at 1155, dropping flares for the gun crews to fire at. Among them was *Ardent*'s newest PO, NAAFI manager John Leake, enlisted for three months to fire the GPMG cartridges Cliff Goldfinch loaded for him.

On the Flight Deck, holes had been punched into the bright orange MBG chemical drums flown on at Ascension. They'd do a useful final job as machine-gun targets. Russ Goble and Scouse Wharton had to be ruthless with them. No one wanted Belisha beacons left bobbing around to mark *Ardent*'s passing.

By 1200 – in the heart of the Roaring Forties at 45 10S 39 21W – the Morning Watch's brief, clear, black meteor backdrop had turned grim, grim enough for *Ardent*'s scheduled RAS rendezvous with the stores ship *Stromness* to be cancelled. So, from 1500 and 1800, the Lynx conducted a vertrep instead.

In the Ops Room, there was a mix of excitement and tension. Three days before, the Task Force had caught an Argentinian 707 snooping. It had returned each day like clockwork. The plan was to scramble two Sea Harriers from *Atlantic Conveyor* and, with *Ardent*'s help, vector them in to attack. For two nights they'd waited, keyed up. A kill before they even reached the Total Exclusion Zone.

At 1630, the 707 was spotted again but, in the hushed, green-tinted catacomb of the Ops Room, they were thwarted. The weather was so bad that, even if the Sea Harrier had been able to take-off, landing back on its tiny patch of *Atlantic Conveyor* would be another matter. The mission was called off.

In fact, the weather wasn't just bad for Sea Harriers. With winds gusting to 40 m.p.h., in sea state 6, and with visibility growing worse by the minute, the Amphibious Group separated. By the evening, a Force 9 gale was blowing spray so high that *Canberra*'s radar couldn't even see *Atlantic Conveyor*, the fleet's theoretical guide ship, on radar. All it could see was sea.

In his cabin, Alan West considered the facts. His intelligence chart told him how many aircraft the Argentinians could call upon, their ships as well, except that it was becoming clear that the enemy fleet was staying in port, unprepared to risk the same fate as the *General Belgrano*. On 1 May there'd been attacks on *Glamorgan* and *Alacrity*, and an unexploded bomb had punctuated *Glasgow*'s war three days

earlier. But nothing else near the islands. They were obviously waiting.

If the weather was good enough, West calculated, the attacks would come thick and fast. But none of the Argentinian jets had all-weather capability. He thought ahead to the 21st. He didn't need weather like the stuff lashing *Ardent*'s Upper Deck right now. Cloud would be enough.

◆◆◆

If she made it there. In the Roaring Forties, the Flight Deck had temporarily became a popular place with word of a gliding bird with an enormous wing-span following *Ardent*'s wake. The buzz had swiftly run its course, but old sea superstitions would have to do better because, in their eyes, nothing could stop them. Until now.

Down below, 'if and when' were the least of the thoughts, for *Ardent* was in trouble. Her engines wouldn't accelerate. The filters on her Tyne engines were clogging up. Instead of cleaning them once a day, Terry Pendrous's stokers were cleaning them twice. They looked at the fuel system and discovered why. The chemicals that had killed off the microbiological growth had turned to grit. If *Ardent* was going to make the gunline, they'd have their work cut out.

While Tony Ray and Mick Cox assessed the damage, Jan Joyce and Brum Serrell began cleaning the fuel tanks, way down on 4 Deck. If they didn't make the best job, they'd be out of it. The job was evil. Stripped of the earphones which kept them in touch with the SCC, they spent hours in the steel tanks – the size of a living-room – wiping them down, the big tank doors left open so that they could step outside, pull off their breathing apparatus masks and gasp fresh air, and keep their senses. It was part of the gossip in every corner of the ship.

The Hangar became a magnet for the chewing of fat, as the Flight Deck had at Ascension. Still convinced he'd walk away unscathed, Bill Bailey welcomed the visits of people like Lenny Yeatman, Richie Gough and Cliff Goldfinch. But, then, everyone curried the PO Cook's favour.

'We all shared the same fears,' Bailey says. 'That bond, knowing what the other person's thinking.' The Flight kept its spirits up the same way as they all did, joking and laughing. The noisier ones were a little bit noisier, Bailey thought, and the quieter ones were a little quieter.

In the Chiefs' Mess that night, Dave Lee took out another bluey. The letter would arrive home with a 26 May postmark, five days after their date in Falkland Sound.

THE THIN GREY LINE

One   South Atlantic to Total Exclusion Zone
            (16–20 May 1982)   119

Two   Falkland Sound (0001–1230hrs, 21 May 1982)   147

Three   Falkland Sound (1259–1744hrs, 21 May 1982)   163

Four   Falkland Sound (1744–1806hrs, 21 May 1982)   185

Five   Falkland Sound (1806–1815hrs, 21 May 1982)   219

Six   Falkland Sound (1815–1835hrs, 21 May 1982)   235

Seven   HMS *Yarmouth*, Falkland Sound
            (1835–1854hrs, 21 May 1982)   247

Eight   HMS *Yarmouth*, Falkland Sound to SS *Canberra*,
            San Carlos Water (1900–2359hrs, 21 May 1982)   259

ONE

SOUTH ATLANTIC TO TOTAL EXCLUSION ZONE

(16–20 MAY 1982)

Andrew Gordon Lennox stood on the Bridge and studied the sky. The clouds were low, no more than two or three thousand feet, the sea grey, no greyer than the night before. Even so, it had pegged *Intrepid* and *Fearless* to 12kts, fast enough to have brought this part of the Task Force back together with the dawn at 1100, around 600nm east north-east of Port Stanley, slow enough to have missed their rendezvous with the remainder of the Amphibious Group soon after.

Now, at 1740 on a Sunday, the three strung-out lines of COMAW Mike Clapp's higgledy-piggledy amphibians moved west, *Canberra* ungainly in the left-hand lane, to the Jimmy's eye.

But not for long. Out of the murk, on *Ardent*'s starboard bow, an escort appeared. Then another. And another. Then the outline of something bigger. And something else. The rest of the Amphibious Group slowly emerged. Gordon Lennox stared as most of the Operational Royal Navy passed through his vision and then on into the murk beyond. It was the moment he knew who was going to win.

As the invitation went out for anyone to come and look for themselves, Radio Operator John Foster was already feasting on it from the back of the Bridge, his heart racing with every shape that appeared from this Second World War movie, ship, ship, ship, ship, tanker, ship, ship, tanker, ship, ship.

About an hour after sunset, 700nm south-east of Mar del Plata, the last ship slotted into place with *Ardent* and *Antrim* at their head. And the ships started to head almost due west. To the Falklands.

In the Ops Room, concentration overflowed to tetchiness when PWO Mike Knowles bollocked Scouse Flynn for some simple error, and ended his lecture by using Flynn's name, not his rate. Offended, Flynn pointed it out. But he didn't leave it there. He knew Knowles hated the smell of Juicy Fruit gum. By next Watch, John Leake's NAAFI store had sold out, the whole room was chewing and Flynn's revenge was both sweet and sickly.

Perhaps, after all, the strain was telling. Alan West and Tom Williams had stuck to their need-to-know tack after Mike Clapp's news that San Carlos Water was where the landings would happen. Even then, they hadn't been told everything. Until Clapp had said which Type 21 would be on NGS duty, the Thin Grey Line's

most southerly outpost, they'd been left to fill in the gaps. They'd have to wait for the Funnel of Fate to narrow again. But only a day.

◆◆◆

On Monday, 17 May, Alan Maunder's notebook had described a familiar South Atlantic day by around 1200, the time that Alan West and Tom Williams flew back to *Fearless* to find out exactly what Clapp had in store for the 21 Club's Canteen Boat: '0600Z-0730Z: RAS (L) with *Pearleaf* Station 4 during Morning Watch; 1125Z: Lynx airborne for surface search, not for exercise; 1200Z: 49 35S 49 08W.'

Around the time they stepped on board the Amphibious Assault Ship, the convoy was about 330nm east north-east of Port Stanley, just a hundred miles from the Total Exclusion Zone. On *Canberra*, the luxurious carpet in the Stadium Room was being ripped up and the floor scrubbed clean, operating theatre clean. The cruise liner's role had been fixed for weeks. Within minutes, *Ardent*'s was too.

West's educated guess was right. F184 would lead the way into Falkland Sound as the second hand ticked into Friday, 21 May, then she would head for the gunline in Grantham Sound and wait for the Call for Fire. Andrew Gordon Lennox recalls West's words when he returned. 'I've seen where we're going,' he told the First Lieutenant. 'We're going to have an exciting time.'

Then he outlined two concerns. First, *Ardent* would be the first ship into Falkland Sound, but no one was sure whether the Argentinians had sewn mines in the channel. Secondly, he was worried about being out on his own without mutual support in a ship that wasn't well-equipped for air defence.

It wasn't music to the Jimmy's ears, but the logic was flawless. Did Clapp need to close Goose Green? Yes, he did. Was it worth risking an escort to do it? It was. What was the threat to the escort, apart from fast jets from the mainland? Actually, the planes at Goose Green. Gordon Lennox completes the reasoning: 'Until I have a lot of people ashore, I need Goose Green. Therefore, it must be *Ardent.*'

West would tell his Chiefs and POs the next morning. Then they'd brief the Lower Deck.

◆◆◆

If the blurred overlap of watches, drills and calls to action stations hasn't clouded Pete Brierley's memory over the years, then the Flight had already sent John Sephton and Brian Murphy up once for a surface search when he straightened in his seat at the sonar contact on his Ops Room screen. He called Dave Croft, his leading hand, to look. They couldn't make head or tail of it. The intelligence chain fed them morsels, enough to know submarines were still reckoned to be a threat and then let them fill in the gaps. But this. They couldn't say categorically this was a submarine. And they couldn't say it wasn't.

'I shit myself and I was excited,' Croft admits drawing a deep breath. 'A whale? They would normally dissolve. But this thing was there. It was putting out metallic sounds.' They could normally decipher a whale within a few minutes.

But they didn't have a few minutes. They called Lt Tom Williams across. He quizzed Brierley. But Brierley was adamant. Williams left the Ops Room and signalled Northwood to tell them what they thought they had. Was it one of ours? If not, could they wake Moscow and ask if the Russians had a sub in the area? 'If you have, get away!'

After his Watch, freshly showered cook Jon Major was playing Scrabble in the 3 Deck S&S Mess.

'Hands to action stations,' the Tannoy changed the course of the game.

Round the ship, men pounded the decktiles in another manic two-minute race. Within a couple more, they were stood down. It was a whale, spotted by the Lynx. They didn't know whether to laugh or cry.

'It wasn't funny at the time,' Major confesses. He went back to his game.

In the Aft Engine Room at about the same time games or sleep were far from their minds. For two days they'd still been changing filters twice a day, instead of once, hoping they wouldn't have to strip the Tynes' finely engineered fuel system down. In the end, they had no option. One Tyne went first. They worked into the night and, eventually, ran it up. An hour later, the second went. It was like painting the Forth Bridge, and a job to give the CO what he wanted.

Tony Ray and Mick Cox spread blue paper over a clean bench in the Engineers' Workshop, just forward of the SCC on 2 Deck, and Cox set about the most concentrated and delicate job of his life, stripping the units slowly, painstakingly writing every setting down, so many turns on this screw, so many turns on that nut, spraying the fine debris with detergent and brushing it off with finer brushes.

It was going to be a gruelling few hours. They knew speed was of the essence. On both Tynes, *Ardent* would burn a ton of fuel an hour. With both Olympuses going, it would guzzle ten.

Every two hours, tests were done on the fuel. In the empty tanks, armed with buckets and cloths and breathing apparatus, Brum Serrell and Jan Joyce were wiping down, grabbing any spare hand to help. Apart from the flow of scran from the Galley, they fed off pride. *Ardent* would meet whatever lay ahead of her.

At around 0530 the next morning – Tuesday, 18 May – Sephton and Murphy were roused from their pits again. Tom Williams's Ops Room Watch had detected another unexplained contact on radar during *Ardent*'s patrol east of the Falklands. It was *Hydra*, the 260ft-long survey-vessel-turned-hospital ship. Geneva Convention rules said they, as a warship, couldn't even communicate with her, without threatening her status. So they left her well alone.

Half-an-hour later, still well before dawn, having briefed his officers, Alan West gathered his Chief Petty Officers in their Mess and hung a map on the bulkhead. On it was a label: 'Top Secret'.

His men looked around at each other and held their breath.

Then he read out his War Orders.

Ardent would be leading the landing force into Falkland Sound. He pointed to its entrance on the map. They'd be going in through a gap about 200 yards wide, not the main channel, to keep as far away from Fanning Head as possible. Then they'd swing across the main channel to make sure that, if there were

mines, *Ardent* found them before the big ships came through. Then they'd steam south to the gunline and await the call for Naval Gunfire Support. He didn't tell them exactly where.

Neither did he tell them exactly what he thought: what they were weakest at, what *Ardent* hadn't been designed for (defending her corner close inshore, fighting off attack aircraft); how many they could take on unscathed; the leading edge of an opposed landing which the politicians had consistently told them the Royal Navy would never have to deal with again.

Instead, he simply reminded them that the greatest danger would come from the air, that they'd 'almost certainly have little warning', and they'd have to rely on their eyes, not their electronic systems, to spot an incoming attack.

His flow was interrupted by a roar outside, the sound of rockets being fired up. They looked at each other for answers. In the Ops Room, one deck above, Richie Gough had them.

He'd been doing standard system operator checks on the 3-inch Chaff Charlie decoy rockets but, through tiredness, hadn't isolated the firing circuit before connecting a voltage test box and pressing the firing button. As soon as he touched it, he knew what he'd done. He'd launched the Chaff rockets.

On the Bridge Wing, Mike Lewis and Mal Crane were swigging tea, gawping at the horrible, murky South Atlantic when they heard the roar. Lewis muttered 'Bloody hell!' convinced they'd been hit.

On the Bridge, Tom Williams heard the whoosh and thought 'Exocet' too, but not incoming. He was certain they'd just hit *Hydra*. Beside him, Navigating Officer Alan Maunder thought the same and peered through the Bridge window, waiting for the impact or the splash.

Just aft of the Chaff Launcher, LMA Bob Young was alone in the Diving Store, door open, topping up the breathing apparatus bottles. He wasn't in there long. 'What the fuck was that?' he yelled as he shot out. 'I came out of that Diving Store so quickly . . .' he admits. 'Pants change.'

Back in the Chiefs' Mess, Lenny Yeatman looked around as the roar echoed and saw men thinking the same as he was. Alan West paused and then contacted the Bridge.

'I think we've just shot a rocket at a hospital ship!' Williams reported.

'What the hell happened?'

Gough had already held his hands up. Williams explained. At Portland, the world would have ended.

'Okay,' West said, then called Gough in and asked him what had happened. He hadn't hit anything but he was crestfallen.

'They must have realised it was fatigue,' he says. 'I was fairly honest. I was dealt with calmly.'

From then on, the checks were never made without someone else watching. And, from then on, Eddie Edwards never stopped calling Gough 'Rocket Man'.

✦✦✦

West took his map out again in the POs' Mess – including the newly promoted PO Stoker Bob Lewis – Master at Arms Lenny Yeatman hung it up and the

Captain ran through the plan once more. Again men stood in silence, the sound of their breathing and the distant hum of struggling Tynes the only thing that punctuated the air whenever he paused. When he'd finished, all that was left was for the Chiefs to brief the lads.

'We didn't associate casualties with people being killed. Hurt maybe,' Chief Electrician Taff Lovidge says of the time before West's briefing. It was the last trace of Portland mentality. Afterwards, someone said, 'Casualties means someone's going to get killed.' They thought about it then.

PO Joe Laidlaw was among them: 'I think it was generally acknowledged that the back end of the ship would be in trouble. Seacat wouldn't take a fly out. It would put them off their aim, though. It was better than nothing.' But *Ardent* had an invisible shield, Alan West.

'It wasn't going to be a picnic, but he had a lot of confidence in us. The *Argonaut* might get hit, or the *Antelope*. But it wouldn't be us. He had some sort of divine protection around this ship.'

Fed by a limited sight of intelligence in the Main Communications Office – 'That hasn't got parts,' 'That's on the airstrip,' 'Could fly,' 'Maybe not' – John Foster was extending the belief. 'We'd better be as good as we say we are. Because we might be required to do the business.'

He'd become used to the grilling, especially from the stewards in his Messdeck who'd picked up Wardroom chit-chat, more than they were supposed to hear, and wanted more.

Gary Nelson, *Ardent*'s muscle-bound PTI, was always on at him, usually over a bacon butty in the Junior Ratings' Dining Hall. 'Come on then, you can tell me!' Foster couldn't. 'I'll rip your head off!' didn't work either. It was a laugh, but it barely hid the desperation for news.

'I just used to say, "I can't say anything except we've got the measure of them, I think,"' Foster adds.

Until their briefing, the lads were more than capable of filling in the gaps themselves.

'I always felt that the only thing we were going to do was bombard them, because the Seacat was a pile of pants,' Scouse Phillips insists. 'The bloody planes could fly quicker than it anyway.'

Not everyone shared the view. If he'd asked the Jimmy, Andrew Gordon Lennox would have told him they'd be fine, especially against primitive low-level attacks, so long as they used Seacat properly.

Radio Operator Jeff Gullick and his old mate Steve Kent had already considered the days to come and agreed that, if one of them didn't make it home, the other would visit his family and say the end had come quickly, that he hadn't suffered. Whatever had actually happened.

That afternoon, Pete Rowe told his lads what they needed to know. He was Divisional Officer to most – Bagsy Baker, Russ Goble, Tony Langridge, Sid Norman, Tug Wilson, George Strachan, Scouse Wharton – so they were more than just Upper Deck weapons crews. It was a long talk. 'We're not playing any more,' he told them. 'If you need me, I'll try to get up there, but I doubt if I can, so you must know what you're doing. If we get a jam, we're not at Portland. Slack the lever, ditch the barrel and don't even ask me. Do it!'

PO Caterer Mike Stephens listened to Lt Cdr Rick Banfield's briefing that afternoon too. Banfield was loved by his men – a well-set rugby player who had everyone's respect and spoke to them the same way, 'a nice bloke, easy-going, no airs and graces'.

Like Ken Enticknap's SCC 'doom watch', Stephens's office was a magnet for people holding conversations he didn't want to hear, conversations about not going home, conversations which ended with 'We're doomed!' and, in Leading Cook Mick Beckett's case, a deep-voiced laugh. Stephens listened to Banfield and felt this was it: 'We've got to do it. I have a faith and that helped. If you want me, take me. There was a possibility I might not come back, but my thought was I would.'

In the Stokers' Mess, his spiritual home, Lenny Yeatman watched Terry Pendrous and Tony Ray outline *Ardent*'s task to the men who'd form the backbone of the Damage Control teams. 'The lads were more accepting than we were,' the Joss recalls. He wasn't particularly surprised. This was home to the best political advisors in the world, the best generals and the best prime ministers. They knew what they'd do.

At 1900, the Joss and the First Lieutenant would inspect the ship for cleanliness, expecting someone to be doing something stupid. If it wasn't this night, it was one soon after when they walked in and every member of the Mess was sitting down, bouncing around on an imaginary train. Coxie doesn't know where the props came from, but Ralph Coates had Knocker White on his shoulders, with a hat on, reading the *Daily Telegraph*. Yeatman shook his head in disbelief and left.

The newer Ardents had found their feet too. Steward Shaun Hanson worked in the Wardroom. He walked in to the S&S Mess one night with a bottle of Scotch. Shorts weren't allowed on the Messdeck.

'Anybody want a drink?'

All the killicks scattered. Hanson broke into a smile, his normal condition. It was tea.

Not all was sweetness and light, though. Karoly Nagy, John Bullock and Buck Ryan had already incurred the wrath of Leading Weapons Operator Martin Jones, a former Killick of the Mess, for working out how long the flight time home would be for enemy jets. He didn't want negative talk.

'I'm not being negative. I'm being realistic,' Naggers told Jones in his gulch. 'It'd be interesting to see how many could get up at the same time. Because we don't have any air cover.'

The confrontation didn't stop there. Only hours after being briefed on their part in the operation to retake the islands of his father's birth, Bernie Berntsen blew his stack. After six hours on watch, he wanted to come down to the Stokers' Mess, have a couple of wets and put his head down. What he didn't need was some ex-alcoholic Bible-basher pushing the Word – his way of dealing with the stress of heading to war – and 'banging away all night on his typewriter'.

The tapper resisted suggestions that he should shut it. In the end, Berntsen threatened to shove the machine up his arse. Then he went to see the Joss and moved to the S&S Mess. Just three days before the run in, it was the wrong thing to do. He knew that almost immediately. 'It took me away from the

nucleus of what I'd been with. I fucked up. I should have whacked him.'

Jessie Owens wasn't a happy stoker either. His job took him all over the ship. And, everywhere he went, he thought of home and wondered why Sally hadn't written. Why did he have to listen to Wacker Payne telling him what was going on at home? Or his closest friend, Brum Serrell? Or Jeff Curran?

She'd treated his last morning at home as if he'd be back the same night and said goodbye on the doorstep. Now he didn't know what was going on in her mind, 8,000 miles away. If she did write, it would be accepting that he may not return. God didn't come into it. And she had a baby to cope with.

And, of course, there was 'Lilliburlero'.

'The World Service became crucial,' Chief Stoker Andy Andrew remembers. 'They'd speak about it, and then you'd get some comedy programme from years ago, and we'd switch the SRE off and there'd be debate. As time got on, the conversation got more serious. It's a release. You might have it in your mind and think, "God, I wish somebody else said it."

'Some said it was stupid, the way we were trying to solve the problem, and some felt it was right. If they didn't like what I said, they didn't like what I said. That didn't mean I wasn't going to do my job. You all think, for a start, that you've all got a lot more to lose than the young lads who are single, downstairs. I was worried because I had a family and a home.'

What frightened Tony Ray most was being frightened.

Lenny Yeatman confesses he was afraid of being shot. Even in the Hangar, he didn't always find the brief sanctuary he occasionally craved among the men of the Flight, the world within a world.

'We had some quite serious talks, Mac, Pete Brouard, Scouse Lacey, Wally, the lot of us sat there talking. "What are we doing here? It's got nothing to do with us." So there wasn't the total loyal thing.'

Such private thoughts weren't confined to the Lower Deck.

'People have different things they focus on,' Alan West says. 'Generally, people are much more worried about being injured than killed, strangely. I never wanted to be burned. I'd much rather be dead than burned. That's silly.'

Apparently not. In the brief sleep he grabbed in between the mind-numbing tension of cleaning the ship's fuel system, Mick Cox's desperate hope was that, if he was going to be killed, it would be quick. 'My fear was being damaged, and being in a lot of pain and being left there.'

By now, there wasn't a man who wasn't sleeping in his 8s, his working rig, a thing of horror to a matelot, trading the ache for a shower for being zipped up and ready to close down the ship to Zulu Alpha, to hit your action station, to be there and concentrating, all in a couple of minutes. In a ship where you could walk from aft all the way forward without missing a note on Radio 1, full-blast, suddenly the music was background only. At six-on-six-off, men needed their sleep.

The lads in the Seamen's Mess set up their own 'I'll look for you and you look for me' buddy system, pairing up to make sure that each knew where the other was every minute of the day, still praying it would never be tested for real.

A few men had sought Bob Young out, too, with various manifestations of stress. All he could dispense was Paracetemol, Brufen or sympathy. As the perceived likelihood of disaster developed, he'd cultivated an 'I'm going to

die!' rash on the side of his own chin, a 'bloody great crusty thing'.

Defence Watches hadn't changed his routine much, if at all. He still had a day-to-day Sickbay to run, as well as the evening breathing apparatus round: open cupboard, check air-pressure, tick card, away. And he'd come to the conclusion that his relationship with Simon Ridout would never blossom. 'We were just different.'

◆◆◆

On *Canberra*, there'd been much talk about whether converting the Whale's plush Stadium Room so publicly to an operating theatre would be good for morale. Whatever, as soon as it was rigged its first visitors were Marines and Paras. They wanted to walk through, eyeball the equipment and see the people behind it. They were reassured.

The doctors on board already had an idea of the date of the landings because they'd taken blood days before, knowing its donors would need time to reform their corpuscles, knowing it wouldn't store long. The maths was easy. But Morgan O'Connell, the genial Irish Naval psychiatrist, let his mind wander.

'I remember thinking that we've got an awful lot of stores on the ships and an awful lot of people. They should be distributed among the fleet.'

He mentioned it in passing. An hour-and-a-half later, he was summoned by a Senior Naval Officer. 'Where did you get hold of this classified information?' he demanded to know.

'It's logical!' O'Connell was aghast.

The officer wasn't impressed.

'That frightened me,' O'Connell maintains. 'If some doc should be able to work it out . . .'

◆◆◆

That night, just over 48 hours before the waiting would end, Alan Maunder's pencil was busy: '0455Z: Base course 317. Action stations twice during fore-noon, both false alarms; 0600Z: Rendezvous with *Hermes* for cross-decking; 0936Z: Lynx surface search, not for exercise. Missile gun direction practice; 10W28Z: Action stations, hostile aircraft, not for exercise; 1122Z: Joined east–west patrol line 50 25S 53 34W to 52 10W 200 miles east of Falklands; 1134Z: Action stations, hostile aircraft, not for exercise; 1200Z: 50 25S 52 17W. Launched Lynx twice for surface search; 1742Z–1813Z: Lynx surface search, not for exercise. Missile gun direction practice; Continued to have trouble with the main engines all day due to poor fuel. Lynx at Alert 15 most of the day.'

A busy list, masked by clipped code but one which hardly scratched the surface of the hopes and fears of the men who'd helped to shape it. One brief moment in the long day had escaped Maunder's trusty pen, however. In the midst of it all, *Ardent* had passed the BP tanker *British Esk*, heading north, carrying the *Sheffield* survivors to Ascension. The Ardents had given them a wave, determined that it wouldn't happen to them.

As the clocks and watches still following Zulu time on *Ardent* slid past mid-

night on Wednesday, 19 May, synchronised with home but four hours ahead of the clocks on Port Stanley mantelpieces, she was 230nm east north-east of the capital. At 0250, she took fuel from *Tidepool*, a spiteful job for the RAS teams on the starboard waist, hauling lines across in the middle of a freezing, forbidding night.

By 0445, she was in the Total Exclusion Zone and her flats and ladders were echoing to the sound of steaming boots pounding the heart-stopping, two-minute beat to action stations. But, this time, the thud of hatches being slammed shut, the clunk of clips being fastened, was for real.

In the Ops Room, Weapons Director Richie Gough and his assistant, Able Seaman Jumper Collins, were watching CAP Sea Harriers heading north to intercept what looked like hostile aircraft. The lightning shift from Air Raid Warning White to Yellow to Red left Gough thrilled at his first chance to defend the ship in combat, but dreading the thought that he'd fail to protect his shipmates. Unless he showed his weapons their target, the ship was defenceless. He felt very human.

Forty-five minutes later, *Ardent* detached to join her Devonport neighbour *Atlantic Conveyor*, carrying eight Sea Harriers, five Harriers, eight Wessex 5 helicopters and five Chinook warhorses on her improvised Flight Deck towards the Battle Group, towards *Invincible*.

Almost six hours later, at 1115, they rendezvoused and the giant Cunard container ship began to cross-deck part of her precious cargo. And, as Surg. Lt Cdr Morgan O'Connell had rightly guessed, the rest of the Battle Group began a frantic swapping of cargo and men.

On *Fearless*, there'd been a calculation of likely casualties in a ship as big and white as *Canberra*, if a Skyhawk or a Dagger slipped past the Thin Grey Line. The odds didn't look good so, to even them out, 40 and 45 Commando units were cross-decked by landing craft to *Fearless* and her sister ship, *Intrepid*.

It wasn't easy for Marine or matelot as men swathed in combat gear queued from the Whale's unromantic Promenade Deck, down D and E Deck stairs and corridors to the port E Deck Galley doors, waiting for the LCU to rise on the five-foot swell to the lip of the hatch – and to take their step of faith.

Miraculously, there was only one tense moment. Just after 1400, a Marine lost his footing and plunged into the cold South Atlantic, between the landing craft and the ship. Splashing desperately, he made it to the stern of the LCU before the waves hammered it back against *Canberra*'s hull.

At 1705, while *Ardent* escorted *Atlantic Conveyor* and *Appleleaf* back to the Amphibious Group, cross-decking done, the effort to lick the fuel contamination, and the lack of sleep, were beginning to take their toll. Tiff Jeff Curran was kicking himself for making a basic mistake reassembling a high-pressure shut-off cock, the last valve on the fuel system before fuel's allowed into the engine. 'I actually thought I was losing my bottle,' he admits.

Elsewhere, Chief Electrician Taff Lovidge had briefed his electrical rates about D-Day. He'd told them exactly what Alan West had told the Chiefs, nothing more: 'We're going through some narrows, we'll be NGS-ing for the SAS, then our role will be to cover the landings, we all have to be more vigilant, it will all be for real, there will be casualties.'

But he reminded them how good they were. Everybody knew where all the

interconnector cables were. Everyone knew how to replace breakers. Now they had to do it in a war.

'That's fair enough,' Bernie Berntsen says. He'd returned to the Stoker's Mess for the briefing. 'That's what we were trained to do. I was half listening, because we were always tired. Always tired.'

The Ardents looked at each other as the briefing unfolded, glances exchanged, nods, eyes tightened at the thought of what was to come. They could discuss it between themselves later.

Not far away, Jessie Owens didn't take much in. His action station would be the SCC, doing his normal job, looking after the engines and the ancillary equipment, doing the spot checks. To him, it wasn't an important job. But it wasn't an unimportant job.

As they drifted back to their posts, their minds switched to final preparations.

Soon after, Buck Ryan and Buck Taylor were in the Magazine, working on the torpedoes, when their boss Ian Jacobs walked in. Taylor remembers his face was ashen and he looked flustered. 'You'd better sit down,' he said. 'It's gone way beyond what I thought was going to happen.' Then he started talking about the air threat.

'Hang on!' the 18-year-old Geordie thought . . .

In the Electrical Workshop, on the port side of 1 Deck, just across the Burma Way from the Joss's office, Andy Cox and his L department mates ran through their own damage control drills . . .

In the Sickbay, LMA Bob Young and Surg. Lt Simon Ridout knew there was no more they could do to prepare. Now they were letting people grab rest when they weren't on watch. They'd be busy later. If the worst happened, Ridout expected to be treating men with high-velocity metal wounds, shrapnel or gunshot and, of course, fire-related injuries. But he was happy with the stewards, writers and cooks who made up *Ardent*'s First-Aid parties and manned the Forward and Aft First-Aid Posts. They could look at airways, check breathing, move on to circulation, put pressure bandages on bleeding wounds. Stabilise the situation.

◆◆◆

The emergence of the Amphibious Group from the murky horizon three days before had been a breath-taking experience for those who'd seen it from the Bridge. An even more mind-blowing sight was shrouded in the black of a late autumn South Atlantic night when, at 2215, Clapp's amphibians rendezvoused with the Battle Group. The only people who caught it were the men in *Ardent*'s Ops Room, watching for returns on their radar screens, and seeing them. Thirty of them.

On his plot, PO Pete Brierley was transfixed, following the track of a Sea King helicopter from *Hermes* to *Intrepid*, presumably transferring men. He was tired after days of Defence Watches, his mind beginning to see the pulsing screen as some kind of video game. In a blink, the contact had gone.

He looked at Mick Newby. Both knew what had happened.

Tom Williams looked at the screen. He knew who the Sea King was

carrying. *Ardent* quickly offered her assistance and joined the search for survivors, but there wasn't much she could do.

As the buzz raced through the ship that a chopper had ditched, slowly a picture emerged from the Tactical Net echoing through the Ops Room headsets. It gradually became apparent to Brierley that 20 or more of the best fighting men in the world had been on board the Sea King.

Twenty-two, in fact. Twenty-two men of D Squadron SAS who'd wiped six Pucaras from the enemy's options on Pebble Island four days before. The full story wouldn't emerge for four more days.

The rest of the watch was very subdued. For Tom Williams, though, it simply added to the stress.

As the pressure grew, Alan West was able to find a refuge from the loneliness of command by seeking out Rick Banfield for chats in the Galley, or John Sephton, obviously the First Lieutenant, and Master at Arms Lenny Yeatman, men whose feel he trusted.

As West's Operations Officer, what time Williams didn't spend in the Ops Room or on the Bridge was devoted to cracking the Captain's signals. It gave him a bigger picture than most of what was happening beyond the confines of this claustrophobic fighting machine, but it added to his burden too.

'Alan West played it by the book,' he explains. 'I had to keep all this on file in my cabin. Eventually I didn't have enough room. Not everybody knew everything. I got very, very tired.'

Tired, and the Thin Grey Line's hardest work was to come. On *Canberra*, they already knew that. Capt. Dennis Scott Masson had addressed the ship's company and their non-paying guests that day.

'If there is a landing,' he'd told them, 'I can assure you we will be in the safest possible place and this will be closed and more or less surrounded by land. During approach, which will obviously be under the cover of darkness, we will be impressively escorted by the Navy and other service elements.'

◆◆◆

Fifteen minutes before the Sea King tragedy, *Ardent* had rejoined the *Fearless* group at 50 12S 52 02W, not that 50 12S 52 02W looked any different from any other spot in this inhospitable corner of the world. Fifteen minutes after, at 2230, *Ardent* changed course at 12kts. Slowly, but surely, the Funnel of Fate was narrowing.

On the stroke of midnight, 110nm north-east of Port Stanley, John Sephton and Brian Murphy took the Lynx up from *Ardent*'s gale-lashed Flight Deck for another surface search. Thirty minutes later, they swapped the sight of heavy seas for the rhythmic roll of decks beneath their feet.

By dawn, 11 hours later, the conditions had barely improved, if at all, as the Amphibious and Battle Groups changed from their anti-surface warfare formation to an anti-air warfare screen.

The previous day's hasty game of 'pass the parcel' had delayed COMAW Mike Clapp sending his Op Gen Mike signal, a piece of paper – 'a very long

piece of paper' – giving final confirmation of who'd go where and why, outlining the amphibious assault, its timings, the whole plot.

Now, on Thursday, 20 May, as Alan West read his copy, it became apparent that Clapp and his advisers had been forced into a change of plan. Reports had reached *Fearless* of enemy troops on Fanning Head. Clapp had reshuffled his pack. But *Ardent* would still lead the way. She'd still harass the Goose Green garrison, keep them distracted. She would still provide defensive fire for Brig. Julian Thompson's 2 Para troops on Sussex Mountains at the southern end of the beachhead. And she'd prove or disprove Clapp's informed hunch that the enemy hadn't sewn mines in the northern entrance to the Sound since *Alacrity*'s run-through the opposite way nine days before.

Nine days before that too, remember, the 'Last Pipe' Operational Order Signal he'd received had said minesweepers would be in his force. That, he suspected, may have been some officer quoting a manual which said all amphibious operations must be protected by mine-clearance. Clapp didn't have any.

'The Admiral doesn't see every signal that comes out,' Clapp reasons. 'Me, sitting down south, didn't know if he's seen it or not too. It's got his signature, so it must be from him. It's unsettling.'

He'd already explained his thinking to one of his commanding officers on *Fearless* four days before. 'You're mad! We're all going to be blown up,' the Captain had told him.

Clapp had lost his rag. 'What the fucking hell's the evidence?'

The SAS and SBS had been sitting off Port Howard and in Port San Carlos for a fortnight, under strict instructions to break silence at any sign of mining. SAS intelligence also said the Argentinians were beefing up the Stanley defences, expecting the Task Force to unleash an amphibious assault there.

'If we're going to war frightened about putting one foot in front of the other, we'll never get there.'

So they'd have their minesweeper. An Irish minesweeper. *Ardent*. Clapp presumed Alan West would hit the channel going like the clappers, with everyone above the water. That's what he'd have done.

◆◆◆

Scouse Phillips remembers the moment Captain Bob walked on to the Bridge and wrote himself into *Ardent* legend. John Foster does too.

Alan West swivelled in his seat and extended a hand. The conversation went something like this: 'Good afternoon, I'm Commander West.'

'Hiya, I'm Bob!'

Pause.

'Yes, I'm Commander West. You are?'

'I'm Bob!'

'The way he said it was, "That's all you need to know,"' Phillips remains impressed. 'I remember thinking, "That was cool, or was that cool?"' So did John Foster.

By the time the giant soldier walked through from the Flight Deck, the buzz had gone round.

Jessie Owens, SCC: 'He'd been on *Sheffield*.' Wrong. It was *Arrow* who'd gone to *Sheffield*'s aid.

Cook Jon Major, away from the 'front line' in the Galley, doing his job feeding the people who fired the guns: 'He was in contact with the SAS who'd already landed on the island.'

Andy Cox, Electrical Workshop: 'He was a Captain in the SAS.'

They weren't far off the mark. But, as they looked on him with awe, dressed in fatigues, wearing a bergen on his back and suede boots on his feet, they didn't know this mountain was in 148 Battery Royal Artillery, attached to Special Forces, or that, only days before, he'd scared himself silly by slipping while being winched off the back of a Type 21 in a Force 5. The Flight crew had found it very amusing. So he'd poked one of them in the head with a rifle.

◆◆◆

The Lynx was airborne again at midday, transferring lubricating oil from *Tidepool* to *Ardent* on the west of the main force. Then, at 1400, Sephton and Murphy were up once more, conducting a vertrep with *Stromness*. While they were aloft Darken Ships was ordered early and, as sunset approached on a gloomy afternoon, ships began to take up fresh positions.

Then at 1415, while the Argentinians in their defensive positions dotted around the Islands were thinking about the fiftieth grim midday picnic of their Malvinas occupation, the Amphibious Group detached from the Battle Group and began its long run to the northern end of Falkland Sound, escorted by the Type 42 destroyers *Coventry* and *Glasgow* as radar pickets, their sister ship *Glamorgan* in support and the Type 21s *Arrow* and *Alacrity* as 'goalkeepers'.

The command ship *Fearless* and her 12,000-ton sister ship, *Intrepid*, were each carrying 650 troops. The smaller 5,000-ton landing ships *Sir Galahad*, *Sir Geraint*, *Sir Lancelot*, *Sir Percivale* and *Sir Tristram*, each had 400 more. With them were the stores ships *Stromness* and *Fort Austin*, the two converted roll-on-roll-off ferries, *Europic Ferry* and *Norland*, and the Great White Whale, the *Canberra*, packed with the bulk of the men who would retake the Falklands.

Any of these would make a prize for the Argentinian pilots they'd face tomorrow, but *Canberra* would surely be the greatest. So it would be the Thin Grey Line's job to stop that happening.

The whole of Operation Corporate, and the futures of 1,500 Falklanders, would depend upon seven warships headed by the 6,000-ton County Class guided missile destroyer *Antrim*, armed with anti-aircraft guns, Seaslug and Seacat missile systems, and four Exocet launchers.

The second escort was the 3,000-ton Leander Class frigate *Argonaut*, equipped with Bofors 40mm guns, Seacat missile systems, ASW torpedoes and Exocets.

Then there were the venerable Type 12 frigates *Yarmouth* and *Plymouth* – each with more than 20 years' bow-crunching service behind them, carrying twin 4.5-inch Mark 6 guns, 20mm Oerlikons, Seacat missiles and Mark 10 anti-submarine mortars – and the Type 22 Sea Wolf frigates *Brilliant* and *Broadsword* – 4,400 tons defended by 40mm anti-aircraft guns, Exocet missiles and ASW torpedoes.

Then there was *Ardent*.

On her Flight Deck, Deputy Marine Engineering Officer Tony Ray filled his lungs with fresh air after four days painting the Forth Bridge in the Aft Engine Room. 'It was a real dank day and I thought, "Thank Christ." It was quite a sight. You could see all these ships and they'd loom out of the fog and then the fog would come down.'

Ken Enticknap followed him to the Upper Deck and soaked up the same sight. He didn't hang around. It was the last time he saw the daylight on *Ardent*.

An unopposed landing, with General Galtieri's fliers clag-bound, kicking their heels at Puerto Grande, would be at the heart of many a silent prayer that night.

With his kit safely stowed in the Sickbay, Captain Bob joined Alan West and went through the outline of his work. Then they moved to the Wardroom, to fill in more details for the benefit of PWO Mike Knowles, Chief GI Pete Rowe and the gathered NGS team.

He filled the room. There was silence. He moved to the map spread out on the Wardroom table.

'What exactly will we be going against?' one Ops Room officer asked.

John Foster remembers huge, gnarled hands darting across the map. Captain Bob mentioned Goose Green and Darwin. Then there were secondary targets if they didn't pay off, and even more after that. The Argentinians might top up Darwin. The other thing was the Pucaras. They had to create as much diversionary noise as they could, and take out the Pucaras.

But it would be hit-and-miss. Their spotter would live on his wits. There'd be moments when he'd stop them, run, then surface, breathless, 20 minutes later and send a new, clipped Call for Fire.

Foster watched, amazed at an RO being treated like an adult in the Wardroom, transfixed already by the Naval Gunfire Liaison Officer's presence. In the 18 hours to come, he'd grow accustomed to the softly spoken Captain Bob turning round, asking, 'You got a fag?' Foster would think: 'No, but I'll go and get you one.'

A Royal Artillery Captain was already dug in overlooking Goose Green and Darwin, keeping an eye on troop and aircraft movements and waiting for *Ardent*'s arrival on the gunline.

They knew better than to ask for any more information about the man in the ditch, and Captain Bob offered none. He could have told them their man had been at Pebble Island. Or that he would have been on the ill-fated Sea King flight if his task hadn't been changed. All that mattered was *Ardent* executing her part of Clapp's and Thompson's plan.

Later on, Captain Bob met Alan Maunder and Alan West in the Charthouse. As those fingers brushed over the dots marking the ruined Boca House, on the shore, and Camilla Creek House, five miles north, and a list of other grid references, they decided where a gunline was best drawn for a Mk 8 gun to rain

4.5-inch shells 17 miles on to the enemy's heads – close to the Grantham Sound kelp beds.

Once he knew where *Ardent* was going, and what time, and the fact that they'd be thundering past Fanning Head at the dead of night, PWO Mike Knowles was able to brief his Upper Deck gun crew. He studied the charts with Alan Maunder and discussed what they'd use as radar markers while the ship was switching between the land grid references used for NGS and their more familiar longitude and latitude co-ordinates on the water.

PO Mike Lewis had also studied the charts, though where they ended up would be immaterial to him. His Electronic Warfare team would be looking for planes now, not ships. He was only worried about his kit working, knowing that, if necessary, the tell-tale signature of high-frequency aircraft radar would blip on his screen; that he'd see a series of dots; that he'd be able to line up the bearing and frequency; that his pre-programmed computer would flicker the names of four or five could-bes. An A4? A Super Etendard? Enough for him to alert the weapons crews.

◆◆◆

On the Great White Whale, Lauraine Mulberry, *Canberra*'s assistant senior purser, took five minutes from her hectic day to add to her diary: 'It is incongruous to sit here in the office and glance through the window and see a soldier in camouflage jacket carrying a complete backpack and gun. Normally one would see a middle-aged grey-haired passenger gazing lazily over the rail at the sea.'

The incongruity of eating dinner with a string quartet and hearing conversation of cold-room storage for bodies turning casually to the poetry of Yeats and Wordsworth was apparent. The ship was full of sharp contrasts; warship/cruise ship; helicopter pad/swimming pool; operating theatre/nightclub.

Not far away, within the towering white walls, Surg. Lt Cdr Morgan O'Connell knew well what the Ardents would be going through in the coming hours. Some would retire within themselves, some would play cards, some would just write letters. Most would take it in their stride because they were with their mates. The worst thing would be having nothing to do.

They'd know their way through her blindfold, have faith in their equipment and believe that, if they were hit, the system would swing into action, the firefighting, Damage Control and First-Aid teams. He knew hearts would pump, mouths would go dry and, he kept coming back to it, the strengths or weaknesses of their teams would mean a lot. And they'd have adrenaline. Adrenaline would help them make a superhuman effort, if necessary.

Ardent's DC parties already knew who'd be doing what in the Forward and Aft Section Bases. Surg. Lt Simon Ridout and LMA Bob Young had also settled on their places. Ridout would be in the Junior Ratings' Dining Hall on the run-in, exuding the air of a man unconcerned about the mine threat. Young would stay in the Forward First-Aid Post, in the Sickbay. He'd spent hours rearranging the equipment there, checking and rechecking canvas rolls with tools in, and a

big roll he carried with kit for putting up drips, a big pair of scissors, basic surgical tools.

'If I'm confident, the boys know it and they're happy,' was his philosophy. Why not? They'd trained and trained. He'd taught them the extras. What he couldn't account for was the lack of experience. They hadn't flown search-and-rescue flights, turned up at horrific road accidents, taken bodies off burning freighters, tended aircrash victims, worked in a hospital casualty unit.

'At the end of the day, they were all cooks and stewards, people like that, who'd never really taken it extremely seriously. I don't think any of them had ever seen a real casualty off the sports field.' The Doc himself? He felt he was as good as he could be.

By 1600, the Amphibious Group was ploughing through a heavy swell in visibility of less than a mile. At 1630 the Lynx was launched for a surface search. During the hundred minutes it was in the air, Morgan O'Connell was proved right. Ardents did start taking themselves off to quiet corners. They did look at those around them and make a value judgement.

Young RO Steve Kent shut himself in the Flag Locker behind the Bridge and said a quick prayer. 'Out of character,' he admits, 'but I'd accepted death was possible. I thought I'd get a few credits.'

On the Bridge, a long career past his first draft, the confidence of First Lieutenant Andrew Gordon Lennox remained absolute. 'We knew we were very, very good,' he says. 'Whatever they threw at us we could handle.'

Seacat's limitations were confined between him and the Captain, 'and maybe Paddy McClintock' – the Weapons Engineering Officer – 'and others who really knew enough to think that problem through. That's the way it goes. Don't forget, we were all very young. The average age was 21–22.'

'Young people are invincible,' his young Officer of the Watch, Lt Nigel Langhorn, adds.

In the Electrical Workshop, PO Wacker Payne was thinking the same. 'You've got to remember that we could do anything, anything at all.'

Not everyone shared the faith, though.

'Buck and Buck!' Jake Jacobs yelled from the top of the Stokers' Mess ladder on 2 Deck. The Bucks hurried to the ladder and joined their boss, dressed for the Upper Deck. The Seacat launcher was loaded and growing damper by the minute in the miserable cold weather. The two young weapons engineers needed to cover the system.

Minutes later, high on the Seacat Deck, as Ryan was pulling one of the protective 'condoms' into place, wind ripping through their bodies, he turned to his boss and took a deep breath. 'I had a bad premonition, Jake.' He still doesn't know why he said it. 'We're not going to come out tomorrow.'

'What do you mean?'

'I don't think we're going to survive.'

Jake looked at him, but they left it at that. Seacat. More people had it sussed than the Jimmy thought.

What had they been praying for? A Force 6 would help. Cloud hugging the rising swell. Something to keep General Galtieri's flyers grounded, 300-odd miles away. For a while, it looked promising. For a while.

By sunset, all that was left of the earlier storms were a few, faint, high cirrus clouds. As the sun had dipped in the west, those placed to see it recall a sky bathed in purples, lilacs and pinks, a backdrop to a romantic cruise, not an uncertain advance to war. To make things worse, there was the promise of a clear moonlit sky, too, to illuminate their journey. But 'Lilliburlero' had more.

On *Fearless*, COMAW Mike Clapp had no idea what *Ardent* and *Antrim* were going into. 'I'd hoped and hoped and hoped that we had surprise,' he says. But he wasn't betting on it. He'd switched on the World Service, in Ascension, to hear the BBC alerting the Argentinians to their ill-fused bombs. Now he'd heard them say that the 'troopships have joined the main force of warships'.

There was no surprise. 'They didn't say we were going to San Carlos, but we were going in.'

◆◆◆

At 1955 Steve Kent was on the Bridge-Signal Deck, watching *Antrim*'s outline, trying hard to appear calm, when the destroyer's Aldis lamp started flashing. Kent wrote as quickly he could, a frustratingly slow job at best, but made harder by cold hands, nerves on both ships and the conditions. As he wrote, he sensed Nigel Langhorn and Alan West's impatience. They'd have to wait. What an irony. In a machine bristling with communications, radio silence had put them at the mercy of Morse.

When he'd finished, he handed the message over.

'I was aware that I'd probably just taken part in history. I'd just received the signal effectively marking the start of the Falklands conflict,' he says.

At 2000 – 50 29S 57 07W, according to the log – the gist was straightforward: 'Detach and proceed as previously ordered.' They did.

Bob Young was loitering on the Bridge when *Antrim* sailed past and *Ardent* followed. He recalls thinking that they made a big target.

As *Antrim* went, Lt David Searle called for 'nine-five-lever', 95 per cent power, and the SCC responded. But, in the choppy seas, the big destroyer was pulling through the water better. He watched the gap begin to open, called to Alan West, then piped down for 100-lever. In the SCC, senior rates undoubtedly walked away from the throttles, grimacing. They hated 100-lever. They hated their engines being opened up until they could offer no more. But at least they could give West what he wanted. The fuel problem had, at last, been licked.

Before Searle left the Bridge, West briefed his officers and senior rates about their 'minesweeping' role. Then he sent some off to brief their men and set off on a final walk through the ship himself.

Searle headed for the Junior Ratings' Dining Hall and spoke with the Aft Damage Control Party. He reiterated the routine. Ken Enticknap was in charge until and unless he was taken out. Then Searle would take over. He would also carry the morphine capsules.

For PWO Mike Knowles, living for weeks with the threat of being torpedoed

had more than prepared him for the thought of mines. They were just another 'embuggerance that might not be there'.

Down below, Alan West shared his thoughts with the Damage Control parties. 'There's a perceived mine threat,' Ken Enticknap recalls the explanation. 'So we won't go down the main channel, we'll go to one side or between islands.'

'His intention was to go through at full speed so the mine may go off behind you,' Enticknap says. And if it hit? 'Then it's hard over and run up a beach. That seemed practical in the circumstances.'

Jessie Owens thought about his action station, the SCC. 'I had that feeling that where we were wasn't that safe. If you got bombed, you got bombed in the middle. If you got torpedoed, you got torpedoed at the bottom. Where we were was below the Hangar.'

Little Errol Flynn wasn't too impressed either. 'I was Forward DC. If it gets it, it gets it forward first.'

Leigh Slatter stumbled through the Bridge, feeling his way round because his night-vision hadn't kicked in after his on-watch stint in the Ops Room, then stumbled up to the Gun Direction Platform and could just make out a figure draped over the gunsight, the man he was due to relieve. He tapped him on his shoulder, but there was no response. Then something jumped out from behind the mast and Slatter's heart nearly stopped. The rotten bastards thought it would be funny to put the man-overboard dummy in the seat and hide.

By the time Alan West reached the Upper Deck weapons crews, the cold South Atlantic air had become bitter, even for Slatter, swathed in sea boots, heavy duty white socks, normal socks, Ron Hill jogging bottoms, normal trousers, foul-weather bottoms, T-shirt, shirt, heavy duty sea jersey, foul-weather top, anti-flash hood, woolly hat, anti-flash gloves, respirator, life-jacket, once-only suit, knife and mug. His pockets held a vast amount of nutty and a copy of Terence Strong's *Whisper Who Dares*.

He looked like a pack mule and weighed the same. They all did. Perish the thought of what would happen if there were mines and they had to go into the water. They'd sink like a brick, the lot of them.

West gathered Russ Goble and Scouse Wharton at their LMG stations, overlooking the Flight Deck. 'I accept there'll be one or two attacks to come up from astern,' he told them.

'He didn't say it,' Goble remains certain, 'but he implied that the Argentinians knew Seacat was a load of crap as well. He had a little chat, and off he went.

'What can you think? The skipper says he expects attacks and you think, "Christ! Officers are always economical with the truth anyway so, if he says two . . . yeah. Five of them."'

West moved on to the GDP, then saw the Oerlikon crews and told them to stick by their guns, keep firing, even if they weren't exactly sure where the planes were.

He saw Ginger Nelson too, had a long chat and realised how nervous the PTI was. 'It's exciting for me as well,' he told him. 'I've never been involved in something like this.'

Brian Murphy was nervous, but not John Sephton. 'He didn't have any problems at all. He didn't show it.'

While West toured the weapons crews, Mike Knowles followed in his wake, checking and double-checking the last-minute details thinking, 'Is there a mine or isn't there? Are we likely to be seen?'

'Then you think, "What are we going to do if somebody fires at us?" "The guy on the GPMG on the back end of the Flight Deck, does he know that he's not to return fire unless he gets the command to do so?" So then you try to get hold of Pete Rowe. "Did you brief him?"'

'He had a brief yesterday, sir.'

'And you think, "I'd better fly down there and make absolutely sure he does."'

Back on the Bridge, West had taken Lenny Yeatman and Alan Maunder to one side. Going in, Yeatman would be on the wheel, Maunder scouring his charts, West doing the navigation by radar.

The charts weren't good, so West's planning observed caution. He didn't want to alert the reinforced Fanning Head lookout, so *Ardent*'s side channel would keep them safely west of the giant headland. Once at the gunline, his plan was to stay on the Bridge, where he could see what 21-year-old Sub Lt Richie Barker's GDP lookouts could see, where he could manoeuvre the ship, because the radars wouldn't work so close to land.

A deck below, in the Ops Room, PO Pete Brierley was beginning to worry about his lads, but not himself. They were edgy, so he made sure they all had a share of time off. 'I suppose I was, in my own mind, the least likely person to be missed.' Instead he chatted with Andy Barr, about the young sonar rating's parents, how he wanted to marry back home. Barr was 'likeable, biddable', he recalls, like his Ops Room rating Derek Armstrong. Both would spend most of the 21st out of the Ops Room in Tiff Geoff Hart's Forward DCP.

Some lads had put together little waterproof packets of valuables – passports, money and personal photographs – so they'd have something to hang on to at their action stations. 'I didn't,' Brierley admits. 'Maybe I lacked imagination, or just never envisaged leaving the ship.'

Bob Young knew where to find good company too, and a bacon butty. The conversation with Mick Foote was predictably 'We're doomed!' 'It was like *Dad's Army*. Wandered around. Had a cup of coffee. Had a nervous gut ache.'

He saw Ginger Nelson too. 'He wasn't too impressed about the idea of being in the Tiller Flat, but that was his station . . .'

In the Junior Ratings' Dining Hall, Steve Kent dropped in for a mid-evening meal – bacon butties – with his mates, wondering whether it would be the last one they'd share.

In the POs' Mess, Cliff Goldfinch settled down to write his wife a letter.

'If I come out of this alive, I'll be very lucky,' it was uncharacteristically pessimistic. As he wrote, Peddler Palmer, the stout-legged, stout-hearted Cornishman, drew the bar keys. 'He had his two pints and his three tots, returned the bar keys and that was the last I saw of him.'

In the Chiefs' Mess, everyone not on watch was kitted and spurred, with hardly a word to say. The tension was clear. Jeff Curran decided to break the ice

and announced he was having a pint. 'I remember Mac McAulay saying how much better off he'd be in his goon suit, compared to us in our once-only suits.'

The banter went from there. 'I was on such a high I had to lie down. It was as if I'd consumed several pints,' Curran admits.

◆◆◆

By the time they'd beaten the fuel system grit, Jan Joyce and Brum Serrell had lost touch with time. For the first time in 96 hours, they peeled off their overalls at the top of the Stokers' Mess ladder and slept in their own gulches. It made a blessed difference from curling up on the Workshop floor, but it was hardly good preparation for what was coming up. It was the most tiring thing they'd ever done.

'To feel that tired, you'd have to work in a factory and do a double 12-hour shift, then have four hours kip, then do another double shift, four hours kip, then another double shift,' Joyce suggests.

Still, the ship regarded itself as the best and the stokers regarded it as their purpose to keep it going.

Brum Serrell, a strapping man from Kidderminster, not the Second City, had caught news of *Ardent*'s role, the mine threat, the run to the gunline. It could work two ways. The first one through could catch the Argentinians by surprise, and the poor sods following would cop it. Or, they'd be lying in wait. Whichever, he couldn't change it. So the 24 year old hid behind his headphones and played Led Zeppelin.

◆◆◆

At around 2100, as his family were settling down in their Shropshire home to watch the mid-evening news, Ralph Coates took himself off to the Electrical Workshop, by the Joss's office, to think. It wasn't something he did often. But he figured no one would bother him there. Then Wacker Payne walked in.

'You realise what's going to happen,' Ralph told him. 'We're going to be in the thick of it.'

'Yes,' Wacker answered. Ralph drew breath.

'Well, it's about time I redeemed my position for what I've received.'

He stood up. In seconds, they were fighting, gas masks and everything wrapped around them. 'I had the best of him for a while,' he insists, 'but he got the advantage of me and he was banging my head on the floor. It's hurting.'

He heard footsteps and looked up. It was the Joss. He had his cap on, 'which meant he was regulatory', and his glasses, 'which he always used to wear anyway, probably to hide his deceitfulness'.

'What's up, Sinus?' Lenny Yeatman asked.

'Can't you frigging-well see? He's beating the shit out of me!'

'What, Sinus?'

'He's beating me, can't you see, Master?'

The Joss took off his cap and glasses, knelt down and head-butted the young stoker. Then he stood.

Ralph looked up, rubbing his head. 'What was that for, sir?'

'Next time, don't snitch on your senior rate,' glasses on, hat on, away.

'Not only did I have a bruise on the back of my head, I had one on the front,' he says. 'He pissed off back to his office. End of story. Don't snitch on your senior rate!'

◆◆◆

After writing his letter, PO Cook Cliff Goldfinch went and saw his lads for a chat, and to repeat his order for the two watches to stay apart. He had them all weighed up. 'Bob Sage, not quite 100 per cent. Jon Major, stupid anyway. He'll always be a cook. Lovely. John Roberts, jovial. I only knew him a short time, but he was a lovely guy, "Whatever you say, let's go and do it!" Like Dunkerley. What a character he was. He was another lovely guy.'

He came away laughing, as usual. Then he sought out PO Caterer Mike Stephens. 'How much fillet steak have we got on board?' he asked.

Stephens checked and told him. 'Let's try half-a-pound a man. When we know we're coming out, we'll bring the bastard up!'

In the Galley, Jon Major killed time with Mick Foote – a roly-poly proud of the years he'd invested in a beer belly even Ginger Nelson couldn't shift – and Bob Sage. Dave Trotter, Mick Beckett, Taff Roberts and Richard Dunkerley were forward, heeding Cliff Goldfinch's order to remain divided.

In the Forward Auxiliary Machine Room (FARM), Karoly Nagy was anxious to have a drink in the Mess before they closed up. Garry Whitford appeared and asked him to look at the evaporator. Naggers protested, but he mended it anyway. Then he headed up through the hatch on to 2 Deck and back down the next ladder forward to the 3 Deck Mess.

Already in the Stokers' Mess, Andy Cox gave a passing thought for the Chinese laundryman, Wong Chun Hong, a man also thousands of miles from his country and his family. 'He obviously knew what was happening and, deep down, must have been very lonely.'

◆◆◆

The clock was ticking. At about 2230, back on the GDP, Lt Mike Knowles was making a final round of his weapons crews, standing with Big John Leake, Cliff Goldfinch now back at his side.

'I kept on saying, "All right?"' Knowles remembers. 'And he was just, "Yeah! What's the problem?"'

He'd made his preparations. A box of soft drink and Mars Bars were already tucked out of sight. 'I thought, "If the Galley's going to get hit, we're not going to be thirsty or hungry,"' he explains.

Knowles turned to the younger lads. He was certain some were terrified, and he understood. 'I'd have been too, if I'd been stood there with a gun and somebody might fire at you.'

If Scouse Wharton wasn't terrified before Knowles appeared on the Seacat Deck, he was as soon as he did. The young gunner and Russ Goble were

looking over the Flight Deck with no one else to talk to. Knowles jumped out of the black, shouting 'All right!' and scared the living shit out of Wharton.

The clock ticked on. By 2300, Naggers was sitting with Buck Ryan and John Bullock, swigging cider from a can in the Stokers' Mess. It was probably the only time he'd drunk the stuff. 'It wasn't Dutch courage. This was the last chance of a beer. I don't think anyone was worried.'

Buck Taylor recalls it differently. He looked around the bare surroundings, most clues to the life of this place now stashed or stored, and felt it was subdued.

Ralph Coates joined Naggers with a can. Since the moment they'd met, they'd wound each other up. 'You watch yourself down aft mate,' Nags told him, 'because you'll be going before we do!' Then, out of the blue: 'If you're hit or injured, just remember, get out. Just keep moving.' He still doesn't know why he said it.

In the S&S Mess, for the exiled Bernie Berntsen, the coming 24 hours would have an added edge. 'I'd been in the Navy since I was 16 and I'd been trained for it,' he says. 'It's something you've got to do. Perhaps it's because of the Falklands. My dad was born in Port Stanley. Dad's dad was a ship's Captain. Coxie knew, I think.' But very few others. He looked around him. 'We didn't go in with our eyes shut,' he remembers. 'We knew we were good. We were the best . . .'

In the same Messdeck, Scouser John Foster looked around too and even now rattles off the names. 'Richard Dunkerley. Quite big. Gentle bloke. Curly black hair. Very affable. Shaun Hanson. Another big lad. Young in his outlook. Gary Nelson. Massive. Muscle massive. He was just one of those blokes, you thought nothing would ever happen to him. You know what I mean? I always felt close to him.

'Everybody seemed to get along well, better than before. I can remember taking photos of all the lads in the Mess, with all their war gear on.'

He'd already seen Supply Officer Rick Banfield, who'd spend the 21st as Flight Deck Officer. 'I remember going round and saying "Sir! Take damn good care of yourself!" Only joking.'

The people he didn't think about were his mum and dad.

'I was just aware of the people round me, the situation, and what we may or may not be about to do.'

Confident? 'Let's get on with it . . .'

◆◆◆

As *Ardent* raced closer to the gap, Surg. Cdr Rick Jolly was on *Canberra*, busy with his own last-minute preparations. He didn't know what was coming up. No one did. He could only guess, but he knew what Alan West's 199 men – and the hundreds of others in the Thin Grey Line – would go through between now and the next sunset.

'Before fright and flight there's one more thing that happens, and that's freeze,' he says. 'You see it with grazing animals. They eat a bit, then look up and freeze, because raptors detect small movements. If it comes at you,

you run. And run with a speed that's gifted by adrenaline and the nervous system, which shuts down everything that's inessential, your skin, your guts. The important things are muscles. The cardiac output is doubled with an increase in pulse rate. The nostrils flare as your breathing rate doubles, and you take more oxygen in. Your pupils dilate to take in more visual information.

'That had an advantage billions of years ago, but not now. But it happens when you're frightened. The danger is you get stuck in as a leader of the gang when you should be standing back and directing others to do what they're trained to do . . . the Damage Control Party is exposed then to the worst.'

◆◆◆

The clock ticked on. By 2320, the conversation had dropped a few notes. The lights on the Messdecks were low too. In the Stokers' Mess, the last of the beer and cider was being sipped.

'I remember that like it was yesterday,' Errol Flynn says slowly. 'I felt like I wanted to be quiet myself, you know. I really got a feeling of . . . sombreness. Some are sat in the Mess Square there. People are sitting in the gulch on their own with their thoughts. Coxie I can see. I can see Knocker . . . I was in the gulch on my own.'

'Hands to action stations! Hands to action stations!' At 2330, the main broadcast broke the mood.

'When action stations was piped, we was all in our gear and lifejackets, whatever you have to carry,' the pint-sized Brummie hesitates. 'We was all shaking hands because people went to their different places in the ship. Shaking their hands. "Good luck!" And then, "I hope to see you . . ." That's the feeling you get. This is . . . something's going to happen here. That's what we felt inside. It was in the heart. It was that type of ship's company.'

◆◆◆

At the top of the ladder, they divided and hurried their separate ways.

The men of Ken Enticknap's Aft Section Base Damage Control Party had furthest to go. Their dash took them ten strides down the main passage between the POs and Chiefs' cabins, through a watertight door with the Forward Switchboard on their left and Laundry on the right, 12 paces past the Heads, then through another watertight door where they moved from Forward DCP's domain into theirs.

They ran on. Ten strides between the Olympus intakes and exhausts. Another watertight door. Ten more between the Tyne intakes and exhausts. Another door. Into the SCC Flat, the SCC on the left, the Aft Switchboard on the right, the hatch down to the Aft Auxiliary Machine Room proud on the deck. Through another watertight door into the Junior Ratings' Dining Hall. One by one they arrived.

For Geoff Hart's Forward DCP, the journey was easier. They turned left at the top of the ladder up from 3 Deck and through one watertight door, straight

into the Gunbay Flat. There they divided again into smaller spaces. Everything from the Laundry Flat forward would be theirs.

As the last man went through each door, it was slammed and the wheel was spun to lock it solid. The hatch manholes were closed too. State 1 Condition Zulu. The ship was sealed. If it was hit, the damage or fire would be contained. The vents would be crashed to stop smoke being drawn through the ship in seconds, *Sheffield*'s fate. The firefighting teams would go in to quell any flames. The DC lads would follow with timbers, wedges and shoring to make her watertight again, and pumps to suck her dry.

The DC locker doors were open. Everyone was ready. If the Ardents were cut off from the outside world, ploughing through the heavy South Atlantic swell, they were cut off inside too, save for communications links to all section bases, and Comms to command.

'We regarded it as cold and the penguins probably did too,' Andy Cox recalls of the Gunbay Flat. 'I had everything on, sweaters, socks, T-shirts. Your anti-flash gloves kept your hands warm. The more layers of clothes you've got on, the less chance you have of burning. By then, everyone just wanted to get in there, get the islands back and then head for home . . . Get drunk as skunks, basically.'

Forward Section Base Chief Geoff Hart quickly told them to thin out.

'Stick with me,' Buck Ryan shouted to Naggers. He knew where it would be warm, in the Sonar Instrument Space on the left of the gun. What a mistake.

'We got up on the workbench and we were cuddling each other because it was so fucking cold,' Naggers shakes his head. So cold they soon forgot sleep and started yapping.

'D'you know what, it just seems right for the *Ardent* to go down tomorrow,' he told Ryan. They didn't dwell on the thought. In moments, he'd moved the conversation on, on to what they'd do when they arrived home. His plan was to finish with his girlfriend and go on a hoolie round London.

In the Gunbay, Bernie Bernsten glanced at his young stokers, Florrie Ford and Buzz Leighton, in their firefighting suits, then at the miserable look on Buck Taylor's face and decided he wanted to be Florrie or Buzz. Warm. Oh, did he!

There were men in the machinery spaces too for the first part of the run to the gap, ready for damage control, breakdowns and local control of the engines. Eddie Edwards was in the FARM on 3 Deck, Dickie Henderson was in the Aft Auxiliary Machine Room with PO Mick Langley and J.J. Smith, his sunburn a distant memory.

Jeff Curran was in the Aft Engine Room with 18-year-olds Wyatt Earp and Barry Muncer, a mag-loop headset over his ears so he could listen to Comms from the SCC, one deck above, as well as general broadcasts from the Bridge, a world away, then relay messages to the lads. Normally, he'd have had them positioned port and starboard, by the hull, to take emergency local control of the pitch of *Ardent*'s propellers, while he stayed between the engines, in case local control was called for. Instead, he brought them inboard, between the gearboxes, mainly for added protection, but also to take away the isolation. No one would have been able to see each other.

The First-Aid parties were placed too. In the Forward FAP, the Wardroom, PO Steward Dave Burr had Writer Mark Bogard, Frank Walmsley and Caterer Pete Ottley with him, among others.

In the Aft FAP – the Senior Ratings' Dining Hall wedged between the Servery hatch forward, the Junior Ratings' Dining Hall to the right and the Winch Room aft – were Simon Ridout, Leading Cook Dave Trotter, PO Writer Trevor Quinton and more of Rick Banfield's 'baby caterers'.

LMA Bob Young was in the Sickbay with Gary Gleed, the Captain's steward, worried that *Ardent* would run over a mine any minute and disappear in a flash, but equipped for it nonetheless. His respirator bag hid a knife, a cylume lightstick, a Mars Bar and a length of quarter-inch rope, 20 feet of it, ready to make a sling, ready to lash lifejackets in the water.

He gazed around. The internal lights were low so that, if they were holed above the waterline, the ship wouldn't look like a string of Christmas lights sailing past. He stood up and walked into the Telephone Exchange office, opposite the Sickbay, and put some tape on – 'if we were going down there as an Irish minesweeper, we may as well have music!' – and talked with the lads.

Jon Major, Bob Sage and Mick Foote were in the Galley, mindful of Cliff Goldfinch's instruction to Ken Enticknap that the two cooks' watches should stay far apart so that, if the worst came to the worst, they'd always have a team left to rustle up a snack. Before he left for the GDP and John Leake's side, he'd made sure there were sackfuls of fresh rolls in the Officers' Galley, far away on 1 Deck, and tins and tins of corned beef and soup, just in case.

Given the choice between the Upper and Lower Decks, most of his lads knew where they'd rather be, preparing the night meal and the next couple of meals after that, breakfast, and the action snacks that would keep *Ardent* going, if events allowed them to venture up top, or forward. Goldfinch was welcome to the GDP. If anyone was going to be in the line of fire . . .

In the Engineers' Workshop, a watertight door forward of the SCC on 2 Deck, the Chief Stoker's Party, the mobile patrol – Brum Serrell, Jan Joyce and Andy Andrew – was closed up too, discussing the latest football results.

In 24 hours, 'Lilliburlero' would say whether Spurs or QPR had won the FA Cup Final. Because life went on.

In the Main Communications Office, signals were coming in thick and fast. Some were aimed at Admiral Woodward, far to the east on *Hermes*, but it didn't matter. Alan West didn't want to be cut off, so he wanted to know what was going on.

'Everything was building up,' Lt Tom Williams admits. He found it hard. Even in quieter moments, his mind wouldn't switch off. He remembers replaying the details he and John Sephton had worked out about deploying the Lynx's secret Stingray torpedoes. The instructions had come by signal, because no manual had arrived with the ordnance on the dockside at Devonport.

'He'd flown the serial, but the operational side . . . We weren't going to get a second chance. We had a live £1 million torpedo sitting there and we had to launch it with instructions that had never . . . I was wary of letting Alan West down. It was like this time-bomb.'

He went to his cabin but couldn't sleep, even though he was dog-tired.

The Aft Section Base had been swelled by some of Williams's young Ops Room ratings, raw lads who needed nurturing at the start of their careers, who'd had no time to find their feet in this grey, confined, tension-packed environment.

To the hard-bitten men of Ken Enticknap's Aft DCP, they were just faces. But they could wield a hammer and ram a wedge in a hole, help the likes of Gilly Williams start a portable pump. Young boys like Steve Heyes, 22, learning the ropes of Mike Lewis's clandestine Electronic Warfare world, keen to please but sensitive, looking up to old hands like John Goddard. Boys like 18-year-old Sean Hayward, plucked from HMS *Vernon* on the eve of departure to make up Pete Brierley's sonar team. Or like South Londoner John Dillon, also 18, one of CPO Tansy Lee's radar ratings, a lad who kept himself to himself, buried in action comics. This war had come too early for them.

Amsterdam, 'The Bright Side of Life', sledges in Narvik, gun-busting waves, errant Exocets, dockyard mateys working their parts off, tearful calls to mum, will we, won't we, *Belgrano*, *Sheffield*, firepower demos. Young men tempted from the classrooms and factories of Britain, like Brum Serrell, a long way from Harry Cheshire County Secondary, Kidderminster. Like Knocker White, a long way from Monkwearmouth College of Further Education, Sunderland. Or Shaun Hanson, CI Jenkinson & Son. Or John Foster, Toxteth High for Boys, and shelf-stacker. Or Buck Ryan, in the Mob since he was 16.

The list went on. All that, and now this. The Thin Grey Line. The Funnel of Fate. Leading where?

In *Ardent*'s Aft Damage Control Party, Wacker Payne wandered about, chatting, doubtless finding a reason to smack Ralph Coates's head, a reminder not to snitch on his senior rate, particularly one who'd been in since he was fifteen. Fifteen?

'We had it, didn't we? We had a skipper we all believed,' he says. 'Most officers you take with a pinch of salt. They've got to earn your respect, and then they're okay. And then you had your Chiefs and your POs and your ratings. It all flooded down through the whole ship. We could do anything.'

◆◆◆

1500, Friday, 21 May, Rio Grande Air Base, Tierra del Fuego, Argentina, 381nm south-west of Falkland Sound. Lt Cdr Alberto Philippi knows his men well. They spend a lot of time together, and so do their families. He also knows his new mission will be precarious, but no more precarious than his first of the war would have been on Saturday, 1 May, from the old *25 de Mayo*, leading a dawn attack on the British fleet, located to the north-east of the islands and launching attacks on Puerto Argentino.

Cdr Acosta, the air intelligence officer, had taken him aside. In all probability, of the eight A4s launched, four would be shot down by anti-aircraft missiles, Harrier CAP and anti-aircraft artillery. Of the four that released their bombs on the ships, only two would be able to return aboard safely.

The squadron commander, Lt Cdr Rodolfo Castro Fox, had begged Philippi to let him lead the mission, 3 Squadron's first in combat. They'd been friends

for 20 years. Their mothers were close. If Philippi was shot down, Castro Fox would be the man to go and tell Graciela and the children. And vice-versa. But Philippi kept the roster as it was that day.

Now, 20 days on, he listens to the reports of early missions to Las Malvinas and feels anger rising at the chatter coming from the Etendard pilots next door. As he dresses, Lt Marcelo Marquez, his wingman, appears from the Galley, smiling, carrying some empañadas, gaucho meat pies. He offers Philippi one, but his commander snaps, 'You know what you can do with them!'

'Okay, sir,' Marquez grins, and shoves them in his flight suit pocket. 'You'll miss them!'

Then Philippi receives his orders: 'Attack a British ship sailing to the south-west end of the Falkland Sound in order to neutralise it as radar picket.'

In case they can't find it, the alternative targets are the troop-transport ships in San Carlos Bay.

Ardent's the most southerly ship, but she's not the picket. It's not what the British are expecting.

TWO

FALKLAND SOUND

(0001–1230HRS, 21 MAY 1982)

'You either crept through very slowly,' Nigel Langhorn recalls the options, 'or you said, "Sod it, let's get through as fast as possible."'

Sod it. At 0001, just past eight in the evening for the Argentinians ignoring their night-vision kit high above, *Ardent* left a broad wake as she made a 29kt passage past Fanning Head and through a narrow channel to the west of the two-and-a-quarter-mile wide northern entrance to Falkland Sound.

On the Bridge, most eyes couldn't help shifting left. It was pitch black, yet crystal clear. Surely they'd heard her Olympus engines thundering. Nerves around the ship were on edge, to say the least.

Alan Maunder was glued to his chart table and radar, desperate to spot the tip of the sunken Tide Rock that threatened to upset Alan West's distant charge past the 770ft steeply sloping headland. If Maunder had plotted well, it would pass to port, between them and Fanning Head. Nobody was saying a word, for fear of disrupting his running commentary or any call from Langhorn's lookout.

Oh for Satnav, West thought. The charts of this part of the world were awful. At least Satnav would have told him where he would have gone aground, even if he didn't know what reef it was.

At the wheel, Master at Arms Lenny Yeatman tried to convince himself he was in good hands, not that his faith in the skipper didn't wobble slightly, occasionally – for instance, when heading through a small channel at 29kts. On his anti-flash gloves were the words port and starboard, left and right, the lads' idea of a joke. Something about an anti-submarine exercise back home and a 'sunk' ship.

Suddenly Langhorn called. It was the rock, port side, exactly where they wanted it, the brilliant glow of water breaking over it the brightest thing in the whole world at this very moment.

On the Signal Deck, Steve Kent was still muttering silent prayers, expecting to be attacked from both sides, if not blown up by mines, hoping that, if he died, it would be quick and painless. Nervous? At least he could call on all his senses. Down below, sight had gone already.

PWOs Tom Williams and Mike Knowles were the only ones standing in the Ops Room, the tension rising with each heartbeat. The rest were kissing the matted deck, 30 stressed bodies pressing stripes into their flesh that would leave them like wallpaper samples in the green of *Ardent*'s nerve centre.

Further below, with *Ardent*'s engine and auxiliary machine rooms cleared of men for the time being, this curious game of 'Blind Man's Buff' was already playing tricks. With every minute, the ship's push through the water became

147

noisier. More noise meant shallow water. Shallow enough for something to be churned against the hull. Gravel. Shingle. Just how shallow was it?

Not too shallow from where Nigel Langhorn stood. Piss-poor charts, maybe, but not that bad. Not shingle. Cavitations. The pop-pop-pop of air bubbles being produced by propellers going at high speed.

Bubbles? Try telling that to the guys down aft. Try telling them now. It was eerie.

In the Capstan Flat, PO Paddy McGinnis was anxious, the furthest forward, maybe wondering why he'd gone back to *Ardent* after losing his wife with a brain haemorrhage.

Two watertight doors away, Andy Cox was waiting, second-in-command of the Forward Electrical Repair Party and mentally rehearsing his tasks; boundary searches, checking hatch valves for air coming out – flooding – or air being sucked in – fire – and reporting back to the man running the State Board in the Gunbay Flat Forward Section Base, then who knew what? Running interconnector cables to restore power? Racing aft to check breakers in the Forward Switchboard? Shoring a hole in the ship's side? The waiting was the worst.

Writer Mark Bogard was thinking. Lying down, head pointing forward, toes pointing aft in the Wardroom Forward First-Aid Post, waiting, a five-feet-eight target for the Argies, thinking that, if he lay port to starboard, they'd only have a one-and-a-half-foot object to hit. Then realising that, if he was hit, he'd get hit in the brain or up the arse. So he lay diagonally.

Errol Flynn was worried. Sandwiched between the Bathrooms and the Laundry, almost amidships, he worried about what might come through the side of the ship, and where was the best place to be, feeling his heart rebound off the deck.

Scouse Phillips was terrified, sitting on the SCC floor with Paul Turner, MEO Terry Pendrous, and Jessie Owens. All this business about silence.

'You've got these bloody big Olympuses. These huge waves making all the noise God can send and we'd been wrapping foam round resistors in drawers in the 184 Room. You could bang a drawer and it wouldn't rattle. They'll never hear us, we've got foam wrapped round the stuff.'

Chief Electrician Taff Lovidge was floundering, a man without a base. He'd crashed out in the Aft Switchboard until the backwash from the blades woke him up, 'throwing up rocks'. Then he'd been up to the Forward Section Base and felt even worse. Back in the Aft Switchboard, he bumped into the roving Tony Ray, the man he wasn't supposed to be caught with. 'Are you feeling the same as me?' the Deputy Marine Engineering Officer confessed. Lovidge nodded. Floundering. Fish out of water.

Lt David Searle was philosophical, a 24 year old who was less bothered about the outcome than perhaps a lot of people were – 'As far as I was concerned, I'd done all I needed to do in my life up to that time. I'd just got married . . .' – even if lying on the Junior Ratings' Dining Hall deck in a ship that's rattling around at 29kts wasn't one of the things he'd tried before.

Pete Brierley was grafting. Aft in the 182 Winchroom beneath the Flight Deck, the confined Winch Room, two small blocks of wood propped up the hatch enough for him to see the First Lieutenant, Andrew Gordon Lennox, and the

Buffer, Mal Crane, on the Quarterdeck recovering the Sonar 182 torpedo decoy streaming out on a 400-yard wire, in the pitch black. Grafting and smiling. 'It was funny seeing the Jimmy working for a living, with Mal being his normal crazy self. I could hear the shingle hitting the bottom of the ship, it was so shallow.' Shallow? The 182 normally streamed around 120ft down. So, shingle or mind games?

Yes, gravel. Bill Bailey was on the Flight Deck and definitely heard it against the hull. So did the rest of the Flight. They were all there. Tense. The night was as dark as he can remember. Apart from the noise from the ship itself, there didn't appear to be another sound.

On the Upper Deck, Chief GI Pete Rowe scanned the West Falkland coast through night-sights. He saw a campfire on one beach, then something else. He called Cliff Goldfinch from his GPMG position.

They could see a firefight going on. Goldfinch looked at it too, away to their right. 'I remember watching the tracers going up there,' Big John Leake says. 'I was thinking, "I wouldn't mind being in that firefight rather than where I am now." That was what I was actually trained for.'

Before long, the narrow gap and the threat of mines receding with every yard of wake, Chief Stoker Andy Andrew had sneaked up top as well, spellbound by the starry night, entranced by the silhouette of East Falkland, the place they'd come 8,000 miles to take back, drawn to the phosphor trailing the ship as she thundered on. She was running well. Then he went down to one of the air conditioning machine rooms off the Burma Way, the main passage on 1 Deck, and put his head down.

◆◆◆

Once they left the opening to San Carlos Water behind, they moved into deeper water – definitely deeper water – and turned left into Grantham Sound. Down aft, the noise dropped and the Ops Room began to bring everyone up to date over the main broadcast – the fact that they were through the channel, the fact that they were heading for the gunline. It helped the senses adapt.

By 0100, with sonar adjusted to its lowest settings for the shallow water – definitely shallow water – *Ardent* was on station in Fire Support Area One, an imaginary box just under a mile off the kelp in Grantham Sound, the 'closest point of oggin to Goose Green', according to the Jimmy.

Action stations were relaxed soon after, for some.

On Alan West's order, the SCC had taken *Ardent* down to Tynes, ready for her 12kts patrol up and down the gunline. It was a short gunline, because of the kelp beds, and it was at the extremes of the 4.5 gun's range. Now all they had to do was anticipate the Call for Fire, whenever that might come.

If they were going to answer the request of their hiding 148 Battery spotter ashore, and answer it accurately, there was vital work to be done. It wouldn't simply be a case of hearing the call and keying co-ordinates into a console, then pushing a button. Far from it.

The Fire Control System on the gun needed reams of information to obliterate the X that marked the spot on Captain Bob's list of targets: cordite

temperature, latitude, muzzle velocity (automatically updated from a basic muzzle velocity of 2,852 feet per second every time the gun's fired, from calculated barrel-wear), air density and temperature. But the most vital information, if the 4.5-inch brick was to arrive bang on target, with maybe 150 following it, would be the direction and speed of the wind high above, at the altitudes the shells would spear through. At maximum range, nigh on 17 miles to reach Goose Green, a little less for Boca House and Camilla Creek House, most shells would be screaming through the air for more than a minute.

CPO Dave Lee stood on the Flight Deck, feeling uneasy, preparing to launch a meteorological balloon to gather the vital data. He'd never seen a flight over one minute on the console display before. And he'd never launched a balloon at night either. In the eerie darkness, worryingly close to enemy-held territory, he detailed Pat Norris to prepare for a launch and watched the young weapons engineer and Paddy Samson drag out the filling gear to inflate the bin-bag-sized balloon. They stayed out on the Flight Deck longer than their boss.

The principle was straightforward to a man of Lee's experience. By tracking a reflective net around the balloon through *Ardent*'s 912 radar, a program on the Mark 8 gun – the only reason they'd come this far on their own – would calculate wind speed and direction through every stage of the flight. The 912 radar, positioned in front of the main mast, almost 200 feet away, would lock its 'pencil beam' eye on to the balloon once it emerged into its line of sight, but not before. To keep it tracked until the 912 spotted it, they'd have to use the Seacat Pedestal Site above the Hangar.

The problem was, how would the Ped Site track the balloon? Lee looked across at the shoreline. He needed an answer fast. Norris came up with a stroke of genius. In minutes, they'd attached two cylume fluorescent sticks to the balloon, the plastic markers normally tied to distance lines during a Replenishment at Sea in the dark.

Working as if he'd just 'acquired' a target for his Seacat arcade game, PO Rattler Morgan followed the sticks until the balloon was in the 912 radar's sights. Once that was locked on, the computer was set to start feeding on the stream of data, and they had the most up-to-date wind info in the fleet! When the balloon was tens of thousands of feet up, Lee asked Morgan if he could still see lines of light. He could.

'If the Argentinians saw the green blob, I've often wondered what they would think it was,' Lee says.

With data gathered and stored for the day's activities, all they needed was to hear from their spotter in some ditch.

◆◆◆

In the Ops Room, Weapons Director Richie Gough was aching to start his Naval Gunfire Support, but aching even more for the moment when he could say, 'Turn the ship for weapons arc 2-7-0', or whatever, and feel the ship turn, ready to use the gun in anti-air warfare mode. It wouldn't be, 'Captain, sir, can you please turn the ship?' He was desperate for the second he'd look at something on the screen and make a decision, and maybe the first thing the

Officer of the Watch would know about it would be when he unleashed a weapon. But that would be some time, maybe another ten hours. The Argentinians couldn't fight at night, and it wasn't even 0130 yet.

With the relaxing of action stations, the tension began to subside. No mines. Now they could go back to 'normal' duties. Blow their cheeks out. Stretch their limbs. Laugh.

Tony Ray was a happier man too. Once they'd arrived on the gunline, he'd been up to the Ops Room and asked his old mate Tansy Lee, Chief Ops Radar, where the Argentinian surface ships were.

'There's their ports, and,' Lee pointed to a chart and moved his finger east a fraction, 'there's our subs. When we've finished our NGS the plan is that we go up to the north again, out in the open sea.'

That was good enough for the DMEO. In open sea, your radar can see anything coming for miles.

Ray moved off, a man of broad build made bulkier by his own 'Michelin man' ensemble, gripping a torch that went everywhere with him, labelled with a warning to 'Keep your bloody hands off.' At some point, he dropped in to the Chiefs' Mess and drew a pint, joking that it 'might be the last one I ever have'. Then, if the long minutes of the night and the years since haven't dulled his memory, he went back to the SCC to give the Action Engineering Officer of the Watch, Mick Cox, some respite.

The Scot went off to put his head down in the Mess, but he didn't sleep for long. Adrenaline. So he went back to the SCC, almost totally clueless from now on as to exactly what was happening and where.

The 'what' at 0215 was HMS *Antrim* steaming slowly through the gap. The 'where' was a position six miles from Fanning Head. Within minutes of arriving, her Wessex helicopters began to ferry parties of Marines and SBS ashore. If the reinforced lookout post dug in on the 770-feet headland hadn't yet told Port Stanley what was happening beneath their very noses, they never would.

At 0245, *Fearless* and *Intrepid* followed *Ardent* and *Antrim* into Falkland Sound, escorted by HMS *Yarmouth*. They'd begin docking down at Chancho Point at 0320, giving them 45 minutes to float out the eight camouflaged landing craft units which would take the first men ashore. Forty-five minutes.

❖❖❖

'If you're a pilot and something's firing at you, what do you fire at?' The logic that had fashioned Cliff Goldfinch's gloomy letter home the night before hadn't been lost on his cooks. At around three, he wandered down to the Galley from the GDP and found Mick Beckett's Watch sharing out his kit. When he asked why, they told him.

'They said I was stuck up on the gun. "He's not going to last!" Who was going to have my whites. Who was going to have my gear!'

He went straight to the POs' Bar and put £10 on his chit for them. 'They were in good spirits. I signed for them just in case I didn't make it and they did.'

Taff Lovidge wandered around his lads too, from Wacker Payne, Knocker White, Kev Johnson, Garry Whitford and Ralph Coates, cheerful in the Aft

151

DCP, all the way forward to Geoff Hart's Section Base, and then the weapons engineers relaxing in the S&S Mess, anti-flash off. Lovidge still tuts.

His biggest worry, though, was the laundryman, Mr Wong. 'The guy didn't have a set of No. 8s. He didn't have a gas mask and we were trying to sort all this out. We ended up putting him in the middle section, up with the First-Aiders.'

Soon after, Ralph and Knocker bimbled up to the Electrical Workshop with their first issue of the day. As they supped, they considered the facts. 'We sat there together and we said, "Well, they're putting the *Ardent* in there to come between the Argentinians and the fleet." We knew we were going to get hammered.'

◆◆◆

At 0410, the Thin Grey Line was reinforced by the arrival of the Type 22 frigate, HMS *Brilliant,* in the narrows. About eight miles north of *Ardent*'s lonely station, the amphibious force was growing busier. But, within her grey walls, time was beginning to drag.

Lt David Searle left the Aft Section Base and relieved Nigel Langhorn on the Bridge. Radio Operator Steve Kent tried to grab some shut-eye on the floor of the Flag Store, but couldn't sleep a wink. A deck below, though, Pete Brierley found his spot, a warm corner between the sonar console and the Computer Room door, 'warm but bloody uncomfortable'.

In between jobs in the Forward Auxiliary Machine Room, Eddie Edwards and Les Pearce found time to come up for a rest in the Laundry Flat, and to craft a rather fetching hat from a pink toilet seat-cover in the rag-bag. It broke the monotony.

At 0452, as the second wave of the amphibians moved into position with her Special Forces troops safely ashore, *Antrim* began laying waste to the granite of Fanning Head. More than 250 shells – enough, someone mused years later, to flatten Windsor Castle – landed on the Argentinians' heads.

At 0530, little more than half-an-hour after the dust had settled, the Marines stormed in to see what 1,800 seconds of high-explosive could do. Twelve men were dead. Nine were wounded. The rest had gone. It was anyone's guess what they'd reported back to Port Stanley before they ran, or died.

About the same time, cooks Bob Sage, Mick Foote and Jon Major made their way aft from the Forward Section Base to relieve Mick Beckett's Watch and serve breakfast, a typical English affair, a fry-up, bacon butties, Richard Dunkerley's fresh bread rolls, a mug of tea.

In ones and twos, men walked in, shared a word, grabbed their food and went. John Foster had roused himself from fitful slumber on gashbags in the Main Communications Office to pay his whistlestop visit and see Ginger Nelson, 'doling out the old bacon butties'.

The frozen Upper Deck weapons crews made it down too. Russ Goble remembers a bacon and egg roll. Nectar. He hadn't eaten for hours. A freshly thawed Buck Ryan dashed in, shouted a greeting to Mick Foote, saw Ralph Coates, then walked back through the ship, yelling into the SCC as he passed,

like most people did: 'Bring out your dead!', 'See you in a few hours', 'See you in a couple of weeks'.

For Scouse Phillips, though, the reassurance that the cooks could rustle up decent scran, whatever the circumstances, was tempered by the knowledge that it would be daylight soon, then there'd be a build-up to the inevitable. The Argentinians were going to try to kill them. It was a tiring thought.

The tension was, indeed, beginning to tell. Mike Knowles had survived for 48 hours on adrenaline. Now he was wilting. Standing at the chart table in the Ops Room, Captain Bob and the First Lieutenant by his side, he felt his knees buckle. For a while, he thought no one had noticed.

'Go and shut your eyes for a couple of hours,' Andrew Gordon Lennox sauntered up to him.

'I couldn't possibly,' Knowles replied.

'Mike, I don't want to order you.' Reluctantly, he went.

It would be another two or three hours before Tom Williams left the Ops Room to freshen up. Even then, it would be via the MCO to collect signals. After decrypting them in his cabin, he'd lock them in a cupboard and head back for the Ops Room, feeling as fresh as Knowles looked.

And so it went. Waiting. Waiting.

At 0600, the port Tyne began to have difficulties. But even that didn't rate as excitement to break the tedium. The ME department had anticipated it earlier, so they shut the engine down while Jeff Curran went below to clean the on-engine filters.

Some time after breakfast, cook Jon Major recalls Ken Enticknap taking a call in the Aft Section Base for 18-year-old radar rating John Dillon, one of the youngsters whose unavoidable lack of experience meant he was unlikely to be at an Ops Room display that day. Dillon's wasn't a face or name Enticknap knew at the best of times, let alone swathed in an anti-flash hood. But, says Major, the lanky South Londoner took an age to hear his Section Base Chief.

'AB Dillon?'

'That's me, Chief!' he finally appeared.

'Oh, for God's sake! Our lives depend on you as well!'

At 0730, HMS *Glamorgan* began firing starshell flares from her Mark 6 4.5-inch guns, illuminating the barren Falkland landscape with the light of 500,000 candles, then launching rounds of HE into the positions guarding the long bay of Choiseul Sound, on the south coast, the other side of Goose Green, doing what it could to convince the enemy that the rest of the Task Force wasn't far behind.

At exactly the same time, 2 Para went ashore at the southern end of San Carlos Water. Seconds after, 40 Commando landed at San Carlos Settlement, on the east. COMAW Mike Clapp's Last Pipe was in full flow. The battle to retake the Falklands had begun.

At 1000, the Paras set off south to dig in on Sussex Mountains, overlooking Grantham Sound, the Marines secured the beachhead and, shepherded by HMS *Plymouth*, *Canberra* anchored three miles south-east of Fanning Head, a mile inside Chancho Point, carrying 42 Commando. If everything went to plan, the troops on *Stromness* and *Norland* were 30 minutes behind, with *Fort Austin* and

153

her helicopter cargo following soon after, protected from air-attack by *Brilliant* to the rear.

But it was still an eerily unopposed operation. At 1045, the Marines heading for Port San Carlos, on the north side of San Carlos Water, discovered one reason why. Far from repelling the invading enemy, the Argentinian forces defending Port San Carlos were withdrawing up San Carlos River.

On *Ardent*, ten miles the other side of Sussex Mountains, Alan West's men were oblivious to most of this. In places as far apart as the SCC and the 4.5 Magazine, in the depths of 4 Deck below the waterline up forward, they'd already begun to depend upon what Lt Nigel Langhorn could tell them about the landings. Most of the time, they might as well have been a world away.

There wasn't much the Officer of the Watch could do about it, though. Any information he had was already second-hand, gleaned from 'eavesdropping' Ops Room conversations on the open line. The Ops Room was monitoring the fleet-wide Tactical Net but, even if someone like Richie Gough heard on his headset about the fleeing Argentinians, he'd still have to talk about it before Langhorn could pick it up on his earphones and pass it on via the main broadcast. If Gough didn't, Langhorn couldn't. If he did, well, the Bridge was so busy running up and down the gunline Langhorn might not have time to let them know anyway. So, for all the rest knew, waiting at opposite ends of the Type 21 for something to happen, the folks back home were finding out first.

At 1050, Langhorn was on the main broadcast, though, but this time with a call to action stations and an Air Raid Warning Red, anticipating their ditch-bound spotter's call for fire. After almost ten hours waiting on the gunline, their time had nearly come. Nearly. For there would be more waiting.

A couple of hundred feet away, Brum Serrell broke off from testing the Avcat fuel for the Lynx helicopter – 'water and petrol-parrots don't go well together' – to peep beneath the half-open, roll-up Hangar door.

Mac McAulay, the Senior Flight Maintainer, was chatting over a cuppa with Chief Stoker Andy Andrew on the Flight Deck, anticipating a busy day, watching the ducks and geese fly by, looking at the islands and knowing that, all things being equal, soldiers would soon be heading for Port Stanley. Behind them, the Flight crew were ready to resume their lookout duties. The Lynx was poised, Sea Skua missiles mounted port and starboard, and ready to go.

In the Ops Room, helicopter controller Topsy Turner was waiting to see the Lynx off on its first flight of the day. Behind him, Pete Brierley and his Action Picture Supervisor, Mick Newby, were waiting too. Brierley glanced at Newby. He was such a garrulous character, capable of sleeping in any corner, at any angle. But he looked nervous.

In the Aft Engine Room, Jeff Curran wiped his oily hands on a rag, smiling, stinking of Dieso. He couldn't change, but at least the Tyne was back on line. He told the SCC. The SCC told the Bridge.

◆◆◆

With first light, the landing ship *Sir Percivale* had arrived off Ajax Bay. The smaller 'Sirs' and *Europic Ferry* were due to follow *Broadsword* and *Argonaut*

into what everyone hoped would remain the unmolested waters of Falkland Sound and the dark shelter of San Carlos Water.

Early the previous evening, British intelligence knew, a Canberra bomber crew had told Stanley of *Ardent*'s move. Overnight, 50 miles east, General Mario Menendez could have tried to rush men to snuff out the invasion in the minutes it had taken *Antrim* to flatten Fanning Head. But he hadn't.

Once it dawned on them that this was no feint, this was a beachhead being established, the Argentinians had to come. Surely they had to come, hitting the supply ships, giving the British a day or two on Falkland soil before their food and ammo ran out. At the very least, they had a big white target to aim at.

So, while 40 and 45 Commando set about their business either side of San Carlos Water, and 2 and 3 Para prepared to tackle their immediate targets further south, in the placid waters of Falkland Sound, the eyes of the Thin Grey Line were glued to the sky.

◆◆◆

Shortly after first light, as planned, Surg. Cdr Rick Jolly took off from *Canberra* in an 845 Sqdn Wessex flown by Lt Mike Crabtree for a rapid tour of all the landing sites. For Crabtree's crew – Sub Lt Hector Heathcote, the observer, and his crewman, Corporal Kevin Gleeson – this was far from the start of their morning. They'd inserted *Antrim*'s Special Forces party for the assault on Fanning Head. Now, just after sun-up, Jolly was picking up their first casualty, a Para with a twisted back.

◆◆◆

Ardent's Lynx was soon airborne too, at 1115, flying south to investigate a gunboat sighting. On the Bridge, Alan West was drumming his fingers, scanning the sky, tired of waiting. 'What's going on?' he said to no one in particular.

It's uncertain the lookouts on the Flight Deck shared the sentiment but, within seconds, radar maintainer Bill Bailey had a colleague on his shoulder. He'd spotted movement near the shoreline. They both lifted their binoculars. It looked like a convoy of vehicles in black and white camouflage.

On the GDP, Sub Lt Richie Barker's lookouts had seen the same thing. John Leake was waiting for the order to open fire, itching to release GPMG rounds and tension, but the call didn't come.

The Bridge lookouts had spotted the slow-moving dots too and told Mike Knowles in the Ops Room. 'Find out if there are any friendly troops in that position,' Alan West told them.

Knowles's men checked the grid position on their chart and radioed *Fearless*, reciting the grid reference: 'Are there any friendly troops in that position?'

'Stand by.' The next couple of minutes passed like hours. Finally *Fearless* crackled back. 'No troops in that position.'

'Right,' Alan West looked at his team, and hearts beat faster. 'Let's put a couple of rounds in.'

One level directly below, Knowles frowned. The 4.5-inch gun was

programmed for NGS on a target 17 miles away, not a pot-shot at enemy trucks three miles off. But, with West waiting for the familiar thud of the Mark 8 'two minutes ago', Knowles knew he had no time to follow the textbook. He raced up to the GDP and called to the lookout on the LAS sight. 'Select rifle mode and point straight at that bit of land.'

He'd have to do this in emergency mode, slaving the LAS sight to the gun to calculate a trajectory, normal practice for NGS if you can see the target but have no range information.

'He pulled the trigger,' Knowles recalls, 'and there's a sodding great bang, and clouds of smoke.'

They waited for the distant crump, but saw a plume of water about 200 yards from the ship instead. They adjusted their sights and fired again. Clouds of smoke swept across the GDP, but the round disappeared over the horizon.

By the third round, they were pasting the side of the hill.

The frightening crump of the first brick had sent the convoy into dead ground, a classic military move, but the lethal accuracy of the third now brought them scurrying into the open again.

On the Bridge, Lt Tom Williams let the smoke clear and lifted his binoculars. He spoke to his radio. 'GDP, Bridge,' he said quietly. 'Do cows carry guns?'

'You can take this in two ways,' Andrew Gordon Lennox says now. 'In direct fire, we engaged until these cows turned into cowards and ran away. Or you can take what the official history says, that we engaged troop positions in support of the SAS.'

It didn't matter either way. It had been a morale-booster. The 4.5 was working. Soon they were talking about it all over the ship and there was an extra spring in steps as they moved about their duties.

◆◆◆

The Ardents were still waiting though. They'd locked the 4.5 gun's radar on to its beacon, a physical object on the landscape that wouldn't move when the ship did. They had 14 rounds of high explosive shell sitting in the vertical feed ring running from the Gunbay on 2 Deck, and 200-odd more spread over the ship, from the 4.5 Magazine down on 4 Deck to a store behind the Hangar.

All they needed was the Call for Fire, then PO Richie Gough's dream would come true. He'd be the conductor of this 3,250-ton orchestra, he'd be fighting the ship, and he wouldn't hurt so much. Fresh from a short rest, around him he had the team who'd make it possible: his assistant, AB Jumper Collins, Gun Controller PO (M) Rattler Morgan, Seacat Controller LS (M) Sid Norman, and the NGS Radio Operator, RO (G) John Foster.

They'd been there for what seemed like hours, a 'God-awful long period with nothing happening,' Foster remembers. 'That's when it's very, very hard to keep your concentration going.'

Foster would be key to the coming hours, *Ardent*'s voice to Captain Bob's spotter, responding to the man-in-the-ditch's slow, deliberate requests. It would be like Alloy Express, except this time he had a gun to fire: Call for Fire – target number – Pucaras on airstrip, or whatever – grid, a six or eight-digit number

map reference – number of rounds – fuse, air-burst or exploding on impact – Out! The information would be repeated and fed into the Action Information Computer, and then the bombardment would be 'indicated' to the gun by the Bombardment Control Officer. More often than not, Richie Gough would already have the data in the computer before the written details reached him.

As the boom echoed around Grantham Sound, Foster would send a 'shot' message to the man in the ditch and, as the bricks approached the target, he'd follow it up with 'falling'. It's a fair bet that the incoming scream of the high-explosive shell was as good a warning as any.

Captain Bob would be behind, waiting for the voice, ready to give Foster a confirming tap on the shoulder at the appropriate moment. He remembers it well. He'd already told his spotter to keep the ship informed of what was happening beyond the horizon. But it wasn't the man ashore he was necessarily worried about. 'We were somewhat bloody isolated weren't we? She stuck out,' he says. But there was some comfort. 'She had a good skipper, she was a well-drilled ship. They were jacked-up and trained and motivated. You can't get a better tool to go to war with than that.'

At 1126, the Funnel of Fate narrowed finally. The call came. In his ear, John Foster heard the words he'd been waiting for: Fire mission. Target number. The number of ranging salvoes required. Once the bombardment was on target, he'd hear '36 salvoes, fire for effect', or whatever the number was to be.

As the SAS launched a diversionary raid on Darwin, she began firing. Every two seconds, until 14 or 16 rounds had been unleashed and the call came to cease firing, another 2.53kg warhead was punched high into the sky. Every two seconds, Buck Taylor, Dave Daley and Nigel Broadbent would lift a fresh shell on to the 4 Deck hoist. Every two seconds, the Gunbay crew would frantically replenish the 12 ring-feed slots, trying desperately to feed the gun's insatiable appetite for round after round after round.

On the Bridge, the first ranging shot made Alan Maunder jump. The first one always did. In the 60-odd seconds between that bellow of smoke and the brick's arrival, maybe 17 miles away, Maunder watched the gentle fall of dust from the Bridge deckhead and his mind went to names like Boca House – already a ruin, but what now? – Camilla Creek House, Darwin, Goose Green, as the whiff of cordite wafted through the vents. The sound of a 4.5-inch shell departing may have changed the further aft the Ardents were, but that acrid smell told the same story. This time, it was accompanied by words. The men closed up at their DC section bases were treated to a running commentary about their targets.

While the young WEMs toiled in the Magazine up forward, taking caps off shells ready for the hoist, hands weren't spare aft. Between calls for fire, a line of Ardents was busy hauling shells forward out of their 1 Deck storage, down to 2 Deck and along the Burma Way to the Gunbay Flat.

Back in the Ops Room, PO Mike Lewis looked across at his leading hand, John Goddard, on the Incident Board about ten feet away, poised to record information about the ship's state in the event of it suffering damage. He was looking grim, so Lewis wandered over. 'This is just like Portland,' he said, hoping it would lift the gloom.

He needn't have worried. It wouldn't be long before the reluctant killick and

his EW pal, Steve Earnshaw, were lobbing chinagraph pencils at Captain Bob: 'Hey, look, I've just had the SAS bloke!'

At 1154, one of *Ardent*'s salvoes hit the runway and had its first kill of the day, destroying a turbo-prop ground attack Pucara as it taxied towards its take-off point. The bombardment was checked after 20 rounds while the SAS pulled out from Darwin.

At the same time, *Brilliant* took up station close to the West Falkland shore, watching the sky with her Sea Wolf missiles poised. South of her was *Yarmouth*, in the middle of Falkland Sound, doing the same, with *Plymouth* facing south-east, ready to fire straight down the wide, open San Carlos Water.

The reply to *Ardent*'s Goose Green score wasn't long appearing. Within five minutes, a Pucara had dodged the shower and taken off. In his relief, though, its pilot strayed too near the mountain lair of an SAS troop having a brew and, crucially, equipped with a hand-held Stinger missile launcher. On *Ardent*'s Bridge, they watched the Pucara rise and fall, the last evidence of its short war a parachute swaying in the early morning breeze.

On *Canberra*, psychiatrist Surg. Lt Cdr Morgan O'Connell's view of the same was quickly followed by coming face to face with the war – the troopship's first casualties, a straggle of Argentinian soldiers. The British medics dressed their wounds, fed them, then washed them. O'Connell watched their swift, deliberate work and decided to allocate his own specialist skills to the T4 area, where those too severely injured to treat were put – with the dead. It seemed an appropriate place for him to be, supporting the nursing staff and doing whatever he could for the dying. When the alternative was thinking of the consequences of a hit on the Great White Whale, a giant ship with no prospect of any damage control, he was glad of something to occupy him, even death.

If Captain Bob had ever wondered why, during his eventful time on board, the engineers on HMS *Arrow* had tried to fashion odd decoy weapons using rocket-propelled flares to deter attackers, a Blue Peter approach to war on a multi-million pound fighting ship, he was about to find out.

At 1230, Nigel Langhorn grabbed the main broadcast mike and shouted: 'Take cover! Take cover!'

Two Pucaras were closing *Ardent*. They came within about 2,000 yards before Richie Gough switched from NGS to anti-air warfare mode and unleashed both the Seacat and the 4.5.

The Pucaras turned tail. As they did, the Seacat lost the race.

'We wanted to put them off at the maximum possible range,' PWO Mike Knowles says, then confesses, 'I wanted to see planes falling out of the sky in bits, but that was a high-risk strategy. I was a bit disappointed that we didn't hit them. The fact is, they didn't hit us. That's the important thing.'

The instant switch from NGS might have left *Ardent*'s spotter querying why the 4.5 storm had subsided, but it proved that Knowles's Ops Room gunnery team had the mental agility and manual dexterity to respond to the air raid warning without losing the 4.5's vital Goose Green target data.

In the Aft Engine Room, Jeff Curran had developed his own take-cover drill, sitting up with his feet tucked in so he was less likely to lose his legs or feet.

He even managed to skylark by banging the plates, just in case Wyatt Earp and Barry Muncer had dropped off to sleep. They hadn't.

Lying on the floor of the SCC hadn't done much for Scouse Phillips either. 'When you hear planes going over, you'd be lying there, thinking, "Where are the bombs? Where are the bombs? Are they coming?"'

As soon as the threat went, Karoly Nagy wandered through the forward section to the Gunbay Flat. To his optimistic eye, the eye of a young stoker told by his mother that the ship would sink but he'd survive, everyone seemed in pretty good spirits, considering. 'I was just outside the Gunbay and I was thinking, "This is all right. This is not too bad!"'

In the 4.5 Magazine, on 4 Deck, with condensation from four warm bodies trickling down the hull, Buck Taylor, Nigel Broadbent, Dave Daley and one other WEM were oblivious to it all.

If they'd been able to hear the main broadcast, one of the next voices they'd have listened to was Alan West's. On the Bridge, he called his steward, Gary Gleed, and asked him to fill his silver tumbler with Coke. Then he spoke to those who could hear. 'We've just seen a Pucara, over the hill. It was a little bit surprised to see all these ships here. We had a shot at it, but we didn't get it,' he reported. They could relax. Maybe.

◆◆◆

The switch to air defence had coincided with Richie Gough being pulled off NGS. Now on his headset he'd either be holding conversations or listening to them, six or seven of them: the Air Warfare Co-ordination team on HMS *Antrim*, Open Line to command, Gun control, Seacat control and Weapons Net. Not only were his ears encased, he also had his Upper Deck weapons crews on speakers.

AWC was probably the most vital, and the words he hoped to hear most were 'air warning green', no perceived threat. But he wasn't fooling himself.

For the next seven hours, or so, the least he expected from *Antrim* was 'air warning yellow', aircraft known to be approaching but not yet an immediate threat. 'Air warning red' he was dreading. Attack imminent. Three chilling words normally broadcast between the Ops Rooms of the Thin Grey Line, then passed on to the ship's company over the main broadcast.

If they came, everything would escalate rapidly. Whoever spotted the intruder first, radar operator or lookout, would call 'alarm aircraft red nine-zero'. Everyone else would be praying for supplementary information, elevation and distance, anything to give them a split-second start in eyeballing the threat, or diving the right side of a substantial object. 'Red' or 'green' would indicate the direction – left/port or right/starboard – and 'nine-zero' would turn heads towards the plane's bearing, 'zero' being the bow, 'one-eight-zero' the stern. Then it would be 'Take cover!' barked by the Officer of the Watch on the Bridge the moment he considered it prudent, normally when the aircraft was about to start firing cannon or dropping bombs.

There was one thing the Ops Room team always knew. They were talking to people on the speakers in the depths. Of these, the Emergency Quartermaster –

PTI Ginger Nelson or the Leading Regulator, Ken Chapman – was the worst job in the world, alone in the Tiller Flat at the back end of the ship.

Within 15 minutes, they were back on the deck. The men of *Argonaut*'s Electronic Warfare team had picked up a tell-tale signature, run through the list of could-bes and seen Agave radar. If the Leander-class frigate was right, a Super Etendard was heading the amphibians' way. Super Etendard. Exocet.

Ardent's Ops Room responded by firing blooms of Chaff Delta from the two-inch rocket launchers between the foremast and the mainmast, spreading a blanket of foil in the sky to confuse the incoming jet's weapons systems. But the alert came to nothing.

Minutes later, John Sephton brought the Lynx back in to land on *Ardent*'s Flight Deck. As Flight Deck Officer Rick Banfield guided her in, a disappointed Bill Bailey saw that the port Sea Skua missile was missing. He'd loaded the starboard missile.

Sephton and his observer, Brian Murphy, were all smiles as the Flight secured the helo and set about routine checks and replenishments. The two quickly made their way to the Ops Room. When they entered the green-lit nerve-centre, they could hardly contain themselves. Why not? They'd just hit an Argentinian merchant ship in Fox Bay, 40 miles south-west.

'It worked!' Sephton told Tom Williams. The PWO put an arm round his shoulder. 'I'm going to tell the Captain!'

Leigh Slatter looked round sheepishly. As they were engaging the enemy ship, the helicopter controller had mistakenly warned Sephton and Murphy that jets were closing 'from red 90', at 90 degrees to *Ardent*'s port side, instead of 'from the south, south-east, range not known'. How, in heaven's name, would they have known which way the ship was facing?

But Sephton walked past Slatter as Mike Knowles looked up briefly from his plot. 'You hit the target?' Sephton nodded. 'Okay, excuse me.' Knowles turned back to his work.

'Suddenly the thought must have hit him that we were bows-under here,' Knowles says now. 'He did extremely well. Everybody knew that, but we never really had a chance to tell him.'

He didn't see Sephton or Murphy again.

The Ops Room was buzzing, though. On the NGS console, John Foster's confidence was rising. 'I remember the CO saying we'd taken a couple of aircraft out on the deck at Goose Green,' he recalls. We thought, "Hey! Is this something?" We could have sat there and done it, day in and day out.'

The trick now was to remain at a peak. The alternative meant they'd be vulnerable.

The air threat, when it finally appeared, was expected from the west or north-west. The 500-feet high Campito ridge and the Verde Mountains took care of the north and south of the beachhead. If the Argentinians didn't want to run the Thin Grey Line gauntlet to hit *Canberra*, they'd have to swing in from the south-east, over the tricky contours of East Falkland. They'd also need to time

their runs to avoid the Harriers controlled by *Antrim*'s Ops Room, even though they were 200 miles from their carriers east of East Falkland and perilously, worryingly, restricted by the capacity of their fuel tanks.

On the southern side of Stanley Airport, Tenientes Horacio Talarico and Guillermo Crippa climbed into their Aermacchi MB339A jet trainers for a mission slated a day before, when intelligence had decided that the eastern shore of Falkland Sound, especially San Carlos Water and Grantham Sound, looked ripe for a counter-invasion. They'd fly low overland to Port San Carlos, then follow the coast south to Darwin, turn east and head home with whatever information they could gather.

Crippa waited nervously in his M339 while reports of British movements were studied. The damp conditions had already grounded many planes, condensation drowning the electrics in the wings of some of the two-seaters, batteries giving up the ghost in the freezing night air in others where ground crew hadn't taken them out to store in warmer conditions. As the two were set to taxi from the apron, Talarico's M339 failed. Crippa asked for instructions and was given them. You're on your own.

◆◆◆

Back in the Ops Room, though, the tension was rising. With the Camilla House bombardment in full swing, in the middle of describing their next target and reading its co-ordinates, *Ardent*'s spotter had gone quiet. Eyes framed by anti-flash masks looked at each other. After an excruciating pause, he broke silence – to say he could hear Argentinians closing in.

Bob wasn't too concerned, but he could see everyone else was. He knew his spotter well, knew that enthusiasm would be the most likely thing to kill him, knew from his own Army experiences in Northern Ireland and Aden that a soldier under fire can leg it, move. You couldn't do that on a ship.

He watched concern ripple through the Ops Room and then beyond. What's going on? Is everything all right? How close are these enemy troops? All they could do was wait, heads down, no whispering, just the sound of machinery. Waiting. They'd become good at it, but this was something different.

THREE

FALKLAND SOUND

(1259–1744HRS, 21 MAY 1982)

After about 20 minutes, *Ardent* sucked in a huge breath. Their spotter resurfaced, safe now in a new hide and ready to pick up where they'd left off, if she was ready. She wasn't.

At 1259, she was approached by a Mirage 5 running rapidly towards the sun from the north-west, the first fast jet. *Ardent* pumped a line of smoky 4.5-inch full-stops behind it until HMS *Yarmouth* arrived in the backdrop to her arc and forced Richie Gough to check fire.

'Approached is a pretty nebulous term,' Andrew Gordon Lennox admits. 'There was an aircraft. We were trigger-happy. We had no chance of hitting it.' And they didn't. A minute later, two Pucaras which had evaded *Ardent*'s NGS took a sniff at the Type 21 too. On the GDP, Big John Leake watched them near, listened to the 4.5 thump and then watched a Seacat swerve through the air. The Pucaras swerved better.

In the Junior Ratings' Dining Hall, Ken Enticknap heard the Seacat go first, then the digga-digga-digga of machine-guns, and sat in trepidation. Alan West watched the Argentinians flee, then turned back to Captain Bob, matter-of-factly, and suggested they switch back to the bombardment. Bob laughed.

In the shadow of the Seacat Launcher, Russ Goble was doing anything but laugh. 'If it had been a Sea Wolf on the back, we'd have been as happy as a pig in poo,' he says. 'There was no way they were going to acquire an aircraft, trail it and shoot it. It just wouldn't happen.'

Bob Young had listened to the same Seacat whoosh: 'We all knew we were up shit creek.'

◆◆◆

A curtain of mist greeted Crippa's M339 as he reached Falkland Sound at 1315. The glare was so bad that he headed north for Foul Bay, to make his run over the Sound with the sun behind him. Minutes later, wave-hopping towards the mouth of San Carlos Water, he saw a line of grey off Jersey Point, West Falkland. As he did, a Lynx emerged from the shimmer and instinct took over. Easy meat. Then he saw something behind it, HMS *Argonaut*.

The switch cost him. He fired all eight five-inch rockets and raked the frigate's decks with 30mm cannon. But only one rocket hit, striking *Argonaut*'s Seacat Deck, injuring three men, one losing an eye and another, Master at Arms Connie Francis, falling with shrapnel an inch from his heart.

On *Ardent*, seven or eight miles away, Lenny Yeatman watched the drama unfold. Crippa had gone before a Blowpipe missile from *Canberra*, a Seacat from *Intrepid*, and 4.5-inch shells from *Plymouth* were fired in reply.

Zig-zagging through the hills behind Ajax Bay, Crippa gathered his thoughts, then turned north again to count the ships. Now it was up to the intelligence channels to pass the news to the eager fighters on the mainland.

Soon after, too, the Ardents heard over the Tactical Net that *Argonaut*'s Joss had been wounded. Lenny Yeatman drew breath. He knew Connie Francis. This was a bit close. His adrenaline was up.

In corners of the Thin Grey Line's most remote outpost, thoughts varied. But in *Ardent*'s forward Damage Control Party, Karoly Nagy had already put his own perspective on the *Argonaut* news: 'We've outlasted them lot.'

◆◆◆

At Rio Gallegos, halfway between Rio Grande and San Julian, the day had dawned murky and cold.

The Argentinians knew a counter-invasion was underway in the San Carlos area, not Port Stanley. Beyond that, the one other certainty was that they had to do something. Their response was simple. They'd launch a strike of six Group 5 Skyhawk A4Bs from Rio Gallegos and eight Group 6 Daggers from San Julian and Rio Grande, then swamp the British defences with wave after wave of aircraft.

As Crippa fled San Carlos Water, Cuna flight was already on its way from San Julian, two Daggers, each carrying two 500lb bombs and three 1,300-litre fuel tanks, sufficient to deliver a massive punch and see them home again. The plan was to announce their arrival with 30mm cannon-fire, then hit anything they could.

Shortly after they took off, Nandu flight departed Rio Grande with orders to seek and destroy British shipping, assault ships and transports wherever possible. Perro flight aimed to form up within 1,000 yards of Nandu over the choppy waters of the South Atlantic. And, soon after they began their high-altitude outward leg, the Leo and Orion flights departed Rio Gallegos in clear weather, each Skyhawk carrying a single 1,000lb bomb.

The eight Group 6 Daggers from San Julian and Rio Grande were still 110 miles west of Falkland Sound, though, when HMS *Brilliant*'s Ops Room detected them. Lt Cdr Rod Frederiksen and Lt Martin Hale took the call and pointed their 800 Sqdn Sea Harriers in the direction of Cuna, Nandu and Perro flights above Chartres. Two against eight. Not good odds. Would they make the interception in time?

As they raced off though, unseen, the six V Brigade A4Bs of Leo and Orion flights sneaked by on their approach from the northern coast of West Falkland.

Having already slipped the Harrier net, the two Cuna Daggers followed their northerly path and saw the British fleet strung out, eight ships, one slightly isolated from the others. It was *Antrim*.

At roughly 1325, the Cuna Daggers dropped into line and followed their pre-planned attack, cannon-fire first, bombs after. *Antrim* was off-guard, but luck

was with her. In seconds, 30mm shell holes dotted her superstructure, but none of the 500-pounders hit. She breathed a sigh of relief.

British and Argentinian records of who was responsible for what, in the next five minutes, remain at odds. What seems most likely was that, having evaded Frederiksen's and Hale's Combat Air Patrol, Nandu flight emerged from the cover of Mount Rosie, West Falkland's high sentry point, and dropped until the wavetops were just 50 feet below. Then they raced for the gap between Fanning Head and Chanco Point, at the mouth of San Carlos Water.

Argonaut was an obvious target, already damaged by Crippa's rockets. The Cuna leader's wingmen immediately made a beeline for her. Before they even came within two miles of the scarred frigate and *Intrepid* – 14 seconds flying – both ships had unleashed Seacats. But it was *Broadsword*'s Sea Wolf which turned the Dagger on the right of the formation into a fireball as it entered the anchorage.

With two more missiles heading his way, the lead Dagger jinked into the vacant hole and saw *Broadsword*. Twenty-nine 30mm cannon shells ripped through the frigate's Flight Deck and Hangar, wounding 14 men and damaging *Brilliant*'s visiting Lynx. But, mercifully, both his bombs missed.

The remaining wingman veered south and went for *Antrim*. His 1,000-pounder slammed into the destroyer's Flight Deck, then bounced through the flash doors at the aft end of the Seaslug Magazine, glancing two missiles on its way to the aft heads. Again, mercy was with *Antrim*.

As her crew clicked into their damage control drill, the bomb failed to go off. So did both Seaslugs. There was only one casualty, caused by flying splinters. As fires broke out, Captain Brian Young sped north in search of cover and help from *Broadsword*. She didn't make it.

The air was littered with the remains of the first Dagger as Perro flight's leader speared left for *Antrim*, perilously close to the rocky edge of Cat Island, three and a half miles south of the landings. The thousands of men either pouring ashore or providing the ferry services were oblivious to what was happening, but in his wake were his two wingmen.

With Seacat out of action, and her crew ditching damaged missiles overboard, *Antrim* had time to throw up one hopeful Seaslug and turn to the 4.5-inch gun. Every available machine-gun opened up in chorus. The onslaught split the attack up but, to Capt Young's horror, the lead Dagger was not put off. It missed with its bombs but sprayed *Antrim* with cannon-fire, starting fresh fires in the Seamen's Heads amidships and some living quarters, wounding seven men, two seriously.

The second Dagger then turned its attention to *Fort Austin*, the big, near-defenceless supply ship. Twenty-four riflemen and two machine-gunners opened up. It looked hopeless but, to their amazement, the Dagger disintegrated before their eyes, blown apart 1,000 yards away by a *Broadsword* Sea Wolf.

Argentinian records don't acknowledge the loss, but it was witnessed by millions on British TV. For her sins, *Broadsword* became the next target. The third Dagger made for the Type 22, spitting 30mm cannon-fire and releasing a 1,000-pounder. Some shells hit, but the bomb missed.

Too late on the scene to have a reasonable chance of wiping out the Daggers,

the Harriers of Frederiksen and Hale both gave chase as soon as the Argentinian cleared the no-go 'box' into which the picket-line was hurling its fire, unleashing one Sidewinder. *Ardent* let off a hopeful Seacat as they fled south but couldn't stop the remains of Perro flight heading home.

It had been a costly few minutes, though. The Thin Grey Line had been reduced to six with *Antrim*'s limp towards *Intrepid*, in San Carlos Water, but it could so easily have been four.

Brilliant assumed *Antrim*'s role in control of the CAP Sea Harriers. Capt John Coward wasn't idle. He swung *Brilliant* round and hurried north-east, instinctively, to hog the middle of the entrance to San Carlos Water. If Argentinians were en-route with ideas of adding to the carnage, they'd have to pass *Brilliant*'s Sea Wolf first, to brave a pheasant shoot.

Antrim's radar worked well over long distance, but not in Falkland Sound's tight confines. Coward's plan was to see incoming attacks on *Brilliant*'s radar as early as possible, then have the Harriers drop on them leaving the 'box'. But he'd have no time to polish his act, for the six Leo and Orion Skyhawk A4Bs which had slipped by Frederiksen and Hale were even now clipping the waves of the north coast.

Lt Mike Crabtree's Wessex was busy in the anchorage with Surg. Cdr Rick Jolly on board, almost a lone witness to the mayhem as they took *Argonaut*'s wounded to the Whale, close to Fanning Head.

The A4Bs were looking for a tempting target as they tore through the narrows towards San Carlos Water at well over 500kts, and *Argonaut* was a perfect choice. The frigate saw them very late and opened everything she had. But it was too little, too late to stop all six Skyhawks. Five made it. Ten 1,000-pounders fell towards the stranded warship. Eight exploded in the water close to her. Two hit.

The first hit forward, ripping through a diesel fuel tank and coming to rest in the Seacat Magazine. The second tore through the bulkhead between the engine and boiler rooms, shattering *Argonaut*'s steering and reverse gearing. Neither bomb went off. Amazingly, the flames ignited by the first hit were doused by cold diesel spewing from the tank. But that's where *Argonaut*'s luck had run out.

With no way to change direction, and nothing to stop her, she was perilously close to Fanning Head. As she approached her jagged fate, Sub Lt Peter Morgan and two ratings raced from the Bridge to the Fo'c'sle and managed to let go the anchor. Seconds later, with two men dead in the Seacat Magazine and her insides ripped and bloodied, *Argonaut* lost all power. Her war was over.

❖❖❖

In and around San Carlos Water, an uneasy calm took over, giving the ships time to tend their wounded and put out their fires, and allowing the landings to go on – with them the arrival of the Rapier systems and the big 105mm guns which would, eventually, defend the beachhead. Eventually.

If many of Alan West's men weren't exactly sure what had been going on eight miles north, there'd been enough to keep their senses on overtime.

Weapons Engineer Iain McRobbie had tried playing games with PO Bob Lewis to take his mind off what was happening but the moments between an air raid warning and *Ardent*'s guns opening up seemed like hours. Then there was the noise of the aircraft. Real fear.

Mick Cox had fought the urge for the toilet during the early air activity, but mind over matter finally found its limit and he'd parked his backside when the chilling call broke his blissful, solitary moment. The echoes of 'Take cover!' were bouncing off the bulkheads when his mind went to the ceramic WCs that had disintegrated 'under attack' during HMS *Amazon*'s sea trials. Pulling his overalls back on, the Scot flew back to the SCC Flat and found everybody on the deck.

Scouse Phillips knew the feeling. Earlier, he was securing the door from the Junior Ratings' Dining Hall back to the SCC Flat after running a message to PO Wacker Payne in the Aft Section Base . . .

'Take cover! Take cover!'

All he could see were tiles, red and white tiles, staring at him, nothing to hide behind. He dived on the floor and covered his head. And waited. It was horrible.

He's a Liverpool man. But, since that day, he's never been a big fan of red and white.

Not everyone felt the same. Brum Serrell busied himself with planned maintenance, putting fresh tanks on-line, changing a dripping hydrant seal. Otherwise, to him, it was like the boy that cried wolf. 'After the first two or three, and nothing happens, you start getting a bit blasé.'

Not Cliff Goldfinch, at Big John Leake's side on the GDP. The PO Cook had spotted a helicopter hopping up and down behind a rise close to the shoreline, maybe a mile or two away. Each time, it seemed to him, 20 minutes later there'd be a raid. Word was passed to the Bridge and Sub Lt Richie Barker's weapons crews waited for orders. Word soon came back. Leave it. It was one of ours. Goldfinch still isn't convinced.

There were other things to be happy about below, though. PWO Mike Knowles had been fastidious with the data fed to the Mark 8's computers, checked it, double-checked it and checked it again. Now the news from *Ardent*'s relocated spotter was encouraging – 'Targets destroyed' coming back down John Foster's headset. It meant they were doing the job.

'When somebody's telling you you're actually destroying enemy planes, you're doing air-burst, with shells exploding overhead to damage the aircraft, and he's actually there looking at it, you think, "If he's going to give me corrections of 200 yards, he must be close enough to do that." It's incredible,' Knowles says. 'To start getting results was gratifying. We were putting bullets in the right place. It was just a sense of relief really.

'Teamwork. Whether they were killing people wasn't something anyone wanted to dwell on, even if it occurred to them. It was distant and impersonal. That's the way they were happy to keep it.

'I don't know and I don't want to know. It's just best to technically do the thing correctly. It's very detached. It's not nice.'

It wasn't hard to stay detached, though. Everyone in the Ops Room was

playing his part, even if the struggle to concentrate often meant they thought they'd seen things which weren't there. Someone 'saw' an Exocet looming and unleashed a full pattern of Chaff. The Exocet was then reclassified as geese, flying low and straight. A couple of ratings also saw torpedoes.

'Penguins,' Lenny Yeatman recalls. 'They were everywhere. They can move, I tell you.'

At least they had something to look at. Unshackled from his headset and the loneliness of the machinery spaces, Jeff Curran had just headed forward for a quick splash. He only met two men on the way. They were looking depressed, as depressed as they could look in anti-flash. On the way back, he was in the Forward Engine Room Flat when he heard the whoosh-whoosh-whoosh! 'Being on my own, I was close to having a baby,' he admits.

He ran back to the Workshop and phoned the SCC with a request to go back down below. At least he knew the Engine Room. The reply from his old mate Mick Cox was negative, if not scornful.

Down below, halfway through the day, the feeling of invincibility was growing. Perhaps it was only Cliff Goldfinch's men who didn't completely share it. They felt as if they were the last to know what was happening. In one of the frontline jobs, maybe they'd have known where the next one was coming from. It was tiring.

◆◆◆

On *Canberra*, Lauraine Mulberry was taking in sights and sounds that she'd later record in her diary:

> Casualties have been coming in by helicopter, but how many I don't know. Seems 3 Para, who were sent to take the highest ridge surrounding San Carlos Bay, have encountered more resistance than expected – possibly tanks – so 42 Commando have now been sent ashore to help. The idea is to hold the complete bay and to make it safe for the Task Force therein and to stop any route for troops of the Argentines to come across from Stanley . . .

> We have just heard that *Antrim*, which is 200 yards off us, has taken an unexploded bomb. She is transferring casualties to us and then is going out to sea. Someone will have to try and defuse it. We have also lost a Scout helicopter and her crew are now lying by the map of the world.

◆◆◆

Lt Tom Williams was at Alan West's side on the Bridge when he shared a thought: as soon as they started dropping bricks on an airfield, some planes were going to take off and come and have a go.

At 1410, *Ardent* was approached by two 3 Brigade Pucaras. In the SCC, the 'Take cover!' call merged with the 'clang-clang' of the telegraphs demanding full power. Eyes swivelled as two men jumped up and pushed the throttles, then hit the deck again, still watching the gauges.

Insulated on 2 Deck, with no idea of what was really going on in the outside world, all they could do was listen to the main broadcast and picture it in their minds. In the Forward Engine Room, though, they couldn't even hear the main broadcast, they just had the Comms link to the SCC. They heard the distant 'boom-boom' of the 4.5 as the Pucaras came within range but, at 2,000 yards, the Argentinian planes turned away. Seacat wasn't troubled this time. Then there was a lull.

Watching the SCC machine panel, Mick Cox was feeling weighed down. So he threw his lifejacket, once-only suit and respirator in a corner. He was part of a worked-up team. Nothing was going to happen to them.

◆◆◆

At Rio Gallegos, 480nm to the west, however, the Argentinians had plans to ensure the lull was only temporary. As *Argonaut* felt the force of the Leo and Orion flights, Capitan Pablo Carballo had been preparing to lead his Mula Skyhawks towards Falkland Sound.

◆◆◆

As *Antrim* limped to shelter, two more ground-attack Pucaras made it into the air, flown by Major Carlos Tomba and Primer Teniente Juan Micheloud, and briefly showed interest in *Ardent*. This time Seacat was part of her reply, in tandem with the 4.5. To Alan West's joy and relief, they 'chickened out'. But he was under no illusions. They'd be back.

First, Tomba and Micheloud flew to Darwin and rocketed a derelict house the Argentinians had identified as an observation post being used by *Ardent*'s spotter. From there, they went to attack a second OP then, at 1505, they returned.

As *Ardent* prepared to give them a second dose of high-explosives, *Brilliant* came to her aid. The Type 22's Ops Room had seen a slow-moving contact over land and alerted the CAP Harriers flying high overhead. They were either Argentinian helicopters or ground-attack aircraft. It didn't take the three CAP Harriers long to find out which.

About ten miles off, Lt Steve Thomas was the first to see the Pucaras hugging the terrain. He set his Harrier's nose at the lead Pucara, Tomba's. Wingman Lt Alasdair Craig wasn't about to be left out. He fired his cannon in unison with Thomas, ripping up the ground ahead of the Pucara.

Tomba almost clipped the dirt as he jinked for his life, but he couldn't stop Lt Cdr Nigel 'Sharkey' Ward's first 30mm burst hitting his starboard engine, then his port aileron, almost sawing off his wing-tip. With ripped metal peeling past his cockpit and Falkland soil looming, Tomba's day was over. But his ordeal was not.

Thomas and Craig dropped back on him, then Ward – at times no more than ten feet from the ground – repeated the attack. Thomas hit him a third time and,

as Ward lined up for another run, pieces of wing, fuselage and canopy tore off the doomed plane, and Tomba ejected. The Pucara ploughed into the ground, ten miles south-west of Goose Green. Seconds later, after one gentle swing of his chute, Tomba's feet were also on Mother Earth. By this time, Micheloud had gone. *Ardent* breathed again.

For the next 45 minutes, maybe an hour, there was little for her to do. The DC parties were looking for jobs in the No Man's Land of the gunline, in the No Man's Land of the clock. Most of the day's work was done, but they weren't close enough to dusk to think of tomorrow.

In the lofty confines of the Forward Engine Room, Garry Whitford dropped by with some food for PO Joe Laidlaw's crew. Whitford was fine, Laidlaw remembers, 'a bit quiet, but he obviously knew what was going on. We didn't. So me and Jock Porter, we weren't particularly bothered.'

There was a sound reason. They hadn't been hit!

In the Ops Room, NGS over for now, Capt Bob turned towards the door and spoke to Scouse Flynn on the surface plot. 'I'm off to get my head down,' he said. 'Give me a shake when the ship's sinking!'

◆◆◆

While Tomba and Micheloud were being seen off, Capitan Pablo Carballo's Mula flight was edging nearer, though now numbering just three after the refuelling probe on one Skyhawk had iced up, forcing it to head home to Rio Gallegos.

Then, as Mula's northerly course took it lower and closer to Falkland Sound, and the depleted Thin Grey Line, the auxiliary tanks on a second A4B stopped feeding its main tanks properly so, after breaking radio silence for a clipped conversation with Carballo, he turned back too.

The remaining twosome passed between Mount Adam and Mount Maria, to pounce from the north, but thickening cloud forced them south in search of a glimpse of something to tempt them on. South was where *Ardent* lay.

Breaking cloud cover, they spotted a cargo vessel close inshore to West Falkland at Port King. They made a careful run-in, both firing 30mm cannon before a low-level bombing run but, at the last moment, Carballo realised there was no return fire. He called off the attack. Too late. Carmona's single 1,000lb bomb was on its way.

The *Rio Carcarana* was unmanned, wiped out days earlier by a Harrier attack, but half of Mula flight's bomb-load had gone. Now Carballo was on his own. He headed north-west, towards Grantham Sound. There he saw an isolated silhouette.

◆◆◆

Ardent, the lonely Type 21, was taking a breather, glad to be at Air Raid Warning Yellow, not Red, relieved at *Brilliant*'s view that the air threat had reduced. White would have been heaven-sent after a busy day, the call every man craved, the chance of attack very slim. Red they were already intimately acquainted

with. It meant that either an attack was imminent, or it was happening. Yellow sat between the two. If they couldn't have White, Yellow would do. They still needed to keep their eyes peeled, but the chance of kissing a deck tile was reassuringly distant. On this Yellow, though, *Ardent* had dropped her guard.

On the Bridge, binoculars were not so constantly aimed at the sky, and cups of tea and ki (hot cocoa) were being handed out. PWO Tom Williams walked up the ladder from the Ops Room with a cup given him by Pete Brierley. He squinted with the change to daylight, put his ki on the window ledge and began chatting with Sub Lt Jerry Bernau, on the wheel, and Captain Bob and Alan Maunder, about the battle 'going on over there', a minute's flying time away, about the cows incident, and about how the day was going. It felt good to laugh.

After a tense few hours, a knackered Richie Gough had left the Ops Room and gone up top. He sucked in the crisp air and wandered to chat with Tony Langridge and AB Steve Strachan on the port LMG. It was good to be in the open. The Jimmy was up there too, feeling the breeze on his face.

Just below the three, gun loader Jeff Gullick had finished his tea and strapped himself into the port Oerlikon 20mm to let gun-aimer Topsy Turner take a break, swapping dits with his old mate Steve Kent as he did. On the starboard Oerlikon, Mick Newby had just put Trevor Hawkes on his 20-mill.

If the enemy was coming, he'd come from the west. But it was Yellow. He wasn't expected.

Carballo's attack was swift and direct. All Gullick saw was the dark shape of a plane hop over the hill and head straight at him. No more than 30ft above the waves. His heart pounded.

'Alarm! Aircraft Red Nine-Zero!' he yelled and started firing.

Kent dived for cover but recalls clearly seeing Carballo's helmet as the Skyhawk pulled up.

The Jimmy thought he was dead. Wall-to-wall A4B. Zero feet. Out of the blue. Out of the east.

On the Bridge, Jerry Bernau managed one word – 'Aircraft . . .' – but it was enough to make Alan West drop his pasty and send Lt Nigel Langhorn grabbing at the main broadcast microphone.

Argentinian records have Carballo's payload at one 1,000lb bomb, but Williams counted two dropping from the rail, bits flying off as Gullick squeezed the port 20mm's trigger, and watched the first bounce off the water before he headed past a rooted Alan Maunder for the ladder. He landed in a heap in the Ops Room, 'Air Raid Warning Red!' drowned by the thunder above.

Mike Knowles looked, muttered, 'A bit fucking late!', and heard the digga-digga-digga of a 20mm.

In the split second after the bombs dropped, time froze for the men defending the invincible *Ardent*.

Russ Goble's mouth was watering at the prospect of his first bite since 0600 when he heard gunfire from the Flight Deck, looked down and saw John Sephton emptying his 9mm pistol. Sephton looked up at Goble, then the young gunner turned and saw the A4B about 300 yards away. And closing.

The man bringing his buttered bun and aluminium jug of lukewarm tea threw the delivery at him from the ladder and, shouting 'Fuck this!' disappeared.

Goble fired about 15 rounds, then saw a big cloud of spray and thought, 'It's our turn.'

John Leake and Cliff Goldfinch heard 'Red nine-zero!' and twisted towards the port side. They saw the bombs drop and followed the Skyhawk as it flew over the ship, seeming to clip the main mast as it went, then opened up on the starboard side. But the gun stopped firing. Leake lifted the feed tray and saw the links were jammed. He quickly cleared the jam, put the belt back in, fired again, then ran out of ammunition. Time to hit the deck. As he and Goldfinch took cover, Leake landed on his back and watched the two bombs sail between the masts, green bombs with stripes on them, in slow motion.

A level below, Mick Newby shoved Trevor Hawkes off the Oerlikon and started firing, 66 shells ready to punish Carballo for his rude arrival, but the magazine jammed after two rounds. End of shoot.

Down below, John Foster was oblivious to the danger as he stepped out of the Main Communications Office and saw men lying flat on their faces.

'John, get down!' someone shouted. He dived back into the MCO, then heard a roar and gunfire.

On the deck of the Junior Ratings' Dining Hall, Taff Lovidge discovered that the cheeks of Tony Ray's behind twitched during an air raid.

'If I could've crawled underneath deck tiles I would have,' Ray admits. 'I thought, "I can't die, I haven't paid for the caravan yet." I was petrified and anyone who says they weren't is a liar.' At the same moment, Lovidge had been trying to spread himself as thinly as floor polish.

In the Ops Room, John Goddard watched his screen start dancing as the departing Skyhawk's jet-stream blasted the mast-top 992 radar.

◆◆◆

Within moments, Richie Gough was back and being greeted by a new Call for Fire. The job wasn't over. Neither was the day. But it had come close. Some knew just how close. Others didn't. The wideness of Andrew Gordon Lennox's eyes told anyone who looked how close.

Men started to think of things they could hide behind next time. The Jimmy poked his head round the SCC door a short while later. 'We've been straddled!' he told them.

Mick Cox had no idea that a bomb had just bounced over *Ardent*, from one side to the other, but he made a mental note. When information did reach the SCC, they'd been passing it on to the guys stationed down below, in the machinery spaces. He decided not to mention the straddling. No point worrying them. But some people had been scared. Scared silly.

Jon Major had started praying. He hadn't known what to say.

Andy Cox had waited for the moment he was bounced off unforgiving metal, trying to count the bombs, willing them not to come near the Gunbay Flat, to go the other side, port side and aft. 'Your mates are there but you think, "Don't come near me, go near him." They're thinking the same.'

On the GDP, Cliff Goldfinch had started the day feeling pessimistic. But now, the feeling of invincibility was further away than ever. 'How long can a

drowning man hold his breath? That's the feeling I had,' he says. 'We were laughing and joking, but you only laugh and joke because it's a release. It was so . . . everything was like something out of a war movie. We didn't expect it.'

Young Richie Barker, less than a year out of training but in charge of Goldfinch and the others on the GDP, couldn't believe the two bombs he'd clearly seen hit the water hadn't gone off. The split-second image of the angry Skyhawk had left an imprint in his mind for life.

Captain Bob stood on the Bridge and the faces around him told him all he needed to know. He'd been mortared and blown up once in the back of a vehicle in Aden, but being in a ship when someone tried to drop a bomb on you was a bit different. 'We'd been a bit gung-ho,' he confesses. But now the talk was 'If their aircraft can do this to us . . .'

◆◆◆

Carballo was as swift in his departure as he'd been arriving, but his daring was the undoing of two of the four Skyhawk pilots originally due to have flown the mission alongside Mula flight.

As he fled, the 800 Sqdn Sea Harriers of Lt Cdr Neill Thomas and Lt Cdr Mike Blissett were dropping low over West Falkland, near Fox Bay, expecting to see Carballo close to Chartres. Instead, Blissett spotted four other Skyhawks passing from left to right below, three miles west of Chartres, 45 miles from the landings. In an instant, the A4Cs switched from attack to defence, ditching their bombs and drop-tanks and splitting up.

Blissett fired one Sidewinder first, destroying one A4C on impact. The pilot's body was never found. Thomas's Sidewinder whistled past Blissett's Harrier as a second Skyhawk tried desperately to reach the sanctuary of the only cloud available. He didn't make it.

The plane caught fire as the missile struck. Its pilot ejected but his parachute failed to deploy and, as his wreckage exploded on impact south of Christmas Harbour, close to the first A4C, he hit the ground.

Blissett went after a third kill with cannon, but the plane fled, trailing smoke.

◆◆◆

Alan West strode to the GDP, dragged his weapons teams and lookouts together and bollocked them.

'You should've been shooting by the time you saw it,' his tone was terse. There'd be no second wake-up call. This wasn't open ocean. The Ops Room screens were practically blinded by cluttered radar returns. They had to keep their eyes glued to the horizon.

He returned to the Bridge and told Officer of the Watch Nigel Langhorn that the 'Take cover!' pipe had to be quicker. Men had to be given the chance to hit the deck before the attacker fled. Then he turned his attention to the 992 surveillance radar aerial blasted by Carballo's turbulence.

The news wasn't as bad as it might have been. The aerial was 12-degrees out and locked beyond the end-stop that helped to keep it scanning the same steady

173

piece of horizon when the ship pitched or rolled wildly in bad weather. Fortunately, as Carballo's wake settled around *Ardent*, the 992 was still active.

PWO Tom Williams looked at his display and sighed with relief. The main air activity picture was still coming in. Every plane was there. He couldn't shoot at them, but at least he knew exactly where they were. Alan West discussed the problem with Weapons Engineering Officer Paddy McLintock and decided they'd live with it until they could put the aerial right.

In normal circumstances, in heavy seas, McLintock would have left it in its cock-eyed position until it was safe to send someone aloft and physically push it off the end-stop. It wasn't a break in the weather they'd need now, it was a break in the air activity.

McLintock called CPO Brian Goulding into the Ops Room and waited for Peddler Palmer, the man whose section looked after the 992, to arrive from Ken Enticknap's Aft DCP. The stout Acting Petty Officer arrived and listened to the order. He knew what was needed anyway. He volunteered. When the air threat subsided, he'd climb the mast and free the aerial.

McLintock and Goulding – and Alan West, for that matter – knew they could rely on the popular, trunk-legged 26 year old, whenever the moment arrived to go aloft. The 992's picture said it would be some time, so Goulding asked if he was staying. Palmer declined the invitation. He'd be safer back aft.

It was the last they saw of the big Cornishman with the big heart.

1630, Rio Grande Airbase, Tierra del Fuego, Argentina: Lt Cdr Alberto Philippi walks the 1200 yards along the apron to his Skyhawk with his wingmen, José Arca and Marcelo Marquez. As he nears his A4B, its 3-A-301 callsign painted in dark foot-high markings on the gull grey of each air intake, technical officer Lt Vitte gives him bad news. The plane has a fault and isn't ready to fly. It's a blow, but not one Philippi can dwell on. He shares the plane with squadron commander Rodolfo Castro Fox because it has a VLF Omega navigation system. The others don't. He tells Vitte to assign them the three first planes ready to fly. Lt Benito Rotolo and his two wingmen, Lt Carlos Lecour and Lt Roberto Sylvester, will have to follow on as soon as the other three planes are ready. The two sections will fly 15 minutes apart and rendezvous in-flight or over the target.

Finally, Philippi says goodbye to his ground crew and climbs the ladder to the cockpit of his replacement plane, 3-A-307, his heavy boots clanking on each of the seven rungs. Before climbing in, he says the same prayer he's uttered since his first flight, 22 years ago.

'Lord, let me accomplish the mission and come back safe.'

Then he closes the cockpit and forgets everything. Graciela, the children, his mother, the plane he should have been flying, his friends. Everything except the mission.

The Ops Room was catching its breath soon after the straddling when – 'Exocet! Exocet coming inboard!' – Leading Seaman Tony Langridge's voice screamed down the Weapons Net.

Alan West was on the ladder from the Bridge and looking at Richie Gough. 'Fire Chaff all round,' he yelled, but Gough's hand was already flying over the control panel.

'Reload all Chaff!' Gough ordered his Upper Deck weapons crews as the thud of rockets rumbled. Then he looked at his screen for the Exocet but, almost immediately, Langridge called again.

'Disregard, it's a bird,' the Lookout Aimer Sight Operator's voice was calmer this time, but the tension had been cranked up another notch. Gough looked around the Ops Room. They were growing very tired.

Around the same time, Dickie Henderson and Knocker White took a few seconds out for a short conversation in the Aft Section Base. One needed to take responsibility for flooding and pumping at the next Watch change, the other would don a fearnought suit and join the firefighting teams. No one wanted to put a fearnought suit on, so they compromised.

The coin fell for Henderson. 'I'll do pumping and flooding, you're in a fucking fearnought suit,' he laughed.

◆◆◆

About 1700, nerves just settling, John Leake dished a handful of nutty from his secret GDP store to the Upper Deck weapons crews, then looked around surreptitiously and slipped a cigarette from his pocket, the first of a long day. It hadn't gone unnoticed.

'You're not allowed to smoke!' someone shouted.

'Piss off,' the big Brummie NAAFI manager thought. He took a drag and it went straight to his head.

In the Junior Ratings' Dining Hall, Richard Dunkerley, Taff Roberts, Mick Beckett and Dave Trotter were busy handing out action snacks, 'helped' by PTI Ginger Nelson and Doc Young, discussing life and the universe and anything else that came to mind. Young had his First-Aid Party there; Mark Bogard, Trevor Quinton, Junior Caterer Pete Ottley, and Mike Stephens, Ottley's boss – men whose job was to wait until someone else was damaged. Kev Johnson was there too, ready by the State Board, a sectional diagram of the ship. Garry Whitford was also in the Aft Junior Ratings' Dining Hall, now a familiar place after his switch with Andy Cox at Ascension. They were nearly all young lads.

In the Aft Engine Room, PO Blood Reed looked at the action snack rolls chucked down and showed them to his young stokers, Wyatt Earp and Barry Muncer. They'd been down in the AER for hours.

'This is all we've got!' he told them, apologetically.

'It's all right,' they replied. 'We've brought our own!'

Earp dipped into his respirator box, pulled out a handful of sweets and handed Reed a share.

'Do you want to go upstairs?' the PO shrugged. He didn't need to ask twice.

After a day below, they shot up the ladder to the Junior Ratings' Dining Hall, while Reed stayed with the Mobile Repair Party in the Workshop and CPO Jeff Curran went down with a couple of ratings to take over.

Earp opened the Dining Hall door and a sea of faces looked up. He glanced into the Galley and saw Geordie Derek Armstrong's familiar eyes among the cooks looking back from behind anti-flash masks. Round the corner, all the Damage Control lockers were open. He looked back at the small space between the Catering Stores and the Galley. It was crammed. He was shocked. He and Muncer hadn't heard any air attacks or anything. This lot had been through it all day. He looked again at Florrie Ford and Buzz Leighton, sitting alone, in their fearnought suits, tucked up like two lonely sardines in a vast ocean.

Earp and Muncer stepped over the bodies to join them, then watched a steady stream of visitors to the Galley pick up their scran and head back to their action stations so that someone else could come and replenish.

John Foster walked in around 1700 from the Main Communications Office. Ginger Nelson handed him a bread roll. Foster was due to relieve Leading Regulator Ken Chapman in the Tiller Flat, everybody's idea of the loneliest, scariest place on the ship, on Earth.

'Get that down you!'

'Only one?'

'I'm going to eat the rest!'

Foster laughed. 'I'll see you later!'

Give or take a minute, PO Joe Laidlaw pushed the SCC's stable door open and had a shock. The Tannoy was rattling out information. It was another world, compared to the Forward Engine Room. Suddenly, he could hear what was going on, and he thought 'Shit!'. He sat down at the throttles and realised this was just as lonely a place to be as the FER.

In the Ops Room, John Goddard, the reluctant leading seaman, was trying to contact his young Electronic Warfare colleague, Steve Heyes, in the Aft DCP, to see if he wanted to take a break too. He caught Steve Earnshaw's eye. The friends read each other's minds. They were both dog-tired.

At Rio Grande Naval Air Station, in the southern reaches of Tierra del Fuego, Lt Cdr Alberto Philippi taxis his Skyhawk A4B to the runway. Behind him are Teniente Jose Cesar Arca and Marcelo Marquez. On the apron, Tenientes Benito Italo Rotolo, Roberto Sylvester and Carlos Lecour are waiting to follow in their wake 15 minutes later. Each plane carries four Snakeye MK82 bombs, 500-pounders with retarded tails.

During the taxi, Philippi sees his ground crew saluting and cheering. It's an emotional sight.

Brimming with 9,000lbs of fuel, weighed down with four 500lb Snakeye bombs, Philippi's battling crosswinds on Rio Grande's long runway, watching its last yards rifle nearer but unable to lift his Skyhawk's nose off the tarmac. In his wake, Arca and Marquez are on their own endless take-off runs. They make it into

the air eventually, but the tarmac's within feet of running out when they do.

Downtown, in the small school of Rio Grande, Graciela stops teaching and walks to the window to watch her husband's plane take off in the cold, cloudy distance. She has a knot in her throat, but she's unaware how close he's being dragged to disaster.

As they finally leave Argentinian soil behind, Philippi can begin to think again of the coming task. He has 4,609 flying hours behind him in a career spanning 22 years. His mission in the next few hours will be to 'attack and neutralise any British ship steaming south-east in the Estrecho de San Carlos' – Falkland Sound – 'acting as radar picket for the British forces'.

◆◆◆

At 1715, with his fire missions complete and Goose Green closed, Alan West spoke with COMAW Mike Clapp's staff on *Fearless* via the Tactical Net and asked what they wanted *Ardent* to do next. The reply was clear: move into the centre of the Sound to cover air raids from the south.

West walked to the main broadcast mike and broke the news to his men. From now until the approaching darkness clipped the Argentinians' wings, they'd be 'splitting up air attacks'.

'In my mind, I thought we were drawing fire,' West explains. He pauses. 'Our job, ideally, was to make things attack us so that they weren't attacking the amphibians.'

At the southern end of the Thin Grey Line, West knew they'd be 'pretty exposed' and easily seen. It was ironic. On the gunline, they'd been out on a limb and lacking close mutual support. But at least they'd had the protection of land, even if it did confuse their radar.

For Clapp, the move wasn't especially alarming. He needed someone to watch the southern approach and, if the Ardents felt a little more detached than some of the others, well, they weren't. It was just the shape of the area. They'd be three or four miles from the others. Not a lot of flying time.

Around the Type 21, Alan West's words set men thinking.

On the Bridge, Navigating Officer Alan Maunder was anticipating a livelier time. Alongside him, Master at Arms Lenny Yeatman was at the wheel, confident the can-do attitude was intact. Down below, in some quarters, they weren't so sure.

'The mood changed when we were told we were being put further down the attack area,' Chief Electrician Taff Lovidge says.

DMEO Tony Ray felt let down. Hadn't his old mate Tansy Lee pointed to the Ops Room charts the night before and told him that, NGS done, they'd head for open sea? He'd felt reassured. Not now. In open sea, you could use your radar and see it coming for miles. In a second, he'd been robbed of a hope which had sustained him through a difficult day. He felt very frightened. Around him, men were passing knowing glances. 'This is it,' he thought.

For others, though, the move meant as little as anything else so far. Maps had been pinned on noticeboards to give everyone a general idea of what was what, but there wasn't one in the Workshop, so Brum Serrell and the rest of the

Mobile Repair Party really had no mental picture. As far as they were concerned, they were moving from point A to point B.

The open water at the heart of Falkland Sound would give them a chance to see, rid them of clutter. Only nightfall could help them more. Men were already looking at their watches.

So, as *Ardent* moved on full-power Tynes towards her new position – Tynes rather than fuel-guzzling Olympus engines – everyone began to adjust their thinking for the coming hours, however long it would take for the sun to set. Maybe another hour and a half.

PWO Mike Knowles was another, on balance, who was more relieved than perturbed to be heading for open water. He listened to the Ops Room chat – 'We're doing all right so far. It's going to get dark soon and we'll be okay' – and began to prepare.

Seacat. It would be more effective out in the middle of the Sound. They'd already loosed off two hopeful missiles at those Pucaras, so his first priority was to fill the two blanks high up above the Hangar. He spoke to Alan West. They decided to reload them when they weren't under attack. Now was probably as good a time as any.

Mick Cox looked at his watch and turned to Ginger Nelson. Ken Chapman had been in the Tiller Flat, the emergency steering position, behind the Flight Deck, most of the day. 'Come on, Ginge,' the Scot called across the SCC. 'It's time you relieved him.'

'Sure, Chief!' Away Nelson went.

The muscular PTI had caught young Scouse Phillips muttering The Lord's Prayer during an air raid warning and, five or six years older, had tried to calm him.

'We're going to be all right, Scouse,' he'd whispered. 'Don't worry.'

Now Scouse watched him go and his heart sank. 'Christ, Ginge,' he thought. 'There's no one down there for you to talk to . . .'

With the end of *Ardent*'s NGS, Richie Gough had taken over as Anti-Air Warfare Director from his boss, Pete Rowe, and was reporting to the Visual Directors on the Upper Deck. The two Seacat missiles they'd already fired in emergency mode, controlled and loosed off from the Seacat Deck, had reassured him a little. At least local control was working. PO Johnno Johnson was proving to be fast at detecting targets and responding to them.

Gough looked at his screens. He'd know where the gun was pointing from a row of Gs on his display, and he'd know where the launcher was pointing from Ms. If the Lookout Aimer just aft of the Bridge-top GDP saw a target and made a switch, he'd see Ls. And, if the Seacat Pedestal Site overlooking the Flight Deck saw a target and pulled his switch, it would be Ps. In an ideal world, his Ps and Ms would cut each other. Target spotted, Seacat locked on. Maybe not, though. In an ideal world, of course, they'd all be anticipating a night at the Grand Theatre . . .

As *Ardent* raced closer to her new station, Pete Rowe went up aft to the Seacat Control Room, just forward of the Pedestal Site, for a breath of fresh air. 'Look,' he said to AB Steve Strachan. 'Beautiful clear blue skies. Why can't it be like yesterday?'

Back below, he stopped to natter with Rick Banfield by the Wardroom

178

Galley. The Supply Officer was in good spirits. When they parted, Banfield headed aft for the Flight Deck, Rowe to the Ops Room.

About the same time, Jeff Curran, Ches Chesterson and another young stoker left the Aft Engine Room, heading for a break in Ken Enticknap's Aft Section Base, the Junior Ratings' Dining Hall. The idea was for Enticknap and two others to replace them but, as it turned out, three men from the Mobile Party went down instead. Curran had been below in one machinery space or another most of the day. His headset was heavy and buzzed constantly. He was glad of the break.

◆◆◆

By early afternoon, the Argentinian command knew the San Carlos landings weren't a bluff.

Forty-five minutes after Carballo's 1600 solo run, three Daggers of Laucha flight left San Julian. They were followed, a minute later, by Raton flight, also three-strong. Around the same time, 400 miles south, Cueca and Libra flights took off from Rio Grande. Thirteen planes in all. Their mission was simple: put so many planes into Falkland Sound, and from such different directions, that the Thin Grey Line and its Sea Harrier guard simply wouldn't cope.

Cueca was led by Capitan Mir Gonzalez, with Teniente Bernhardt and Primer Teniente Hector Luna his wingmen. Libra's four-man formation, however, was reduced by half even before it was airborne, leaving just Capitan Cimatti and Capitan Robles to follow Cueca flight.

The mission soon hit a second hitch. En route, Cimatti's Dagger began to lose oil and he turned for home. Robles moved up to make a foursome with Cueca flight. They flew on in radio silence but, before they could descend below the Thin Grey Line's radar blanket, *Brilliant* had already called in an 800 Sqdn CAP to greet them.

As the Daggers turned through 60 degrees to split Mounts Robinson and Maria, Luna's day was about to go horribly wrong. North of Chartres, with two smouldering Skyhawks below, they were spotted by the Sea Harriers of Lt Cdr Rod Frederiksen and Sub Lt Andy George. Frederiksen was first on the trigger, wrecking the nearest Dagger's control surfaces with a Sidewinder, causing it to roll wildly beyond Luna's recall. He had fractions of a second to call a warning before ejecting near Teal Inlet. But his cry had been stifled by a broken radio.

So, as the three remaining Daggers dropped below the mountain clouds, none were aware of the Harriers' efforts to add three more scalps to the tally. Still unaware that death had breathed down their necks, Robles broke radio silence to tell his flight leader that he feared Luna had flown into a mountain, then he fell in to line astern through a small ravine.

◆◆◆

Twenty minutes behind Cueca flight, Lt Cdr Alberto Philippi's mission is going almost as planned. The hours flying together have given the 43 year old and his wingmen Jose Arca and Marcelo Marquez an almost telepathic understanding,

so the radio silence imposed to thwart the Thin Grey Line's EW operators is no problem. But, now, he should be picking up last-minute details from a S2-E Tracker plane. He's called it twice without reply. He presses on. It doesn't worry him.

His altimeter alarm, set at 30ft, has sounded frequently since the descent from Isla de los Pájaros, Birds Island, before his formation turns right to the south-east, looking first for the entry to Falkland Sound, then for the radar picket below.

♦♦♦

At 1740, thirst had the better of caution as the Flight decided it was Scouse Lacey and Bill Bailey's turn to make a brew. Bailey asked who wanted one, then the pair left John Sephton, Brian Murphy, Mac McAulay, Pete Brouard and Rick Banfield on the Flight Deck.

In the SCC, Jessie Owens was feeling good. Well, not good, but better than for most of the day. Dusk was near and they'd made it. They had a shield around them. They were the best, after all.

In rare breaks from the brain-crushing Ops Room EW screens, the straddling had proved to PO Mike Lewis that there was a chance they could be hit. On the other hand, if Carballo's open goal was an example, maybe not. Conflicting thoughts? No, on reflection. The Argentinians were useless.

His thoughts were broken by a crackling voice through his headset. 'They're coming to you *Ardent*! They're coming to you!'

♦♦♦

On the 650ft-high Sussex Mountains ridge, overlooking Falkland Sound ten miles away, Major Tony Rice and Lt Col H. Jones paused amid the 2 Para rifle companies and took up their top row positions.

The day had been good for 2 Para. They'd been the first battalion ashore in San Carlos, to the eternal annoyance of the Marines, and moved swiftly on to the mountain because British intelligence had lost the Argentinian reserve and there were fears they might be at Goose Green, ready to move.

Distance was hard to judge through the clear air, but Rice could tell the ship the planes were after was a 21, even if he didn't know it was the one that had kept the enemy's heads down most of the day.

In *Yarmouth*'s Communications Room, 19-year-old AB Mike Roe thought the four planes were Etendards. It already felt like he'd spent hours looking for the safest spot in the Sonar Control Room to take cover, hoping his younger brother Dave had managed to do the same in the Ops Room. But the threat wasn't coming their way. Heads turned on *Yarmouth*'s GDP as the Daggers raced past her position on the east of the patrol line and made for *Ardent*, steaming to the west.

♦♦♦

Beside PO Mike Lewis, John Goddard tensed. He was watching the radar,

relating the tracks on his screen with the green bearing given to the incoming threat, working out what kind of distance they were at, but still unable to resist a joke as the 'Alarm aircraft!' call went out.

'No rock cakes to be eaten in the Ops Room in the middle of an air raid!'

Up forward, PO Paddy McGinnis was moving towards the FARM with little Errol Flynn, on his way to relieve Eddie Edwards and MEM Les Pearce when Goddard halted them in their tracks.

Jon Major, Bob Sage and Mick Foote were about to go aft to relieve the on-watch cooks at 1800.

'Air raid warning,' McGinnis told them. 'You're not going anywhere.'

The burly Foote wasn't having any of it. As soon as the POME's back was turned, he went. Major and Sage stayed put, but Cliff Goldfinch's firm order had been broken.

Wyatt Earp and Barry Muncer were sitting with Florrie Ford and Buzz Leighton, both firesuited, on the pipes at the back of the Junior Ratings' Dining Hall, asking, 'Has it been like this all day?'

'You're joking!'

Earp looked around and something said to him, 'Get out!' He turned to Muncer. 'I'm not staying here! It's like a fucking morgue!'

'You can't just leave!'

'I'm going down.'

'You've got to tell someone.'

The pair stood, stepped back over everyone, opened the door and walked out. Back at the Engineers' Workshop, they bumped into PO Blood Reed.

'D'you want to go back down?' he asked.

Their masked eyes gave him their answer. So far as Earp was concerned, if the Aft Section Base was anything to go by, they were better off not knowing what was going on. Reed called the SCC.

'Permission to go back down to the Aft Engine Room.' Reed paused. The SCC told him to wait. Something was happening. They'd call back.

On the Bridge, Captain Bob was peering through his binoculars, extra eyes after the straddling, when they saw the three silhouetted Daggers circling. Alan West asked him what he thought they were.

'Aircraft,' he replied. 'And they're angry!'

West called down to the Ops Room. 'I have the ship . . .'

It was as well. PWO Mike Knowles's men were trying to find the Daggers on radar, trying to sort out the identification friend or foe ticks. But it was a jumble still because of the land round the ship.

Lt Nigel Langhorn grabbed the main broadcast mike and calmly called out the crucial information to every corner of the ship with the means or the chance to hear. For most, it amounted to 'Take cover!'

'Take cover!'

Dave Croft had departed the Deep Seacat Magazine after a call to leave

his runner, young Nick Carter, on his own and return to the Ops Room to relieve Jock Greer. He'd reached the flat by the Joss's office when the call came and he hit the floor, face down . . .

'Take cover!'

Jon Major knew Portland and Alloy Express had been leading them up to this situation but, now it had come, he was helpless . . .

A few feet away, Andy Cox had been talking to Ralph Coates on the green line, just a normal conversation, giving him a hard time, 'I'll catch you in a minute.'

'Take cover!'

Coxie and Buck Ryan raced to the DC lockers, one flat forward from the Gunbay Flat where *Ardent*'s bow began to narrow to its razor point. Naggers tried to join them, running through the hatch, yelling, 'I'll come in with you!' until Coxie pushed him back down to 3 Deck – 'Get back out there with the bullets' – closed the hatch, pulled the clips down and then grabbed Ryan in a bear-hug.

Ryan found it really funny. Nags might have another day. Instead he was thinking, 'I don't want to go up with it on my own.'

Cliff Goldfinch stood by John Leake on the GDP, plane-spotting, watching the Daggers roll through the last, long, lazy turn of their figure of eight. There wasn't much else they could do.

Wyatt Earp and Barry Muncer stood in the passage, waiting for Blood Reed to give them the nod to return to the sanctuary of the Aft Engine Room.

'Take cover!'

Earp jolted and looked at Muncer. It was the first time they'd heard the call. 'Fucking hell!' was all he managed to say. The Malvern teenager was lost. For a split second, he didn't know what to do. Then he saw everyone else hit the deck. So he hit the deck too.

'Take cover!'

In the Junior Ratings' Dining Hall, between his office and the Galley hatch, PO Caterer Mike Stephens hit the floor by Peddler Palmer. If the giant Cornishman had been right two hours earlier, the slightly built Stephens was better off here than in the Ops Room. Now they'd find out.

Just feet away, Dickie Henderson crammed into the 'safe' space by the Scullery, with most of the other Aft DC men. He looked up. Knocker White was in the Dining Hall, a few feet away. Ralph was on Comms over by the open DC lockers, shielded from the Senior Ratings' Dining Hall on the port side by a partition, Kev Johnson beside him. Everyone else was on the deck.

On the Bridge Wings, as Alan West rang down to the SCC for maximum Tynes, about 18kts, and began to manoeuvre to open his 4.5 and Seacat weapons arcs, Oerlikon gunners Mick Newby and Topsy Turner followed the Daggers round.

Below, Pete Rowe watched as Richie Gough reminded the Upper Deck weapons crews to fire at will and he heard the loud dunka-dunka-dunka of the Oerlikons and the chatter of the GPMG.

West wanted his guns side-on to their target, to start pumping 4.5 bricks at the rapid jets. But he couldn't bring it to bear. The three planes flew on with a clear intention, to attack *Ardent* from the rear, narrowing her weapons arc, leaving themselves with just Seacat to worry about and the Type 21 heading away, an easier target than if she was crossing the line of fire.

'Take cover!'

Jessie Owens and Scouse Phillips hit the floor side-by-side in the SCC, Mick Cox dived for the starboard quarter by the fuel section of the control panel, and the telegraphs clanged. PO Joe Laidlaw stood up, pushed the throttles to full ahead and dropped again like a stone.

On the Bridge, Alan Maunder was trying to keep track of *Ardent*'s ever-shifting position, struggling to stay up with the man at the wheel as *Ardent* ran a manic course, trying to give her weapons as wide a field of fire as Alan West could carve out. But first he lost touch with the ship's path, and then the Daggers overhauled them, and it was obvious they were coming in for a run.

'Hit the deck!'

Maunder yelled a warning and already knew where he'd go next, between the pelorus and the chart table, a big enough gap for two people, the only place where anyone could hope to survive the Bridge roof crashing in. As he fell, Alan West landed on top of him, a big man. But Maunder's mind was racing to other things. 'What am I supposed to be thinking about now?'

Then it all went quiet . . .

On his way to make a brew for the Flight, Bill Bailey was securing the hatch in the Hangar Workshop when Nigel Langhorn's agitated voice boomed from the Tannoy. 'Take cover!'

Bailey didn't have time to look for Scouse Lacey. He hit the deck just forward of the Hangar access hatch. Behind it were John Sephton, Brian Murphy, Rick Banfield, Pete Brouard and the rest of the Flight. Behind them, the Funnel of Fate was closing. The Daggers were queuing for their final run . . .

FOUR

FALKLAND SOUND

(1744–1806HRS, 21 MAY 1982)

1744: In the eerie light of the Ops Room, PWO Mike Knowles's eyes are straining to pick out the incoming aircraft on the search radar. For a fleeting moment he thinks he has them, then they're gone. They're beginning to lose the fight to lock on to whatever's heading their way. It's a horrible feeling.

At the Seacat console, heeding calls for emergency local control of the missile from the Ped Site above the Hangar, Richie Gough scans Johnno Johnson's target track line on the computerised display. But where are the Ms to show the Launcher's slaved to Johnson's control? In the Seacat Launch Control Room, behind Johnson's left shoulder, the launcher hasn't been switched to emergency. Oh Christ!

Gough looks back to the Ops Room Seacat Controller's panel, desperately hoping to see the panel light glowing. It isn't on. In his headset, Johnson is already screaming. Gough starts screaming on the Weapons Net too, for Pat Norris to make the switch in the Launch Control Room.

Gripping his LMG on the port side of the Seacat Ped Site, Russ Goble's concentration on the circling jets is broken momentarily by the sound of Johnno's voice, screaming louder and louder, 'I've lost control! I've lost control! Give me LOF control! Give me LOF control!'

Goble looks back at the incoming Daggers and looses off an entire magazine. He looks down. At the door of the Hangar, pilot John Sephton is firing his 9mm pistol in the same direction.

Back in the Ops Room, Knowles hears the familiar *Portland* cry, 'Seacat to local control, your engagement' rapped out on the Weapons Net, a plea now almost. Across the display, Tom Williams stares at his colleague and waits. Waits for the whoosh! which says Johnno's locked the arcade game's crossed wires on its target and fired. They don't hear the whoosh! They don't hear anything. Somewhere deep in his mind and his stomach, Williams thinks, 'Shit!'

And the most awful thing occurs to Knowles. *Ardent* has lost control of her own destiny.

From the Tactical Radio position, RO Steve Kent hits the floor with almost everyone else, covering their heads, praying. Leigh Slatter hauls young Sam Saxty from the wrong side of the radar plot, no warning, and the bewildered 17 year old must think he's being strangled by a madman. Slatter hits the tiles, looks at a photo of his daughter Kelly for the last time, asks God to forgive him, and waits. The only people left standing are Gough and his young colleague, Jumper Collins.

Outside, with Johnson's desperate screams still echoing round his head,

Russ Goble aims his LMG and squeezes the trigger again. The gun clicks. He assumes it's empty. But he doesn't know. He turns to the ammunition box by the Seacat Ready-Use Magazine, behind him, then realises, 'Fuck, I'm not going to have time.' He runs and crash-tackles starboard gunner Scouse Wharton, blind and deaf to the danger, and catches sight of Pat Norris taking cover in the Launch Control Room.

Then the whole world erupts.

Two hundred feet away, the grim silence of the Ops Room is broken by a dull thud, then another, and another. Tom Williams feels 3,250 tons lift out of the water. It never occurs to him that someone might have just been killed.

❖❖❖

1744: 'Alarm aircraft!'

Mick Newby shouts from his starboard Oerlikon and waits for the lead Dagger to come into range. But, each time he fires, the Dagger rolls through 90 degrees and Newby's 20mm shells scorch past into fresh air. Jeff Gullick listens to the ratchet cannon-fire but the Daggers' calculated figure of eight leaves his port Oerlikon impotent, and him too. It's all happening so fast.

Cliff Goldfinch looks aft from his Bridge-top GDP position alongside Big John Leake and watches the planes scream closer and closer, thinking, 'Here we go again,' until he sees bombs drop, and then he thinks, 'You miserable shits', and the bombs disappear and, 'Fucking hell!' . . .

A stride away, 21-year-old Sub Lt Richie Barker doesn't hear the noise of the first explosion, but the orange and black fireball and the heat searing his face etch an indelible image on his mind and, from the same big mushroom, Goldfinch sees the Seacat Launcher cartwheel through the air.

1744: The urgency in Nigel Langhorn's voice echoes through Ken Enticknap's mind as he lies on the floor of the Aft Section Base. This is going to be different. All around, men are covering their heads. Instinct. Enticknap's near Knocker White. Ralph Coates, Wacker Payne and Kev Johnson are by the DC lockers, Peddler Palmer and Mike Stephens are between the Catering Office and the Galley, Dickie Henderson is just aft, crammed in the 'safe' spot by the Scullery with Garry Whitford, Gilly Williams, Sean Hayward, Steve Heyes and John Dillon. Taff Lovidge and Tony Ray aren't roving now, but lying, alongside the watertight door into the Canteen Flat, with Lt David Searle hugging tiles nearby.

In the Galley, Doc Young and Cook Taff Roberts have the treasured spot between the Servery and the range. They only have the ship's violent swing beneath their bellies to tell them something's coming, only their ears to tell them it's upon them. Their ears and their imagination and their fear.

Then there's a huge noise and the ship lurches and they bounce off the deck, flesh and bone hitting deck tiles, a much louder bang than Portland scare charges, then – whoosh! bang! – another and – whoosh! – another impact, separated by seconds, and the Dining Hall lights go out and the Galley shutters spring up and rolls they haven't had a chance to eat appear, flying.

❖❖❖

1744: Scouse Phillips is lying by Jessie Owens on the deck when the ship lurches and the room fills with noise and the bottom half of the SCC's metal stable door is blasted off its hinges into his head.

Owens hears the crump, then endures a horrible moment's delay before water begins pouring in to the SCC from overhead and blood rushes from Phillips's skull. PO Joe Laidlaw begins to stand and sees the young weapons engineer lying deathly still and feels sick.

❖❖❖

1744: As they hit the deck outside the Engineers' Workshop, beyond a watertight door, forward of the SCC Flat, Wyatt Earp starts telling Barry Muncer a joke. He's more scared than he's ever been and he starts telling a joke. Someone shouts, 'Shut up!' and then all hell breaks loose and something falls on him.

'The bulkhead's come down on my legs!' he yells in panic.

❖❖❖

1744: Inside the Engineers' Workshop, Brum Serrell and Jan Joyce are on the deck, wondering, 'What the bloody hell's happening now?' as the shockwave lifts them both 18 inches off the floor.

They bounce heavily but Joyce feels nothing as his chest meets the deck again. The ship settles and dust from the deckhead lagging flutters down over their battered bodies. Through the snow they look at each other. 'Fuck me! They've got us,' one says.

❖❖❖

1744: Buck Ryan and Andy Cox are hugging, listening to the distant roar of jets and the vain dunka-dunka-dunka of Newby's Oerlikon, both thinking the same thing, feet from Cliff Sharp and Bernie Berntsen, but a million miles away, willing these things not to hit the Gunbay Flat, but go somewhere else. Then there's a huge jolt, and a shudder. Then another jolt, then it settles. Then the whiplash.

Ryan squeezes his eyes shut as they bounce, feeling like they're in the bottom of a kettle that's being thrown around, but feeling worse than that, much worse.

With Mick Foote missing, Jon Major and Bob Sage are out of their environment, terrified, unable to see what's happening, just to hear and feel.

❖❖❖

1744: Buck Taylor, Dave Daley and Nigel Broadbent feel the shudder in the depths of the 4.5 Magazine on 4 Deck and the distant rattle of the diesel generators in the Forward Auxiliary Machine Room is replaced by deathly silence.

❖❖❖

1744: Minutes ago, Chief Stoker Andy Andrew had been chatting with the Chippy, Roger Fenton, about the muck his lads'll have to clean before rounds in a couple of hours, once it's dark. Now he's alone, outside his 2 Deck cabin. A hollow boom. The ship's shaken like a puppy dog. Dust falls and some lights go out.

◆◆◆

1744: Alan Maunder tenses himself, hoping the slim gap between the pelorus and the chart table will save him, trying to count the planes as they roar overhead, reaching three – or is it five? – amid this incredible noise, guns firing, then three, four, maybe half-a-dozen clanking sounds, then a sudden bang, and another, and he realises the clanks were just the bombs ripping through *Ardent*'s steel skin.

Whiplash shakes dust from every crevice, a rapid earthquake through Lenny Yeatman's boots that almost throws him off his feet. It's bad. He can feel it through the wheel. How bad? He looks over his left shoulder and the sky above *Ardent*'s arcing wake is full of debris, and the sound of alarm bells echoing round the Bridge begin to replace the horrible thud of God knows how many explosions.

As the Daggers flee south, Captain Bob shakes himself down. 'Christ, we survived that one!' But, like Yeatman, Nigel Langhorn knows different. He stands and looks past the port Bridge Wing and his eyes tell him more. The debris is neoprene and air bottles, all sorts of crap littering the air, and he thinks, 'The bastards have got my Diving Store.'

Alan West clambers to his feet and moves to the Bridge window and yells, 'Turn the bloody alarms off!' He knows his ship's damaged. He doesn't need bells to tell him. What he needs is to know where, and how badly. But no one's telling him.

By West's side, Maunder looks over the Fo'c'sle and, for a moment, thinks, 'No damage', the ship's escaped. Then he realises he has to find out where they are on the face of the planet and plot the chart.

West pipes down to the SCC but information's scarce. Lenny Yeatman listens in on the conversation and realises how scarce. The SCC's having difficulty talking. There's water everywhere. At least he knows the ship's answering the helm. She has steering. And she still has her engines.

Through the dust, Captain Bob asks permission to leave the Bridge, disappears down the ladder to 1 Deck, and heads aft for the Sickbay, to find his revolver and do something, anything. Anything but stand and watch . . .

◆◆◆

1745: The whipping subsides and PWO Mike Knowles staggers to his feet and knows the look on other faces is 'Jesus, what was that?', like it is on his. His eyes dart round the Ops Room and he sees the ASW box, kit to simulate submarines, off its mountings.

Chief GI Pete Rowe, convinced he's heard the Seacat go, checks for injuries.

None. Richie Gough, knowing the Seacat never switched to Johnno Johnson's hands above the Hangar, gathers his wits.

◆◆◆

1746: Russ Goble rolls on to his back and checks himself. There's a razor cut on one glove, but not a mark on his hand. His neck's sore. The fireball's scorched the imprint of his necklace on his skin. His ears are ringing. The Seacat Pedestal Site's bent over but there's no sign of Johnno. He looks back to his LMG position on the port side. There's a hole where his gun was.

'What do we do now?' he looks at Scouse Wharton.

'Fuck this, I'm off!' the starboard LMG man shouts. Before they climb down the ladder by the whaler and on to the starboard waist, they gaze into the twisted, fiery mess below. No sign of life.

◆◆◆

1746: John Leake and Cliff Goldfinch have already seen the 4.5-inch gun pointing to the sky as Goble and Wharton emerge from the smoke aft and tell them the horror story. Flames are licking out of the Hangar and news starts to trickle through that the ship has lost all power. Leake knows he's lucky. On the GDP, he can see what's going on. Down below, back aft, it must be horrendous.

◆◆◆

1746: A light shining from near the door to the SCC Flat, ten yards forward, catches Ken Enticknap's eye. He's ankle deep in water, feels a flutter of panic and shouts 'Go!' to his Aft Damage Control men and hopes to God they move. If they don't, they've lost it.

They move. It's dark, it's wet, it's cold, the shocking cold that catches your breath, but at least the geography of the Aft Section Base is the same as it was seconds before. Now it's instinct and training.

Lighting's not important. They can rig a couple of portable floodlights. Flooding's the problem, from above, from Christ knows where. They need to find out where, isolate the system, pump it dry.

Pandemonium – ratings dashing round with boxes of wooden splinters under their arms, trying to find holes in the hull until Enticknap shouts to put them away. He looks up. One deck above is the Flight Deck. Above the SCC Flat, those ten short yards away, is the Hangar.

Guesswork. It's all he has, but he points his men in that direction.

What he needs more than anything are the damage reports from Wacker Payne's blanket search team – information Kev Johnson can chinagraph on the Incident Board. Ready to tell the Ops Room. Ready for the Ops Room to tell Command. To plot the progress of repairs. To keep the ship as a level fighting platform. To restore power. To stay part of the Thin Grey Line. Right now, Enticknap knows nothing.

Alongside Johnson, Ralph Coates is on Comms, on the green line, yelling to

189

Buck Ryan a mile away in the Forward Section Base, 'For fuck's sake, get your First-Aid parties down here,' his ears ringing, his feet feeling the ship listing, his sore eyes picking out shapes trying to restore order from chaos.

A few paces away, Dickie Henderson sees the big fridge outside the Scullery's awash and realises his home-made action bedding's still behind the pipes. He looks through the deluge and Enticknap calls over, 'Go up and see what's going on!'

Lt David Searle takes a lead and wades through the food and timber-strewn water towards the SCC Flat, sending men forward to fetch portable pumps as the tide rises, spewing out of the eight-inch firemain running above what used to be the SCC door.

Doc Young rubs the back of his head and hears seawater blasting into the SCC Flat at 90psi. The noise is alarming, but it's only noise he can go on. In the blast, his glasses have flown off.

The clips on the SCC Flat door are a struggle because the door's buckled. Once they prise it open and step into the Canteen Flat, Taff Lovidge sees the contents of John Leake's NAAFI, Kit-Kats, lighters, cameras, T-shirts floating past. Lovidge's chest's already telling him he's been very, very frightened.

Alarms are going off somewhere. He looks up and round and back into the SCC. It's grim. A fog's hanging on the water of the Dining Hall, the inch-thick 'soft' patch – the wide access hatch through to the Hangar – is bowed down and spilling water on top of their heads, and MEO Terry Pendrous is shouting about electric cables being soaked.

Amid it all, Gilly Williams is on his knees, trying to coax a portable pump to life, the misfit stoker, the first man to react while everyone else is still wondering what to do. 'Christ!' Lovidge thinks, then he and Tony Ray head into the Ship Control Centre to see . . . to see whatever's waiting for them.

Then he turns left and looks in the Aft Switchboard, and thinks, 'Christ!' His nightmare begins then. So does Tony Ray's. As they step into the SCC, water's pouring across the door. It's red.

The two step through the high-pressure shower and duck beneath the top section of what had been a stable door, peering through the smoke at the mess, but MEO Terry Pendrous has already ordered a blanket search and left to find out how Ken Enticknap's isolating the fractured firemain.

The first thing Ray sees is a lad lying badly injured but alive, Scouse Phillips, dragged to one side and left bleeding all over the floor by Officer of the Watch Mick Cox seconds before. Smoke alarms are going off. So are the SCC control panel alarms. So's the steering panel. There are no lights on the console from the Switchboard, across the SCC Flat, either. This isn't panic. This is hell.

'We've been hit! We've been hit!' Cox hears through the smoke and noise. 'Christ!' the Scot thinks, what a ridiculous thing to say, but he mutters, 'Okay!' and gathers his thoughts.

There's no Comms. They've lost the 24-volt circuit. Cox and Lovidge stoop at the back of the SCC control panel to reach the 24-volt transformer rectifier, but the bulkhead's come in. They can't reach it.

Lovidge grabs a young rating, LWEM Eric Samson. If the Aft Section Base

has no Comms link with the rest of the ship, use a runner. The genial Ulsterman. Lovidge wants Wacker Payne, the Aft DC party's electrical PO, to go out, see what's damaged and come back and tell him.

Cox and PO Joe Laidlaw have already scanned the control panel, Jessie Owens too, almost transfixed by the flashing lights and alarms, almost convinced it means everything's failed. Bad news. The ship's lost power aft and the fuel pump and emergency air turbine have both stopped. Cox has already grabbed the main broadcast microphone and gives orders to the Aft Engine Room, a deck below, to de-isolate the fuel systems, restore the flow of fuel. In the AER, someone has already responded.

Cox looks at the console again. Not everything's failed. The engines are still running, the power turbine gauges tell him that. He has propulsion. That's his priority, to keep this ship moving. But they've also lost both aft generators, down in the Aft Auxiliary Machine Room.

Lovidge isn't surprised. He's already seen big Tansy Lee standing in the devastation of the Aft Switchboard. It's a miracle the giant CPO's still alive.

'I've got no power aft, Tansy,' Cox yells over to him.

'I don't know what I've got,' Lee shouts back.

'What are you doing?' Lovidge turns back to look at Big Tansy.

'Drawing an underground map.' Lovidge doesn't know why.

In the corner of the SCC, Jessie Owens and Paul Turner have ripped an action dressing off Taff Lovidge's lifejacket and wrapped it round Scouse Phillips's head and pulled him to his feet. Mick Cox looks round quickly for the wounded teenager and sees the bandage. The next time he looks, he's gone.

In his haze, as they leave the SCC, Phillips thinks he sees Knocker White in the NAAFI store, trying to stem the tide of water. He can't be sure. It's the last thing the young weapons engineer remembers.

Moments later, Joe Laidlaw wades into the smoky SCC Flat and grabs a pump, leaving Cox in the SCC trying to sort out the AAMR power failure. The only answer's to send someone down to see.

◆◆◆

1745: Paint and dust are dropping to the deck outside the Engineers' Workshop. Wyatt Earp's panicking, convinced the bulkhead's fallen across his legs. Barry Muncer reassures him. 'It's the fucking noticeboard, you prat!'

They look up. It is. Then someone shouts, 'Search for damage! Search for damage!'

Jan Joyce hurtles out of the Workshop with Brum Serrell in his wake, tool bags rapping their sides, hearts racing, instinct on tap, ready to blanket-search, down in the vast machinery spaces, even though they may be manned, in case they've been wiped out and no one can say what's happening.

Serrell's on automatic, drawn by some predestined force to race to 3 Deck, until – 'Help me!' – he hears a call from the top of the ladder outside the Workshop door.

He never finds out who it is. Instead of following his old pal, he turns left, up the ladder to 1 Deck, right and left through the gas-tight NBCD airlock door,

swivelling again through 180 degrees and out through another into the Hangar. In a split-second, the Kidder tankie's mundane job, maintaining CO2 extinguishers, greasing nozzles up, takes on its true meaning. He knows everything works. Someone thrusts a hose in his hand. He doesn't look back.

◆◆◆

1745: Jeff Curran picks himself off the Workshop floor as Serrell and Joyce disappear. So much for his take cover drill, tucked up on the Workshop bench. The blast's blown him clean off it. He runs into the passageway and bumps into Nick Carter emerging from the Deep Seacat Magazine and breathes one sigh of relief. At least nothing's gone off in there.

Then speckles of paint float down from the hatch and he calls to others to follow. Debris is scattered along the passageway near the Aft EMR when he reaches 1 Deck but, where Serrell's found a way through, all Curran sees is a distorted watertight door. Then he finds an injured airman in wreckage.

With his way blocked, breathing heavily, he doubles back and spins open the gas-tight internal airlock door. Then he opens the next door to the cleansing station, then the door to the stripping area, another to the aft NBCD Citadel and another into the Hangar. What's left of the Hangar.

The noise is horrendous, a screaming hell, high-pressure air ripping God knows where, a banshee, and thick, black, sometimes purple smoke . . .

◆◆◆

1745: A deck above, CPO Jake Jacobs and young steward Shaun Hanson rush out of the Electrical Machinery Room. The bloodied shape of Pat Norris coming from aft through the 01 Deck Olympus Flat confronts them, shouting that the Hangar's been blown up, the Seacat launcher's gone.

Among the Upper Repair Party electricians and engineers, Hanson's confessed to feeling out of place. Now he has no time to worry. The pair run through the open door, down the passageway and, possibly with two others, go into the Air EMR about 15 yards away, grabbing a firehose on the way.

Uncertain what awaits them after Norris's warning, they force the Hangar door open to reach the walkway. Then it hits Jacobs. The roof's gone. He looks down on the devastation. Fires. The worst on the port side near the Torpedo Magazine. Then he realises the ladder's gone too, so they start tackling the fires from the balcony.

Maybe 1746: It seems like a couple of minutes before the noise subsides and debris stops landing on Bill Bailey. Then it dawns on him. As far as he can tell, he's in one piece. A shout breaks the moment. 'Anyone in there?'

Bailey yells back, suggests he can do with some help freeing himself. He stands, shakily, and spots the Aircraft Workshop hatch embedded in the forward bulkhead and wonders how it missed his head. He looks around, but Scouse Lacey's gone. He's already back in the Hangar, trying to help.

In moments, Captain Bob appears and enlists Bailey to take Andy Schofield forward for First-Aid. The young Flight mechanic can't breathe. Bailey doesn't

know it, but Schofield's just extricated himself with broken ribs from a small, twisted space between the Sea Skua torpedoes and the Hangar wall, just yards from where one bomb's gone off. Bailey puts an arm round his young colleague.

❖❖❖

1745: Naggers feels the ship rock, then settle. Instinctively, he lifts the hatch in front of him and looks down from the Capstan Flat into the No 2 Naval Store below on 2 Deck. There's no water. He rushes back to the Gunbay Flat and finds Coxie and Buck Ryan still locked in a hug of terror.

They separate and Ryan looks at the Comms link and thinks, 'Fuck! Ralph's down!' He panics. 'Ralph, what the fuck's going on?' he yells down the phone.

'For fuck's sake, get your First-Aid parties down here . . . it's a disaster. It's black.'

Buck can hear the devastation, the sound of men's voices screaming, not petrified screaming but yelling. Ralph's trying to explain. Firefighters. First-aid. The pleas last a split second, but it seems ages to Ryan, then . . . nothing. God knows why, but he begins struggling to remember what Ralph's said.

In the frantic seconds after the hit, Coxie offers a passing thought to Iain McRobbie. 'They'll have to send us home now!'

❖❖❖

1746: Eddie Edwards and Les Pearce gather themselves in the Forward Auxiliary Machine Room as the shockwaves ebb and they begin to look for damage. Water. Before long they see water. Not much, not gushing, dripping. From behind the sound-proofing. Outside one of the diesel generators.

Little Eddie flashes his torch below the deckplates, where the bilge comes up, and sees there isn't much water, but calls the SCC for permission to put an inductor on, to suck it out. He's not certain. It'll rob the firemain of pressure. He doesn't want to rob some poor bastard of a hoseful.

❖❖❖

1746: Chief Stoker Andy Andrew turns into the Laundry Flat, but passes the hatch down to the FARM and pushes open the stable door into the Laundry. To his relief, Mr Wong's in one piece.

❖❖❖

1746: In seconds, PO Mike Lewis has gone through the lot. He's felt the hit, felt the lurch, felt sheer terror, anger and frustration. In seconds. He's realised a human can only be scared for so long. It's a moment of absolute certainty that he's going to die. He accepts it. Then the fear's gone. Then he's just bloody angry. He wants to shoot at them, but his team's totally passive. It's frustrating.

Blue smoke's starting to drift into the Ops Room as John Foster kicks a little

access hatch through from the Main Communications Office and crawls in and sees PWOs Mike Knowles and Tom Williams, disorientated, staring at screens that have shifted, what-do-we-do-next looks on their faces, oblivious to the horror down aft and wondering what they have left to fight with.

Chief GI Pete Rowe's snapped from the horror by the sound of one of his young rates starting to lose it. He smacks him round the ear. He mustn't start the rest off. It works. The lad pulls himself together.

Richie Gough and Pete Brierley are into system checks and quickly discover there's no power to the 4.5 gun. And there's no Seacat. Gough's convinced. The ship's dead.

As they struggle to regain control, Yeoman Chris Evans speaks with Alan West on the Ops Room Net and passes instructions to young Steve Kent, alongside him. Twenty-one hours earlier, the young signalman took the Morse message that set this whole thing rolling. Now he's on the Tactical Net, ignoring the rulebook, ignoring codes, ignoring logging procedure, repeating messages in plain language to anyone who cares to listen, 'This is GQID. We've been hit!' straight out over the air. He doesn't have time to stand on ceremony.

◆◆◆

1748: Jan Joyce stares at the torrent gushing through the drooping deckhead. Then he turns right, through the gas-tight door into the airlock that'll take him down to the Aft Auxiliary Machine Room. He begins to check the test plug – air rushing out says there's water below, air rushing in, fire – and the clips start coming off. Someone's coming up. He stands back and yanks the manhole up and he sees PO Mick Langley's eyes looking back at him from behind grimy anti-flash, followed by a young rating.

'There's a bomb in there. It ain't gone off,' Langley gasps. 'There's a bloody hole. One of the diesels has been knocked against the other and one of 'em's working.' There's no mention of water. Langley turns round, locks the hatch and dives for the SCC.

A big shape looms at Joyce out of the smoke. Dickie Henderson. The tossed coin with Knocker White's left him pumping and flooding, a win that's come down to, 'Where the hell's this water from?'

If they can find a portable pump they can discharge it through the Beer Store, aft of the SCC, on the starboard side, where the list of the ship's shifting the deepest water.

'Where's the Beer Store key?'

'Why? We havin' a party?' someone shouts. Across the Dining Hall, one of the injured lads laughs. It hurts, but he can't help himself.

'Let's just knock the padlock off,' someone else yells to Henderson.

'We've got the key!' Joyce tells him as he approaches.

◆◆◆

1746: 'Blanket search! Blanket search!'

PO Bob Lewis screams the order, but it's already been anticipated. The staccato thud of seaboots on decking beats a hollow echo around and out of the Gunbay Flat Forward Section Base, hot breath drifting through anti-flash masks, panting lungs and pumping hearts, but still eerily silent for Andy Cox in the dimly lit passages, the most horrible silence he's ever had to come to terms with.

There's no time to fix the lighting. It's check test plugs – air sucks, fire; air blows, water – boundary search, check Comms, report back to Tiff Geoff Hart and record it on the Incident Board.

Buck Ryan's mind's racing with his feet. He works his way back to the Forward Section Base, blanket-searching each compartment. Comms have gone. No PA. No amplification, he thinks. But the lights are on. Just. So there's power from somewhere.

He manages to raise Ron White, midships, next to the Electrical Machine Room that Jake Jacobs and Shaun Hanson have just left. The picture he paints is sickening. He describes the smoke, what he can see, more important, what he can't. He can't see the Flight Deck. He can't see the Seacat. For the man who's cheered every time Seacat's gone off, it's enough. 'Ron, I'm just wasting my time talking to you,' Ryan says.

'No,' White replies. There is a point. The 4.5's barrel's pointing to the sky. It's lost power.

'Karl. Lost power to the 4.5,' Ryan breaks off and shouts to Naggers, and the pair start to run cables. No one tells them to. No one hands a chit out. They just do it. Get power to 4.5. Get power to 4.5. Never mind Comms, Ryan has to get power to the 4.5. He's not doing anything constructive, just decides he's going to help run the cable.

◆◆◆

1748: In the FARM, Paddy McGinnis joins Errol Flynn running torches round the areas checked by Eddie Edwards. Around the same time, Bernie Berntsen scours the same space. If little Eddie's found water, McGinnis can't see any damage. Neither can the old hand.

As they go, Flynn's mind's in flashback, looking aft from the Bathroom Flat through the Olympus Flat towards the SCC – a fog. McGinnis tries to report back to the SCC on the main broadcast, but no one answers. In seconds, the hatch opens and Edwards and Pearce clank hurriedly back down the ladder, with a message that McGinnis and Flynn should return to their FDCP stations. They go.

◆◆◆

1748: In the 4.5 Magazine, in the bowels of 4 Deck, the deathly silence enveloping Buck Taylor – and, he assumes, Nigel Broadbent and Dave Daley – is broken by the sound of running water. 'Get behind the rack!' he shouts to Broadbent. 'See if there's any damage.'

Taylor goes port side, sliding into the gap between the back of the rack and

the flare of the bows, the other WEM the starboard side. They can't see anything, but Taylor's convinced there's water and suspects the whiplash has broken a seal on the 184 sonar dome, beneath the ship. He's tight against the rack when the hatch opens and Steve Arnell's face appears.

He's fast fetching his four lads out of this box. Earlier in the day, someone's put a peg through all the Magazine hatches, as a joke. But this isn't funny. Not remotely. There's been no smell of cordite, no smell of burning, just the jolt, then the silence. But Taylor's never so glad to see a hatch open as this.

The young Geordie hurtles through the open hole and lies down in the narrow void alongside the shell hoist on 3 Deck. Kids. Just kids. Feeling like kids, now.

◆◆◆

1748: It's devastation, like someone's grabbed hold of this sardine can from the port side and ripped it open. Unaware that the soft patch amid all this carnage is leaking torrents of detritus into the SCC Flat below, Brum Serrell dashes into the Hangar, dragging his heavy, charged hose, and gasps.

Five fires. At least five fires. One on the walkway, by the Wafus' hampers. Another by the Avcat filter he's checked this morning, primed with fuel. One on the starboard walkway. One port side by the door. Another mid-Hangar, three or four feet in from the Hangar door.

He climbs over the debris and sees a body. Then one of the Flight appears, a finger hanging off his hand. Get out of the way. He can't stop for either. Portland training. Fire hose, hose fire. The problem's the Avcat Pump. We've been hit. That's all he knows. The last thing we want's 200 gallons of aviation fuel going up. 'Get this lot under control and we've made it.'

◆◆◆

1748: Glad to be out of the FARM, Bernie Berntsen races aft, not a decision, just instinct. Within seconds, he's running a hose through the Laundry Flat with another stoker, 32 feet aft to the Olympus Flat door, another 34 to the Tyne Flat door, another 24 to the Workshop Flat, up the ladder Brum Serrell's just vaulted up, through the aft starboard airlock and into the Hangar. They walk in and wade through the debris. One of the first things he sees is a body. 'Oh Christ! He's dead!' He doesn't know who it is.

◆◆◆

1748: A whistle stiffens Buck Ryan momentarily and he twists to the sound. By the Forward Section Base Incident Board, there's a figure grasping a clipboard, writing how much air's in the breathing apparatus bottles on the two firefighters, their bodies wrapped in protective fearnought suits, testing the whistle that'll warn them they're running out of air. The figure pulls his own suit on. It's Andy Barr, Pete Brierley's willing sonar rating.

With a link restored between HQ1, in the SCC, and the Ops Room, Big

Tansy Lee's called for Forward DC to 'Get 'em down here ASAP'. Pete Rowe's spoken with Section Base Chief Geoff Hart.

Naggers is back from his cable-run, and realises most of the Forward DC's back in the Gunbay Flat. He makes out Buzz Leighton and Florrie Ford. He hears Cliff Sharpe shout to the 18 year olds, 'Go down and give aft a hand.'

Ryan hears the same, assumes it's coming from Hart and, thinking they haven't heard, turns. 'You're down there,' he yells to Florrie. The order's Hart's, but Ryan's passed it on. There'll be times when he imagines the lad walking down a corridor thinking, 'What the fuck am I doing here?'

It strikes Naggers as unusual, Forward DC going aft. That's all he remembers.

'Go and check the Forward Engine Room,' Bob Lewis grabs him. 'Then check for power supplies.'

FER? Now Naggers will have to cross the dividing line between Forward and Aft DC too.

◆◆◆

1748: Blind to what's happening elsewhere, no information being broadcast, and annoyed that he doesn't know, Chief Stoker Andy Andrew breaks his roving search route at the Forward Switchboard and flashes his torch inside, the whiff of cordite filling the midships area of 2 Deck.

He can call the SCC from the sound-powered phone by the Fuel Manifold, just across the Laundry Flat, like he does when he's fuelling the ship. But he doesn't. He still doesn't know why. Instead, he heads that way on foot, moving aft past the Heads and Bathrooms, 24 feet aft, to the next bulkhead door and spins it open. Then he moves another 33 feet through the Olympus Flat to the next door, and then into the 2 Deck Tyne Flat, heading for the mayhem of the SCC Flat, ten or twelve paces away.

Opposite the Deep Sea Cat Magazine he turns left and checks his own office, then doubles back past the Tyne exhausts and into the Air Conditioning Unit compartment on the port side to check for damage. There's no point in crossing the Burma Way, squeezing into any of the airlocks down to the machinery spaces, because he knows men are there already.

◆◆◆

1748: While the searches go on, Bob Lewis spins the door to the S&S Mess open, runs down the passage with Ordinary Seaman Brad Vallint, past the battened hatches down to the Stokers' Mess, through another door and into the Forward Switchboard. Lewis reads the gauges, then turns. 'Whatever you do, if you see the meter moving like that, don't interfere with this' – he points the voltage regulator out to the 17 year old – 'just leave it. At the other end . . . they'll play with it from the other end. If you see the generator dying and nothing's happening, grab hold of it and bring it back and wind it up. Maintain the generator on the board. Don't move.'

Then the giant PO turns on his heels and heads aft alone to find out what's

happened, stopping only to spin the locks on the bulkhead doors, haul them open, then close them again . . .

About 1748: The 'Search for damage!' cry in the 2 Deck Tyne Flat has shaken Wyatt Earp out of his panic and he heads forward ten yards on legs he'd lost minutes before. He turns left into the Air Conditioning Compartment and sees Chief Stoker Andy Andrew under a unit. Their eyes meet. The senior rate speaks first.

'Is everything all right in there?' Earp recalls him asking.

'Fine. It's all right up here,' the 18 year old answers, then leaves . . .

Is it 1747? 1748? Jeff Curran tries to tell his lads to run firehoses out into the space which used to be the Hangar, but he can't speak. He grabs a nozzle instead. Thank God! They take over from him. In a second, though, his heart's in his mouth. One of his young lads dashes into the Hangar without thinking, unfurling his hose, legs churning knee-deep through the bloated lagging that's dropped to the deck. But he's all right. Curran feels the kick of the hoses charging with water. Then the smoke begins to ease and he realises what's made it appear purple. It's the sunlight. Where's the Hangar roof?

There are bodies in the vicinity, but he pays little or no attention to them. Is he callous? The seeds of doubt for future years begin to sow themselves in his mind. But he's here to put fires out. He takes in the rest of it. The port bulkhead's missing. So's the Diving Store. Torpedos are lying around. The whole place is alien. Somewhere in the middle of all this is Brum Serrell, convinced he's on his own.

Beyond the gaping hole that used to be the roll-up Hangar door, there's a peppered can on the Flight Deck, blades drooping. It's the Lynx. What's left of it. Next to it are the remains of the Seacat Launcher, and Rick Banfield, *Ardent*'s Supply Officer, injured but alive. Members of the Flight are milling, Scouse Lacey with a head gash, in severe shock. They all are.

He can have them evacuated, but doesn't. More seeds of doubt. The fires are more important. Then Jake Jacobs's hose appears from the door at the forward end of the Hangar, next deck up. Curran can't work out how the fires go out, then re-ignite. Whatever, there's nothing more he can do.

Deciding everything's under control, he tells his team he's off, to the SCC, to give them a sitrep. On the way down to 2 Deck, he passes Wyatt Earp and shouts, 'The Hangar's gone! We need firefighters!'

Earp runs up, one of the first to go. He turns the corner, through open doors, and all he sees is blue. He hasn't seen blue sky for days. Then he realises he's not meant to see it, not inside the Hangar.

♦♦♦

1750: There's a point where you have to go back to square one to recover, and Ken Enticknap's reached it. He has Command screaming for a sitrep. He can see people fighting to beat the flooding, to find out what systems are down. But it must be five minutes now, and no one's coming back into the smoke-laden Junior Ratings' Dining Hall to tell him what's happening. So he can't tell the Bridge.

The hardest job's doing nothing. He decides to go and find out for himself. A gaping hole in the ship's side is what greets him in the Switchboard, and cables dangling in the water. He recoils, frightened about being electrocuted, then realises how ridiculous he's being.

Jan Joyce strides back to the Dining Hall, give or take a minute, and knows too that the priority's isolating the 8-inch firemain, stop this deluge, give them a chance, wrestle control back; isolate the main, maybe cut off a hydrant somewhere up on 1 Deck, where they're trying to put five fires out. Can't be helped. Isolate the split. Run a breech to bypass it. Restore firemain pressure. Give them all the water they want up top, stop it spewing down here. Give the pumping teams, the bucket-chain, a break. Stop this list. That's the theory. He walks into the SCC and they're poring over plans already.

Around 1750: Bernie Berntsen walks through the torrent pouring through the SCC Flat soft patch. Through the open door to the Junior Ratings' Dining Hall he can see Knocker White shoring up the hatch down to the Fridge Space below. Knocker says something about flooding.

'See you later!' Berntsen yells through the bedlam.

'Okay!'

✦✦✦

1750: Ken Enticknap wades out of the Switchboard to MEO Terry Pendrous outside the SCC, and tells him what he's seen. Then he hammers the padlock off the NAAFI door. There's an isolating valve in there. Stop this damned water flooding from the fractured firemain and maybe they can get back to square one, come up with a plan.

They have seawater spearing at 8-bar, four times the pressure of a car tyre, from a gash between No 3 and No 4 risers, two of the four eight-inch mains sucking it out of the Sound. They have to stop it pouring into the starboard quarter, with all the water flooding through the soft patch, adding to the list.

In the 'calm' of Portland, they can spread the plumbing map out and begin playing chess, see which section between which risers supplies which hydrant, and follow the hose to the man on the nozzle.

If his hose runs back to the section that's split, he can move it to another hydrant, so long as someone reconnects him, so long as there's enough hose. In theory, he can run one from the Fo'c'sle to the Quarterdeck. The permutations multiply with every pipe running to every hydrant to every hose. As long as one of the three pumps is working, forward, midships or aft, he's laughing. He'll find water somewhere. If one hydrant won't work, try the next, it's not being supplied from the same section.

If his hose isn't feeding off a split main, no problem. The men below can crack on, run a 3-inch 'breach' pipe round the split, isolate the leak, then bring main pressure up again and hope everything's connected properly, because you don't want the solution becoming a problem, another 'flash' flood.

It's a game of strategy in the English Channel, where all that rests on it is a tick in the box. It's a game of chance when you don't even know what time

it is, let alone how much time you have left. When you don't know who's fighting the fires up top, let alone which hydrant they're plugged into.

When you hope that poor bastard blasting the seat of a blazing Avcat Pump's remembered – as their hose goes limp – that your priority below is to breach that split. Too bad. Go and find another hydrant.

When you can't just let the water pour on down through a hatch to the AAMR, shifting so much dead weight deeper into the hull – 'A pint of water, a pound-and-a-quarter' – cutting the chance of the ship becoming top-heavy above the waterline and turning turtle. Even if you do have the power to run an adductor, to suck the whole shitty mess out, you can't do it because there's a bomb in there.

Kit-Kats float out of the NAAFI door; Ken Enticknap turns the isolating valve and goes back to Kev Johnson at the Incident Board. There's hardly a line of chinagraph on it. He looks at the Leading Stores Accountant's eyes, framed by anti-flash, and sees he's shit-scared. He can't blame him.

They start trying to write down what they know. Five minutes, maybe six, maybe seven, after those three heart-stopping hits, they know precious little. If the water starts draining, they're getting on top of it. Maybe they are anyway. Who knows? They're beginning to lose track of time . . .

About 1750: Back in the SCC, Taff Lovidge is slotting pieces into place. The bomb in the Aft Auxiliary Machine Room. He's been guessing so far from the damage to the Switchboard. Now he knows from Mick Langley's description. This unexploded bomb's knocked the port generator clean off its mountings, a huge lump of throbbing, power-giving metal, and straight on to the starboard generator. Lovidge is starting to lose track of time too . . .

It could be before, it could be after Jeff Curran sees Scouse Lacey wandering the Flight Deck that the young PO's head looms through the escape scuttle to the starboard waist from the SCC deckhead, demanding help for Rick Banfield. The SCC passes the plea to Command. Then they return to the crisis. Tony Ray and Mick Cox consider the picture.

If Alan West wants to move and fight, at least they can give him movement. The SCC gauges tell them they still have propulsion and telegraphs. The shafts are still turning and there's nothing to suggest that the steering gear's been damaged. But the unexploded bomb sitting in the AAMR is causing the most problems. It appears to have slammed through the Diving Store on the port side of the Hangar, then penetrated the deck and speared straight through the Aft Switchboard before coming to rest against the port diesel generator, severing its cable on the way.

Curran arrives and adds to the picture. The water gushing into the SCC Flat is from the firemain supplying the Hangar. Bypass the gash! He's not aware, but he may be telling them something they know. Whatever, he's feeling pretty good, in the circumstances. Then Mick Cox ruins the feeling. 'Jeff, get yourself down to the Aft AMR.'

Curran leaves the SCC and sees Bernie Berntsen.

The grimy, soaked shapes battling God knows what, and for how long, might feel they're slowly taking control in the Aft Section Base and the SCC Flat but, to Bob Lewis's eyes, it's mayhem. It stops him in his tracks as he runs to the

open door from the 2 Deck Olympus Flat. He has to reach HQ1, in the SCC itself, because the only people left to do anything might be the Forward DC. At the moment, that's him. He steps into the SCC Flat and cracks his head on a salvage pipe. Even at his height, he should clear that.

The place stinks of Avcat and Dieso. He wades in and looks into the Aft Switchboard. No water in there. The list to starboard's taking it away. He hesitates at the SCC door because going in means he's going to be drenched, but goes in anyway. Inside, Taff Lovidge and Tansy Lee are looking at drawings. Lewis grabs the Chief Electrician. Reports are already coming in by runner. 'What's happening?'

'Can you go and check forward?'

Lovidge and Lee are operating on training, experience and instinct. With the Switchboard in tatters and the AAMR wrecked, they need Lewis and Wacker Payne to check for electrical damage elsewhere. To follow the back of their hands through her smoke-lagged passages. To bring back the clues that will solve the power puzzle and keep *Ardent* alive.

Until, what, seven or eight minutes ago, her ring main was split in sections with alternative supplies fed from her two FARM and two AAMR diesel generators through the Forward and Aft Switchboards, each switchboard supplying different parts of the ship in case of power loss.

In theory, they can move power how they want. Damage forward? In theory, they can supply it from aft. Damage aft, they can supply from forward, running emergency cables that conduct fewer volts than the wrist-thick interconnectors between switchboards, but still enough to run fire pumps, emergency pump sockets, the gun. With the Aft Switchboard gone, they've already lost vital supplies.

They need to know how healthy the interconnector cables are. If they can't trust them, they'll need 30 minutes to rig a temporary solution, at Portland. But where are they going to buy 30 minutes here?

Bob Lewis races out of the SCC and begins the most vital minutes of his life. This is where his nightmare starts. This is where he starts to doubt his own memory . . .

Jan Joyce takes a deep breath and sets to work, knowing the breach will isolate one of the hydrants in the Hangar, one on the waist and one just outside the Airlock, convinced whoever's up top – his young tankie pal Brum Serrell – is running off the latter. Someone finds a length of 3-inch hose and Jessie Owens sets off to turn the right stopcocks, then run a bypass from aft of No 3 riser to a hydrant.

It doesn't take long. They stand and watch. The gush subsides. It's working. Now they need to be sure firemain pressure's back. Joyce finds out, by tripping over a hose heading up. It's either pressurised or the man on the other end hasn't opened the nozzle. Not much chance of that.

Jeff Curran, Bernie Berntsen and Cliff Sharp step gingerly into the AAMR and stop dead.

'God, it's light down here. There should be no lights,' Berntsen thinks. But there are no lights. It's daylight. Streaming through a bloody great hole as big as a kitchen table.

Curran recalls the opposite – a dark compartment, the air thick with dust particles and, in the port aft quarter, right enough, a hole in the deckhead but, oddly, no damage to the chilled water plant beneath it. One generator's running as he shines his light, wondering what a bomb looks like. Berntsen's seen it, under the dislodged diesel. But before Curran can see it, he's distracted by the generator stopping. He looks at it but can't work out what's happened. He tries to call the SCC, to ask if they want it starting again. There's no answer. So they head back, thank God.

◆◆◆

Doc Young gathers his First-Aid team together. There are casualties on the Flight Deck.

Up on 1 Deck, Young tries to reach the Hangar and Flight Deck through the starboard pocket on to the waist. But the door's twisted. He turns back and heads for the Air Electrical Maintenance Room instead, relieved as the sliding door opens. Straightaway he's confronted by a casualty walking towards him, blood pouring through his fingers from a wound on the top of his head. It's Scouse Lacey.

Young puts a shell dressing on the wound and details a First-Aider to take him to the Forward First-Aid Post. Then he turns aft and opens the door to the Hangar. What he sees is impossible to describe. He's expecting a dim cavern. What's there is the shock of sunlight, burning his eyes. Even without his glasses, it's devastating. The Hangar wall on the port side's about six feet high. To starboard, it's 12.

The Hangar floor's strewn with walkway wreckage, a Naval scrapyard. A few feet away, he sees a body, face down. He searches for a pulse and quickly realises he's dead. No evidence of injuries. His attention's snatched by the Flight Deck. He looks to his right and sees more casualties beneath wreckage, the legs of one visible, clad in aircrew overalls. There's nothing he can do.

He pauses to put his lifejacket on, then continues aft towards the Flight Deck, torpedoes standing high in the air. He turns and sees the Diving Store air reservoir's been blown up. Now there'll be nowhere to recharge the fire teams' spent air bottles. They could try it off the main engine bottles, but the point on the Fo'c'sle's out. It's fed from the Diving Store. It looks good on the drawing board.

In the middle of the sea of crap on the Flight Deck are the remains of the helicopter, still fixed to the deck by its restraining harpoon. He can't believe his eyes. There's smoke and fumes everywhere.

As he appears, PO Flight Maintainer Pete Brouard calls him to someone trapped beneath the Seacat Launcher. It's Rick Banfield, his head inboard, semi-conscious, blood running from the leg of his heated Flight Deck suit. To Young's hazy focus, the launcher still appears to have two live missiles attached. He smiles at Banfield and passes a greeting. Banfield smiles back. Then the Doc turns to send one of his First-Aiders to find a stretcher, ready to evacuate the 30-year-old Supply Officer forward. The look on Mark Bogard's face, and Pete Ottley's, says it all. This is their boss. Amid all the noise, they

can't comprehend that such a very, very likeable man's lying badly injured on the deck.

◆◆◆

On the Hangar walkway, Jake Jacobs's boys are fighting the flames roaring in all quarters. After a couple of minutes, he's called out to sort a problem on the starboard torpedo tubes. He looks at his fire teams. They seem to be on top of it. Shaun Hanson's busy fighting with the rest of them. A few moments ago, the big Sheffield steward told Jake that he's found his role.

Below, Jessie Owens struggles through the escape scuttle in the SCC deckhead because there's too much going on outside the door for him to get through. He emerges less than ten yards from the Flight Deck, by the cutaway, and thinks, 'Bloody hell!' This is a disaster.

He takes the first chance to find a way back inside, keeps going, putting as much distance behind him as possible, as quickly as possible, telling the Wardroom First-Aid Party, 'They need you aft,' as soon as he arrives, then moving on to the Forward Section Base with an equally short message, 'They need you aft. I've come from the SCC. Water damage down the back end. They need somebody down there.' Then he comes back up through the hatch to 1 Deck and heads for the Bridge.

In Forward DC, no one's thinking about the clock, no one's keeping time, most of what they know about what's happening aft is the echoing sound of distant shouting, wherever it's coming from.

Paddy McGinnis grabs Iain McRobbie and tells the Scot to take four spare hands aft and report to Peddler Palmer. Florrie Ford and Buzz Leighton have already gone forward, fearnought-suited. The softly spoken Scot picks four men at random, Mick Mullen, Andy Barr, Geordie Armstrong and Sean Hayward – ages 24, 20, 22 and 18.

On the way, they come across one of McRobbie's messmates, with what looks like a head wound. His dilemma begins. Look out for your messmates first. Tradition. He tells the four he'll catch them up.

◆◆◆

Maybe 1750: Chief Stoker Andy Andrew has reached the Electrical Technical Office, feeling isolated, checking bulkheads, meeting no one, hoping the main broadcast will give him a sitrep.

Jessie Owens, breathless, nervous, salutes Alan West and recites Terry Pendrous's vital message. 'We've lost the After AMR. We don't know what people we've got. We've got no communications. What do you want?'

'Start and select both Olympuses,' the Captain replies.

Owens isn't certain the SCC can deliver. But it's not his place to say. It's what the skipper wants.

PWO Tom Williams remains at the Ops Room command display while Weapons Engineering Officer Paddy McLintock disappears to the Bridge with the bad news. Sitreps are starting to trickle in. As they do, a young rating

goes to pieces. He can't do anything. Williams sits him down, out of the firing line, and moves someone else in. And the reports go from bad to worse. Fires.

'What if one comes in here? We'll be gone,' he thinks. He's not a church-goer, but he has Christian values and reckons now's a good time to pray. The thought's chased by another. He looks round. 'If I pray now, just because I'm in trouble, God's going to think I'm a hypocrite.' So he doesn't.

The sound of coughing tells him smoke's drifting more densely into the Ops Room. It's frightening him, and he's damn certain it's frightening everyone else. He closes the Ops Room door and opens the escape hatch to the Bridge, to vent it out. An arm's length away, about the same time, Alan West calls PWO Mike Knowles. Clearly Seacat's out. They have to restore power to the gun.

Above their heads, West's pacing the Bridge, desperate for damage reports, to see how long it'll take to lick their wounds and meet *Ardent*'s date protecting the Thin Grey Line's southern end.

They know Seacat's gone, but not why it failed to operate, why it left them defenceless as the Daggers raced beyond the 4.5's arc to attack from the rear.

Nigel Langhorn's spoken with Ginger Nelson on the sound pipe telephone in the Tiller Flat, and he seems to be in one piece. Then, as the smoke begins to clear, there's word that a couple of men are dead. And they can't raise Ken Enticknap's Aft DCP. And reports from the SCC are erratic.

First Lieutenant Andrew Gordon Lennox appears on the Bridge and begins to add to what Paddy McLintock's already given West: a thousand-pounder's gone through the Aft Switchboard and burrowed down into the Aft AMR, severing cables, all but wrecking the two aft generators, taking the power to the gun and one of the ship's two steering motors with it. The Hangar's wrecked and on fire. Torpedoes are hanging out of the STWS tubes, perilously close to flames. The Lynx is smashed. And there are a number of casualties and Rick Banfield's lying amid the Seacat Launcher. And men have died. John Sephton and Brian Murphy are two.

Most of what he's reporting are things he's seen himself. The shock of the hits has crinkled the corner of the soft patch in the Flight Deck. The Damage Control parties are dealing with a deluge of water, some of it red, probably ox blood from Hangar FBIOX extinguishers, and nasty, nasty debris, the nastiest, practically dropping on to their laps. It's not good news. Psychologically not good news.

No one knows yet that it was Gonzalez's 1,000lb bomb that bounced off the calm waters of the Sound and slammed through *Ardent*'s hull in the vicinity of the port STWS torpedo launcher, then exploded in the Diving Store.

No one knows yet that Bernhardt, a split-second behind Gonzalez, smashed a 500lb Snakeye bomb against the base of the Seacat Launcher, flinging it violently into the air, demolishing the helicopter and the Hangar in searing orange and black, bringing it down again on Rick Banfield.

No one knows that Robles has run in third, pieces of *Ardent*'s aft end twisting in front of him, to drop his thousand pounds of HE, wrecking the aft power supply but failing to go off in the AAMR.

West takes a breath. He's lost two of his major weapons systems, the helicopter and Seacat, three if the STWS can't be salvaged. But it's clear that

the damage isn't fatal to the safety of the ship. The fires are serious, yes. But she can survive.

Navigating Officer Alan Maunder turns to the chart table. He's already plotted a course that'll keep *Ardent* on her new patrol line.

◆◆◆

In the Sickbay, Surg. Lt Simon Ridout and his Forward FAP are beginning to field casualties. With worrying news of what's happened aft, he decides to open the Wardroom, one flat forward on 1 Deck, as a temporary casualty unit. The First-Aiders are probably tending Rick Schofield's perforated eardrum and damaged ribs, with a battered Bill Bailey doing what he can to give help and comfort, when Captain Bob appears and adds to the news. There are men down on the Flight Deck.

◆◆◆

About 1750 (he doesn't know): Wyatt Earp's still catching his breath at the sight of blue sky where the Hangar roof should be when Barry Muncer arrives on his shoulder, maybe only a second behind him all the way from Jeff Curran's cry into the Workshop flat. Who knows?

'Get the hose!'

They turn back down the Burma Way and grab a hose. It's funny. At Portland, he's always forgotten the nozzle. Not now. It all comes together and they run back into all the water, eyes turning to a fire in one corner, stepping over everything, whacking the nozzle, and Earp shouts, 'Turn it on!'

Muncer rushes out, within moments, water's kicking out of the hose and he starts to fight the fire. Then everything goes into slow motion. He's kneeling down, looking around. The helicopter's on the Flight Deck but it's just, well, burnt out, one of its blades rolled up.

The words 'Fucking' and 'Hell!' are echoing in Earp's head as Brum Serrell runs past. He watches the big tankie go, and it's only then he sees a torque wrench on the floor, then a glove and other items of Flight Deck clothing. He puts them together and realises who's lying there, face down. Earp thinks: 'Them bastards at Portland have got it wrong!'

Training might be good, but they forgot to tell Brum Serrell the holes would be bigger than six inches and they appear more than one at a time. He's walked into what earlier in the day's been a Hangar. Now two-thirds of the roof's missing, there's daylight: 'Something's not right here.'

The AS12 Magazine beyond his right shoulder's full of 4.5-inch shells, unless Jim Watt's WEM chain's cleared it. There are two Stingray torpedoes on the rack on the port side. In Portland, there'd be two people on this hose. He's on his tod. He needs support if he's going to carry on holding this full hose and kill these fires. The Stingrays are the right height. Serrell parks his arse. Stupid, or what . . .

Some days, Bob Lewis thinks the next thing he does is struggle through the water in the SCC Flat to the Forward Switchboard, to make sure Brad Vallint's

still in one piece, glued to the gauges. Then he heads aft to find clues for Taff Lovidge.

Some days, he thinks he wades forward to the Workshop Flat ladder then up a deck and left, right, right into the Hangar, picking out the bulky shape of Brum Serrell tackling fires, then retracing his steps, left, left, right, four paces, left, two paces to the 1 Deck Load Centre.

Vallint or Serrell? Switchboard or Hangar? Maybe he does one. Maybe he does both. It's mayhem. It's already becoming a haze . . .

◆◆◆

No Seacat. No gun. A Weapons Director with no weapons. Richie Gough leaves the Ops Room and runs to the Bridge-top GDP and the Weapons Director Visual, PO Dave Taylor, explains why. All he has left are the two 20mms, the GPMG and the LMG. Gough hammers aft, down the port ladder to 02 Deck, as far as the Upper Deck ammunition lockers, and sees a group by someone on the deck. Johnno Johnson. Gough kneels. He looks awful. The blast that's ripped Seacat off the Hangar, 20 feet from his Ped Site action station, has hurled him another 20 into the Cheverton, now tilting like the ship.

'Can you make it to the GDP?' Gough asks Johnno.

'Of course I fucking can. I got here, didn't I?'

◆◆◆

To Mick Newby, it seems like the attacks were two seconds ago. It's five minutes, probably more, as Russ Goble and Scouse Wharton stagger past the starboard Oerlikon on the Bridge Wing. 'All right, Russ?' Newby twists against the shoulder restraints of the 20mm. No response.

'All right, Russ?'

No response.

'All right, Russ!'

Goble turns, makes eye contact, then points to his ears. To Newby, he's walking like a lost man.

Navigating Officer Alan Maunder stares at the man staggering into his sight. Something in his mind says, 'Look at the state of him!' It's Johnno Johnson.

He grabs some morphine and sprints out of the Bridge, still thinking, 'My God!', mild panic welling in his chest. He doesn't want to do this, put this thing into him. 'Are you all right? D'you want morphine?'

Johnson looks at him and mutters something he takes to be 'No'. Maunder smiles. In his mind, he's saying, 'Great!' He returns to the Bridge and Johnson lies down.

Seconds later, possibly, Goble sees something from a cartoon lying on the starboard Bridge Wing deck. His clothes are shredded. There's smoke coming off him. Goble wonders what part of the sky he's dropped from. It's Johnno. 'You all right?' the gunner asks, then he looks forward and sees Alan West's

eyes peering out of the rear-facing Bridge window. They're wide. Shocked.

Another few seconds, could be, and the Jimmy takes Goble aft, pumping him for information as they go: 'What happened?' 'Don't know.' 'Anyone injured?' 'Might be someone in the Hangar. Don't know who.' They rush on, boots clanging, the Jimmy's long legs maybe pounding out three frantic drumbeats to every four the small man of Gloucester can manage.

◆◆◆

In his effort to help paint Bob Lewis's power picture, Naggers's path's taken him into Aft DC territory, to the Forward Engine Room – head down the hatch, lights on, seems all right – and on towards Ken Enticknap's Aft Section Base. He's not certain what he's going to find there.

What he finds looks almost theatrical, unreal. 'Blimey! They're all sitting in the SCC. Blimey! They're pumping water from the Aft AMR.'

At least they're pumping. The hoses are charged. If they're pumping, they have some sort of power.

◆◆◆

A masked face appears behind Wyatt Earp at the Hangar hatch. He doesn't recognise the eyes. 'Anyone injured?'

The 18 year old knows they're already treating someone on the Flight Deck. 'There's someone dead here, but you can't do anything for him.'

The man in the mask doesn't stop until he hits a bulkhead forward. That's what Earp's told, later.

◆◆◆

Errol Flynn drags his short legs through about a foot of water towards the SCC Flat to help bale. He thinks he might see his old pal, Dickie Henderson. He doesn't. He steps to one side to let someone through with a face wound. It's Mick Foote. He looks at his injuries and thinks, 'God!'

By the SCC, he can see shapes moving. The devastation's shocking. He can't see the Dining Hall through the waterfall. It's black. It's as if someone's gone along the deckhead, ripping a gash as far as they can. He looks up and thinks . . . that's the closest he comes to Aft DC. A step in . . .

It's as shocking for the next man as the first. Ken Enticknap tells Dickie Henderson to go up and see what's happening in the Hangar. A minute later, he's there, at the Workshop hatch. No Hangar roof, no nothing. All peeled back, water on the deck. Where's it coming from? This is above water level. Above the split SCC firemain. Must be from somewhere else. There's one guy in there, five or six feet inside. He shouts. It's a brief conversation, maybe two sentences, possibly no more than eight words: 'We've got two BA firefighters!'

A shout back. 'It's under control!'

The shape's almost certainly Wyatt Earp, though Henderson doesn't know it. Behind Henderson, Earp sees his 'little brother', Florrie Ford. He knows the

eyes looking back at him. Ford shakes his head. Earp sends him away. It'll be 15 years before he and Henderson consider the consequences.

Henderson rushes back down to 2 Deck and finds Enticknap. 'There's nothing we can do. There's no Hangar up there. There's flood water.'

'Can we isolate the firemain to stop it?'

Henderson turns to Florrie Ford and Buzz Leighton and sends them away. 'Go and wait.' Then he tries to fire a spate pump into life.

◆◆◆

1750: Alan West's already heard *Argonaut* on the Tactical Net, telling *Fearless* she can fight but not move. *Ardent* can move, but not fight. Until now, even though he has no Seacat and the 4.5's pointing, impotent, to the sky, he's thought of nothing other than following the last order, to patrol the southern end of the Thin Grey Line, to 'split up air attacks' from the south, to draw fire, all the rest of it. But he's had his damage reports and contacts *Fearless* by call sign, laying it all out, serious fires, casualties, no Seacat, no gun, it'll take an hour or so to regain control, expecting to be told to stick it out.

Fearless orders him back to San Carlos Water. To even the most untutored staff officer, *Ardent*'s no longer capable of splitting anything, except perhaps herself. Nevertheless, it's a shock.

Alan Maunder plots a zero-two-zero course to sanctuary, siting North West Island at the northern end of Grantham Sound, then laying ten degrees off. *Ardent*'s nose, now prouder of the chilly Falkland waters with her starboard quarter listing, cuts through the early evening light at 16kts, on Tynes.

Alan West picks up the main broadcast microphone and gives the news to those who can hear – about the damage, the bomb, the Flight Deck, about licking their wounds in San Carlos Water.

1751–1755: PWO Mike Knowles is in the Ops Room, walking round his young crew, telling them, 'Just calm down', because some people are saying, 'Let's get out,' coughing in the smoke, or, 'The Seacat's gone and I'm a Seacat operator' and wanting to head aft, or, 'I haven't got a gun, I'll make myself useful down there.'

Richie Gough's already done it. No Weapons Net working, all systems showing faults, too many Weapons Directors doing nothing. So confusing. Other people are just slipping out, having asked Chief GI Pete Rowe. In the past few never-ending minutes, Knowles has realised he's beginning to lose it, no longer sure whose eyes are staring at him through grimy anti-flash masks, whose eyes aren't.

There's nothing for them to do in the Ops Room. On the other hand, he doesn't have a clue whether they're going to be bombed again, or if he might need them.

Now Knowles is saying, 'Let's stay put, it's not that bad yet,' beginning to realise why people talk of the fog of war, that no matter how many times you practise, when it happens for real, it's like letting Mohammed Ali take a swing at you and trying to do your ten times table. You can't.

Larking about in the Seamen's Mess during *Ardent*'s trip to America during 1980. Picture courtesy of Ian Turner.

We four kings: (from left) John Goddard, Scouse Flynn, Fluff Garnham and Trev Barnes in an Amsterdam Burger King. Picture courtesy of Steve Flynn.

On duty, off duty: (from left) Knocker White, Mark Bramwell, Kev McDonald, Tug Wilson and Mick Mullen pose on the Quarterdeck alongside at Devonport. Picture courtesy of Dave Serrell.

Inset: *Ardent* alongside at Narvik during Operation Alloy Express. Picture courtesy of Dave Serrell.

Kev Johnson (left) and Ginger Nelson in the Supply & Secretariat Mess. Picture courtesy of John Foster.

Greyhound of the seas: Brian Murphy's pictures of *Ardent*, as she powers away from Narvik. The images arrived on the *QE2* as the Ardents made their way home from Ascension. The lower shot is the one that hangs on the walls of many homes to this day. Pictures courtesy of Lynn Dridge.

(From left) Kev Johnson, Phil Jackson, Peddler Palmer and Buster Brown relax in the Seamen's Mess. Picture courtesy of John Foster.

No turning back: (left to right) POWEM(R) Chris Waspe, POWTR Trevor Quinton, POMEM(M) Robert 'Paddy' McGinnis, MEA2 John 'Blood' Reed, MEA2 Paul 'Joe' Laidlaw and APOWEM(R) Andrew 'Peddler' Palmer pictured in the POs' Mess as *Ardent* prepared for her run in to Falkland Sound. Picture courtesy of Chris Waspe.

Third Attack Naval Squadron pilots on the tarmac at Rio Grande during the Falklands War. Picture courtesy of Alberto Philippi.

A thoughtful-looking Lt Cdr Alberto Philippi with his children, Manfred Otto, Cristina (centre) and Verónica. The picture was taken on the evening of Thursday, 20 May 1982. A day later, he was missing. Picture courtesy of Alberto Philippi.

Ardents dressed in their 'once-only' survival suits line the port waist of the burning Type 21 as HMS *Yarmouth* manoeuvres alongside. Picture courtesy of Mike Roe.

Fluff Garnham's picture of *Yarmouth* hands waiting to catch Ardents as they jumped off their burning ship. Picture courtesy of Mike Garnham.

Caught by chance: the silhouette of CPO Ken Enticknap bending forward to pull 18-year-old Able Seaman John Dillon from the burning remnants of *Ardent*'s Flight Deck. The detail is from a general shot of the scene taken from HMS *Yarmouth*'s Wasp helicopter as the Type 12 closed *Ardent*. Enticknap's outline was not spotted in the picture for some years. Crown copyright, Ministry of Defence, Fleet Photographic Unit, Portsmouth. FKO.58/7

No going back: HMS *Yarmouth* steams away from *Ardent* in Grantham Sound as dusk gathers on Friday, 21 May 1982. Picture courtesy of The Trustees of the Imperial War Museum, London. Crown copyright. FKD 144

Pictures from the family albums: the *Daily Express*'s line-up of lost Ardents days after the terrible events of Grantham Sound. (Top, left to right) John Sephton, Simon Lawson, Andrew 'Peddler' Palmer, Shaun Hanson, Sean Haywood; (bottom, left to right) Brian Murphy, Andrew Barr, Allan 'Mac' McAulay, Stephen 'Knocker' White. Ian Boldy (bottom, right) was killed when the frigate HMS *Argonaut* was hit, 29 minutes before the first attack on *Ardent*.

Sunday, 8 August 1982: A group of Ardents, dressed in No 1 rig to please Val Wopling, at the Grand Theatre after the Remembrance Service.
Picture courtesy of Val and Dave Wopling.

Acting Leading Marine Engineering Mechanic (Mechanical) Stephen 'Knocker' White. Picture courtesy of Mrs Brenda White.

Acting Leading Marine Engineering Mechanic (Electrical) Garry Whitford. Picture courtesy of Alan Whitford.

Ardent's crest.

The Load Centre door's so twisted that Bob Lewis has to kick it in. Inside, the bulkhead's moved and the 24-volt breakers have jumped. The 24-volt system's vital to lots of things, but mostly the gun. He knows there's general power and lighting, but nothing's fuelling the gun. So the bulkhead and breakers and the gun must be related. The breakers are vital.

The 24-volt battery back-up hasn't kicked in. Whiplash. That's what's caused this, cutting the cables. Completely buggered. He tries to hold the breakers in with one huge foot, but he can't. He must find the SCC, tell them. Major bulkhead movement. They've lost all minor cables aft. Give them a picture. Then Taff Lovidge can make a plan, find a way to fix it. Decide how he's going to use his manpower. Unless you can plan, you're like a blind man in a snowstorm. He lifts his foot . . .

◆◆◆

1757: Lt Cdr Alberto Philippi has doubts about going on. The ceiling's 500ft, he can only see a mile and it's raining. His wingmen, Arca and Marquez, have been forced to close their formation so they don't lose sight of him. It means they're more vulnerable. They have a larger radar echo, and less space to twist and turn away from any missile heading their way.

Philippi knows any ship will be able to detect them 20 miles off and unleash a missile at five, four miles before they'll even see it. Nobody says a word, but Arca and Marquez are thinking the same.

There's worse. The tracker plane that's supposed to feed them a last-minute fix on the lone frigate's position isn't there. Tactically, the odds are against them.

◆◆◆

Stomachs churning, Richie Gough and Russ Goble climb the vertical ladder to the remains of the Seacat Deck. The Seacat Control Platform's been pushed back and bent in towards the funnel. To their right, a single LMG's pointing lifeless in the air, Scouse Wharton's LMG.

Gough's aching to man the gun, but he has to take a sitrep to the Ops Room. It's a hard urge to resist. Before he goes, Goble goes on to what's left of the Ped Site. It's a total . . . there's a gaping hole into the Hangar. On the Flight Deck, he sees the Seacat launcher. To his horror, someone's under it.

They survey the rest. The LMG's intact and, as they make it safe, Gough tells Goble to find a new crew. While he speaks, he hears shouting from the Hangar. The man's anti-flash hood means Gough can't tell who's calling, but he can hear him ask if there's anyone injured on the Seacat Deck. Gough pulls his hood down, shouts 'No'. He has no idea who it is.

Forward again, down the starboard ladder from the Signal Deck, and then aft. In front of them, the Hangar roof's peeled back over the Ship Torpedo Weapon System launcher. A torpedo's hanging from the top tube, trained outboard, ready for action, held in only by its propeller guard.

The First Lieutenant's by the STWS launcher, with the Buffer, PO Mal

Crane, and motions to them to help him release the trapped torpedo. They try, in vain. The Jimmy climbs on it as Goble grabs the back of his shirt, kicks it, trying to make it go over. Kicking it. Hitting it. It won't discharge.

Jake Jacobs arrives and sends one of his weapons engineers to find a long piece of wood. His idea's to push it out from behind. While he goes, Jacobs rushes to his grot next to the EMR, to fetch his keys to fire the compressed air chambers at the back of the tubes. Gough leaves too, telling the First Lieutenant he needs to go back to the Ops Room and brief Command.

◆◆◆

1758: As their Rio Grande flight plan would have it, after reaching Cape Belgrano Philippi and his men start an easy turn left, course 0–9–0, to cross the Sound from the west, praying there's no incoming missile, each straining to pierce the rain and clouds to spot danger early and avoid it.

At 450kts, 50 feet up, they're seven and a half miles closer to their target every minute. The crossing will last about eight minutes. In the loneliness of their cockpits, every minute will seem like an hour.

A moment later, Philippi breaks radio silence. His first words in 45 minutes of flying are brief – 'What a long trip this is!' – but Arca and Marquez, his wingmen, know what he means.

The east coast of the Sound appears, and the planes turn left again then, according to the flight plan, decide not to find the frigate. They'll go for the troop transport ships in San Carlos instead, about 45 miles to the north-east, six minutes' flying time away.

◆◆◆

1800: With the split firemain finally breached, Jan Joyce heads straight back for the SCC.

'We're starting to list,' Terry Pendrous tells his tankie.

'What d'you expect?' Joyce says to himself. He knows what's coming next.

To return to a level fighting platform, ready for fresh power to shock the gun back to life, the ship needs trimming. Water's swilling about in the starboard quarter of the Dining Hall. God knows what's below. The freshwater tanks hold 34 tons each, one per cent of the ship's weight. The Tiller Flat's three times as big as that. Then there's the Avcat tanks. They need to fill tanks forward to balance her out.

It's another dilemma that has to be faced, a compromise with only one possible course of action, like the need to risk robbing the Hangar firefighters of their pressure to stop that flood deepening aft.

With the Aft Engine Room and Aft AMR firepumps out because of the power failure, the whole ship's working off the only one left, in the Forward Auxiliary Machine Room.

Joyce doesn't need telling what to do, or how to do it. While Bob Lewis, Naggers, Coxie and whoever else continue checking cables, and trying to run replacements from the Forward Switchboard, he sets off on a race forward, a

divided loyalty, turning cocks as he goes to split the firemain supply between the ballast tanks forward and the hoses fighting fires in the Hangar and the Flight Deck.

The further he goes, in theory, the less likely he is to be robbing. In theory. But at least one hose snaking into the Hangar runs all the way to the FARM Flat, so who knows what'll happen up top when he knocks the vital cock with a wheel spanner and, the inside of freezing, sopping anti-flash gloves like sandpaper on his skin, spins it with two hands. Big hands. Big wheels.

There are a few ways to shift water around the ship, to counter-balance her. Most are easy alongside in Devonport, where you're sure there isn't someone with an Exocet 100 yards away, or a Skyhawk coming your way. But Alan West wants this ship upright. It's another unreal game show, Beat the Clock: 'Jan Joyce, you can normally do three ballast tanks, up and back, in three minutes, spinning the door wheels and pulling handles as well. This time you don't have three minutes! Start the clock . . .'

◆◆◆

1800: While Jan Joyce begins his heart-stopping race, the Thin Grey Line's busy too. The three Daggers of Laucha flight jump HMS *Brilliant* in the neck of the San Carlos anchorage, raking her Ops Room with 30mm cannon-fire. But they're seen off by a hail of fire from the amphibious fleet, led by a Sea Wolf missile from *Broadsword*, before fleeing home.

In his haste to escape a rising cloud of tracer, one Dagger breaks off and straightens up and heads directly for a casevac Wessex helicopter taking cover on the shoreline while the air attacks go on.

The twinkling lights from the leading edge of the Dagger's wings spell horror for Surg. Cdr Rick Jolly. Instinctively, while crewman Cpl Kevin Gleeson cocks his GPMG and fires, Jolly dives head-first into a ditch, waiting for the blinding flash and agony that will end it all. It never comes.

With a wet leg and a jammed, muddy helmet visor, Jolly climbs back into the cabin, ashamed to have run while the others stayed, worried that Gleeson's ignoring him as he makes the gun safe, convinced of it when he hears Mike Crabtree's first words as he plugs his headset in: 'You back with us, Doc?'

It's not been a good day so far for 26-year-old Gleeson. After inserting *Antrim*'s Special Forces detachment on Fanning Head, 15 or more hours ago, they've been called to a downed Gazelle and found that one of the dead crew's a good friend of his, Cpl Brett Giffin. Thoughts of his friend haven't left Gleeson's mind all day, and they won't for a few years yet, if ever.

Jolly? He needn't worry about letting the side down. What he doesn't know is that, as he hits the ditch, Gleeson's thinking, 'Very sensible.' The cold shoulder's nothing of the sort, just a man intent on being ready for the next threat to his life, to Jolly's, Crabtree's and co-pilot Hector Heathcote's.

Within a minute, Raton flight's three Daggers are expecting to add to the carnage below, but they're even less successful. *Brilliant* gathers her wits and vectors two Sea Harriers in to meet them. They do. In moments, all three Daggers are spread across a mile of Mount Caroline's slopes on West Falkland.

On their way back to *Invincible*, though, the two Harriers spot three Skyhawks spearing low towards Falkland Sound. There's too little fuel left in the tank to pursue them, so they radio ahead over the no-go box to Lt Clive Morrell and Flt Lt John Leeming, the next CAP due on station.

◆◆◆

1803: Brum Serrell's battling to put out the last fire as Jeff Curran emerges in the smoky remains of the Hangar and grabs J.J. Smith, sending the stoker to run a hose from the Quarterdeck in case any more firemain isolations threaten to cut their water. Another of Curran's young ratings jumps on the hose with Serrell. It's the first back-up the tankie's had since he stepped into this fiery, misshapen place, God knows when, maybe not long ago. He hasn't a clue.

The Jimmy's head appears, white overalls long past their best. Serrell gives him a thumbs up, shouts, 'Just finishing off,' before he disappears again, leaving Serrell vaguely aware of people moving around the Flight Deck – someone wearing a First-Aid jacket chasing after wounded Flight Mechanic Pete Brouard, someone shouting, 'Go and patch him up.'

◆◆◆

1803: As they near the southern outline of Grantham Bay, the weather begins to clear and Alberto Philippi has his first break – the mast of a ship, at eleven o'clock, behind a small island. He doesn't have time to share the sighting with his wingmen before the familiar tones of Arca's voice fill his ear: 'Un buque a las 11! A ship at 11!'

Philippi smiles inside. Jose Arca, a very skilled pilot, a very good cook, on top of everything going on around him, never missing a detail.

◆◆◆

1803: Richie Gough rushes into the Ops Room, briefs the Captain and the PWOs on the damage aft and requests a permanent move to the Upper Deck. They agree.

Leading Seaman Sid Norman goes too. Up there, the port weapons crews are going spare because they haven't been able to bring their weapons to bear, the straps are stopping them. Gough turns. 'Start charging the Oerlikons,' he shouts to Norman. 'Start charging some more magazines.'

The Oerlikons are all they have left, them and the GPMG of Cliff Goldfinch and John Leake.

Gough looks at Norman. He's nervous at the best of times, but he looks terrified. Gough can see. He knows the feeling. He gives the missile man a verbal slap. It works. He turns to set up the Oerlikons.

◆◆◆

1803: It's only taken an instant for Simon Ridout to know that the shape lying face down beneath debris in the Hangar is a body, not an unconscious person. It's intuition. He hasn't seen many like it before. The sort of thing you see at a roadside accident, not in an A&E department.

It's taken an instant for Doc Young to give him grief for not having his lifejacket on, and for being in the same place. Now he looks at Rick Banfield, lying on the Flight Deck, and tries to assess what needs to be done to save this man's life.

✦✦✦

1803: Taff Lovidge is still desperate for information, to find out the extent of the damage. Are the aft generators written off? What other essential machinery's been lost? They need the fire pumps back on, and quickly. Knock off everything that's not essential.

He calls Wacker Payne to the SCC, ready to pool Bob Lewis's information when he comes back from his hunt for clues. Then they can come up with a plan.

✦✦✦

1803: Ken Enticknap acknowledges Peddler Palmer's arrival in the Dining Hall, covering for the departed Wacker Payne. The water level's dropped now. They seem to be in control.

Florrie Ford and Buzz Leighton drift into the Aft Section Base, not needed in the Hangar. Now Enticknap has all four fearnoughts. He sits them down in the oddly angled, unwelcoming Junior Ratings' Dining Hall, waiting for news, the heat of their breath mingling with the remaining smoke particles in the emergency lighting. Waiting for a plan.

It's still smoky by the NAAFI, just a few feet forward through the SCC Flat door, as Joe Laidlaw bumps into Knocker White watching water still running out of Big John Leake's store. A box of Mars bars floats past. It's a moment Laidlaw will never forget. He bends down and picks up a couple of bars, gives one to his young Geordie pal, then turns to put a pump in the Beer Store, immediately opposite.

✦✦✦

1804: After flying a motor bomb-hoist to *Antrim*, to help rid the destroyer of its UXB, *Yarmouth* switches its attention to *Ardent*. Two of the Type 12's Seacats have already failed to defend the 21, though no one on board's surprised. Now, with *Ardent* struggling at 16kts towards North West Island, then San Carlos Water, to the protection of the Thin Grey Line after her day on its most southerly edge, *Yarmouth* turns to provide her with firefighting help. As she does, it's increasingly hard not to start thinking about the time. The Argentinians are running out of daylight.

✦✦✦

213

1805: Philippi orders Arca and Marquez to deploy for attack and starts an easy turn to the right to fly over the coast of Grantham Bay during his approach to the ship. His purpose is simple. An indirect approach may not alert the ship's radar. It gives him his best chance of surprise.

He glances at the Skyhawk's instrument panel. He only has 5300lbs of fuel left. His loiter, the fuel he needs to see Rio Grande again tonight, is 5000. He has just 300lbs to pick his spot, attack and escape.

On the weapons rails beneath his wings, four 500lb Mk82 Snakeye bombs, with retarded tail and fused for anti-ship strike, have been selected since take-off. All he has to do is hit the master armament switch.

1805: The faces around PO Mike Lewis all look wrecked. On his headset, the Tactical Net tells him the last thing he wants to hear and thinks 'Not again!', wondering for a moment who they're going for, but knowing in the back of his mind. Men down below are oblivious to what's been going on. But he knows what's coming, and he knows what to expect.

1805: Richie Gough hears there are planes coming in and runs as fast as he can to the Bridge to grab the rifle, intending to jam a fully loaded 20-round Magazine in it and do something this time. But it's locked away. It's the worst moment. For the first time, he feels totally useless. It's as if he's been running on Ever Readies, then nothing. He looks at Alan West. He's standing there. Then he looks at these things in the sky, and it's just like looking in slow motion.

◆◆◆

1805: Alan West starts to throw the ship left, right and centre to throw the three Skyhawks off the trail, but the Tynes are running flat out and they start to close in. This time, Alan Maunder has a better sight of the looming danger, but his gaze is broken by the sound of the Captain's insistent voice. 'Hit the deck!'

Maunder feels deck tiles on his face first, in his favourite place, between the chart table and the pelorus. He looks to one side and sees Lenny Yeatman lying flat. Then he realises no one's told the rest of the ship's company. He'd better make the call. But the microphone's beyond his reach. He half stands and manages to clutch the handset and lift it up and tries to speak, but nothing comes out. He tries again. This time, he croaks, 'Hit the deck!' He's aware it's hardly gung-ho.

◆◆◆

1805: The feeling of fear won't go away. Andy Cox doesn't like his life threatened like this. It's only natural. So is 'What'll I do if I lose limbs or my eyesight?'

He lies in the Gunbay Flat, feeling Alan West's every violent move of the wheel, wondering where Naggers is, because Nags's mum's wrote and said he'll survive, so anywhere Nags goes, he ought to go too. He manages another

thought, 'I'd rather be tucking into a curry, a few pints and sitting there opposite a stunning blonde.'

✦✦✦

1805: Jessie Owens is near the Olympus Flat, maybe 20 running paces from the SCC Flat on 2 Deck when he bumps into PO Bob Lewis and shouts, 'I'm going back to the SCC.' Lewis has other ideas. 'Hit the deck!' So Owens does.

✦✦✦

1805: Jake Jacobs has the air compressor keys in his hand, retracing his knackered steps back to the starboard STWS Launcher when he hears 'Air Raid Warning Red!' crackle in his ears. He hits the deck with a handful of others in the 2 Deck EMR Flat.

✦✦✦

1805: There's a mass of bodies hurtling towards Bob Lewis, rushing out of the open SCC Flat door, when he drops to the bottom of the Workshop Flat ladder, hurrying to tell Taff Lovidge about the bulkhead damage in the Load Centre. One nearly pushes him over in the panic to escape. They're running because they know what's coming from aft, and what can happen next.

He pushes some back and pulls someone to the ground and sets off a lifetime of regret about whether he was right or wrong. He thinks it's the Bathroom Flat where he eventually hits the deck. It's survival. He ends up sitting on Errol Flynn, six feet two, maybe six feet three, playing five feet four in his thickest socks.

✦✦✦

1805: Jan Joyce's spin-the-valve dash sees him hurtle back into the SCC Flat about the same time, wondering where the rest of the Mobile Party are, Brum and Jessie, his old drinking mates, wondering what Terry Pendrous wants him to do next.

The MEO's stepped beyond the lip of the SCC Flat door into the Workshop Flat when Maunder's call comes through. He looks at Pendrous. He isn't going to move, is he? He's going to stay on his feet. The leading stoker slams the door shut and crash-tackles his boss to the deck.

✦✦✦

1805: As they make their final approach, Philippi takes centre stage with Arca spread wide to his left and Marquez to his right. They've trained this way so many times against their own ships.

Each man will attack on a different arc, giving the ship's weapons crews

215

three parts of the sky to watch, three parts of the sky to aim at; putting enough time between each plane to avoid the shrapnel and debris from the bombs of the preceding aircraft, Arca and Marquez from their leader, Marquez from his close friend. If the gunners below decide to concentrate on one plane, well, the other two will have more time to take aim.

◆◆◆

1805: All this frantic effort to keep *Ardent* in the war has left her wide open. They're about on top of it all, but she's in no state to take any more attacks. She's not closed down properly. How can she be?

Tony Ray hears the call and tries to put space between himself and Taff Lovidge. But he only has time to duck under the sagging soft patch before throwing himself to the SCC Flat deck.

◆◆◆

1805: Alan Maunder doesn't know it, but some of those who've heard his warning have taken the voice as a bad sign. If they've had that much damage first time, this is going to be worse. He drops the microphone to reclaim his slot in the haven between the chart table and the pelorus, but it's been filled. So what? In a split second, he's burrowing. He doesn't care. He's thinking, 'Anytime now, one's going to come in the Bridge and we're not going to have a chance.' There's no panic, just a very clear observation. 'Should I think about my family, my job or what?' Just completely clear.

◆◆◆

1805: Jeff Curran's watching J.J. Smith, just about level with the remains of the Lynx, heading for the Quarterdeck hydrant to run a stand-by hose. The stoker turns and hurtles past him into the Hangar, shouting, 'Take cover!' Curran doesn't need two invitations.

At the same time, Wyatt Earp hears what for everything in the world sounds like gunfire and someone yelling, 'They're coming again!' then the unmistakable roar of aircraft and, in one blur of movement, ditches his hose and crashes to the deck, landing in the wash of debris next to a body.

Something flashes through his mind, something like, 'If you don't want to wind up that way, run!'

He starts running before he's properly on his feet, racing past Brum Serrell and diving head-long into the Hangar Workshop, thinking there's no one there, then hearing voices round the corner. It's only now he starts thinking of his family.

◆◆◆

1805: To Ken Enticknap, it seems like 22 seconds since the sickening sound of explosions started this whole, horrible business off, not 22 minutes.

216

Ralph Coates hits the deck beside the Damage Control lockers and the partition separating the Senior and Junior Ratings' Dining Hall. Kev Johnson dives down one body width further in from the port quarter. Lt David Searle is just forward of Ken Enticknap, the Aft Section Base Chief the last to hit the deck, desperate to find somewhere left that resembles dry, with Peddler Palmer's stout Cornish frame next in this odd sardine line, in the middle of the deck.

There are others around them in the rest of this space, just 27 feet square, all cold, all soaked to the skin through heaven knows how many layers of clothing. But Enticknap doesn't know where and doesn't know who. Lads like AB John Dillon, MEM Gilly Williams, Garry Whitford, Florrie Ford, Buzz Leighton, maybe Simon Lawson, Sean Hayward, Steve Hayes, Mick Mullen, lying tense, praying for this one to go over and let them stop for the day.

Ten feet away, where the floodwater's still creeping up the listing deck outside the Canteen, Dickie Henderson kneels down on all fours and braces his feet against the bulkhead.

Ten or twelve feet aft, beyond the lip of the Dining Hall door, Knocker White and Joe Laidlaw are continuing with their tasks, setting pumps up. 'I'll go in the Galley,' Knocker shouts through the haze. It's not five feet away.

'I'll stick one in the Scullery,' Laidlaw yells back, and turns as Knocker's shape disappears round the door.

◆◆◆

1805: From somewhere among the roar of burning fuel or metal on the Avcat line, and the deafening hiss of water being vaporised by its heat, and the shouts of Curran and Earp, Brum Serrell hears the last thing he wants to hear screamed from the Hangar Tannoy, 'Air Raid Warning Red!'

He turns and sees what he doesn't want to see – Curran's back disappearing through the Hangar Workshop door – and thinks, 'Curran, you bastard!' and carries on his desperate firefight, alone.

A few yards the other side of the spitting heart of black and orange, by Shaun Hanson's side on the Flight Deck, Mark Bogard looks at Rick Banfield, at his boss's torn No 8 jersey and legs, his half-open eyes, and the picture imprints itself on his mind and he tells Banfield, 'You'll be all right, sir.' Then someone yells 'Take cover!' and he flees instinctively past Serrell in what's left of the Hangar.

With the taste of burning plastic, diesel, soot, engine exhaust, burning aviation fuel and blood in his throat, and the sounds of runaway engines, high-pressure water and the ringing in his head from the hit, Bob Young works on quickly to save Banfield's life.

They can keep his airway open. Stop him bleeding. Maybe even work on his wounds. Given time and space. But before he and Ridout can even start, Young looks up and sees men legging it, in great detail for the first couple of steps, then blurred to infinity. His glasses are somewhere on the Galley deck. Ridout and Hanson stay with him.

A noise to starboard distracts them and they see three aircraft, setting

themselves up like Young's seen them do on the ranges. He almost thinks they're Hunters from Yeovilton. Then they spit their nose cannon and a ripping noise adds to the overload of his senses. He feels like a rabbit in the road.

In the lead Skyhawk, Philippi's cannons jam as *Ardent* makes a hard turn to port, and he thinks, 'This guy knows his trade,' stares at the smoke and the devastation of the Flight Deck, and frees his retard bombs. Ridout watches the first second of the bombs' fall and crouches back down to cover Banfield. As Young does the same, Ridout looks at the Supply Officer again. He has died.

They turn again as Philippi's bombs shatter the water in dirty brown plumes off *Ardent*'s starboard side. Young's life flashes before his eyes. He doesn't know what Ridout and Hanson are thinking, but he tries to cram in a couple of thoughts of home. He tries to cling to something familiar.

As Philippi passes the corner of Young's eye, Ridout turns further and sees two of Arca's bombs and thinks, 'These aren't going to miss.' The Funnel of Fate.

FIVE

FALKLAND SOUND

(1806–1815HRS, 21 MAY 1982)

From the moment Philippi's straining eyes picked out the lone frigate through the gathering gloom, *Ardent*'s been in little shape to defend herself. About a mile from the ship, the three Skyhawks climb to 300 feet, release altitude.

'Not yet, John. Not yet, John. Not yet, John . . .' Russ Goble stands rooted to the GDP behind John Leake as Cliff Goldfinch urges the big Canteen Manager to pick his moment. 'Not yet, John . . . now!' Leake's body shakes with every 20mm round scorching from the barrel to form a wall of lead and the shapes of these black dots grow bigger and bigger in Goble's eyes, until he knows he has to save his life and throws himself down the wooden ladder behind the vacant port Oerlikon.

Philippi begins his run in the centre, running like a bullet at *Ardent*'s turning, listing starboard quarter, Arca to his left, Marquez right, trying to ignore whatever's spitting from the smoke, aiming his sights over *Ardent*'s bow, knowing he'll spit 30mm fire back before he squeezes the bomb release.

Not this time. His cannons jam, as usual, so he switches straight to his 500lb bombs, waiting for the sight to cross the bow, waiting, waiting, then – 'Now!' – feeling them drop in the sequence governed by the intervalometer, separating each Snakeye by 50 yards, increasing the chances of at least one hit. As the last one goes, he pulls sharply on the stick and accelerates in a wild skydance to put time and distance between him, the blast, his wingmen and any missile heading his way. Any Seacat missile.

As Philippi rips right into fresh air, Mick Newby twists his starboard Oerlikon 20mm right and has time to see three of the four free-falling Snakeyes crash into the water about ten or 12 yards away. Amid the brown plumes, he doesn't have time to register the margin by which he's escaped death.

'Very good sir,' Arca's clipped voice tells Philippi at least one bomb's hit its target. Then the wingman follows Philippi, choosing an angle to avoid his leader's flight path, listening to the ratchet of his 30mm cannon-fire as he waits for his sights to tell him – now! – and four more Snakeyes begin their parachute-retarded descent towards *Ardent*'s devastated Flight Deck.

On the GDP, John Leake abandons his wall-of-death plan and decides to take Arca on head to head, hoping the Argentinian will spear into his line of fire as he attacks from the port quarter. He does.

The Brummie watches chunks of nose and starboard wing rip off the Skyhawk, then the world starts somersaulting, his head hits metal, and he feels a pain in his neck, and the rest becomes vague.

As it does, Cliff Goldfinch is trying to burrow a hole next to PO Dave Taylor at the rear of the GDP.

As they drift, Russ Goble's bouncing behind the port ladder, seeing the port Oerlikon ready-use magazine fly 50ft into the air. Then things become even vaguer.

As they do, a 30mm shell rips into *Ardent*'s aluminium superstructure to the left of Mick Newby's head and the gun-aimer feels the ship lift from the water and plunge back down and he's soaked by the splash that comes with it. In the violence of the moment, Newby recalls seeing metal lift from the Bridge roof, then things become vaguer still.

As they do, the ARMADA logo on the flanks of Philippi's scorching Skyhawk adds to the images etched on Sub Lt Richie Barker's mind, that and a deep, rhythmic sound. He realises he's being strafed by cannonfire.

On the Flight Deck, Bob Young's already surrounded by fireworks. Christ! He's being singled out for a 30mm shoot. He's somehow aware of men falling around him. The third A4, Marquez, is the best, more aggressive, more accurate. Young puts his head in his arms, expecting to wake up very dead.

'Another in the stern,' Marquez's voice crackles through Philippi's and Arca's helmets. At least two bombs must have hit, the formation leader thinks. Neither sees the results of Marquez's run, but neither doubts he'll have added to the carnage. It's the last either hears of their friend's voice.

'*Escapamos por la misma!* Escape the same route!' Philippi orders his wingmen to flee the same way they came, a route they know is clear. By the time Marquez rips into his own turn, Andrew Gordon Lennox has lost count of the bombs, and the planes, though he's certain there are five, not three. For a split second, his eyes fix on a red helmet, red with black bits. Marquez looks up and the Jimmy raises a middle finger. The Argentinian doesn't know it, but he has only moments to live.

On *Ardent*'s Flight Deck, Doc Young sees flash after flash after flash. Then a bigger explosion. No noise. Just orange. And a sensation of flying through the air. And pain as he hits something hard.

Wyatt Earp sees those same orange flashes and starts to think of his family. He counts two massive explosions and feels his body lifting off the Hangar Workshop Deck, twice, then the heavy weight of feet running up his legs and across his head, and his nose being rammed into something very hard.

They're not Brum Serrell's size God-knows-what feet. He's hanging on to his firehose for dear life, a bagatelle on his own in the remains of the Hangar, still cursing the sight of Jeff Curran hurtling past.

Spread out on the floor just feet below, and separated by the thickness of what remains of the Flight Deck and Hangar floor, are Ken Enticknap's Aft DCP men, being bounced about with each thud.

He's not sure which blast does what but, at some point, the open Damage Control lockers collapse over Ralph Coates and he's knocked out, blood running from wounds in his chest and leg and back. Just inboard, Kev Johnson's buried beneath them too, ears robbed of his protective headset. Next in, debris falls on Ken Enticknap's back and knocks him out. Christ knows what else has happened in that unbroken line of men, or further aft, in the dark, listing corner that, minutes ago, was full of Ardents.

At the same moment, one massive bang, Joe Laidlaw's flung forwards ten feet, up in what remains of breathable air and back to his knees. Knocker's nowhere to be seen.

Beyond the SCC Flat door, a spate pump hits Dickie Henderson. His take-cover position's as pathetic as everyone's, after all. Feet away, deafened, Tony Ray's white overalls are ripped by raining debris.

For Taff Lovidge, fear's grip came with the sound of bombs coming closer and closer, Big Tansy Lee and Wacker Payne lying on top of him, waiting for it all to go up. A long wait, then an uncountable accumulation of impacts – thump! thump! thump! thump! thump! thump! thump! – then a surreal calm. Lovidge looks at Lee and thinks, 'This is strange,' then looks at Wacker. The PO's staring down.

An arm's reach away, Mick Cox has stopped counting at three. For all he knows, there are 20 planes queuing to take a kick, like some bar-room bully. He stands up in the middle of the attack as smoke drifts into the SCC and looks at the open hatch above his head. Then – thump! – another, and he's back on his knees in the water, watching the smoke being sucked out of the escape scuttle.

Two decks up in the EMR Flat, clutching the STWS keys, wondering if the next one's for him, wondering if he'll see Chris and Lorna again, Jake Jacobs knows the vague direction the violence is coming from, somewhere below. Bang after bang after bang. When they stop, he's just glad to be alive.

Bang after bang after bang.

Lenny Yeatman's lying in his safe haven, behind the screen by the ladder to the Ops Room, trying to scrabble beneath the tiles, certain Alan West and Nigel Langhorn are trying to do the same, listening to cannon shells ripping into the Bridge, listening to knife-sharp shrapnel whizzing through the air above his head, and wondering how the hell Richie Barker's GDP weapons crew are managing to stay alive.

And, amid it all, Able Seaman Fluff Garnham's still on his feet at the wheel, trying to alter course.

Bang after bang after bang. The Ops Room shakes, lights go out, electronic boxes flex on their mountings and John Goddard hears a voice like Frank Gilmour's on his headset, echoing from somewhere back in the Aft Section Base. It says, 'Oh shit!' In the background, there's the sound of explosions and panic.

Then he hears Rattler Morgan shouting things like 'Are you all right? Are you all right?' as he hits the deck by Goddard and Steve Flynn, maybe even on top of them.

'No, I'm fucking not!' Well, he isn't. He's been so tired for hours and he's been thinking, 'Kill us or get out of the way.' That and, 'I'm never going to have another shag!' Not 'I'm not going to see my mum and dad again.' It may sound trivial now, he admits.

Bang after bang after bang. As they bounce, John Foster looks at his old mate John Newton, and Mal Crane scrambles through the door, past Dave Croft's hunched shape, grabbing the legs of Pete Brierley's stool, agitated.

Brierley shouts above the din, 'We're okay! We're okay!'

'Thank fuck for that,' Crane breathes heavily. 'I thought you were all dead!'

In the Forward DCP, it seems like an eternity. For Bernie Berntsen. For Cliff

Sharpe. For Buck Ryan. For Andy Cox. Time for a mind to race, to make choices – 'If this hits, I'd prefer a direct hit, I won't feel anything' – and time to realise that, back aft, whoever's left is taking a pasting. Time to feel the air sucked out of every corner with every Snakeye 500-pounder.

Iain McRobbie's lying in the black SIS Flat just forward of the S&S Mess, listening to one bang after another, feeling the ship list further to starboard with each one, convinced the next will be it. He's sharing the confines with maybe ten others, but he's never felt so alone in all his life. Jonah Jones grabs his hand, a born-again Christian, and the Scot thinks, 'It's okay for you. If we get blatted, you're going where you want to go. You can't lose.' He can't help it.

'Why don't you leave us alone?' Steve Arnell shouts. Young Buck Taylor listens and it feels like a pub fight, when you're begging, 'Don't kick me, I'm on the floor!' But the kicking goes on and on.

Brum Serrell's dragged himself to his feet and tried to drag his hose to a fresh Hangar fire by the time Teniente Benito Rotolo lines *Ardent* up, wingmen Roberto Sylvester and Carlos Lecour taking a textbook station either side. How long after Philippi's overkill? No one's looking at a watch. There's precious little daylight left, but dusk is already too late to save them. So it doesn't matter.

✦✦✦

On the distant crest of Sussex Mountains, Major Tony Rice is morbidly transfixed, not seeing a human tragedy happening, just watching a wounded ship dying slowly in front of his eyes, circling, besieged by waves of aircraft, a pack of wild dogs cornering an animal, then going for the kill, the kind of thing you see on television, not in real life.

✦✦✦

The sight that greets Serrell as he struggles to the Hangar door is shocking. It's the same one greeting Mark Bogard, though neither knows the other's there. Where there were people moments before, working to keep *Ardent* alive, working to keep Rick Banfield alive, now there are none. The Flight Deck's been swept empty. No people. No helicopter. No Seacat launcher.

There isn't enough hose to take him into the open, nor enough pressure to push the water through the wind rushing across the empty deck. It's just adding mist to the cool late afternoon air. Water, water, everywhere . . . He's frustrated, so he turns his attention back to the Avcat filter, a fresh glow of orange and black. It probably saves his life. He returns to the Hangar and hears a new sound, 30mm shells ricocheting round what remains of the four walls.

His heart sinks. Aren't bombs enough?

His answer isn't long in coming. He hits the deck and looks up through the Hangar roof and sees three or four retard bombs sailing past, their fins fanned out, in a line, like someone's suspended them from a piece of string. 'Fucking hell!' He braces himself for the inevitable but, amid all the chaos, for all he can remember, they don't hit. In the Hangar Workshop, Jeff Curran's started running forward when the next hit sends him flying again.

To Dave Croft, it's a blur by the time he reaches the STWS, sent aft to the starboard waist by lights glowing in the Ops Room gloom, and hears the Jimmy yelling, 'Get these torpedoes back in the tubes!' Coming out of the Ops Room, he's convinced he's seen daylight, and the funnel. Where's the hole?

'Get these torpedoes back in the tubes!' the Jimmy shouts.

'What with?'

'I don't fucking care! Get them in!'

Croft grabs the man overboard pole and climbs on to the STWS launcher, desperate to hook the torpedo and pull it back into its tube. He snares it, then the noose slides off, then, for all he can remember, someone yells 'Air raid red nine-zero!' and he's certain he sees three black dots, two low, one high, and he dives for the Chief Bosun's Locker, hurrying the clips off, pulling the hatch open, shutting it, diving under ropes. Then, for him, the ship does erupt. And it's a big, big one.

Still on the Upper Deck, Andrew Gordon Lennox is equally convinced he's seen just two Skyhawks in Philippi's tracks, one from port, one from starboard.

Fifty yards away, Mike Lewis has given up counting. He feels two distinct hits, then it all begins to merge. He thinks they've had it. He's very frightened.

Two planes or three? Five or six? One wave or two? Hit or miss? It's academic. The Ship's Log records eight hits, midships and aft. It doesn't matter who's put them there. As Rotolo, Sylvester and Lecour flee north at low level, all that matters is that time's running out for *Ardent*. And for Marquez.

◆◆◆

Philippi, Arca and Marquez have covered the first ten miles of their own long, lonely flight home to Rio Grande south-west down Falkland Sound when *escapamos* goes horribly wrong.

Alerted by the departing Sea Harriers of Sharkey Ward and Neill Thomas, Lt Clive Morrell and Flt Lt John Leeming see a warship exploding as they drop through 10,000ft over pock-marked Goose Green, maybe ten to 15 miles away. Morrell's on his 14th sortie. Until now, he hasn't seen an enemy plane. Now he feels anger well inside and knows there's no time to feel anything else, no time to waste in finding the men who've done this, and destroying them.

In seconds, the 33 year old sights Philippi's formation, three A4Bs running low like thieves south, then adrenaline kicks in, tuning every nerve and muscle for revenge. He's not aware of dwelling on the possibility of death – other than being acutely aware of his vulnerability to an unseen fourth Skyhawk.

The G forces are relatively low as they come in from behind and above.

◆◆◆

In the SCC, Taff Lovidge climbs to his feet and looks at the horrible mess flowing past his feet. Wacker Payne's all over him – 'Taff, you've just saved my life' – all over him.

'What are you talking about?' Lovidge thinks. Wacker doesn't know what's

happened back aft. He just knows he's been there minutes before. It's the start of his nightmare. 'Let's go and sort things out,' Lovidge tries to calm him down.

They move into the SCC Flat, the three of them, Lovidge, Payne and Lee. The ship seems hollow . . .

Jessie Owens is thinking, 'Put me out of this misery.'

A foot away, the look on Errol Flynn's face says he doesn't want to be here any more. They've lost it. Owens turns to Bob Lewis in the Bathroom Flat and knows the only way he can control his fate is by doing what he's been trained to do. And if he can't reach the Upper Deck and firefight . . . 'I'm going back down there, Bob!' he says.

Richie Gough's moving too, having dragged from the depths of his mind the fact that Russ Goble and he have left the LMG unmanned on the Seacat Deck. He has to retrieve it. As he leaves the Bridge, Alan Maunder's surveying the scene. Nigel Langhorn's voice breaks the spell as the Navigating Officer tries to assess the damage. 'We'd better put that in the log,' Langhorn suggests. They haven't put anything in for the 1744 hit.

Maunder's still in control of his hand as he writes a rushed entry against the time 1806: 'Attacked.' One word. In truth, the darkened Ops Room effectively knows little more.

Lt Tom Williams has some of the picture from the State Board opposite. Flooding, fire, listing to starboard, then news that they're counter-flooding, and he assumes she's been hit somewhere forward.

Most of all, he knows he doesn't want to be in this horrible place, he wants to run away from the alarms, people telling him there's flooding aft. But, if he does, so will 30-odd men. It's not an option.

Lt Mike Knowles wants to run too. And his men. The room's filling with smoke. There are words like 'abandon ship' floating around. No way!

'Sit here until you're told!' he barks. He feels bad about that, and tormented. He's telling them all to stay, even Chief GI Pete Rowe, who's anxious to move aft, convinced there's still a locker full of 4.5 shells waiting to go up, knowing that, in his office, there's a photo of himself and Ginger Nelson laying the Narvik wreath, desperate to salvage it while he has time. Don't ask him why.

'Sit here' but, inside, Knowles is thinking, 'If it goes over, we'll drown. How am I going to get out?'

Get yourself to a position where you can go hand over hand to the nearest exit. He holds on to the display, working out his route, yet still telling his men 'Stay put.' What else can you do? 'When I can't breathe, then you're going to leave the Ops Room and I'll tell you to go before me,' he tells them and, in his mind, he's resolved the dilemma.

An arm's length away, PO Pete Brierley's trying to make contact with someone on the radio, anyone, any Net, calling out that they've been hit again, his kneecaps going up and down like jackhammers. He can't hear the rest of the Thin Grey Line telling him to shut up. The receivers are damaged. He's terrified. He's not alone, even if he feels he is.

A foot or two to his right, Mike Lewis's mind has switched to survival. He looks right and imagines the Exocet shields beyond the Fo'c'sle Screen. The torment's spreading. 'If I get behind there, I'm going to be safe . . .' Then, 'You

silly bastard! You can't leave your men.' He's ashamed for even thinking it. It's all beginning to come apart.

The near-deafening sound of water gushing down the filling trunk greets Paddy McGinnis's return to the Forward Section Base from the bottom of the Wardroom ladder. The valves from the firemain system are open. Seawater's flooding the ballast tanks below. He rushes up to Section Base Chief Geoff Hart, but they'll hardly be able to hear each other speak until they're shut off again.

The same noise echoes round *Ardent*'s grey walls as Iain McRobbie completes his blanket search, confident from checking the inspection valves – air gushing out, water; air sucked in, fire – that there's no major flooding below. Not between the Gunbay Flat Section Base and the Laundry Flat, on the aft extreme of FDCP's domain, anyway. He doesn't open any hatches to check. The risk's not worth it.

Back up in the Wardroom Flat, Chief Stoker Andy Andrew runs into a straggle of Ardents dragging wounded men from the direction of the Hangar. They're all bleeding. He asks if he can help, and where.

'It's not worth going aft. There's no firemain pressure, Chief!'

There's no this, there's no that. And 'there's no bloody Hangar left'. He turns round and moves on.

Inside the Wardroom, *Ardent*'s makeshift casualty centre, it's all happening too fast for Jon Major. The young cook's used to Portland. You know it's not for real there, so you keep going at it. Now, he wants to do something. He knows he has to do something. What?

Bill Bailey's so desperate to find something he leaves the Wardroom and moves aft. What's the point in staying? In seconds, he bumps into Captain Bob coming the other way.

'There's nothing you can do down there,' the Army man doesn't waste words.

◆◆◆

'Harrier! Harrier at six!'

Marcelo Marquez was the first to see the two Sea Harriers attacking from the rear and shouted a warning to his comrades. Philippi didn't need two invitations. As Marquez yelled, he told his wingmen to drop their auxiliary fuel tanks, then started a break turn to the right to face the interceptors. Too late.

A Sidewinder AIM-9L missile was already chasing his tail.

◆◆◆

Karoly Nagy's heart's thumping as he nears the SCC Flat and sees a figure emerging from the chaos and emergency lighting beyond. It's Mick Beckett, on his own. 'I've been flying and they're all dead!' the leading cook's deep voice reports, something like that.

'What d'you mean, they're all dead?' Naggers doesn't understand.

'They're all dead in there.'

Beckett drops his overalls. 'Look at my arse! It's all bruised.'

Naggers shouldn't laugh, but he does. Then he makes sure Beckett reaches the Sickbay.

Two flats back, Lt David Searle's coming round, in the pitch dark of the Junior Ratings' Dining Hall, with debris lying on top of him. For a second or two, he can't feel his legs. He runs his hands down his sides and, relief, they're still there.

He struggles to his feet and becomes aware of flames aft, then sees a shape no more than an arm's length away. He reaches for it, but misses. He doesn't have a second chance because whatever it was disappears. There's no call, no noise apart from the sound of flames, and it's so difficult to see.

Jan Joyce asks Marine Engineering Officer Terry Pendrous what he should do, then takes himself off to test the inspection plug on the Aft Auxiliary Machine Room hatch, just off the SCC Flat. Then he remembers there's an unexploded bomb down there and realises. It's pointless.

He turns and starts striding the ten paces to the hole that used to be the watertight door into the Dining Hall, but something, maybe a voice from the SCC, maybe a sixth sense, says, 'It's a shambles in there,' and he steps back. He doesn't know why.

'It's time to leave.' Back in the SCC, Mick Cox, the Action Engineering Officer of the Watch, turns to the sound of the MEO's voice and sees his familiar shape – short, stout, black-rimmed glasses framing his eyes behind a grubby anti-flash mask.

Cox catches his breath. He assumes they'll head for the Bridge, then send someone down to take local control of the engines and bypass this disfunctioning nerve centre. Men start wading up the deck towards the battered stable door. Just 30 minutes ago, this place was pristine. It seems hours.

Cox begins to follow the straggling group, then remembers his lifejacket and respirator. He's thrown them on the floor. They're there somewhere, under eight inches of water. He splashes around but can't find them. There's nothing he can do except pull himself up to the escape scuttle in the deckhead, to the daylight beckoning beyond. He launches himself towards freedom, past the Incident Board, and realises it's almost blank . . .

Wyatt Earp hurtles down the ladder from 1 Deck to the Workshop Flat, blood streaming from his nose, and hears raised voices. He peers towards the SCC Flat, just aft, and sees the MEO shouting at someone. The words he thinks he hears are 'You've lost your ship! Save your men,' and he's stunned.

Then the 18 year old's conscious of men moving past, most looking grim, all looking relieved to be swapping barely breathable air for something infinitely fresher. Pendrous turns and sees him. 'Help people up the ladder,' he says; then, 'I told you this was how you were going to come back.' Then he moves off. As he does, he turns again. 'I told you, didn't I?' Yes, he did.

✦✦✦

Lt Cdr Alberto Philippi felt the heat first as Morrell's Sidewinder exploded close to his tailpipe. The rear of the aircraft broke away from the cockpit

section, and the 43 year old ejected. Before Philippi's parachute was swaying in the late, low afternoon light, Morrell was scenting his second kill, and Arca was his prey. He squeezed the button, his second Sidewinder, but it refused to fire, so he resorted to his cannon, hitting the second Skyhawk several times on its wings. Then the Sidewinder launched on its own and whistled past Arca.

Marquez wasn't as lucky. While Morrell was punishing Philippi and Arca, Leeming had the 28 year old in his sights. Diving from the rear, he hit the Skyhawk with gunfire as it fled dangerously close to the waves of Falkland Sound. It exploded and disintegrated. 'Loro' Marquez was killed instantly.

In the distance, the moment was watched by Andrew Gordon Lennox.

◆◆◆

On his way forward, Terry Pendrous bumps into his SCC stoker, Jessie Owens.

'The skipper wants Olympus,' Owens says, still trying to make his way back.

'Forget it! He won't get them,' the MEO says. 'Go on the Upper Deck. I'll go and see the skipper.'

Pendrous moves quickly up before pressing on and runs into Dave Croft. The Radar Operator's still quivering from an eternity buried in the Chief Bosun's Locker, then seeing the Hangar roof gone. 'Where are you going?' Pendrous calls. 'You aren't going down there. Get back up top.'

◆◆◆

Simon Ridout struggles as he resists the urge to gasp for air and battles to reach the surface. The water's cold. As he makes it, he gulps and gulps and grabs hold of some wreckage. He feels for his lifejacket pouch, takes it out and blows it up. Then he looks up and sees *Ardent* steaming away, on fire.

◆◆◆

When he comes round, the first thing Bob Young hears is water rushing, somewhere below. He looks down through the net skirting the forward edge of the Flight Deck and the sea's racing past.

Beyond the Hangar wall, Brum Serrell's in trouble too. There's no one to put extra hose on and now he's losing pressure. Has Jan Joyce's heart-stopping, valve-turning, counter-flooding run minutes before Philippi's attack robbed him after all? He doesn't even consider the chance, because he's still oblivious to what's happening below. The limits of his world are here, deformed and pressing in towards his shoulders. Then the hose flops completely. With it, the fight inside him starts to wane.

He looks round. There are extinguishers in the Hangar, he knows. He maintains them. But where are they? He can't even tell what he's looking at, let alone where. A figure looms from the Hangar Workshop. It's Jeff Curran. The man who sprinted past him, the bastard, minutes ago. The pair pick their way back to the Flight Deck and Curran sees Bob Young struggling like a trapped fly in the netting. The Doc rolls on to the deck and tries to stand up, but he's

227

dazed and his right leg's dead. All that's left is the Lynx harpoon. The rest has been wiped away. Absolutely wiped clean. No helicopter. No Seacat launcher. No Rick Banfield. No Simon Ridout. No Shaun Hanson. End of story. He has another problem. There's a massive fire just forward, a colossal fire. He doesn't need to guess where it is – the Avcat Pump Space, and his Medical Store next door . . .

PO Joe Laidlaw's instincts have switched from 'Save the ship' to 'Save yourself'. He's gone from the SCC Flat, and not being able to see three feet in front of his face, to the Hangar Workshop Flat and the Chippies' Workshop on the starboard waist, and not being able to see what's in front of his nose. The Hangar. Flight Deck. Not there. Like a giant's ripped it up. There's fresh air where they used to be. 'Christ! That can't be true,' he thinks. He climbs a ladder and hurries forward as fast as his bruised joints allow. Men are already dressing in their once-only suits. That Flight Deck. It's unbelievable . . .

Mick Cox gasps fresh air as he climbs out of the SCC escape scuttle and on to his feet on the starboard waist and looks aft and catches his breath again, this time without being able to help himself. There's a torpedo hanging out of its launch tube practically above his head and the ship's lying over towards land. The water only looks like it's four or five feet away.

He's accepted the damage down below, the destruction in the SCC and the Switchboard, but this isn't his environment. He starts to lose it. He stumbles aft a few paces until he can see on to the Flight Deck and the full scale of it hits him. Then he sees movement in the port quarter, where he knows the 182 Winchroom should be, two figures, struggling through the smoke and flames. Then he's really scared. He stands transfixed for what seems like hours, gazing at the water, gazing across at the islands they've come all this way to liberate.

Then the sound of another struggle behind him breaks the spell and he turns to find Taff Lovidge jammed in the scuttle, trapped by the 'Michelin man' volume of gear round his waist. It's what he needs, a task. He runs back and grabs Lovidge's left hand and yanks him free.

In seconds, Lovidge has gone, up the ladder by the starboard bollards to 01 Deck.

'I've got to get to the Bridge, got to get to the Bridge,' is the message running through Cox's mind. Eventually he crawls beneath the peeled-over Hangar roof and follows Lovidge up the ladder . . .

If PO Mike Lewis can believe his ears, the Ardents are being left to save themselves. He's felt in control of his part of the Ops Room until a few minutes ago – the second hit – as much in control as he can from his passive Electronic Warfare console. Even the loss of Comms to the DC parties hasn't stopped a flow of info. They've been assuming everyone aft's coping. In the Ops Room they are, after a fashion. It hasn't crossed his mind that someone might have been hurt. But now he feels isolated.

He's had his headset on and heard what for all the world sounds like *Hermes* or *Invincible*, God knows how many hundred miles east, give the Harrier patrols what for all the world sounds like orders not to intercept *Ardent* again. They put us out here and they're not even going to help us, he thinks. 'Where are those fucking Harriers?' he shouts out to himself . . .

228

Lt David Searle gropes around the gloom of what was the Junior Ratings' Dining Hall, searching desperately for the shape he's seen a moment ago. He still can't find it. He looks back for Ken Enticknap. That's his only recollection, lying down by the Section Base Chief. He can't see him either. He shuffles through a full circle. He can't fathom it. What was on the port side before the hit now seems to be on the starboard. The geography's changed.

There's a fire raging in the port quarter. There's no sign of anyone else. This is his nightmare, being stuck below decks. If he'd wanted this, he'd be a submariner.

He walks forward again and sees light. Daylight! He's not sure where it leads, but anywhere's better than this. He tries to squeeze through the hole, but he can't. He pulls the once-only suit off his waist and tries again. This time he manages. He peers through the hole and sees fire on the Flight Deck.

◆◆◆

DMEO Tony Ray's on his way to the Bridge when he turns back in the Sickbay Flat and races to the Hangar Workshop, to see what's what, and finds out. Peering aft through the Hangar Workshop screen door, there's smoke and flames everywhere. He knows immediately he dare not go any further. He turns on his heel and runs into Captain Bob as he hits the Sickbay Flat again. The giant liaison officer's busy shuttling men from the Sickbay forward to the Wardroom. It's only 20 steps forward, but it's still distance between them and the arse end Bob's convinced will be the target for the next hit.

'We need a fearnought team aft to make an entrance to the Hangar,' Ray's message is simple. Then he jinks left and heads straight for the Bridge to arrange taking local control of the engines. He doesn't know that both fearnought teams were already aft when the last wave came in . . .

One minute Dickie Henderson's frantically trying to pump out the SCC Flat, the next the alarms have stopped. There's no one near him. No one in the SCC. Nothing. They've run. It haunts him still. Suddenly the Aft Auxiliary Room hatch lifts, the one Jan Joyce has tested minutes ago. The 21-year-old leading stoker dives across and pulls it up and PO Mick Langley's face appears from below.

'They've all gone! They've all gone!' Henderson shouts, and Langley tells him to calm down . . .

Chief Stoker Andy Andrew heaves the Forward Auxiliary Machine Room deck hatch open and takes two or three cautious steps down the ladder. No lights are on, there seem to be no diesels running, but he can hear water running. It sounds like it's coming from the starboard hull, and it's running hard. He doesn't know what it is. A split firemain? A sprung pipe? A seam gone when those Skyhawks' bombs, God knows how many, lifted this lump of metal out of the water and shook it like a cocktail shaker?

He peers further in, but decides against going down. One slip and there'd be a man lying injured in the FARM and a hatch open to 2 Deck. He steps back, shuts the hatch, battens it and turns to the sound-powered phone by the Fuel Manifold. Nothing. No one answers. So he heads for the Bridge instead.

'If I'm still here and everyone else is going . . .' Wyatt Earp's had enough of

this, standing at the foot of the Workshop Flat ladder, sucking air that tastes of cordite and Dieso and fear and flames and chaperoning men up and forward like some fucking air hostess. So he steps into the queue himself and leaves 2 Deck and the gagging smoke behind . . .

Lt Tom Williams's intense discussion with Weapons Engineering Officer Paddy McLintock about when the gun will be back is interrupted by the sudden appearance of Chief Bosun's Mate Mal Crane in the Ops Room, yelling: 'Have you given the order to abandon ship?' People are beginning to muster on the Upper Deck.

Chief Ops Tansy Lee and Chief GI Pete Rowe look at Crane. It's the first Williams has heard of it. 'Have you just given the order to abandon ship?' He calls the Bridge on the intercom.

'Certainly not!' Alan West's answer is curt. Williams sends Crane away with a flea in his ear. But he's totally oblivious to the fact that there isn't a back end of the ship any more.

Rowe feels the deck listing beneath his feet and tries to calculate how far, then reassures himself, 'She's not going very quickly. There's only a bit of water coming in.' But he knows he has no power left in his weaponry. That's gone. All he has are the Oerlikons. 'What's the state of play with ammunition?' he calls down to the Turret Room.

'I've got a Gunbay full,' the reply comes.

'Get the lads out of the Magazine. Bring them up into the Gunbay'.

◆◆◆

Andy Andrew arrives on the Bridge and walks straight up to Alan West. His briefing is short: there's water flowing into the FARM and he believes the ship's in danger of listing further and further to starboard. He doesn't know the full picture, because he's met no one who knows what it is . . .

The look on Terry Pendrous's face makes a deep impression on Richie Gough by the starboard ladder to the Seacat Deck. The MEO's anti-flash hood's down. He's sweaty and smoky and ashen, in a daze. He asks Gough where the Captain is, so the 23-year-old PO abandons his mission to salvage Scouse Wharton's LMG and the pair walk back together via the starboard Signal Deck to the Bridge.

The scene that follows forms a picture in Gough's mind. Lenny Yeatman's in it. So is the WEO, Paddy McLintock, and Andrew Gordon Lennox. Gough stands between Pendrous and the Captain, knowing full well what *Ardent* has left to fight with. No gun. No Seacat, two Oerlikons, one LMG and a GPMG. Rag-bag. Great in a field, but not if you're a massive grey target.

◆◆◆

Lenny Yeatman's on the wheel but the ship's not answering to the helm. The engine telegraphs are hanging down, useless. There's no way he can ring down to the SCC to stop the engines. The rugged edge of North West Island's looming, at 18kts.

'Stop the ship!' West orders his Navigating Officer. It's no time to panic, but Alan Maunder can feel it. The ratings he's sent aft with messages are back. They can't get through.

So Maunder's only half listening when Terry Pendrous arrives on the Bridge. 'Give me a sitrep,' Alan West turns to meet him. The Tiller Flat's effectively been taken off, the ship's in danger of plunging by the stern. Maunder doesn't catch the MEO's exact words, but the gist alone comes like a bolt of lightning. The ship's lost and we'd better leave.

He looks straight at the skipper and, for the first time, he sees him as Alan West, not as CO. West pauses, maybe only for three or four seconds, but Maunder's transfixed for all of them.

'Get me the First Lieutenant,' West says.

Maunder turns back. The rocks are hurtling nearer. Then his eyes drop on the control console. The engine revolution counter! It's there to tell the SCC what revolutions the Bridge wants. If the switch is flicked to Full, it's maximum speed, no matter what. If it's Stop, you stop. He snaps the switch down, praying that, four decks below, the SCC will be echoing to the familiar ding-ding-ding of his command, his plea. Praying there's someone there to hear it and do something.

Mick Langley and Dickie Henderson are already in the SCC, Langley piping down to the machinery spaces below – 'Anyone below, you've got to get out!' – Henderson ripping off his respirator and lifejacket and desperately trying to ram his muscular frame through the escape scuttle.

Ding-ding-ding! Langley drags the young killick stoker back.

'Look, let's not panic.'

He turns and trips both Tynes, heeding someone four decks up. The subliminal hum of the two small gas turbines fades. Now *Ardent*'s free-wheeling towards the rocks. Then he directs Henderson back to the battered SCC stable door and they slosh uphill and turn right, without as much as a glance back into the black smoke filling the Dining Hall, and head forward. How Henderson regrets not looking back.

On the Bridge, Alan Maunder feels the distant throb of Tynes running at full tilt subside. If Alan West wants to start the engines again now, he'll need pneumatic air. For pneumatic air, he'll need compressors. For compressors, he'll need a supply of electricity. He has to hope the Forward Auxiliary Machine Room generators are still running. Now all they have to do is stop the ship.

West doesn't wait. He tells the Ops Room to muster an anchor party, to brave the Fo'c'sle and release the anchor cable. If it doesn't rip out of its Cable Locker mountings at this speed.

◆◆◆

Jeff Curran surveys the carnage as the lame man approaches. It's as if someone's changed the scenery. There's a large gash in the port side, and the only hose not buried under debris has a gash too. It's not long enough to go far anyway. Brum Serrell already knows that.

231

They badly need more firefighting equipment, and more men. Curran, the senior man, dashes round to the starboard waist. There's an FBIOX foam branch pipe there. As he arrives, he sees two stokers evacuating the SCC near the escape scuttle. It's about this time that Dickie Henderson and Mick Langley emerge. If it's them, no one knows who's speaking to who.

'What's happening?'

'Nothing left,' they tell him.

Curran can't take it in. He tries to open the firemain valve, but it won't budge. He looks back at the two POs and asks them to tell someone they're still back aft, when they reach wherever they're going. Then he watches two perfect candidates to fight an oil fire disappear. It doesn't occur to him. All he wants is to feel the valve turning, to hear water rush. For years to come, he'll think of them going and ask how hard he tried to open the valve, how much he assumed water had been isolated in the Hangar.

Henderson's still not thinking straight. As he and Langley head forward, the big, dark-haired leading stoker tries to climb through the V-cutout and up to the Upper Deck. Langley pulls him back.

'The ladder's still there,' he shouts. 'Use the ladder!'

✦✦✦

Mick Newby sees a familiar face on the starboard Bridge Wing. It's Dave Croft. 'You all right?' Newby asks as his close friend wanders up from the Flag Deck.

'Yeah! You?'

'I'll see you after.' It's obvious what's going to happen . . .

Lame and blind beyond a few paces, Bob Young knows they're operating on instinct. The Avcat Pump fire's still roaring. There's no spare hose. The gash in this one needs closing. They're beaten. He does the only thing he can. He sees a once-only suit on the deck. He assumes it's his, so he ties it round the hose to stop the spray of water soaking him. He can do without. He's cold enough.

On the Upper Deck above, Taff Lovidge looks at the remains of the Flight Deck and fear takes over. He feels vulnerable. Some of the machinery fans are still working. Then he hears the engines go . . .

Sighs of relief ripple round the Bridge. On the Bridge-top GDP, NAAFI manager John Leake feels the ship twist beneath him and watches a wave of thick, acrid smoke engulf the starboard side of the ship. 'I can't see anything,' he shouts to Sub Lt Richie Barker. 'Can I move to the other side?'

Barker waves him on, then Leake and Cliff Goldfinch lift the GPMG the few paces to the port side.

Leake's struck dumb as he looks aft, beyond the lines of men in their orange once-only suits . . .

Jeff Curran climbs through the wall of debris in front of the Hangar and his mind's racing. From the devastation of the Flight Deck, two frayed, shuffling shapes appear, in a bad way. Curran knows one. It's LSA Kev Johnson. Both his eardrums are blown out. The other's in overalls that used to be white. Not now. He has something wrong with his left hand. It looks broken. Bob Young's already spotted it. 'You're going to lose that finger,' the LMA tells him.

232

Lt David Searle looks at his ring finger. His first thought's his flying career. He's supposed to start flying in the summer. He looks at Curran and starts telling him about it, but Curran cuts him short, tells him to help with the hose – take his mind off it – then clambers through the Hangar Workshop to find foam-making equipment at the foot of the Workshop ladder, a deck below. He only makes the hatch before belching smoke tells him there's no way through. For the first time, he thinks about home.

As he does so, in the devastation of the Junior Ratings' Dining Hall he's just escaped, a waft of fresh air breaks through the thickening smoke.

◆◆◆

It might be before he heads off to muster his anchor party, it might be shortly after, when the First Lieutenant appears to complete the grim picture for Alan West. He's as brief as the Chief Stoker. 'The Flight Deck's been taken out,' Andrew Gordon Lennox says. 'Her back's done to bits, she's sinking and she's burning.' In essence, she's no longer any use as a frigate.

Terry Pendrous reasserts his view. There's no firefighting capability left, the stern's taking water and there's a danger that a bulkhead will go and the ship will plunge and 'I fear we're going to lose her.'

Lt Nigel Langhorn and Alan West stare at each other. Langhorn's thinking, 'What is the man on?' He suspects his Captain's thinking the same. Yes, they know they've been hit but, until now, because it's all aft of the funnel, they've had no idea how bad the damage is. Isn't everything under control?

West listens intently but, with every word, he's thinking, 'Right, is the assessment correct?' He double checks with Gordon Lennox and Pendrous. They repeat their fears.

No power? The answer soon comes back. The FARM's out.

He pauses. In the distance, beyond the shattered outline of *Ardent*'s Bridge window, the last of the day's raids are still going on in the mouth of San Carlos Water. West can easily say, 'No, we'll carry on.' But what with? If there wasn't an air threat, if he were in mid-ocean with no way of evacuating his men, if enemy-held territory wasn't 400 yards away. Deep, deep down, he knows it's a decision that will haunt him. But, if the ship's lost, he can save his men.

'Is it your advice that we leave the ship?' he looks at Gordon Lennox.

'Yes,' the First Lieutenant replies.

West takes a breath. At his side, Richie Gough's heart sinks. For the first time, he's afraid.

Lenny Yeatman watches West's mouth move but, even as he listens, he's thinking 'We don't do that. Not *Ardent*. We don't do that. We're still afloat.'

But they do. The Captain's spoken. 'We must abandon ship.'

SIX

FALKLAND SOUND

(1815–1835HRS, 21 MAY 1982)

'Let me know when every single person's off,' Alan West tells Master at Arms Lenny Yeatman. Then he turns to Lt Tom Williams. 'Get on the Tactical Net.'

Williams doesn't hesitate. As West heads for the port Bridge Wing, he hurtles down the ladder. The Ops Room's already almost deserted. Smoke's belching in.

LS Scouse Flynn steps past John Goddard with Williams and looks for the call sign. It's changed every hour, religiously. Where is it? No book. No nothing. Everything on the Tactical Net's supposed to be in code. But the Yeoman's already stripped the place of its secrets, locked them in the safe. Tansy Lee or Pete Rowe have bagged what's left, all but the Chief GI's gunnery notes. He's put them in a folder, then left them on his console, forgotten them.

Flynn grabs a microphone and takes a deep breath. '*Yarmouth*, this is *Ardent*!'

Every ship in San Carlos is listening. In years to come, Flynn's voice will echo round Navy classrooms as the way not to do this. But he has no choice.

'Use proper call signs on the circuit!' *Yarmouth*'s Ops Room isn't impressed.

He sits there, hoping the Type 12 realises he isn't pissing about, not realising she's on her way. '*Yarmouth*, this is *Ardent*! Take my people off.'

He waits a second longer . . . 'Roger, *Ardent*!'

On the Bridge Wing, following the skipper's orders, Radio Operator Jeff Gullick rattles the Aldis lamp handle in *Yarmouth*'s direction, another plain-English message blinking through the gathering gloom. 'T-A-K-E O-F-F M-Y M-E-N,' it flashes in Morse.

Gullick sees a message flashed back. 'A-A. Who are you?'

He realises. He hasn't identified the ship. He hasn't given the call sign. He thinks of the only alternative available, and hopes his counterpart across the water understands: 'F-1-8-4.' They do.

Below Gullick, Lenny Yeatman's detailed Leigh Slatter to rush round with him, putting fenders along what's left of the port deck. The radar operator's been chasing things to do, firefighting, boundary-cooling, ferrying men to the Sickbay. Now he cuts lanyards off fenders and ties them over the side. The Joss doesn't want *Yarmouth* damaged. Straight from the Ops Room, Scouse Flynn joins them. As they work, Slatter sees the frigate heading their way. And he sees two men in the water.

◆◆◆

A slight figure staggers through the smoke, leaving the inferno behind with every shaky step. Every turn leaves a photo in his mind, the dim glow of the emergency

235

lighting he's maintained – sometimes after a whack from a red-handled screwdriver – guiding him away from this fucking hell hole.

No 8s and everything beneath in tatters, lacerated by shrapnel, he turns right and instinct tells him it's the Galley on the left. Through the half-mangled SCC Flat door. Apparently walking past bodies, but without realising. The Workshop Flat, cables hanging on the right. Walking from memory . . .

'There's nothing left!' the Chippy, Roger Fenton, tells Bernie Berntsen and Cliff Sharpe as they head aft from the Aft Engine Room Flat. No need now. So they climb the ladder to 1 Deck, away from the devastation. Berntsen's taking his second step when he sees a figure limping from the void. He turns. It's Ralphie. He's a mess.

Ralph looks at Bernie, standing there in his 8s, soaked to the skin, no survival suit in sight.

'Right, get yourself dressed!' Ralph tells him. If he's heard it, Bernie ignores the order.

'Is there anyone back aft alive?' he shouts back.

'Don't know.'

Ralph's ready to turn back with them, until Captain Bob appears and yells 'Everyone forward, we're getting off.'

Bernie regrets not saying 'Fuck off, I'm going back aft!' He follows the last order instead.

'I can't walk,' Ralph complains. So Captain Bob picks him up . . .

◆◆◆

Surg. Cdr Rick Jolly can't hear the Tactical Net. It's not shared with the Wessex 5's cabin passenger. Nothing personal. Nothing to do with his ditch dive. It just isn't wired that way. He's just about recovered from his moment of shame when he sees smoke in the sky, south. 'Something's been hit,' he calls to Lt Mike Crabtree, Hector Heathcote and Kevin Gleeson.

As the column of smoke drifts higher and higher, Crabtree glues himself to the Net. It's some time before he overhears a conversation and a 4-letter call sign. It's *Ardent*. Crabtree starts the rotors and tells Jolly he's refuelling first. It's not a detour Jolly has in mind, but at least he can grab a couple of stretchers. They've used all theirs. They fly straight to *Fearless*.

◆◆◆

The Jimmy's scratch Fo'c'sle Party hurries down to 1 Deck and out through the screen door, where they meet a handful of Forward DC hands emerging from the Gunbay hatch.

The cold air hits Andy Cox's lungs as he races with Russ Goble, PO Pete Brierley, Topsy Turner and maybe three or four others to the anchor brake on *Ardent*'s rising Forepeak. The guardrails are down.

Brierley and Turner struggle to undo the salt-crusted rope lashing the cable. Without their seamen's knives, they find an axe from God knows where and let go the anchor strop, brake and bottle-screws, but the anchor won't budge. They

look for something and, as hawsers thrown from the newly arrived HMS *Yarmouth* thud on to the deck, Brierley picks up 4.5 cartridge cases, and starts using them to wedge and hammer. No good.

Turner steps into the 18 inches of deck space left between the cable and the ship's side and swings his axe at the the anchor fluke, a two-inch target, as Brierley smashes the cable between the hawse pipe and the capstan, trying to force the cable to surge and flow under the anchor's weight. Turner's first swing misses. His second coincides with Brierley's next kick and, finally, it starts to move, slowly at first, gathering speed with gravity until the cable's spewing up from 3 Deck, a deafening snake. Scared witless, Turner lets go of the axe and watches it hit the water, then – sod health and safety – jumps over the cable.

There's no instructions about how much cable to free, so they let most of it go, then secure it in a seamanlike manner. It's a source of pride on a desperate day. Then they race back again and it bites, slowing 3,250 tons first, then stopping it dead, her port quarter twisting slightly into the wind.

◆◆◆

Jeff Curran, Brum Serrell and Bob Young finally find more hose in the Hangar, and try again to shut the hydrant off. But now that's buried in thick smoke too. Curran looks round for the umpteenth time. The Avcat Pump's burning well. There are hundreds of gallons of Avcat below. It could go up at any time. But still no one's coming. What can his tattered lot do on their own? They all know the answer . . .

'Tell your guys to make their way up top, calmly and quietly,' Cliff Sharpe tells Iain McRobbie.

'What you telling me, Cliff?'

'Just make your way up top calmly and quietly, that's all.'

McRobbie doesn't need to know any more: 'What about aft?'

'That's already taken care of.'

The Scot heads forward to the ladder down to the Magazine, to let the lads on 4 Deck know their day's over. The Magazine's empty. He should have known. He's just spoken with young Buck Taylor.

Back on 2 Deck, there's little conversation. It's time to get off. They move in near silence, only the sound of steaming boots on metal decks echoing round the grey confines. The walking wounded lead the straggling Forward Section Base Party. In the middle of the queue, baby stoker Oscar Wild's chaperoned by Andy Cox, bleeding. Cox had heard the 17 year old yelling 'Help!' somewhere in the darkness, and gone back and found him, injured, disorientated.

The thin line makes the short walk to the base of the S&S Mess ladder adjacent to the POs' Mess, then haul themselves wearily up to the Wardroom Flat, across the narrow passage, then up another deck to the Ops Room passage and another to the Bridge.

As they go through to the port Bridge Wing, Alan West looks at every one of them in turn. Before he walks out into fresh air, 18-year-old Buck Taylor looks down at his gas mask and wonders why he's carrying it. He hurls it in a corner of the Bridge, amid the shards of broken glass.

Behind the junior ratings, Paddy McGinnis and Chris Waspe move

methodically, rechecking each compartment from the Forepeak back, the
Capstan Motor Space and No 1 Naval Store, the No 2 Naval and NBCD stores,
into the SIS Flat, left into the Gun Hydraulic Room, out and left again to the
Gunbay, then the 4.5 Power Room and the Sonar Instrument Space opposite.
And back, and back.

It's a thorough search. It has to be. As they proceed – heave! clank! thud! –
they lever all the doors and hatches shut with samson bars and clip them. No
one else will be able to use this route now. By the time they've finished, the rest
are on the Upper Deck . . .

Jessie Owens looks at Terry Pendrous and realises that he's escaped aft by
being sent to the Bridge with a sitrep after the first hit. The MEO's visibly
shaken. It's the skipper's ship, but it's Pendrous's too.

By the time Owens steps off the Bridge Wing, his mind's switched to survival.
He walks forward, helping men into their once-only suits, Belisha beacons
bobbing, moving, standing rooted against the warship's dull paintwork. Someone
has a gashed ankle. Scouse Phillips wanders into view, a bloodied bandage
swathed round his skull, muttering, 'Why are we doing this?' He's lost it.

Up on the GDP, the damage has horrified Lt Mike Knowles. A plume of
smoke's obscuring the aft end, the ship's leaning over at a crazy angle. Up
forward, the barrel of the gun's gone crazy too . . .

Down on the starboard Oerlikon, Mick Newby's left the aimer's position, a
tight 12-inch gap between the shoulder restraints and the gun. He sees a chunk
of shrapnel on the chequered plate beneath his feet. It's been blasted off God
knows what and speared between his legs. He picks it up.

'Bloody hell!' he thinks. 'How close was that?'

Chief Stoker Andy Andrew strides from the Bridge to the Fo'c'sle, checking
for his lads. He's already gone aft through the straggling line of men, some
wounded, to where the Hangar was, looked in the gaping holes, tasted the
cordite, a quarter of the ship destroyed, realised the Argentinians have done
their job, and done it well.

As he moves around, it's dawning on him how many faces he can't see, and
where they might have been. He scans the mustering men and realises that, at
least, they're still alive. He clings to the hope that the grapevine's not playing
cruel tricks, that the Harriers are, indeed, seeing off the last raids . . .

Buck Ryan knows what it felt like when the bombs went off, but he never
expected this. He looks aft from the port Bridge Wing, watching heaving lines
being secured to the Waist, and his thoughts race to his mates. His eyes dart
from man to man, trying to dig beneath the grime, putting shapes and sizes
together to make sure the lads are there in one piece. If not in one piece, there.

People around him are dumbstruck. He's thinking, 'What could I have done?
What am I doing?' He sees the Deputy Weapons Engineering Officer, Jim
Watts, dressed in combat gear. 'Don't panic,' the Fleet Chief tells him.

He looks aft again and thinks, 'Fucking hell! All those will be dead!' He
can't help himself. Where the bomb's hit. That's where his big mates are. He
grabs Ron White. Where's John Bullock? He's been in the Torpedo Magazine,
two compartments up from the Diving Store. The Diving Store's gone.

And Ralph. The last time he heard Ralph's voice was just after the first hit,

screaming for First-Aiders. He looks around. How many Aft Damage Control Party faces can he see?

'Where the fuck's John Bullock? Where's Ralph?' he asks White . . . 'Shit!'

Naggers walks up to his shoulder. At least that's one safe.

Around them, the Joss is continuing his headcount. Everyone's doing their own anyway . . .

John Bullock is a very touchy person, but Buck Ryan couldn't give a shit. The two hug. Bullock's great big grin's what the young Seacat engineer's seen first. His great big teeth. Not a scratch on him.

'How the fucking hell did you get out?'

'This thing went off and I kicked the emergency hatch. I was away.'

There's no time for them to say much more before Jake Jacobs grabs Buck. The CPO has keys. Keys mean they can fire the STWS torpedoes from their tubes. They go down the port side, the bad side for Buck, because he can see the damage. The port STWS aren't there. Nothing he can recognise is.

Then over the Signal Deck to the starboard side. He sees the torpedo hanging from the top of the triple-launcher. Then he can see where his Seacat launcher used to be. It's not there either. His pride's hurt. Beyond the shredded Hangar roof – the Seacat Deck – he sees Bob Young's balding head moving.

Jake turns the key. His hands move automatically, and suddenly – bang! bang! bang! – off they go. Buck looks at Jake and Jake looks at him. Their expressions share disbelief . . .

With the best will in the world, the efforts of the rag-tag firefighting team in the Hangar to contain the Avcat fuel blaze are pathetic. One peppered hose, bandaged with Brum Serrell's survival suit, and a trickle of water. There's nothing more they can do, other than piss on it. So they give up.

They pick their way out of the back of the Hangar, leaving it to burn, and go up Dickie Henderson's escape ladder to 01 Deck. The first thing they see is a torpedo hanging out of the top STWS launcher. Serrell takes one look at it and, 'Fuck!', decides to be somewhere else. They press on to the Boat Deck and work their way to the port side and can't believe their eyes.

'Cheers, guys!' Brum says to himself as he sees the rest of the ship's company, either in their once-onlys or just stepping into them. Heads turn. The expressions are revealing for the big Kidderminster tankie. These men have assumed that everyone down aft has gone, lost in the debris, lost in the fires. Yet here they are. Serrell, Young and Curran. Bimbling out of the void.

Lt David Searle's already moved on ahead, to the Bridge. But Young surveys the same scene and thinks, 'Why are we doing this?' Then he walks to an Upper Deck locker and grabs a new once-only.

Curran surveys the scene. People have given up. People are crying. Someone's wandering round, saying, 'We've lost . . .' and he says the first thing he thinks of, 'You didn't like him anyway.'

Then someone else walks up to him and says, 'I thought you were dead.'

' I nearly was . . .' He knows it's callous. He can't help himself now, but he'll live to regret it.

Bill Bailey's mind flashes back a few days to the conversation about how they'd clear the Flight Deck if the worst came to the worst. Now he's carrying

Rick Schofield to the Boat Deck from the Wardroom Flat. The young Wafu still can't breathe properly. He needs attention fast. But Bailey's struggling to climb past the safety chains across the top of the Upper Deck ladders. He doesn't know what's happened to the rest of the Flight.

'I've lost it. It's been blown off!'

By the time David Searle sees Mike Knowles, he's beginning to panic about his left hand. He walks past the PWO clutching it, in a terrible state, as white as a sheet. The sight's shocking. 'All right, David,' Knowles tries to calm him. 'Let me have a look.'

He lifts the hand carefully. It's all there. He looks Searle in the eye. 'Look, old son, you're all right. Don't panic. You haven't lost anything. The worst it is is a break.'

Knowles doesn't know where Searle's been, or where he's come from, just that he's appeared from nowhere, petrified that he's lost his hand. That pretty well sums it all up. Nobody really knows what's happened. Alan West's men are completely disorientated . . .

PO Blood Reed's carrying an injured stoker when he sees Eddie Edwards in the Bathroom Flat. 'We're getting off!'

'You what?'

'We're getting off.'

Stunned, Edwards rattles back down to the FARM, to grab Les Pearce. And leave. He scans the Forward Generator Space. How can they be doing this? Nothing's happened down here, really, apart from them being chucked around a lot. And a bit of water coming in.

Before they leave, they hastily check oil levels on the diesels. He passes the firepump on his way to the ladder back to 2 Deck. Is it running? In the years to come, he'll wonder. Of course it was. If it hadn't been, the guard would have been shut. He'd have noticed. Wouldn't he?

At the top of the ladder, they pull the hatch cover over and batten it down. In seconds, Pearce has gone. Edwards doesn't know where. He steps through the gas-tight door from the FARM hatch into the Bathroom Flat, turns right, steps through the next watertight door, past the POs' Mess and up to the Wardroom Flat, ripping his magloop headphones off and throwing them into one of the CPOs' cabins on the passage, clearing his pockets of tools and chucking them the same way. Then he dumps his gas mask. He won't need that in the water. Before he moves on, MEO Terry Pendrous sees him. 'What's going on down the FARM?'

'Nothing,' Edwards shrugs. 'There's a bit of water coming in.'

Pendrous seems shocked, but the PO doesn't have time to dwell before he hears his name called.

'Eddie. The bastards got me!' Johnno Johnson's walking up the Wardroom Flat, supported by two people. His knee's badly cut. The two swap quick notes, then the tattered Seacat aimer follows Edwards up to the Bridge. Johnson moves gingerly down to the port Signal Deck, still complaining that one of his knees hurts, and tries to step into his once-only suit. He can't manage.

'Somebody help me!' he calls and looks round. There are people dashing all over the place. John Foster makes his way past the line of men already filling

the port waist and gives him a hand. Then Foster sees the Jimmy on the port
Chaff Sponson, sorting out people who aren't dressed.

'D'you want volunteers to go down aft?' Foster joins a gaggle of men asking
what they can do.

'No, the Master at Arms has got all that.' The answer's the same to all of
them. And he has.

Lenny Yeatman's standing at the top of the Boat Deck ladder as 18-year-old
Wyatt Earp steps off the final rung and stares at the mass of orange bodies
spread forward.

'I need two volunteers to go and check down aft,' the Joss shouts. Hearts
sink, heads tilt towards the deck, as if they haven't heard. Earp looks at him and
the Master at Arms looks back. The young stoker's eyes must have 'Please, not
me' written all over. Yeatman guides him on to the Boat Deck. The next thing
he remembers is someone calling for a knife, to cut the ropes binding a
lifejacket locker.

In the seconds that follow – maybe the seconds before – Ken Chapman grabs
hold of Yeatman. 'I'm worried about Ginger.' If it wasn't already the Joss's duty
to go back down, it is now.

He looks about and sees Mick Cox stepping into a once-only, feeling guilty.
In his mind, he's seeing two figures climbing out of the smoke enveloping the
port quarter, down by the Quarterdeck Tiller Flat hatch, Ginger's well-practised
escape route.

They don't need to exchange many words. They just hurry aft, towards the
Cheverton seaboat, towards the Flight Deck. One of the first people they see is
Andy Andrew.

'We're going to get off,' Yeatman says, then asks the Chief Stoker to check
the Senior Rates' and POs' cabins, up forward on 2 Deck. Yeatman and Cox
leave Andrew to his task, then continue a few paces aft past the port Tyne
intake, smoke drifting from the blackened grilles.

Cox pauses and finds himself staring into what used to be the Aft Auxiliary
Machine Room. Somewhere in it, there's an unexploded bomb. He sees water
gushing in. It's not from the sea. The list's lifting the hole away from the waves
with every second. It's from shattered systems deep inside *Ardent*.

The Master at Arms looks aft and sees nothing but mess. He hadn't realised
how bad . . . He stares on, thinking he's looking down into the Dining Halls.
Beyond the smoke is the Tiller Flat. Ginger Nelson. There's no point. He can't
make it back there. He turns to Cox and there are tears on his cheeks . . .

Down on the port side, Richie Gough's beyond the Boat Deck, trying to sort
out once-onlys for those who don't have them. The heap round his waist is
beginning to annoy him, snagging, restricting his movement, his gasmask box
most of all. So he cuts it loose and ditches it. Gone. Good riddance. He won't
think until later, but his camera's in it. Every photo he's taken on the way south,
and today. It'll break his heart when he realises . . .

Mick Cox and Lenny Yeatman turn back and enter the ship beneath the
Cheverton and move as quickly as they can down the ladder to the Ship's Office
Flat on 1 Deck. Yeatman's driven by an echo in his head. Ginger. If they can't go
aft, they can go down, then sweep forward. They turn for the next ladder, the one

down to the Workship Flat, the ladder Wyatt Earp's just spent long minutes guarding. But there's no way they can descend. Smoke and flames.

Instead, they stand there for God knows how long, shouting. All Cox can hear in return are things happening down below, crackling noises, lots of things. But not voices. Yeatman leaves him by the ladder hatch, after extracting a promise that the Scot will warn him if another air raid comes in . . .

Dickie Henderson and Mick Langley arrive on the Boat Deck and everyone's there in orange suits. The two stokers are still in their 8s, drenched to the skin. Chippy Roger Fenton takes them back to the once-only container beneath the Cheverton and grabs a couple of suits. The port Tyne intake's on fire. They don't waste time returning to the Boat Deck.

Someone tells Henderson to be careful putting his once-only suit on. Get the air out of your feet. If you don't, when you're in the water your legs will hit the surface and your head will go down. He heeds the advice, then shares a moment of relief when he bumps into Errol Flynn. The pair swap notes, but not much. Time and fatigue. In seconds, the Jimmy's walking Henderson's way.

'We need a ladder to get down to the *Yarmouth*,' he shouts. Henderson finds his adjustable spanner, but it's too small for the securing nuts. For a moment, he thought he'd have something to do . . .

Lenny Yeatman turns aft again, one last time, to try to go in through the Hangar. The smoke and flames have beaten him on the Workshop Flat ladder. This is his last hope. But there's no way through here either. The doors are blocked. It's no use. All he can do is hope Ginger's escaped by himself . . .

Bill Bailey's standing, waiting for *Yarmouth* to arrive alongside, watching the helicopters buzzing round the dying ship, when he spots two familiar faces, Wally Wallington and Speedy Ball. Then he sees Scouse Lacey. He makes his way towards him. He's distressed. John Sephton and Brian Murphy are dead. And there's no sign of Pete Brouard or Mac McAulay.

Lacey fears the worst. Bailey looks back towards the Flight Deck. It's pretty obvious. If they aren't here now, they're not coming . . .

Blood's streaming down Dave Trotter's leg on the far end of the Boat Deck. His lower back is in tatters. Wyatt Earp looks at it.

'What about my stereo, what about my stereo?'

Someone puts an arm round him, and says, 'Come on, let's go.'

Then someone else suggests they help him on with his lifejacket. So they do. Earp watches them lavish care on Trotter, and he feels his heart sink. He regrets trading his gas mask for nutty space. The covert supply of sweets had kept him going in the Aft Engine Room, but now?

He opens the small sack carrying his once-only suit, trying to lift the flaps as carefully as he can. Fumbling, more like. The suit flies out and rolls down the side of the Boat Deck. His heart races again. He runs and grabs it. He opens it. Then he realises he doesn't even know how it's meant to go on . . .

Everyone's in once-only suits as Jan Joyce walks to the Fo'c'sle. Everyone except him, it seems. 'You'd better put your once-only suit on, Jan,' Terry Pendrous shouts to him.

'What for?'

'We're going to abandon ship.'

This isn't what Joyce had in mind. He looks at the MEO, then down at the rising swell. 'I ain't going in there!'

'If you've got to, you've got to . . .'

On the GDP, Andrew Gordon Lennox has already taken a minute to break the bad news about Rick Banfield to Cliff Goldfinch, two words, 'He's gone,' and the PO Cook's thankful for being told, but upset. How many men on board didn't like the Supply Officer? Not one.

Now the sight greeting Goldfinch, as he looks down on to the port Bridge Wing, is horrific. It's something he's never going to forget. The last time he saw Dave Trotter, he was sharing Cliff's belongings out among Mick Beckett's half of the cook's party. Now half of Trotter's back seems to be missing, he's soaking wet and there's blood all around him. Trotter looks up to his boss. 'They're all gone, Cliff.' That's all he says . . .

Everyone's on the port waist, a disjointed line beneath the Bridge Wing and the Fo'c'sle Screen.

'Sod it!' Dave Croft knows the starboard side's quiet, so he and Mick Newby wander between the Exocet launchers, Croft ditching his respirator as he goes to the top of the Fo'c'sle ladder, pulling his lifejacket on, thinking, 'Don't break your ankle,' taking care not to rip his survival suit.

Then Newby starts clambering up the ladder beneath the Bridge, towards the ship's crest . . .

The door to the Main Communications Office is smashed, as if someone's been determined to make sure no one's in there. The 'bip! bip! bip! bip! bip! bip!' from the Scot satellite console greets John Foster, Buster Brown, Phil Udy and John Newton as they step in. It's more than Brown can take. He picks up a hammer and swings it, ready to smash it to smithereens, emergency destruction drill, rip the plugs, everything, wreck it. Brown's always hated the thing anyway, Foster knows.

'No Buster!' they yell. Foster grabs him before he can slam the weapon down.

'Scrub round it,' Udy shouts. 'It's in shallow water. They'll be able to recover everything . . .'

If Tom Williams needed therapy, he found it. Who the hell packed these damn things? He glances round. Men are sitting like idiots, trying to undo knots that someone tied in some once-only factory. You can't use it without undoing the knot. Suddenly, everyone has something to do . . .

Ralph Coates hobbles through the Bridge, past Buck Ryan. The weapons engineer takes one look in his direction and opens his mouth. 'Fucking hell, Ralph!'

He smiles. There's a grandad not far from the surface in Ralph, Buck's always thought. He doesn't think much about the limp. Not for the moment. The wounded stoker walks out towards the Fo'c'sle, towards the other injured men, and sees Scouse Phillips sitting there, blood pouring down his head.

'Ralph, am I bleeding?' Scouse asks.

'No.'

Phillips instinctively feels for his head, then looks at his hands.

'You lying bastard! I am fucking bleeding!'

Ralph looks again. Scouse has split his head open. That's all he remembers.

Buck watches Ralph hobble away, then turns his gaze to John Goddard, busy picking bits up off the Bridge deck, bagging them. For Goddard, picking up stuff that's not glued down isn't so much a professional occupation, more a personal obsession. Only, this time, he reaches down and grabs the Ship's Log. He gives it straight to Alan West.

An arm's reach away, Alan Maunder's gathering things too – his calculator, for some reason, and a felt tip he uses to mark his charts, and his notebook. His entries have been economical today. In the middle of his trawl, he glances out of the window. The ROs are still signalling on the Aldis lamp, by the vacant port Oerlikon. There's something else beyond them. *Yarmouth*, steaming closer.

Buck Ryan sees *Yarmouth* too, then looks up. Big John Leake's staring down, sunglasses on, like something from a war film. That's when Buck's attention's drawn to men shouting and pointing. Then he sees two men in the water, and a chopper clattering towards them. The news ripples along *Ardent*'s port waist. Suddenly, they don't know which way to look. At the men? At *Yarmouth*? At the smoke?

John Foster joins the line of men in time to see one of the figures fighting to stay afloat. In a split second, he starts to hope it's Ginger Nelson. A split second further on, he's muttering, 'Excellent! Ginger, what the hell are you doing?' to himself. It's wishful thinking, but it might just be the PTI.

Then the Liverpudlian grabs hold of John Newton, and pushes him in front because, remember, Jan Newton's made him responsible for bringing her husband home.

They move down to the Fo'c'sle, one by one, taking care not to rip the once-only suits. As they go, Foster looks up at the aerials, the ones he built, and thinks, 'You bastards!'

'Take cover!'

Jon Major's eyes dart to Scouse Phillips at the cry they don't want to hear. 'It can't possibly happen again!' the young cook decides.

On the Bridge Wing, Alan West tenses and shouts to John Leake on the GDP. It happens so fast, he can't count them, but they look like Daggers. One fires cannon, he's sure, and one drops a bomb, he's sure too, but there's no explosion. He looks round. Only a handful of his men have seen it.

Captain Bob's one. For him, the digga-digga-digga-digga ratchet of cannon-fire's becoming personal. One moment he's been thinking, 'I've got away with this,' the next it's 'They're not giving in.'

Someone on the Flag Deck's seen as well, judging by the desperate shout of 'Oh God, they're coming again.' Russ Goble looks up. Two or three of them. He doesn't see cannonfire or bombs, though he knows how much trouble they'll cause if they pick either. He's so tired . . .

Chief Electrician Taff Lovidge has been down below, with Chippy Roger Fenton, to try and find Mr Wong, and anyone else. There are lights on down there, but they've only been able to hunt as far as the Battery Shop before the smoke's driven them back. Now the final fly past . . . He's not feeling too good.

Neither is John Goddard. As the Daggers make their final run, they remind

244

the Londoner of a Japanese Airfix model he had when he was a boy. The Joss finds him and Danny Byrne on the Bridge Wing. There's glass everywhere underfoot from the shattered Bridge windows. The 20mm gun's unmanned.

'Get on the Oerlikon,' Lenny Yeatman tells them.

Goddard's aghast. 'I don't know how to fire one,' he says. He sees the Daggers coming closer. He doesn't consider himself chicken, but he'll do all he can to resist being put on the 20mm.

◆◆◆

Willie Quate's already grabbed Mike Roe from *Yarmouth*'s SCR by the time the Argentinians try their final run. Roe's not unhappy. Eight men in the SCR's a couple too many. So he's in the bowman's position in the Seaboat as the Type 12 closes *Ardent* and opens up with everything she has, both 4.5s, both Oerlikons, and a Seacat unleashed more in hope than expectation.

◆◆◆

There or thereabouts, he can't remember where, Bob Young's doing what he can to treat the casualties as *Yarmouth* comes alongside. Dave Trotter has a piece of Formica as big as your hand sticking out of his rear end. But Young's rapidly becoming useless himself.

He's put the dead-leg down to a pen in his trouser pocket. What he won't know for a few hours is that he has shards of metal behind his ear and in his shoulder too, and all down his leg. What he won't know for another 12 years, or so, is that there's a thumbnail of shrapnel in his right femur. Right now, though, his head's swimming, he's starting to shiver, yet he's sweating like a pig . . .

The orange queue's stretching from the Fo'c'sle Screen back beyond the Boat Deck as *Yarmouth* nears, so orderly they might be lining up for scran in the Junior Ratings' Dining Hall, except they're wearing one-size survival suits and grim expressions. One by one, once Alan West tells them to go, they'll make their way on to the old Type 12 frigate.

Iain McRobbie's on the Bridge Wing as she edges closer, pulling the zip on his once-only suit as he prepares to slide down to the port waist and take his place in the queue. In a second, he's in trouble. The cord that's supposed to seal off the hood has snagged a cleat and it's tightening round his neck, choking him. And no one's seen him hanging.

He feels his face turning red, purple, and he's beginning to panic when he suddenly feels the garotte loosen. A seaman's seen him dangling, legs dancing, he doesn't know who, and cut the cord. Robbie's relieved but annoyed. If they have to hit the water, this thing's now as useful as a chocolate fireguard.

Nags is in the same thin orange line, gradually accepting with every noise he can hear from deep within that it was the right decision not to sneak back down to the Stokers' Mess on 2 Deck to grab the £56 and the new jeans he's left in his locker. He looks round and sees faces he knows well, John Goddard, Coxie, Buck Ryan, the rest. He even begins to count heads because

he's been hearing suggestions about who's still back there, beyond the wall of smoke and flame.

❖❖❖

Surg. Cdr Rick Jolly's heart sinks as Lt Mike Crabtree brings the Wessex 5 nearer to *Ardent*. He's sad and angry. Beautiful lines but grossly under-protected against air attack. A gun at the front, some Exocets, and that dreadful Seacat missile. Seamouse, the Marines call it. Utterly useless.

Beside him in the Wessex's noisy cabin, Cpl Kevin Gleeson looks down on the listing Type 21. He can see her men pointing frantically to the water and starts scouring the waves. At more or less the same time word comes over his headset and they see what they're looking for, two shapes. They need winching on board as quickly as possible.

❖❖❖

In the freezing water of Falkland Sound, too far away to swim, too far away to shout, Surg. Lt Simon Ridout's somehow pulled the once-only from its waistband pouch and put it on. Impossible. It's hard enough on a listing deck. Now he's clinging to a pipe, resisting his instinct that it's a periscope, clinging to that and the hope that someone's seen his orange arm waving desperately in the swell.

It doesn't look good. *Yarmouth*'s gone, though he's certain someone waved at him as she passed.

He's not aware of any injuries, nothing that stops him trying and trying to attract someone's attention anyway. If he's injured, his chances of survival in this situation will be slim. He knows that. Then his hopes begin to soar. First the sound of a helicopter, clattering louder in the fading light, then coming into sight, flying towards him... and banking away so that all he can see is its bottom.

As it banks, it flies on and Ridout watches helplessly as it hovers and prepares to pluck someone from the water. Someone, but not him.

SEVEN

HMS *YARMOUTH*, FALKLAND SOUND

(1835–1845HRS, 21 MAY 1982)

'Further air attack has put out *Argonaut* – badly damaged – and *Ardent*
is so badly hurt we are expecting her complement to transfer over to us
. . . Hopefully with darkness at 4 p.m. things may go quiet.'

Lauraine Mulberry has spent most of the day with Helen Hawkett, taking cover
beneath a table in the troopship *Canberra*, resting on lifejackets. As she adds to
her diary, there are three people dead, 16 people in Bonito Ward and heaven
knows how many waiting for surgery.

Mike Roe's transfixed by the smoke belching from *Ardent*'s port quarter as
Yarmouth comes alongside at 1835, quite far aft to begin with. He doesn't know
why, maybe because what he's seeing's so unbelievable, but he can't help taking
his camera from the haversack that's supposed to hold his gas mask and fires off
five shots. It's as well one of the older lads sees someone else do the same first.
So it's not Roe's camera that's ripped from his grasp and ditched over the side.

A shout causes Roe to look up at the orange bodies scurrying around
Ardent's Cable Deck, and he hears an officer shouting across for a maul,
presumably to complete the anchor party's work. A Yarmouth goes off in search
of one, but it doesn't stop the Ardent yelling and yelling.

Off the Type 12's port beam, HMS *Brilliant*'s protecting her two
preoccupied companions, her Seawolf missile launcher alert, swivelling in the
dimming light.

Andrew Gordon Lennox is the first to slip down, anxious to find her First
Lieutenant – his old school friend Jonnie Plummer. Can he provide firemain
pressure and hose parties? Can he at least help stabilise the situation? Then he
moves to *Yarmouth*'s Bridge roof to warn Capt Tony Morton of the fires
burning near *Ardent*'s port magazines. If they go off, that'll be two ships lost.

Morton looks at the Type 21's blazing stern but, although the fires aren't his
major concern until all Alan West's men are off, he heeds the First Lieutenant's
advice. As he edges *Yarmouth* forward, she snags her starboard propeller on the
anchor cable trailing beneath *Ardent*'s bow. At the same time, the boiler safety
valves lift in her Engine Room, letting off steam. Along *Ardent*'s port rail, men
duck, scared stiff.

As *Yarmouth* creeps forward, Mike Knowles is heading aft on *Ardent*'s port waist and he's horrified. He's on the lip of a volcano. The Flight Deck's a crater of deep red fire. The fires of hell. That's what it is. Tangled metal, nothing that's recognisable until his eyes run forward of the funnel. He looks back at the Bridge and sees Nigel Langhorn, arms behind his back, surveying the scene. In an instant, nothing occurs to Knowles except escaping what he's seen, but he doesn't know how.

On *Yarmouth*'s Flight Deck, 30-odd feet below, men are shouting, 'Go on, jump!'

Knowles registers the drop. Thirty feet. 'Right,' he turns to the line of men leaning on *Ardent*'s port rail, 'can we get some ropes?'

Somebody has. They start tying them to the rails and throwing them over the side, but nobody's going. He stares at the men below and realises why. *Yarmouth*'s propeller's thrashing the water lazily.

Not sure what's possessing him, he tugs the rope, then, like the first child plunging into the pool, he commits himself to fresh air. As soon as he leaves *Ardent* metal, he regrets it. He should be waiting till everyone else is off. As soon as his feet hit *Yarmouth*, he looks up and sees others following and begins clinging to a hope that will ease the guilt he'll feel for years to come. Maybe he's led the way.

By the 3-inch Rocket launchers, Captain Bob surveys the Yarmouths below, yelling, 'Come on! Come on!' For the first time, he feels helpless, thinking, 'If they hit us again, there'll be a lot of lives lost.'

Alan West moves across the photograph that's becoming embedded in Bob's mind, and what it records is a man who's lived and died in a few hours. Until an hour ago, things were going well. He had a cracking crew. Now they're calmly waiting to go to *Yarmouth* because there's nothing else to do.

At 1840, the 27 wounded men on *Ardent*'s Fo'c'sle take a step to salvation, helped by messmates and Yarmouths, Dave Trotter – his once-only holed by an over-zealous helper – Mick Beckett, Scouse Phillips, Ralph Coates, Kev Johnson, Johnno Johnson, Pat Norris, Rick Schofield, Scouse Lacey.

Bernie Berntsen's with Cliff Sharpe and Captain Bob by the 3-inch Rockets in front of the Bridge Screen, ready to hand Scouse Phillips and Ralph down the ladder. Ralph's the problem.

'We've got ours on, get yours on!' He's intent on making sure Bernie has his once-only on. The old man of the Mess isn't really interested, even though he's frozen to the bone, craving warmth. 'Oh, for fuck's sake!' he dismisses the order. 'You're wounded, aren't you?'

Ralph grunts 'Yeah,' but he doesn't understand the question.

'Fuck off, then!'

In seconds, he's off. So's Bob Young, helped by Captain Bob and Bob Lewis, the big PO innocently gripping the medic's wounded thigh. By the time he hits *Yarmouth*, Young's sense of humour is back.

'We'll have to spend a long time in dry dock to fix this!' he tells someone. As they lead him inside, he's feeling more sceptical, something on the lines of, 'What chance do we stand on this old thing?'

Back on *Ardent,* down below, far aft on 1 Deck, Lenny Yeatman joins Mick

Cox again and they move forward, through the engine flats, striding further from the Aft Section Base and the Tiller Flat with each step, checking compartments. On the way, Yeatman sees someone in white in the Cabin Flat ahead.

'You've heard the order,' he can't tell who it is. 'Get out!' There's no mistaking the voice. They go.

◆◆◆

Back on *Ardent*'s Bridge Wing, ashen, covered in what looks like firefighting foam and nursing his injured hand, Lt David Searle's passed control of his emotions to Nigel Langhorn. While the orderly queue of Ardents behind him waits to be called forward, Searle's looking at the rope connecting the two ships, certain that shinning down it's a non-starter, a complete non-starter.

He doesn't know how it happens but, a moment later, he's on *Yarmouth*'s starboard waist.

For Jon Major, the impetus to leave is simple. His turn to go comes just after the reassuring sight of Mr Wong, the Chinese laundryman, has greeted him.

'Shin across,' the Yarmouths can see Major's not keen.

'There's no way I'm going across on that!' the young cook shouts back. He's shaking.

'Jump! Just look aft!' He does and a strange power seizes his body. One by one, men follow.

Mark Bogard's glad he's heeded the Ardents who've told him not to jump into the water before *Yarmouth*'s arrival, rather than the ones who have. Glad, but already feeling lost and dispossessed.

Richie Gough finds time to wedge the bright orange 'man overboard' dummy on the starboard Oerlikon, then grasps a horizontal railing bar on the *Yarmouth* and swings over like a monkey.

Still thinking of the man he's seen spinning on the end of the Wessex helicopter's winch, Russ Goble's jumped from the Bridge Wing on to a liferaft rack on *Yarmouth*'s starboard waist.

Jan Joyce and Brum Serrell have gone too, the killick tankie with his heart in his mouth, thinking 'Jesus!' at the sight of the 20ft drop, his 23-year-old stoker knowing the Type 12 will be his salvation, focusing on being out of hell, but wishing they'd allow him one final look back as he's ushered below. But not everyone can find what's needed to wait for the queue to reach the Bridge wing.

Buck Taylor twists and watches in disbelief as Terry Ducker takes a run and leaps into the void.

The young stoker flies from *Ardent*'s Boat Deck and hits the coconut matting on *Yarmouth*'s Flight Deck with a thud. Taylor's convinced he'll have broken both legs. He hasn't. The 18-year-old Geordie's still not persuaded to follow him though, not even by the smoke and flames consuming *Ardent*'s port quarter, maybe 40 yards away. He'll wait. So will Naggers.

Buck Ryan thinks about doing the same as he hits the front of the queue, close to last. One moment he's watching Mick Newby halfway up the Bridge Screen, trying to prise *Ardent*'s crest off, the next he sees *Yarmouth* start to drift and, 'Fuck it! I'm going!', he doesn't hang around to find out why.

He lands on *Yarmouth*'s Flight Deck and picks himself up and looks at his new surroundings. Beside him there's an injured man. Very badly injured. Shrapnel. He can't see who it is.

The orange stream of Ardents continues. Wyatt Earp's lifted over by a stoker, even though he's not injured, and is caught by someone big on *Yarmouth*. Errol Flynn takes his chance. It's intimidating for Dickie Henderson crossing from the Fo'c'sle, but for the little Brummie – all five feet three-and-a-half of him – it's terrifying. Mind you, if it had been 20 feet, he'd have jumped. Thirty even.

Pete Brierley swings down to *Yarmouth*'s waist. Someone with Flight Deck training's told him to try ten chin-ups before letting go of the liferaft stowage. He manages two. He arrives on *Yarmouth*'s waist in his action working dress. All he has on him is sixpence and a pen.

John Leake and Cliff Goldfinch watch man after man find their way off. Eventually, there's a shout.

'All those on the GDP go now.'

Leake clambers down by the Exocet launcher, his GPMG cradled in his arms. He turns to Sub Lt Richie Barker as he pauses to watch Mick Newby and Andy Cox grappling with the ship's crest.

'Shall I take the gun?' Barker nods. Leake passes it to Captain Bob. He hands it down to *Yarmouth*.

'Did you do much firing?' someone asks. Stupid question. The GDP's awash with spent cartridges.

As Leake prepares to follow his GPMG, the ship lurches. His mind tells him it's a bulkhead going, but who cares? A few men around him mutter words about the ship turning turtle. It's enough.

As he lands, his cine-camera falls from his respirator bag and smashes. He's been wrestling with the idea of recording the scene. He's already decided he can't bring himself to do it. Now he can't anyway.

At least the GPMG will bolster *Yarmouth*'s close-quarters weapons stock though. The Type 12's already sent a scavenging party across. They won't find much.

It's too much for Iain McRobbie, this waiting. Waiting for one of the two ropes to have his name on it. So he leaves the line and finds a rope of his own. He ties it to a cleat, then realises the last time he did any ropework was in training at HMS *Ganges* in 1973. The facts are simple. If it takes his weight, he has his own escape route. If it doesn't, he'll fall between the ships' hulls.

Before he can pluck up the courage, Captain Bob leaps over the rail and slides down it, convinced that all matelots can tie knots, blissfully ignorant that this one probably can't.

McRobbie's about to give him the benefit of his opinion, something along the lines of 'Find your own rope!' when he realises the giant soldier's safely down. The knot's held his weight. It's probably the biggest risk he's taken in the entire campaign, the Scot muses. How little he knows.

High above, still on *Ardent,* Alan Maunder's mind's spinning, Alan West's calm voice echoing in his ears, telling him, finally, 'You'd better go.' It's not what he wants. In the queue, he feels agitated. Who are these people? He doesn't know. He can't recognise one pair of hooded eyes staring back at him,

not one name, not one trade, not one rank. There are plenty of people to talk to, but no one's talking. How do you start a conversation with someone you don't recognise?

Down on 1 Deck, Lenny Yeatman and Mick Cox have continued their lonely search, past the Officers' Heads, past Brian Murphy's cabin on the right, past John Sephton's cabin just after it on the left, then Rick Banfield's, then Terry Pendrous's, until they twist past the Wardroom and reach the Officer's Pantry. If they choose the ladder to their right, they'll go up to the Ops Room Flat. If they choose the one to the left . . . well, without doubling back, it's their last chance to go deeper.

'I'm just going to nip down to 2 Deck,' Yeatman turns to Cox. He disappears from Cox's view.

The seconds pass slowly again. Then Cox hears a groaning noise. A chilling sound.

'Come on out!' he shouts to Yeatman. The Master at Arms doesn't need two invitations.

They meet again and, this time, head up, up to the Ops Rooms Flat, up to the Bridge. The light there's dull but bright, and they pause to adjust to it. There are, what, a dozen men left. Slowly, the Ardents are being divided. Those on *Yarmouth*. Those waiting to cross. Those still back aft.

Back in 3 Mike Mess, next to Yarmouth's Tiller Flat, about half the surviving Ardents are gathered, trying to calm each other but desperate to feel safe. Jan Joyce looks up as he hears Terry Pendrous.

'How's Knocker?' the MEO asks.

'Don't know,' Joyce answers. 'I haven't seen him.'

'I saw him on the Fo'c'sle.'

Joyce pauses, but 'I don't think so' is running through his mind.

'I thought he was in the Aft Section Base,' he tells Pendrous.

The same kind of questions are being asked in low tones around the Mess, 'Where's so-and-so?'

Joe Laidlaw listens. Until now, he hasn't thought that some men might have been killed.

'Where's Knocker?' someone asks.

'He was with me down the NAAFI Flat,' he says. 'I haven't seen him since. There was so much smoke. He's probably all right.'

But people keep saying they haven't seen him. Then he thinks, 'I haven't seen him either.'

❖❖❖

It's taken all the courage Dave Croft can muster to leap off the Fo'c'sle, just behind the gun. The cries of 'Jump!' from *Yarmouth* have only made him more uncertain, that and 'We won't let you fall.'

He thinks, 'Oh yeah?', but goes anyway. The lad who catches him is PO Bungie Edwards. The last time they met was on the *Scilla*. Never met since. A larger-than-life character. 'Hey, Crofty, fancy meeting you here!'

Croft smiles, but the good feeling doesn't last long. He turns and sees the

devastation of the Flight Deck, and it all comes flooding back. He starts sobbing. He feels an arm round his shoulder and hears a soft voice. It's meant to console him, but it doesn't.

'Come down below, son. Don't worry about it.'

The trouble is, he can't help himself. The smoke and flames mean they haven't done their job properly. He lets himself be guided away. It's the last time he'll see *Ardent*, like the rest.

On *Yarmouth*'s 3 Deck, Bob Lewis is taken to one side. So are three or four others. They're considered a health hazard. They reek of diesel and Avcat. The Yarmouths hand them individual cardboard boxes. One by one, they open their survivor's kits and burst into laughter.

God knows what shape the packers thought they'd be, but Lewis has never seen a six-foot matelot squeeze into 8s with a 36-inch chest and a 30-inch inside leg before – certainly not from a survivor's kit with size 11 pumps and a sweater that's somewhere in between. Everyone's kit is just about as useful.

It's still not perfect when they finish swapping, but it's better.

By now, only the stragglers are left on *Ardent*. Andy Cox has given up on the ship's crest. He has his locker keys, so at least the ring his folks gave him on his 18th will be safe. So will his Walkman. His letters. Otherwise, he's left with just what he stands up in. Then he ditches his tool roll, and he has even less.

He slides down a rope, glances aft, thinks, 'Bloody hell!' and heads off. He doesn't know what's taken him this far. But he's run out of it. He's cold. He doesn't know who's survived and who hasn't.

He's given a tot of rum and 20 fags. It calms the surface. Then an old friend on *Yarmouth* comes up.

'Coxie! Lost your ship again?' Cox laughs, but he's not interested any more.

Nor Buck Ryan. He's in the Senior Ratings' Mess, separated from his messmates by men who are simply anxious to know if he's all right. He's not aware, but that moment of concern is already starting a chain of events which will turn his family's lives upside down in the next 24 hours.

◆◆◆

After scouring *Ardent*'s Ops Room for documents, PO Mike Lewis arrives on the Bridge with John Foster. It's a mess – a sea of glass, gasmasks, tool rolls, all sorts. Foster bends and picks up something from the debris. Lewis watches him dust it off and hand it to Alan West. It's the Captain's blue, braid-covered baseball cap. Foster walks out of the Bridge onto the Fo'c'sle, up to the Jimmy.

'Sir, is there anything you want me to do?'

'No,' Andrew Gordon Lennox tells him. 'Just leave.'

Back on the Bridge Wing, Lewis struggles to put the smoke billowing from aft together with the order to leave the ship, berating himself for not being able to put on his once-only properly – 'Pull yourself together!' – as he heads aft with Foster to sling classified books on to *Yarmouth*. The uncertainty about what's happening remains until he arrives on *Yarmouth*, until he goes to retrieve the books from the Type 12's Flight Deck and looks back at *Ardent*.

'Christ!' he thinks, and wonders if they'll ever be able to put the fires out so

that they can go back on board and start again. But that's not going to happen.

When *Yarmouth* first came alongside, the two ships seemed to be in the same attitude but, by the time Nigel Langhorn leaves, *Ardent*'s well over, and sliding down the ropes has become a hard task.

He feels the level Flight Deck of *Yarmouth* beneath his feet and joins Lt Tom Williams and Captain Bob. The three stand for a moment, absolutely silent while, all around them, the Yarmouths toil.

Then it dawns on Williams that they've lost men. He's terribly tired and suddenly very cold, looking around at the faces near him, thinking, 'Where's John Sephton? Where's Brian Murphy?'

Back on *Ardent*'s Bridge, Lenny Yeatman walks up to Alan West and Andrew Gordon Lennox and gives them the information they've been waiting for,

'Everyone's been accounted for, apart from the dead.' Then he leaves the ship too with the Jimmy.

West walks on to the Bridge Wing and sees Mick Newby, still trying to wrest the ship's crest from the Bridge Screen. He's not amused. 'Newby get down from that,' he shouts.

'But I want to get it.'

'Forget it.'

Newby climbs down, closes his eyes and, seconds later, he's walking away from *Yarmouth*'s coconut matting, his legs trembling. Now Cdr Alan West's on his own.

Navigating Officer Alan Maunder watches the glow in the black heart of *Ardent*'s stern, then looks back and sees him, pacing from Bridge Wing to Bridge, not yet in his survival suit. He has nobody to talk to, nobody to give orders. Maunder's desperate to go back, but he can't. The guilt starts now. He should have waited. Overhead, the clatter of helicopters seems a distant thing.

◆◆◆

Ken Enticknap opens his eyes and feels panic welling. First an almighty bang, and now this. Smoke and flames and the stench of burning Avcat are gagging the space around him and there's something lying across his back, something heavy. As his head clears, he realises how much trouble he's in.

His hand's damaged. Through the remnants of his anti-flash glove, he can see that he's lost a finger on his left hand, his ring finger.

There's a throb in his left temple. He instinctively reaches to it and feels Formica sticking out of his skull. He pulls it out. Then he tries to stand up.

He can make all-fours, but no further. He's trapped by a section of ventilation trunking.

He pauses for a moment, trying to think what to do, and hears voices echoing from somewhere. Where? He can't work out. Then he hears a distinct voice and looks up. There's a tall figure beside him. Where's he come from?

'You all right, mate?'

'Get this off my back,' Enticknap coughs, 'and I will be.'

The figure pulls as hard as he can, but an arm injury's hindering him. Eventually, Enticknap feels the weight lift and he stands, slowly, breathing in

lumps of thick, black smoke, and looks at the face of the young rating as they hug.

He doesn't recognise him. He's not one of the regular Damage Control guys. He's just someone who comes down to the Section Base on his stand-off period. It doesn't matter, anyway.

In his mind, Enticknap's thinking, 'I'm too young to die.' But he manages to cling to something. The belief that, at any moment, a firefighting team will come bearing down on them and they'll be out.

The pair straighten and try to move forward, the natural way to go. But there's so much debris they can't see a thing. Soon they're back at square one, wherever that is in this unrecognisable space. And it's dawning on Enticknap. The odds on finding a way out are slim. Maybe 28 isn't too young to die.

Then he feels a wisp of fresh air from the port side and sees the wall of flame grow. If the fires are being fanned, it must be from outside. He looks at his young companion.

'We'll head this way,' he shouts, and they battle aft straight away, taking hope and relief from the wafts of hot air, and arrive in an area that's reasonably clear. But there's still no obvious way to escape. All the bulkheads are deformed and there's a mass of debris to trip and confuse them.

Then there's another rush of air and Enticknap glimpses a gap beneath a winch. He stares. It's the 182 Sonar Winchroom, without the wall that should divide it from the Senior Ratings' Dining Hall.

His broad shoulders are a tight fit, his head and hand are throbbing, but he goes first and, with a push from the unknown matelot, and the whiff of fresher air enticing them on, he manages to crawl through the gap. The rating follows and is hauled to his feet on the Quarterdeck by the Section Base Chief.

Below them, through the drifting black, he can see water.

Between coughs from his smoke-logged lungs, Enticknap inflates his lifejacket. It's next to impossible. The young rating's is punctured, so he hits the water with nothing but his arms to save him.

After the heat of the Aft Section Base, it's freezing. But Enticknap's not bothered. He's out. Alive. Any moment now, someone'll see them. Drag them to safety.

The young matelot's struggling to keep his head above water as Enticknap looks back at the burning ship and he can almost count the men in the thin orange line, gathering along the port waist. Then he sees another ship steaming towards him and thinks it's coming for them. It isn't. When the swell lifts him, he can watch it slow alongside *Ardent* and start taking men off.

He's not sure how much longer he can last in the water. His body's beginning to feel warmer, but he's losing blood and he can hardly stay afloat, not without dragging the other man down.

Then the boy who's saved him lets him go, and drifts out of sight.

Then he hears the sound of a helicopter approaching. Then it hovers.

◆◆◆

Corporal Kevin Gleeson leans from the Wessex cabin and watches the winch and strop drop towards one of the floundering bodies in the waves. In a

moment, the thought of Brett Giffin's body lying beside the shattered Gazelle recedes from his mind.

If they'd been able to raise a Sea King, well, Christ, this would've been easier. There'd have been a dope on the rope too. Instead, one of the men in the water can't catch the strop. He's too tired. It's all he can do to save himself from drowning.

Gleeson talks to the intercom as Surg. Cdr Rick Jolly stuffs his camera in a pocket and shuffles across on his knees. He looks down and sees the man looking back up, the downwash of the rotors breaking over his face. He knows instantly the only thing that will save this man's life. He's fouled up once today, shown his true colours by jumping into a ditch. Now, in his heart of hearts . . .

He taps Gleeson on the shoulder. He points at himself and then down. To Jolly, Gleeson looks at him as if he's crap. Then the winchman speaks rapidly to Mike Crabtree up in the cockpit.

Gleeson's not sure. But the only other option's for him to jump in and keep the two afloat until a Sea King arrives. And all the time he's there, there's the chance the Wessex will become the next target, and the risk that the fires raging against the dark seascape might rip *Ardent* apart, and take them with it.

'Yeah, let him go!' Crabtree says, and Gleeson beckons the Doc.

Jolly slips into the single-man strop. He has no lifejacket on. No immersion suit. He forgets he's just put his camera away. Speed's the only priority. Whoever it is down there is drowning.

The 26-year-old Royal Marine studies the look on Jolly's face as he prepares to leave the cabin. For all the world, it seems like he's taking it very matter-of-factly. Then Jolly steps out and the world changes. As he descends, he's vaguely conscious of the Ardents looking across from their burning ship.

He hits the water between two waves and – bang! – static electricity rips through his flesh and bones. Horrible. Then he feels a second shock, the shock of immersion. The water's just above freezing. In a split second, his heart rate slows and his peripheral vision turns grey. He struggles to breathe. But there's nothing he can do. The big man will have to rely upon his diving experience. His bulk. His natural insulation. He splashes water on his face and begins to regain his senses.

High above, Mike Crabtree drops the Wessex's nose slightly and drags Jolly gently through the water, about ten yards or so. The waves are five or six feet high and the young matelot's about to disappear as he grabs him. He goes limp straight away. Another ten seconds, 15 maybe, and he'd have gone.

Instinctively, the Doc swims behind the young sailor, threads his arms underneath his armpits and clasps his fingers in an 'S' grip in front of his chest. Now all he has to do is hang on.

Gleeson stares down and waits for Jolly to finish his work. Jolly looks up. If the corporal uses the winch to lift them out of the water, the jerk will loosen his grip. But Gleeson's already ahead of him.

Jolly feels the cable tighten. Crabtree lifts the helicopter five or six feet and the Doc's body gradually leaves the waves. The water cascades down his freezing legs as they dangle in chilly evening air.

He hadn't expected this, though, the size of the man in his arms, and his enormous unconscious weight. He has to hang on as, inch by inch, foot by foot,

Gleeson raises them. Gently. Gently. Using muscular movements of no more than two or three pounds on the winch control, he watches the two bodies edge nearer, terrified that Jolly's grasp will slip in the violent, icy downdraft from the rotors.

Jolly's hurting so much. Then he feels a muscle pop in his shoulder and he hurts even more.

'Come on, come on,' he begs himself. 'Keep going!'

When they arrive beneath the winch motor, Gleeson leans carefully out and grabs the strop and pulls them in. As he does, Jolly remains a passenger. He's alert enough to know that, if he tries to help, the young lad will fall, spear straight back into Falkland Sound. And they won't see him again.

Eventually, he feels the solid cabin floor and the pair flop in a big heap. His arms are almost numb. Utter muscular exhaustion. But his work's not over.

He looks at the young Ardent. Without pausing, he bangs a fist hard on his back. The sailor's sick everywhere, coughing seawater all over the floor. He's not in a good way. But at least he's alive.

'Thank God, we've got him,' Jolly rocks back and sits on his heels and thinks 'I've done it!'

The feeling of inner peace and contentment's like a wave. He's been asked a question and managed to answer it. Now he feels part of the crew. He looks at Gleeson, hoping this feeling of redemption's matched by the look in his eyes. It is. Gleeson looks back with a big grin on his face and a thumbs up.

Jolly puts his thumb up. Then the winchman grins again and points down out of the door. Jolly's heart sinks. There's someone else to go and fetch. He looks back at Gleeson. Gleeson returns the glance. He has a slight inkling that the Doc's not as keen this time. He's not.

Jolly crawls across again, wriggles into the strop and steps back into the void. The difference this time is that he knows what's going to happen when he hits the water, and he's almost a spent force.

Like some mad fairground ride, the scenery goes round and round as Jolly's winch spirals on this second descent, land followed by sea followed by burning ship, followed by sea and more sea.

Below, there's a man floating, looking up, a trail of blood pouring from his head and his hands.

Bang! Jolly hits the water. The static shock rips through his body again. Then he grabs the next man.

Ken Enticknap's just about had it. He thinks he's dying. He feels like he's lying in a hot bath, which is a bonus in a way. Except that his mind's playing tricks. His body's cooling so rapidly his brain still thinks he's warm. So he is dying.

This time, there's no way the Doc can hug this man back to the Wessex. Then he has a stroke of genius.

His eyes fix on the small becket on the front of Enticknap's lifejacket. It's not going to be that strong, so this man's life will have to hang on the safety margin the Navy's sewn in to this bit of kit.

They're almost at the limit of the winch cable as Jolly lets himself drop underwater, grabs the becket with his left hand and tries to drag the strop hook to it with his right.

THROUGH FIRE AND WATER

The first attempt fails. Jolly surfaces and gulps air. In his receding world, Enticknap's wondering whether the Archangel Gabriel's come to save him or kill him. The becket's there for pulling you into a boat, not supporting dead weight. This man has no idea of procedure. But he's the only chance he has.

At the crucial moment, Kevin Gleeson gives Jolly some slack and, on a rising wave, he tries again. This time, he feels the hook click into the becket and looks up, waiting for Gleeson to lift them.

As they inch clear of the water, the strop cuts into Enticknap's back. It hurts. Then he spots the Commander's stripes on Jolly's tunic and, that's it, he thinks he's dead already. Every Commander he's ever known – with the exception of Alan West – is old. It's one of the last things he remembers, that and being laid down on the helicopter deck, the agony of being warmed by the cabin heater, then Jolly shouting 'Get these to *Canberra* quickly.' Then he drifts off.

Gleeson shuts the door and the deafening clatter of rotors subsides. He looks at his two new passengers and then at Jolly. It'll be 15 years before Gleeson knows the names of the men he's helped to save. It'll be 15 years before Jolly finds out that, if Gleeson had been able to take the 'sensible' option, he would have joined Jolly in that ditch those few hours before.

◆◆◆

Cdr Alan West's sure, given everything he's been told, that it's the right decision to abandon ship. He's pacing the Bridge Wing, racking his brain for something he hasn't done, something he hasn't checked or accounted for.

The ship's about to plunge. There are strange movements down below as water shifts around, inside and out. If the 4.5 was still working, if they were still involved, then, yes, he'd keep his men on board. Yes, on balance, they might lose a hundred men . . . But actually, if he did, he'd feel guilty all his life.

He looks around. The light's failing. Too late. He doesn't want to go, but there's nothing more *Ardent* can do for this campaign. It's the right thing to do. The Funnel of Fate has closed.

He hesitates.

Then, at 1854, like many of his men already, he walks to the Fo'c'sle, and steps off. He has tears rolling down his cheeks.

257

EIGHT

HMS *YARMOUTH*, FALKLAND SOUND TO SS *CANBERRA*, SAN CARLOS WATER

(1900–2359HRS, 21 MAY 1982)

They exchanged a few words, then Capt Tony Morton left Alan West with Andrew Gordon Lennox on *Yarmouth*'s port Bridge Wing, surveying his ship and feeling distressed.

West's conversation was barely longer with his First Lieutenant, but it lives with both men.

'Why the hell hasn't she sunk?' he asked his right-hand man.

Neither had an answer. Gordon Lennox had left because *Ardent* was on fire, the Captain because he'd been told she had no power either, couldn't fight, and was about to plunge. For one moment, both were tormented by terrible doubt.

Below deck, the ship's company was tormented too. The tea, the nutty, the rum, the fags were all welcome. But, among the 175 men scattered about the ageing Type 12, for every sigh of relief that they'd made it this far, there were a hundred moments when someone said, 'Have you seen . . . ?' and their chests tightened. This wasn't the way it was meant to end.

In the POs' Mess, the whole enterprise had lost its charm for John Foster. He just wanted out. 'From being the master of all you surveyed to all of a sudden being reliant on other things, strange ship, strange people. Not *Ardent*,' he says. 'Not how we were.' Vulnerable and defeated.

'You feared the worst,' Andy Cox admits. 'If you don't see their face, you assume they're dead. You panic. No one knew who'd been lost.'

In the bundle of despair packed into the Aft Seamen's Mess, it was just beginning to dawn on Mike Lewis that people had actually been killed, close friends.

'Where is he?' he quizzed Bill Bailey about Pete Brouard. 'Where's Pete?'

'Don't ask him,' Terry Pendrous said quietly. 'Don't ask him.'

But he already had. Scouse Lacey, he thought, had heard that the Wafu had been blown over the side. It all kick-started a headcount in Lewis's mind. Where's Pete? Where's Steve Heyes? But you can't count. You daren't believe the good news. You don't want to believe the bad.

Then someone says, 'No, I saw so-and-so go off . . .' and, in the end, it all descends to frustration.

An arm's reach away, maybe, Buck Taylor was next to Bernie Berntsen in the Junior Ratings' Messdeck too, searching the faces he could see from his slim vantage point, too tired to do anything but sit and look – for one face in particular. Word had begun to filter down.

'Have you seen Knocker?' Bernie asked the young Geordie. Buck wished he had.

A moment or two later, Bernie took up the offer of a shower. He wandered from the Mess, stripped off and, for the first time in what seemed like a lifetime, felt warm water. Then his mind wandered.

The only way to salvage hope was to believe – as Naggers did – that, if *he'd* come through, maybe the guys missing aft would have escaped with a trip to the Sickbay. Maybe, but no one was betting.

Not Leigh Slatter. The day he'd joined *Ardent*, 18 months before, he'd found the Queen's Head and been confronted by the drunkest matelot he'd ever seen. Mick Mullen. In minutes, the Scouser had bought everyone a drink. In hours, he'd explained the art of out-drinking, out-singing and black-catting anyone in the 21 Club – and how to lie in the name of pride, and in the face of failure, when you arrived back on board. In months, he'd become an accomplished drinking partner.

Mick Mullen. One of those guys who really didn't care about promotion. Give him a can of paint, leave him to it. A heart of gold. Generous to a fault. Loyal to his friends. A pain in the arse to others. Now no one was answering his name in the Joss's roll call. Nor Stretch Armstrong's. Nor Ginger Nelson's. Nor Andy Barr's. Nor Mick Foote's. It was devastating.

❖❖❖

At 1905, as Capt Scott-Masson's *Canberra* crew prepared space in the troopship's Meridian Room to receive survivors, while *Plymouth* hooked up to *Argonaut* to help weigh the battered Leander's anchor, as *Broadsword* guarded the San Carlos narrows, *Yarmouth* began to move. Or, at least, she tried.

In the half-hour alongside, her starboard screw had remained entangled with *Ardent*'s anchor cable. Capt Morton couldn't go astern, the most seamanlike move, because of the danger posed by *Ardent*'s burning Torpedo Magazine. He had no option but to go ahead.

While a Fo'c'sle party prepared to cut the cable, Morton tried all he knew to edge his ship to safety. It took valuable time. The fires spread closer to *Ardent*'s ordnance, but he eventually succeeded.

On the Flight Deck, Nigel Langhorn and Tom Williams stood arm-in-arm, shocked, almost crying. Eighty minutes before, Langhorn had witnessed his Diving Store filling the sky on the ship's port side. But it was only as *Yarmouth* pulled away that he had his first sight of the damage that had forced them to leave her. It was his last sight of *Ardent*, Williams's too.

Not many paces away, a tearful Lenny Yeatman saw *Yarmouth* slip the lines bonding her to *Ardent*, then watched as, wave by wave, the sea between them opened up.

'Joss, you'd better get down below,' one of *Yarmouth*'s Flight tried to suggest quietly.

'Have you got a big enough team to make me?' Yeatman snapped. But, of course, he had to.

It was his last sight of *Ardent*. If that was grim, though, the task ahead was grimmer.

He'd known his lads for a year or more. He'd lived with them, laughed with them, asked many of them to hold his glasses, required some to stand and receive their summary justice, but there were still moments as he trawled the Messdecks when he looked at his list, then studied the face, and could he remember the name? Could he hell. It was upsetting.

In the Aft Junior Ratings' Mess, Wyatt Earp saw the look in the Joss's eyes and knew whatever he'd seen down below on his final, sweeping search of *Ardent*'s Lower Deck, had totally changed him.

Yeatman read names from the list and waited for a reply. Two made Wyatt Earp look up. 'Stephen Ford? Alistair Leighton?'

His young mates' names echoed round the grey bulkheads. The last time he'd seen them was from the Hangar, in their fearnought suits, a thumb in the smoke-logged air, 'It's under control.' Then they'd gone back down to Ken Enticknap's Aft Section Base.

No one answered the Joss's call.

'Fuck!' The 18 year old's heart sank and he trudged out of the Mess Square and lay down in one of *Yarmouth*'s gulches. Within seconds, the very worst thing happened.

'Air Raid Warning Red! Air Raid Warning Red!'

Not again!

The vents were crashed immediately and the rumble of them slowing sounded like a bomb dropping.

The call, the hum, then the silence. To a man, the Yarmouths hit the deck. There was enough room for everyone to take cover, but not everyone could summon the will.

In the middle of it, Mike Lewis ripped off his anti-flash mask. 'Bollocks to it! It's going to get me, but I'm not wearing this any more.' He'd given up.

Dickie Henderson had just taken up smoking again after five years, just heard the Joss asking, 'Have you seen . . .?' and realised the names were Aft DCP lads. Then the air raid warning.

Lt Mike Knowles was thinking about this as well. He was with Alan Maunder, surrounded by most of the ship's company, aching to walk forward because aft was where *Ardent* had been savaged. But there wasn't a damn thing he could do about it. This was what it was like to be hunted. It had become personal. They were after J.M. Knowles. He looked at Maunder and the Navigating Officer was absolutely ashen, already despairing from the realisation that, if names hadn't been answered from Lenny Yeatman's call, they were still on board. And if they were still on board . . .

'God, you look awful!' Knowles muttered.

'You want to see yourself!'

Fate had been kinder to Lt Tom Williams. With nowhere to rest, he'd taken up Captain Bob's offer to join him in the wood-panelled Wardroom as the Tannoy yelled: 'Air Raid Warning Red! Air Raid Warning Red!'

The giant soldier was pouring them brandies as *Yarmouth*'s First Lieutenant walked in. What else could Williams do? It wasn't his ship. He didn't have a job. It was the worst moment.

On his own, he'd have been thinking, 'Oh shit!' Like everyone. But Bob had said, 'Bugger it! If I'm going to be shot at . . .' That was good enough for the Welshman. So they clicked glasses, and waited.

Many of the Ardents squeezed into the Aft POs' Mess were still pulling off their soaking overalls. The chilling call meant significantly different things to men who'd been caught aft at 1744 and 1806 than it did to those who'd been forward.

'Air Raid Warning Red! Air Raid Warning Red!'

Bernie Berntsen was jolted from the soothing warmth of the shower. He could run, or he could lie down. He just stood there instead, convinced they couldn't hit the Ardents again.

Iain McRobbie was in an Aft Messdeck, asking about Eric Samson, the life-loving Ulsterman.

'He's in the Dining Hall,' someone answered.

'Air Raid Warning Red! Air Raid Warning Red!'

McRobbie remembers the response.

'The bastards ain't gonna get us now.' He now wonders if any of them really believed it.

There wasn't enough room for everyone to hit the deck in the Dining Hall, so Dave Lee stood where he was, like most Ardents.

'Air Raid Warning Red! Air Raid Warning Red!'

For Big John Leake, the moment was shocking. As those four words bounced off the bulkheads, he realised he was stuck below, feeling what the rest had felt when the bombs were falling on *Ardent*.

'Air Raid Warning Red! Air Raid Warning Red!'

'For fuck's sake!' Brum Serrell felt helpless. Haven't we had enough for one day?'

Lt David Searle was halfway through being undressed, and was bruised and cut, but aware there were people around him much more badly carved up than he was.

Ralph Coates was one. He had shrapnel in his leg, back and chest, and his eardrums were burst. But he was oblivious to his injuries and the terror the warning was bringing to his mates. He'd just come round in the Sickbay. He recalls killick chef Dave Trotter lying right next to him, his lower back split wide open, oozing God knows what. But he remembers nothing else.

On the Upper Deck, Andrew Gordon Lennox had his ship's company roll in his hand, ticking off names but seeing a lot of blanks staring back at him, confirming what he already feared. The echoing call stopped him. For the first time, he had time to be scared. He doesn't know why, but he ran to the Bridge faster than he'd ever moved in a ship before.

All available eyes on the Bridge were welded to binoculars, all pointing at the sky, desperate to pick out black dots traversing the grey–green backcloth of Falkland Sound with the speed of a bullet. If there was ever anything there, it never came close enough to engage with close-range weapons.

That was no consolation to Wyatt Earp. The silence greeting Florrie and

Buzz's names had sent him to some Junior Messdeck gulch. He flopped down and looked at the bottom of the bunk above and saw faces staring back, a girlfriend, maybe family, photos meaning something to the man who slept here.

Then it hit him. He didn't know who they were, but he began replacing all the faces with his own family. He started sobbing, thinking, 'What a waste.'

'Air Raid Warning Red! Air Raid Warning Red!'

The Malvern teenager didn't move, even when someone raced in saying, 'You need to take cover!'

The young Ardent was still in his ovies and gloves, soaking. He had a nosebleed. He was in a mess.

'You need to take cover!'

'They can come and get me.'

Back in the Seamen's Mess, bodies were still taut, waiting. But nothing happened.

The 'not again' look on Lenny Yeatman's face must have been obvious.

'Don't worry, Joss,' a young Yarmouth turned to him and smiled, 'our PWO panics at shitehawks.'

The Master at Arms laughed. It was just what he needed.

When they opened the hatches again, that's what Russ Goble needed. To be out of there.

He squeezed through the tight manhole cover, breathed deeply and began watching the line of men moving from the Sickbay and Forward First-Aid Post to the Flight Deck, ready to go to *Canberra*.

One face stayed with him. To this day, he's convinced he saw Knocker White in the queue. Then he went one way, and they went another.

Bob Young was among them. He knew he was badly hurt because the leg of his once-only suit was filling with blood. The shivering and shaking was the shock that had set in on *Ardent*. For one horrible moment, he thought he was losing his marbles too. There in front of him in *Yarmouth*'s main passage was Surg. Cdr Rick Jolly, dressed in flying overalls. What was he doing there, dressed like that?

It would be some hours before Jolly's heroics became apparent. For now, the big RM medic's cool greeting was all Young had. The tale of Enticknap and his young saviour would come later.

Jolly moved swiftly to the Sickbay and wasted no time trying to decide if any casualty needed immediate transfer, stepping from man to man, hooking his arms beneath theirs, declaring 'Okay for winching' as he eased them back down. None needed moving straightaway.

Minutes later, as he was winched into an 846 Sqdn Sea King, Young was greeted by Smiler Grinney, an old Yeovilton mate. It was as if everyone he'd known in his career was helping him to survive. The pair exchanged smiles.

Minutes later, the Sea King approached *Canberra* and Young's heart sank again. They weren't planning to dump them on this bloody great white thing, were they? They were.

✦✦✦

Lenny Yeatman stepped on to *Yarmouth*'s Bridge, then stopped in his tracks. All he could see were white-clad figures in anti-flash gear. Their eyes turned to him, but who was who? He was thrown, totally, until Alan West stepped from behind a screen.

Minutes later, the Captain left the Bridge and went down to see his men. Some were in a bad way, distressed at leaving their ship and their mates behind. It upset him to see them like that.

'You'd come from this pedestal where you'd gone through COST, you'd gone through JMC and then, suddenly, you've lost the thing you thought was . . .' Mick Newby's voice trails. 'Some people might say, "We came home without a bullet hole." Well, where were you? We didn't come home with the ship. It's all about what you achieved during the time you were there.'

'You all right?' In one of *Yarmouth*'s grey passageways, Lenny Yeatman bumped into Tony Ray.

'I'm bloody well not. All I want to do is go home,' the DMEO replied, or words to that effect. All he could think about was Ken Enticknap. 'Are you going to tell Frankie or am I?'

As the missing Aft Section Base Chief's boss, Ray felt it was his job. But it could equally be the Joss's responsibility. So the pair tossed a coin. Neither remembers who won.

Eighteen-year-old Buck Taylor was wrestling with a similar dilemma. It didn't matter who said what about Knocker. 'He's made it.' 'He hasn't.' How many railway-platform promises had been extracted back home? All Buck could think was, 'I've got to go and see Brenda.' He had to see Knocker's mum.

✦✦✦

At about 2000, the Ardents mustered once more in the cold air of Falkland Sound. Behind the low-slung clouds, the sun was going down. The Ardents watched landing craft pull alongside *Yarmouth*'s Flight Deck, ready to transfer them to *Canberra*.

At 2006, the sun set. Too late. Two hours too late.

As they waited to leave the Type 12, Mick Cox talked to Tony Ray. The man they couldn't account for was Ken Enticknap. Him and Ginger Nelson. Cox was convinced he'd seen the PTI escaping from the Tiller Flat, through the smoke and flames, with another man.

Then, one by one, the Ardents left *Yarmouth* too, a straggling line lost in thought, filing into a couple of LCUs. Some found the step simple. For others, the vulnerability was more than they could handle.

A Royal Marine reached up to guide Mike Lewis down the ladder.

'Christ, I can do this on me own,' Lewis thought. But he couldn't.

John Foster stepped on board having difficulty seeing. He'd never put a once-only suit on before. Next time, he vowed, if there was a next time, he'd put it on the right way round.

For the first time since they'd separated at the foot of the Workshop Flat ladder a minute after the first hit, Brum Serrell set eyes on Jan Joyce, just a thumbs-up, but it helped him put a piece into place.

AB Mike Roe and other Yarmouths up top exchanged waves and good wishes, convinced that only a couple of Ardents had been hurt. Maybe.

Leigh Slatter had just bumped into Eddy Bogey, an old shipmate from his HMS *Blake* days, and told him Mick Foote was missing. Bogey couldn't believe it. He and Foote had been drinking partners. He swore vengeance. Slatter looked at him. He didn't know what Bogey thought he could do, but if it made him feel better.

While one LCU set off for *Canberra* via *Fearless*, the other headed straight for the Great White Whale in San Carlos Water. As they did, Slatter looked back and caught sight of Bogey, standing on *Yarmouth*'s GDP, yelling obscenities at the sky. Suddenly, the firepower demo seemed an age away.

Minutes later, in his world, Jon Major watched the cruise ship grow bigger. To the cook, only a week out of his teenage years and unaware that Foote might have gone aft to his death, the Whale was lit up like a Mississippi ferryboat. 'Why did they hit us?' It didn't make sense.

At 2030, while everyone at home was half an hour from the *Nine O'Clock News*, the surviving Ardents boarded *Canberra*. After escorting her to war from Ascension, now she would protect them.

◆◆◆

The Thin Grey Line had taken a bad beating. As the men of 3 Commando prepared to swap places in the LCUs, Capt Chris 'Beagle' Burne explained to *Canberra*'s ship's company just how bad.

'This has been a day I shall never forget,' his voice echoed round the liner. 'It has been marked by courage, humour and sadness. One of the sadnesses is that we have on board at the moment the ship's company, the gallant ship's company, of HMS *Ardent*. Be aware of the fact that some are injured and others lost. In fact, there has been a bitter air battle going on throughout the day in the Falkland Sound and sitting here watching the Naval frigates do it has made me proud to be a Naval officer.'

So had it all been worthwhile? That depended on where you'd spent the day.

As the 'Beagle' spoke, CPO Michael Fellows and his Damage Control parties had cut a tunnel through *Antrim*'s twisted spaces and were edging the destroyer's unexploded bomb towards the water.

On the frigate *Argonaut*, Lt Cdr Brian Dutton and his team were achieving the same miracle in the Seacat Magazine. While Dutton sweated, within six feet of the device, Chief Stoker Michael Townsend was welding a four-feet square steel plate over the hole near the waterline. Fellows would win a Distinguished Service Cross for his work, Dutton a DSO and Townsend a DSM.

To Admiral Sandy Woodward, the signals returning to *Hermes* made grim

reading: *Ardent* was sinking; *Argonaut* and *Antrim* were severely damaged; *Brilliant* and *Broadsword* had slight damage; only *Plymouth* and *Yarmouth*, the oldest ships of the force, were unscathed. In 50 sorties in and around San Carlos Water, the enemy had lost three Pucaras, six Daggers and five Skyhawks.

Ardent had been in a seven-strong line of defence. Her men had stopped counting when the number of attacks hit 17. But the troops were ashore on their most perilous day. Not one casualty had been·inflicted on the landing troops by the Argentinians. The Thin Grey Line had done its job, and *Ardent* had paid the ultimate price.

Alan West's men climbed the accommodation ladder which led from the ship-side port to a small pontoon she'd been using for troop movements all day. Then they stepped through a gun port door high on *Canberra*'s side, many still in their 8s and woolly pullies, smelling of fire and smoke, feeling very sorry for themselves, lost and a long way from home.

They filed past lines of fighting companies waiting to go ashore, laden with ammunition and backpacks, faces blackened with camouflage cream, weapons cradled in their arms, clapping quietly. They connected these grimy and exhausted men with their own safety. *Ardent* had fought for them.

On the sidelines, Rick Jolly watched the line move slowly and looked at virtually every face in it. He was moved. Trapped in their troopships, the soldiers had placed their faith in the Royal Navy's willingness to put themselves between the landing forces and the enemy. Men like these.

Like Brum Serrell. As the new arrivals shuffled on, someone behind him offered a request to the pongos: 'Go on. We've done our bit. Give them some shit back.'

Like Andy Cox. He swears there was blood in their eyes before the last Ardent had passed.

With nothing more than they stood in, they formed a new queue for the Meridian Room and collected their tot of rum, can of beer and 20 fags in return for their names to go on a survivors' signal home.

Like Joe Laidlaw. He waited patiently, listening as the solemn applause rippled down the corridor. 'Okay, we've lost four or five people,' he thought. 'It's sad for us, but look what it did.'

Cliff Goldfinch waited too, feeling nothing but respect for the P&O crew. They were doing far more than the Ardents, he thought. He'd done a job he'd signed on to do. The merchant crew had not.

Like Topsy Turner. He owed John Dillon 50 pence. Now Dillon, the lanky 18 year old who'd spent his day in the Aft Damage Control Party, was missing. Turner took a 50 pence piece from his pocket and hurled it into the sea.

Iain McRobbie saw a face he knew before long: Taff Cooper, a Marine who'd served on *Nubian*.

'What are you doing here?' Cooper asked.

Then a steward moved towards him, pushing a trolley loaded with packets of fags and paper cups full of Four Bells rum. The Scot downed three before someone convinced him it was their turn.

He wasn't the only one whose past appeared. Richie Gough bumped into Ed Candlish.

'I survived a Gazelle being shot down today,' the former *Mohawk* flyer told him.

'Yeah? I survived the *Ardent* being sunk.'

One by one, the Ardents stepped forward to Lauraine Mulberry and Helen Hawkett.

'What's your name?' one of them asked John Foster.

He sat down and his mind went blank. 'Leave that one with me,' he paused, 'I'll get back to you!'

'Can you remember what your name is?' she pressed him gently. Foster started to well up.

'John,' someone behind cut in, 'it's Foster!'

One by one, they moved on. Not on to head-counting, because that was pointless in this shifting sea of men, but to look for faces, many still shaking. Bang! Bang! Bang! Bang! Bang! Then they were sitting there and a lot of others weren't.

As the last Ardent cleared reception – around 150 of them according to Lauraine Mulberry's count – Andy Andrew gathered his stokers and Pete Rowe did the same with his gunnery teams. There were big holes in Andrew's ranks, but Rowe was able to find all his men. The Chief GI thought he detected an urgency among them to help *Canberra*'s crew to man the guns, but there was no need.

Mike Lewis soon saw Chris Evans, the Yeoman. Great. But he was still concerned for Mal Crane because, the last thing he'd heard, the Buffer was heading aft. On the other hand, he still hadn't given up hope that Pete Brouard would stroll round a corner any second.

In the mêlée, Wyatt Earp found himself talking to men of 42 Commando who'd been frustrated in their ambition to go ashore because some of their kit had left with 45 Commando. While the problem was sorted, they shared a bottle of whisky and asked the baby-faced stoker what the islands were like.

What could he tell them? He hadn't even seen the place.

Tom Williams felt little better when a man in Army fatigues sauntered up to him, drawn by a face which was white and green in patches from the stresses, the successes and the horrors of the day. 'What was it like?' he asked.

'Busy!' Williams told him. 'There were guys on the Upper Deck who fought like tigers.'

He mentioned the name John Leake, and they continued to pass what was left of the time of the day.

Eventually, the bootneck departed for whatever lay ahead of him.

'D'you know who that was?' a *Canberra* crew member wandered up to Williams as he left.

Williams didn't. The man wasn't a booty, he was a journalist. For years, Williams thought it was Brian Hanrahan, but it was the BBC's radio man, Robert Fox.

'They fought like tigers.' Those four words would reverberate round the world in the coming couple of days, until the news agenda pushed on with the landing troops, and left the Ardents behind.

◆◆◆

Left behind with what? The drills of a thousand endless Portland hours had given them their best chance of survival. Amsterdam, Narvik, Union Street too. Fight, float, move. Systems, procedure, luck, adrenaline. In whatever order, at

whatever point, they'd proved to be fallible, or simply run out. And no amount of discipline, desire, pride or spirit had been enough to change that.

Now there was no clock to watch any more, no schedule to meet, no job to do. A void.

So, by 2100, cabins allocated, they mustered again in the Meridian Room, ready to be pointed in the next direction, another chance to compare head-counts and wonder what was in store. It wasn't what Errol Flynn, for one, wanted. He just wanted to be alone. He didn't want to know who hadn't made it.

For a strange moment, Jon Major's mind turned to the bread rolls they'd left baking in *Ardent*'s ovens, then his attention was diverted by some good news. He hadn't seen Shaun Hanson since before the first hit, but now it seemed he was in the hospital. Knocker White too.

'Thank God for that!' Major remembers Bernie Berntsen saying.

In truth, Berntsen wasn't certain how much hope to hang on second- and third-hand information. Still dressed in his 56-inch chest, 46-inch waist Second World War survivor's kit, and the boots given to him by a Yarmouth, he was coming down now. Literally. In the past couple of hours, he'd heard it all.

'Have you seen Knocker?'

'No. Not since so-and-so. Have you seen Knocker?'

'Not since so-and-so.'

'Buzz Leighton? Where is he?'

'Florrie Ford? Where is he?' To the 33 year old, they were kids.

'What about Ginge?'

'Has anyone seen Mick Foote?'

'Simon Lawson?'

'Micky Mullen?'

'John Dillon?'

'Peddler Palmer?'

'What are you talking about? They've got to be here somewhere!'

In odd corners, in plush corridors, the names of 50-odd Ardents were muttered. What did 'missing' mean? Where else would they have been taken? Most of their questions were soon answered.

At 2100, Alan West cleared Lower Deck and stood in front of his men. He faltered occasionally, but he was determined to pick them up, tell them what they'd achieved, let them know who the casualties were, and who wasn't accounted for, and assure them it hadn't been in vain.

'They'd done a bloody good job,' he thinks back. 'In the final analysis there was one person who made the decision to abandon ship, and that was the Captain, not them. I wanted to make that clear.'

Groans greeted every name. There was nothing he could do. There were more names on the list than he'd lost, he was certain. But, until the stragglers were accounted for, no one could say they'd survived.

Once he'd finished addressing them, he wandered from group to group, trying to keep the spirit together. At 34, he was younger than many men he commanded. But not everyone was keen to listen.

'I didn't really want to hear any more, at that stage,' Russ Goble admits. 'I knew there'd been a death in the Hangar. I'd seen someone. I presumed there

were deaths down below. But then we heard that Knocker White had gone, and Mick Mullen. He was a nice lad. Thick-set bloke. Sturdy. Reliable. Andy Barr too. Andy slept above me, and Mick slept above him.'

Iain McRobbie thought of the day he and Peddler Palmer joined up together at HMS *Ganges*. Was there ever anyone as proud to be a matelot than the giant Cornishman? Not many, Robbie admits.

But the bad news was rapidly laced with good. Ken Enticknap's name was among the missing but, as soon as West's briefing was complete, Tony Ray had word that he was in the Sickbay.

As Ray strode into the makeshift casualty ward in the ship's casino, he didn't know what to expect. The wounded Aft Section Base Chief looked dreadful, but at least he was alive. Then the DMEO went to find the cabin he'd share with Bill Bailey.

The Flight Weapons Engineer had already been mesmerised by his new surroundings. The change of clothing into a white boilersuit had been arranged with the efficiency of a Butlin's holiday camp and the cabin was the most luxurious room he'd seen in his life.

But two things would remain in his memory forever. The cabin had a bath, and a steward asked him if he could fetch a selection of books from the library. From the fires of hell to the lap of luxury. It was too much. As Tony Ray tried to start putting the day into perspective, Bailey broke down in tears.

Contrast. Conflict. Emotions. Dickie Henderson was in a cabin with Errol Flynn – a big man who didn't want to be here sharing the hardest moments of his life with a little man who didn't mind the surroundings but wanted to be a million miles from any reminder of the day.

'You were ecstatic that you were saved,' Henderson admits, 'and you thought you were going home, because they hadn't actually said what they were going to do with us. I didn't want to stay there.'

But, even as he wondered, he was thinking 'It'll be great when we get home, because we'll be heroes.' Then he felt guilty. He couldn't win.

Bit by bit, the descent into uncertainty was matched by inactivity and more of the absurd. While the junior ratings ate in the Atlantic Restaurant, the officers and senior rates dined in the Pacific. Men who'd last eaten a rock cake on the run from Carballo's Skyhawk faltered on the steps down to the vast room. The lamps cast a soothing glow on menu cards and silver service, not Ops Room screens. This might as well have been the Caribbean. Chill out. Come down. Limbo.

One by one, like refugees, some picking shrapnel from their legs, they were shown to their seats.

'There was I, dressed like an off-watch gipsy, in survival kit for a 16-stone, small-footed man, and a snapper of a waiter attending to me as if I was Royalty.' Jeff Curran still doesn't believe it happened.

While some risked the steak and crab, Cliff Goldfinch was less adventurous. He stuck to corned beef – Argentinian – boiled potato and salad.

At one stage, a few buns dropped to the floor and their waiter started picking them up.

'Don't worry,' Goldfinch tried to reassure him. 'Put them on the plate. We haven't eaten all day.'

A few tables away, bewildered in Fantasyland, naïve to journalistic ways, Pete Brierley found himself with two scruffy-looking civilians, talking freely about what had happened – sea dits like firing on cows, or loosing off chaff at geese, oblivious to the timebomb fuse he was lighting.

The names John Leake and Cliff Goldfinch peppered the chat, the NAAFI manager and the PO Cook who'd claimed a Skyhawk kill, if the rumours were right. The journalists were attentive, but not attentive enough.

As the meal wore on, men split off in ones and twos and Surg. Cdr Rick Jolly took the opportunity to speak with Ardent's Captain. West looked shocked. He was pale and stinking of smoke as the ebullient medic described the breathless moments of Ken Enticknap's and John Dillon's rescues. As they spoke, the First Lieutenant came up with a blue nylon bag.

'What have you got there, Number One?' West asked wearily.

'Some mail, sir.'

'Well, you've got more than I've got.'

Jolly saw West's tired eyes, and it dawned on him. Here was a man who had nothing, someone no Royal Navy commanding officer wanted to be – a Captain who'd abandoned his ship.

◆◆◆

The first thing Ken Enticknap remembers of waking on *Canberra* was being covered in field dressings, then seeing Tony Ray and Andrew Gordon Lennox peering at him. At least, he thinks it was the first thing. Minute by minute, the night was becoming a disorientated blur of faces and information.

'You're all right. You're on the *Canberra*,' Tony Ray said.

Enticknap took it as a good sign, but he didn't have a clue what *Canberra* was.

'It's all right, I've put you on the seriously ill list,' the First Lieutenant tried to reassure him.

Before long, his view of the world changed with the arrival of a couple of packing cases and he was lifted on to a mattress. Around the same time, he assumes, Pete Rowe appeared at his 'bedside'.

'That AB did a good job getting you out,' the Chief GI said.

That AB? The name 'DILLON' on white tape above the left breast pocket of the young radar rating's 8s, was in Enticknap's mind, if only deep down. Rowe looked towards the 17 year old, then beyond, to a young Argentinian lying in the next bed, Miguel Garcia.

Minutes later – it might have already happened, for all he recalls – a doctor came to tend Enticknap's wounds and apologised. They were going to have to put a couple of homeward-bounders in his head, large stitches to pull together something awful, the kind of thing you'd expect to see in a sail, not flesh.

If they weren't too busy in the next few days, he promised, they'd do the proper job. They never did.

'I'm not that pretty anyway, so it didn't matter,' Enticknap laughs now.

He may have looked like he'd been through a mincer, but his sense of humour was still intact. If the rest had had their survivor's tot, he wanted his too. He was due for theatre so, much to Morgan O'Connell's annoyance, when Rick Jolly

270

appeared, he rubbed a drop of rum on Enticknap's lips. The big medic wished him a speedy recovery, then downed what was left. He was on a high.

A few days later, O'Connell would prescribe a tot of whisky himself, to help his patient sleep.

◆◆◆

Their meal over, either defeated by nervous belly or not, cabins found, plusher than a Section Base deck tile, the Ardents sought refuge.

Blagging possessions wasn't too hard. *Canberra* crew and Commandos almost fell over themselves to share what they had. Pete Brierley ended up with some old socks from a Marine sergeant and a pair of white overalls with cut-off arms from one of the ship's company. For days, he'd wonder why he was given funny looks whenever he wore them. Eventually, he'd find out that they'd belonged to the biggest queen on board.

Another Marine took Bernie Berntsen to the ragged edge in the Purser's Office, as he was queuing for money. The bootneck chomped through: bergen, rifle, helmet, cammed-up, and stopped.

'What you waiting for?' he asked the slim, short stoker.

'Some money.'

The Marine put his hand in a pocket. 'Here you are, boy,' he handed him a bundle of cash. 'I won't be needing that where I'm going.'

A former sonar rating who'd joined the Marines – a Welshman called Taff, unsurprisingly – hunted out cabinmates Andy Cox and Mick Newby. For the two Ardents, the drinking had started with their paper cups of Four Bells rum as they'd left the landing craft. Now Taff weighed in with a supply of booze, and underpants too.

By this time, Newby had already taken Karoly Nagy to one side and given him the benefit of his opinion. This was his mother's fault. He was fuming.

'For God's sake, it's only a letter!'

'She put a curse on the ship!' Newby told him.

With each mouthful of beer, in some quarters, the reluctance to share the sights and sounds of the day receded. They broke off in threes and fours, or moved from man to man, grabbing morsels, hoping the next word would carry hope, desperate to feel unburdened by explaining to someone what it was like.

'Knocker was in the Dining Hall. He didn't come past me and he couldn't go anywhere else, because he was in the SCC Flat so, more or less . . .'

Or 'I knew instantly about Florrie Ford . . .'

Or 'He was a scally. I've always thought of him as my little brother . . .'

Or 'What was it like back there?' then 'It's hard to explain,' then 'Christ! I didn't know that.'

Men who hadn't seen their mates killed disbelieved the news, even after Alan West's solemn early list of missing. It had been so quick.

'One minute we were together. The next, half of us gone, with no bodies to say that they were ever there.' Bill Bailey.

'You try and tell them that the back end's been blown off. It was an

incredible ship. Wrecked. Opened up with a razor blade. That supreme confidence . . .' Joe Laidlaw.

'It's like "I'm All Right Jack." That's the hard way of seeing it. You looked around and you just knew you were never going to see them again.' Karoly Nagy just tried to accept it.

A lot of the young stokers stayed up that night, playing cards and working out who wasn't alive.

Navy life. The wind-up. Go with the flow. But it would still probably never sink in. In Bernie Berntsen's cabin, Wyatt Earp, John Goddard and Wolfie Price were coming to the same conclusion.

'Well, Buzz is missing,' Bernie ventured, and Wolfie began to cry.

'I'm with his sister,' he sobbed. He'd recently met her. They hadn't known.

The junior officers sought refuge in alcohol too. After dinner, Nigel Langhorn sought David Searle in the makeshift Sickbay, conscious of his promise to Searle's new bride, Jenny, that he'd look after him. They talked and Langhorn came away with a new insight into what had brought Searle to within inches of his life.

After he left, he bumped into an acquaintance and took up the invitation to share a bottle of whisky in his cabin. Tom Williams and Mike Knowles joined them and, while they weren't revisiting their repertoire on a borrowed guitar, they trawled over the day, a roller-coaster of guilt, frustration and anger. When the anger came, their glasses suffered, smashed against the bulkhead.

Separated from his Wardroom companions, David Searle's chat with Nigel Langhorn had been a vital chance to start gluing together what events he could remember. There was precious little.

◆◆◆

At some point, the Watch and Station Bill had to tally with the names on the lists Lenny Yeatman and Andrew Gordon Lennox were carrying round. The two retired to the Master at Arms's cabin. They ran down the lists and, when they'd finished, there were 30 people unaccounted for. All the men left to be checked, one final time, were those who'd been 'casevaced from *Yarmouth*. So, the conclusion after their next visit to the surgical wards would be inevitable. If the missing weren't there . . .

When they arrived, Ken Enticknap and John Dillon were in surgery. Then Lenny Yeatman heard word that Bob Young had been with Simon Ridout in the seconds before the 1806 hits.

Young was pleased to be in the ward, rather than the casualty reception area. He'd been greeted there by more people he knew, but the room had glass walls. Not good. Not good at all. So, lying on a stretcher, he'd distracted himself by watching a pool of blood spread on the floor beneath his leg.

Scouse Phillips was already in the ward by the time Young had arrived, still not totally aware of where he was or what had happened, and nursing the mother and father of all headaches. They all were.

Before long, the Jimmy appeared at Young's side to see if he could account for anyone. 'Was Simon Ridout with you?'

'I think he went over the side.' He couldn't tell him any more.

So Ridout was lost as well. His name went on the missing list.

272

THROUGH FIRE AND WATER

At around 2200, as the nightly *News at Ten* vigil began at home, Dave Lee found a pen and paper:

Friday 21st May

My Dearest Darling Catherine,

Today has been a day which will live with me for the rest of my life and yet it is a day that I would gladly erase from my memory, if I could, as it must be the worst day of my life in terms of fear and the acceptance that it could only be my last day of life.

It has only been a few hours since the terrible happening so please excuse me if I convey what I feel in this letter now instead of leaving it to the morning. I would be but one place now if I could and that would be home with you, not to talk about it, but to talk of other things.

I am, thankful to God, fully well physically but at the moment mentally drained. I can only think of you my lovely and how you had to contend with those hours before you knew that I was well. I couldn't possibly sleep just now even though I've had little for two days.

My last letter to you is still in the Ardent where it now belongs because I had written to you about my fear of the 'next few days' although I could never have comprehended what was to follow the day after. I wrote it because I had to 'talk' to someone and there was nobody I could find comfort from apart from you. After a couple of days have passed I will write again my lovely, probably when the full force of today has subsided a little.

My thoughts are now that you're well my darling, ready to receive me home for the 'last' reunion, that the children are well and happy; all of you waiting for me.

Those families who have lost their loved ones today I feel such close sorrow for them, such a waste, such a loss of happiness. If I read this letter tomorrow I might tear it up but we are allowed anyway just this one letter so it will probably stay. I just want to be home now with you my darling, no more, no less. Until then my love stays with you. David.
XXXXXXXXX

XXXXX Stuart XXXXX Sharon

The letter would arrive home on Friday, 4 June.

✦✦✦

They might have had the Pacific Restaurant and the Crow's Nest Bar to call their own but, that night, most of the senior rates headed aft to be with the lads.

It was here and in the Sickbay, and in the passageways between, where the what-ifs began. For some it was a purge. For others it marked the start of the

search for answers to ease the guilt, to calm the fear of ever being out of control again, because look what happened when you lost it; the conviction that, if they'd done this first, or that after, or hadn't turned left when they might have turned right that, somehow, it might not have happened. The what-ifs.

Why had Seacat failed at 1744 when it had gone off three times in emergency control? Richie Gough couldn't understand.

Could Command have done more for the people down aft? Lt David Searle didn't know.

Why didn't the guys leaving the SCC tell Dickie Henderson they were off, and not leave him on his own until Mick Langley's head appeared from the AARM hatch? They only had to turn round and yell 'Get out!' or whatever. And why, why, why hadn't he taken one look, just one look, back towards the Junior Ratings' Dining Hall when he and Langley hurried the same way minutes later?

For every second of every minute between 1744 and 1815, there were a million what-ifs.

Henderson walked nervously up to Ken Enticknap's bedside after he came out of surgery. He had to ask about Knocker. As they talked about the fires, all he could think was, 'Right, did I do everything I could have done?'

Then Henderson saw Ralph Coates, and realised he'd come out of the Dining Hall. He saw the young stoker's wounds and said, 'What are you doing here?'

He looked up and down the rows of men and saw John Dillon next to a young Argentinian. Then it began to dawn. People like Knocker weren't upstairs in the big room, and they weren't in the hospital.

Eddie Edwards ventured in with Joe Laidlaw and soon made the same calculation, and it dawned on him too that Knocker was dead. Or, if he wasn't, he was still on the *Ardent*. It amounted to the same thing.

Laidlaw looked at the Argentinians and thought, 'You bastards!'

Cliff Goldfinch stood at the door not long after and made a mental note of where men were. It would stay with him for years. The lighting marked the room as a casino. Mick Beckett was on the left-hand side, with Bob Young next, and the rest of the superficially wounded in a row, Scouse Lacey included.

Then, in the centre and the right, lying motionless on packing cases and mattresses, where all the main lights were, he saw the men who were gambling for their lives. Among them was Ken Enticknap. Goldfinch walked up to him. He looked like shit but, like the rest, the PO Cook tried to let small-talk deal with the shock.

'How you doing?'

'Can you write this letter?' Enticknap replied.

'What's that?'

Breaking the news to Frankie, that was what. But he'd had time to work out how to do it gently. He began to dictate.

'I wish to report the loss of one wedding ring!' he recited. 'I know where it is. My finger's with it!'

The trickle of visitors went on, and so did the search for faces. Among them, late that evening, oblivious to where Naggers had gone, Buck Ryan wandered into the Sickbay looking for Ralph Coates.

'He's over there,' a nurse pointed.

Like the others, Ralph was on a timber frame and drifting in and out of consciousness. It was the start of a long vigil, broken only by trips for scran, which would last a number of days.

Ryan could see the devil-may-care stoker was in a bad way, but he never asked the obvious, 'Is he going to be all right?' He was Ralph. Of course he'd be all right. As for the others . . . well, he was starting to focus, hoping that, just because he couldn't see their faces here, it didn't mean the worst.

Knocker. 'What if he's escaped like Ken?' It seemed logical. Florrie and Buzz were two others.

'Into the water and picked up elsewhere?' He had no way of knowing.

Bernie Berntsen came in too, to see Ken. The Chief was chirpy, he recalls, but it didn't stop him turning at the sight those homeward-bounders etched on his eyes. They also saw Ralph. He was chirpy too. Then they sauntered up the ranks chatting, one last chance to prove to themselves that someone had seen Knocker on the Fo'c'sle, after all, or on a stretcher.

'We were looking. Just looking,' he thinks back. 'But it never happened, did it?'

❖❖❖

In a landing craft heading for San Carlos at about 2230, the most dramatic words of his next despatch forming in his mind, BBC reporter Robert Fox saw a huge blue and red flame on the western horizon. It lit the sky for more than a minute. Then there was a distant rumble.

❖❖❖

It wasn't as soon as Alan West had thought but, while he was writing his report for Admiral Woodward, the fires finally reached *Ardent*'s Torpedo Magazine, six miles beyond Wreck Point. The explosion was huge. He saw the flash to the right of the 800ft ridge and knew what it was.

❖❖❖

Surg. Lt Cdr Morgan O'Connell was prepared to see anger among the *Ardent* survivors. He knew that was part of grief. But it needed to be addressed, because it wouldn't go away on its own. And it could run out of control. He was frightened about intervening, in case he tipped the scales himself. Finally, he went to Alan West and asked for permission to help his men. West agreed.

❖❖❖

Captain Bob – Captain Robert Harmes, 148 Battery Royal Artillery, attached to Special Forces – was in his bunk on *Canberra* before he started to think what the hell had happened. The poor men who'd been killed. The ship. They'd lost the ship. That's when it hit him.

He'd been given his survivor's pack, as all Ardents had, and a pair of Marks & Sparks pants, then acquired a bottle of brandy. He'd also spent a few minutes with Morgan O'Connell and, in reply to the genial Irishman's polite enquiry, he'd asked for the first thing that came into his head, 'A beer!'

He'd had one. It tasted great. Now, though, he was lying down, alone in his cabin, and he didn't want to go back to war. But he had to. He wouldn't be able to live with his guys afterwards if he didn't.

❖❖❖

On *Hermes*, on the eastern fringe of the Battle Group, Lt Clive Morrell sank back in a chair and reflected on the day. He and John Leeming had landed on the carrier at 1845, around the time most of Alan West's men were sliding down ropes to *Yarmouth* or taking a brief, heart-stopping leap of faith into the empty southern air. It was the 800 Sqdn Harriers' last CAP of the day and, on their return, they'd been greeted with the news of *Ardent*'s fate. It wasn't a good feeling. They hadn't been able to prevent the ship being hit. But now there was tomorrow to think about.

The signal was going to come to *Canberra* sooner or later. It was simple and direct. In essence, off-load all your remaining troops and leave the anchorage by midnight, local time, 0400 for the battered *Ardent* body clocks. It gave them five hours.

Major Ward, the Amphibious Operations Officer who'd controlled the off-load all day, didn't have enough hands to do the job. In minutes, the main broadcast was making an appeal to the P&O crew.

'Would anyone off-watch please report to D Deck Flat forward.'

Within minutes, he had his men, a snaking chain, winding from D Deck, humping Kompo ration cases, baggage and ammunition towards the cargo doors and into the cavernous shape of the LCUs. Almost every able Ardent was there, boxes bouncing off bodies already battered by deckplates.

They just went for it. Balls out. It was what they needed, to stay busy, to keep focused, the rhythm of routine, to carry on playing a part in the war.

❖❖❖

'You either screw yourself up and say, "We'll never do it again," in which case, you've lost the war, or you just say, "Perhaps that was a reasonable trade-off. Let's get going."'

The difficulty for COMAW Mike Clapp, the man who'd sent *Ardent* to the gunline, was assessing what was a trade-off and what wasn't. Round a chess table in Whitehall, rules of engagement are easy. The enemy's going to behave this way or that. Then you plan on probability, expectation.

So why hadn't they gone for the high value units, *Fearless*, *Canberra*, instead of the escorts?

Clapp had endured anxiety for the whole operation that day, for the entire Thin Grey Line and their wards. He'd expected to lose more. But that was no comfort to Alan West.

'They concentrated on poor old *Ardent*. She did more than just get hammered. She wasn't put there as a decoy, but she actually was the decoy, unwittingly.'

He didn't have the chance to say 'Well done!' to Alan West and his men. He had his head down. In years to come, he'd realise how much they needed him to tell them that the Thin Grey Line had saved the amphibians, that *Ardent* had done all it could too. Instead, he was left to grit his teeth and reflect that at least she'd closed Darwin and Goose Green, kept 2 Para safe on Sussex Mountains. There was day two of Operation Sutton to consider. The Last Pipe was now consigned to the history books.

◆◆◆

In *Canberra*'s radio room, late that night, Alan West spoke with Captain Jeremy Larken, who'd spent his day with his gunnery teams, exposed on *Fearless*'s Gun Direction Platform, then he sent a personal signal to Admiral Woodward. It contained a list of lessons from the past 24 hours of his life: the value of anti-flash gear; the belief that the ship which kept up a steady and heavy stream of fire would put the enemy off; the fact that, the closer a ship was to shore, the harder it was for all but the truly suicidal pilot, or the phenomenally brave, to stick to his wave-hopping final attack. And there had been many.

It was far from easy. It wouldn't become any easier.

'I found it very difficult indeed for months after that to sleep. Not because people had been lost,' he says now, 'but much more: "What if I'd done this? Should I have done that? How did that happen?"'

So had *Ardent* been a sacrificial lamb? He pauses. 'That thought didn't occur to me,' he says. 'I suppose we were in the most exposed position. They must have known the damage we'd been doing ashore with our NGS. I suppose it was inevitable that our chances of avoiding being hit were very small.

'But, remember, not one man or landing craft was lost going ashore, and *Canberra* wasn't hit either. What *Ardent* and the other picket-line ships did that day was very special. Not many people know.'

His next task was to tell his men how they'd done, to begin giving these 24 hours a context for the rest of their lives and, after the Master at Arms's and the First Lieutenant's heart-breaking search of *Yarmouth* and *Canberra,* to tell them who wasn't going home.

◆◆◆

In one of *Canberra*'s aft bars, chairs upturned like an out-of-hours working men's club, Lenny Yeatman called the ship's company to attention and the Captain and First Lieutenant walked in. Both looked harrowed. West told them to sit down, then gave a brief résumé of their day.

'I don't want any one of you . . .' Alan West began speaking, then hesitated. 'You will go through periods of feeling guilty. You mustn't do that. I am the Captain and, if what we did was wrong, I'll be court-martialled. It was my responsibility.' His final words were, 'Thank you very much. I was proud to sail

with you.' Then he read his list of possible fatalities:

Derek Armstrong (22), Richard Banfield (30), Andrew Barr (20), Peter Brouard (31), Richard Dunkerley (23), Michael Foote (24), Stephen Ford (18), Shaun Hanson (20), Sean Hayward (18) . . .

. . . at some point, he faltered. For a moment, the room was silent. The First Lieutenant stepped towards him and took the list . . . Stephen Heyes (22), Simon Lawson (21), Alistair Leighton (19), Allan McAulay (36), Michael Mullen (24), Brian Murphy (30), Gary Nelson (25), Andrew Palmer (26), Simon Ridout (28), John Roberts (26), John Sephton (35), Stephen White (21), Garry Whitford (23), Gilbert Williams (21).

As he spoke, young men grew up, others started trying to picture their mates. Other minds, unavoidably, drifted to the Junior Ratings' Dining Hall, to the Ship Control Centre, the Flight Deck, the Hangar, flashes to moments on the opposite side of the world, in another age, with backdrops like the Grand Theatre, the 25 Ikkies Bar, sledging in Narvik, moments captured for posterity on the Gronk Board, gone but not forgotten. Never forgotten.

All that was left was to send the names home.

Andrew Gordon Lennox and Lenny Yeatman were joined by Tom Williams in *Canberra*'s hair salon to put the next-of-kin casualty signal together. When they were as certain as they could be, they called up John Foster and, after a change to white overalls, he went to the radio room and began typing.

Canberra's rudimentary off-line equipment meant it would take hours to key, encrypt and check before the list reached C-in-C Fleet in Northwood.

He wasn't looking for names. They leapt at him. 'Missing.' He could forget the buzz now.

Wham!

'He's not dead!'

Wham!

'Gary's been killed.'

He typed on.

Wham!

The Flight.

Peter Brouard, John Sephton, Brian Murphy . . . He'd spoken to them all just before it happened.

Rick Banfield. 'Sir, take damn good care of yourself!' Only joking.

He typed on and felt as if he'd put a curse on them. As if he'd gone round and touched them.

Take damn good care of yourself.

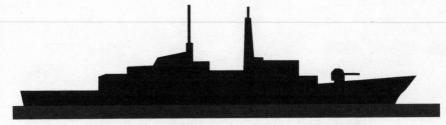

THOUGHTS OF HOME

One   SS *Canberra*, San Carlos Water to Total Exclusion
       Zone, South Atlantic
       (0242–1600hrs, 22 May 1982)   281

Two   SS *Canberra*, Total Exclusion Zone, South Atlantic
       to *QE2*, Cumberland Bay, South Georgia
       (22–28 May 1982)   295

ONE

SS *CANBERRA*, SAN CARLOS WATER TO TOTAL EXCLUSION ZONE, SOUTH ATLANTIC

(0242–1600HRS, 22 MAY 1982)

At 0242, as the last stored landing craft slipped away from her side, the Great White Whale weighed anchor in San Carlos Water. Thirty-three minutes later, according to the clocks on her Bridge, her giant propellers began thrashing the cold water and, slowly, followed by *Norland* and *Europic Ferry*, escorted by the battered *Antrim*, she moved towards Falkland Sound. As she sailed, the sky beyond Wreck Point was still glowing orange.

One by one, the cross-decking complete, the Ardents found their cabins and lay down.

Some, like Lt Mike Knowles, were totally exhausted, but found it hard to sleep.

Some, like Chief Stoker Andy Andrew, talked of the horror of the day.

Some, like his cabin-mate Jeff Curran, listened and felt sick, then gave in to total exhaustion.

Joe Laidlaw, at least, realised people had died, but knew there wasn't a damn thing he could do about it. He felt selfish. Very selfish. And guilty. Then again, he'd been there, seen it. His parents died when he was young, then his grandparents. So he watched his mates break down and thought of his family.

Like Buck Ryan at Ralph Coates's bedside, some kept up their hospital vigil. The dark of the night had more in store for some Ardents, though.

At 0125, the Bridge had broadcast an Air Raid Warning Yellow. For those not asleep, the last yellow they'd heard had been the one before Pablo Carballo's Skyhawk straddled them at 1600, the one that had fooled them into thinking that, if the chances of attack were slim, neither were they imminent.

Taff Lovidge, for one, had just slipped into his luxury hot bath in his luxury cabin when it came.

'This is it!' he thought, then, 'I don't really give a shit!' He stayed.

Ninety minutes later, maybe, Bob Lewis was sleeping peacefully . . . Bang! The crash was enormous. Before he gathered his wits, he was grabbing his lifejacket. Then he realised it wasn't a bomb. *Canberra* must have hit a wave. The open wardrobe doors had slammed shut.

At the same moment, the sound of his toilet door rapping its frame was

painting a picture story in Mike Knowles's subconscious mind. He woke feeling hunted again. He'd only just dropped off.

It was the hot water taps on Mick Cox's bath that had Jim Watts diving for cover – judder! judder! judder! – rattling the pipes, sounding like an Oerlikon pumping 20mm shells into the ceiling.

If they were in the cabin next door, maybe it was the same moment that convinced Cliff Goldfinch and Pete Rowe to try crawling under the carpet. Goldfinch was already very drunk when they'd hit the sack, milking one joke for all it was worth in these absurdly plush surroundings – 'Hello, are you still awake over there?' – when the pipes juddered. But they couldn't lift the carpet. It was so funny.

'You all right?'

'Yeah, fine!' They weren't, though. They were both shaking.

◆◆◆

At eight on the Friday evening, Brenda White had become agitated. She felt something was wrong. Ian had phoned and reassured her. 'Don't be silly, they won't be anywhere near yet.' But, as the night wore on, those fears had grown stronger. Around midnight, she'd picked up the receiver and dialled 0383 412191, the emergency line in Rosyth. They had no news.

An hour later, 0383 412191, she'd rung again. Still no news.

And again an hour later. And an hour after that. 0383 412191. No news. 0383 412191. No news.

She didn't know – no one at home did – that, in the cramped Military Signal Office near *Canberra*'s Bridge, Andrew Gordon Lennox was trying to clear the casualty signal. It had taken hours to obtain the best information about where the helicopters had taken those who hadn't ended up in *Yarmouth*.

But now the list was as accurate as it could be at this stage. Approved by a disbelieving Alan West – was it really that many who'd gone or were missing? – it now had to be encrypted by the liner's old equipment and transmitted through the difficult radio static conditions without disrupting the urgent operational traffic required to recover from the day of warfare. *Ardent*'s time might have passed, but the dawn would bring fresh problems to the Task Force survivors.

After four hours, the message had gone. Then Gordon Lennox met with another old friend, Naval psychiatrist Morgan O'Connell.

'For you I prescribe this and a bed,' the genial Irishman handed him half a bottle of Courvoisier brandy. It sounded like good doctor's advice to the Jimmy. 'Where's your cabin?'

'I have no idea,' Gordon Lennox told him. 'I haven't stopped since I reached *Canberra*. Nobody's mentioned cabins!'

They found one and oblivion followed. It had been a long day.

◆◆◆

At about 5.30 a.m. in Widey Lane, Crownhill, the thing Iris Andrew had

dreaded all night happened. The phone rang. She picked it up. It was one of her Link Wives. She'd been trying the number given on the TV newsflash the night before and, finally, managed to speak with someone. It was good news. *Ardent* wasn't involved. Iris told her sister, Jenny. They could breathe a sigh of relief. But Iris didn't.

✦✦✦

At 0600, HMS *Broadsword* sailed past *Ardent* off North West Island. She was blazing from stem to stern, the windows of her Bridge glowing like a warehouse in the Blitz.

✦✦✦

Nine-year-old Stuart Ray was sound asleep in the caravan at six that morning, completely unaware that his mum was on her way home to Plymouth to begin dialling 666666, the HMS *Drake* number.

Twenty-four hours before, she'd been in her bedroom, in tears, pulling the covers over her head. What else would she do with Tony 8,000 miles away?

At 0700, *Canberra*'s Bridge broadcast another Air Raid Warning Yellow.

At 0732, it was reduced to White. One by one, in the next hour, Ardents emerged from their cabins, most hung-over. While they'd slept, or talked, the Falklands had been left behind. If they hadn't taken a look while they waited for *Yarmouth* or, like Eddie Edwards, hadn't been tall enough to see over the landing craft walls on the ferry to *Canberra*, well, maybe they wouldn't see them at all now.

✦✦✦

At 0857, the emergency smoke detector alarms sounded on *Canberra* and her fire parties mustered and searched all the holds and spaces. It was a false alarm.

✦✦✦

About nine, Brenda White heard a knock. It was Larry and Judith Irvine. They'd heard the news.

'I've been up all night. I can't get this out of my head,' she told them.

'Come across and have a coffee,' Larry said.

It helped. Within minutes, they were sitting and laughing about how daft she'd been, sitting up all night. Laughing the way you do. Trying to brave the whole thing over.

✦✦✦

At 0930, Lenny Yeatman mustered the ship's company in the new ship's office – *Canberra*'s hair salon – and told them what they'd be doing. It amounted to this. Whether they wanted to stay south or not, Queen's Regulations said they had to stay together.

283

They signed forms to say whether they were prepared to take an emergency draft to one of the other warships, but most realised what would happen. Like the Sheffields, they'd be going home. For some, it confirmed what they'd been feeling. They'd failed. For others, home couldn't come soon enough.

Then the Master at Arms started finding them jobs.

◆◆◆

At 1100, Capt Tony Morton took HMS *Yarmouth* past *Ardent*'s last known position. It didn't surprise him, but it was a sad moment. She'd gone.

◆◆◆

As dusk had turned to black night, 12 hours before, Maj. Tony Rice had looked up from 2 Para's Sussex Mountains position and seen *Ardent* on fire, listing further. As the night went on, she'd burned and burned. Now, with dawn, he looked back and she was gone.

◆◆◆

The main television was on BBC in Christine Rowe's lounge, starting the build-up to the Spurs v QPR FA Cup Final. The portable was showing ITV in the kitchen. Both had the sound down. Somewhere between the two, the radio was on in the background. But eleven o'clock came and went . . .

Carol Ray almost dialled the six off her phone but *Drake* couldn't tell her anything. Eventually, Mick Requier, a steward at Mount Wise, called round and offered to drive down.

In the gym, there was a blackboard for every Task Force ship. On each the names of the ship's company were chalked, next to a contact number for the next of kin. But the news on the QT was good.

'HMS *Ardent*? Oh, she was nowhere near there,' someone told him.

He called Carol with the news. She was relieved. In the next ten minutes, she called one of her Links, Andy Barr's mum, to tell her. Then she went back to the television. And the newsflash came on . . .

Cathy Lee couldn't face watching the news on her own, so she'd gone round to a neighbour, Jean Green, for a cuppa and company. Before they switched on, Cathy caught sight of her close friend Ann Smith running past the window. Her husband was on the *Antelope*. Her face was ashen . . .

Since *Sheffield*, the radio and TV news had become a magnet in Pete and Renee Hanson's neat home in High Street, Ecclesfield. This Saturday was no different, except for the uneasy feeling Pete had had through the morning, a feeling he couldn't explain or shrug off.

Just before one o'clock, he turned on the radio and waited, as he'd done a thousand and one times since that grim Tuesday, 18 days earlier. The voice said *Ardent* had been sunk, with 'some loss of life'.

Renee was working at the butcher's. Pete put his coat on and drove straight there.

'Come on, we're in trouble here,' he said as he walked in. She was devastated. They rushed back home and began dialling the emergency number. Total waste of time . . .

In Hull, Jon Major's dad, Ken, was already phoning and phoning, but with no luck either. The line was constantly engaged. His mother, Betty, was frantic. One by one, the family gathered. It would be the start of a long wait . . .

After a few cups of coffee, a knock at the door interrupted Brenda White's chat in Larry and Judith Irvine's Washington home. Judith opened the door and another neighbour looked beyond her at Brenda.

'Have you heard?' he asked. 'She's been sunk.'

'You're joking!' She started to say it but, before she'd finished, she realised nobody would joke like that. She ran home and rang Rosyth again.

'Yes,' she was told, *Ardent* had been sunk, but 'in shallow waters and calm conditions, though there has been some loss of life'.

The voice on the other end sounded young, but she was so shocked she couldn't remember any more.

She tried to calm herself. 'Oh, he's a White and he's a Knocker,' she thought. 'He'll come bobbing back to the surface.'

At Northwood, the signal naming *Ardent* as sunk had arrived in the bunker of Fleet Operations and been passed very quickly by the watchkeepers to the On-Watch Duty Commander, who'd just left the Ops Room and was talking to his superior about the briefing which Defence Secretary John Nott was due to be given within the hour.

As the Duty Commander returned to the room, his assistant picked up the scrap of paper and handed it to him gently. The Ops Room was strangely quiet as Cdr Michael Gordon Lennox, the elder brother of *Ardent*'s First Lieutenant, digested its contents.

After the briefing, Nott made it clear to the Commander-in-Chief that he intended to name the ship as soon as he returned to Whitehall. He wanted to do it before the Argentinians did.

Michael Gordon Lennox couldn't afford to wait for the casualty signal, but he left what he had to do as long as possible before calling his sister-in-law at her little cottage, near Portsmouth. He broke the bad news that the ship had been sunk but, as so many would over the coming hours, tried to hint that, although there were 22 dead, the news about Andrew could be good.

Julia Gordon Lennox and Rosie West spoke on the phone. Rosie already knew that her husband was alive. It would be hours before another call from Northwood gave Julia Gordon Lennox her news too.

❤❤❤

Beryl Yeatman walked into the Fleet Club just before one o'clock. Wives and girlfriends were already gathering to film a video packed with messages to send

out to the ship. The media were there to record the event. She walked up to the first woman she saw.

'Do you know Sally Banfield?' she asked. They'd only spoken on the phone.

'Yes, I'm Sally Banfield.'

She introduced herself, then asked: 'Is Rosie West here?'

'No,' the Supply Officer's wife told her.

'D'you think she knows something we don't know?' Beryl joked. As they spoke, a radio journalist by them turned round and started to walk out.

Minutes later, as Beryl walked round the other women, he came back in and walked straight for Sally Banfield. Beryl saw Sally look across the tables and her heart sank. She went over to the reporter. He looked bothered. She could see a piece of paper in his hand, upside down, and whatever he'd written on it he'd gone over and over, an unmistakable impression carved over faint blue lines. She read it.

It said '*Ardent* sunk.'

And, underneath, '22 dead.'

She looked round. There were people still laughing and talking.

Sally Owens was there, ready to tell Jessie, 'Here's Katie, she's doing well. I'm not sleeping but, apart from that . . .' It was reassuring to have all these things in common in the middle of all this chaos.

Then, before Beryl could say anything, another woman came in and said, 'They've sunk the *Ardent*!'

The room went quiet. Until now, Sally had kept herself together, even after *Sheffield*. She'd even written to Jessie. But now she burst into tears. She wasn't alone. Beryl was soon at her side.

'You haven't got time for that. You've got a young daughter to look after!'

'What?' Sally held four-month-old Katie tightly.

'Pull yourself together!' It was abrupt, but she needed it.

Beryl rounded Paul and Joanne up. He was more shocked than his sister. Then she found someone from another ship to go home with Sally Owens, and headed for the door. As she did, Jill Maunder and Sally Banfield rushed to the club's two phones and Lesley Palmer, Peddler's wife, walked in,

'You'd better get home to your phone,' Beryl told her. 'The ship's sunk.'

Then she hurried to the car, an arm round each of her children, telling them not to worry, 'Your dad'll be all right.'

◆◆◆

Apart from standing sideways and giving a 'Here we are,' Frankie Enticknap knew there wasn't anything she could say to Ken on the tape. He'd understand. So she'd relaxed with some gardening, smiling to herself every time the Plymouth Sound DJ handed over 'to the London studio' for the Ministry of Defence statement, heard nothing but burble and played another record. Typical.

In the end, she went inside to make a burger – well, she was pregnant – and turned on the TV instead.

She'd taken one bite when the Ministry's spokesman, Ian McDonald, said it. *Ardent* had been sunk.

She froze. She froze and needed someone to talk to, but not her parents. Or Ken's. So she headed for her neighbour, Dawn Goard. Dawn was already heading the other way. Within a minute, she had the kettle on. It would boil non-stop in the coming hours . . .

Christine Rowe had put the last piece of bacon in her mouth, a late breakfast after a late, late night, when McDonald said *Ardent* had been sunk. She knew the first thing she had to do was ring Pete's parents in Bude.

They asked her over, but she said no. 'If any information comes, it comes here.' From then on, she was desperate to go outside, but she couldn't. The phone wouldn't stop ringing . . .

Iris Andrew and entourage had made it as far as the TVs in Debenhams when she caught Ian McDonald's dour face on a bank of screens. Pictures, but not sound.

She rushed to a set, pushing buttons, but couldn't work out how to turn it up.

'My husband's on one of the ships,' she grabbed a salesman. 'Can you turn it up, please?'

He wouldn't. She couldn't believe it. She was frantic.

They hurried to the car, parked some way from the town, then she sat in the back with Debbie and Jenny's two and waited for two o'clock. Her brother-in-law Bob reached forward and turned the radio on.

'. . . HMS *Ardent* has been sunk with some loss of life.' Debbie burst into tears . . .

Lesley Sephton hadn't heard the Friday night newsflash. So her sister ringing her Dorchester shop, saying, 'Have you heard the news?' came out of the blue. What news?

'John's ship's been hit.' She went cold and her knees weakened.

'What else?'

'Nothing. It was on the *One O'Clock News*.'

She rushed out to her assistant, gathering baby Harriet's bits on the way.

'John's ship's been hit. I've got to go home.'

She rang her parents, put Harriet in the car, and drove to them. Her father was waiting as she arrived.

'Don't worry,' he tried to reassure her. 'They'll have got the helicopter off. That's the first thing they'll have done. He's fine.' She wished she could believe him.

'I'm going home,' she said. 'That's where they'll phone.'

'I'm coming with you,' her mother said . . .

Five ships hit, including *Ardent*. Alan Whitford hurriedly dialled his parents' number. Engaged.

He knew straightaway it was serious.

Eventually, he caught them. That's when his mum said she'd heard the flash the night before but hadn't wanted to worry them. He went straight round.

Stuart Ray had spent the morning on train rides round the Dobwalls park, waiting to hear from his mum, who'd gone home after hearing the news the night before. Liz was with some of her friends. She was too old for trains.

When he went back to the caravan for lunch, it was locked, so he sat on the stool. Yards away, some family friends were talking quietly. But not quietly enough to stop him hearing 'So that's Tony's ship.'

Panic began to rise in his chest, but he managed to convince himself he'd misheard.

About five minutes later, Margaret Harvey saw him sitting on the stool and called him over for a bite to eat. Her husband, Roy, had gone off to find Liz. While she put a bowl of soup in front of the hungry nine year old for lunch, the news came on. She reached quickly to turn it off, but not quickly enough.

'That's my daddy's ship,' he said, and burst into tears.

'Well, he'll be all right, he can swim,' Margaret put her arms round him. 'They'll be near shore . . .'

She was running late. Worse still, Carole Leake's mum and dad, Marjorie and Leonard, had turned up early to go Saturday afternoon shopping.

'You can come in but I'm not ready,' she laughed. Her parents looked at each other.

'My God, she doesn't know,' her dad said.

'Doesn't know what?' They looked at each other again.

'The ship's been sunk,' her mum said.

It was like a knife. Everything began turning. Carole collapsed to her knees and started shaking, trying to grab the phone, not thinking who she'd call. She wasn't John's next of kin.

The first person she rang was his mum, in Birmingham. She knew. After that, all Carole could do was wait, hoping to God no one would bang the door, gripped by terror every time the phone rang . . .

The grapevine from HMS *Drake* to the Grand Theatre had fed the odd bit of news about Val's Boys to supplement what the lads themselves had told her and Dave in their occasional letters. They knew the trip south wasn't a party, even if they'd joked with Knocker, Ralph and co. that last night, more than a month before. But this time, the call wasn't from the Naval Base.

Dave was serving in the bar when Val walked through, white. Her sister had phoned. 'You'll never guess . . .' was all she said.

◆◆◆

How Christine Rowe wanted to step outside, leave the phone behind. But she couldn't. She was a Link Wife, the wife of a senior rating, a woman with a separate life when Pete went to sea. But now Pete's ratings were hers and she found herself dispensing comfort to the sick. The sick with worry.

'Have you heard anything?'

'All I can tell you is what I know.'

'I can't get through to *Drake*! What should I do?'

'The best thing is sit at home. They're going to come to your home address first.' All she could do now was wait.

And wait. The phone was ringing as Iris Andrew opened the door and walked in. It didn't stop all afternoon. She feared the worst, believed it was going to be horrible. The Cup Final kept brother-in-law Bob and little Stewart occupied. What else could they do? Apart from wait.

And wait. By two o'clock, Brenda White was in knots. Between calls to Rosyth, first she'd called the sister on Dawn's ward at South Cleveland Hospital

– 'Could she be sent home? Her brother's ship's been sunk.' – and then, eventually, she contacted Mandy's headmaster and asked him to arrange for her to be driven back from a school camping trip to the Lakes, 'But please don't let her hear the car radio.'

One side of her kept saying, 'He'll pop up like a cork.' The other said, 'They need to be home.' She sat down and waited.

And waited. Roy Harvey had broken the news to Liz Ray by the time they arrived back at the caravan. She was sobbing. Margaret comforted her, then they packed her into the car with Stuart and tried as hard as they could to keep their spirits up on the drive back to Plymouth. But it didn't work.

Waiting. Carol Ray had already discovered that was the hardest part. Who could she phone? Should she ring the others to find out? She didn't even know where Tony's office was. Whenever she'd been on board, it was always down two hatches, into the Chiefs' Mess, drink, laugh, out of the Chiefs' Mess, up two flats, home. That's all she knew. How could she tell herself he'd be safe if she didn't even know where he worked?

While Stuart and Liz were on their way, she busied herself in the kitchen and called Tescos.

'Can I speak to Helen Ray, please?'

'Is it important?'

'Yes, it's very important.' They brought her to the phone.

'Oh, Helen, come home. It's Dad's ship that's gone down.' They put her in a taxi.

The oven was sparkling by the time the Harveys pulled on to the drive. She gathered the children in her arms and gave them a hug. And the tears flowed again.

Mick and Sandra Requier were already there. While the rest sat down in the lounge, with the Cup Final on the TV and a pom-pom-making chain to keep them distracted, he drove down to *Drake*.

Within minutes, Helen's taxi pulled up outside. When she stepped out, she had a bunch of flowers. Her mum's birthday had started the minute *Ardent* steamed into Falkland Sound, the day before. It was almost more than Carol could take. One wait was over. Now there was another.

And another. Information trickled into the Grand Theatre in dribs and drabs. The mood was terrible. Lads who used to be on *Ardent* were dropping in. The TV was on. Then they started to hear that some had been killed, and that was the worst of all. They didn't know who, and they had no way of finding out.

They were Val's Boys, but the Navy didn't know that. So she'd have to wait.

And wait. 'Let me tell you, no news is good news,' the voice on the Yeovilton information line told Lesley Sephton, 'so I'm sure everything's fine.'

She put the phone down, walked into the sitting-room and said she was going to change.

'Do you want a coffee?'

She nodded but, halfway up the stairs, something made her pause at the landing window. A car. There was someone in it. She watched. The person stepped out and, as he walked up the drive, she could see he was a clergyman. She didn't know him, but she knew what he'd come for.

Her mother took over. She put her straight in the dining-room, on her own,

and pulled the curtains. She took the dog and Harriet away and left her there. Lesley couldn't stop crying, but she didn't want to be alone, so she went back into the sitting-room and talked to the clergyman, and waited.

And waited. The TV was on at the Yeatmans, but hardly anyone was watching. The children were playing games.

Among the stream of visitors and the relentless dialling, 666666, Beryl Yeatman's phone went. It was Rosie West. As she'd been about to leave home for the Fleet Club, someone had been to see her with a list of the dead. Beryl held her breath.

'I couldn't read it properly upside down,' Rosie said, 'but I couldn't see Len's name on it.'

She had seen Rick Banfield's, though. She felt guilty, finding out her husband was safe and in one piece before most of the others even knew the ship had been hit. No waiting for her. Just that guilt.

Beryl didn't know how to feel. Then she decided the Navy was contacting officers' families first. So if Rick had died, where was Len? Officers and Bridge went together, didn't they?

And didn't stokers work in the Engine Room? Sally Owens's parents had just arrived as she walked towards the house. She fell apart.

'I've got nothing left now,' she sobbed in their arms. 'They've taken it all away. It's all gone.'

'Don't talk like that! You've got Katie,' her dad told her.

In minutes, despair had turned to anger.

'It's her fault. She brought this about. I'll kill her,' she shouted.

She didn't need confirmation. If Jessie was working with the engines and the ship had been sunk, then he was gone. And it was Thatcher's doing. Not the Argentinians'. It wasn't their fault they'd had to bomb our ships. It wasn't the *Ardent*'s fault that they'd had to kill Argentinians. She should have stopped it. And she hadn't. All Sally needed was a gun.

Waiting. Frankie Enticknap and Dawn Goard had it down to a fine art as the afternoon wore on. Whenever the phone rang, Dawn would leap over the low wall between their gardens, rush into Frankie's house and answer it. Frankie would follow at a more sedate pace.

Ken's parents, Les and Mary, were one of the first to ring. In minutes they were on their way down from their newsagent's in Aldershot. Eventually, at three o'clock, Dawn also managed to contact *Drake*, but they wouldn't tell her anything. So she held the phone while Frankie listened. It wasn't a lot, but it was something. The ship had gone down in calm waters. There was every expectation of a lot of survivors.

Survivors? 'The longer this goes on,' Alan Whitford reasoned, 'the better it'll be.'

His parents had been trying all night for news of Garry, without luck. That was good, wasn't it?

The Rowes lived in a cul-de-sac so, every time a strange car appeared, Christine prayed.

News? She'd had no luck with *Drake*. She'd had no luck with Pompey. So she tried 0634 812771.

'We know as much as you do. We've got no names,' the Chatham rating said. She called a friend of Pete's who was a Regulator in Portsmouth.

'I'll go in and see,' he said. The minutes dragged until he called back. 'His name's not on any list.'

'Does that mean it's only the dead that have come through?'

'No, they're coming through in no particular order.' She knew what that meant. She'd have to wait.

Carole Leake's mum and dad sat in her front room and stared at the clock, watched it go round and round and round, and made endless cups of tea. Every time the phone rang, it made her jump. The longer it went, the more agonising it became.

About four o'clock, a couple of miles away, Sally Owens's dad was doing the phoning while she made the tea, convinced that, if three people turned up at the door, then Jessie was dead. Two and he'd been injured severely. One and it wasn't much to worry about. The doorbell rang and the silhouette was alone.

'He's all right!' she thought, and rushed to open the door. It was Margaret Redman, from the flat next door, a lovely lady with a baby and a husband who was a Royal Navy gunner.

'Have you heard anything yet?' she asked. It wasn't what Sally wanted.

'No, Margaret. If I know anything, I'll tell you. But just go away!' She shut the door.

◆◆◆

Lesley Sephton thought the next call would be to say sorry, it had all been a terrible mistake. If they couldn't tell her that, she didn't want to know. She didn't have a body, so what proof was there? On the other hand, if he'd been badly burnt . . . He was very proud and wouldn't want to come back. So she wanted to accept it too. Mostly, she didn't want to know he'd suffered.

After what seemed like hours and hours of dialling, at four o'clock Pete Hanson heard the emergency line finally ring out at the other end. The conversation was short, but it was sweet. Shaun was alive.

'I don't know who I were talking to,' he says. 'The person just said Shaun was a survivor. I put the phone down and, by then, the family had gathered. We was in absolute celebration. Arms in the air . . .'

It was late afternoon when Brenda White saw a priest, a young chap, walking towards the house.

'Here it comes,' she said.

Her elder son, Ian, was already on his way home from Devonport with an escort. Another young lad with a rotten job.

She invited the priest in and sat him at the side of the kitchen table. He was ashen and shaking.

'Do you need a drink?' she asked.

'Yes, please.'

She gave him a whisky. She felt sorry for him. He stayed a long time. But he never actually said, 'Your son has been killed.'

In the Hanson household, after five minutes of screaming, laughter and tears,

the relief and celebration were a heady mix. Then Pete Hanson looked out of the window and saw his nephew walking down the drive. The Hansons weren't Catholic, but behind him was a priest. Pete knew straightaway.

The priest still didn't have Shaun's name exactly right but there'd been a mistake. Their strapping, big-hearted son was dead.

At about 4.15 p.m., a man from the Soldiers', Sailors' & Airmen's Families Association arrived at the Whitfords' door with a scrap of paper. He said Garry was believed missing. He didn't say, 'Missing believed drowned'.

That wasn't definite enough.

'Is there a chance that he could've been picked up by another ship?'

He couldn't say. All he had was what was scribbled on the scrap of paper.

Alan wandered round the house again, in a daze, playing percentages, 200 on board, 22 dead. There was a good chance he'd have been picked up, wasn't there?

His dad disappeared upstairs and lay on the bed, curled up in a ball. He couldn't talk. But his mum kept going. It was her way of coping.

Later that day, the phone would go again – Isabel, Garry's fiancée, a girl they'd never met.

'He'll turn up,' she said. They wanted to believe her.

At about five o'clock, Frankie Enticknap looked out from Dawn Goard's front room and saw Arthur Norton, her boss from RAF Mount Batten, and his wife Mary, walking down the drive.

She hadn't met Mrs Norton before. She took them in and they were drinking tea when the phone rang about an hour later. She stood up in trepidation – Dawn had done all the answering in this house so far – and it was *Drake*. They had news. Ken was a survivor, but they didn't know any more. She put the phone down and breathed deeply. It had never occurred to her that he might have been killed, but now it did . . .

Eventually, Mandy White arrived home from the Lakes. Her teacher had told her that Steve's ship had been sunk, but he'd kept the radio off. Now Brenda had the hardest job of all. How do you tell a 13 year old that the brother she idolises is dead? Brenda White took her into the living-room and tried.

Mandy sobbed. 'He can't be dead. He can't be dead.'

Somewhere deep inside, Brenda thought the same. Steve was a White. He'd bounce back. Family bonds were too strong to let anything happen. Somewhere deeper, though, she understood what those feelings had been through the night.

The knock. The call. The lone car driving slowly from the end of the road. In homes across the length and breadth of Britain – in Redditch, in the Forest of Dean, in South Shields, Hemel Hempstead, Chatham, Liverpool, Hull, wherever – a long afternoon had seen them all, again and again and again.

In Gloucester, Russ Goble's mum and dad were no exception. They saw a

vicar walking down the path, carrying a note. Their hearts sank. This time, though, the tidings weren't bad. Russ was alive. They were so relieved, they opened a bottle of whisky. The vicar stayed for one. Then another.

By six, the Cup Final over, there was nothing on the TV worth watching. Well, nothing to interest Iris Andrew. She kept thinking of the young lads. She couldn't help it. Then the phone went and she wouldn't let anybody else answer it. After a brief exchange of details, she turned and smiled. Andy was on the list of survivors. She thanked the caller and walked back into the living-room and told her sister Jenny. In seconds, the family was jumping for joy. But not Iris.

'Mistakes are made and you don't know,' she told them.

At exactly the same moment, fixed in his hallway vigil, Ken Major finally heard the phone ring out at the other end. The rest of the family listened with their hearts in their mouths. A few seconds later, they heard him swear for the first time.

'Thank fuck for that!' he sighed.

Sharon was by the kitchen door and started crying. Jon's mum, Betty, was in the kitchen, just out of earshot but close enough to see her daughter begin weeping. She collapsed on the floor. Her boy was dead. When they brought her round, they broke the good news.

About an hour later, maybe a little sooner, Christine Rowe had a phone call with the same news.

'Oh, well!' was all she remembers saying.

'I don't care whether he's lost a leg, as long as he's still alive,' her mum answered, but Christine wasn't so sure Pete would have shared the view.

The call came to Cathy Lee around the same time, maybe a little later. The numb feeling hadn't gone all afternoon. Stuart was taking it badly. Sharon hadn't realised what was going on.

The news was good, the voice on the other end of the line told Cathy. But she wanted to be certain.

'Can you check, please. There are three Lees in the Mess.' The line went quiet for a moment.

'Yes,' the voice said, finally. 'He's safe.'

Beryl Yeatman found out at about eight. Len was alive.

'Any injuries?' They didn't know. It was that brief.

A short ride away, Frankie Enticknap rushed out as she saw Ken's parents arrive. Their faces were white. They still didn't know. She couldn't wait to meet them, so she shouted as she ran. 'He's okay! He's okay!'

Then she spent the evening trying not to phone Cathy Lee, her Link Wife, in case her news had been bad. In the end, Cathy phoned her. She'd been doing the same.

Carol Ray and the girls found out at about 8.30 p.m.

'Thank God for that!' she yelled. Then she called Stuart at his friend John Peters's house and told him. He was already enjoying himself, but this made it better. He asked his mum if he could stay the night. She said yes.

Then she had a call from Jim Watts's girlfriend, Kay.

'Have you heard anything about Tony?'

'Yes, he's a survivor.'

'So's Jim.'

Sally Owens's dad picked the phone up when it went, at about nine o'clock.

'I can't speak to you,' the young rating told him. 'I have to speak with Mrs Owens.'

He asked her to confirm who she was and Jessie's service number.

'I'm Sally Owens. His number's D142826P.'

'I have some good news for you. He's fine.'

'You're absolutely certain?'

'Yes!'

She put the phone down.

'Thank God for that!' her dad said.

'God's got fuck all to do with it!'

She meant it. It had taken eight hours to find out her husband was alive. It should never have been on the news until they'd all been told.

A couple of miles away, the news was trickling into the Grand Theatre. Val Wopling would dry her eyes after one phone call, then start again when another of her lads came in and added to the names of the dead. She felt lost. She'd never seen so many grown men cry.

About ten o'clock, Frankie Enticknap slid between the sheets and looked up at the ceiling. She hadn't thought about the baby all day, but now she did. Ken was all right. But what would she have done on a widow's pension? It was an academic thought.

The longest ten hours of Carole Leake's life ended bang on eleven o'clock. The phone rang. She ran to pick it up. It was John's brother, David, and he was euphoric. John was safe and well, no injuries.

It was a short conversation, but her mum and dad knew from her reaction what the news was. It would be a while before they'd find out that 22 men had died. Then they'd realise how lucky they were. They weren't alone.

One by one, 178 families had endured the worst and found joy in a word from a stranger.

One by one, 22 families had endured the worst and then found something worse still.

Late that evening, with his escort in tow, Ian White turned his key in the front door of the family's Washington home. At least one of Brenda White's sons was home safe.

That night, Brenda went to bed but found it hard to sleep. She couldn't help thinking that Steve might have been trapped inside *Ardent*, alive.

TWO

SS *CANBERRA*, TOTAL EXCLUSION ZONE, SOUTH ATLANTIC TO *QE2*, CUMBERLAND BAY, SOUTH GEORGIA

(22–28 MAY 1982)

Alive. Ken Enticknap was alive, even if he was only just beginning to remember how.

In ones and twos, they'd arrive at his bedside to fill in a little more, conversations which normally began, 'Young Dillon did a good job getting you out'.

The 18 year old was two beds away, close enough for the pair to spend odd minutes reliving the part they'd played in each other's survival, rare moments when Dillon's painful shyness allowed him to open up, a junior and senior rating separated by years of life and experience, but bonded forever.

The others found it just as hard to penetrate the barrier. All Richie Gough can remember is the young AB inisisting: 'I was looking after myself and there was someone in my way.'

Amid the onerous task of compiling next-of-kin lists, Lenny Yeatman was a visitor too. He wouldn't need to go and see Frankie now, but the faces of the injured who hadn't yet been moved from the Island Room to the Meridian for safety told him his grim list might easily have run to more than 22.

At 1600, as dusk fell, memories of those 22 were never far away when the bulk of the surviving Ardents gathered solemnly on *Canberra*'s Upper Deck. Below, 200 people had congregated in tightly packed, orderly rows aft on D Deck for the burial at sea of Lt Kevin Francis, Cpl Andy Evans, Lt Cpl Brett Giffin and Cpl Doc Love, the first three killed when their Gazelles were shot down early the day before Doc Love when the SAS Sea King ditched on *Ardent*'s screens two days before the landings.

With dusk falling, *Canberra*'s side doors were opened and, as a seabird wheeled by, the dark, strangely placid sea surged past. There were readings from the Bible, a prayer and the Naval hymn, 'For Those in Peril on the Sea'.

After a moment of silence, the Royal Marine buglers played 'Last Post', then 'Reveille' and the rising swell of South Atlantic at 51 01.8S 54 43.4W took the

shrouded bodies. The Blue Ensigns which had covered them flapped sadly. No one spoke. With dignity and tradition, *Canberra* left them to their final rest. It was a committal none of Alan West's missing Ardents could be given.

In the hours after the solemn service, the enormity of the past 24 hours began to haunt West more and more. Other than *Ardent*'s chummy role on the passage south, Capt Chris 'Beagle' Burne hadn't known the 34 year old or his ship until they'd embarked *Canberra*, weary and defeated.

In between, they'd proved the truth of the lore which says that, when a Royal Navy warship goes into action, it either sinks or wins. There's no third way. With one in four of her men killed or wounded, the 'Beagle' already knew the scale of *Ardent*'s sacrifice. The rest of the war would prove it to be the heaviest of any British fighting unit but, for now, he was only concerned with her young CO. There was no one else for the lost frigate's Captain to talk to so, in the seclusion of his cabin, he sat while Alan West poured out his doubts. He helped him take the day apart and put it back together again. For an hour or more they spoke until, finally, West was back on his feet.

In *Fearless*, Cdre Mike Clapp – Commander Amphibious Warfare – was reflecting too. If the punishment taken by the Thin Grey Line had continued for a second day, the Marines and the Paras would have been stuck on shore with enough food to last them two days and ammunition for one. Sitting ducks.

But, for reasons he couldn't fathom then, the enemy had been absent on the 22nd. Not that he was complaining. From being knackered and fearful, he'd been given the chance to regroup. He'd taken it.

Capt Bob Harmes took his too, though it felt like running away, running from what the Ardents were facing. On the other hand, if he'd stayed, he'd have never lived with himself. So, after arranging a trip to *Fearless*, with his pistol but no bullets, carrying a brown paper bag and wearing the tropical gear he was going to defeat the Argentinians in, he paid his final respects. On a scrap of paper, he wrote, 'Share this with your officers.' Then he stood a bottle of Scotch outside Alan West's cabin and left.

◆◆◆

By 0700 on the Sunday, *Canberra* was 170nm north north-east of Port Stanley, inching further from danger and ready to start a vertrep with RFA Resource. It would last all day.

Back in San Carlos Water, the story of *Ardent*'s one-day war was about to make its brief appearance on the airwaves. With permission now granted to mention her destruction, and armed with his flawed account from the lips of disorientated survivors, Robert Fox joined his BBC colleague Brian Hanrahan and ITN's Michael Nicholson in RFA *Stromness*'s Wireless Room just after breakfast.

The three pooled their information. Fox was first on the satellite link back to Britain, his despatch measured if imprecise. Nicholson was typically rapid-fire, lifting chunks of Fox's *Ardent* testimony, repeating the story of John Leake's sprint from below to the GPMG and taking out a Skyhawk (Arca's). The big Brummie NAAFI manager, of course, had been up top by Cliff Goldfinch's side all day.

Still, the reoccupying forces had paid tribute to *Ardent*, Nicholson told the

296

millions feeding off his words back home: 'I must pay tribute, public tribute, as certainly the troops would wish to, to the crew of *Ardent*, the frigate that went down, sunk last night. They had a gunline over the British landing troops. They had to stay in position, or else the troops were totally unprotected. *Ardent* was in a totally vulnerable position in the Sound, could not move, did not wish to move. Without *Ardent*, they could not have got ashore. Had they got ashore without *Ardent*, they could not have stayed protected ashore. So let's just make that tribute very public.'

With that, their looking back was done. While they moved on with the campaign, on *Canberra* the price of protecting those grateful troops would go on being paid.

The Ardents had already started gathering in the hair salon, a cold wash of the ship's final day in a corner accustomed to blue rinses and warm gossip. No idle chat of sun-kissed ports, but conversation about what had happened. Not which horizon they were heading for, but the one they'd left behind.

◆◆◆

Working with the victims of the Harrods bombing had nurtured Surg. Lt Cdr Morgan O'Connell's growing interest in the problems of people who'd been involved in disasters. Then, he'd met a group of Far East prisoners of war and found that more than one in four of them had some sort of cardiovascular disorder. Most were in their 60s, so that was no surprise. But what he hadn't expected was the 48 per cent who had a psychiatric disorder, all relating to their experiences as PoWs.

'We were treating patients for depression and alcoholism, phobic anxieties, schizo disorder and the rest,' O'Connell admits, until a junior doctor at Royal Naval Hospital Haslar began reading American literature on something called Post Traumatic Stress Disorder (PTSD). 'Then we began to look again and realised, shit . . .'

There was a common thread between Haslar's patients. At their moment of horror, already feeling control slipping out of their hands, their senses had been bombarded with information, too much to take in, so much that the brain had locked the overload away, waiting for the moment when a sound, a word, a smell, a sight would bring it all flooding back. The tilting of a deck could do the same.

At 2030 two nights before, O'Connell had seen Alan West's refugees shuffling on to *Canberra* and he'd known he had to bring them together again quickly, mates talking with mates, to kindle the belief that what they were feeling was normal. He knew full well that how they handled their reaction would dictate whether or not they'd become casualties to PTSD, like those Far East PoWs.

O'Connell's background was in bereavement, but he'd never done anything like this before, so he gathered them together, officers, senior ratings and junior ratings, and explained what would happen, and why. They'd start with the guys who'd been aft.

'What goes on within the group should stay within the group,' he told them. 'It's confidential. It isn't about a Board of Inquiry and it's not to point the finger of blame.'

In his own mind, he was already expecting certain questions to echo round the room. Like, 'Could we have searched the ship one more time?'

Within half-an-hour, a pattern emerged and his eyes opened. Someone would start talking and, after a couple of minutes, he'd be interrupted by someone who'd say, 'That's not quite right, because I was on the Flat and this happened.' At times, he thought they'd come to blows and, 'Wind your neck in,' it wasn't always the most senior person there who defused the situation.

In that half-hour, he saw the things he was expecting: guilt, searching, anger, denial, the great big question 'why?', the things he knew they needed to work through. But what he hadn't anticipated was how quickly their memories had distorted.

In the coming days, his sessions would follow the same thread. From time to time, someone would say, 'So-and-so should be here,' and they'd disappear to the ward and bring them in on a stretcher.

Some felt like John Goddard, as if they'd been told they were going to be executed, they'd been blindfolded, then, 'No, we're not going to do it now,' and the blindfold came off. Then it went on again. The whole day had been like that. Hit the deck. Bang! Bang! Bang! Bang! Out of the water. Check arms and legs. Back down.

'That's how me and Steve Earnshaw felt. We just wanted to die. We were that tired,' he says.

Some felt like Mike Knowles, the guilt, the wanting to go back, not knowing where he'd been in the chain of things.

'Whether you like it or not, you're not going to forget this,' O'Connell had told them. 'My advice to you is to go out and get drunk' – or words to that effect. Not everyone found both parts of the trick easy.

Neither was it simple to choose 30 words to tell their loved ones how they were. But 30 words were all they had when the chance to send familygrams came round that Sunday. Some resorted to code – 'The roof's still on' – others were more direct: 'Hello. Most of us are okay. Don't know what will happen to us now. Expect to be coming home on the next ship north. See you soon. Love.'

Some didn't bother. Amid a homeless ship's company on someone else's ship, Mike Lewis, for one, didn't see the point. No one at home would have a clue there was anything wrong, so why worry them?

Little did he know. The young sailor who handed Iris Andrew her telegram was unaware his knock on the door had, in fact, given her the confirmation she'd prayed for. Andy was alive and well after all.

Frankie Enticknap too. Her signal, read by a caller from *Drake*, said Ken had severe scalp wounds.

'How severe is "severe"?' she asked.

'If it meant life-threatening, it would say so.' That was good enough for her.

Buck Ryan sent his 'I'm all right' message off with the rest, unaware that, for 24 hours, his family had believed he was missing, a hideous mistake. The telegram didn't arrive home either. It would be another week, or so, before he'd hear back from his dad. When he did, he'd realise why. You don't send a telegram to a dead son. Until then, he'd feel very lost.

While the Ardents composed their thoughts, and their words, Lauraine

Mulberry continued recording the events going on around her. At this point on Sunday, 23 May, she was pessimistic:

'There is talk of us going back into San Carlos tonight; the *Ardent* survivors don't wish to, and neither do the patients. (Crew ain't too happy! 150 per cent or not!)'

◆◆◆

The Ardents collected about £120 for Mr Wong, their dispossessed Chinese laundryman, feeling desperately sorry for a man who'd told his wife he was in the Mediterranean. Within days, he'd set up another Laundry and started making more cash, the bastard! As for themselves, they were becoming proficient at taking their minds off things, running round volunteering for anything that had to be done.

'If we'd been left to our own devices, we'd have cracked up,' Lenny Yeatman recalls, so they mended washing machines wrecked by bootnecks and pongos, humped stores from the bowels of the ship all the way to the nets slung beneath the waiting helicopters and wore their arms down to the bone doing it, glad, nevertheless, of the reassuring width of steel sides, and the fresh air of the Upper Deck.

John Leake was part of that human conveyor belt when somebody came down from up top. 'Hey, John, you've just had a mention on the World Service,' he shouted.

'Oh yeah!' He thought it was a wind-up. They'd been told not to talk to the Press.

When he finished, he went back up to his cabin, switched on the radio and had a shower. Then he heard it too. It wasn't the only thing he found difficult to believe.

Alan West had agreed to the Revd Noel Mullin's suggestion of a Service of Thanksgiving, something the Catholic chaplain hoped would meet a host of spiritual needs, a time for the combined ships' companies to acknowledge the great loss, to pray for the repose of the souls of those who had died, and to reflect on what they'd achieved through their courage, dedication and sacrifice.

'I can't go to a thanksgiving,' Leake thought. 'Give thanks for something that just killed 22 shipmates? What have I got to be thankful for? That I'm alive?' No, he had no reason to go.

But many did, willingly, in search of God knew what, or because they just found themselves there.

The men and women of *Canberra* stood solemnly and respectfully, among them Lt Bob Horton – the young pilot of the Sea King which Pete Brierley, Mick Newby and Tom Williams had watched disappear from their screens four nights before – in a wheelchair, his ankle broken with the force of smashing his way out of the sinking helo.

The Ardents gathered at the back, a sea of sombre faces in white P&O overalls among so many different uniforms, not people they knew, not the ones with happy smiling faces they'd seen on runs ashore.

The Revd Mullin led their prayers for the injured and the bereaved, especially

299

families and friends. They also gave thanks for the rescue of so many. Then Alan West stood and read the Roll of Honour: Derek Armstrong, Richard Banfield, Andrew Barr, Peter Brouard, Richard Dunkerley, Michael Foote, Stephen Ford, Shaun Hanson, Sean Hayward, Stephen Heyes, Simon Lawson, Alistair Leighton, Allan McAulay, Michael Mullen, Brian Murphy, Gary Nelson, Andrew Palmer, John Roberts, John Sephton, Stephen White, Garry Whitford, Gilbert Williams.

At the end of the service, a large number of men received Holy Communion; a larger number than Noel Mullin expected. In the coming days, he'd spread his pastoral care far and wide, administering the sacrament of the sick to the seriously injured, spending a huge amount of time with the Ardents, hearing their stories, providing what words seemed appropriate as they tried to make sense of it all.

Whether the Catholic chaplain knew it or not, he also helped to keep Morgan O'Connell on an even keel when the isolation of his psychiatric work reached its loneliest.

Back home, Lesley Sephton received another visit from the Revd Bill Taylor, the man who'd broken the news of John's death. He didn't say, 'He's gone to a better place,' or anything like it. That helped.

Elsewhere, families took their comfort where they could, and gave it where they were able.

It took all of Christine Rowe's courage to call her Link Wives, not knowing what their news had been. The last person she rang was Lesley Palmer, Peddler's wife.

'Hello Lesley. How are you?'

'I'm all right. Have you heard how Pete is?'

'Yes, he's a survivor. Have you heard how Peddler is?'

'Oh, he's dead.'

That's how it came out. She'll never forget the conversation.

'Are you sure?'

'Yes, they said.' The padre and a neighbour had been round.

'What are you doing?'

'I'm just sitting here.'

'Have you been all night on your own?'

'No, my mum stayed here. She's gone home. I'm going to sort one or two bits out and then go over.'

It hadn't sunk in. She wrote her a letter and rang her mum, but there was nothing more she could do.

In Plymouth, little Stuart Ray managed to keep a brave face going at the Perrys until the *Sunday Independent* arrived. On page three there was a picture of *Ardent* beneath the words 'Give 'em hell' – a sub-editor's summary of a message for the Task Force from the widow of the only survivor of the Narvik *Ardent*, Lilian Hooke. Beneath that was a picture of Leigh Slatter's wife, Chris, and little Kelly, alongside 'Agony of the wives who wait'. That was when Stuart became upset.

In the days to come, Brenda White would find herself comforting friends who couldn't believe what had happened any more than she could: John Cocker, and Alan, the man she'd chosen not to marry until all the kids were grown up, if he asked her again. Knocker had worshipped him.

For now, the Whites were still trying to come to terms with the fact that Knocker hadn't been indestructible. He hadn't come bouncing back, that irrepressible grin on his face. Not this time. But, if Knocker couldn't come to them, they'd go to Knocker.

So, that Sunday, Brenda, Ian, Dawn and Mandy, and three or four close friends, drove to Seaborne on the bracing north-east coast, a packet of multi-coloured condoms tucked safely in Brenda's pocket.

'We wanted to be near the sea. That sounds crazy, doesn't it?' she laughs. 'We had a beach party. We had this fire. We blew up the condoms and sailed them out to sea for him. As these condoms sailed away . . . I never look at a pack of coloured condoms now, but it amuses me. Mind you, I'm not certain they always used them.'

The anticipation of a Board of Inquiry didn't trouble Alan Maunder much until one heart-stopping discovery. The Ship's Log had to be up-to-date and signed by the Navigating Officer and the Captain before it went off for scrutiny. His preparations went well until it was stolen from his locked cabin.

Suspecting a key-holding trophy-hunter, he reported the theft to the First Lieutenant.

'Build up your diary. You need hard evidence for the inquiry,' Andrew Gordon Lennox told him. Then he instigated a search. It would be 24 hours before Maunder found the courage to tell Alan West.

He took a deep breath and knocked on the skipper's door.

'Sir, I want to tell you about the Ship's Log,' he said.

West walked off and returned with a puzzled look on his face with something familiar. It was the log.

At 1250, in Falkland Sound, *Ardent*'s tormentor returned to haunt the 21 Club. On another lone run, Capitan Pablo Carballo came across HMS *Antelope*. This time, he didn't waste his day's work. Instead of straddling the frigate, he slammed a 1,000lb bomb through her port side, just beneath the Bridge. It didn't explode, but it left one man dead and one seriously injured.

Not long after the call went out for blood donors, Jessie Owens went up to the ward, but could they find a vein? His arm was like a dartboard. The slightly built stoker had gone into shock. Not far behind, there was probably more in an armful from his six-foot drinking partner, Brum Serrell, anyway.

It was the first time the tankie had given blood so, once the Tony Hancock gags were done and the nurse had asked him how he felt – 'Fine' – and did he want a cup of tea – 'Stupid question' – he bimbled across to see John Dillon. The trouble was, he wasn't feeling fine at all.

Level with the end of Miguel Garcia's bed, he felt himself going, knees first, ankles next. He went out like a light.

'Aaagh!'

The young Argentinian was convinced some hairy-arsed stoker was going for him. In seconds, someone rushed to pick the Ardent up and, gradually, in the space of a few hours, a wink or a smile here, a pair of scrounged plimsolls there, the fear etched in the soldier's eyes eased. He didn't know the matelot next to him was not much older, far less what path had brought him here, or why so many glanced their way. A 19-year-old South London lad and his companion of fate from Cavaria, the enemy, not much older, if at all – like lots of the lads they'd left behind. It was hard not to glance.

Not far from Scouse Phillips in the Ballroom, a couple of Argentinian 16 year olds looked equally frightened. The 'wodging great hole' in his head, and the throbbing skull were small beer, Phillips realised. He had his mates too, even if they didn't believe that his neck was sore.

He couldn't remember the hits, he couldn't remember the helicopter ride so, in true Ardent style, they reminded him. How he'd told Bernie to go back down below and fetch his music centre, even though it was at Bernie's mum's. How he'd been singing rugby songs no one recognised. The business about the blood on his forehead. Everything else, 'You fat bastard!'

Lt David Searle was never short of company, either, if nothing else because Navy rules didn't allow him to be alone. As soon as he moved out of the Sickbay, he shared a cabin with Paddy McClintock.

Then he was reintroduced to the social setting of the Wardroom, Morgan O'Connell at his side.

It was one of those bar room encounters. The rest were fine. The only person who wasn't was him, seeing divisions where they didn't exist, on morphine and whisky with his arm in a sling.

It was only when he saw Ken Enticknap that he faced the emotional difficulty of understanding why he couldn't have done more, and the next few pieces of those missing minutes fell into place.

The mending of Enticknap went on, meanwhile. He'd become accustomed to the ball of bandage wrapped round his left hand when a doctor came and told him he'd be going to theatre.

'We can't give you anaesthetic. You've ingested so much smoke. We'll do it under a local.'

It didn't bother him. He'd survived. So he spent the operation watching three casualties being put back together. There was plenty to see. Even if his war was over, it hadn't stopped outside.

At 1715, to prove the point, the unexploded 1,000lb bomb erupted in one of Antelope's Air Conditioning Units, killing Staff Sgt James Prescott, the 37-year-old Royal Engineer trying to defuse it, and injuring six others. Eighteen-year-old steward Mark Stephens had already been killed by flying debris when the second 1,000lb bomb, Carballo's, crashed through the hull three hours or more before.

Her DC parties ran from the icy wind of the Flight Deck but, like Ardent, her firemain had been shredded. At 1840, consumed by flames, her Seacat

Magazine exploded too. Five injured Antelopes were on their way by air to *Canberra* when Lauraine Mulberry settled down to add to her diary:

> Actually spent a civilised quiet evening; changed into my blue dress (brazen); a drink before dinner, a leisurely dinner, a drink after dinner in the Cricketers. Sat with a young helicopter pilot with a broken ankle. He was pilot in the SAS on the Pebble Beach raid – 25 SAS men – completed raid, no injuries, and when flying between ships with them the helicopter plunged into the sea. Twenty of the SAS men drowned. He was the only one of the crew who escaped and is now living in an agony of guilt and remorse. All that to cope with at 23 years of age.

That was only half of it. Some of the SAS men flying on the 846 Squadron Sea King from *Hermes* to *Intrepid* had already survived two crashes on South Georgia's Fortuna Glacier. The story filtering back to *Canberra* said that, in near darkness, the helo hit an albatross, lost power and hit the sea, losing an automatic flotation bag and starting to sink. In seconds, the pilot found himself trapped underwater.

Gasping for air in the dark, icy water, he kicked out in desperation and broke his ankle as it freed. He prised himself through the cockpit window and, almost unconscious, burst to the surface. When he came round he was in his liferaft, alone. Then more men appeared in the water. Then a ship's boat.

It wasn't only the Ardents whose minds were on constant rewind but, among the giving of blood and thanks that day, at least the majority of them had found something to keep their minds occupied.

By the time they hit the sack that night, they'd helped to move 61 pallets of compo rations and 101 pallets of stores and ammunition towards the islands. They'd worked out that D ration packs were lighter than C, they'd learned not to flinch when a Wessex wheel landed by their crouched bodies on the Flight Deck and another net-full of cargo went. In some small way, they were still playing a part.

It had been a busy day beyond the horizon too. Early that morning, Sea Harriers had attacked Goose Green airstrip and seen the remains of the Pucara destroyed by *Ardent*'s NGS. *Antelope* had gone, but the Argentinians had lost a Skyhawk and six Daggers. Now it was a question of who could last longest.

Back in Plymouth, Carole Leake had watched her brother Alan run through Milehouse in the Plymouth Marathon during the afternoon. Watched, but with unseeing eyes. That evening, she sat down with her parents as Michael Nicholson came on the ITN news and told his version of *Ardent*'s story. Suddenly, he said, 'the NAAFI manager, John Leake . . .' and the phantom sprint from Canteen to GDP took root in legend.

'Oh my goodness,' she shrieked. 'I told you he'd do something like that.'

At around midnight, Christine Rowe caught her last news bulletin of the day on radio. The Argentinians were claiming to have sunk *Canberra*. She didn't need that.

Swing the pendulum 170nm north-east by east from Port Stanley and *Canberra* was no further from the occupied capital when early breakfast was

served at 0930 on Monday, 24 May, than she'd been 24 hours before, just a few minutes further north and west, still loitering while the destoring went on.

Lauraine Mulberry recorded the aims of the day:

> This morning, all ammo, supplies and remnants of 3 Para, 40/42 Commando are being transferred to the stores ship *Resource*, so perhaps she is going in and we will be reprieved. Low dependency patients will also be going into cabins from the Meridian Room hospital.

So, the Ardents wouldn't be heading back for the Falklands after all. For one, as he heaved ration packs up stairs that morning with Jeff Curran and Geoff Hart, Mick Cox was still feeling guilty. He still wanted to go back and, from what he could tell, so did others. But it wasn't going to happen.

'We came south as a ship's company and we're going back as one,' the First Lieutenant told them.

◆◆◆

At 1100, Pablo Carballo's 1,000lb bomb ripped what was left of the heart out of *Antelope* in San Carlos Water. Soon after, 22 hours after being hit, her back broke and she sank. The images were to become the most enduring of the war, but not in the way the photographer had hoped for Leigh Slatter.

Ardent's 26-year-old helicopter controller was helping PO Smudge Smith on *Canberra*'s Bridge when a journalist arrived at his shoulder, itching to show him the picture he was about to wire home. If he'd pushed his delight much further, the world would never have seen Martin Cleaver's dramatic shot, because Slatter would have shoved it up his arse before it reached the drum.

◆◆◆

In *Fearless*'s Wardroom, Capt Bob Harmes was reconsidering the wisdom of returning to the fray when he heard a familiar stutter and thought, 'It can't be!'

He turned round to see a dead man walking in and said, 'What are you . . .?' It was Simon Ridout.

The two sat down and *Ardent*'s Medical Officer relived his story.

After watching *Yarmouth* steam past first, then Mike Crabtree's Wessex pluck two men from the water, Ridout had realised he had little time left. His once-only was full of water, he was growing cold and it was becoming harder and harder to stop his face being turned into the freezing waves.

He'd tried to pull his lifejacket waveguard down, but only managed to yank the whole thing over his head instead. Letting air out to put it back on, and blowing it up again only robbed him of more energy.

In the end, he gave up trying to turn his back to the waves. He didn't really care any more.

Dying never really entered his head but, if *Broadsword* hadn't arrived to give *Ardent* air cover, or if she'd sailed past too, God knows what he'd have felt.

But *Broadsword* did stop. Her Swimmer of the Watch leapt into the water,

attached to a rope, and swam to him. Ten sailors hauled Ridout aboard until he was hanging from a rig, too heavy to handle, a Michelin Man dressed in orange. Killick of the Watch Terry Lee took his rigging knife to a leg of the Doc's watterlogged survival suit then, drained, they laid him on the deck.

The First-Aid Party couldn't work out why he wanted to know the name of the ship's MO, Surg. Lt Gerard Woodruff, until they cut his once-only and saw his overalls. Then they carried him to Capt Bill Canning's cabin and, in return for a hot bath, he stank the place out with diesel fumes. A cup of tea continued the therapy. Apart from bruising all over his body, the only damage was a broken ring finger.

Before long, they decided to move him to *Canberra*. Walking down *Broadsword*'s Burma Way, he was gripped with fear. He'd only just learnt his way round a Type 21. If this one sank . . . he couldn't go through that again. It didn't bear thinking about.

Eventually, he found a seat on a Lynx flight off the frigate. But it didn't take him where he wanted to go. By the time it reached *Canberra*, it was too dark to land. He'd have to make do with *Fearless*.

His lodgings there were in the Sickbay. He was told of *Ardent*'s fate, heard how the landings were going and then overheard Surg. Lt John Ramage, *Antelope*'s MO, talking to Surg. Capt Young.

A few months previously, Ramage had left one of the Royal Marine Commandos. Now he was anxious to rejoin them ashore. But Young had bad news. Queen's Regulations. He'd have to go home. Ramage wasn't happy. Ridout was.

That night, with the Antelopes who'd been moved to *Fearless*, he was transferred to the North Sea ferry *Norland*. All that remained was *Norland*'s final rendezvous with *Canberra*.

◆◆◆

'Christine, the *Antelope*'s gone down! The *Antelope*'s been sunk.' Dr Nicky Cutler came rushing in to Christine Rowe's office at Launceston General Hospital and threw her arms around her. Her boyfriend, David Mugridge, was a Lieutenant on the Type 21.

'Have you rung the number?' Christine asked.

'They haven't heard anything.'

'They'll let you know as soon as there's news. Have they said there were any casualties?'

They hadn't. 'They'll contact you.'

Every half-hour she'd be back: 'They haven't rung, they haven't rung.'

'Give them time.' It was all Christine was qualified to say.

In Plymouth, Frankie Enticknap received Ken's familygram. He'd be in hospital a while, but he was all right. He hoped 'Little E' and she were well. He didn't mention the lost ring, or the finger in it.

Carol Ray received hers too. 'Okay, no injuries' and, on the bottom, 'Tell Kay that Jim's fine.'

Up the road, after a roller-coaster weekend, Beryl Yeatman was more

concerned that Paul's teacher would think he was making up war stories if he mentioned dad's ship. She rang just to make sure.

Down in Milehouse, Carole Leake ran the media gauntlet on the way home from school, then pressed on with decorating and thinking what to wear when John came home.

They were the lucky ones. In Blackburn, the Whitfords were still clinging to the hope that 'missing' meant Garry had survived, somewhere, despite what the Sunday papers had said, and the Monday papers too. Deep down though, his brother Alan admits, they'd known since 4.15 p.m. on Saturday.

In Ecclesfield, Shaun Hanson's last letter dropped through the front door too that Monday. His dad opened it. It was typically cheerful, like the one he'd sent his sister Carol for her 18th birthday, with a key drawn on it. But Pete immediately began to clutch at straws.

He went down to the Navy recruiting office in Sheffield and unfolded the letter on the desk. 'Look,' he pointed at Shaun's handwriting and spoke to the officer there, 'I've had this letter from my son saying he's on this RAS, but I've been told he's lost his life!'

The man explained. An RAS wasn't another ship, it was a Replenishment at Sea. Pete went home.

◆◆◆

On *Canberra*, Jon Major still couldn't believe Shaun was gone either. Three or four hours a day opening tins in the cruise ship's Galley only delayed him thinking about his best mate.

Despite the day's poor visibility, at 2000, just before 4 p.m. local time, the Ardents completed the destoring of *Canberra* to *Tidepool*. Without them, the Royal Marine bandsmen and P&O crew would have taken days longer to do the job.

Around three hours later, they received their next bag of mail from HMS *Leeds Castle* while the Antelopes did the same on *Norland*. With helicopters in the air, Simon Ridout took the opportunity to hitch a lift and reintroduce himself to his shipmates.

Lt Mike Knowles was with Alan Maunder in the Crow's Nest Bar, talking about their lost MO, when the Nagivating Officer's jaw dropped. Knowles turned to see what had stopped the conversation and thought he was seeing a ghost. There he was.

The three hugged. Then they drank and listened to Ridout's story – the miracle of putting a once-only on in the water without drowning – and he to theirs, the lost battle to save the ship.

Ridout knew he'd been reported missing in action. In fact, it was *Fearless* who'd rapidly signalled Fleet to say he was alive. Eight thousand miles away, his family soon found out, but the message never arrived on *Canberra*. All they'd had was 'missing'. Later on, Ridout walked into one of Morgan O'Connell's clinics in the Meridian Room and Bob Young did the same double-take.

'I thought you were dead!' the LMA stood, amazed. They embraced. A far cry from Devonport.

He saw Alan West as well and, gradually, more of the horror of those final minutes on board became apparent. The two would meet and talk from time to time during the coming few days, and West's guard would often be down. The what-ifs. Had he done all he could to save his men and his ship? Ridout remembers the question being asked time and time again. To him, the answer was clear.

♦♦♦

With no more stores to be manhandled up top from *Canberra*'s cavernous hold, all that Tuesday, 25 May, could offer was grim and grey and frustrating. While efforts to transfer her wounded passengers to the hospital ship, *Hydra*, alongside the port side were wrecked by the rising swell, Lenny Yeatman paid a visit to the Purser's Office to find something, anything, for the Ardents to do.

After weeks running their lives by clocks timed to match those on mantelpieces in Britain, now they had little in the way of routine to govern their days. One minute was like any other. One hour and the next. Not even the arc of the sun across the sky could measure time passing. It was overcast.

So, here they still were, 170nm east north-east of Stanley, three days effectively steaming round in circles. Despite the Joss's best efforts, Eddie Edwards's most reliable memory of such times probably works for the majority of them.

Although he shared a cabin with Taff Lovidge, he didn't always sleep there. If there was an empty one on his way back from the bar, it would do. He could work out where it was when he woke up. And, if he missed muster, he'd just say he'd been up top working.

Morgan O'Connell had told them to get drunk. The trouble was, he'd told them to do it for a couple of days. With the assistance of their newly found P&O friends, most had a couple of weeks in mind.

They maintained the tradition, telling jokes, and, for a time, they'd put a can of beer on the table for a lost friend, keep a seat empty, 'Cheers, Knocker!' have a drink to him, and be thankful it wasn't them.

Scouse Flynn found himself with a handful of others in John Goddard's cabin – no surprise there – when someone offered the toast to 'absent friends'. It didn't go down well. Raw nerves spilled over into harsh words, until they realised how pointless it was.

Little Errol Flynn didn't mean to swamp his pit that day but, even through his swimming head, he could see Dickie Henderson wasn't too impressed, not even when he offered to clean the mess up.

'I'm not having that in here!' his disgusted cabin-mate shouted, and made him go and tell the cleaner. Apart from Villa winning the European Cup, it's all the pint-sized Brummie remembers about the week on *Canberra*. The Joss wasn't happy.

A few cabins away, Mark Bogard's frustration erupted with Gary Gleed, over something forgettable. The writer didn't hit the Captain's Steward, but he did put his fist through a mirror, cutting his hand. Leading Regulator Ken Chapman heard about it and gave him a bollocking too.

Fuelled by half-truths, supposition dressed up as substance, with time to kill and enough alcohol to keep them oiled, it was inevitable minds would race. Then

opinions and fears wouldn't be far behind. By the time the knock came on the Joss's hair salon door, he thought he had a mutiny on his hands. They'd heard the Old Man was going to be court-martialled. The youngsters, especially, were livid.

Lenny Yeatman straightened them out. It was a Board of Inquiry. When you'd lost God knows how many millions of fighting kit, there were lessons to be learned. Could she have been saved? Had they done enough? The questions they'd asked themselves. It sorted them, for a while, but it worried the Joss, so he went to see the First Lieutenant and voiced his fear that some of the lads were drinking too much. Andrew Gordon Lennox shared his concern.

Alan West knew the dangers. In the seclusion of his cabin one night, just one, withdrawing into his shell, he'd been 'absolutely ratted' himself. He promised them that he'd speak to the senior rates and remind them that only one person would carry the can, but that the rules demanded an inquiry.

Back in the hair salon, though, the fruits of the Joss's and Jimmy's efforts to nurture morale were beginning to show. The ship's company was mustering every day. The salon had become a gathering place where wandering souls would sit under driers and talk. The youngsters' knock on his door had shown that the *Ardent* spirit still burned somewhere.

Lenny Yeatman sat down with Tony Ray and a handful of others and the idea of an HMS *Ardent* Association was hatched. Whatever happened between now and returning home, they'd stick together.

Whatever? The question wasn't long being answered. With the destoring done, 'Beagle' Burne had to decide what to do. From the odd signal he'd received, and his own reading of the situation, he believed *Canberra* would be needed at South Georgia to collect 5 Brigade from *QE2*. So that's where they'd go.

Some wanted to stay. But, for others, it was the news they were waiting for. John Foster was one. He hadn't dared to think of home until someone said, 'We're on our way to South Georgia.'

The buzz had terrified him. There'd been people killed on the other ships. Men were needed.

He was praying, 'Please, I don't think I could handle it.' He wanted to think about the ship. He wanted to be with the people he knew, and go home with them.

For some, the men who couldn't bring themselves to believe that lightning didn't strike twice, the worry was still being in the Total Exclusion Zone. Like Tom Williams. He was managing to stay honest by filling in on the Bridge, but a visit to the ship's cathedral-like Engine Room had rattled him.

'If any bomb comes in here, I'm finished!' he thought. So he practised finding the Upper Deck from his cabin, right up forward, and slept with his seaboots and 8s on. The once-only suit hanging on the back of his cabin door was a worry. One of the cleaners had already asked him what it was.

'All RN people are issued with one. Haven't you got one?'

'No.'

He kept his eye on it after that.

That night, Lauraine Mulberry's diary added her own speculation to what the Ardents knew:

We are now 200 miles east of Stanley and steaming for South Georgia where, we believe, we will rendezvous with *QE2* and probably take on her troops. The survivors of *Antelope* are now on *Norland*, and it is thought that they and *Ardent*, plus well-enough patients we are carrying, will all go over to *QE2* and she will probably head for Ascension and then home . . . '

Then she added:

Argentine news report states that we have sunk. Obviously didn't realise we had sailed away under the cover of darkness or else some pilot missed his target but claimed a hit!

What she didn't know was that the Task Force had, indeed, lost another ship. At 1419, north of Pebble Island on West Falkland, HMS *Coventry* had been hit by three bombs from two Skyhawks in a formation led by Capitan Pablo Carballo. Within 15 minutes, she'd rolled on to her port beam and 19 of her 282 men had been lost.

Worse still. At 1641, 60nm west of *Canberra*, *Atlantic Conveyor* had been hit by an Exocet missile aimed at *Hermes* and abandoned. Twelve of her men were dead, including her master, Capt Ian North, the bearded sea dog who'd welcomed the Ardents on board in Devonport ten weeks before.

◆◆◆

Time was beginning to blur for everyone on board. Wednesday, 25 May, was probably the first day Ken Enticknap felt something resembling alive again. In his condition, it's unlikely to have been before. He remembers it because he met the NAAFI man with his trolley in the ward.

'D'you want anything, Jack?'

'I'd like a toothbrush and some toothpaste, please.'

'That'll be 67 pence.'

Sixty-seven pence? All he had were the pyjamas he was in. The man looked at him and said, 'Oh!'

It was a strange moment. Back in the land of the living, yes. But what a lot he'd lost on the way. A few hours later, if that, the docs decided Enticknap was well enough to join Morgan O'Connell's sessions – and Ralph Coates was well enough to wheel him there, on the road to recovery from penetrating upper body wounds, and with a limp his messmates would never let him forget.

The rest of the Ardents had adjusted to the purpose of the Irishman's gentle probings, either that or given up on them for good. He asked them about their experiences, then dropped in the odd question.

'How are you going to cope when you get back home again?'

'How will you cope when you see the families of the bereaved?'

'Your mother's fussing?'

There were no answers. Enticknap knew there weren't supposed to be. O'Connell wanted them to find their own way to deal with the unavoidable.

309

Mike Lewis was one of those who wouldn't see the psychiatrist. But he did increase his drinking, though even that didn't stop him feeling more dislocated every day.

Cliff Goldfinch was another who'd found a ready supply of drink in the Galley, unsurprisingly. He didn't suffer any pain for days but, when it came, it was bad.

'Every night you'd see somebody go down. I went down. We all did.'

That night, it was someone else's turn.

As usual, the senior ratings were drinking too much, all of it masking different thoughts, listening to the Royal Marines' band knocking out a non-stop string of the old songs, the old Navy songs.

Taff Lovidge was drinking with Big Tansy Lee, Bob Lewis and Wacker Payne when, he recalls, Wacker suddenly called him Carole and lurched back into the band, sending the drums flying.

Lenny Yeatman was already looking after Connie Francis, on the surgeon's understanding that his wounded *Argonaut* counterpart would have one drink and then go back to the ward.

Instinctively, the Joss rushed towards Wacker, anxious to put an arm round his shoulder and reassure him. The more he tried, the more Wacker fought him off.

'You'll frighten him,' Jim Watts shouted.

Yeatman backed off and the young PO wandered across the Ballroom alone, leaving the drums rolling about on the floor. Lovidge walked over and did the only thing he could think of doing.

'Carole's here,' he said softly. 'I'm here.' Then they walked him somewhere quieter.

'It was so sad,' Lovidge says now. It shook them all up. But Yeatman's night was far from over.

'Come on, Connie,' he turned to Francis after two drinks. 'I've got to get you back,'

'Just one more!'

He had one more, then the pair set off back to the ward. On the way, though, the Argonaut heard the merriment coming from one of the Mess rooms. Francis decided to investigate. He knocked on the door and it was opened by the man who'd filleted the bomb shrapnel from the edge of his aorta.

'Connie! Come in,' he greeted his patient. 'What are you going to have to drink?'

There was no way Yeatman could manhandle a man who'd had surgery, was there? He eventually wheeled his old pal back into the ward and tucked him in. As Yeatman was about to leave, a surgeon commander appeared and read him the riot act. He took it. He had no choice.

Back home, his wife was going through the mill too, and she had no choice either.

Beryl Yeatman watched the *News at Ten* half-time headlines, then felt the blood drain.

'. . . ships have been hit, one seriously,' she heard Defence Secretary John

Nott admit, 'but I'm not prepared to say what it is.' End of part one.

Part two didn't give her any more, except that it was a 'big ship'. Big ship? What was it? *Canberra*?

End of part two came and she still didn't know. It was the late, late bulletin before she found out that it was *Atlantic Conveyor*. Little did Beryl know – little did anyone know – but *Canberra* was well out of Exocet range, more than 700nm east of Port Stanley, and heading for South Georgia. Slowly.

◆◆◆

The bright red paintwork of HMS *Endurance* stood out against the mountains of South Georgia beyond the starboard bow as she rendezvoused with *Canberra* at 1100. On the horizon, a line of clouds turned out to be snow-covered peaks. It was a clear but cold day, bitterly cold.

There was a poignancy about the meeting of the giant cruise ship and the tiny, 3,600-ton Antarctic patrol vessel, less than a tenth as big, which was almost certainly lost on the Ardents.

Endurance was skippered by Capt Nick Barker, the son of the late Lt Cdr Ben Barker, the ill-fated commanding officer of the last *Ardent* before Alan West's, the man whose ship they'd paid homage to in the Norwegian Sea just weeks before.

After one of *Endurance*'s Wasps flew over on an errand, the big ship pressed on. At 1242, *Canberra* altered course for Cumberland Bay. At 1315, the port anchor was let go at Grytviken while the Great White Whale waited for the *QE2*, still way north, delayed by thick fog and ice. At 1345, the Hull trawler-cum-mines countermeasures vessel HMS *Cordella* made fast to *Canberra*'s port side.

And, at 2000, the *QE2* arrived.

◆◆◆

Sleeping, resting, drinking, talking. But mostly drinking and talking.

Saddened by the news of their sister ship, *Antelope*, and the stricken *Coventry*, the Ardents were safe now, ready to take what for many meant the final step away. Many, but not all.

Inside some cabin, thwarted in their plan to smuggle a makeshift Devonport dockyard anti-tank missile launcher ashore, Richie Gough and Tony Langridge were plotting again. The plan was to kidnap a couple of Scots Guards, swipe their uniforms and head back to the war.

They'd had a couple of drinks too many, of course, but they were only half joking. They'd made it through, but there was unspent adrenaline to deal with. And that wasn't fair.

In the small hours of Friday morning, the Ardents' last night as guests of Capt Scott-Masson and his grateful crew, the minesweeping trawlers *Cordella* and *Arnella*, and the tug *Typhoon*, continued cross-decking from *QE2*. In total darkness between 0100 and 0515, the Welsh Guards were first to cross, lugging 90lb packs and rifles with them, just six hours after arriving in Cumberland Bay.

At 0800, the rest of 5 Brigade followed – 2 Battalion Scots Guards, Naval

Air Force and Royal Air Force sections and other minor units – while the Gurkhas embarked the North Sea ferry *Norland*.

It was a long day. In their week on *Canberra*, the Ardents had revisited hell a million and one times. They'd felt the desolation of their loss. They'd begun the never-ending what-ifs. They'd started nursing their wounded. They'd shifted a cruise-liner full of war stores in a sinew-wrenching effort to play a part in whatever was happening back in the Falklands. And they'd made a ship-full of friends along the way. They'd remained *Canberra's* chummy ship.

While *Debbie Does Dallas*, or something an equal shade of blue, entertained a few matelots for the umpteenth time in one corner of the Meridian Room – the lounge they'd first stepped into a week before – Cliff Goldfinch, Tony Ray and Roger Fenton were watching *The Life of Brian*, crying their eyes out. Knocker White. The bright side of life.

Before long, Scots Guards officers were starting to hunt the men of *Ardent* out, to renew old acquaintances, to ask what it was like to be under attack. And, around the Great White Whale, gifts were being left for those who'd be heading back for the war zone, rather than home.

Pete Brierley and two young ratings had found solace in the linen store, deep in the bowels of *Canberra*. It was an excellent way of having the laundry done for nothing, Brierley laughs. But it was much more. The store was full of fluff so, while they reminisced with the Whale's old hands, they systematically cleaned it out for them. It was their parting gift, a thank you.

Tom Williams left his once-only suit hanging on his door for the cleaner, John Foster and a handful of others handed their anti-flash gear on. They wouldn't be needing it again.

At 1300, Lenny Yeatman told the ship's company to gather their paltry possessions and what they'd been given – someone's shoes, someone else's trousers, paper underpants, that kind of thing – and muster in the Ballroom.

At 1500, eight minutes after HMS *Leeds Castle* came alongside to collect the surviving Ardents, Ken Enticknap and his fellow 'sickies' were transferred to the *QE2* by helicopter. He'd been wheeled outside his makeshift ward to watch the sun rise over Grytviken that morning. The spectacular sight had reassured him that, at last, they were safe and heading home, thoughts still tinged with the sadness.

Half-an-hour later, after a frustrating series of false starts, the rest stood up to follow and pulled open the doors to go. What they saw took their breath away. The stairs on both sides were lined with soldiers, clapping. The line stretched through the Galley and along all the corridors to the ship's side and the ladder down to *Leeds Castle*. They clapped all the way.

In the chilly Antarctic winter air, as Lenny Yeatman checked heads, there was a shout from above. He looked up and two bottles of beer hurtled past, followed by Mick Newby. The beer had been launched by a former Naval sonar rate called Taff. He wasn't the only familiar face Newby had met.

As he was walking past the line of applauding soldiers, the 26 year old had seen 'Uncle' Ray Durbin, a family friend he'd known most of his life, waiting to head the other way. They hugged. Durbin was glad he was safe. Mick told him what to expect and wished him luck. Durbin would make it home.

Then, on *Leeds Castle*'s Flight Deck, the Ardents heard a familiar sound amid the echoing applause. On the Promenade Deck, the Royal Marine band, the men they'd spent so much time with during the past six days, were playing, first 'Hearts of Oak', then 'Rule Britannia', then 'A Life on the Ocean Wave', finally 'Hootenanny'. The Ardents replied the only way they knew. They sang 'The Oggie Song', the rocky walls of the harbour soon echoing 'Oi! Oi! Oi!', chanted first by the Ardents, then returned by the thousands lining *Canberra*'s rails in salute.

On one of *Canberra*'s aft decks, Morgan O'Connell took in the scene, snow falling gently, the lights from a couple of warships bathing Cumberland Bay in an icy glow, its glass surface reflecting little ships moving about the harbour, and the mountains behind, and the glacier. It was, he says, the most emotional thing he's ever seen. On *Canberra*'s Bridge, Capt Scott-Masson felt the same. Tears were already falling on *Leeds Castle*.

The moment was still uneasy for some, though. As Jan Joyce stepped on to the Flight Deck, the surroundings looked too similar to the Falklands for him. Buck Ryan couldn't see much to ease him either as the band played on. Bill Bailey, tears streaming down his face, felt completely alone too. Somewhere nearby, Eddie Edwards looked at the glow of lights across the bay and felt exposed.

John Foster was among those who glanced back at the giant P&O liner and a thought jolted him: 'Some of these guys aren't going to come back.'

Leeds Castle pulled away. As she did, her Marine Engineering Officer, Pete Rigg, walked on to the Flight Deck in case there was anyone he knew. Amid the motley scene, he spotted two familiar faces.

Taff Lovidge was miles away, deep in thought, when a big hand stretched in front of him. He looked at his old mate from HMS *Fife*. The two embraced.

Rigg turned to Mick Cox and then back at Lovidge.

'Have you had a beer?'

'No.'

'Come down the Mess.'

The three were joined by Jeff Curran and Geoff Hart, Lovidge recalls. Rigg gave them a beer, then another, and another. He didn't ask them what had happened, their scraggy state told him all he needed to know. They talked, instead, about *Canberra*. And drank.

Not all the Ardents took the *Leeds Castle* ferry ride, however. On HMS *Arnella*, Pete Brierley had bumped into Lt Bob Bishop, his old *Ardent* Divisional Officer. Bishop seemed surprised his former charge hadn't been promoted. The small-talk was what Brierley needed.

On *Northella*, David Searle met Lt Eric Fraser. The last time they'd been in each other's company was about a month before, in Reigate, at Searle's wedding. The contrast couldn't have been greater, the routes their lives had taken in the six, short weeks since, betrayed by what they stood up in, no gold braid, but working rig and oversized white P&O overalls. Fraser handed him a pair of black trousers.

Back on *Leeds Castle*, the echoes of a hundred and more hearty voices were beginning to fade and eyes were starting to dry when something more filled the chilly air.

Drifting across the waves came the haunting lament 'Flowers of the Forest'. Alone on *QE2*'s deck, Pipe Major J.J. Riddell was bidding 2 Battalion Scots Guards' farewell to the friends they'd never see again, those heading north, those who would never go home. Men who'd bitten their lips minutes before now gave in to their deepest feelings.

Chief Stoker Andy Andrew scanned the distant shoreline. He saw the shape of old, abandoned whaling ships lying alongside the jetty, and the crippled Argentinian submarine, *Santa Fe*. He listened to the pipes but the applause was still echoing in his mind.

'I've never been a hero in all my life,' he says. 'They were starting their journey and we were just finishing ours. It was strange.'

◆◆◆

Leeds Castle's slide alongside the rust-stained hull of *QE2* wasn't easy, but no one noticed. Its radio aerials scraped Cunard paintwork off the luxury troopship's protruding Bridge Wing, then, one by one, the Ardents took their next steps closer to home.

The reception committee was no less gracious in welcome than *Canberra*'s had been in departure. Lines of men applauded. After a week adjusting to the lap of luxury, so soon after leaving their burning warship, these new trappings of civilisation still took their breath away.

The Flight Deck was empty and, as *Leeds Castle* prepared to manoeuvre, a stoker knocked on the door of the Chiefs' Mess. *Ardent*'s men looked round and, in seconds, they'd raced on to a deserted Upper Deck. Beer and conversation. Two great Naval traditions had nearly given Mick Cox his wish to return to the Falklands.

By the time their feet trod *QE2*'s passageways, everybody else had gone to a lounge. They found it, too, eventually. But by then the others had moved again, already issued with their cabin keys.

◆◆◆

In the moments before they'd left the Scots Guards on *Canberra*, Alan West had found himself with Major John Kiszely, a man he knew well. Before they parted, Kiszely had uttered a promise.

Now, on *QE2*, Tom Williams was holding a signal from *Canberra*. It was from 2 Battalion Scots Guards. It read: 'To HMS *Ardent*: we will avenge you.'

Sixteen days later, Major Kiszely would win the Military Cross after a bayonet charge in the final assault on Mount Tumbledown, a charge he completed with only three unwounded men and, legend has it, an enemy bullet lodged in the compass on his belt. His promise? 'I'll get them for doing this!'

If *Ardent*'s end had graced her motto so spine chillingly, so the men of 2 Battalion would live up to their own declaration of intent: *Nemo Me Impune Lacessit* (No one molests me with impunity).

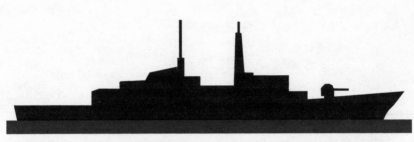

THE BENEFIT OF HINDSIGHT

One   *QE2*, South Georgia to *QE2*, Ascension Island
          (28 May – 5 June 1982)   317

ONE

QE2, SOUTH GEORGIA TO *QE2*, ASCENSION ISLAND

(28 MAY – 5 JUNE 1982)

It wasn't the *QE2* nursing staff's fault. They'd been used to administering to rich old ladies with bunions, and seasick Gurkhas. Her Sickbay had proper beds, but the way the curtains were suddenly drawn around Ken Enticknap, and the other wounded men as they were checked, was cold and clinical.

'We weren't sick, just a little incapacitated,' he recalls.

With every panelled door heading aft, the *QE2*'s accommodation grew more luxurious. Up forward, the four-to-a-cabin bunk beds were as close to a Junior Messdeck as fare-paying passengers could come. Amidships, the best part of 150 yards further back, there were king-size beds and walk-in wardrobes, plush carpets and telephones. Not the kind of place to throw up in.

The senior rates stood at the front of the queue for keys and were given them. They headed forward. The lads waited until only the keys for cabins aft were left. Then, in their pairs, they turned and went in search of the place they'd call home for a week, until they reached Ascension; Iain McRobbie with Eric Samson, Coxie with Barney Barnard, Naggers with Buck Ryan, Jan Joyce with Jessie Owens, Scouse Phillips and Kev McDonald, Brum Serrell with John Leake's NAAFI sidekick Nigel Woods, his old Kidderminster Boys Brigade pal, Steve Kent and Jeff Gullick, John Foster and Kev Johnson, Errol Flynn with Dickie Henderson, Dave Croft and Mick Newby, Paul Behagg and Mark Bramwell, Topsy Turner with young Nick Carter, Scouse Flynn with Fluff Garnham again, the list went on – like on *Canberra*, becoming dependent on each other.

Bernie Berntsen, the old man of the Messdeck, found himself with Buck Taylor. Between the beds were switches to turn the lights off, or the radio on. The TV was missing – 'Miserable bastards!' – but on the wall was a painting by El Crappo, so at least they had somewhere to hang their once-onlys.

Two by two, the other Ardents turned keys in locks for the first time and gawped. This was absurd. There were baths in en-suite Bathrooms. The beds were as wide as a gulch, and so were the walk-in wardrobes. Walk-in wardrobes? They laughed. All they had was what they stood in.

Further forward, the likes of Eddie Edwards and Richie Gough were viewing a scene less opulent, but no less welcoming, and so were Mal Crane and Pete Brierley, and Joe Laidlaw and Blood Reed. Further forward still, Tom Williams was choosing beds with Paddy McClintock, David Searle was in with Jonathan

Cody and Tony Ray was cheek-by-jowl with Jim Watts. It wouldn't be long before the senior ratings realised how Cunard's architects had arranged things. Some were niggled. Most weren't.

Lenny Yeatman, though, wasn't too happy to start with, but not because of the unexpected reversal of Royal Naval pecking order. He found himself baby-sitting a young sailor who'd tried to beat the boredom of sentry duty on the ammunition ship *Elk* and, like a prat, started dissecting a hand grenade. The detonator went off and blew his hand apart. It could have blown the ship up.

Yeatman was having none of it, though. His misguided charge was only sharing a few minutes before he'd been switched with Connie Francis. The two Jossmen had some catching up to do.

Within an hour, Russ Goble was running up a slate in the Pig and Whistle – and he wasn't the first. Elsewhere, Pete Brierley, Mal Crane and Clem Clements had been taken in hand by an old acquaintance and deposited in the Chippy's cabin with a pile of blue movies and beer.

Scouse Flynn and Fluff Garnham went one better, several better. They wandered into the NAAFI and asked how much beer they could have.

'As much as you like,' the Canman told them.

That was good enough for them. They went back out, stole a porter's trolley and started to move crates and crates of the stuff to their cabins behind the Joss's back. Literally behind it, on one sortie.

It didn't take Mick Newby and Dave Croft long to settle either, not in a cabin like a state room. The first thing Crofty did was pick up the phone to ask if they could call their mates next door. A telephone exchange, presumably, meant women.

'You girls sound quite nice,' he smarmed. 'Where are you?'

'We know where you are,' the voice on the other end giggled. It wasn't what he'd been expecting.

'Come on, tell us where you are,' he laughed.

'Come out of your cabin, turn left, turn right and you'll see a curtain . . .' They went.

The girl Crofty'd been talking to was Sue Crozier, but it didn't take him long to spot her friend, Jane Broomfield. They chatted for a few moments and he thought nothing more of it.

◆◆◆

The mood was still solemn when Alan West's officers sat down for their evening meal. It stayed solemn until a waiter glided up to Nigel Langhorn with the sweet trolley.

'A Manchester tart, sir?' he asked.

'I don't care where she comes from,' Langhorn replied, dead-pan. 'Wheel her in.' It did the trick.

The lads were already doing their own thing. Despite Lenny Yeatman's best efforts after evening meal, they were trying to drink *QE2* dry in the Pig and Whistle and at various parties being thrown for the intriguing new passengers

318

– 'Hey, we had some of those boys down our cabins' – even if it meant wading through Piper beer. Awful.

It didn't take Bernie Berntsen long to join Russ Goble in the Pig and Whistle, nor much longer for him to bump into a butcher who lived not far away from home in Desborough Road.

'Are you hungry?' he asked.

'We're starving!' Berntsen answered. A few minutes later, they were liberating a Galley of its tastiest contents. A few minutes later still, they were back in the Pig and Whistle, washing it down. It was also the Pig where Buck Ryan and Berntsen met Steve Jackson, a small steward befriended by Knocker on Portland. He quickly sorted out an illicit beer supply that would last the duration. Food and drink. Things were looking up.

From then on, to Bernie's knowledge, the only abberation of note would come when, somehow, he and Buck Taylor ended up in another bar and didn't suspect where they were until the 18 year old was confronted by a seaman's nice fingernails. His hunch was confirmed by a glance round the dark corners of what a significant proportion of the QE2 crew knew mockingly as the Blue Oyster Club.

The Geordie would swap looks with Berntsen, offer some advice – 'I think you'd better sling your hook, pal' – and then they'd leave and not go back. For now, though, they could drink unbothered.

So could Crofty and Mick Newby. They turned the key in their cabin lock after eating and were confronted by a crate of ale on one bed. The note on it said: 'You don't know where this comes from, but there's more if you want it!' They just drank.

But not everyone was happy. Karoly Nagy had been supping with John Bullock and Kev Ryan until they were invited downstairs by some Welsh Guards, and went. Naggers wasn't asked, not personally, so he didn't go. He went back to his cabin instead, locked the door and took his hump with him.

◆◆◆

Pete and Renee Hanson and the girls had found a routine. It consisted of empty days followed by sleepless nights. Friends were trying to do their best, but the family already knew it would be up to them to cope, to stop people running away from them into shops when they were down in the village, things like that. They did it by waiting for them to come out again and making them speak.

That Friday, while the Ardents prepared to leave their 22 shipmates behind, the congregation in Ecclesfield Parish Church stood as the Hansons walked up the aisle at a memorial service for Shaun. The church was full. It reminded Pete of the service they'd been to for the Sheffields three weeks before. For days afterwards, his mind would remain blank, he'd start drinking – 'Have a spell at that' – and he'd become accustomed to feeling very, very tired.

Alan Whitford found himself sitting on the canalside in Blackburn around the same time. He'd called at his parents late, but decided not to disturb them. Now it was raining hard and he was thinking about Garry's last letter home. It had arrived a couple of days after the SSAFA man and his slip of paper, and his

mum had given it to her sister, unopened. As he walked home, at about three or four in the morning, all he could feel was anger at whoever had let all this happen. He had an idea who it was.

◆◆◆

That night, far west of the Ardents, men from 2 Para were gathering their thoughts as well. They'd finally taken Goose Green after a fierce battle, but at the price of 35 men wounded and 17 dead, including Col H. Jones, the man who'd stood with Maj. Tony Rice and watched the first attack on *Ardent*.

By the time the Paras mopped up, they found the Argentinian garrison had grown to about 2,000 troops, many of them rain-soaked, demoralised teenage conscripts. More sinister was the discovery of dozens of napalm bombs near the remains of the Pucaras taken out by *Ardent*'s NGS. What the Argentinians might have been able to do to the landings didn't bear thinking about. Not that any of the Ardents would find out, though it might have given them a way to measure their own loss.

◆◆◆

Not many of the junior ratings felt like a game of hide-and-seek the next morning, but they had no choice. Once he'd woken up Bernie Berntsen and Buck Taylor for muster, the Joss had evidence everywhere in front of him.

'Last night was abysmal,' he told them. 'There were people crawling on all fours to their cabins!'

He banned them from *QE2*'s bars for three days and told them there'd be cabin searches for beer.

In the cabin next to an under-the-weather Berntsen, Mick Newby had been 'ill' too. So had Eric Samson, who tried to blame Iain McRobbie. But it wasn't him. And there was Buck Ryan, less than fresh from his Welsh Guards party.

Most of the lads didn't resent it, even though they thought they'd done enough to deserve some slack. They'd done wrong. There were regulations that said three cans per man per day. But these were the men who'd unscrewed ventilation louvres in the Stokers' Mess and slid back-up supplies out of sight so, on the basis that they had nothing else to put there, they'd already stowed beer everywhere – in every drawer, under their beds, in Bathroom cabinets. These were men who, in days, would arrange for catering to arrive from Mac in *QE2*'s Galley, and then start their cabin parties anyway, a different venue each night to keep the Joss on his toes.

After muster and a bite of breakfast – what they could stomach off their printed menu cards – Croft and Newby returned to their newly cleaned cabin and found another note: 'Did you enjoy your beer?' They had. 'D'you want some more?' They did. The penny dropped.

◆◆◆

At sunset on Saturday, 29 May, *QE2* weighed anchor as snow fell and set sail. But few noticed.

Scouse Phillips walked into Mark Bramwell's cabin, opened the Bathroom cabinet and started counting. He stopped at 28. Twenty-eight cans of beer. For an afternoon's drinking.

The lifejacket stowage was already full of empties, safely beyond the range of the Joss's roving eye. Phillips didn't know where they'd hide 28 more, but he sat down anyway with Bramwell, Kev McDonald and Paul Behagg and began supping, oblivious to the consequences.

The night before, rumour had it, Mick Hallam, *Ardent*'s Chief Weapons Radar Engineer, had lost it in the Galley, kicking shit out of a dishwashing machine. Now it was Bramwell's turn. With no warning, he leapt on Paul Behagg and 'went nuts', Phillips recalls, trying to throttle him.

'It took a shed full to hold him. Too much to drink and a lot of thinking.'

They calmed him down, but not before Lenny Yeatman heard about it. Phillips tried to make himself scarce, but McDonald had already locked him out of their cabin and collapsed, comatose, on his bed.

Phillips swivelled and broke in to the cabin opposite, locking the door behind him.

The next morning, he prised his eyes open and saw the Master at Arms standing over him.

'Right, you Scouse git,' the Joss growled. 'You were with Bramwell last night, weren't you?'

Phillips said the first thing that came into his throbbing head: 'No, Master!'

'I'll see you in half an hour!' Yeatman walked out and Phillips struggled to his feet. Then his heart sank. There was mess everywhere. All over the bed. All over the table. All over the floor.

'I'd just told Lenny . . . looked him right in the eye and told him, "Nothing to do with me!" I thought, "How am I going to talk my way out of this one?"'

He wouldn't. The Joss had opened the lifejacket stowage and found what remained in the Bathroom cabinet. The confiscated cans ended up in the Sickbay and ward, all donations gratefully received.

The beer ban didn't bother Phillips, though. The scar on his forehead was a reminder that he didn't have anything to forget, lucky man. Beer was beer. But not to the others, the ones who remembered, the ones fighting emotions and injuries, as well as the emptiness of a ship's company without a ship.

'That must have hurt people most of all,' he says now.

So, whether the Joss liked it or not, the ban was only a temporary inconvenience.

'We got up in the morning at eight, had breakfast, went to muster and then back to bed,' Bernie Berntsen remembers a simple routine, rather than the Joss and Jimmy's work in keeping men, morale and discipline together. 'You got up for lunch and then went back to bed. Got up and had supper and then,' eventually, once the ban was over, 'in the bar. That's all you did.'

The muster meant news from the war zone and home. It would have helped if there'd been boxes to shift from A to B. But all Yeatman could find before the unions intervened were passageways and cabins that needed cleaning.

The main concern on Monday, 31 May – not that anyone could have named the day – was rumours that an Argentinian Hercules was looking for them, ready to lob bombs out of the back door. The buzz spread. Those who heard it knew they'd already been on a ship which hadn't been able to defend itself.

At one stage, they were called to action stations and found themselves in a dance hall, surrounded by glass panels. Several of them slipped away. Taff Lovidge was one. He joined a handful of others heading for the Engine Room, 'You can't do this' echoing in his ears as they strode off.

'We're not staying up here, boy!' he shouted back, and carried on.

There was food. There was alcohol. And there was banter. But the food wasn't the Forces scran they'd become accustomed to on *Canberra*. The *QE2* food was rich, chosen from a menu printed daily, the kind of fayre matelots weren't used to, not even after Cliff Goldfinch's culinary revolution, and soon they were 'shitting through the eye of a needle', according to Jan Joyce.

But food was still the least of Lenny Yeatman's problems. The beer was still flowing too fast and there was insomnia, the odd fight, the occasional argument. It wasn't long before Buck Ryan found himself sitting alone in a corridor, feeling very lonely. Bob Lewis would find himself in the Laundry.

Somewhere else in the indistinguishable confusion of days, Russ Goble and Bagsy Baker missed muster in the Ballroom one morning. The Leading Regulator, Ken Chapman, found them.

Goble had already been caught with Wolfie Price and Barney Barnard, if the rumours were right, with a massive poker pot waiting to be won. The Master at Arms stopped the game, but didn't take any action. In the Yeatman scheme of things, Goble's and Baker's crime was punishable, by two days cleaning up 13 Deck. They accepted their fate and headed below. But, when they arrived, their jaws dropped. It was massive. There were lorries ferrying stores around. They reported back to the Joss.

'It's like the M4 down there,' they told him, no place to run a broom. 'We'll be killed.'

So he sent them to the bakery. That was massive too – a 3,000-rolls-and-loaves-a-day place.

'We've got to help you clean up,' they walked in and told the master baker.

'What for?'

'We're under punishment.'

'You're under punishment from *Ardent*? You've been sunk!'

He took them through the section until they were facing a big steel door. He opened it. Three-quarters of the shelves were ingredients. But at the bottom there was beer.

He disappeared and came back with two milk churns and a plank, built a bench and the pair drank themselves stupid again. At the end of each day, they were sneaked back to their cabins in a dumb-waiter. It was the best punishment they'd ever had. It would be 15 years before the Joss found out.

In the cabin next to Bernie Berntsen and Buck Taylor, Mick Newby, Crofty, Fluff Garnham and John Goddard were regular drinking partners. That didn't go unnoticed either.

Goddard's Divisional Officer, Mike Knowles, pulled him aside and told him

he had a drink problem. Goddard tried to defend himself, all the while thinking, 'What else is there to do?' Newby agrees. 'It was a ship that got us from A to B,' he says. 'We hid behind it. Lenny handed out most of the bollockings, and rightly so, but we didn't know what he got up to behind closed doors.'

He drank spirits. The stewards in the Senior Ratings' Mess rarely poured less than a treble, then the likes of Andy Andrew, Tony Ray, Jim Watts and co. would look out over the ocean and talk about what had happened, and how. They all had different stories.

If memories had begun distorting in the space of hours after they'd left *Ardent*, as Morgan O'Connell had witnessed, finding a common account was going to be impossible, no matter how hard they tried, talking among their groups, in twos and threes, on their own.

Talking. The days passed and the more he listened, the more Lt David Searle realised he'd made a relatively rapid exit from the Dining Hall. So what he couldn't accept were the versions of events that would materialise in the Wardroom – people saying how far they'd been aft, what they'd seen, and who. To the 24 year old, the timings didn't add up, and he fell out with the First Lieutenant in saying so.

Talking. Tom Williams lost count of the times Paddy McClintock reasoned that, if he'd had five more minutes, he'd have had the gun back. It was just the tactical decisions that had overtaken him.

Talking. Chief Stoker Andy Andrew's solo blanket search between hits had robbed him of a big picture. But now he could see men thinking, 'Well, we spent all morning in training saving the ship . . .', knowing that, when 'for real' came, it hadn't all come together. Some things just didn't happen in training. You could switch a fire pump back on at Portland.

Portland. It was a thought Bernie Berntsen kept coming back to. Years going balls-out, playing their games. If your weapons go, do something before you're hit again. But it hadn't worked. He'd been petrified. Then there was Jan Joyce.

In theory, that manic three-minute valve-turning, counter-balancing six o'clock dash didn't need to rob Brum of his firehose pressure in the Hangar. In theory, you pick your permutation of hose and hydrant. But he'd been operating on instinct. There'd been no time for chess.

Or Mick Cox, convinced there was still power up forward when he'd left the SCC, following the principle that section chiefs worry about their own patch and leave the wider picture to others.

'I often think that, if I'd been able to get the guys up forward to come back aft, the outcome would have been different, because they . . . That's played with me for a while.'

On the other hand, 'There was the Senior Rates' Dining Hall, the Avcat tank was on fire. We weren't in a proper state . . . Comms were out . . . It's probable . . .'

The fires? 'That's true. They were very close to those torpedos. Nobody will ever know, but maybe we should have tried.'

The what-ifs. The great what-ifs. Somehow, they had to sift and sort their memories, because the Board of Inquiry would be asking questions, and expecting answers.

What if Iain McRobbie hadn't paused to help a wounded messmate on his run aft with Mick Mullen, Andy Barr, Sean Hayward and Derek Armstrong? They'd all have been killed.

What if Eddie Edwards had gone aft when he'd had the chance? They wanted to confirm what had happened to everyone. All he'd heard about Knocker was that someone had seen him in the Dining Room, with chest injuries. Why hadn't Eddie gone back? That's all that bothered him.

That and maybe the flooding in the Forward Auxillary Machine Room? It wasn't flooding when Eddie left. It was just a trickle.

What if the cooks had stayed apart, like Cliff Goldfinch had told them? He didn't know Mick Foote had gone aft alone. That was cooks for you. See a problem, disregard what you've been told anyway.

Where had Shaun Hanson been and what was he doing? Jon Major still didn't really know. A little later on, he'd start thinking of Pete and Renee. They'd be devastated.

Or Mark Bogard. 'Why did others die and not me? I'm only a Writer.'

Or Bill Bailey. Because of his total faith in his own ability to survive, he'd told Pete Brouard there was nothing to fear either. Now Pete was dead. Had that chat helped? He'd never know.

Or Dave Croft on Sean Hayward. 'He was a young guy plucked from a class. He was a bright guy and because of that he was . . . He was in the wrong place at the wrong time.'

Or Wyatt Earp, 18 and resentful. Resentful that only the Ardents were mustering to be sent off in ten-minute cleaning parties. Resentful at three cans a day. Resentful at having to write a report so that a Board of Inquiry could decide whether they'd done enough to save the ship. He wrote whatever he could remember. When he finished, he showed it to the man he happened to be playing cards with.

'You can't put that,' he told Earp. The Malvern lad argued, then rewrote it.

To this day, he doesn't know whether the final version was the truth. Not the truth as he saw it.

For Andy Andrew, the thoughts were of *Ardent*'s move to open water, the design of the ship, no diesel-driven firepumps, of feeling like he was the only man left on the ship after that first hit until Earp, his young stoker, appeared in the Air Conditioning Unit and their eyes met through anti-flash masks. Earp recalls the look as terror.

'It wasn't terror,' the Chief Stoker explains. 'Shock. What to do next. Where to go . . . All the practice in the world . . .' Then Andrew sighs. Terror? 'Yeah, he was probably right.'

For CPO Dave Lee it was Seacat. Why hadn't it fired? The signal to *QE2* telling the Ardents that they'd won the Fleet Seacat Trophy only rubbed it in. The best bet, for Lee, was Seacat's Achilles heel. When the launcher followed its target, using instructions from the 912 radar or the Ped Site arcade game, it would stop training if the ship's structure appeared in its sights.

The Ops Room man on the launcher control console should spot that and hit the launcher resector switch, swinging the launcher back through 180 degrees to find its target again. Ground clutter could have the same effect. So why

hadn't the PWO realised that those Daggers had to be taken out by the Ped Site operator in emergency control?

He didn't know it, but that's exactly what Johnno Johnson had been screaming for – 'Give me LOF control! Give me LOF control!' – in the seconds before the Seacat was blown God knows how many feet in the air and back down on to the Flight Deck. Who, where, why? What if? Questions, questions, questions.

From the position he'd now accepted on the outside of the close-knit *Ardent* company, flying doctor Simon Ridout could see what was happening. With every mile they steamed north, and the warmth growing on their skin, maybe this sea voyage was the best thing they could have asked for.

No. Not from where Brum Serrell sat. Zero activity. It was the worst time of his life, even if he was methodically placing the pieces of his own jigsaw together, as complete as he'd need them so he could start again when they arrived home. For others, it was soul-destroying and unproductive, no information to tell them how they'd done, just a screen of booze and acting like hooligans.

Richie Gough felt unfulfilled, guilty, not because they weren't bringing their ship home, but because it had been sunk. It was a wound. It said he hadn't done his job well enough.

John Foster was only thinking about what would happen to the team when they finally arrived home. It was preferable to looking back. He hadn't actually witnessed Rick Banfield fighting for his life, or seen the Lynx as a smouldering mess. He'd seen most of it through other people's eyes, and he really didn't want to know about it any more. When he did think back, it was to Gary Nelson laying the wreath over their predecessor in the Norwegian Sea. Now, here they were.

Otherwise, he'd noticed that, when anyone looked around for a Chief, there'd be nobody there. The ship's company had fallen back into officers, senior rates and junior rates, all except the likes of Tony Ray and Lenny Yeatman, to Foster's eyes.

'All the time people were "Master this, and Master that". They were always about, doing things for you. I imagine that was to the detriment of himself, because he needed a quiet few minutes too.'

There was only one man going through it alone.

'We had rules and chose to break them,' Mick Newby admits. 'We mustered, did an hour's work, then got on. When we were told not to go to the bars, we went. But only the skipper was on his own.'

On his own and depressed. Depressed and preparing for the Board of Inquiry and, inevitably, finding evidence of things he hadn't known about when he made the decision to leave *Ardent*. It was a period of information-gathering and soul-searching, and writing letters to the children of the men he'd lost, letters they could open on their 18th birthdays to tell them things he thought they should know about their dads' lives. But the isolation would leave him with one regret.

'I think I let them down a bit by not being more . . . by not talking to them,' he says.

'What did I do wrong? What should I have done for Loro to be alive now?'

The what-ifs. After four hours in the freezing water off Port King, and four days living rough ashore, Lt Cdr Alberto Philippi had been found by Tony Blake, the manager of North Arm Farm, and handed back to the Argentinians. The what-ifs had already taken root.

By the time he'd been reunited with Graciela and the children in downtown Rio Grande on Sunday, 30 May, she'd spent four days inconsolable after Rodolfo Castro Fox had broken the news that Alberto's Skyhawk had been shot down, and he was missing.

He'd had a hero's welcome at the airbase from his fellow pilots and crew members, a warm salute from them all. But he'd come back pessimistic as well as sad, as well as grateful. He'd seen lines of trenches, a lack of mobility, poor communications and low firepower, enough to tell him that, in the face of the British and the Americans, diplomacy would be Argentina's only hope.

Above all, though, he had Loro's voice echoing in his mind – 'Harrier! Harrier at six!' – shouting the warning that had allowed him and José Arca to twist and turn and, somehow, save their own lives.

Loro, 28, clever, dedicated, the perfect wingman, like Arca. The right word for a tense moment. A brilliant sportsman. An *empanada* stuffed into his flight suit pocket. But always the what-ifs: the what-ifs when Philippi visited Loro's parents, amid rumours that he was alive as a prisoner of the British, to tell them that, no, their son had been killed fighting to the last minute and that his death was swift.

The what-ifs. From then, every year, on 21 May he'd send them a telegram: 'Always close to you.'

♦♦♦

John Foster walked into his cabin with a cup of tea and called to Kev Johnson in the bath. No answer.

He called again. Still no answer.

He went into the Bathroom and found him asleep, slipping beneath the water, quietly drowning.

Foster managed to stir him and helped the Aft DCP Incident Board man out. As he'd dozed, water had gone through Johnson's perforated eardrum into his throat and his lungs. It gave them both a fright.

Once the Yorkshireman had recovered, it also gave them a topic to fill the endless drinking hours between muster, ten-minute chores and meals. In Foster's close circle of messmates, they'd already exhausted life stories and ended in hysterics when he'd finished regaling them with his, 'the bastards'.

Otherwise, even if they didn't know it, things were falling apart. They needed to be occupied, but there was nothing to do.

They needed to know how well they'd done their jobs back in Falkland Sound, but no one outside their number was telling them.

They needed to know there was nothing more they could have done to save the ship and their friends. Their preparations for the Board of Inquiry provoked plenty of questions, but few answers. Men who'd been to war needed more than three cans a day, not to have to beg, steal or borrow. Men who'd taken O'Connell's

advice to drink for two days needed to realise it had been almost two weeks, and maybe they should stop, sleep, deal with two big problems, insomnia and alcohol.

Men who'd cherished being part of *Canberra*, and *Canberra* being part of them, needed the *QE2* crew to stop boasting openly how much money they were making on this cruise, to stop looking at them as if they were desecrating their sacred ship. The Canberras knew what war meant. Not this lot.

They needed to step off at Ascension and fly home, like the Sheffields had. But no one knew what would happen to them once they reached Tracy Island.

And they needed to stay away from the Coventrys and the Antelopes because, whether the Wardroom or Senior Ratings' Mess knew it or liked it, the rivalry on which the Navy thrived when Guzz met Pompey on the sports pitch, or on exercises, didn't mix well with alcohol and feelings generated by the very different wars the three ship's companies could talk about if they wanted.

For people like Iain McRobbie, the animosity some Ardents had for the Coventrys stemmed from the very first encounters on *QE2*. It left a deep hatred which would fester for years. Still does.

'They were going to run the show,' he recalls. 'We were constantly reminded they were a Pompey ship' – the Glory Boys, as Buck Taylor describes them – 'and they'd show us how to enjoy a cruise.'

It was a 'them and us' situation from Leigh Slatter's perspective, a courteous nod at best when he passed an Antelope or Coventry on board. Shut-up shop.

From where PO Pete Brierley stood, the Coventrys seemed rudderless, an impression strengthened by reports that one Ardent had been chased to his cabin by a group of Type 42 ratings one night and beaten up. He never found out if it was true and, if it was, why.

In his customary seat on the fringes, Dave Lee swapped salty sea tales easily with the *Coventry* and *Antelope* senior rates, but the Pompey junior rates did seem hyper.

'These guys really think they've done something,' he recalls telling himself. 'I didn't think, and still don't, that having your ship sunk makes you some kind of hero.' The impression didn't stop there.

At a race night in the Wardroom one evening, Weapons Engineering Officer Paddy McClintock took a swing at one Coventry. After that, it was very hostile.

'These warriors from *Coventry* who, after all, were survivors like us,' Tom Williams shakes his head. 'What had they done to deserve special recognition?'

If the bonds of 21 Club membership often kept the friction between Plymouth and Portsmouth, it didn't always work that way.

'I did think, "We're better than you" when we went on to the *QE2*,' Karoly Nagy admits. Then he bumped into an old face from Raleigh and was told, 'Your lot have been fighting with my lot.'

Naggers has a theory.

'The Antelopes walked off the ship in Procedure Charlie, in 8s, with all their kit. That was the big bone of contention, like. It's not our fault that it went up. The way I feel we're projected as a ship is second-class. Hidden.' But not every encounter was bitter, or remembered with regret or sourness.

Blood Reed and Eddie Edwards sat with two Antelopes one night and listened to how they'd been sent to put chocks beneath Carballo's unexploded

1,000-pounder. One of them admitted he wouldn't bend over the bomb to slide a chock on the other side, not that it would have made any difference if it had gone off then, rather than later. It was a good tale. It was a good night.

Elsewhere, Bob Young had teamed up with Andy Till and, among other things, while the two old pals drank for Britain, *Antelope*'s LMA told him how the other 1,000lb bomb had gone in through the POs' Mess and blasted a gas bottle into young steward Mark Stephens, sitting next to him.

Young had tales to tell, too, but he didn't notice any animosity, not even during his own therapy – manning the surgery he had set up with Till and *Coventry*'s medic, Taff Lewis, for the three ships' companies.

Back in harness, if still bruised from something akin to a car crash, Simon Ridout was a frequent visitor in his role ensuring the continuity of medical care to the wounded, 'a little disappointed' at not feeling as if he'd become an Ardent, but accepting it. From where he stood, the Antelopes felt untested.

'They hadn't really gone down fighting, as *Ardent* and *Coventry* had,' he says.

Trouble and tension between the ships? There were some, like John Foster, who simply didn't care.

'I was aware of it,' he says, 'but I'd just finished fighting. All I wanted to do was get home.'

◆◆◆

If most of them believed the first step onto home soil again would be the tarmac apron at Brize Norton, like the Sheffields, they were mistaken. And resentful.

The SAS men who'd swapped tales of survival would be spirited off at Ascension and flown home, a hop from Wideawake to Oxfordshire countryside and on to the anonymity of Hereford. But not Jack.

They'd have the sun on their backs for another week. In return, there'd be the chance to be filmed steaming up the Solent in the *QE2*, the pride of the British merchant fleet, an armada of boats in their wake before a tearful reunion, the troops home from war. Except the war was still going on, and they'd have preferred to be heading for Devonport, in their own ship. It was political, and many didn't like it.

'Are they going to make us pay for it? Divide it 178 ways,' Simon Ridout wondered when he found out. There were a hundred other thoughts, but they amounted to the same thing.

So there'd be another week of drinking. Another week of wondering, 'What are they going to do with us when we arrive home?' Another week waiting for 'Lilliburlero' to bring them morsels of information on what was happening back south. The sun was scant compensation for all that.

Pete Brierley was one who didn't mind much one way or the other, though. When they'd been heading the opposite way from Ascension, harassed for the gas-bill money by his estranged wife, he'd decided there wasn't a lot to come home for. Five weeks on, nothing had changed.

Antelope's Jimmy, Lt Cdr Bertie Guy, had been Brierley's Divisional Officer on the *Puma* and asked him to run a task book training session for some sonar

rates, then compile a set of exam questions. Brierley was glad of the diversion and set about it with typical thoroughness.

Most of the rates passed, but there were no Ardents among his students. There was no call. His newly built sonar team had been a mix of experience and youth. And four of them – Derek Armstrong, Mick Mullen, Andy Barr and Sean Hayward – had been killed.

◆◆◆

It wasn't like cutting yourself on a knife and going to hospital for a couple of stitches. Some of the injuries sustained in those 22 minutes from exploding bombs, or razor-sharp shrapnel, or falling debris had been contaminated. The treatment hadn't been pretty. Some wounds had needed cleaning and having dead tissue cut away before being packed with gauze and left open to make sure there was no infection. Other casualties had been luckier, if not lucky.

Dave Trotter's lacerated back and backside left a deep impression on Simon Ridout, though it was Ken Enticknap's survival that surprised him most. His wounds were one thing with the loss of blood, but staying alive in the water was another. To do that, you needed to be fat and Enticknap wasn't.

The Aft Section Base Chief's first outing on *QE2* was to see a video as a guest of the ship's company POs' Mess, a cautious and curious bunch, but very hospitable.

Soon after, he was allowed up to join the senior rates, as long as he was wheeled there and back by 2200 and disciplined himself to a couple of beers. It was difficult for a dreadful timekeeper whose ability to count had been compromised by the loss of his wedding ring and the finger in it.

There were highs and lows on such evenings as more pieces dropped into place, and the need for consolation before the night duty sister loomed in the bar and took him back – after a drink herself.

Scouse Lacey complained of headaches until he was given an X-ray and the medics saw the cause, a chunk of shrapnel embedded in the back of his skull. Simon Ridout and Bob Young were there when a trapdoor about two and a half inches wide was cut in his skull to remove it.

Lacey would be the one Ardent to fly home from *Wideawake*. No one begrudged him, though Bill Bailey, the Flight Mechanic's tea-making pal when that first hit had wrecked the Hangar Workshop, did fret: would Lacey's docs worry about his mental state without realising he was bonkers before?

Ralph Coates was back though, even if he wouldn't talk to Buck Ryan because he was sharing a cabin with his old rival in love, life and the stoking branch, Naggers. And after those 24-hour bedside vigils on *Canberra* as well, Ryan thought. He couldn't win.

Ralph's arrival did liven things up for Coxie and Wacker Payne, though. The shower in Coxie and Barney Barnard's cabin wouldn't drain and they finally called an engineer, though not before the Damage Control Party had let themselves loose on it. Eventually, the cabin flooded. So they moved.

Ralph was also someone new to stumble back to the cabin with after a drink, or someone to share a Laundry basket when the journey to Coxie's cabin seemed longer than the walk from the Grand Theatre.

In the daytime, the monotony was broken by games of hide-and-seek, good fun for big kids on a ship the size of Birmingham. Coxie remembers dashing out of a lift one day and seeing the *QE2*'s Master, Captain Peter Jackson, walking round. Their eyes met. The Ardent hesitated.

'They went that way,' Jackson pointed down the passageway.

'Cheers!'

When it came to the chase on one occasion, he also recalls, Ralph was running normally.

'He was limping a minute ago!' Coxie turned to his PO. 'Why's he all right now?'

'There's nothing wrong with you!' Wacker flicked his wounds. Then they continued the game.

'You'd been sunk, you were trying to get your life back in order, we were stuck on a ship,' Cox explains. 'It made you feel better.'

With the air enticingly warm now, Leigh Slatter tried his hand at clay pigeon shooting off *QE2*'s stern and missed just about everything. Maybe hitting that flare during the *Canberra* firepower demonstration had been a fluke after all.

For some, though, Naval life went on as if nothing had happened. The Divisional Officers met Alan West in his penthouse suite every morning and kept him in the picture. West had hardly left his accommodation since leaving *Canberra*, if at all.

His preparations for the Board of Inquiry went on, and so did writing to the families of the men he'd lost. The grim task was completed with the help of his officers and senior rates, a duty Navigating Officer Alan Maunder found especially hard when he drafted the letter for Mick Mullen's parents.

Maunder knew that everyone except Ginger Nelson had been accounted for first-hand, but he still agonised about how to tell the Mullens about their son, a man he'd only just come to know. In the end, he learnt enough of the unassuming, hard-working 24 year old's death to tell them, 'He was killed carrying out his duty to the last minute,' or words to that effect.

The letters went off when *QE2* reached Ascension on Saturday, 5 June. In return, the Ardents received their first mail since *Canberra*'s mid-ocean rendezvous with *Leeds Castle* a week before, tons of it. It was as welcome as the covers being taken off the portholes, the end of the Darken Ship routine which meant she was no longer at risk, and that her passengers could, at last, afford to think of home.

Brum Serrell's letters from home normally ended 'Love Carol and Tigger', but the one that arrived this time read 'Love Carol, Tigger and Ninky'. There was no explanation about Ninky.

Buck Ryan heard from his folks for the first time since sending his telegram from *Canberra*. It was the first thing to stop him feeling lonely.

A well-wisher sent Tony Ray a willy-warmer – a little late, in the circumstances – but, more appropriately, Jan Joyce opened his mail to find a pair of swimming trunks. There was something for everyone. Everyone except Mike Lewis, it seemed.

'Perhaps she didn't get the telegram,' he was thinking. 'Does Tessa know *Ardent*'s been sunk?'

'You'll get some mail tomorrow,' Mal Crane tried to reassure him. And he did. About ten letters, from his family and from people he'd never really kept in touch with, saying 'I'm sorry', but how glad they were. How little they knew, he thought.

Once the heads of department and Divisional Officers had pooled their thoughts, Lt Nigel Langhorn had the citations for nominations for bravery awards that Alan West had asked for. It might have included dozens of names but, in the end, the list he saw was this:

> Lt Cdr J.M. Sephton, Distinguished Service Cross (posthumous); AB (R) J.E. Dillon, George Medal; MEAM (M) 1 K. Enticknap, Queen's Gallantry Medal; PO J.S. Leake, Distinguished Service Medal; Sub Lt R.J. Barker, Mention in Despatches; MEM (M) D.J. Serrell, Mention in Despatches.

One by one, the surviving nominees were either visited in the hospital or called up. For Brum Serrell, being told to report to the Captain's cabin was the worst moment of the deployment.

'Brum, get your arse upstairs, the skipper wants to see you,' Tony Ray told him one morning. The DMEO didn't say why but, after walking most corridors, he eventually found his destination.

'Come in,' Alan West replied to his knock on the door. He bimbled in, wetting himself.

'Sit down. How are you feeling?'

Serrell offered an appropriate pleasantry, but he couldn't stop shaking. Then West spoke again.

'It's my pleasure to inform you that you've been recommended for a bravery award. Well done!'

Serrell was thrown. As he left the room, the 24-year-old tankie was still shaking. When the citation eventually came through, months later, on a piece of A4, it would have his name spelt wrongly. But the oak leaves would be there on his South Atlantic Medal.

Sub Lt Richie Barker, the baby-faced GDP director, was also called up. He was nervous too, honoured as well but, as West told the 21 year old that he was sending a signal recommending him for an MID, he couldn't help thinking of the last time the skipper had spoken to him about a signal, the one going back to Northwood carrying the names of the dead. It was a sad reminder.

As the ship steamed on north, no one could work out how Ken Enticknap had turned out to be the second man to be allowed to make a call home after Captain Jackson, *QE2*'s master.

As soon as Frankie heard her sister-in-law's voice on the phone at the international telephone exchange in London, where she worked, she knew. Jane

had been on duty when Capt Jackson's call had come through for Cunard. The rest was simple.

The first thing Ken did was tell Frankie he'd lost a finger. She was so shocked by hearing his voice that all she could say was, 'That was careless,' but, to be honest, even when it sank in, she thought, 'What's a finger?' She knew she'd find out how he'd lost it, when he came home, in his own time.

For many of the men who followed, after all they'd been through, it seemed strange to be speaking with mums and dads, brothers and sisters from the radio room of a British institution; a couple of minutes when the need at home to know everything was almost overwhelming, but the feelings on board were still very private.

Carol Ray had wondered so many times about how she'd have paid for the caravan if Tony had died. She felt sorry, bitterly sorry, for the families, but at least she wouldn't have to cope alone. When Tony called her at the salon on the Tuesday, he might as well have been ringing from home.

'Hello dear!' was his familiar greeting. She could have screamed.

Beryl Yeatman had grown accustomed to walking through town, watching everyone go about their normal business, desperate to yell, 'Don't you know what's going on?' at them. It made her angry.

She was so relieved to hear Len's voice again, but not too impressed by having to spend what precious time they had arranging to call Margaret, Connie Francis's girlfriend. He wanted her to drive the Granada down to Southampton so that he could drive it back again. Beryl wasn't certain, but she couldn't recall Lenny mentioning anything about heart surgery.

◆◆◆

First there'd been the *Yarmouth*. Then there was *Canberra*. Then there was the *Leeds Castle*, *Arnella* or *Northella*. Then *QE2*, then Ascension. Back on the liner, Alan West's Ardents were about to take another step away from their war, another step closer to whatever normality awaited them.

Along with a form asking for their banking details, their plans for travel once they were home, the size of their chests and length of their feet, they were asked to make a list of the personal possessions they were going to claim for, what was in their lockers: Walkmans, King Crimson tapes, walking guidebooks, Levi's, fishing rods, 18th birthday signet rings, badminton rackets, ceremonial swords, morning suits, a pair of football boots that used to belong to Trevor Whymark, portfolio pictures of Denise Collins, naked and otherwise, cameras containing the last photos of Knocker White, semi-naked or otherwise, doing something disgusting with the barrel of the 4.5-inch gun, and laughing.

Possessions, clues to the men they'd gone south as, but not the men they'd come back as. Among the bags of mail brought on at Ascension, though, there had been some compensation, an unexpected item, even if some didn't know.

In an envelope addressed to Brian Murphy, *Ardent*'s lost Lynx Observer, there was a packet of photos. Among the pictures was one of the ship steaming out of Narvik. Copies of it would become the most treasured possessions of the men on board, then and now.

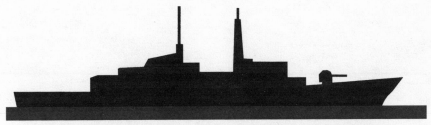

A KIND OF HOMECOMING

One   *QE2*, Atlantic Ocean to various locations
        (9–14 June 1982)   335

Two   Damage Repair Instructional Unit, HMS *Raleigh*,
        Saltash, Cornwall (5 December 1996 to present)   351

Three   Present   357

Four   Present   385

Five   Present   393

ONE

QE2, ATLANTIC OCEAN TO VARIOUS LOCATIONS

(9–14 JUNE 1982)

Robbed, reprieved, condemned. Past, present, future. How far do you look ahead? How long do you look back? As the Ardents edged closer to the Channel, in solitary hours soaking up the sun, or snatched moments between pints in the Pig and Whistle, or in the lull between hiding and seeking again, one thought rarely came without the other.

'My anticipation of arriving home . . . it was excitement, freedom, sorrow. I felt, in a way, that we'd let people down because we were returning without our home,' Andy Cox admits. 'And how lucky I was . . .' The leading electrician had been in Ken Enticknap's Aft Damage Control Party until the run south from Ascension, then moved forward, swapping action stations with Garry Whitford.

Fortunate, yes. Coxie was coming home. But luck? How many throws of the dice between Ascension and Falkland Sound before it was impossible to connect his survival with his young messmate's death?

How many times between 1744 and 1806 had someone, anyone, turned left in the grim, dim, confines of the listing Junior Ratings' Dining Hall, when they might have turned right and changed the course of that chaos, saved a life, cost another? They all had some cause to ask.

◆◆◆

The clatter of helicopter rotors over the gentle waves of Mounts Bay was a reminder of a thousand moments from the last eight weeks. Take your pick. Ascension, TEZ, *Canberra*, Cumberland Bay. But, this time, it wasn't a gash disposal unit, a liberated GPMG, a cargo net full of ammunition, or a sick messmate they were moving from A to B. The choppers were ferrying in around 30 men and women with everything 600-odd matelots could want to step ashore looking the part; fresh 8s for everyone, blue cotton work shirts, trousers and seaboots rather than the size 15 pumps and boiler suits they'd been in, and new ID cards and cheque books too, and travel warrants to take them wherever they'd chosen to go next, if a choice was what they had.

It was a slick operation.

If there were people like NAAFI Canteen Manager-turned-Petty Officer

John Leake who appreciated the chance to look the same as everyone else when he stepped ashore, there were others who despised it.

Lt Tom Williams would walk off *QE2* the next day wearing the same socks he'd worn since Ascension – a pair a doctor had knitted him with tassels. He looked at the people around him being transformed into something that suited the British Empire and he thought it was a sham.

If he heard it, around the same time, the Tannoy would have merely confirmed Williams's thoughts.

'You are, in the eyes of the British public at the moment, heroes. You're going to have a lot of attention,' the Ardents, Antelopes and Coventrys were told.

A sham for Williams, at least. For others, it sent a shiver of pride down their spines or a sick feeling to the pit of their stomachs. There'd be thousands and thousands on the jetty when they pulled alongside, not just their families. They'd also be doing a sail-past of the Royal Yacht with the Queen Mother aboard. Flashing bulbs, cheering, colour, noise, fuss. Hip-hip, hooray.

To make that rendezvous though, their timing had to be perfect – the final insult, sacrifice, imposition. If it hadn't already been bad enough sailing on from Ascension, they were soon to start sailing round in circles off the Cornish coast, practically close enough to smell the grass on the rugged cliff tops, spinning the journey out even further.

Bob Young, among others, stood on the Upper Deck that night and watched Plymouth go past and wondered why they couldn't have slipped home quietly to Devonport, why it was being made to look like they were coming back in victory when, he knew, they were just survivors.

Up Channel Night. Outside the regulations. Tradition. The *Ardent* junior ratings were already in the Pig and Whistle, sipping from their three-can issue before working their way down to the cabins, drinking more until the small hours, sometimes falling out, more often doing what homeless Ardents did when drunk. The senior rates and the Wardroom could add port or Scotch to the choice, but the effect would be the same. Most would wake with baggy heads. If anyone went to sleep.

Crofty would normally have expected to be part of it. Not this night. He was already in a starboard cabin, 'something special' put aside by the young telephonist, Jane Broomfield, who'd provided him with beer – and other distractions – for the duration of the voyage from South Georgia. They'd spend their last night on the ocean wave as they'd spent a few others.

How COMAW Mike Clapp could have done with a little TLC, 8,000 miles south. As the Ardents steamed slowly up the Channel, a conversation with Northwood would have been something. He was still receiving every signal, but no one was returning his calls. The isolation and ambiguity that had prompted the Last Pipe had gone right through to the very edge of victory. But now he was exhausted, as well as bemused, in no shape really to second-guess his masters or make long-term plans for backing up the troops ashore. And, for God's sake, running everywhere, to boot.

'Shit! You're showing it,' he scolded himself that night. So he forced himself to straighten out and walk and fixed a big smile on his face, though inside he

harboured a fear that everyone could see through the façade. He was so tired. What he'd have given up to help the soldiers win this bloody war 'and get it all over with'.

How Dave Wopling could have done with a gun at about the same time. He'd put a Union Jack up outside the Grand Theatre to welcome Val's boys home, but someone had stolen it.

If he'd seen the person, he'd have shot them, he promises. 'How could anyone be so hard-hearted? After what they'd gone through.'

And how the evening of Thursday, 10 June, would stick in Frankie Enticknap's mind. She could have done with a map, then a drink, by the time she checked in to her hotel that night. She'd driven up with PO Writer Trevor Quinton's wife and two children, leading a convoy of four cars all the way from Plymouth. Southampton wasn't too hard to find, but the hotels the Navy had paid for were.

They'd arrived by seven o'clock, stopped at a police station to ask the way, then she'd plodded round the city, dropping the others off. It was eleven o'clock when she finally found her own hotel. The night porter let her in, but either couldn't or wouldn't find her anything to eat or drink.

The hotel room was small and airless too, like a broom cupboard. It had one window, overlooking the dustbins. In the coming hours she couldn't sleep. Every so often she'd look at the clock. Three. Then four. Then five. Wishing it were seven, so she could go down for breakfast.

Christine Rowe was also safe in her hotel room, safe and hoping husband Pete, *Ardent*'s Chief GI, would want to talk about what had happened. Earlier that day, Peddler Palmer's young widow, Lesley, had phoned her to say she'd be thinking of them all, and to assure her that 'everything will be fine'. But Christine was just beginning to realise something of what they'd all been through. She'd switched on the TV and had seen the first pictures of *Ardent* burning, taken from *Broadsword*. It was horrible.

Iris Andrew didn't go to bed that night, however. She was too excited. So, by ten to four, she was sitting in her Toyota Corolla outside Plymouth Garden Centre, with Debbie asleep in the back, waiting for Beryl Yeatman to arrive so they could drive up to Southampton in tandem.

As she waited, a police car pulled up behind. The driver climbed out and wandered over.

Iris wound the window down.

'Are you all right?' the policeman asked.

'My husband's one of the Falkland survivors,' she said. 'We're waiting for friends, to go and meet the *QE2*.' She couldn't wipe the smile from her face.

'Good luck!' he said, and shook her hand.

Half-an-hour later, Beryl pulled on to the car park in Connie Francis's Granada with Margaret, his girlfriend, in the front and Paul and Joanne in the back.

By seven, they were sitting on another forecourt, pouring cups of tea from a flask and eating sandwiches, waiting for a petrol station to open. Thirty minutes after that, they were sitting in the car in the dockyard, changed and talking, watching the dockers arrive for work and everything else that was going on,

desperate not to miss anything on a day they'd remember for the rest of their lives, not knowing whether those lives would ever really be the same again.

By eight, a convoy of six coaches was on its way from Plymouth, carrying those wives, girlfriends and families of the Ardents and Antelopes who hadn't found their own way to Southampton. The party mood was more noticeable with some than others and, when they stopped at the services, other travellers realised who they were. For people more accustomed to driving down the hill to Devonport to see the ship come home, this was a little strange and a little too public.

◆◆◆

The last time some of these Ardents had stood on a ship's waist and watched so many vessels fussing, they'd been 400 yards, maybe a few more, from the rocks of North West Island. Now another armada of small craft was gathering around them as they made their way towards the Solent in a stately fashion, at leisure, if not at peace.

Some saw the bobbing, weaving sea of colour before others. Some not at all.

The books holding one corner of Buck Taylor's bed weren't the only worry for the 18-year-old Geordie and his 33-year-old cabin-mate, Bernie Berntsen, when a steward arrived to inspect.

A day or so after Buck's hooligan steeplechase over the furniture, Coxie had burst in and started throwing his weight around. There was only one thing Taylor and Berntsen could do, so they did it.

They threw him against the bulkhead and, tinkle, tinkle, heard the sound of glass as the El Crappo picture fell. Now it was covered by a once-only. Would the steward see the books or the picture first?

It was the picture. The steward looked at it and smoothed a hand across the paper on his clipboard.

'That was like that before,' Bernie lied. The steward glanced at him, then the picture.

'Okay,' he said. He didn't look at the bed.

But Crofty didn't escape as lightly.

Bang! Bang! Bang! After a night of passion, he was woken by loud thudding noises. He rubbed his eyes and realised what they were, a gun salute. In seconds he was out of bed, pulling his clothes on. A few seconds more and, after a quick 'See you!' to his companion, legged it aft.

They'd been given orders to clear cabins, strip beds and put dirty linen outside, then gather their gear and muster on the Flight Deck. By the time the Sonar Operator ran into his cabin, Mick Newby had gone. So had the epaulettes off his shirt, so had his pullover and his beret. And all his gear. He cursed.

The last time he'd done a two-minute sprint was to action stations. Now he raced through the corridors and up the stairs to the Aft Flight Deck, out into all the noise and colour of the Solent, his heart pounding, in an unavoidable state of undress, trying desperately to find Newby, not the Jimmy.

'Croft! Come here!' He failed at both.

After handing the *Elk* grenade man over to military police for court-martial,

Lenny Yeatman called the ship's company to attention and prepared them for disembarkation in a final Both Watches. It wasn't intended but, for many, it was where they said their collective goodbyes.

They could either go through the blue channel, with nothing to declare, or through the green, where there'd be hundreds of cameras and press from round the world. Then they were briefed by Alan West.

'When you go off,' he told them, 'I don't want anyone hitting cameramen! You owe these people a story. They need a story. If you're asked, keep it precise and to the point, but tell them.'

It was their last order from the Captain.

As they fell out, the First Lieutenant passed Pete Brierley and called him 'Chief'.

The PO whipped round: 'Are you on drugs, sir?'

Andrew Gordon Lennox smiled and made a show of calling PO Writer Trevor Quinton over to present Brierley's promotion order. It had been issued on the return journey. Then Alan West offered the 29 year old his congratulations too.

A few minutes later – with the Antelopes elsewhere on the Aft Flight Deck and the Coventrys maybe 200 yards away on the Forward Flight Deck – 95 Ardents gathered again for a final picture. On their right they held a banner cobbled from a Cunard bedsheet. It read 'Falklands First World Cup next'. To the left was something a little more substantial, but the same size and home-made too, a White Ensign with 'HMS Ardent' at the top and, at the bottom, 'Through Fire and Water'. The words '. . . and Alcohol' might have brought the ship's story up to date, but the motto on the crest which Newby, Cox and co. had fought to prise from her Bridge Screen was a truth to be proud of.

Gradually, men broke off into smaller groups, a couple here, a dozen there, 20 or 30 somewhere else, and took their own pictures. As they did, the noise and colour buzzing about on the waves way below grew and grew, water cannon pushing great white plumes high into the air at a pressure of about 8-bar.

Most of the Ardents gazed around and either tried hard to let it soak in, or wash over them. It was all a little different from the cheering thin line of dockyard mateys who'd seen them off from Devonport, a world removed from 'We're on our way, we are Club 21 . . .' blasting out of the Tannoy as they'd steamed into Plymouth Sound and prepared to turn right.

The pristine navy blue outline of the Royal Yacht sat serenely amongst it all as the *QE2* continued up the Solent. As they sailed past *Britannia*, they could make out the tiny, white figure of the Queen Mother waving a tiny white-gloved hand in their direction.

'Three cheers for the Queen Mum! Hip-hip-hooray! Hip-hip-hooray! Hip-hip-hooray!'

The massed, spontaneous reply to her distant gesture of welcome and thanks was probably lost on the Solent breeze, but tradition demanded it all the same. Not for her 'The Oggie Song'.

Within minutes, as the *QE2* edged closer and closer to home, frustratingly slowly, another vessel moved up on her seaward side and, in a second, men

who'd been scouring the shoreline were rushing across her decks to study a boatful of Page Three models in full glory. Splendid.

The greeting was matched as the returning heroes edged close to the jetty and, here and there, women – lovers, wives, girlfriends – let go of their banners and balloons and lifted their blouses and unhooked their bras. It was a bonus. For some, though, it was too much. More than they'd expected or wanted.

Jon Major and Frank Gilmour missed the Flight Deck photo, sitting almost alone in one of *QE2*'s vast restaurants eating fish and chips, their last Cunard meal.

Mike Lewis was relaxing after having breakfast with Mal Crane. The Buffer had gone for a stroll, but came back almost in tears, shaking.

'What's up?' Lewis asked, but Crane couldn't explain. They went up top and Lewis saw. Millions of people and boats. He still hadn't put the loss of 22 friends into perspective. This didn't help. Then some silly bastard in a red jet roared over and, in a split second, men were hitting the deck.

For God's sake, what was it all for? They hadn't come back in victory. They'd left their ship behind. They'd just as readily have crawled in under the red carpet rolled out in one of the big customs sheds. The banners, balloons and flags too. It just made it harder to spot familiar faces.

John Leake wasn't at all happy with the fuss. Like Jon Major and Frank Gilmour – and possibly 83 others – he'd seen no reason to stand for a photo. Now he saw no reason to be euphoric. Instead, he went up top and tried to pick Carole out from among the thousands. She wasn't there, though. Her coach party was finding it impossible to move through the cheering crowds.

◆◆◆

They also serve who only stand and wait . . . and wait, and wait. For Stuart Ray, first there'd been fussing and bothering and packing and phone calls. Then the long drive up from Plymouth with Mum and Helen and Liz, and Jim Watts's girlfriend, Kay. Then there'd been the diversion to drop Kay off at her friend's. Then on to Joan and Norman Jefferson's (Dad's old *Aurora* boss) for the night. Then, after breakfast, they'd been to pick Kay up again and, even though Mum had said she didn't need to have her hair done, she'd ended up sitting in the salon next to Kay, trying to kill more time before the ship docked. And that was still only nine o'clock.

Now it was after 11 and, as Mum chatted with Beryl Yeatman and Iris Andrew in the family enclosure, and the band played, and flashbulbs popped, if he'd had to ask once, he'd had to ask a million times, 'How much longer?'

Iris didn't help. Trying hard not to be too excited because not every wife had a husband coming home, she yelled, 'It's the *QE2*! It's the *QE2*!' and they all twisted and stretched on to tip-toes and saw a ferry. A big ferry, but only a ferry.

Eleven. Five-past. Ten-past. A quarter-past. Sixteen minutes past. Then Stuart saw this big, black-and-white shape grow larger out in the estuary.

As it moved closer, the indistinguishable line of bodies hugging her port rail slowly began to clear, enough for them to believe they'd now be able to make faces out, and the excitement went off the dial. They hoisted their banner high

340

between broom handles: 'Welcome Home Ardent Crew', soaring into the sea of home-made messages.

'Can you see Andy?'

'Can you see Len?'

'Can you see Dad?'

But they couldn't. Then they were gathered and shown into a big customs shed, Ardents in one group, Antelopes in another, Coventrys in a third. Not everyone was there, though. Outside, no one was telling six coachloads where to go. They could see the crowds bouncing with excitement and the cliff-sized sides of *QE2* nudging the jetty and the men on board preparing to tie her up. And panic was beginning to well inside them.

'Where's our Carol?' The agitated north Worcestershire tones were unmistakable to Carol Serrell. She turned to them and saw her dad, Ivan, shouting, 'You go this way!'

'This way!' Carol turned round and yelled and, in seconds, dozens of others were following her, women and children running into the throng like something from St Trinian's.

They were just in time. At midday, *QE2* pulled alongside.

In the vastness of the customs shed, Frankie Enticknap looked through the open doors at the huge slab of metal and saw the massive, rusting white letters against their weather-beaten black background, C-U-N-A-R-D. She'd been peeled away from Cathy Lee and, with the families of the other wounded men, was waiting to go on board. Rosie West, the Captain's wife, was there too.

Eventually, they were allowed up the gangway and she started walking towards the hospital, footsteps tapping a measured beat on the hardboard still protecting the ship's plush carpets.

She didn't know what to expect, but her first sight was a pale man wearing a large pair of light blue pyjamas, size 11 pumps on his size 9 feet, and a stubbly beard. At the end of his left arm was a huge bandage pierced by a pin supporting his middle finger. They embraced, gently. Ken was home.

'You're extremely lucky to have him back,' a doctor told her. She'd already realised. Then she helped him dress, in civvies, and they sneaked off.

Waiting, waiting. At 1230, the first matelot stepped on to the gangway. Frustratingly for the *Ardent* families below, predictably for the Ardents on board, he was the youngest Coventry.

Waiting, waiting. He was followed by the remainder of the Type 42's survivors. Pompey first again.

At least they didn't have to wait as long as the Antelopes. Once the last Coventry had gone, the Ardents began taking the last steps of their journey, smart in their new 8s, looking like men who'd done their bit, even if some would have stayed in ragbag overalls, tatty socks and used Marks & Sparks knicks they'd been wearing a day before, given the choice. Then they'd look like they'd been to war.

In ones and twos they stepped ashore and were handed a single red rose by waiting children. Some knelt to kiss the ground, others paused in a desperate search for familiar eyes looking back, still more drove through the crowd to hug and cry.

With each man, there'd be another shriek, the sea of bodies would ripple, the tide would shift as bobbing, tip-toeing waves of anxious, excited mums and dads, brothers and sisters rolled forward.

Errol Flynn was home, feeling very emotional as he fell into the arms of his mum, dad and brother. Proud, honoured, lucky and thankful too, but not desperate to continue his Naval career.

Brum Serrell was home, almost crash-tackled by Carol as she raced his dad, John, for the first hug. Brum caught her, just about, then asked a question that had been bugging him: 'Who's this Ninky?'

Jan Joyce was home, greeted by his step-mum, brother, fiancée Lynne and an old friend, Steven Thornhill, and his schoolmate's sister, and a dilemma. Did he go home to Chippenham with his mum, or Cannock with Lynne? The decision had already been made off Mounts Bay, when he'd asked for his rail warrant to take him to Staffordshire. He apologised to his mum.

'I understand.' She smiled.

John Leake was home. His brother Ian spotted him first. The big Brummie Canteen Manager pushed the barrier to one side, dropped his grip and picked Carole up. When he finally put her down, she stood back and looked at him. He was drawn.

Richie Gough was home, expecting to have to make his way by train to Falmouth in his stiff new 8s, but pleased to see the welcoming party, his parents, sister, two brothers and an uncle and aunt. They hugged and made small talk about how well he looked, but his mum couldn't hold the tears back long. He was safe. But she'd convinced herself that he'd been hurt and hadn't had the heart to tell her.

If he was hoping for a swift getaway, though, he was mistaken. Within five minutes of leaving the customs shed, he'd been stopped by three papers and a camera team. The intrusion wasn't that welcome, but at least he was polite, as the Captain had ordered.

Bob Young wasn't. He was home, carrying his white canvas bag with his stolen towels, arm-in-arm with Linda and his sister, Elaine, when some prat from the *Sun* shouted, 'Give us your photo, mate.' Someone should have told the photographer the paper was far from top of the *Ardent* popularity stakes.

'Fuck off!' Young replied, and continued walking.

Dave Croft was home too, thinking, 'That's it! I'll just get on with my life,' agreeing to pose for the press with Jane Broomfield on *QE2*, the returning hero who'd found shipboard romance.

His dad Dave was waiting ashore, with Denise Collins, his pin-up. They embraced, then Crofty told his dad about the problem he had with his car, parked in the dockyard at Devonport.

'Dad, I've lost my keys,' he said.

'Where are they?'

'Falkland Sound!'

The jolt for John Goddard, as he and Steve Earnshaw walked down the gangway, relieved to see their families, was being handed a red rose by a young black schoolgirl. He can't explain why. Then he took his girlfriend Kate and his mum in his arms and their stories started to pour out. How Kate had been

watching the Cup Final when she heard about the sinking. How his mum had been told he was missing, presumed dead until, an hour later, she found out he was alive.

He'd already given the *Daily Telegraph* his time on board, before the ship had docked. All he wanted to do was go home. So no more interviews.

Nor for Brum Serrell. They were walking out of the shed when a camera was shoved up his nose and a female reporter asked him if he was off *Ardent*. He said 'No,' and they walked on.

Nor for Scouse Phillips as he met his mum Beryl, his brother Chris and sister, Helen. Tearful hugs.

Nor Leigh Slatter. The day they'd sailed was their wedding anniversary, and he'd forgotten to give Chris a card. He bumped into them before he saw them and the first thing he realised was that little Kelly was walking.

Nor Russ Goble. The flashlights, the shouting and the screaming were too much once his mum burst into tears. He turned round and walked the family back on board to escape the claustrophobic noise and attention. He was desperate to see Gloucester, but they'd wait till the madness had died down.

These people deserved a story, Alan West had told his departing Ardents. Maybe. But, even if he expected his men to be brief but polite, no one had said the order extended to the waiting families.

'Are you pleased to have him back?' the *Washington Post* man asked Taff Lovidge's wife.

'What the hell do you think?' she asked him back.

For West himself, though, there was no choice. Lt David Searle, *Ardent*'s impromptu Press Officer, tried hard to keep the question-and-answer session brief as cameras and microphones pressed in.

West kept it together as he offered economical facts about Friday, 21 May, and their consequences. It was when he was saying how well his men had done that it became too much.

'I think that's enough,' Searle interrupted, off-camera. But West took a calming breath and continued. Someone owed them a story.

On-camera, Buck Ryan and John Bullock drifted into shot behind Charlie Oscar and began mouthing, 'Hello Mum!' For Ryan, it was impulsive but pointless. His mum was only a few yards away, waiting.

The young Weapons Engineer greeted his family, then introduced his wife Teresa and little son Kevin to the Jimmy. Then his regrets started. How do you deal with being a hero? He didn't know.

The *RAF News* asked if they could take a picture of the family, but his dad stepped in. 'You need to be quiet. You need to reflect,' he told his son. So Buck didn't play. Now he thinks that, maybe, he should have.

Andy Cox found himself being greeted by his separated parents Val and Jim, and his older brother Steve, as well as a Union Jack-covered girl who planted a kiss on his lips for the waiting camera. Page three of something or other would be his the following day. He'd keep the cutting. Like Crofty.

Jon Major had a black binliner in one hand and a duty-free bottle of Bailey's in the other when he heard his sister Sharon shouting. Could he find her? He could, eventually, with his mum and dad, and his brother, and the bus

driver friend who'd ferried them down in a minibus, and the driver's wife.

Street cred being the most important thing, Scouse Flynn and his cabinmate, Fluff Garnham, had made a pact not to shed a tear when they stepped ashore. But the Flynns weren't known for being reserved or patient.

The whole family – seven brothers and sisters, assorted spouses, wife-to-be Mandy and her family – had heard the request to stay behind the barrier, in an orderly fashion. It lasted as long as it took to see him, then the barrier was vaulted and Scouse forgot all about the cabin pact.

He began to cry. His family began to cry. Then they began to take the mick. He didn't expect anything different.

All John Foster had wanted since they'd left the Falklands was to move clear of the war zone, then see his fiancée, Jane, then his family. In that order.

He walked off, carrying a brown paper bag with 'Falkland Islands Tours' scrawled on it and some gizzits inside and Jane was the first person he saw. Before long, a *News at Ten* camera was with them.

'What did you first think when you saw *QE2*?' the reporter asked Jane.

'I felt like being sick!' she told them. Then the couple retired to a hotel room.

With every pair of shaky legs on the gangway, another homecoming began. A kiss, a hug, a shriek, a tear, a look, an unspoken word. Some or all, multiplied maybe 178 times. The one other thing they had in common was uncertainty.

The return wasn't the one Karoly Nagy had been expecting or had planned. In the icebox of the Sonar Instrument Space during the run-in past Fanning Head, he'd decided to finish with Jane, then go on that Soho hoolie with Buck Ryan. There was more to life. It lasted as long as it took her to greet him.

'I'm glad you're back,' she said. 'I'm pregnant.'

'It kind of destroyed me,' he admits. He didn't have the heart to follow the hoolie route after that.

Pete Brierley was hardly feeling better. He'd walked down the gangway hoping that, somehow, his estranged wife Christine and three-year-old daughter Karen would be waiting for him. They weren't.

Instead, he had to wait for his mum Evelyn and brother Mick. They'd been delayed by a blown head gasket. When they finally arrived, his nephew Michael and niece Angela were there too. It was very emotional, but a little unreal.

Joe Laidlaw had just found his stepfather John, and sisters Denise and Lesley, when a man stuck a mike under his nose and said: 'A few words for *Newsround*?'

Coxie was behind him. Laidlaw gave the man a few words, but not the ones he was expecting.

'What do you want?' his stepdad asked him.

Within a few minutes, they were in a pub. His dad passed him his pint, but he couldn't hold the glass. His hands were shaking. It would be the only reaction he ever had.

It didn't take Wyatt Earp long to sit down with a drink either, once the 18 year old had been reunited with his folks and they'd drifted away from the emptying customs shed and found somewhere to eat.

They didn't expect him to talk much, and he didn't intend to. But then someone asked him what it was like, and he couldn't help himself. It poured

out. The more it did, the more he listened to what he was saying. And, the more he listened to himself, the more he started hating the people in charge.

When he arrived home in Welland, his family and friends had organised a party in Worcester – on the River Severn.

'A welcome home party, on a fucking boat!' he shakes his head. 'I just thought, "These people don't understand." No one understood. And they don't.'

But people still wanted information he couldn't really give. Soon, he couldn't sleep at night. Then he sought refuge in the *QE2* cure-all, and spent almost every waking hour in the pub, and all his money.

Bernie Berntsen would spend the entire coach journey back to Plymouth with his mum and brothers, determined not to speak to anyone, and succeeding. The house would be full when they arrived but, eventually, he'd tell his mum and have a good cry. There was no hiding from the war and its consequences anyway. Among the small piles of personal possessions left behind in Mrs Berntsen's house on Monday, 19 April, were the contents of Knocker's locker.

One by one, then, they'd appeared. And slowly the shed emptied. And still Stuart Ray was waiting for his dad, well past bursting point.

At around ten to one, the long wait ended. The children saw their returning hero and he heard them yell. Carol Ray caught sight of him too, walking down the gangway, arm-in-arm with Lenny Yeatman – home the sailors, home from the sea. She dropped everything and ran. The children weren't far behind. Neither were Beryl Yeatman, or Joanne and Paul.

Five minutes later, with Connie Francis hurrying on ahead to be reunited with his beloved Granada, Beryl saw a young Ardent sitting alone on a wall.

'Who's that?' she asked Lenny.

'Davis I.F.,' he told her.

'Hello!' The rating, too young to be allowed out on his own, looked up and saw the Joss's wife.

'Your sister's coming to meet you,' she said.

'Thank you,' he said. She bent and gave him a kiss. And, within minutes, they were all gone.

But gone to what? The question was lurking in most minds as they headed home, whether that was Bob Young heading back to *Drake* with Linda and the children, a sheep being led, starting to dwell again on the green fields and landmarks passing the coach and the people who hadn't come home.

Whether it was Eddie Edwards, looking so ill his mum and dad thought he'd had a rough time down south – even though it was a fortnight's alcohol abuse etched across his face – but determined not to be put on show as some kind of hero. Because he wasn't.

Whether it was Scouse Phillips, wincing at the 'Welcome Home' posters in everyone's front window on the last part of the journey back from Lime Street,

not wanting any of it, just aching to sit down and have a pint, but putting up with it for his mum's sake. All that.

Whether it was the sight of his Nan sitting outside when Jon Major arrived home in Hull, big red, white and blue pop socks on, the street decked in bunting. He opened the bubbly but never tasted a drop. He went to the working men's club opposite, and the band stopped halfway through a song as he walked in, and everyone stood and cheered. He wanted the ground to open.

Whether it was Naggers, a father-to-be who'd just learned his own mum and dad had been told he was missing. A dad-to-be watching his grandad unfurl South Atlantic maps when he arrived back in Hemel, but not in the mood. And he wouldn't talk. He'd been told to say nothing, so he didn't. It had been near sunset. That was all he said about the dying moments of Friday, 21 May.

Or Buck Ryan, trying hard to be cheerful after driving home to Chatham with his family, not Portland, all the flags and banners and a wife who, understandably, wanted the party stopped because, 'Look, I've not had you for six months.' No hoolie, then. He couldn't find a way to deal with it.

Big regret. 'At that time . . . if I'd got it all out then, things would probably have been better.'

Or Pete Brierley, about to be divorced, shopping for clothes, one of the hardest things he'd had to do.

Or Richie Gough, occupied, for the moment, in trying to lure his homeless mate, Brierley, down to Falmouth, using his divorced sister Teresa as bait. But still feeling unfulfilled.

Or Christine Rowe, wanting to know what had happened, and trying to work out why *Ardent*'s Chief GI wouldn't answer her questions. It wasn't like him.

Or John Leake. He and Carole went up to Birmingham to see the family, for a huge reunion the reluctant hero didn't know anything about. Not until he drove down the road in Erdington, then the flags and bunting and reporters and camera crews gave the game away. He took one look, waved and drove past. Everybody was horrified. Until he turned round at the top of the road.

He put up with the booze, booze, booze, and everyone wanting to talk. But, by the time they'd returned home, all he'd wanted was quiet. They'd look for it at Badger's Holt, on Dartmoor, and there'd be two or three of the ship's company there, doing the same thing. They'd nod and smile, then all sit apart.

◆◆◆

The Yeatmans had no choice about where they stopped on the drive back to Plymouth. Beryl had thought to pack a picnic but didn't object to pulling in to the car park at the Cat and Fiddle, in the New Forest, because Connie had insisted on driving the Granada and she was frightened.

By chance, minutes later, the Rays walked in. If the dockside welcome had measured the relief of families seeing their men again, young Stuart saw the gratitude of ordinary people as Dad walked to the bar. The barman didn't say much, but knew who he was serving. The drinks were on the house.

What 22 other families would have given to be like them.

Alan Whitford watched the homecoming on the news, heart-broken. He still remembers the feeling.

'It was all about Garry that day. For us, it had all finished,' he says. 'That were for everybody else to think about, whether it was worth it.'

◆◆◆

Captain Bob Harmes had been on HMS *Arrow* when it went to *Sheffield*'s rescue five long weeks before. Then he'd known the death of *Ardent*. After a brief respite, he cashed a cheque on *Coventry* the day she went down. And, but for the instincts of Capt Hugh Balfour, HMS *Exeter* might have succumbed to a ground-fired Exocet while the artillery man was preparing the Type 42 destroyer for work on the Stanley gunline. He was already aware what a charmed life he was leading.

At 0237 that Saturday morning, he'd just closed his charts and left *Glamorgan*'s Ops Room when – bang! – he felt the sickeningly familiar thud and ripple. She'd been hit by an Exocet.

Men flew past him from the Ops Room, yelling 'We've been hit by gunfire!'

Harmes knew different. *Glamorgan* was doing 15 or 16kts.

'There's no fucking gunner in the world that's as good as that!' he shouted at them.

Then – whoosh! – the sound was terrifying and he thought they were being hit again.

Talk about horror. The noise was Seacat missiles being fired into the water as the flames neared, and Harmes quickly joined the Damage Control parties heading aft, into zero visibility.

The rest of the night wasn't good. The effort to save her went on and on. He saw and felt things he'd rather not have added to his Falklands war. But, by daybreak, they'd saved her, the only ship to survive an Exocet. *Arrow*, *Ardent*, *Coventry*, *Exeter*, *Glamorgan*. All he had to do was hope his luck held out.

The *Glamorgan* news wouldn't arrive on British TV screens for a few more hours, maybe a day. When it did, it would be a potent reminder of the Ardents' war.

Until then, after their first night between familiar sheets for 63 days, the news pictures brought other reminders of what they'd left 8,000 miles away. It was an odd experience. Eight thousand miles. For some, it may as well have been a million. For others, it was still close enough to touch.

As the sun bathed Britain on Saturday, 12 June, the pictures were of British land forces taking Mt Longdon, Mt Harriet and Two Sisters Ridge, overlooking Port Stanley, and of Welsh Guards rowing their injured comrades ashore after attacks on the RFAs *Sir Galahad* and *Sir Tristram* at Bluff Cove. That was hard to accept. Just two weeks before, they'd swapped places with the Guards on *QE2*.

Not that news-gathering was top of everyone's list.

On the train home from Southampton with his family, Scouse Flynn picked up a copy of the *Sun* and saw a familiar face.

In Leigh, near enough the same time, Dave Croft woke to the sound of his

little sister Jacqueline knocking on his bedroom door. He rubbed his eyes a moment later and saw the *Sun* on his bed, opened at page three. For once, it wasn't Denise Collins who filled it, as he recalls. It was him, and Jane Broomfield, smiling beneath a headline which read: 'It's not the ships that pass in the night, it's the nights that pass on the ship!'

Within a day, though, he'd receive air tickets to Bournemouth. His survivor's leave would be spent living the high life in Devon and Dorset, horse riding, messing around with Jane, out of his league.

❖❖❖

Tony Ray hit the road north, back to Birmingham, to see his 84-year-old dad Harold in a home in West Heath. The family hadn't told him about the ship but, if *Ardent*'s Deputy Marine Engineering Officer was wondering how to break the news, he needn't have worried.

While he'd been on *QE2*, his sister, Eileen, had taken their father up to the Lickey Hills one morning and sat with him looking across Worcestershire. Out of the blue, he turned to her. 'That was Anthony's ship that sank,' he said. He'd known all along. She took his hand and told him.

That night, Buck Taylor did the hardest thing he'd ever done. With his parents beside him for support, he drove from South Shields to see Knocker's mum, Brenda, in Washington. He was composed until he saw her, then he lost it completely.

'What do you say? "I'm sorry. It's not my fault, but I'm sorry"?' he still asks himself.

He started to feel his heart racing and his eyes moisten, but Brenda didn't need him to say anything.

'He was just a youngster. Nobody wants to make a visit like that,' she says. 'I actually felt I was to blame for the final parting shot. I just took it that they were big enough and daft enough to look after themselves. I can still see myself patting them, like this, as they stepped on to the train.'

Buck's dad quickly saw the look on his 18-year-old son's face.

'We'd better go,' he said quietly. Once they'd left, Buck turned to his dad.

'Drop me off at a club,' he said. 'I need a few drinks.' He never saw a bed that night.

By the time his head cleared that Sunday – 13 June – the Scots Guards were preparing to take the 500ft high Tumbledown Mountain, five miles west of Stanley, and 2 Para were doing the same with Wireless Ridge, on the north side of Stanley harbour.

By first light on Monday, 14 June, both were in British hands. Tumbledown had fallen after grim hand-to-hand fighting which left eight Guards dead but their pledge to *Ardent* fulfilled. Wireless Ridge was won after a battle resembling the inside of a fireworks display, with NGS support from *Yarmouth* and *Ardent*'s sisters, *Ambuscade* and *Avenger*. It took the number of 2 Para men killed to 17.

By the time Captain Bob unfurled his charts on HMS *Plymouth*, the venerable Type 12 had been patched up after an attack by five Daggers in open

water beneath Fanning Head that had threatened to end her war. Her funnel had taken superficial damage, but a depth charge had gone off on the starboard edge of her Flight Deck and a bomb had passed through her Mortar Handling Room.

Now she was proceeding up and down the gunline, waiting for the Call for Fire.

The sound of voices chattering on the Net made Harmes straighten. They were supposed to be silent.

'What's going on?' he asked curtly, but the words in his ears weren't the ones he was expecting.

'They've surrendered!'

Surrendered? 'Are you sure?'

'Yes! We're above Stanley and there are white flags going up.'

Suddenly, the whole Net came alive. He turned to Capt David Pentreath, a man looking forward to exacting some revenge of his own for the damage they'd had to patch up.

'I've got some bad news and some good news,' Harmes told him. Pentreath raised his eyebrows.

'The bad news is that you're not going to do a bombardment tonight,' the giant artilleryman said. 'The good news is that they've surrendered in Stanley!' Harmes saw the CO's masked eyes smiling.

'They knew I was coming!' Pentreath quipped. Then he turned and lifted the main broadcast mike.

'Attention all hands, Captain speaking,' he said. 'I have an announcement to make . . .'

❖❖❖

Life without Knocker. Brenda White doesn't remember the specific moment she heard the war was over. By now she couldn't watch television without retreating upstairs in tears.

'Dawn and I both wanted to shout at the world that we'd lost a son and brother. For months, she still expected him to come home on leave. Mandy couldn't accept what had happened. Ian took a real shaking. They were very close. Friends, as well as brothers. He really was very special . . .'

'You know you have to go back,' Mick Newby recalls feeling lost. 'You have to face the outside world. You can't go on the piss with Dave. You can't get a bollocking off Lenny, because he can't bollock you at home. "What am I going to do about that?"'

He had no answer any more than he knew why the minutes between 1744Z and 1815Z on Friday, 21 May had unfolded as they had. An Ardent without his ship, heading for an uncertain future. An Ardent who'd cheated death, bonded for life to an unexplained past, and the men who'd shared it.

But a life without Knocker, Shaun, Ginger, Florrie, Buzz, Gabby, Peddler, Muncher, and all the rest.

And life without *Ardent*. This wasn't how it was supposed to end.

TWO

DAMAGE REPAIR INSTRUCTIONAL UNIT, HMS *RALEIGH*, SALTASH, CORNWALL

(5 DECEMBER 1996 TO PRESENT)

The room's on fire. I'm cocooned in an oil-stained, yellow suit, heavy boots weighing my feet down, a smelly rubber, full-face breathing mask clamping my nose, mouth and eyes. I glimpse men moving near me, but only if the searing orange glows from their hoses. The rest I know by sound. Hearing's the only sense I can depend upon. The roar of flames. The odd distant shout. But mostly the sound of my own breathing. Rapid. I don't want rapid. Rapid means my oxygen will run out too soon.

The man who's led me in to this raging firebox shouts an inch from my ear. I can barely hear him.

'Stay exactly where you are. I'll be back. If you move, I won't find you.'

I never see him go. I weld my feet to a girder on the floor and the visor starts to steam up . . .

The room's flooding at 600 gallons a minute. I've been in here about two minutes and I still haven't caught my breath, my hands are freezing already, and I've dropped my hammer.

All I have to do is ram three wooden wedges into a shrapnel hole in the metal wall to stop the water spearing in, the first wedge in the middle, the others either side, so I wait for the roll of the ship to throw the rising tide away, desperate to grab the hammer before I'm submerged again. Jesus, I can't.

Five minutes. Ten. Fifteen. Just one damned hole and three damned wedges and two of us trying to stop the deluge. Six hundred gallons a minute. Past my knees, then my waist, then my chest. I can't feel a thing. My dark blue 8s weigh a ton. Then my shoulders. Then, as I'm gasping for a lungful of air, the water slaps and my head's slammed against a ladder. I laugh. I think of laughing like a child, in frustration. A laugh, then a sigh. That's it. Sod the wedges. Drink it! Twenty minutes. I've failed.

I crawl up and out of HMS *Raleigh*'s clanky, evil damage repair simulator and the bitter cold of 5 December 1996 rips heat out of my body in spirals of

steam, teeth like castanets tapping out a manic Morse message that reads, 'What in God's name am I doing here?'

Twenty minutes. It's all the Ardents had between hits. Fire and water. They've taken me one per cent closer to knowing what it's like to try to save your ship. I don't want to know the rest.

◆◆◆

'I didn't really know what to expect and I didn't really prepare for it,' Chief Marine Engineering Artificer Mick Cox was the first man called before the HMS *Drake* Board of Inquiry to find out why millions of pounds of Royal Navy warship had been lost, and to decide whether it had been avoidable, to learn lessons for next time, picking their way, man by man, through the Ardents until they had a complete picture. Queen's Regulations. Tradition. But Cox admits it was an ordeal.

'I went with the attitude to tell the truth. It was still fresh in my mind. I was still thinking about it.'

Eight thousand miles from where *Ardent* lay, though, they mainly wanted him to tell them what had happened to systems and power supplies. It didn't take the men in gold braid long to home in on what Marine Engineering Officer Terry Pendrous had said to cause the evacuation of the Ship Control Centre, minutes before Cdr West gave his order to leave the ship.

'They implied he'd told me to abandon ship,' Cox recalls. 'He never said that. I was on my knees when he said it was time to get out. In my mind, we were going to continue from somewhere else.'

The die was cast, and so were his memories of the inquisition.

'Did you try to contact the Bridge?'

He'd tried both intercoms. He'd tried the other communication systems. They were all dead.

'Why didn't you try the exchange telephone?'

Well, he could have, but . . . to sit calmly and ring the Bridge, when what was going on back aft.

'You could have tried it.'

'But I didn't. I just didn't have the time.'

It didn't take long for the what-ifs to haunt his mind again.

'The Forward AMR fire pump, providing we could have got firemain pressure from that pump, which I'm almost certain was running when we left the SCC, and firemain pressure was still in the forward section of the ship . . . it must have been from the ballast . . . so there was firemain pressure and the lights were on.' The lights were on?

It dawned on him in a split second as he spoke. It came like an express train. Cox felt the blood drain from his face. There had been power. Unless he was mistaken.

Taff Lovidge stood as Cox left the Inquiry Room, still ashen, and glanced at his colleague.

'That was shit,' the Scot told the Chief Electrician. Lovidge had been in the SCC too. He walked in.

'It may seem we're getting at you,' he recalls one of the Board reassuring him. 'We're not.'

He didn't stay reassured long. When they said, 'Why did you do so-and-so?' he began to doubt whether he'd done the right thing. When they asked pertinent questions, he began to feel guilty.

His defence mechanism in those days was to attack. Alan West was sitting beside him, keeping his counsel, doodling as the exchange continued, until Lovidge bristled once too often.

'Taff, just answer the question,' West told the Welshman.

'I got it back together,' Lovidge says. 'But, God, it was nasty.'

Weapons Engineer Buck Ryan wasn't far behind, a man who'd spent his Falklands War in the Forward Damage Control Party, but his mind went blank.

'I was just totally lost. Bewildered, to be quite honest. It was a very difficult time.'

LMA Bob Young soon knew the feeling.

'They had this great list of questions. They asked what you did. A lot of it I glossed over because I took it for granted that people would know what I'd done and how I'd done things,' he remembers the inquiry well. 'You kept getting battered and you never really got your head up off the canvas.'

If men like Mick Cox and Taff Lovidge had found the gold braid and the cold, calculating questions hard to take, how could an 18 year old be expected to cope, an 18 year old ready to wrap his hand in?

'I went in and never looked at anyone's face. I was looking down,' Wyatt Earp admits. 'They had the microphones on the table. Then they read out my statement. This was to 'help us in the future'. Suddenly they started asking about what I'd written, what I'd done.'

So far as he can recall, they started with the body he'd seen near the Hangar door as he ran, shocked, to fight the fires with Brum Serrell.

'In your statement, you refused medical attention because the person was dead,' one of his inquisitors said. 'How long did you spend in medical school?'

'Well, I've never been to medical school,' the youngster replied.

'Then how d'you know he was dead? Would he have been able to survive if he'd been given medical attention which you denied him?'

'It was like that,' Earp says now. In the corner, he could see Alan West was moved. 'I was just this young lad. He was dead. He was dead. I said, "He was dead." They told me he was dead.

'He said, "Let's get this man into the medical side." He was taking the piss. I came out thinking . . . No one expected the second or third attack after the first one.'

Andy Andrew expected the Board of Inquiry to say, 'Thank you for what you've done and what you helped to do as a team. Just tell us what you know.' He soon changed his mind.

'Their first objective is probably trying to get somebody's neck for this. The thing that got up our noses more than anything else . . . when I stepped into the room, I took my hat off and stood to attention. When I sat down I could have been some bit of trash off the street. The way they were speaking to me.'

To help paint the big picture, the one denied Alan West until those crucial

THROUGH FIRE AND WATER

couple of minutes on the Bridge, they quizzed the Chief Stoker about the flooding in the Forward Auxiliary Machine Room.

'The ship was lying to starboard,' he reruns his evidence. 'You'd perceive there wasn't anything flooding forward in the ship by looking at the photos. It may have been a contentious point with the Board, but I maintain there was water flowing in forward. And it was the Forward AMR.

'I knew the ship like the back of my hand. A lot of the lights were out, there was a smell of cordite. It was quite gloomy in the ship. It was the quietness I remember . . .'

They kept coming back to the flooding forward.

Buck Taylor, all of 18, was asked. He'd been in the Magazine all day. They'd checked some for water they could hear during their boundary searches.

'What did it sound like?'

'It was running water. It wasn't a torrent, but it was running water.'

'Define running water.'

'How the fuck do you define running water?' he still wonders. 'You're still a kid and you've got admirals . . . and the size of that table.'

If the men in gold braid didn't want to appear hostile, or seem as if they'd already decided – 8,000 miles away – that the ship could have been saved, few Ardents remember them trying hard.

'The Board of Inquiry said everything you did was wrong,' is how Dickie Henderson remembers it.

'They said that, no, there was just two attacks.'

He can clearly remember four bangs.

'Maybe you only heard three bangs.' No. Four.

Unlike some, the giant stoker had written down everything he could remember and he'd resolved to stick to his guns, whatever, even if it dropped others in it, like his belief that Mick Cox and the others had left the SCC without telling him and POME Mick Langley they were going, leaving them to shut the engines down. Bernie Berntsen was less helpful.

He couldn't tell them much else. On the day, he'd been on auto.

'What was going through your brain was "I've got to run a hose. I've got to do this. I've got to do that." You're not thinking "What's happening here?"'

Some found the challenging questions particularly difficult to handle.

'Why did you turn that off?' one asked Jessie Owens to explain how he'd set about isolating the firemain valve to stop water drowning the SCC Flat at 8-bar.

'Because if I'd turned the other, we'd have had no water aft at all!' All it did was fuel his doubt.

Some men, it has to be said, found the chance to chew the fat after weeks of dislocation at home like a purge. Others, like PO Joe Laidlaw, came away unmoved and unimpressed.

'I didn't prepare for it. All they were really worried about was the hole in the NAAFI and water coming through. I showed them where the hole was, and that was it.'

For still more, questions linger because they seemed so absurd.

'Were you frightened?' Captain Bob Harmes was asked. He still shakes his head.

'Of course I was bloody frightened! Everybody was frightened.'

He was challenged on why he'd moved men from the First-Aid Post. He shakes his head some more.

'They were terrified! They were minor injuries and this was not the place to be. They were bombing the arse out of the ship! It was the contact point for the next bloody hit.'

Lt David Searle had already come to the conclusion that he couldn't have done much more, even if he'd tried, but he knew little of what had prompted Alan West's decision: 'Were you told this?' 'No.' 'Did this happen?' 'Nope!' 'Was the place flooding?' 'No.' 'Were you sinking?' 'Not as far as I'm aware.' – so he learned more from his time at the long table than the Board did.

Ignorance. And resentment. CPO Dave Lee fell into both categories. He found the Board 'more like an inquisition' as they homed in on why the Seacat system had failed to operate just before the first hit.

'My answer was that I didn't know,' he concedes.

Ignorance, resentment and fear. Bob Lewis was one of the last to go in and trawl through the worst day of his life, worried about what he'd do if someone had mentioned his name, asked to remember what he'd told young Brad Vallint to do after the first hit. He's not certain he was much help.

'Why didn't you ask me to write this down the day after?' he thought. And he still does.

'Until that Board of Inquiry reported, nobody on the ship knew whether or not they'd be judged by their peers as having fought their ship to a standstill,' Surg. Cdr Rick Jolly acknowledges.

A standstill? A 1,000-pounder through the Aft Switchboard and on into the Aft AMR, severing cables, all but wrecking the two aft diesel generators, and taking the power to the gun and one of the ship's two steering motors with it? Another 1,000lb bomb ripping past the port Skua torpedo launcher and exploding in the Diving Store? A 500lb Snakeye bomb flinging the Seacat launcher in an orange and black fireball on to the Lynx and the Supply Officer? The Hangar wrecked and on fire? Torpedoes hanging out of the STWS tubes perilously close to flames? A deluge of firewater, some of it red, pouring through the Hangar soft patch? She'd survived that, for 22 minutes.

Then two more planes or three? Five or six? One wave or two? Hit or miss? It was academic. The log said eight hits, midships and aft. It didn't matter who'd put them there.

Queen's Regulations, tradition, inquisition. For one, Jolly didn't need to wait for the verdict.

'In a sense, I was a privileged witness, having come to the hover off her port quarter just after she was hit,' his mind rewinds the tape of Friday, 21 May 1982, and the frame freezes. 'The ship had had it. She was listing, hugely on fire.'

In the end, the Board agreed. *Ardent* had, indeed, been fought to a standstill.

But the damage had already been done, the seeds of bitterness sown.

They'd called Buck Taylor to the Inquiry, an 18 year old who'd spent his entire day in the Forward Magazine, to describe the sound of water. So why not leading stoker Jan Joyce, the man who'd run that three-minute Race of Life to spin stop-cocks and counterbalance *Ardent*'s plunging stern in the

heart-stopping seconds before Philippi, Arca and Marquez struck?

From the way the Board asked its questions, it seemed its mind had been made up long before the *QE2* brought the surviving Ardents home, hadn't it?

And hadn't their ship, the Falklands fighting unit with the greatest losses, one in four of them killed or wounded, forgotten by the British public, been stuck out on a limb – a sacrificial lamb to draw Argentinian fire in the first place?

And another thing. Why hasn't anyone ever told them what they achieved by pounding Goose Green and Darwin? Just how many of the enemy did they pin down? How many Pucaras distracted or destroyed?

'It might have seemed very harsh, but their job was to get to the truth. In a sense, the country deserved that,' Alan West reflects now. 'But, sitting in an office with hours to look at things, they appeared to be making judgements on young men who were trying to do their best in very difficult circumstances, the hardest day of their lives. I know the lads felt bitter at the time.'

The names change, depending on who's talking, and the fingers point in different directions. But there are still so many questions and too few answers. If they're still bitter, it's not hard to see why.

THREE

PRESENT

'I have three stories I can tell,' Ken Enticknap says after two or three hours. 'I have one story, I can hold court in the pub over a couple of beers and tell everybody. Then you have a more serious story, the likes of which I tell you. The third story you can only ever discuss with the people who were there. You don't want to tell it to anyone else.'

He says it to summarise the bond that's grown between Ardents over the years, not to mark my card for the conversations to come. Still, at least I know there's a line drawn. There'll be moments in the coming 30 months when I'm aware I've been taken to the horizon, some when we pause and I think I've been allowed to accompany someone beyond it, and others when I blunder past without realising.

Minutes later, Enticknap starts to think about his last round of golf before duty takes him for a two-year draft with the Royal Navy of Oman. The fingers missing on his left hand – two now – won't hinder his grip, he insists. Nor, judging by the gap, will he have a problem measuring a tot at the 19th.

He stands and fills the door frame and I can't help wondering how an 18 year old could carry this 40-something matelot here and now, let alone soaked, wounded and dead-weight. Three stories.

Three stories? 'He did have a couple of nightmares,' Frankie explains when he's gone. 'The only one he's ever told me about was in Aldershot. There are two main roads and, in between, there's a huge field, Queen's Parade. He dreamed he was in the middle of Queen's Parade in a shed, surrounded by Argentinians, and all he had to fire at them was baked beans. This bore no resemblance to anything, as far as I can tell. He woke up. He didn't shout or anything, but he was hot.'

◆◆◆

After five hours stretching the skeleton of the story out on Tony Ray's dining-room table, pictures and notes scattered among the beer cans and breadcrumbs, *Ardent*'s Deputy Marine Engineering Officer and her Master at Arms have almost finished adding their share of flesh to the bones.

'What do you feel now about not coming back with your ship?' I ask Lenny Yeatman.

'This is where it'll get difficult . . .' he pauses. It's been a long day. I catch his right hand moving to his left eye, but I'm not sure whether it's a gesture to complete the sentence or something else.

'You were part of the ship, of course, and you feel a sense of responsibility for it,' he says. 'I can feel remorse but not blame. The only way to have saved her would have been to put the fires out and had support alongside. What would we have achieved? We'd have saved a few rounds of 4.5. You'd have saved the torpedoes. You might have had some bodies for the families to grieve. That's all.'

The two close friends, 50-odd as we speak, have spent the day completing each other's sentences, though there've been times when the ground between their memories hasn't closed, no matter how many miles of coastal path they've pounded together since. Ray takes up where the Joss leaves off.

'We'd have never got her back,' he sits up, then, 'I don't think you can ever say the end justified the means. But what you can say is that our role within that whole day was something to be proud of.'

A couple of months later, I'm at the same table, eating lasagne with Carol Ray and Beryl Yeatman, wives of Navy men, never Navy wives, with their roots in the beautiful heart of England.

Three stories? Maybe there are four.

'Not long after they got back,' Beryl explains, 'they had a party down the Mess and I said something to upset him. He said, "Right, that's it, I'm going home." So we did.' She doesn't know what it was she said. 'Connie Francis didn't stay long afterwards, because Margaret had said something as well.'

Carol nods. 'He has a nightmare when 21 May comes. It starts in the middle of April. By the 21st, he's unbearable. He's in the main passageway and he's trying to get through . . .'

She's not being disloyal. I just ought to know. But nightmares don't only come at night.

Mick Cox's soft Scottish tones rise one notch on the volume control, only one, as he leans forward, a hint, maybe, that there's something he needs to say, even if the smile stays on his face.

'I went to Phoenix, to the NBCD school, a wee while after. I'd just been promoted. The Falklands was part of the scenario, and this guy asked, "Was anybody here in the Falklands?" I stuck my hand up. "I was in HMS *Ardent*."'

'You might not like some things we're about to do,' he was told. 'Could you have saved the ship?'

'Well, yes, I suppose we could.'

The guilt was immediate. For the benefit of the class, he described how they could have saved her. But, deep inside, he was telling himself, 'If everybody's thinking we could have saved the ship . . .'

He pulls himself back, but he admits his thoughts still shuttle from pole to pole, feeling a failure, but then reflecting that 'people who weren't there look at the damage, and they don't know what was happening, and they sort of say, "You could have saved that ship." That plays on me.'

In truth, he has enough questions of his own. He doesn't need anyone else's.

'The spirit was great,' he says. 'You get the guilt as a result. The what-ifs. I made the ship my life because my marriage was disintegrating. Not shutting the engines down. There's a page about me – in the Board of Inquiry report – and it has a sentence in it that I left the SCC when I was ordered, but I didn't shut

the engines down. That plagued me as well, because the training was never shut the engines down without permission.

'I couldn't get it, and I wasn't prepared to take the decision on my own. We had no information. We knew the first attack was coming, but no one mentioned the second or third. We knew they were coming when we were thrown round.'

Nightmares don't only come at night. Soon after resuming what amounted to a normal life, he went to Portland and found himself, he recalls, in *Amazon*'s Tiller Flat doing a war scenario. The engines revved, the rudder went hard over and the Tiller Flat shook and, over the din, he heard 'Skyhawk!'

'For 30 seconds, I nearly lost it,' he admits. The only other thing he remembers about the fright was seeing Ginger Nelson's face in his mind.

Andy Andrew can still see the lads he lost as well: Knocker, Florrie, Buzz, Gilly Williams, Garry Whitford, and he still hears them some days too. Above all, though, it's the guilty-till-proven-innocent attitude of the Board of Inquiry that doesn't sit well. I think his biggest criticism is his biggest desire.

'For the work that we did on 21 May, for eight hours,' he says, 'nobody ever thanked us.'

Although he had another ship after the Falklands, it finished him. He and Iris provided Debbie with a brother, Ben, and suddenly family became more important than the Navy. But he's still another who can set off on one stream of thought and meet himself coming back. Not confused, just unresolved.

'I don't think I'm wrong,' he says of Alan West, a skipper still worshipped by his men. 'On the *QE2* I don't think I saw him once. That was 14 days. I do say that's the Navy's fault. They train Captains to be somewhat aloof, but it would've been nice to have seen him and felt his presence.

'We were all shocked. None of us had been under fire before,' he goes on, then, 'it was a lot for him to comprehend. To look at his ship burning. Stopped in the water. Couldn't fight. It was a nightmare. I rode it quite well. I can't say the Captain did. He'd looked after us for so long.'

◆◆◆

Three stories? The fog on the drive south to Sussex is so thick that even the birds are walking. Not a journey to take as an omen for a day with two stokers who can't remember meeting each other since they stepped off *QE2* and, though they'll do their best, can't promise to add much to what I know.

It's only fate that's brought us together here. Geography, to be precise. Steve Earp runs a hotel near Worthing, Dickie Henderson has his own company in Hove.

While one talks, the other sits back and feasts on pink wafer biscuits, listening, a 33 year old who used to be an 18-year-old stoker, a 36 year old who was once a 21-year-old leading hand in the same trade, reminiscing about Amsterdam, Portland, Narvik, Devonport and Ascension, about Gilly Williams, and family, and friends. Common ground, common tales, but never part of each other's 21 May memories.

Not until Henderson goes back to the Hangar after the first hit, sent up into that twisted mess to try and stem the tide pouring through the soft patch into

the SCC Flat, and to see if the men up there need any help with the fires. The masked figure in the middle of the carnage shakes his head as he shouts, so Henderson turns to the two fearnought-suited firefighters behind him and sends them back below.

Then Earp takes his turn stepping back into the Hangar after the first hit, seeing blue sky again where there should have been a roof, describing the moment he sees a body in the debris before he picks up a hose and starts fighting the fires.

'Someone came in,' he recounts, 'and shouted, "We've got two BA firefighters!" and I said, "It's all under control. No need." They turned round. Florrie Ford was one. He looked at me and he shook his head. I sent them away.'

Henderson stiffens as the penny drops. 'Someone came in.' Henderson and Earp are talking about each other.

'In my mind, for all those years, I can remember coming down from up top and saying there wasn't really a fire to deal with. I always remember Florrie because we were in the same gulch. They said, "We've been sent from forward." I always thought the other one was Andy Barr. It's one of the things I wanted to clear up in all this. They came and I said, "There's nothing you can do. Go and wait in the Dining Hall." A couple of minutes later we got another bang, and that was it. The guilt I had . . .'

For a moment, reunited by the convenience of the Black Rabbit, the significance of that five-second exchange ricochets round his mind. But it'll take more than the next few minutes, more than the rest of the interview, for him to close this chapter and move on.

The fact is that both believe they sent Florrie Ford and Buzz Leighton into the heart of the next raid, though Earp appears to accept the part chance played. It'll be months before another conversation throws a third dice, when Ken Enticknap recalls quizzing the teenagers on their return to the Aft Section Base, then telling them to 'wait there', in the disarray of the Junior Ratings' Dining Hall.

It's not the only what-if Henderson has to resolve. Until he'd heard the story of Ralph Coates's escape from the Dining Hall, he adds, he'd always maintained that nobody came back out through the ship after he and Mick Langley fled the SCC. Nobody could. That's why he hadn't even thought about searching aft. Not any more.

'You *could* go all the way back,' he insists, partly kicking himself, but mostly taking some kind of blame. 'All these bulkheads *were* all right. The only thing I knew of the Dining Hall was it was just pouring black smoke. You couldn't see anything. I wasn't going to go back in there.'

It was 1990 before he saw a doctor, and even then it was an American psychiatrist and done privately, for fear of being labelled a 'nutter' by the Navy. In the eight years between, he'd switched careers to field sports, channelling his concentration into muscle-wrenching, mind-sapping physical torture so there wasn't time or energy to think of other things: Florrie and Buzz; the guys abandoning the SCC without telling him and Mick Langley; not looking back.

He's also been back to the Falklands, ten years to the day, on the

Campbeltown. They went over the *Ardent* and he laid a wreath. But it only laid so many ghosts.

'Every Christmas,' he admits, 'every occasion, out of the blue, it'll come. The doctor was brilliant. I had to talk. I'd always put it off because I wasn't sure who it was. I was almost sure it was Florrie. They said, "You've got to talk to his mother or father."' In 1996, after he left the Navy, he finally did.

By that time, Earp had long since left the Mob. The final straw for him was being drafted to *Hecla*, the survey ship which had gone south as a hospital ship.

'They said, "We've already got your hero off *Ardent* on here,"' he says of his welcome. 'Then they asked, "What did you do?" and I said, "I didn't do anything. I just stayed out of the way." Then I never spoke to anyone about where I was.' And he decided to quit. When he left, he threw his watch away.

It was a couple of years before Mick Newby had had his fill of the Navy. He was drafted to the shorebase *Dryad*, failed his PO's course, then moved to the Leander-class frigate HMS *Penelope*, waiting all the time for the service to provide him with the support he needed. The final straw came in Plymouth in 1985, just before *Penelope* returned south as a guard ship. It still makes him angry.

'We was about to go. We had this sailor from *Raleigh*, a week out of training,' he explains. Beside him in a Wiltshire country club lounge, Dave Croft looks at his old pal. He knows what's coming. 'He'd only done six weeks in the Navy. As a killick, you tell them they have certain jobs. Scrubbing flats was one. He told me to fuck off. I said, "No, no, no! Me chief, you Indian" type of thing. I told him again. He said, 'I didn't join the Navy to scrub decks."'

'I said, "Come on, we're going down the Chief's office." I explained the situation for ten minutes and he said, 'Wait outside."' Newby leans forward. 'Then he had me in and said, "We'll forget it this time."'

'Totally blew everything. I walked out of there, walked round the corner, saw my Divisional Officer and put 18 months notice in. That just did it for me.' He went south and came out in September 1986.

◆◆◆

Scouse Phillips shuffles forward in his chair. His reward for a war he remembers only to a point was Inskip, a godforsaken corner of rural north-west England with a radio mast sticking out of it, working shifts for a year, four on, four off.

'I'd gone from *Ardent*, that wonderful group of guys, through that trauma, to a farm in Lancashire.' But there was worse. 'They drafted me to a Leander.' He laughs.

He also counts himself lucky that his head was in the way at 1744, Friday, 21 May 1982, when 1,000lbs of tank-busting bomb, properly fused, blew the bottom half of the SCC's stable door in.

'In a way, I sometimes feel left out because there are certain memories I want to know about. But, on the whole, yes, I'm very fortunate. I haven't had to go through the psychological traumas some have.'

And, to prove that matelots remain the world's best pundits and

commentators, even when they've given up life in a blue suit, he still thinks long and hard about why it all happened.

'I'm no fan of Mrs Thatcher,' he shuffles further forward. 'I don't think many people are. But, as much as I don't admire her, I don't believe she went to war to get herself elected. She did it because of her personality. She's very bullish. A very determined person. Probably a very British person.'

John Foster's spent most of the past couple of hours leaning forward too, older than his years, owing his sanity after Friday, 21 May 1982, to Jane – now his wife – and his family. His fierce pride in *Ardent* underlines almost every word he chooses, and his pride in men like Ginger Nelson, and Alan West. All the Ardents. All except one.

He didn't see the RO Chief sent home by Tom Williams from Ascension again until he joined HMS *Ajax* after the Falklands. The man's first words to the craggy Liverpudlian, when he walked in the Main Communications Office, were, 'How did the war go?'

'I felt like somebody'd slapped me across the face,' he says.

They went to Portland soon after. Things didn't improve. In the ship's first exercise, Foster was taking cover, 'back there' in his mind. He looked up and saw the man standing, oblivious.

Foster shakes his head. 'He was an arse 'ole.' Give him Nelson, Banfield and West any day.

◆◆◆

On the one hand, David Searle puts the midnight run past Fanning Head, mines or not, into perspective like this: 'I was less than bothered about the outcome than perhaps a lot of people because, as far as I was concerned, I'd done all I needed to do in my life up to that time. I'd just got married. There was nothing else on the agenda. So I wasn't aware of any special concern.' Nonchalant. Together. A shrug of the shoulders for most of the day where Alan Maunder, our host, mops a brow at the same questions. However, you listen to the tape again, and you hear it differently.

One story: 'When I did my flying training in September and October, I was handbagged by this RAF wife at a function. She was telling me how the RAF were doing at Ascension; her husband was there; how jolly brave they'd all been. I was dreadfully polite until I finally lost my rag, and told her exactly what I thought. I was called in front of the Senior Naval Officer the next day.'

Two stories: 'Brian Murphy lent me his sword for my wedding,' his voice drops a note. 'I drove there, some weeks after we got back, and gave it to his wife. She was quite grateful, because it was the only thing she had of Brian. As far as she was concerned, Brian had it with him.'

Three stories: 'The thing I found hardest, subsequently, was when I was doing my medical survival training. I was to go into a darkened house. They turned on the smoke and you had to go in, find this casualty and sort him out. I just couldn't go in.' He did, eventually. 'It was actually pretty terrifying.'

Then there's Lt Mike Knowles, a Commander 15 years on as we talk of not bringing your ship home.

'That was what happened,' he says. 'The ship was too badly damaged. But most of us got back, and that was it, until we got reunited with our families. Sadly, some didn't. That's the way I talk about it.'

Then, a few minutes later . . . 'For a long time, I couldn't say the words of the Naval Prayer, "that we may return in safety to enjoy the blessings of the land, with the fruits of our labours . . ." I still have difficulty because it's to do with coming back. That's the guilt I have. I came back, but others didn't.'

The man who sat across the Ops Room from Knowles, with no way to defend the ship, sits opposite me with a picture of his 17-year-old son David, proud in his HMS *Raleigh* cap, on the wall behind.

It somehow fits that, whatever sustained 34-year-old PO Mike Lewis during the long, painstaking hours at *Ardent's* passive Electronic Warfare plot, sustained him as a driving instructor when he left the Navy. Methodical. Patient. Considered. To the point.

In the absence of a true picture, he fears that any sense of achievement will never compensate the sense of loss. 'The healing's slow,' he says, 'a process of elimination; eliminating the bad memories.

'I remember coming back and being in the garden and a jet flew over and I was down on the grass thinking, "I hope no one can see me!" A couple of years later, I was on a ship which did NGS and I couldn't bear the 4.5 firing. People were looking at me, thinking, "What's the matter with him?" I said to myself, "You're being stupid."'

I ask about the Ardents being broken up twice in three weeks, once by the bombs, then by the Navy.

'All gone,' he says. 'Into a vast emptiness. It was hard. You try to picture the faces, and that's terrible when you can't. I feel guilty today when I can't think of the names. The mind blanks things out.'

◆◆◆

It's the change in Jan Joyce's voice that's so noticeable as he explains when he started to look forward again, not back. The note drops, just like it will when I ask Errol Flynn if he can tell me about the Stokers' Mess the moment action stations was piped that Thursday night.

Joyce is back on the hillside overlooking Falkland Sound when he answers. 'I thought the sooner I go back to sea and the sooner I go down to the Falklands, now it's finished, and try to ease the memory, go past the point of no return . . .' He did, a couple of years later, on *Battleaxe*.

'There was about eight of us. We walked up the mountain to have a look. One of the lads was talking to me for half-an-hour and I didn't hear a bloody thing he was saying. I was down there. I was talking to the lads I knew.'

He was thinking of wrapping his hand in at the time, but he swears blind an answer came back from the Sound, like they were saying, 'Don't give up! Stick with it.' So he did.

◆◆◆

Iain McRobbie's hazy to begin with. In his first letter, he recounts a conversation he's had in his local the night before with a guy who's worked in the Clyde shipyards for 40 years, including Yarrow, where *Ardent* was built. But he can't say he's heard of her. *Sheffield*, *Antelope*, *Belgrano*, yes. Even *Yarmouth*. But not *Ardent*.

Hazy to begin with. But, by the third page, he's blank, like Mike Lewis, and frustrated.

'I have a major problem with four of the other guys who died. I've never told anyone this before, but I feel responsible for their deaths,' he writes. Then he paints a picture, of Paddy McGinnis telling him to take four spare hands aft to report to Peddler Palmer. He's confident Mick Mullen and Richard Dunkerley are two, but that's all. On the way, he's distracted by the sight of a messmate with a head wound. You look out for your messmates first. Tradition. He tells the four he'll catch them up.

I write back. Mullen, maybe, but Dunks was already in the Galley. Florrie Ford and Buzz Leighton?

He replies. No, not Florrie or Buzz. They'd already headed aft.

I write again. That leaves Andy Barr, Simon Lawson, Taff Roberts, Derek Armstrong, Steve Heyes and Sean Hayward.

'I know it wasn't Simon Lawson or Taff Roberts,' he comes back. 'So, by a process of elimination, there are now only four names left in that list.'

But four into three won't go. Hazy? Blank? We rely on someone, anyone, to recall with certainty but, in the end, we're left with elimination: 'Mick Mullen definitely, almost certainly Andy Barr, most likely Geordie Armstrong and Sean Hayward. 24, 20, 22 and 18.' It's close, but . . .

For me, it's frustrating. For Robbie, I suspect it's tormenting, but I never ask.

Russ Goble has unfinished business too.

'Someone high up, above our Captain, should have come to us and said, "This is what you did. You were here because we were protecting this. You did a fantastic job," or "You did a crap job," or "Sorry you lost 22 of your mates," instead of just carrying on as if nothing happened.'

It's all he ever wanted. Instead, he has a Falklands medal, handed over in some other Captain's cabin. Handed over, not pinned on. He nearly gave it back.

A short time after, he was at a service in Tewkesbury Abbey. As he was coming out, in uniform, a couple approached him.

'We're Mr and Mrs Barr,' they said. 'Do you remember our son?'

'Yes,' he told them. 'He slept above me.'

'Can you tell me how he died?' Mrs Barr asked.

'I thought, "Christ!"' he pauses. 'I said he didn't suffer because, where he was, the bombs came through and devastated the room.'

Meeting Pete and Renee Hanson for the first time after coming home wasn't something Jon Major looked forward to. What do you say? In the event, it was Renee who broke the ice and walked up to him at a reunion to say, 'How are you?' Since then, they've helped him to cope.

He was on HMS *Cornwall* when the 1991 Gulf War began and heard one of his messmates echoing the cries of 1982: 'Let's get down there!'

'I said, "Why d'you want to go?" He said, "I want a medal!" So I went to my locker and got my South Atlantic Medal out and said, "If you want one so badly, have that!" He did apologise afterwards. He was about 20, the same age as me when I went down the Falklands.'

It took another couple of years for it to hit him. The Majors and Hansons had returned to the China Fleet Club and opened a bottle of whisky his mum had won at the reunion. Jon went outside, sat on the steps and broke down. He doesn't know why. The person who came to sit with him was Shaun's mum.

◆◆◆

Dave and Carol Serrell had never met Peggy McAulay until they arrived home in Kidderminster on his survivor's leave. His path had often taken him into the Hangar and past Mac McAulay, but he didn't know *Ardent*'s Senior Flight Maintainer that well. Peggy had called Dave's folks after reading about the young tankie in the local paper, wondering if he could phone or make the short trip to Droitwich.

'We said, "We can't really phone her up," so we bimbled across, found the house and went up to the front door. The finger was there, on the button, and it was, 'What do I do now?''

She welcomed him with a hug and sobbed on his shoulder. From then on, until she died after being knocked over, they rang her almost every week.

Bob Young didn't meet Mac's mum until he went on board *Cunard Countess* from HMS *Penelope* in San Carlos Water, the next April, and met the families of the men they'd left behind. He stood with them as wreaths were cast on the water. *Ardent*'s aerial and a small oil slick a reminder of what had happened. He talked with Mrs McAulay and Pete Brouard's sister but, as he stood there, the quandary was still about Mac. Had he checked him properly? In his heart of hearts, he knows he did.

It was a low point in a year he'd rather forget. He'd struggled to cope as a medical instructor at *Raleigh*, because part of the training involved playing a tape of the action alarm klaxon, and it used to crack him up. On *Penelope* it was hardly better.

'There was a Task Force South video where the credits start with a klaxon,' he laughs now, 'and I lived in the Sailors' Mess and they used to say, "Watch the doc" and put it on. I'd be out of my bed like a shot. Not good. And so, really, I hid it away.'

He worked in the Patient Services Department at the Naval Hospital too, but his poor short-term memory let him down and he'd forget to do things. It wasn't advisable.

'Anything in life, you've got to take your right decision at the time and stand by it,' he says now. 'Everything you do in a split second you stand by forever, don't you? You can't step back and say, "I should've done this or that." That's what mostly tears people apart. I was better equipped to do my work because I'd dealt with real casualties.' But the ones he's talking about were also his friends.

'That's one of the big things,' he concedes. 'You identify a person who's badly injured or dead, you know them by their first name . . . and you take two seconds to check them and go on.' Like Mac.

He paid a price. For being a professional medic who should 'get on with it', he stuck to his plan to have a drink with the rest of the guys and get on with life, rather than do things Morgan O'Connell's way. He kept it private. He shed a lot of weight. And it took years to 'burn out' of him, if it ever has.

◆◆◆

Pete Rowe says he told the drafting committee he wanted to go back to sea straight away, to see if he still had his nerve. Buck Taylor admits that, even before the Falklands, his first experience of the Royal Navy for real had been hard, typically hard, even if he wasn't old enough to appreciate it. Eddie Edwards tells you that he knew Navy life would go on, somewhere, whether he liked it or not. Bernie Berntsen likewise, though he doesn't say so. It's something you pick up from his manner.

Within months, they all ended up on *Active*, *Ardent*'s sister ship. Danny Byrne too. Berntsen, the old man of F184's Junior Messdeck, was fine for a few days after he and Taylor joined the 21 at Portland, until a couple of sea-riders, two Chiefs, tried to tell him what would happen if an Exocet hit the ship.

'There'd be smoke everywhere,' they assured him.

'No there wouldn't!' he remains indignant as he replays the scene. 'There wouldn't be any at all.'

'How d'you work that out?'

'The ship's going forward, isn't it?' They nodded. 'There's a hole in the ship. It'd be sucked out.'

'No it wouldn't!'

'Fair enough . . . but it would.' He turns his back on me.

They went straight south from Portland, and that's when it hit home. He was put in the Aft Engine Room, and he handled it until the first Air Raid Warning Red and they closed up.

'I was frightened. I nigh-on cacked my pants.' He leaves it at that.

Eddie Edwards knows what his mate went through, because he admits feeling the same when the first call to action stations came. A little later on, there was another reminder when he walked into a NAAFI Canteen on the Islands and thought he recognised one face among the customers. They'd met before, but Edwards couldn't place the man until he said who he was. He was Charlie Ford, Florrie's dad.

A year almost to the day after the sinking, if Pete Rowe remembers right – almost, it was April – *Active* also escorted the *Cunard Countess* at the Falklands.

'We sat over and put her on sonar and we could see the ship, all the outlines,' he says. Then the Ardents moved out into the open air just off North West Island. 'The rest of the ship's company was cleared and nobody came out on to that Flight Deck. After that, they flew us all up to the memorial.'

'He had a very harrowing two or three days,' Christine interrupts. 'The impression I got was that he was finally able to say goodbye to his friends. In a proper way.' He nods.

As a special concession, he remembers, he and Bernie Berntsen were

allowed to yomp the couple of miles from Campito Ridge down to Port San Carlos, to meet Bernie's cousin. They had roast lamb, then Rowe left his colleague overnight and returned to the ship.

Leigh Slatter went ashore at the same time, from HMS *Cardiff*, and visited Goose Green with a shipmate. The owners of Camilla Creek House – once an *Ardent* NGS target – welcomed them with a warm meal. As they sat, Slatter noticed a sheet of bent metal by the fireside. Blue metal. Their host had found it washed up on the shore, further up Grantham Sound. He looked closer, intrigued, and then something made him jolt. It was the figures 3-4-0. This was a chunk of *Ardent*'s Lynx.

Alan Whitford talks of the visit as if he has a camera rolling in his mind. He was beginning to come to terms with Garry's death when his family climbed on to a crowded train at Blackburn on Monday, 4 April, then travelled through Mill Hill Station, the place where he'd waited for his young brother's final wave 352 days before, and he began to shake like a leaf.

Four days later, they were in Falkland Sound, passing the spot where *Ardent* lies. A buoy was supposed to mark the spot. His mum and dad, Jack and Teresa, were pointing it out to him, but he couldn't see it. Still, the moment put pictures in his mind, and that's what he wanted.

For five years, his folks kept their heartbreak to themselves. It was six, possibly more, before his mother opened Garry's last letter. It was just like he was talking about his holidays. After Jack died in 1992, she slowly began to talk more, but still as if Garry was just away.

Around the same time, one night, the phone went in her Blackburn home. It was Isabel, Garry's fiancée. She said she'd just thought of him.

'You're being silly,' Mrs Whitford reassured her. 'It's just something you're thinking about.'

They kept it at a phone call.

'That's the thing that's disappointing, really,' Alan says when you ask for his memories of his younger brother now. 'I can't remember that much about him, because he was six years younger. I remember when he had his Slade stuff, his blue pants and tank-top, that kind of thing.

'Did he get away with things? It was just accepted. I remember me mother getting angry with him one Christmas. He was on leave and she came down one morning to find he'd cleared the house of all the drink she'd got in.' The lads would be proud of him.

Each year, 21 May is marked privately, within. There's no grave to tend, so Alan normally finds himself with flowers at the war memorial at Belthorn, the only place Garry's name could be engraved, where their dad lived his early life.

'With Garry being 8,000 miles away, I don't feel I need to be in any particular place,' he says. 'I don't really think about why it happened. I just think about Garry. And the ship.'

The bungalow where Pete and Renee Hanson live now is called Shardent. It's neat, almost every wall has a Navy connection, and there's a huge map of the world on the end wall of the conservatory, above the stereo Shaun bought with his first wages. We drink tea almost endlessly. Every cup hits the spot.

'Do you know what Shaun was doing when he was killed?' I ask when the time seems appropriate.

'The First Lieutenant, he came to see us,' Pete says. 'He said, "I'm going to be perfectly honest with you," and I've never had reason to doubt what he told me. "Your son died instantly. I can assure you he didn't suffer." He survived the first wave and the back end was hit a second time, and that took him.'

It comes as a relief. What I already know of the strapping steward who'd stayed alongside his mortally wounded boss on the Flight Deck meets their understanding too.

The Hansons spent the first couple of months visiting 'Welcome Home' parties for other *Sheffield* lads, putting a brave face on for Shaun's sake, but life was far from easy. They visited the Falklands a year on, met 21 other families in similar circumstances, made new friends, and time began to heal.

'It were tremendous,' Pete says. 'I did a bit of a story. I sat up every night, while two or three o'clock in the morning. It's what I was feeling at that particular time. D'you want to see it?' I do.

'Everybody has different ways of grieving. Some people have been here and said it's a bit like a shrine. I don't regard it as that. That map on my wall. I bought it for Shaun and put it up. It said: "Wherever you go in the world with the Navy, put a string across." He didn't get very far with it.'

A couple of days after our conversation, still overdosed on tea, an envelope arrives with a Sheffield postmark on it. It's Pete's journal. It follows the family's route from Ecclesfield to the South Atlantic and, after 35 lines of Heathrow, Barbados and Montevideo, it arrives at Thursday, 7 April 1983.

Thursday, 7 April 1983

Our point at noon was latitude 40 degrees 17 minutes south longitude 53 degrees 16 minutes west. Distance to go 697 miles. The weather was still fine and sunny but as we moved further out into the South Atlantic wind increased and the ship started rolling in the huge swell. It was a funny sensation to be staggering all over and be quite sober. Earlier in the day we met the other 21 families of HMS *Ardent*. Introduced ourselves and made ourselves known to people.

Friday, 8 April 1983

Our position at noon was latitude 45 degrees 44 minutes south longitude 56 degrees 16 minutes west. Total distance 852 miles, distance to go 344 miles. Had a bad night, ship was rolling and could not sleep, a lot of creaking. The tension is beginning to build up not only with our family, but amongst other families and widows. Everyone knows we are nearly at the Falkland Islands.

The ship is due to rendezvous with HMS *Cardiff* north of Pebble Island at 1045 hours on Saturday morning. We had to collect the poppy wreaths which had been ordered by our family and we have decided to

place three wreaths on the water over HMS *Ardent*, the other two we are placing at the memorial overlooking Ajax Bay and San Carlos. Carol and Lisa are placing a Sheffield United pennant and scarf at the memorial. The weather is still holding quite good, warm if you find a sheltered deck.

Saturday, 9 April 1983

Position at 0700 hours approx some 45 miles north of the Falklands. Breakfast at 0730 hours and all service people wear their respective uniforms for the first time on the journey. The ship is flying the Union Jack for the first time and at 0930 hours we spot a helicopter approaching. At 1030 hours HMS *Cardiff* approaches from the Falklands. As it comes alongside the *Countess* emotions are running very high with a mixture of being proud to be British and sadness that Shaun is not amongst the sailors lined up on the *Cardiff* deck. At 1130 hours we stop for the memorial service of HMS *Coventry*, 12 miles north of Pebble Island. Mr and Mrs Tonkins, from Eckington, invite us to attend the memorial for their son Stephen. Another very emotional time for everyone concerned.

HMS *Active* has now joined the *Cardiff* to escort us. At 1415 hours we are nearing San Carlos and Ajax Bay, and at 1430 hours, we stop for the memorial service for HMS *Antelope*.

Mr and Mrs Stevens, from Mansfield, invite us to attend the service in honour of their son Mark.

The position of HMS *Antelope* was marked by two buoys and very close to the shore at Ajax Bay. After the ceremony we came right up to San Carlos Bay and dropped anchor. On the top deck we could see the tiny settlement of San Carlos with the war graves cemetery clearly visible. On the other side across the bay on top of a high ridge we could see the erected memorial in honour of the brave men of *Ardent* and *Antelope*. All around you could spot missile sites.

Our first impression of the Falklands was one of perfect peace and tranquillity. In some places we even spotted what very much resembles the Filey Brigg.

At 1700 hours two of the crew from HMS *Active* came on board the *Countess*. These two officers were ex-HMS *Ardent* and all the *Ardent* families sat down and had a drink with them and made them welcome for the hour that was allowed. Throughout the day the weather has been good, visibility was clear and fine with a strong breeze. A very emotional day, retired to bed very tired.

Sunday, 10 April 1983

Up at 0645 hours and on the top deck to witness sunrise at 0715 hours. Beautiful setting with the tops of the hills shrouded in mist. HMS

Endurance sails in alongside us. At 0930 hours we set foot on the Falklands for the memorial service at San Carlos cemetery. Plaques are mounted on the wall at the head of the circular resting place. A stone wall about five feet high runs round the perimeter. Every serviceman who has lost his life has his name inscribed on the plaques. Before the service begins at 1130 hours we have time to walk around the small settlement in San Carlos. We meet and speak to one of the islanders. He came from Scotland 25 years ago, his wife is from Manchester, they run a sheep farm with 27,000 head. At 1415 hours after the service and lunch we board a helicopter which takes us across the bay and to the top of the ridge, a distance of approximately two-and-a-half miles. The ridge is the highest point in the area and overlooks the position of HMS *Ardent* in the Falkland Sound and HMS *Antelope* in Ajax Bay.

A memorial cross has been erected in honour of the men from *Ardent* and *Antelope* who lost their lives. Our wreaths, flowers and mementoes are placed and a short service is held. Magnificent views are all round from this point. During the day we collected keepsakes, such things as one or two stones and rocks, Falklands soil, grass and wild flowers. A day never to be forgotten.

Monday, 11 April 1983

On the top deck at 0715 hours to witness sunrise, clear skies and a sunny morning. At 0815 hours we sail from San Carlos and into the Falkland Sound to head south escorted by HMS *Cardiff*, HMS *Active* and HMS *Fort Grange*. Time is drawing near for what we have come 8,000 miles to do.

Decided to put Shaun's suit on for the ceremony and at 1005 hours we take up our position on the Flight Deck for the service. At 1015 hours the *Countess* and escort ships stop engines, flags are flying at half mast, the service begins and halfway through the service over the position on HMS *Ardent* we cast our wreaths.

Over the water, saying prayers for everyone back home. Do not remember much after this except to say that we stood on the very end of the Flight Deck and watched the position of HMS *Ardent* slowly begin to disappear, gave a wave of farewell to our Shaun. After 30 minutes or more HMS *Cardiff* and HMS *Active* passed us in silent tribute, the decks lined with sailors holding their caps.

We continued down Falkland Sound and headed east of Port Stanley out to open sea. At 1715 hours we attended the service and act of remembrance where HMS *Sheffield* had been hit. Later there were ceremonies for people lost on *Hermes*, *Sir Galahad*, *Glamorgan* and *Sir Tristram*. Each time we stopped and paid a tribute to every man lost. All in all a very heartbreaking day.

Tuesday, 12 April 1983

Very busy day ahead, dawn we dropped anchor in Port Stanley harbour.
Breakfast at 0700 hours. HMS *Cardiff* and *Active* berthed alongside the
Countess. At 0930 hours we went aboard the *Active* for a full tour of the
frigate, very impressive. We saw the exact place on the ship where
Shaun lost his life. After the tour we went down further narrow
stepladders into the 129 Mess where we sat and had drinks with all the
survivors from HMS *Ardent*. At 1145 hours we had to say our farewells
to the lads. In respect we were saluted off the ship by every officer.

At 1900 hours the following message from HMS *Active*: 'It has been
a great privilege and an honour to be your escort during this unique
period. We are most grateful for the kind hospitality you have shown all
of us who visited your fine ship. Please tell the families that we have so
enjoyed meeting them and being able to share in their pilgrimage. God
bless and a safe journey home.'

Wednesday, 13 April 1983

0815 hours we attended the service for the *Atlantic Conveyor*, this was
the last act of remembrance in the Falklands. Throughout the ship you
could talk to people and if one did not feel like talking, fair enough, you
understood. Everyone had their own story of fate, bad luck, and
hardship. No one's family life can ever be the same again. There were
divorced people meeting and sharing the same meal table. One man had
his ex-wife and new wife, along with two sons and daughter all together
throughout. They appeared to get along very well. There were widows
who could not get along with their in-laws and kept away from one
another, others who got along very well, and shared their grief together
as a family.

Friday, 15 April 1983

People will ask have you found peace of mind on the pilgrimage. Our
family's answer is yes, we paid our last respects to Shaun at the place
where he lost his life. We have found answers to lots of unanswered
questions, and learnt a lot which we previously did not know of. We've
been and seen for ourselves and it is no longer in our imagination. I
could go on forever but here's a brief example.

My family, friends and people locally all knew Shaun was a hero.
When we stepped ashore that clear morning at San Carlos, walked up
to the cemetery and saw Shaun's name, rank and ship inscribed on one
the plaques alongside 254 other men, we knew then he was a hero of
the nation and of the Falkland Islands. As such his name will be
honoured and treated with respect for all time, a long time after we

ourselves are dead and buried. I could not wish for anything more for him.

This is a true account of the Falklands pilgrimage, each night I have sat down and wrote of the happenings and feelings of the day we have been a party of, and I am not ashamed to record that many times I have had to wipe the tears away as I have put pen to paper.

In a final conclusion, this Falkland pilgrimage has been a unique experience. It is one for all time that will never be repeated in our lifetime. To be a party to this experience you must have lost someone very close to you. The irony of it all is we have lost our only son. God bless him.

Shaun's name is on the cenotaph in Ecclesfield Church, memorials on the Hoe and the China Fleet Club in Plymouth, and at St Paul's Cathedral. But his parents have no grave to tend. And that's been difficult.

It was George Palmer, Peddler's dad, who persuaded Pete and Renee to go to the annual reunion. 'We get a lot out of it,' Pete says. 'We go for the service. I like to hear my son's name read out.'

◆◆◆

Another conservatory, another quenching drink, but this time an unspoilt view of Portland across the shimmering bay.

'Alan West came round,' Lesley Sephton explains, soon after telling me she'd put her desire to know much behind her, 'and I asked him, "Was John killed outright or did he suffer?" He said, "No, he was killed instantly," and that was enough. Apparently, the doctor had gone to administer whatever and he said it was too late. I accepted that, because that was what I wanted to hear. I often wonder whether that was said to soften it. I used to say to John that, when I died, I wanted a grave with white flowers all over it. He just used to say, "Send me out into the open sea on a burning ship."'

After five weeks, she went back to work. One morning, she saw a helicopter flying parallel to her, its pilot looking down until they reached a junction where there was a man in a car with a clipboard. As she arrived, the helicopter would peel off and the man would write on his board. It went on for days.

'It was as if someone up there was making sure I was all right,' Lesley smiles, but her eyes are not aimed at me. 'I know it meant nothing, but it was a great comfort to me.'

A little later, over lunch, Harriet beside us, she disarms me by asking where John's body is now. We think of the final blasts that cleared the Flight Deck, the movement of the ship, and settle on a possibility. She smiles.

'Harriet and I, we've talked about him virtually every day, "Your father would have done this or that." She can only refer to what her friends' fathers are like. I'm sure her father would have been perfect. He would have adored her too.'

◆◆◆

The kitchen of Ardent House, a two-up two-down cottage deep in Weardale is cosy. Outside, the snow that's been falling since I left Buck Taylor and Naggers outside the Chichester Arms in South Shields, three hours before, is now threatening to strand me. It could be worse. I'm supping tea and eating a cheese-and-potato casserole with Knocker's mum, and she's made far too much. She's already stood at the window, watching the snow fall, not resting until I've arrived safely.

At the end of one letter to me, she's written: 'Steve is watching over me while I type this. It is a photo of him taken pulling a funny face. One taken in Jerusalem.'

Jerusalem, Mombassa, Amsterdam, Portland, Ascension, Falkland Sound . . . Ralph, Wacker, Coxie, Bernie, Buck, Nags. All their stories about Knocker have ended in laughter. They miss him. He'd be 38 if he were here. Instead, he's 21 and still making people happy. I wish I knew his voice.

'I coped because Steve would not have wanted me to fall to pieces,' Brenda says. 'I talked about all the funny things he'd done.'

We start to talk about some of them, but mums aren't daft. She can sense that I'm not sure which of the stories should be paraded in front of her.

'I probably know them all,' she laughs. 'The ones I don't wouldn't surprise me.' So we talk.

'Lt Cdr Gordon Lennox visited us, a wonderful man,' she says later, 'and told us Steve had been killed when bombs hit the aft part of the ship. He'd been seen to be dead. This was a relief. The night after the sinking I couldn't sleep for a long time thinking he may have been trapped inside alive.'

And: 'We all wrote letters. The last one I wrote was returned to me with "Deceased" on it.'

And Knocker's records: 'They were left to Mandy. She still has them. We don't use them. There's nothing that will ever be disposed of. It's part of Steve that's still with us.'

In among all the chat, I talk about 'Always Look on the Bright Side of Life'. It's one of those stories Brenda hasn't heard, and, fortunately, one I wouldn't mind telling any mum.

The snow's receded when the conversation ends, the next morning.

Eighteen months on, on the phone, she tells me Mandy's just moved into her first house. She's decided to call it 'Bright Side'.

✦✦✦

John Leake can remember his older brother Alan telling him, 'You've got to talk about it.'

But the big Brummie thought no, he didn't. He didn't have to talk about it to anybody. He didn't have to explain why *Ardent* was 'a sprat to catch the mackerel', something that had to be sacrificed, the friendliest ship he's ever been on. Eventually, he gave up trying to explain why he should never have been awarded the DSM, because there were far more deserving men than him and because it drove a wedge between him and his old drinking partner and GPMG loader, Cliff Goldfinch.

'I feel with Cliff . . .' he pauses. 'Every time I tried to say "Cliff Goldfinch did exactly the same" . . . In the end I got so fed up, I just didn't talk about it . . . I don't think it was out of the ordinary. People thought I was a civvie . . . I was putting my military training to good use . . . It was said I ran from below and there were dead or dying and I carried on. That story got out. I don't know where it came from.'

It was an innocent old sea dit, so far as Pete Brierley's concerned, and he's mortified. He didn't think twice when those two scruffy-looking journalists joined a bunch of Ardents for breakfast on *Canberra* early on Saturday, 22 May. Not that he knew they were journalists at the time.

'It was like telling a dit about the firing on the cows, or Chaff at the geese. The story of John and Cliff was just part of a conversation,' Brierley rues.

He's now happily married to Richie Gough's sister Teresa, but it was years before he found out how his story of a NAAFI Canteen Manager who'd enlisted to man a machine-gun – and had spent all of Friday, 21 May 1982, on the GDP – caught fire and turned in to that fictional, divisive sprint from below to take out a Skyhawk. The media loved it. They drew cartoons of it. Admiral Sandy Woodward even repeated it in his own memoirs. But it wasn't the story Brierley had told. Because it wasn't true.

'If it was because of my conversation,' he says now, 'I can only say I'm truly sorry for starting something that's given them so much grief.' Leake and Goldfinch didn't speak for years before the big man lost his final battle, to kidney cancer, in 2000.

◆◆◆

'There was going to be a few bangs, and we'd all go aft and have a cup of tea and an almighty piss-up in the evening. That's the bottom line.' Cliff Goldfinch can only guess how many lives hinged on the difference between what he expected and what he saw. What any of them saw. His life did.

It's the end of a working day on a cold, misty, late November night when we meet in his Lutterworth dry-cleaning business, his fresh start away from the West Country. There are reasons for me to be apprehensive, despite the warmth of an hour in the pub first: 'Mr' Leake, the length of time it's taken me to arrange this conversation, his PTSD, Eileen's polite point that she doesn't want him dredging up the past, the fact that he keeps calling me Martin. But he has more reason to be apprehensive than I do.

Lucky me, though. Lucky Ardents, too. The food's exquisite and, chain-smoking, he rolls back the years in remarkable detail, a precise memory for dates – but not always faces – even if we're on egg-shells from time to time, until he sighs and begins to paint a sketch of his life since Friday, 21 May 1982.

'Do you count yourself lucky that you know of the problem?' I ask him about the shadow of PTSD he's first told me about on the phone, more than a year before.

'Oh, yeah. I'm extremely lucky. Because, prior to leaving the Navy, I knew I had a serious problem. Let's face it, I was drinking ten or 12 pints at lunchtime, then the same in the evening and driving home.

'Then one night I had that one too many. I said to my wife, "Whatever happens, whatever I say, promise me you'll ring my boss at nine in the morning and tell him I have a drink problem."'

This was five years after the Ardents arrived home. But it wasn't only drink. It was something else.

'How long were you still in the Service after you got back?'

'I finished in 1988. I was a horrible bastard, but I worked harder than anyone else and I made sure my product was 100 per cent,' he says. Then he goes on to talk about something a dozen or more Ardents can nod to, spending time at RN Hospital Haslar, on Morgan O'Connell's 'basket-weaving course'.

'Did they put anything back when they took your problem away?' I remember a conversation with the genial Irish psychiatrist months before. Cliff draws on his cigarette, but I've guessed the answer.

'They never did. There was one of the Wafus with me on the course' – he incorrectly names a member of *Ardent*'s Flight. 'I was almost at the point of telling my story and he came in and they pursued his. Everybody else walked away and I was still there. I'm still there . . . They've never let me unburden myself. Nobody's ever sat and talked and thrown questions in. Asked about feelings . . .'

And so it goes, minute after minute, out with the lighter, an apology for rambling, a look at the watch for Eileen's return, a patient pause while I read shorthand notes of John Leake's conversation, a man who needs to talk but – I'm beginning to realise – knows that four hours will only be a start.

Then he seems to divert. 'Very few people could ever get my father to talk,' he says. 'I could. I'd listen and throw a few titbits in. One night, me and the old man went into Southampton and we went round a few of the old pubs he remembered from the war. We went to places I didn't even know existed.

'We was sat there and there was a little old boy in the corner, alone, 90-odd. The old fella said, "You're old so-and-so!" My old man said, "How d'you know?" "I was one of those rough matelots in the war!"

'They went and talked. We went on to another pub and you could see he wanted to tell me so much. And yet he told me more that night than he's ever told anybody in his life . . . But I've never had that.

'There was the doc off the *Sheffield* who tried for 45 minutes to revive a WEM and . . .' he's back at Haslar, 'they all cried, but I never cried. To this day, I've sworn blind, if I'd only been allowed to finish off, maybe my life would have been different.' Maybe.

By the time we part, Eileen's home, the fog's freezing, it's gone midnight, and 'Mr' Leake is 'John' again.

Four stories. The one you don't regale your drinking mates with, the one you don't mention to friends because you all have dark secrets, the one you even resist discussing with others who were there, the one you can't talk about with your closest confidant.

Bob Lewis has known all four since 1982 but, when it looks as if Taff Lovidge isn't coming, we set off on the path he's wound himself up to tread, starting almost as the first hit comes in. It's fragmented, but we can assemble the pieces in the right order later.

When Lovidge arrives, 15 minutes on, Lewis's introductions are warm and the instant Amsterdam dits are recalled with joy, though I'm sure that, somewhere, he's feeling a stab of despair that he'll have to trawl through the ordeal again at some point. That's the problem with PTSD, managing the stress so you don't end up on overload, or lacking control. They can both tell you about it, if they choose.

Lovidge's long spiral of drinking, dreams and weeks away from home caught up with him four or five years after the Falklands. He ended up a quivering heap. Then, after talking with a welfare officer at HMS *Drake*, and trying to arrange a date with Morgan O'Connell, he came to a conclusion himself.

'I'd been worrying about everybody else, but I'd forgotten about me,' he admits. 'The whole incident and the drinking and the other things. I knew I'd bottled out of it.'

His way of coping now is to avoid the Navy. He stopped going to *Ardent* dos a long time ago.

Lewis too. We try to pick up his thread after Lovidge departs, but it's not easy. Little has been since May 1982. After the Board of Inquiry, he went from internal drafts within *Drake* to Portsmouth, helping to repair the Exocet damage on *Glamorgan*. Then he went to start bringing the Tribal-class frigates out of mothballs to replace the ships that had been sunk. From there he went to Rosyth maintenance, then to the minesweeper *Keddlestone*, then back to Rosyth.

After that, he went to Faslane nuclear repair, then, after a short draft elsewhere, back to Devonport and *Alacrity*. The more he needed to purge everything building up inside him, the further he was taken away. His problems started.

'There was no mechanism to offload it,' he says. 'The Navy didn't want to know the downside of it. All they wanted was, "How was it on the way home?" "Great party! Lovely to be home." That's what everybody wanted us to do. You tended to conform.' He put up with it for two and a half years, slowly slipping under, until he was medically discharged. He'd made it as far as Chief Stoker.

'It was shit. It was a bloody awful time,' he insists. 'Even O'Connell said that. If he'd had time to debrief each one of us individually, we'd probably have had very few cases of stress disorder. It changed everybody. Boys who were boys were now men. Men were boys. Their ideas of life had changed. What they wanted had changed.'

A year later, Bob Lewis eventually settles on a sequence of events for 21 May. The delay can't have helped.

What did it for Jessie Owens was joining the first Type 21 that came back from the Falklands after the Board of Inquiry. It was *Active*. He bumped into Knocker's brother, Ian, straightaway. He'd come back thinking he was invincible. In a week, he was phoning Sally from Haslar. She thought he'd broken a leg.

'No,' he told her. 'I've gone mad.'

He was the only one from the Falklands in the ward and, after six weeks, they told him he could go. When he arrived home, Sally knew he was different

but not why. Slowly he withdrew. His friendship with Brum Serrell evaporated when he joined the *Beaver* and discovered his old drinking partner had left the stoking branch to become a Regulator. It was something you didn't do.

'I didn't want to know anybody, especially somebody who'd left what we had.'

But while he tormented himself – 'the job I had in the SCC, having to go up to the Bridge and back . . . I could have gone quicker . . . Why didn't I go quicker?' – Sally didn't have time for him to feel sorry for himself. She just made him angry and fight back.

He's out of the Navy now, long since, and earning a living making expensive beds. Lenny and Beryl Yeatman are godparents to their eldest daughter, Katie. Like many *Ardent* children, she was christened in the ship's bell, and she's proud of it. He still hasn't resolved the big question in his mind, though.

While he tells you that, 'To us there was no logic. At the end of the day we walked off that ship and they didn't. What could we have done? Why did we do it?' Sally asks him to show me the jar of pills he still has to open every day, her proof that he hasn't finished with the war yet.

'He gave up his career, his way of life, his friends. Gave up everything for the Navy, and they said, "Sorry, you're just damaged goods. For all you've done, the Falklands Fund is giving you £1,500. Thank you very much, piss off!" They had a duty to care for these servicemen. They were prepared to lay down their lives for the benefit of these people at home, and the people on the island. They threw him away.'

◆◆◆

On the face of it, Buck Ryan hardly seems a candidate for PTSD. You can see why Jake Jacobs recalls him as a hard worker, and a good talker, 'Quick with it, which meant he was occasionally classed as cocky', to be exact.

The hoolie with Naggers never happened, but the rapport did. After his marriage broke up, after he tested his talent for banter running a pub on Portland, he joined the same company as his pal. And the two ended up married to sisters, Nags to Veronica, Buck to Joan. It's only when he describes hearing Ralph's panicking voice on Comms line after the first hit, then dwells on his part in sending Florrie Ford and Buzz Leighton aft, that it even occurs to me that he's sought Morgan O'Connell's advice.

The hard thing after that was Joan. She wasn't around when Buck came back. She was never part of the family conversations which dealt with the Falklands, Teresa was. So how should he have explained to someone who'd given up her life in Ireland the reason for the bedsheets being kicked all over the place some nights. What had caused the sweating and screaming? He doesn't know. He never tried.

That's why he doesn't really want to see Ralph. If he does, they'll just bang on about the old days.

'It's overpowering,' he admits. 'We've got to live the next chapter. I feel like I want to break into tears now, but I can't. Men don't do that. I couldn't confide in Ralph for that. Couldn't confide in Karoly for that.'

377

John Goddard reckons the drafter had a sense of humour when he was sent to Pompey to join the *Glamorgan*. He'd often find himself wandering on the Flight Deck, examining what a repaired Exocet hole looks like. He left the Navy six months after. When we speak, he's working for the Post Office, and he's turning up at all the *Ardent* dos and keeping them entertained, loudly.

In one breath he says it wasn't the guilt that eventually took him to Morgan O'Connell, but the anger. He was angry with Thatcher, angry with the politicians. In the next breath he feels the reason he has his problem is because of Gabby, Stephen Heyes.

'In half an hour, I could have gone down,' he thinks back to the Ops Room. 'My mum keeps telling me it's fate. Had I gone down there, he would have escaped.'

'Look, you were there to do a job and you did that,' O'Connell has told him.

'It's easy to say,' Goddard answers. It probably is. 'It was like you put yourself in a film. It was like me and Earnie [his old Ops Room mate Steve Earnshaw]. I remember looking in his eyes. Years after, I said to him, "You know when we looked at each other that time . . .?" He said, "I felt exactly the same." We just wanted to die. We were so tired. What an incredible thought.'

Ken Enticknap had dubbed Wacker Payne, Andy Cox and Ralph Coates 'The Beastie Boys' before I arranged to meet them in the Archers. As it is, there's Five Nations rugby on the telly, Ralph's wearing the red jersey of Wales, and they seem to think there's some kind of drinking race going on as we retrace their *Ardent* steps.

Three stories.

Wacker, I know, has dredged courage from the soles of his boots to make a contribution to a story he wishes someone had told years ago. I already know he blames himself for Peddler Palmer's death, and why. I know about his breakdowns on *Canberra*, and a two-year bender in Hong Kong, continuing the therapy where they left it on *QE2*, that ended with him seeing Morgan O'Connell and leaving the Mob.

What I don't know, and what he doesn't offer, is covered every time I excuse myself and head for the gents. To begin with, I can't work out why Ralph follows me in every time, until a pattern emerges.

'If you want to know about so-and-so, ask me. It'll save Wacker.' That kind of conversation.

Before the half-time whistle, no one's watching the rugby, they've swivelled on their stools, listening to tales you wouldn't tell your mother. We should have charged them. That night, we adjourn to the Woodland Cottage, Wacker first, then Coxie, but not Ralph. He's comatose on Coxie's floor, having locked them out first. Coxie ends the night wondering where he's left the long-handled screwdriver.

Wacker's guilt is simple: if he hadn't left the Aft Section Base just before the second hit, Peddler wouldn't have been standing in for him. Guilt overwhelms logic. Logic says he was called away by Taff Lovidge. Logic says that, even if he hadn't been, any one of a million other changes of direction during the day could have ended in something different, maybe something worse, for him or Peddler.

Then a letter arrives from Dave Lee, describing the moment after the big Cornishman volunteered to climb the mast and right the 992 radar after Carballo's straddling: 'Peddler was asked by Brian, his CPO, if he was going to stay where he was or go back to his Aft Repair Party. Peddler said he felt "safer back aft" and retired there.' So, he needn't have been the man who took over from Wacker.

I leave it to Scouse Phillips to judge the time for telling him, hoping it'll help, wondering how different Wacker's lot might have been – and Carole's and James's – if someone had told him years ago.

Months later, Scouse has apparently picked his moment. A call of gratitude comes from Wacker, unnecessary, but understandable. He's been having a hard time again. Now he stills feels bad, but it's a better bad, the feeling that comes with the thought that you've been robbed of 16 years of your life.

Three stories. Richie Gough hasn't sat down with an analyst yet because it would 'scare the shit' out of him. There are no real ghosts. He saw the carnage, he had a picture, unlike a lot of men who heard bangs and had to leave the rest to their imagination.

There was a time after they arrived home though, when *Ardent*'s gung-ho Weapons Director – 'so gung-ho it hurt' – sought psychiatric help from the Navy, fearing PTSD too. But that wasn't it. The stress he was suffering had been building since he was a 19-year-old rating and realised he was gay.

He lived with this shadow through the Falklands War, and beyond on three more ships, until he couldn't suppress his feelings any more and put in 18 months notice at the age of 31. His ambition had always been to be the Navy's best missileman. He's always been convinced his sexuality had never affected his ability to fight. But leaving nearly broke his heart.

◆◆◆

Three stories? Too many stories, so far as Morgan O'Connell's concerned. At the outset, we sit in his RN Hospital Haslar office and he marks my card, about the dozen unnamed Ardents he's seen, about telling them the truth and then not worrying about treading on toes, his or theirs. It sounds so simple.

'PTSD's a form of grief,' he tells me. 'It's something that continues with you for the rest of your life. We were just travelling a short distance on the road to recovery. Some of them will be travelling on that road for the rest of their lives. They had to find, back in their own community, whatever they needed to support them. For some, that would be virtually nothing.'

There will be times when particular words of warning or advice come to mind during conversations, and it's unnerving to be stranded in this No Man's Land between theory and practice as the men roll back the years. Like Cliff Goldfinch and 'Mr' Leake: 'It may be he's still searching for that missing piece of the jigsaw. I'd say that those guys need to get together for each other's sake.'

Like Jessie Owens: 'One of the sad features of the British way of life is they'll send their young men to war and, then, when they come back, they'll put them on the scrapheap, provide no real aftercare.'

On how it's harder for a close-knit team to cope with grief. Like Wacker

Payne: 'You can't have it both ways. It's part of the price you've got to pay. We wouldn't wish to change it, but we need to say to people . . . We're in the business of killing people. Some of us are going to get killed.'

So why are some still suffering? 'We should have protected them from the media. And welcome-home parties. That's where we got it badly wrong. They represent relief to the people at home but, to the people who came back, they're not in the mood for a party. They were preoccupied with the people who didn't come home.' Then again: 'Really, it would be wrong for them to slink home at the dead of night and for there to be no public acknowledgement at all of what they'd been through.'

Their loss? 'If half of the airstrikes which hit *Ardent* had been diverted to *Canberra* . . .' he pauses. 'She really did fulfil that role of the sacrificial lamb. It's the ultimate sacrifice. That's what they did.'

Their guilt? 'Not to come home with your ship, there's a great big gap in your life.'

Their pride? 'You don't need to be a psychiatrist to see that it's important for them to feel this proud. How you'd cope with something when you don't have that pride? Well, you just wouldn't. The fact that there were really so few casualties from *Ardent* is a reflection of their pride. They suffered, but they did what was required of them. No one else could have done it, but I think they all know that.'

They know that, but do the men who sent them to the gunline, rather than *Antelope*, and then asked them to guard the back door to Falkland Sound? There's more than one answer.

'I can't remember when I next saw Andrew Gordon Lennox,' the Commodore Amphibious Warfare, Cdre Mike Clapp, explains. 'He'd served with me on one of my ships and I liked him. He came up to me and said something to the effect of, "Are we talking?"'

'I hope we are,' Clapp was taken aback.

'We're pretty resentful,' *Ardent*'s First Lieutenant went on.

'I can understand that. From my point of view, you did a bloody good job and you couldn't have done it better and I'm sorry you became the decoy.'

'Is that how you see it?'

That was the end of it, but Clapp admits that the thought that the Ardents hated him was troubling.

'There's nothing I can do about that,' he says now. 'I've got to live with it. I still think the decision I made was the right one with the information I had.'

He's already covered the ground leading up to that decision – the risk assessment, the fact that the enemy 'took the first ship they saw', the fact that the men planning on *Fearless* 'didn't know how the Argentinians were going to approach', but 'didn't expect them to concentrate on the escorts'.

It was, he knows, a 'very thin grey line'. And he understands now the bitterness of some that no one thanked them, told them what they'd achieved for the operation, for the troops, or the islanders.

He admits it should have been him. 'I'd like to hav e seen Alan and said, "I'm terribly sorry, but thank you."' The chance never came. He was head down at the time.

So, 14, 15, 16, 17 years after the war ended, among a thousand million words devoted to the war, Britain's first instant-replay conflict, the Ardents still have no context, no yardstick to measure their day or their sacrifice, apart from the one they've given themselves. Without a context, there's no conclusion.

From the outset, Capt Jeremy Larken, the Commanding Officer of HMS *Fearless* and Cdre Mike Clapp's right-hand man, makes it clear that he can't subscribe to the implicit assumption behind the statement that *Ardent*, effectively, saved the rest of the Amphibious Group by becoming the focus of enemy attention. He starts by explaining what COMAW Mike Clapp and Brigadier Julian Thompson, the man in charge of the operation once the troops were ashore, didn't know.

They didn't know whether Argentinian forces at Goose Green would counter-attack the beachhead if they didn't send *Ardent* to the gunline. So they took no chances. The troops were a threat.

'In light of what we know since of the inflexibility of the Argentine land forces,' he says – about 1,100 bedraggled Army and Air Force personnel, well-armed and napalm-equipped by the time 2 Para persuaded them to give up the fight, seven days after *Ardent* sank – 'I now doubt it. None of this cold hindsight detracts from *Ardent*'s gallantry in doing what she could to take care of this flank.'

It's hindsight, too, which tells him why the Argentinians didn't go for *Fearless* first, then *Canberra* and the other troopships, and then the store vessels. His theory's simple. The enemy gave too much respect to the British air defences in San Carlos Water. They didn't know the defences were far from complete. The Rapier missile system wasn't even in place. Instead, they went for the Thin Grey Line.

'It's my understanding that it was toward the end of the day that the Argentines settled on *Ardent* exclusively as their prime target,' he goes on. 'It's my impression that they did so because she was damaged, the only ship remaining outside the direct cover of the San Carlos defences and because they were desperate for at least one major success – to chalk up for the first day and atone for the losses.'

But that shouldn't detract from *Ardent*'s gallantry either, he adds. 'It seeks simply to put her martyrdom in perspective.'

He understands the rest, even if some of it didn't happen: the need to explain the immediate loss to survivors; the importance of keeping the ship's company together for some time, giving them a chance to adjust and relive their experiences together, before rejoining their families and friends, the people who'd take on the burden of helping them adjust to the new circumstances.

'A ship's a community with its own personality, and the loss of the ship constitutes a long-lasting bereavement to her company,' Larken adds. 'This confronts those in command, in this case Alan West, with a task that will moderate only with time, and probably only end with his own eventual passing.'

It might have been *Antelope* on the gunline, courtesy of a gun that could lob 4.5-inch bricks 15 miles, but it was *Ardent* who paid the biggest price. If there are 178 other versions of her story to be told, how close did the rest, *Antrim*,

Argonaut, Brilliant, Broadsword, Plymouth and *Yarmouth*, come to providing another thousand like them? We'll never know.

'They did their very best,' Jeremy Larken gives the Thin Grey Line a context too. 'None was designed to fight to best effect in inshore waters. Examples from history don't come readily to my mind. The fate of the previous *Ardent* excites sympathy, lost as she was attempting to protect the *Glorious* from the *Scharnhorst* and *Gneisenau*.'

Brigadier Julian Thompson agrees: 'I consider the landings got off amazingly lightly on 21 May, especially in view of the fact that we didn't have one of the prerequisites for amphibious operation – air superiority. *Ardent* played a major part in holding off the Argentine Air Force. The Thin Grey Line was absolutely critical to the success of the landings and the operations after.'

Thompson confesses to being little in the way of a Naval historian, though his peers disagree. He puts the Royal Navy's achievement in the Falklands alongside that of the operations off Crete in 1941.

Four battleships, one carrier, 11 cruisers, a minelayer, and 32 destroyers were deployed to Crete. Two battleships and the aircraft carrier were badly damaged, five cruisers and seven destroyers were damaged, while three cruisers and six destroyers were sunk, a 49 per cent loss over several days.

There were seven warships protecting the amphibians, RFAs and troopships in the vicinity of the beachhead on Friday, 21 May 1982. Four were damaged, one sank, a 71 per cent loss in one day.

'Watching our ships slugging it out toe to toe with the Argentine Air Force was a most inspiring sight,' he thinks back. 'It hasn't been recognised by the British public.'

He thinks it would be appropriate for the nation to mark the anniversary of the surrender each 14 June, to complement the dinner he and his fellow commanders hold each year to commemorate 21 May.

◆◆◆

The Argentinian government were happy for the importance of 2 April, the invasion, to die quietly after the war, but the public wouldn't allow it. Now the nation remembers its dead in defeat, and the Aviación Naval – the Fleet Air Arm – like other forces, marks every parade with 'The Malvinas March'. It has, Alberto Philippi says, a 'very nice melody and very sensitive words'.

'You should study the history of diplomatic claims, already now 167 years, after the British invasion of the islands to decide if Argentina had another way of recovering its property,' he writes to me, then cites Julius Goebel Jr's *The Struggle for the Falkland Islands* as a starting point in understanding the conviction that remains – that the islands were an inheritance from Spain after independence in 1816; that Britain took them by force in 1833; that Argentina exerted a legitimate right to recover them by force in 1982, after many years of unsuccessful diplomatic claims.

But there's a more important date than 2 April for Philippi and the men who flew together in those dangerous days. They gather on 21 May each year and toast 'the presents, and the absents'. At home, his children celebrate their

father's 'new birthday' that day too. They're all considered heroes of the nation, but he prefers to regard the 700 men buried on the islands and at sea as more deserving of the honour, 'because they gave all'.

Philippi didn't know it was *Ardent* when he lined up for his attack, his only thought was neutralising an enemy warship. It was a piece of steel, electronics and guns firing. It was days before her name became part of his life, years before he and his comrades learned about the human losses.

'It didn't make us happy,' he says.

'Did my bombs hit?' is the first question he asks after he introduces his wife, Graciela, when we finally meet, in Stratford-upon-Avon, one warm June night. At first, I have to tell him that I understand they did. It's not the answer he's hoping for. The conversation goes on long into the night.

Months later, Mick Newby describes those same 500lb Snakeye bombs hitting the water off *Ardent*'s starboard waist. So they didn't.

On New Year's Eve, a few months later still, a letter arrives from Argentina with bad news. After all those years following him from base to base, bringing up the family, coping with the long days of worry when he was flying, planning for his new life of retirement, Graciela and his mother Margarethe have died within weeks of each other.

'I have lost my compass and my rudder,' he writes. He sounds a broken man.

FOUR

PRESENT

On Wednesday, 7 July 1982, Tony Ray stood on the jetty at Devonport and watched HMS *Arrow* arrive home. He'd watched other ships come in, but this was the most poignant, a Type 21.

'I thought, "I wish that was us,"' he admits. 'That should have been us. It's like losing your house and family. That's what it's like.'

On Friday, 19 November, he was there again when *Amazon* came in, waiting at the bottom of the gangway as Mick Brain walked ashore. The old friends greeted each other, then Brain took Ray to show him something. It was *Ardent*'s bell. Divers had found it in the wreckage of her Hangar.

Some come up with unexpected answers, some with the obvious when you ask them to share their strongest memory of it all. Some offer a token instead, to be polite, to keep the conversation flowing. Something tells me Tony Ray's floats in between. Three stories, don't forget.

So, story one, two or three? The first thing that comes to Jessie Owens's mind is Scouse Phillips being hammered by the SCC door in the first hit, always, always the first thing he sees.

'Me and Joe had switched seats. I was on the left, he was on the right and Scouse was next to me. So when we hit the deck, we just went the way we were . . .'

Story one, two or three? Errol Flynn goes back to the Bathroom Flat, 1806Z, hearing 'Air Raid Warning Red', feeling his heart beat off the deck. That's fear.

One, two or three? It reminds Naggers of his brother. They were very close, but he'd given him a life of hell. Until they were being hit, then he thought, 'This is it,' and decided he'd better make amends. Otherwise, he doesn't talk to people about the Falklands.

'Why mention it? They're hardly going to talk about their worst time.'

For Mick Cox, it's the lost moments between taking cover first time and standing up again. The explosion had turned the SCC into something different. What never registered? What's been erased? Was it a bigger bang? A blast? He often wonders. That's what's missing.

For Bob Young, it's what's not missing, but the smell of burning plastic, diesel, soot, burning Avcat, blood and the sound of runaway engines, water escaping from the firemain, the ringing in his head.

'We were the best then, yes,' he says, 'but no amount of training can prepare you for the real thing. At the time, I was deeply upset when some of the First Aid team disappeared off the Flight Deck. I couldn't understand why

they'd left the Doctor and I to deal with Rick Banfield, although they'd have probably been killed if they'd stayed. Is it wrong to want to be somewhere else when someone's shooting at you? Probably not, with the benefit of hindsight.'

But there's worse, 'the feeling of helplessness as Rick was slipping away, having all that taken away from me'. And Mac McAulay, 'Did I check him properly? In my heart of hearts, I know I did.'

It goes on. Russ Goble. If someone talks about the Falklands, he sees the first formation of Daggers running at *Ardent*'s stern, wishing he wasn't there, then witnessing the consequences. Most of all, he wishes they could have sailed home with the ship, buckled or whatever, with the 22 dead.

Pete Brierley. He wishes *Ardent* had seen Devonport again too, but he's never been one to look back, he says; he accepts what happened and thanks God he was spared. Mind you, three or four years after, he was driving between Falmouth and Portland and 'We're On Our Way' came on the radio. He had to pull up because tears were streaming down his face.

Brum Serrell? Once he and Carol had rediscovered the joy of being man and wife, they went home to Sutton Road, Kidderminster, for a big party he didn't really want. There were relatives he hadn't seen for years, a cake made by an aunt and a ten pence piece from one of his nieces, her pocket money, because he'd lost almost everything. He still has it.

At about two o'clock one night, maybe that night, a sound half woke him. There were thin curtains at the window and a single lampshade hanging above. As car lights flashed past, shadows raced across the ceiling. He looked up and thought, 'Fuck! Retard bombs!' He was back there. He jumped, heart pounding, and woke Carol.

'Are you all right?' she asked. He was, soon. And that was it.

Simon Ridout, the Flying Doctor. He mentions bombs too, the ones he looked up and saw, thinking, These aren't going to miss,' before the world turned black and he was blasted off the Flight Deck. But his eyes moisten when he says his strongest feeling is great pride in the Navy putting 3,000 soldiers and Royal Marines ashore without losing one.

'We did our jobs,' he says, but insists that, above all, they were lucky. 'We lost more than 10 per cent of the ship's company. The previous *Ardent* lost 90-odd per cent. What I get angry about is people who try to say we were heroes. We were doing our job.'

The tears catch me off guard. Later, I think, maybe my surprise has only added to his distress.

'Can you understand the public's reaction, though?' I wonder.

'Any other ship's company would have done the job as well. Different, but no better or worse.'

'In that case, does the British public have a need to admire you?'

'If they admire you for doing it, does it mean we did something more than they expected of us?'

Alan West spent a long time afterwards thinking about whether he should have asked more questions before giving the order to abandon ship and, if he had, whether the outcome would have been very different. The first time our conversation explored the ground, 15 years on, he wasn't absolutely sure.

'Looking at it now,' he leaned back on his couch, 'I think it was the right decision. But sometimes, at night, I still think maybe I should have . . . you know what I mean. Probably I could have left it later. We knew *Yarmouth* was close. I knew I could move a large number of my ship's company off without having to get into the water. It was certainly the hardest decision I've had to make.

'If I'd left the gunners on board, and another attack had come in and I'd lost more, then I'd really have felt guilty all my life. If I had my gun working, and we were still involved, then I'd keep men on board because, on balance, yes, we might lose 100 men but, actually . . . I probably did the right thing.'

When he offered that view, back in 1997, he'd just been promoted from Rear Admiral to Vice Admiral and taken up his appointment as Chief of Defence Intelligence. The three years that followed would involve Operation Desert Fox in Iraq, the conflict in Kosovo and operations in Sierra Leone. The two years after that – as a Knight Commander of the Order of the Bath, promoted to full Admiral – would be spent as Commander-in-Chief Fleet, NATO Commander-in-Chief East Atlantic and NATO Commander Allied Naval Forces North, streamlining the Navy's command and management structure and leading the maritime response into Afghanistan, post 9/11. Then he'd be appointed to the ultimate role, First Sea Lord, the man responsible for £19 billion worth of assets and 40,000 employees, the man accountable to the Prime Minister for Britain's nuclear deterrent force, the man in charge of the world's second-largest Navy at a time dominated politically, socially, militarily, economically, culturally and morally by the response to 9/11, the war in Iraq, and its consequences.

By the time we speak again on the subject of 1982, nine years on from our first conversation, he's retired. After 41 years serving Queen and country, his CV is as rare as it is remarkable, every step followed with pride but no great surprise by those who still refer to him as 'the Boss'. He has left high office convinced that the Navy's at its weakest for years, and concerned about the effect that defence cuts, MoD spending plans and the Government's growing focus on anti-terror campaigns will have on its ability to defend the interests of an island that still depends on the sea for 95 per cent of its trade.

'I think the nation has lost sight of the Navy,' he says. 'They're working their best when they're not being used. When they're being used, they've actually failed. The Navy's always been one jump ahead. What really worries me is that we haven't got great numbers any more. Twenty-five destroyers and frigates is too few. Assuming we get the carriers' – the Strike programme to build two carriers by 2015 – 'and assuming we get the Astutes' – the nuclear attack submarine force that's been cut from twelve to ten to eight – 'the Navy's in good shape. We need the nation to think that we need these things. The world is a dangerous and chaotic place. One fears that it isn't going to be sweetness and light. Whenever we've forgotten the Navy, the nation has suffered. I still believe that's the case.'

Twenty-five years on from the Falklands, it's not hard to imagine the same voice enquiring as to the availability of experimental Stingray torpedoes for *Ardent*'s journey south. He has always regarded the Distinguished Service Cross he won on 21 May 1982 as the kind that recognises your men have done a very good job, not the sort you're awarded if you've been amazingly brave yourself. So, 25 years on, it's also unsurprising when he says there are still moments when he reflects that there were things they 'could have done better' and that there's rarely been a day when he hasn't thought of his boys.

'When I'm at the reunion, I see them as they were. And the lads who were lost, I see them too, but not necessarily that day. My memories of them are of other moments on board. It's one of the strangest things. You serve on a number of ships, but when one of them has been sunk, it's frozen in time. I think the nation has acknowledged us. We were a small frigate and did our best. I'm proud of them.'

The feeling's mutual. John Foster still refers to him as Charlie Oscar and insists that, if the phone went and the voice on the other end said the skipper was taking a ship to the Gulf and wanted his boys to go with him, he'd be there.

Iain McRobbie has always thought there's a 'bit of the Mountbatten in Banjo' and tells a story of the tenth *Ardent* reunion, in 1993, when he was a three-badge AB in the Royal Navy Reserve, standing outside the China Fleet in full No. 1 rig, with his medals on, cap on the back of his head, swigging from a pint when Rear Admiral West arrived, acompanied by his Flag Lieutenant.

'"Hello, good to see you again!" says he, not at all bothered that I didn't stand to attention or salute,' Robbie recalls. 'His Flag Lieutenant was turning purple.' It's a story he likes to tell. There are many.

Andrew Gordon Lennox knows why most of the Ardents worshipped West and still do. 'People looked up to him and will continue to look up to him as a very fine leader but, having said that, if *Ardent* was still sailing around . . . The fact remains, we didn't make it and that's the way it goes.

'*Ardent* wasn't the best ship I served in, by any means. *Avenger*, which I went to afterwards, holds a dearer place in my heart and actually, as ships' companies and competence go, *Battleaxe*, which I went to after that, beat both of them, hands down. If *Ardent* hadn't been sunk and was in Pakistan now, like the other 21s, would we be eulogising about her? Possibly. Possibly not.'

It's academic. The fact is she was sunk. That's how Jan Joyce deals with it when his part in the war crops up in conversation. 'Yeah, been there, got sunk, didn't stay long, came home.' Then it's back to the consequences of the early evening of Friday, 21 May 1982, when all but a couple of the reporters were digging in ashore, looking towards Stanley, not back to Falkland Sound. When he tells them he was on *Ardent*, people struggle.

'Everybody remembers the *Antelope* because she split in two, Atlantic *Conveyor* because she was civilian, *Sir Galahad*, *Sheffield*, *Coventry* . . . But nothing's been said about *Ardent*.'

The Forgotten Frigate? Not in Captain Bob's mind, nor Major Tony Rice's, nor Rick Jolly's. It comes back to Harmes whenever he tries to tell another soldier what it's like to be on a ship under attack. He can never explain.

'You can't run away. You're there. You've got to be part of what's going on.

That's the thing. That's a terrifying thing. You haven't got open plains to get across.'

It only dawned on Rice the day after *Sir Galahad* was bombed in Bluff Cove. The memory of his grandstand view of *Ardent*'s mauling from Sussex Mountain was still fresh when he found himself stuck at sea in an immobilised coaster.

'On the battlefield, the second-to-second events are, to an extent, in your own hands. Run, crouch, jink, fire and so on. In a very, very thin-hulled ship, you're a bean in a tin with absolutely no control over your immediate destiny,' he says.

After *Ardent*, ships didn't close the coast until after dark to answer the Call for Fire. They were away to the ocean before dawn. *Ardent*'s fate had made one thing plain: ships had to be preserved at all costs if the loss of heavy metal wasn't to be rapidly followed by the withering of the land campaign.

The abiding memory for Rick Jolly is being with his wife Susie and his late son James on the Grand Staircase at Buckingham Palace, one day in February 1983, after receiving his OBE. As they waited to advance, he realised he was standing next to a young sailor who couldn't have been more than 18. Jolly glanced to see what medal he was wearing. It was a George Medal. It was John Dillon.

'He was on my left and I nudged him,' Jolly recalls. 'He looked at me and saw I was a Naval officer. I grinned at him and he said, "Are you . . .?"'

"Yes, Doc Jolly."'

Dillon's face burst into a smile, and he grabbed his mother on his left. 'Mum! This is the doc who pulled me out of the water.'

'I gave him a hug, which was a strange thing to do when you're in a Naval officer's uniform and he's a sailor in rig,' he laughs.

But there's regret, mystery and vague thoughts where Dillon's concerned; tales of bullying on his next ship, a 'hero' whose place was mopping the Junior Ratings' Dining Hall; of men who bumped into him ashore and recall a troubled youth; of others who served with him before he wrapped his hand in.

For Ken Enticknap, he's a name and face he'll remember for the rest of his life. Their mothers swap Christmas cards.

For Tom Williams, he's the junior rating they didn't have the time to teach in the Ops Room, the one they sent aft 'to be killed', the one who, by a stroke of luck, had presence of mind and lived.

For John Goddard, Dillon's the one who left a George Medal in his locker for four months, didn't want it, never asked for it back, a cockney kid, quiet and modest, who wanted to make a new start.

For Rick Jolly, he's the source of sadness, the reluctant hero who found it all too much, left the Navy and sold his George Medal.

◆ ◆ ◆

John Foster has a picture in his loft of the ship on fire. When things seem bad, he looks at it and life isn't so bad after all. Little could possibly be worse than feeling so utterly vulnerable at the Service of Thanksgiving on

Canberra, having people round him but knowing everything had been stripped away.

'Defeated,' he replays the tape in his mind. 'Losing the ship. Losing mates. Knowing that feeling when I came off the *Canberra*, thinking, "Some of those soldiers aren't coming back." And there they were, thanking us in their own fashion . . . *Ardent* was a young ship. We came away old. Alive, but old and very aware of how short life is.'

Sometime later, he went south on a patrol ship. It gave him a context for the first time; he was able to see some of the development, and he walked to the cemetery.

'I looked at one of the stones and it said "Marine such-and-such, aged 17". That summed it up. I had a good cry on the bench looking out over San Carlos Water. It was as if we'd just picked up and left.'

First thoughts and final memories. Scouse Phillips's are nearly always the same.

'I remember guys who aren't here any more, who always gave me joy when I knew them,' he says. 'Then I feel guilty because I can't remember the 22 names. That makes me feel a bit inadequate.'

Jon Major's final memory is nearly always the same too: Shaun Hanson walking into the S&S Mess, grinning, with a bottle of 'whisky' in his hand. 'I'll remember that forever.'

For Buck Ryan, it's the look in Florrie Ford's eyes, baby-faced, tall, curly haired, when he passed on Geoff Hart's order for him to head aft with Buzz Leighton just before the second hit.

'Just that look,' he says. 'I see it all the time. "Go back." I've felt like crying for the past five years, but I still haven't found it. They're the fellas I always see. Getting dressed in their fearnought suits.'

Bernie Berntsen sees them too.

'I was 33,' he thinks back, 'and all the kids had died. I thought, "Why me?" I don't know the answer. Florrie and Buzz were 18 and 19. The two kids had been to Portland, Milford Haven, Amsterdam, and that was it. Nowhere else. I'd been round the world and robbed most places. "Why me? Why did I survive and not them?" I was in the right place at the right time.'

Dave Croft sees faces too, four of them – Mick Mullen, Derek Armstrong, Andy Barr and Sean Hayward, 24, 22, 20 and 18 – but he doesn't talk about it unless someone asks. His biggest memory of all, though, is leaving Devonport on Monday, 19 April.

'I was stood on the starboard waist singing "Always Look on the Bright Side of Life". It was windy. It was a nice morning. We went out of there with high hopes, in such high spirits.'

In a letter, I ask Scouse Flynn if he remembers when he saw Mick Mullen the last time.

'I'll tell you this in private, when we have a pint one day,' he replies, then reels off a list of mates who shone, like Muncher did – Goddard, Slatter, Croft, Garnham, Newby – and recalls that, whatever was going on outside, most of the chat still managed to involve women.

'On the day of the race, Mick Newby showed me the meaning of bottle,

manning an Oerlikon on his own. I don't think many people know how brave he was that day.'

Then there's Knocker. Dickie Henderson's lasting image of the happy-go-lucky stoker is tossing that coin for firefighting or flooding. But it could have been any of a million-and-one pictures in his mind.

Knocker. 'He's the one I miss the most of all,' Eddie Edwards admits, and he isn't the only one. 'I don't think anybody didn't like him. He could be a pain sometimes, but he was just such a bubbly guy. We had some good times together. Boobs especially.'

Russ Goble received a letter one day from Donna, the girl Knocker had been with the night before they sailed, the girl with 'Knocker White, HMS *Ardent*' tattooed on her arm. She'd heard about him being killed. She was devastated. Buck Taylor, too.

'I think it was a bit of a shit ship,' he confesses, the scars of being an overworked junior hand struggling on his first Portland apparently still fresh, 'but that doesn't detract from what we did. I'm glad I made a contribution. But by the same token, I wouldn't want to waste it on people who don't understand. I was young and I detached myself from everyone.

'Nobody knows at work. Nobody knows I was down at the Falklands. I never, never talk about it.'

But, when he picks a paper up, his recollection isn't the event. It's Knocker's mum, Brenda.

'That always sticks with me. I think it's wasted on people who don't understand.'

'At an *Ardent* reunion, a few years later, it was Ken Enticknap who told me the story,' Brenda White explains near the end of our conversation. 'I was so very grateful to be told. I know it was very hard.'

The story? 'You've touched on that third story that's difficult to tell,' Enticknap confides. 'I was one of the last people to see Knocker alive. In the mêlée down aft, it wasn't pretty and I dearly wanted to tell Brenda that he didn't suffer.

'Knocker was a great character. He was the killick of my part of the ship and one of the most capable, loyal and trustworthy fellows I've known. Most of all, though, he was a tearaway, living life to the full, always on the edge of acceptability. A run ashore with him was fun, full of energy and a guaranteed hangover the next morning – if you made it back to the ship! I think my conversation with Brenda went along those lines.

'Knocker's the person I miss most from *Ardent*. He was a good mate. There are some tales I could tell you that his mother would definitely *not* want to hear!'

FIVE

PRESENT

How many times had they staggered through this door and turned left for Boobs, or lurched right, back to the ship? And how many times had Knocker been with them, apart from that last night, when he hung back to say goodbye to Woppers? Too many to count, but not too many to care about.

Now Brenda White and the girls stood outside the Grand and watched them roll in, not out.

They'd driven down to Plymouth and Ian was collecting Knocker's gear from Bernie's mum's house. The Ardents were in uniform, on their way back from the Remembrance Service at HMS *Drake*.

Sunday, 8 August 1982 is a day Brenda will never forget. She told me so 16 years after she last saw her youngest son, and nine years later still I know nothing has changed.

'I remember standing outside the Grand with them, laughing and crying at the same time,' she smiles. 'There was a lot of people coming in, all pretty plastered. I suppose it was the way they coped. Getting drunk's all very well but, at the end of the day, it really only makes things worse.'

That night, they all went to Boobs. Instead of Knocker, stripped to the waist and going wild, the Ardents danced with his mum, danced themselves silly. It helped.

'It was very traumatic for us,' Brenda says, 'but I felt it was more so for the lads to have us there on that day, because here we were, without, and the rest of them were returning. I don't know. I feel it must have been a very hard day for them for us to be there.'

The Woplings had done a lot of laughing by that Sunday, and felt like crying too. They'd hardly been able to wait for Val's boys to appear again, to act stupid, and they'd done it the night before, a night the Grand's landlord and his wife will never forget.

'You'd seen these lads play around and you'd never think they could go and do what they did,' Dave explains. 'I was so proud of them. I remember when they came back. It was like your child coming home. Their lovely faces coming in. They gave us a great smile.'

The night ended on a familiar note, with Dave drenched in mild and his treasured polished floor swimming in the stuff, so much so that, for the first time, he couldn't open on time the next morning.

But there'd been low points that night as well. Val had seen some already bottling things up. 'You couldn't believe some of the lads,' Dave says. 'They

just lost everything. Dreadful to see, it was. It was lovely to see them, but some was such jolly blokes and they'd gone into their shells.'

It was the last time they were all together. With the heart of the pub ripped out by *Ardent*'s sinking, and the other Devonport frigates either coming or going, trade fell to a trickle. Eventually, civvies started using the pub again, bringing trouble with them. It wasn't what the Woplings wanted. The following March, sad and struggling to make ends meet, they finished.

'We was quite proud to have been part of it,' Val says. 'I had the last *Ardent* plaque. I'd never part with it. One of the lads gave me his hat, too, and they all signed it the day they came back.'

It went up in the middle of the pub, until they packed it away with the other mementos.

The next time they went in, the place had changed. Dave's long bar, built from ship's wood, had gone. So had the rows of sparkling glasses. In their place was plastic. Modern. Heartbreaking.

'All my memories hit me in one go. It was horrendous,' he admits. 'I couldn't believe it.'

It has flaking paint now, and shrubs grow in the gutters, and the Ardents only turn to look as they go up Union Street towards HMS *Drake*. The Grand, Plymouth's third-oldest pub, closed in 1994.

◆ ◆ ◆

Not every Ardent goes to the Remembrance Service at St Nicholas Church on Whitsun bank holiday weekend every May, or the reunion organised afterwards by the HMS *Ardent* Association. Not everyone wants to stir demons. Some don't think others should either.

The ship's bell stands at the front of the congregation during the service and again at the back of the dance floor later on. It no longer sparkles as it did when it hung on its bracket beside the Hangar door whenever *Ardent* was alongside. It's scarred, the way the Ardents preferred it to remain after *Amazon*'s divers found it, and now engraved with the names of *Ardent* sons and daughters who've been christened in it.

There are a hundred-and-one reasons why people travel miles to be there. Pete and Renee Hanson go with Carole and Lisa and their grandchildren because Pete likes to hear his lad's name read in the Roll of Honour at the HMS *Drake* service. The occasional infant's cry is now the sound of a grandchild, not a son or daughter. And each year more of them reach for an inside pocket – or a wife's bag – give a nod of admission and understanding to the shipmate by their side, and put on their reading glasses before singing as ill-timed and as tunelessly as they did that bitter, happy December day in 1981, in Amsterdam. A few hours later, the families and friends gather for the reunion and watch men who used to be 18, 19, 20, or 25, 26, 27 roll back the years.

Scouse Phillips goes to feel the spark again and to keep moving forward, accepting that, as the years go by, he forgets more names, loses more hair and takes longer to recover from a baggy head.

The Ray children go too, when they can; Helen and Liz with their own

children, Stuart now with a family of his own, and a career in the Army, serving his country in war zones like Afghanistan and Iraq. His mum deserves a medal.

The list goes on.

After the Navy, life as a prison officer kept Lenny Yeatman's sixth sense sharp enough to divert him from his organising duties, alongside Tony Ray, and bring the odd wayward Ardent back into line with a sharp word about setting a bad example to children. Eventually, the two handed the reins over to Pete and Teresa Brierley. They now run the association with the help of a posse of husband-and-wife teams, while Carol and Tony, and Beryl and Lenny – the latter now an MBE – have a more relaxing weekend. If some of it is a little slower than it once was, the beer still goes down like it did, and the families know the telltale signs that say their men have passed the point of no return.

Fifteen years on, Mick Newby and Dave Croft plucked up the courage to spill the beans to the Joss about that Portland car trip, the one that had him ringing round Portland's Paint Store, Rigging Shed and a dozen other places. Lenny looked at them.

'You bastards!'

A year later, Alan West – by then a Vice Admiral and Chief of Defence Intelligence – broke his heavy Whitehall schedule to read the Roll of Honour at the Remembrance Service and address his men at the reunion. He told them about a trip he'd made to the Falklands a few months before, his first return to the islands since the day, and described the moment his helicopter had hovered over *Ardent*'s resting place, her outline clear beneath the placid waters of the Sound. I'd wager there wasn't a soul in the room who wasn't painting a picture in their mind as he spoke. You could hear a pin drop.

Not long after, four of these 40-somethings mooned for another camera. Lenny didn't see. However, even now, you'd be hard pushed to tell whether you were looking at a picture of the bald heads of Bernie Berntsen and Eddie Edwards, or the cheeks of Pete Brierley's arse. Around the same time, Ralph and Coxie were on the dance floor, less dressed than they'd been, a strange grace in their drunkenness that's not apparent when they're sober, improvising a moving tale to Celine Dion's 'My Heart Will Go On'. Torvill and Dean meets Laurel and Hardy.

◆ ◆ ◆

Lesley Sephton twists in her chair and smoothes a hand down the immaculate crease in her trousers. 'I went to the tenth reunion and I had to stop because it was taking over my life,' she smiles at me. 'Harriet was that bit older, but it didn't do anything I wanted it to. I wanted it to be all the boys getting together, a few drinks and a meal. Then I could say "how typical". It wasn't like that at all.

'It wasn't a question of trying to put it out of my mind. I realised they haven't forgotten. Whatever they saw, whatever they went through is with them for the rest of their lives, not just me, even though it ruined my life totally. Whatever visions they had are with them.'

Nine years after that conversation, Lesley Sephton's still right. For some,

approaching the 25th anniversary, life goes on. For a few, it has started again. For others – maybe most of the 178 who came back damaged or outwardly unscarred – the past has a habit of tightening its grip, now and then.

◆ ◆ ◆

There are three constants in Ralph's mid-40s life where *Ardent* is concerned. There's his self-perpetuated place as one of the junior members of the Stokers' Mess. There's the protective arm he instinctively throws around Wacker Payne. And there's the irresistible temptation to tell anyone, in any pub, at any time, what it's like to be abandoned, alive, conscious and seriously wounded, below decks in the twisted, burning devastation of a sinking warship.

The night before the 2005 memorial service, I was on the end of a drunken chest-jabbing at the bar in the St Leven's Arms. He wanted to know why a 19 year old had been put on the Incident Board in the first place. Why Tony Ray hadn't been there with them. Why he'd been left to his fate as the rest fled. And this. If he'd been able to stagger forward out of the smoke and flames, on his own, with a lacerated back, chest wounds and leg injuries, how come no one had been able to fight through to find him?

I couldn't tell him, not that he was interested in answers. He wasn't interested in Lynne telling him to shut up either. He wasn't really interested when Brum Serrell suggested he wind his neck in, but he did. Next day, he apologised, then reminded me what a shit time Wacker had been through. Typical.

Typically, too, it's Ralph I call first, 18 months later, to see if he can have a chat to Wacker and judge whether he's ready to talk. You see, Wacker's looking forward as much as back these days. If you catch him with his heart on his sleeve, it's no longer necessarily a sign that he's three sheets to the wind and heading for the rocks. He's a changed man, just past 50 and married to Pauline. What's more, he and Ralph are now back in harness, using screwdrivers of a similar length on the Thames Barrier, saving London instead of the remnants of the Empire.

'I got him the job about six months ago,' Ralph explains on the phone. 'There's no pressure. That's made a lot of difference, in his life and in mine. He could work on the barrier until he's 90, and not feel like he was under pressure. My last job I done for 16 years. The pressure was phenomenal. It made me feel ill. Wacker was the same. The barrier isn't like that. It's there and it's immaculate.'

I tell him of an overheard conversation between Scouse Phillips and Bernie Berntsen, during one Sunday morning dockyard trip a few years before.

'Would you change anything?' Scouse had asked Bernie, as the boat chugged past Wharf 13.

'No,' Bernie had said, then added, 'except for the lads.'

'Sometimes, I feel like I'm grateful that it happened,' Ralph says in response to hearing the story, 'but I live for the day, more or less. It's happening more as I get older. Twenty-five years on, Wacker's a strange person sometimes, but I still feel like I want to make sure he's OK. Does that come across right? If I were to say that Scouse has my will and that he's in charge of it, would you believe it?'

I would. Then I suggest there are things about 1982 that he hasn't yet squared away himself.

'You've got it right,' he says. 'It's every so often. I wish I could get the answer, but I don't think I'm ever going to. I lose it and sometimes I annoy people. I have to learn to live with it.'

There are Ardents he could name, he says, who go through the same. 'I know they do. I think the hardest case is the one you're going to talk to. He's come to terms with it. He's been there, it's happened, and he has to live with it.'

A few minutes later, I'm on the phone with Wacker. It's the first time we've spoken about the Falklands, one to one, since the night he rang to say that Scouse had told him of Dave Lee's revelation about Peddler Palmer, about the big Cornishman deciding he'd be safer back aft after the Carballo near miss, as dusk beckoned *Ardent* beguilingly towards the safety of nightfall. He's already told me by email that he's happy to answer any questions – 'even ones of a bizarre sexual nature!' – and the voice I hear is thoughtful, rather than guarded.

'I've really come to terms with it now,' he says, then rolls back the years. 'I came off *Ardent* and they sent me to the *Plymouth*, off Scotland, which was a bit of a kick in the teeth. Then I got the Hong Kong draft out of that, which was fabulous, but I was drinking so much because I didn't want the nightmares. If I got the nightmares, I woke in the morning without having any sleep. I'd drink to not have the nightmares, then wake up with a bloody hangover. It was a catch-22.

'The problem was that I didn't know what was wrong. It wasn't until I came back to the UK and they drafted me on the *Ambuscade*, and everything was the same as on *Ardent*. Then, one weekend, I was driving home and I didn't even get as far as Gloucester. I pulled over in this car park and burst out in tears. My brother-in-law had come and take me home. I was a wreck. The GP saw me and said, "You've had a nervous breakdown." About three weeks later, I went to the Sickbay in *Drake* and there was a two-and-a-half ringer there and he said, "You've got PTSD."

'The worst thing of all was when they kicked me out. I said, "Don't kick me out. Look at my record." I'd been in since I was 15. I didn't know anything else and I didn't want to know anything else. After that, it was just shit, really.'

After an unequal struggle to find a new life and a new rhythm back in Civvie Street, his marriage to Carole eventually became another of the Falklands War's many, many unreported casualties.

'I'd go off on a binge and she'd be uncaring about it, because it happened so much. I could have done with more support, which wasn't forthcoming. I don't want to run her down. Obviously, my behaviour . . .if the knowledge had been there straight away, who knows what would have happened.'

The marriage was on its last legs when Scouse told him what Dave Lee had said about Peddler.

'It was like a huge weight had been lifted from my shoulders. I'd felt so much guilt about Peddler – and Garry Whitford, because I didn't know where Garry had gone when it all happened. More than anything out of my whole journey, that for me was a revelation. It was like "Fucking hell!" All those years of total guilt that Peddler had taken over from me, and I'd gone away, and five seconds later the bomb had gone through . . . The guilt I felt was immeasurable. That was crushing.'

He still has nightmares, but only when it's coming up to the reunion.

'That's a price that I'm more than willing to accept, because it tells me that I've never forgotten those people,' he says. 'I'll go to the service, and I'll always cry, and it's not because I want to, it's because I have to. I can't forget them. It means more to me, in a lot of ways, that I feel the way I do.'

Occasionally, he says, people have come up to him at work and said, 'You were down the Falklands with Ralph?'

'I just say "Yeah". Obviously, Ralph has talked to them, because you know what he's like. They'll say "Was it bad?" and I say "Yeah," but I don't go into details. They mean well, don't get me wrong, but it's a private thing.'

He met Pauline when he walked out of his flat one day, and saw her putting the kids in the car to go to their dad's. He spent a few days trying to come up with excuses to invite her out and, eventually, she agreed. Then, one weekend, Pete Brierley invited a host of Ardents to the family's Falmouth hotel. They were as unsubtle as ever.

'I took Pauline with me,' Wacker says. 'We had separate rooms and the lads were playing on it. When we came down for dinner, they'd put a table away from everybody else with candles on it.'

It was the lads, not Wacker, who told Pauline about the Falklands. Obviously Ralph, mainly in a drunken stupor. After that, anything she wanted to know, he told her.

'She's been fantastic. She totally understands. When May comes round, she's ready for the nightmares. My life's been totally changed. I bought myself a flat and bumped into this wonderful woman and ended up getting married again, with a couple of kids who are 11 and 12 now. I'm as happy as a pig in shit.'

His main concern now is Ralph. 'Whenever we have a drink and someone else comes into the conversation, he says "This is Wacker, he was my boss in the Navy." They really don't need to know that. As far as I'm concerned, we're just mates. I feel the same way about anybody who was on there.'

That's one thing, but the big problem is the one Ralph knows he has. 'He has everybody else's best intentions at heart. But he needs to step back from it all and look at himself. He's never done a PTSD course, never had someone else tell him that he has a problem, because he will never shut up about it. He'll get drunk and tell everybody. Everybody who knows him will tell him he's really boring. But I will not give up on that man. I've known him for too long. I'll put myself in danger for him in pubs when people want to punch him. I'll say "Please don't hit him because, if you hit him, you've got to hit me as well."'

'He's an excellent sparky and he knows his Thames Barrier. He's been an enormous help to me there, but I do think he should sit down one day with Coxie and Scouse and talk about himself, when he's sober, and take it on board. When he's drunk, he just comes out with all this bleeding rubbish. You can't get the full picture when you're pissed.'

◆ ◆ ◆

As mums and dads, sons and daughters, wives and lovers roll out of the Southampton dockyard Customs shed, Friday, 11 June 1982 etched on their

lives forever, Jim Cox's car edges through the slow-moving tide towards the long road north to home.

Beside him, Andy Cox is starting to provide his dad, his mum Valerie and elder brother Steve with an account of his life since they were last together. It's a selective insight, delivered in typically hesitant sentences, not the story he'll share and share again with his fellow Ardents but one to satisfy his mum's wary need for information, and make her laugh instead of cry. Now, as then.

LMEM (L) AD Cox (D136940C)

Coxie, Wacker Payne's trusty killick electrician.

Cox, the bringer of red screwdriver to Ralph Coates's head.

Big Andy, the man switched with Garry Whitford, from Aft DCP to Forward DCP, before *Ardent* reached Falkland Sound.

Andrew Cox, once of Walkwood Secondary School, Headless Cross, Redditch, Worcestershire. Steve Pullen's classmate.

Andy, 'six-and-out and you fetch the ball'. My cousin.

As Uncle Jim edges on, an elderly couple walk towards the car. Jim stops. They go to the passenger door and smile at the 27 year old, in his crisp new blue Number 8s. He winds the window down.

'Thank you,' they tell him. That's all. Then they walk away.

'Maybe they were Falklanders,' he says now. Maybe they were. But he'll never know.

HMS *ARDENT* SHIP'S COMPANY

(21 MAY 1982)

OFFICERS
Commanding Officer Cdr Alan West

(Other officers named as Department Heads, plus:) Medical Officer Surg. Lt Simon Ridout, Lt David Searle, Lt Jonathan Cody, Sub-Lt Jerry Bernau, Sub-Lt Richie Barker

OPERATIONS DEPARTMENT
Executive Officer Lt Cdr Andrew Gordon Lennox, Navigating Officer Lt Alan Maunder, Correspondence Officer Lt Nigel Langhorn, Master at Arms Lenny Yeatman, Leading Regulator Ken Chapman, Leading Physical Trainer Gary Nelson (KIA), Leading Medical Assistant Bob Young, Chief Bosun's Mate PO (Sea) Mal Crane, L (SE) Bob Clare

Principal Warfare Officer (Air) Lt Mike Knowles, PWO (Underwater) Lt Tom Williams

Missile: CPO (Ops) Pete Rowe, PO (M) Richie Gough, PO (M) J 'Johnno' Johnson, PO (M) Barry 'Rattler' Morgan, PO (M) David 'Buck' Taylor, LS (M) Tony Langridge, LS (M) SW 'Sid' Norman, AB (M) WJ 'Bagsy' Baker, AB (M) Russ Goble, AB (M) Steve Strachan, S (M) Robert Burgess, S (M) M 'Scouse' Wharton, S (M) Keith 'Tug' Wilson

Electronic Warfare: PO (EW) Mike Lewis, LS (EW) Steve Earnshaw, LS (EW) John Goddard, AB (EW) IF 'Dickie' Davies, AB (EW) Stephen Heyes (KIA)

Sonar: PO (S) Pete Brierley, PO (S) AJ 'Clem' Clements, LS (S) MF Carter, LS (S) Dave Croft, LS (S) J 'Jock' Greer, AB (S) Derek Armstrong (KIA), AB (S) Mark Barnes, AB (S) Andy Barr (KIA), AB (S) KA 'Henry' Cooper, AB (S) W 'Granny' Graddidge, AB (S) Sean Hayward (KIA), AB (S) Kev Mumford, S (S) Steve Alves, S (S) Steve Mallon

Radar: CPO (Ops) (R) ND 'Tansy' Lee (obit), PO (R) Mike Paterson, LS (R) RC 'Danny' Byrne, LS (R) Steve Flynn, ALS (R) Mick Mullen (KIA), LS (R) Mick Newby, LS (R) Leigh Slatter, LS (R) Ian 'Topsy' Turner, AB Harry Cliff,

AB (R) KW 'Jumper' Collins, AB (R) G 'Bruce' Curtis, AB (R) AD 'Watcha' Dunne, AB (R) Mick 'Fluff' Garnham, AB (R) Trevor Hawkes, AB (R) RB 'Lemon' Kerr, AB (R) J 'Wolfie' Price, S (R) John Dillon, S (R) J 'Sam' Saxty

Tactical Communications: POCY Chris Evans (obit), LRO (T) AJ Carter, RO1 (T) Jeff Gullick, RO1 (T) Steve Kent, RO1 (T) NR Whyte

General Communications: RS Pete Saward, LRO (G) John Newton, LRO (G) Phil Udy, LRO (G) Simon 'Cheesy' Craft, RO1 (G) Darren 'Buster' Brown, RO1 (G) John Foster, RO1 (G) R 'Paddy' Hayden, RO1 (G) IS 'Jock' McGregor

MARINE ENGINEERING DEPARTMENT
Marine Engineering Officer Lt Cdr Terry Pendrous, Deputy Marine Engineering Officer FCMEMN (P) Tony Ray, Chief Stoker CMEM (M) Andy Andrew, CMEA Mick Cox, (Forward Engine Room) MEA1 Andy Lee, (After Engine Room) MEA1 Jeff Curran, (Forward Auxiliary Machine Room) MEA1 Geoff Hart, (After Auxiliary Machine Room) MEA1 Ken Enticknap, (Workshop) MEA1 Roger Fenton, (Electrical) CMEMN (L) Alan 'Taff' Lovidge

Electrical Sections: POMEM (L) Jeff 'Wacker' Payne, POMEM (L) Bob Lewis, LMEM (L) Andy Cox, ALMEM (L) Garry Whitford (KIA), MEM (L) Stephen 'Ralph' Coates, MEM (L) SA 'Jessie' James, MEM (L) Karoly Nagy, MEM (L) Brad Vallint, MEM (L) GR 'Oscar' Wild

Mechanical Sections: POMEM (M) Dave Brooks, MEA2 Ian 'Eddie' Edwards, MEA2 Paul 'Joe' Laidlaw, POMEM (M) Mick Langley, POMEM (M) Robert 'Paddy' McGinnis, MEA2 John 'Blood' Reed, MEMN3 R Whiteoak, LMEM (M) RE 'Bernie' Berntsen, LMEM (M) Ian Cousar, LMEM (M) Mark 'Dickie' Henderson, LMEM (M) Alan 'Jan' Joyce, LMEM (M) Cliff Sharpe, ALMEM (M) Stephen 'Knocker' White (KIA), MEM (M) R Butters, MEM (M) Paul Behagg, MEM (M) Tony 'Ches' Chesterson, MEM (M) Terry Ducker, MEM (M) Stephen 'Wyatt' Earp, MEM (M) Dave 'Errol' Flynn, MEM (M) 2 Stephen 'Florrie' Ford (KIA), MEM (M) 2 Alistair 'Buzz' Leighton (KIA), MEM (M) Bryan 'Tex' Marshall, MEM (M) Roy McClimon, MEM (M) Barry Muncer, MEM (M) Keith 'Jessie' Owens, JMEM (M) Martin Peacock, MEM (M) Les Pearce, MEM (M) J 'Jock' Porter, MEM (M) Dave 'Brum' Serrell, MEM (M) JJ Smith, MEM (M) 1 Gilly Williams (KIA)

WEAPONS ENGINEERING DEPARTMENT
Weapons Engineering Officer Lt Cdr 'Paddy' McClintock, CWEM (R) Mick Hallam, FCWEA Jim Watts, WEA1 Steve Arnell, WEMN1 Brian Gowland, WEA1 Ian Jacobs, WEA1 Cliff Le Good, WEMN1 Dave Lee, WEA1 Barry Young, WEA2 Adam Porter, WEA2 Steve Palmer, POWEM (R) Chris Waspe, APOWEM Andrew 'Peddler' Palmer (KIA)

Radio ratings: LWEM (R) Iain McRobbie, LWEM (R) Pat Norris, LWEM (R) Eric Samson, LWEM (R) Paul Turner, WEM (R) Mark Bramwell, WEM (R) Simon Lawson (KIA), WEM (R) Stephen 'Scouse' Phillips, WEM (R) CJ 'Tug' Wilson

Ordnance ratings: LWEM (O) Iain 'Pussy' Catto (obit), LWEM (O) Martin Jones, LWEM (O) Stuart 'Soapy' Watson, LWEM (O) Ron White, WEM (O) John Bullock, WEM (O) Nigel Broadbent, WEM (O) Dave Daley, WEM (O) Kevin Macdonald, WEM (O) KF 'Pricky' Price, WEM (O) Kevin 'Buck' Ryan, WEM (O) Kenny 'Buck' Taylor, Weapons Engineer Artificer Apprentice Derek Lincoln

FLIGHT
Flight Commander Lt Cdr John Sephton (KIA), Observer Lt Brian Murphy (KIA), Senior Flight Maintainer AEMN (M) 1 Allan McAulay (KIA), Flight Maintainer POAEM (M) Pete Brouard (KIA), AEMN (R) 2 Bill Bailey, AEMN (L) 2 SP 'Scouse' Lacey, LAEM (M) Mark 'Speedy' Ball, AEM (M) Andy Schofield, AEM (L) John 'Wally' Wallington

SUPPLY AND SECRETARIAT
Supply Officer Lt Cdr Rick Banfield (KIA), CPOSA Alan Curtis

Galleys: POCK Cliff Goldfinch, LCK Mick Beckett, ALCK Mick Foote (KIA), CK Richard Dunkerley (KIA), CK Jon Major, CK John 'Taff' Roberts (KIA), CK Bob Sage, LCK Dave Trotter

Caterers: POCA Mike Stevens, CA Pete Ottley

Wardroom: POSTD Dave Burr, LSTD Bob Brooks, STD Shaun Hanson (KIA), STD Gary Gleed, STD Frank Walmsley

Ship's Office: POWTR Trevor Quinton, LWTR Frank Gilmour, WTR Mark Bogard

Stores: LSA Kevin Johnson, LSA Alan Whitworth, SA Tony Allison, SA Nigel 'Barney' Barnard

NAAFI Personnel: PO John Leake (obit), AB Nigel Woods

Unofficial Chinese: Wong Chun Hong (laundryman)

HMS *ARDENT* ROLL OF HONOUR

FRIDAY, 21 MAY 1982

AB [S] Derek 'George' Armstrong
Lt Cdr Rick Banfield
AB [S] Andy Barr
POAEM [M] Pete Brouard
CK Richard Dunkerley
ALCK Mick Foote
MEM [M] 2 Stephen 'Florrie' Ford
STD Shaun Hanson
AB [S] Sean Hayward
AB [EW] Stephen 'Gabby' Heyes
WEM [R] Simon Lawson
MEM [M] 2 Alistair 'Buzz' Leighton
AEMN [M] 1 Allan 'Mac' McAulay
AL [S] [R] Mick 'Scouse' Mullen
Lt Brian Murphy
LPT Gary 'Ginger' Nelson
APOWEM Andrew 'Peddler' Palmer
CK John 'Taff' Roberts
Lt Cdr John Sephton, DSC (posthumous)
ALMEM [M] Stephen 'Knocker' White
ALMEM [L] Garry Whitford
MEM [M] 1 Gilly Williams

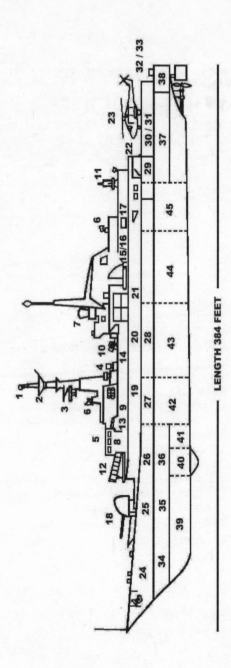

LENGTH 384 FEET

Appendix

HMS *ARDENT* PLAN

F184 HMS *Ardent* (Type 21 frigate, launched 9 May 1975)

	Number	Item / Space
Foremast	1	992 surveillance radar
	2	1010 Interrogation Friend or Foe radar (IFF)
	3	1006 navigation radar
	4	Lookout Aimer Site
03 Deck	5	Gun Direction Platform (external)
	6	912 weapons tracker radar
	7	Scot Satcomms
02 Deck	8	Bridge
	9	20mm Oerlikon guns (external)
	10	Chaff launchers
	11	Seacat launcher
01 Deck	12	Exocet launchers
	13	Ops Room
	14	Comms Room
	15	Whaler (starboard)
	16	Cheverton (port)
	17	STWS torpedo tubes
1 Deck	18	4.5-inch gun (Fo'c'sle)
	19	Officers' accommodation

	20	Sickbay
	21	Offices
	22	Hangar
	23	Flight Deck
2 Deck	24	Stores
	25	Gunbay Flat
		(Forward Damage Control section base)
	26	Senior and Junior Ratings' Messdeck
	27	Heads and Bathroom
	28	Air conditioning plant
	29	Ship Control Centre / Workshop
	30	Junior Ratings' Dining Hall
		(Aft Damage Control section base)
	31	Galley
	32	182 sonar (Quarterdeck)
	33	Hatches to Tiller Flat and Avcat Pump space
3 Deck	34	Cable Locker
	35	Forward Storerooms
	36	Junior Ratings' Messdeck
	37	Aft Storerooms
	38	Tiller Flat
4 Deck	39	Magazine
	40	184 sonar dome
	41	Fuel tanks
	42	Forward Auxiliary Machine Room
	43	Forward Engine Room (Olympus)
	44	Aft Engine Room (Tyne)
	45	Aft Auxiliary Machine Room

FURTHER READING

Max Arthur, *Above All, Courage* (Sidgwick & Jackson, 1985)
Michael Clapp, *Amphibious Assault Falklands* (Orion, 1996)
Capt Chris Craig, *Call for Fire* (John Murray, 1995)
Robert Fox, *Eyewitness Falklands* (Methuen, 1982)
David Wilton, *Falklands: The Air War* (Arms and Arrow Press, 1985)
Capt John Lippiett, *Modern Combat Ships 5: Type 21* (Ian Allan, 1990)
Admiral Sandy Woodward, *One Hundred Days* (Fontana, 1992)
Cdr Sharkey Ward, *Sea Harrier over the Falklands* (Orion, 1992)
Michael Bilton and Peter Kosminsky, *Speaking Out* (Deutsch, 1989)
Peter Way, *The Falklands War* (Marshall Cavendish, 1982)
Lt Cdr JL Muxworthy, *The Great White Whale Goes to War* (Peninsular & Oriental Steam Navigation Company, 1982)
Rick Jolly, *The Red and Green Life Machine* (Century, 1983)
David Brown, *The Royal Navy and the Falklands War* (Arrow, 1987)

◆◆◆

The HMS *Ardent* Association preserves the memory and spirit of the Forgotten Frigate and her ship's company.

For further information, visit www.hmsardent.org.uk.

GLOSSARY

AAMR	Aft Auxiliary Machine Room, containing diesel generators
aileron	control flap on an aircraft wing
anti-flash	protective balaclava or gloves to protect the skin from heat
ASW	anti-submarine warfare
ATC	Air Training Corps
Avcat	aviation fuel
Awkward	operation to deter underwater attacks by swimmers against ships at anchor
A4B/A4C	versions of Argentina's American-built Skyhawk fighter-bomber jet
becket	a small loop of material used as an attachment for ropes
Bn	battalion
Canteen Boat	title bestowed upon the ship among a squadron with the most junior commander
CAP	Combat Air Patrol
capstan	a revolving barrel used for winding cable
casevac	casualty evacuation
Chaff	metal strips fired from ship-borne launchers designed to confuse enemy radars or distract enemy missiles. Chaff Charlie, Chaff Delta and Chaff Echo indicate the position of the launcher on board.
Chief GI	chief gunnery instructor
chinagraph	a marking pencil
Chippy	the ship's carpenter
chocks	blocks of wood used as wedges
COMAW	Commodore Amphibious Warfare
Corporate	British operation to recover the Falklands
COST	Continuation Operational Sea Training to maintain a ship's company's ability to meet all the demands asked of it during peacetime and war
Dagger	Argentinian version of the Mirage jet fighter
dits	anecdotes
DMEO	Deputy Marine Engineering Officer, second-in-command of the ship's propulsion and power systems
draft	a sailor's posting to another ship
draft chit	notification on paper that a sailor is being posted to another ship
DSM	Distinguished Service Medal
DSO	Distinguished Service Order
8s	Number 8 uniform; working clothes
Exocet	French air-to-air and surface-to-air homing missile
FAMR	Forward Auxiliary Machine Room, containing diesel generators

FARM	*Ardent*'s shorthand pronunciation of FAMR
Fearnought	fireproof suit
flat	open area linking passageways on board ship
Fo'c'sle	the Upper Deck forward of the Bridge but aft of the forepeak
FOST	Fleet Operational Sea Training, the Royal Navy branch responsible for organising and executing COST
Gazelle	British Army helicopter
GDP	Gun Direction Platform, sited on the Bridge roof
gizzits	gifts
GPMG	belt-fed General Purpose Machine-Gun manned on *Ardent*'s Gun Direction Platform
grot	a bunk-bed
gulch	a four-bunk sleeping cubicle
gunline	the position at sea from which a ship bombards a target during Naval Gunfire Support
Guzz	Plymouth
helo	helicopter
Jimmy	Lower Deck nickname for the First Lieutenant
Joss	Lower Deck nickname for the Master at Arms
ki	hot cocoa (pronounced kye)
killick	a leading hand (LMEM, LWEM etc). A killick is another name for an anchor
LCU	Landing Craft Utility
LCVP	Landing Craft Vehicle and Personnel
Leander	Class of Royal Navy frigate
LMA	Leading Medical Assistant
LMEM	Leading Marine Engineering Mechanic, sub-divided into the Marine (M) and Electrical (L) branches, one advancement higher than an MEM
LMG	light machine-gun
LWEM	(Pronounced L-wem) Leading Weapons Engineering Mechanic, sub-divided into the Ordnance (O) and Mechanical (M) branches, one advancement higher than a WEM
Lynx	Royal Navy and Royal Marine light helicopter
Master at Arms	the ship's co-ordinator and 'policeman'
matelot	sailor
MBG	microbiological growth
MEO	Marine Engineering Officer in charge of the ship's propulsion and power systems
muster	to gather
M339	Italian-built Argentinian fighter
NAAFI	Navy, Army and Air Force Institutions, run by civilians on board ship
NBCD	Nuclear, Biological and Chemical Defence and Damage Control
NGS	Naval Gunfire Support for ground troops from a ship offshore
Oerlikon	20mm quick-firing light gun used for close-quarters defence
oggie	Cornish pasty
oggin	the sea
once-only	bright orange, one-piece survival kit
Opgen Mike	operational order issued by Commander Amphibious Task Force, bringing together all the maritime aspects of an amphibious landing
Para	Parachute Regiment

Pedestal Site	the position above the Hangar from which the Seacat missile was directed in manual control; known as the Ped Site
Pelorus	sighting device on a ship's compass
POME	Petty Officer Marine Engineering (pronounced pommie)
Primorye	class of Soviet spy ship
pongo	soldier
PTSD	Post Traumatic Stress Disorder
Pucara	Twin-seat, turbo-prop Argentinian ground attack aircraft
PWO	Principal Warfare Officer (pronounced p-woe)
Rapier	ground-to-air missile
RAS	Replenishment at Sea, (L) liquids (S) stores (pronounced razz)
recce	a reconnaissance operation
RFA	Royal Fleet Auxiliary
RO	radio operator
Satnav	satellite navigation
SBS	Special Boat Service
SCC	Ship Control Centre
scran	food
Seacat	short-range, mainly manual Royal Navy surface-to-air defence missile; *Ardent*'s primary air defence system
Sea Harrier	Fleet Air Arm version of the RAF's Harrier fighter-bomber, used mainly for air-to-air combat
Sea King	Royal Navy helicopter
Sea Skua	short-range, helicopter-launched air-to-surface attack missile
Sea Wolf	Royal Navy automatic, short-range surface-to-air defence missile
SHAR	Sea Harrier
Sidewinder	air-to-air missile carried by Sea Harrier
sitrep	situation report
Skyhawk	American A4 attack aircraft used by the Argentinian Air Force and Fleet Air Arm
Snakeye	British-made tank-busting bomb carried by Argentinian jets
squaddy	soldier
SSAFA	Soldiers', Sailors' and Airmen's Families Association
Stanavorlant	standing Naval exercise in Atlantic involving ships from numerous nations
Stinger	US-supplied portable, shoulder-launched surface-to-air missile used by British Special Forces
Stingray	experimental torpedo deployed on *Ardent* during the Falklands War
strop	a band of rope or iron round a pulley
STWS	Ship Torpedo Weapon System (pronounced Stews)
TEZ	200-mile no-go Total Exclusion Zone established around Falklands by Britain
tiff	artificer
Type 12	Class of Royal Navy frigate
Type 21	Class of Royal Navy frigate
Type 42	Class of Royal Navy destroyer
UXB	unexploded bomb
Vertrep	vertical replenishment (by helicopter) of a ship at sea
Wafu	nickname by which a member of the ship's Flight is known to non-Flight members of the ship's company (pronounced Wa-foo)

Wasp	Royal Navy light helicopter
WEM	Weapons Engineering Mechanic, sub-divided into the Ordnance (O) and Radio (R) branches (pronounced Wem)
Wessex	Royal Navy medium-lift helicopter used in support operations
wet	Royal Navy slang for a drink